Four Women

FOUR WOMEN

LIVING THE REVOLUTION
An Oral History of Contemporary Cuba

Oscar Lewis
Ruth M. Lewis
Susan M. Rigdon

UNIVERSITY OF ILLNOIS PRESS
Urbana Chicago London

In order to maintain the anonymity of the subjects of this study, the names of all informants, members of their families, their friends, and their neighbors have been changed. Places of birth, hometowns, details of work histories (but not salary or skill levels), as well as some streets, stores, hotels, and other public places, have also been changed. The names of historical figures and public officials have not been changed except in those cases in which a public figure or official had a personal relationship with one or more of the subjects in this study.

LIBRARY OF CONGRESS CATALOGING IN PUBLICATION DATA

Lewis, Oscar, 1914–1970.
  Living the revolution.

  Includes bibliographies.
  CONTENTS: v. 2. Four women.
  1. Cuba—Social conditions. 2. Cuba—Poor.
3. Cuba—Politics and government—1959– 4. Family—
Cuba—Case studies. I. Lewis, Ruth M., 1916–   joint
author. II. Rigdon, Susan M., 1943–   joint author.
III. Title.
HN203.5.L48   1977   309.1′7291′064   76-54878
ISBN 0-252-00639-9 (v.2)

Contents

Acknowledgments

WE ARE INDEBTED TO THE Ford Foundation for the original grant to do research in Cuba, and for supplementary funds to write up the field data. For additional financial support, we thank the University of Illinois Graduate College Research Board and the university's Center for International Comparative Studies. We also thank the Department of Anthropology for their continued cooperation and generosity in providing office space and other services. We would like to express our gratitude to those in Cuba—the Cuban Academy of Sciences and the many government officials and Cuban citizens—whose cooperation and interest made the research possible. We are especially grateful to the four major informants and their families who appear in this volume.

The preparation of the materials for this publication required the help of many persons whom we would like to acknowledge and thank: Maida Donate for interviewing one of the informants, Muna Muñoz Lee for translating the bulk of the Spanish materials, and Asa Zatz and Claudia Beck for their translations of shorter pieces. For preliminary editing of one or more of the autobiographies at various stages, we are grateful to Cecilia Coles, Barbara J. Sewell, Janet Burroway, Phyllis Murphy Hobe, and Annette Constantine. For editing sections of the manuscript, we thank Mary Heathcote, Ken Robbins, Phoebe Stone, Nina Díaz-Peterson, and Bernice B. Lieberman. For organizing parts of the Spanish materials, we thank Paola Costa and Mabel Casagrande. For typing the many versions of the manuscripts, we thank Terese Follett, Josephine Ippolito, Lorraine Glennon, Barbara Anderson, and Rosemary Decker. For the task of changing the original names to pseudonyms and for many clerical chores, we thank Nina Díaz-Peterson, Alice McMurray, Terese Follett, and Janet Sobolewski. Transcription of the original Spanish tapes was completed in Cuba and we are grateful to Carmen Graxirena and to the several Cuban women who performed this difficult task.

For reading one or more of the manuscripts in this volume, we thank

Jorge Cela, Alberto Domingo Gutiérrez, Nina Baym Stillinger, Berenice Hoffman, Gene L. Lewis, and Judith Ann Lewis. For their many critical comments and helpful suggestions on all three volumes in this series we are very grateful to Diane Levitt Gottheil, Susan Welch, and Alan J. Booth. We would especially like to express our deep gratitude to Fern M. Hartz, secretary to Oscar Lewis from 1959 to 1970 and to the Cuba research project since its inception. Finally, we wish to thank Elizabeth Dulany of the University of Illinois Press for her painstaking editing of the final manuscript.

Introduction

THIS VOLUME, THE SECOND in a series of three, presents the life stories of four Cuban women who spoke at length, in tape-recorded interviews, of their lives and personal experiences before and after the political upheaval of 1959. Their autobiographical data reflect the general purpose of our research in Cuba, that is, to show the impact of the Revolution and its institutions upon individuals and their families and to provide a recorded history of a rapidly changing period. More specifically, these life stories, as well as others in the series, illustrate the changing status, attitudes, and roles of women, their new opportunities, and the conflicts created or resolved by the Revolution. We hope they also shed light on the relationship of the informant's personal history to her degree of involvement or "integration" in the Revolution.

Although these informants were not interviewed specifically for a study of women, it seems logical now, in the light of the great wave of consciousness-raising on women's rights that has been developing in Cuba and in the United States, to group their stories together in one volume. In 1969-70, when this research was being carried out, neither the interviewers nor the interviewed had more than a vague awareness of the women's movements occurring in North America, Cuba, or elsewhere. The direct question, "What do you think about women's liberation?" did not receive very illuminating responses. More productive at that time, and more important to our understanding of Cuban women, were the specific questions about the informants' relationships to their spouses and children, their daughters' futures, attitudes toward women joining the labor force and mass organizations, taking positions of leadership, and so forth.

During the course of the project approximately 150 women were interviewed, of whom about 80 percent were from the urban lower class, 10 percent from the rural lower class, and 10 percent from the middle class.[1] There were significant cultural differences among them and a

1. Because we did not have access to all the field notes (see the series Foreword in *Four Men*), these figures are not exact.

wide range of personalities and life-styles. Understandably, the women tended to interpret the government's programs differently and to react to the social changes with varying speed.

With the Revolution barely a decade old, it was not unexpected that our informants showed little indication of profound changes in their views on sex roles. The government had only begun to deal systematically with these problems, and while most informants were acquainted with the Party's official support of equal rights for women, they did not fully understand what that support would come to mean in practice.

I

The struggle for women's rights in the Cuban Revolution has been as much or more a function of time and priorities as of ideology. Government programs for women have evolved, along with the rising consciousness of the Revolution's virtually all-male leadership, slowly and cautiously over the past fifteen years. During the first decade, when, as Castro has said, the Revolution was struggling just to stay alive, the government gave top priority to defense against invasion and internal subversion and to achieving its basic objective of improving the economic position of *all* Cubans through land reform and industrialization, full employment, universal education, and better housing, health care, and social services. With the demands of defense, agriculture, and the rapid expansion of educational and social services, it is not surprising that the new government's initial interest in women was as an untapped human resource.

The liberation of women, then, has come to have quite a different meaning in Cuba than in the United States.[2] In the North American women's movement the concept of liberation has been rooted in the idea of personal fulfillment or self-realization for women, and inasmuch as this means the breaking down of traditional sex roles, of self-realization for men as well. The emphasis is on individual development, and "liberation" may have as many different manifestations as there are individuals.

In the Cuban socialist context, which subordinates the individual to the group and the community, there is no self-realization except through service to state and society.[3] Thus, the primary impetus for liberating Cuban women from the traditional sex role was to free them to serve, through participation in mass organizations and incorporation

2. That is, in addition to the basic use of the word *liberation* in China, Russia, and Cuba to mean the act of being freed from bourgeois, capitalist domination.

3. Fidel Castro has said, "An individual alone can do nothing, an individual alone is very little, but an individual integrated into the strength of society is everything!" (Quoted from "To Create Wealth with Social Conscience," in Bertram Silverman, ed., *Man and Socialism* (New York: Atheneum, 1971), p. 374.)

in the labor force. This is in sharp contrast to the Western liberal context wherein *ideally* the community is served, that is, strengthened and enriched, through the development and expression of individuality.

In the United States the variety of groups and organizations that form the backbone of the women's movement have been founded not under government auspices but by private citizens. Policy-making and leadership positions in these organizations are held almost solely by women, but there is no one power center. The U.S. government has its own personnel and facilities for implementing equal opportunity laws, but by and large its resources have been spent in responding to demands from outside the government and not in providing a vanguard for the equal rights movement.

In Cuba, on the other hand, the movement for women's equality comes primarily from within the government. The principal women's organization, the Federation of Cuban Woman[4] (whose founding Castro has called the "developing of the women's movement"[5]), is an arm of the government. Since its founding the FMC has been headed by Vilma Espín Guilloys, a revolutionary heroine and member of the Party's Central Committee. As an integral part of the Revolution, the women's movement is ultimately responsible to and dependent for direction upon the official core of the Revolution's vanguard, the Political Bureau of the Party. The achievement (even the statement) of the objectives of the women's movement is, therefore, dependent upon the values, attitudes, and perceptions of the handful of men who make up the Political Bureau and on their sense of national priorities at any given time.

This means that, with the possible exception of Vilma Espín, who is Castro's sister-in-law, the role of women leaders in the Federation has been confined largely to the process of implementing programs and achieving objectives set for them by men at the top of the Party hierarchy. Raúl Castro has said that of all Party and government leaders, Fidel Castro "most clearly understands . . . the problems of women in society and their decisive role in the Revolution. . . ."[6] The idea that Castro understands the problems faced by women in society better than does Vilma Espín, for example, may strain the credulity of some women, but it may help to keep in mind that the Cuban women's movement is not primarily a feminist movement but a movement for equal rights, and

4. The *Federación de Mujeres Cubanas* (FMC) had 1,192,843 members in 1969, or 46 percent of all women between the ages of fifteen and sixty-five. (*Granma Weekly Review,* Jan. 25, 1970, p. 5.) In 1975, 77 percent of all women fourteen and older were members of the Federation. Seven-tenths of 1 percent of all FMC cadre were paid for their work; the remaining 326,450 cadre were volunteers. (*Ibid.,* Aug. 31, 1975, p. 6.)

5. Fidel Castro, in a speech made to the closing session of the Second Congress of the Federation of Cuban Women. (*Ibid.,* Dec. 8, 1974, p. 2.)

6. *Ibid.,* Dec. 7, 1975, p. 4.

that it is much easier for a man to comprehend equal rights for women than it is for him to develop a feminist consciousness.

As an arm of the Revolution—and an organized women's movement would not be allowed to exist in Cuba on any other terms—the Women's Federation has some decided advantages over the North American movement. Because the government has swept from the books most laws based on differential treatment of the sexes, the Federation is freed from the ongoing struggle faced by the U.S. movement, which expends a great deal of energy attacking the existing legal structure and lobbying for new legislation. These two activities alone are very costly and add to the amount of time feminist activists must spend in fund-raising. The government-funded Cuban Federation, on the other hand, is regularly allocated a share of the state's human and material resources for its work. Although the Federation does collect dues (on an ability-to-pay basis), the primary purpose is not to fund the organization but to exact a commitment and provide a continuing reaffirmation of membership.

An especially important aspect of the Federation's link to the government is the access it has to the great symbol-making machinery of the state, which directly controls the press and other mass media, as well as school curricula. In the United States, the women's movement has no direct control over the image of women projected on television, for example, or in advertising or textbooks. Although women have established some independent publications, to reach the majority of the population they must depend to a great extent on the mass media, which are not always sympathetic to their aims and which, in fact, at times have misrepresented and belittled those aims.

Perhaps of greatest importance to the Cuban Federation is that it has behind it the full authority and legitimacy of the state and Revolution. Official approval is particularly valuable to women's movements because they are trying to alter radically some of society's most fundamental precepts. In Cuba, this official support takes on special meaning because the legitimacy of the state has been based precisely on its commitment to radical change.

In the United States, the women's movement has official (but not necessarily wholehearted) support only for those legal actions designed to bring full compliance with the rights guaranteed under the Constitution. But the extra-governmental character of the U.S. women's movement gives it the potential for greater flexibility in the determination and communication of goals and greater control over use of its resources. The U.S. movement is not committed to a single ideological interpretation of women's rights and the feminist struggle, and is not in the position of having to ask women to subordinate their personal objectives to government priorities. Nor is it required to use its resources to defend and implement government programs. The extra-governmental nature of the U.S. movement means, then, that its ultimate goals do not have to be redefined with every shift in national priorities or every change in government administration.

Since its beginnings, the Federation of Cuban Women has been primarily an agency for mobilizing women for education, production, and defense. It has played a major role in encouraging women to attend schools for adults, to enter the labor force, to do voluntary productive labor, and to join the militia. It has also conducted periodic surveys of women's educational and employment backgrounds, skill levels, and willingness to work, and has been instrumental in the establishment and operation of sewing and dressmaking schools, re-training centers for domestic servants, and day-care centers for children of working mothers. Federation-sponsored study groups have played an important role in the ideological training of all Cubans, but especially of women.

Within its delegation meetings, the Federation has sought out the feelings and opinions of women and encouraged the free expression of the disparate views of its members for the purpose of communicating these collective opinions to the top levels of leadership. Still, the basic purpose of the Federation is more that of representing government policy to women than of representing women to government. This is not to suggest that public opinion is unimportant in Cuba, but to point out that it has a greater impact on how (i.e., the pace at which) government implements policy than it has on determination of the country's ultimate goals and objectives.

The single-mindedness of the Federation in mobilizing and politicizing women and in seeking compliance with new laws and programs has perhaps impaired its ability to reach some women. There is a tremendous distance between the subservient, dependent, apolitical, homebound model of the traditional Latin woman and the militant, independent, politicized, and community-minded model of the socialist woman. For women who have had virtually no relationship to the world outside the home and extended family except through their husbands, the achievement of integration in the Revolution may require a very personalized kind of guidance and support.

In the past, the Federation has asked women to get out of the house and into productive labor and volunteer work, with little sympathy—or perhaps not enough time or resources—for those who were unwilling. It has provided many kinds of material support—child-care facilities, adjusted working hours, paid maternity leave, remedial education and vocational training—but it has probably not, at least as of 1970, offered adequate moral support on a personal level to those who are truly threatened by the proposed changes in life-style.

For example, the five women we interviewed for *Neighbors,* the third volume in the series, were housewives who conformed more closely to the conventional female sex role than did the work-oriented, community-activist informants in this book. Each of the five women occupied herself full-time with household chores and refused to look for work outside the home, although four of the five did take in laundry when their families needed extra money. The women spent most of their time at home, had few or no friends of their own, and for the most part were limited to the company of their husbands, children, neighbors, and relatives. One of the women described herself by saying, "Like *mamá*, I live exclusively for my family. I try above all to be a good wife and a good mother." This statement summarizes as well the general life view of the other four women in that volume.

The men of these five families, except for one who was unemployed because of a disabling illness, were away from home a good deal, often for several weeks at a time, because of their voluntary work in agriculture. The women knew little about their husbands' activities outside the home and were not accustomed to asking questions. As one of the women put it, "I'm not in the habit of pestering my husband with questions. I don't meddle in men's affairs." In general, all five women accepted as a basic premise of their marital relationships the necessity of ordering their lives to accommodate their husbands' needs and desires. Wherever the men's work took them, for whatever period of time, these women acquiesced and willingly served them upon their return. "When a husband gives his wife an order," one of them said, "his wife should never answer, 'No, I won't.' Not unless she wants to find herself out in the street." The only woman among the five who asserted herself in her marriage denied that she did and insisted upon representing her husband as the head of the family.

Two of the women, Sara Rojas and Lala Fontanés, spoke with bitterness and resignation about their husbands' extramarital affairs, and when asked about women's liberation, identified the movement with sexual promiscuity and saw it as a direct threat to the stability of their marriages. This confusion about the purpose of the women's movement was remarkable in Lala Fontanés, who, of all the women we interviewed, was one of the most active members of the Federation. It was revealing not only as a projection of her personal problems but also of the Federations's shortcomings as a feminist organization.[7]

In *Neighbors,* all informants were interviewed and observed in their homes, giving a clearer understanding of the resistance to social change in Cuba and the role of the home and family as a refuge from it. All five

---

7. Another example of this problem is in the story of Inocencia Acosta Felipe. An active Federation member for many years, Inocencia still believed that men were superior to women in all things save child-rearing and homemaking.

women were aware of the government's position on equality for women and of its efforts to utilize their labor power in both paid and volunteer work. Although only one of the women expressed any real disagreement with the direction of revolutionary programs, none was ready in 1970 to accept a job outside her home, only one of the five was actively involved in mass organizations, and only one had attended an adult-education night class. Unlike the four women in this volume, they did not have high expectations for themselves but spoke, rather, of better futures for their children.[8]

In addition to the challenge presented by tradition-bound women, the Federation faced even greater resistance from the socially and politically marginal women of Cuba's slums. Most of the women interviewed for the Buena Ventura community study had grown up in the slums of Havana.[9] For them the traditional sex roles had a different applicability than for the women introduced in *Four Women* and *Neighbors*. In the lowest levels of poverty, the standards and role models of the larger society were, for the most part, irrelevant to daily life, even though some, especially those few with hope of leaving the slum, clung to these standards on a verbal level. Economic necessity liberated large numbers of lowerclass women from the conventional standards of behavior; so-called "feminine" characteristics, such as dependency and submissiveness, were liabilities to women who were wage-earners and heads of households. Their economic independence gave them a freedom of expression and movement (within their own subculture) that many middle-class women did not have. Legalized marriages and monogamy occurred less frequently because poor women and men often entered into a series of temporary liaisons out of economic necessity. Child-rearing occupied less of a woman's time as she frequently had to leave her children to go to work, and because, among the poor, childhood itself was abbreviated.

To many women from the slums, "liberation" did not imply independence from home and children and incorporation in the labor force and mass organizations. "Liberation" meant *release* from outside work, taking care of their own homes, and having time to spend with their children. Of the Buena Ventura women old enough to have worked in the prerevolutionary period and who responded to the work-history questionnaire, 91 percent reported holding jobs, mostly as domestics or other service employees, for the greater part of their adult lives prior to the

8. In the summer of 1976 we learned that three of these five women had taken full-time jobs. One woman, a high school graduate, was teaching English in a technical institute; another took a factory job after the death of her husband; the third woman, a sixth-grade graduate, was working in a nursery school full-time while attending a basic secondary school for adults.

9. The community study is not included in this series, although some of the men and women from Buena Ventura appear in *Four Men*. For background information on this study see the Foreword in that volume.

Revolution.[10] In 1969, only 17 percent of these women (or just under the national average of women in the labor force that year) worked outside their homes.[11] Another 9 percent worked in their homes as laundresses (7), seamstresses (1), and candy-makers (2).[12] In addition to withdrawing from the labor force, many Buena Ventura women were reluctant to volunteer for productive labor or neighborhood activities. Almost all of the women had for good reason always been suspicious of government and had no concept of civic obligation. The local branches of the mass organizations had difficulty recruiting volunteers and were relatively inactive compared to those in other neighborhoods of Havana.

In general, we found among all our female informants—but particularly those outside the urban lower class—low self-esteem and little support of women by women. This lack of mutual support manifested itself in preferential treatment by women of their sons and sons-in-law over their daughters, lack of empathy and trust between women, exploitation of women by women, especially of domestic servants, and by mothers trying to perpetuate in their daughters the same restrictions they had been subjected to in their own youth. Because of this, we think the absence in Cuba of small, informal support and consciousness-raising groups, like those that have become so widespread in the United States, was especially important.

The study groups or "circles" sponsored by the Federation and the Committees for Defense of the Revolution (CDRs) were not designed to serve the same purpose as the U.S. groups. The study circles are structured around a group leader, possibly trained in one of the Party's Schools for Revolutionary Instruction,[13] who has been given a set topic for discussion. The study groups are usually neighborhood-based, with male and female participants coming from the block Committees and the Federation's zone-level organizations. Unlike most of the consciousness-raising groups in the United States, the study circles are not made up of women who have sought out each other for reasons of compatibility and mutual understanding. Individual problems are usually not discussed from a personal perspective but rather are re-stated in an ideological context. In Cuba, the pursuit of personal identity at the

10. Sixty-three of sixty-nine respondents. A detailed report on their work histories will appear in the Buena Ventura study.

11. Eighteen of 108 women between the ages of fourteen and sixty-five. Part of the disparity in percentages of women working can be explained by the tendency in 1969–70 to continue education beyond elementary school, thereby increasing the average age at which women entered the labor force.

12. Such forms of self-employment were officially prohibited by 1969, but the law was not strictly enforced. Some work in the home was permissible if it was contracted by a government agency. In *Neighbors*, for example, three of the four women who took in laundry were employed by the state.

13. In 1975 the Federation opened its own ideological training schools for FMC cadre; among other duties, they will lead FMC study groups.

expense of collective identity is considered not simply a luxury but a social and political evil as well.

From the perspective of the Cuban government, the liberation of women is dependent upon the Revolution's success in attaining its primary objective: to establish a wholly socialist economy and society. Women can be free only to the extent that they commit themselves, first and foremost, to that objective. According to this view, women do not have just a right to work, but an obligation to society to engage in "socially productive" labor.[14] (Domestic labor is not considered "socially productive.") Castro has said, in effect, that the achievement of full rights for women is conditional on their willingness to join the labor force:

> ... the whole question of women's liberation, of full equality of rights for women and the integration of women into society is to a great extent determined by their incorporation into production. This is because the more women are incorporated into work—thus helping society, helping their families—the more the need for the solution of all those problems that were recently discussed at the Women's [Federation's Second] Congress ... and the [more the] inequality and discrimination that our women are still victims of in our society [will be] evident. Therefore, to the extent that women are incorporated into work, so will the way to their liberation become easier and more clearly defined.[15]

The struggle to bring women into the labor force, however, has been long and difficult. Only after ten years did the government see significant results from its efforts to educate and re-train women. Among its earliest programs were those to provide vocational training for two of the most exploited groups in Cuba—prostitutes and domestic servants. In 1961 the government began a systematic program for the elimination of prostitution and the rehabilitation of prostitutes. Special schools and job-training programs were set up for them, as well as state pensions to support their dependents while they completed their re-training. In this volume, the story of Pilar López Gonzales (Part III) presents her personal experience with the rehabilitation program. Women in domestic service were offered other jobs or the opportunity for re-training in other skills. Private employment of servants was officially prohibited, but a number of former domestics, among them Inocencia Acosta Felipe, another of the four women in this volume, went back to work as maids for the state—in hotels, schools, hospitals, or protocol houses for foreign guests—but with considerable improvement in status and salaries.

---

14. The distinction between *right* and *obligation* is basic to the whole conception of political participation (as well as social, cultural, and economic participation) as seen in the United States and Western Europe as opposed to the socialist countries.

15. *Granma Weekly Review,* Dec. 15, 1974, p. 3.

Many of the special educational programs for women reflected both the government's good intentions and its stereotypic view of women and women's capabilities. For example, thousands of young girls were brought from the countryside to Havana on scholarships to study, en masse, "feminine arts" such as cooking, sewing, and nursing. In other schools, established for the "improvement" of wives of political prisoners, country women were encouraged to formalize their marriages and taught to curl their hair, shave their legs, wear high-heeled shoes, nylon stockings, and matching accessories.[16] Vocational training schools for women, such as those for former prostitutes, also often had personal grooming classes as part of the curricula.

The drive by the government to incorporate women into the labor force met with resistance from both sexes, and there was no overwhelming demand by women for jobs. Most men did not want their wives away from home, out of their sight and control, mixing freely with other men, forming friendships with women, and gaining economic independence.

Whether to keep peace at home or for fear of stepping out of the sex roles in which they had been so strongly trained, women also often resisted taking outside jobs. The demands of household management, which in some ways became more difficult after the Revolution, also deterred them. With rationing (introduced in 1962) and nationalization of services—such as repair shops, laundries, and dry cleaners—shopping and housekeeping were more time-consuming. Few men were accustomed to helping out at home, and the increased pressure placed upon workers to put in long hours of voluntary labor and overtime meant they were even less available to their families. Unable to hire someone to help with housework, and confronted with insufficient day-care facilities, and with the time demands of volunteer labor and involvement in the Federation and Committees for Defense of the Revolution, many women were reluctant to take on more work. In addition, because of the increase in real income for many after the Revolution and the decrease in availability of consumer goods, some found a second income less necessary.

As a result of these factors and others arising from personal situations, the number of women in the labor force rose slowly, from 14.2 percent in 1958 to 15.6 percent in 1968.[17] A census of unemployed women carried out by the Federation just prior to our field work showed that, of

16. For a description of these schools see Lee Lockwood, *Castro's Cuba, Cuba's Fidel* (New York: Vintage, 1969), pp. 261–79.

17. José A. Moreno, "From Traditional to Modern Values," in Carmelo Mesa-Lago, ed., *Revolutionary Change in Cuba* (Pittsburgh: University of Pittsburgh Press, 1971), p. 480. The government may have recruited more women into the labor force than these figures suggest because the emigration of hundreds of thousands of Cubans between 1959 and 1961 probably caused a decrease in the percentage of women in the labor force, especially of women professionals (teaching and medicine) and clerical workers. The percentage

the women canvassed, only one out of four was willing to take a job. Of those refusing work, 59 percent, or 300,000, attributed their negative response to family obligations and lack of facilities, especially for child care. However, 41 percent of those refusing work did not have family obligations.[18]

During the 1969 drive to reach the goal of the 10-million-ton sugar harvest, the government intensified its effort to recruit women, especially into agriculture and industry, the two sectors of the economy where women's representation had traditionally been lowest. The overall goal of hiring 100,000 additional women was met and surpassed, raising the percentage of women in the labor force from 15.6 in 1968 to 17.7 in 1969,[19] thereby surpassing the combined gains of the nine previous years.

This success was due not only to the patriotic appeal of the harvest campaign itself, but to a decade of vocational and adult night-school training, and to the increasing availability of day-care centers and boarding schools. The government also took steps in 1969 to make household management more convenient and less time-consuming. Store hours were extended and working women were given priority at grocery and department stores and laundries.

The rapid expansion of the educational, health, and day-care systems made available a large number of jobs that traditionally had been held by women. In 1969 women continued to hold a disproportionate number of the nursing and teaching jobs; day-care centers were staffed almost completely by women, which in part explains why, despite the abolition of privately employed domestic servants, women's representation in the service occupations continued to increase—to 52 percent in 1969.[20] However, women also steadily increased their representation in agricultural and blue-collar jobs.

Between 1970 and 1975 the percentage of women in the labor force increased to 25.3.[21] But on the job, women were not being nominated in proportionate numbers by their fellow workers for Vanguard Worker status and for membership in the Communist Youth. Before 1971 this

---

drop could not have been too great, however, because Castro claims that 70 percent of all women employed before 1959 were domestic servants, and it is unlikely that many of these women emigrated.

18. *Ibid.*, p. 481.

19. *Ibid.*, p. 480. Labor statistics do not in themselves reflect the extent to which women were becoming involved in work outside the home, since much of their work was voluntary. During the Revolution's first decade, women contributed hundreds of thousands of work hours in agriculture; approximately a quarter-million women were cadre in the FMC; and according to Richard R. Fagen, by 1963, 17.1 percent of CDR cadre were housewives. (*The Transformation of Political Culture in Cuba* (Stanford, Calif.: Stanford University Press, 1969), p. 83.)

20. *Ibid.*, p. 481.

21. *Granma Weekly Review*, Dec. 8, 1974, p. 3.

dual status was one of the principal paths toward membership in the Party, so that by 1974 women still made up only 12.79 percent of Party membership and 6 percent of the cadre. In the same year they held only 15 percent of the leadership positions in all units of production, services, and administration.[22]

Women were also underrepresented in leadership positions in the Party and in state institutions and have made only token progress at the highest levels of government. Celia Sánchez Manduley, Minister of the Presidency, was the only woman with cabinet rank until 1970, when Nora Frométa Silva became head of the Ministry of Light Industry, the sector that employs the largest percentage of women industrial workers. A number of women have advanced to secondary leadership positions, most notably the Twenty-sixth of July veteran, Major Haydée Díaz Ortega, Deputy Minister of the Interior, and Asela de los Santos Tamayo, Deputy Minister of Education.

Of the 100 members of the Party's Central Committee, only six are women, none of whom sit on the Political Bureau. Three of the six women are heroines of the rebellion against Batista. They are Celia Sánchez Manduley, who helped plan the landing of the *Granma* (the yacht that brought Castro and his followers to Cuba from Mexico) and who fought in the Sierra Maestra with Castro; Vilma Espín Guilloys, who was Raúl Castro's political adviser in the Sierra del Cristal; and Haydée Santamaría Cuadrado, who took part in the 1953 attack on the Moncada Garrison, and is now president of the national literary center Casa de las Américas.[23] Although these women now hold important positions in the government, they represent only a small proportion of the women who took part in the struggle against Batista, either in the women's fighting contingent in the Sierras[24] or in the more dangerous underground in the cities, towns, and countryside, which led to the imprisonment, torture, and/or death of a number of women. Some have gained fame as martyrs, but at large rallies in the Plaza de la Revolución, when portraits of revolutionaries are displayed, it is unusual to see a woman's face

22. *Ibid.*, p. 2.

23. At the First Party Congress held in December, 1975, Sánchez, Espín, Santamaría, and Elena Gil Izquierdo, head of the Ministry of Education's Special Plans, were all re-elected to the Central Committee. Clementina Serra Robleda, member of the old Communist Party and former head of the Federation's day-care program, was dropped from the Committee, but the addition of Asela de los Santos Tamayo and Pilar Fernández Alvarez raised the number of women members from five to six. Five of the twelve alternate members to the Central Committee named at the First Congress were women, but again, no women were elected to the Political Bureau.

24. The Mariana Grajales Brigade, named for the mother of Antonio Maceo, national hero and a martyr of the War of Independence.

among them.[25] Nor are there many women in the hierarchy of the Revolutionary Armed Forces. Although women have played an important role in civil defense and many are now enrolled in the FAR's officer-training schools, there are very few who have risen above the subaltern ranks. Women such as Lieutenant-Colonel Thelma Barnot Pubillones, Sierra del Cristal veteran and now head of the History section of the FAR's Political Department, are exceptions.[26]

The memberships of the national and provincial directorates of the Committees for Defense of the Revolution are a more meaningful indicator of women's progress because, while the military has a history of domination by men, the CDRs were instruments of the Revolution, without precedent in Cuba, and could have been used to set an example. The scarcity of women in high-level positions is even more significant because they are well represented among the activists at the block and zone levels.

In 1974, when the first elections to People's Power (the new system of administrative/legislative assemblies) were held in Matanzas Province, only 7.6 percent of the candidates and only 3 percent of the delegates elected were women.[27] Citing these figures in his closing speech to the Federation's Second Congress, Castro voiced disappointment and concern over the lack of voter confidence in women. The government, however, did not prove much better in its appointments. Only a few women, for example, were included on the various Law Study commissions established between 1969 and 1974 to draft the new Civil, Penal, and Family codes and the new Constitution, and there were no women on the Central Preparatory Commission of the First Party Congress.

Castro readily acknowledged that full equality for women did not yet exist and that women's rights was one area in which, "after more than 15 years of revolution, we are still politically and culturally behind."[28] In 1975, International Women's Year, the de facto position of Cuban women was still in rather sharp contrast to their de jure status. In general, as Castro has said, the laws and programs promulgated to achieve equality for women were in advance of the objective and subjective conditions necessary for their full realization. Much groundwork has still to be done in vocational training and education of women, in opening up

25. An occasional exception, and it usually does not occur in these rallies, is Tamara Bunke (Tania, the guerrilla), the East German who was killed while fighting in Bolivia. A normal school in Pinar del Río has been named for her.

26. Women are being recruited into FAR civilian positions in large numbers. In 1975, 32 percent of all civilian employees were women. (*Granma Weekly Review*, Aug. 24, 1975, p. 5.)

27. Election results appeared in *Cuba Review*, Dec., 1974.

28. *Granma Weekly Review*, Dec. 8, 1974, p. 2.

sufficient jobs of the requisite skill levels, and in the construction and staffing of day-care centers and boarding schools. In addition, the political consciousness of both men and women on the subject of women's rights was still low.

In the first decade of the Revolution, the Castro government was conscious of the dangers of tampering with too many fundamentals at once, and the home, family, and *machismo* come as close to being basic as anything in Cuba. But since 1969, a period often described as one of institutionalizing the Revolution, the government has been trying to bring the attitudes and behavior of Cubans into closer harmony with the new laws and institutions.

Whereas in the past the government tried in more oblique ways to open the minds of Cubans to the possibility of different roles for women, in 1974, with an eye to what Blas Roca has called the "living reality" of Cuba,[29] it attacked the problem head on by launching a nationwide discussion of women's rights and of the relationship between home and community in a socialist society. The discussions were held in work centers across the country in conjunction with the drafting of the new Family Code.

Among the code's many important provisions, some of the more significant are: the establishment of "equal rights and duties for both partners" in marriage, including the responsibility for the education and upbringing of children, and, when both husband and wife are working, joint responsibility for management of the household; guaranteeing to both partners "the right to practice their profession or skill" and charging them to cooperate with one another in order to make it possible.[30] Strengthening of the family is a main objective of the code, and to this end it encourages legal marriages and requires parents to make "every possible effort to provide [their children] with a stable home." In addition, by requiring a judicial decree it makes divorce more difficult to obtain. Either or both parents may be wage-earners, but both are obligated to live lives of service to the community *outside* the home, through participation in mass organizations and voluntary productive labor, and *inside* the home, by raising children who are "worthy citizens."

Discussion of the code aroused underlying anxieties and brought them to the surface. According to visitors to Cuba during the last half of 1974, the code was being discussed not just at work centers but wherever people met—at stores, in social circles, and on street corners. In a speech given by Blas Roca, who supervised the writing of the code, and in

29. Blas Roca Calderío, member of the Political Bureau and head of the Law Study commissions, quoted in *Granma Weekly Review*, Oct. 20, 1974, p. 4.

30. All quotations from the Family Code used here are from the English translation of the full text that appeared in *Granma Weekly Review*, Mar. 16, 1975, pp. 7–9.

another made by Castro in late 1974, each acknowledged the fear expressed by Cubans over some of the changes proposed in the code. Referring to this in his speech at the Second Congress of the FMC, Castro said, ". . . what should really frighten us as revolutionaries is to admit that women still do not have absolute equality in Cuban society."

The code went into effect on International Women's Day, March 8, 1975, when, in a state ceremony, a copy was formally presented to Federation President Vilma Espín. The code may be somewhat of a disappointment to those feminists who maintain that women can be freed from their traditional role only by the demise of the family.[31] Some have believed that socialist systems offered the best chance for this, by destroying man's position of economic supremacy in the family and thereby ending his control over his wife and children. Of course, in China and the Soviet Union the nuclear family has remained strong even though those governments have drastically reduced the man's economic hold on the family. This has been due in part to these governments' acceptance (at least temporarily) of the cultural primacy of the family unit, and to their recognition that the family, as a principal agent for transmission of social and political values, can be one of the state's most important allies.

Cuba's new Constitution and the Family Code recognize the pervasive influence of the family and are, in part, attempts to harness that influence in service to the state. Chapter III of the new Constitution, borrowing from the Constitution of 1940, begins: "The state protects the family, motherhood and matrimony."[32] The family envisaged for socialist Cuba, however, differs in some very fundamental ways from the traditional family. The economic, legal, and political positions of its individual members—husbands, wives, and children—have been changed, so that a new, more equal footing for each is possible. By "defining each member's specific responsibilities," Vilma Espín has said, "the Cuban Revolution has made the family much more solid. . . ."[33]

The new Cuban home is not supposed to function as a refuge from state and society; it is not to be a place of escape for women or men who refuse to take jobs or do community work, nor a place for family members to fall into the old *machismo*-based pattern of human relationships. In other words, human relationships within the family are not to offer alternatives to those in socialist society but to mirror them.

The Family Code does not mention family planning, birth control,

31. Vilma Espín is not among them. She told the International Women's Year Conference in Mexico City that ending sex discrimination was not "a question of fostering antagonistic contradictions between men and women. It's a question of upholding the dignity of the couple, the family nucleus." (*Granma Weekly Review*, July 6, 1975, p. 10.)

32. All quotes from the draft Constitution are from the English translation of the full text that appeared in *Granma Weekly Review*, Apr. 20, 1975, pp. 7–10.

33. *Ibid.*, June 29, 1975, p. 9.

and abortion. These are subjects rarely discussed publicly in Cuba; in fact it is not easy to find an exact statement of official policy on them. Certainly they are not among the Federation's priority issues, and there has been no public discussion by the movement about women's right to control their own bodies. We have seen conflicting reports on the availability of contraceptives and abortion in Cuba, but the most detailed statement (part of an intelligent general discussion of women's liberation in Cuba) appeared in Elizabeth Sutherland's *The Youngest Revolution.*

> Contraceptives were available in Cuba without restriction in 1967. These included the diaphragm and an intrauterine loop . . . the pill was still considered too dangerous.[34] Any woman, married or not, could go to a hospital and be fitted with an *anillo* [IUD]; should it fail and the woman become pregnant, she could have an abortion free of charge. She could also have a free abortion if she reported to a hospital within a month after becoming pregnant—but her family would be notified, which acted as a deterrent. Abortion under any other circumstances than these remained illegal. A woman who was over thirty-eight and had had five children could have a free operation to tie up the uterine tubes.[35]

Many of our women informants mentioned their own experiences with abortion and birth control but did not have any clear understanding of government policy. Among the five women included in *Neighbors,* three practiced birth control but none had ever had an abortion. One woman, however, reported that abortions (self-induced or performed by friends or midwives) had been common in her hometown in Oriente Province. This thirty-four-year-old woman had had eight children, three miscarriages, and a stillbirth, but was refused a tubal ligation and also told that an IUD was not suitable for her.

Among the four women whose stories comprise this volume only one had practiced birth control. This woman, fifty-four years old and a devout Roman Catholic, had an unhappy marriage and did not want to have children with her husband. Only one of the four reported having an abortion, and she had had an uncounted number while working as a prostitute. Two of the four women reported that their mothers had had two or more abortions, and one had even assisted her mother with one of them. The female informants in the Buena Ventura community study, all of whom were former slum dwellers, said that abortion, self-induced or performed by other women, had been commonplace in their barrios. However, none of the women we interviwed reported having had a legal abortion since 1959.

34. Another reason given for the unavailability of the pill was that it was not manufactured in Cuba and the government did not want the expense of importation.

35. New York: Dial Press, 1969, p. 178. On a visit to Cuba in 1976, Carl T. Rowan, apparently basing his report on government statistics, stated that abortion was available on demand and that in 1975 there were 64 abortions for every 100 live births. (*Chicago Daily News,* Dec. 15, 1976, p. 8.)

From the experiences of our informants, we can conclude that prior to 1970, regardless of official policy, the availability of birth-control devices and abortions depended to a great extent on the attitudes of the individual doctor, and to a certain degree on the persistence of the woman in her demands. It did not appear that the government was making any systematic effort to educate women on the availability of contraceptives or abortion or to enforce a uniform policy for all doctors.[36]

Despite progress toward realization of equal rights, government policy still harbors certain forms of sexual discrimination. Castro referred to some of these inequities in his 1974 Federation speech, saying that women are entitled to "certain small privileges" and to "special considerations" and courtesies because nature made them "physically weaker than men." Effort should be made, Castro said, to instill in children appropriate standards of conduct and "proletarian courtesies," such as men giving up their seats to women on buses. Certainly most women and men want to be treated courteously, but questions of courtesy are as irrelevant to considerations of weakness and strength as they are to the struggle for equal rights. It is difficult to say whether Castro really believes his rhetoric or whether he was trying to reassure the Cuban people that not all of the traditional code of conduct is in conflict with the new.

What is important is not Castro's gratuitous remarks about courtesy, but the fact that the belief in women's physical inferiority may have found expression in the new Constitution. In article 41 of Chapter V, sexual discrimination is prohibited, but article 43 states: "In order to assure the exercise" of women's right to work, "the state sees to it that they are given jobs in keeping with their physical makeup. . . ."

The affirmative-action program mentioned by Castro in his 1974 Federation speech seems designed to implement the provision in article 43: "In every new factory built in any Cuban town, it must be indicated *what work is to be given to women* so there will be time enough to proceed with the selection and training of those women" (italics added). It would appear that certain work will be labeled "appropriate for women" and that women will not, as a matter of course, be competing with men for the same jobs, at least not in industry and agriculture. This is not a quota

36. Sutherland said that the government "did not actively disseminate birth control information," although she had seen one 1967 edition of *Granma* that devoted three pages to a discussion of the availability of contraceptives and abortion. (*The Youngest Revolution,* p. 178.) Sutherland also reported that the state had no sex-education program in the schools, and we know from our young female informants that they were afraid to discuss sex with their parents and had learned about menstruation, for example, from their friends. The 1971 Congress on Education and Culture called for "appropriate sex education for parents, leaders and students," and also stated "the need for scientific knowledge of sex in the education of children to eradicate prejudice." (*Granma Weekly Review,* May 9, 1971, p. 5.)

system, which reserves a representative proportion of jobs for female applicants, but a system of freezing certain job categories (e.g., light work in textile factories or in sugar mills) for women, while closing other jobs to them. The policy of giving women protected access to certain "suitable" work may be seen, in the short run, as a method of insuring the most efficient use of Cuba's labor pool, but it is a policy that contains the risk of permanently categorizing the least physically demanding and most unskilled jobs as "women's work." At the same time, this policy denied some women applicants (even if a small minority) access to jobs they were physically able to perform.[37]

The policy of job-slotting was being re-evaluated for some industries, such as sugar, in 1974, because, according to Castro, women of the requisite skill levels were not applying for the jobs. But Castro criticized administrators who were routinely giving jobs to men over women applicants: "First, it is a question of elemental justice; and second, it is an imperative necessity of the Revolution, it is a demand of our economic development, because at some point, the male work force will not be enough...." This statement, coupled with that on "appropriate" work, raises questions concerning the future of women in the labor force. Are women to be considered essentially as supplemental labor for an otherwise male work force? If so, what will happen when there is no labor shortage and the choice is between a man working and a woman working?

In this same speech, alongside his characterization of women as "nature's workshop where life is formed," Castro mentioned briefly the problems created by the linguistic style that has made man the central focus in all things. He cited this as a minor, although not unimportant, problem in the struggle for women's equality, but he did not give examples. However, the phrase "new man," which had such currency when Ernesto Guevara's influence on policy was still strong in Cuba, is much less used now, although the basic idea is still honored. In 1973, Vilma Espín, in an open letter to Fidel Castro, wrote: "... every mother, every woman should be aware of the tasks she must accomplish in raising the new generations of revolutionaries, who will have all the positive qualities of the Communist, of *the new kind of human being* that Che was" (italics added).[38]

That Castro even acknowledged the linguistic factor is some indication of the government's recognition of the pervasiveness of sex discrimina-

---

37. We have no information on wage and income differences between men and women, although we do know men and women received equal pay for the same work. However, in 1970 Cuba did have four wage scales, each with eight gradations (see Inocencia, n. 58), with wage level dependent on sector of employment and skill level. If low-skill jobs continue to be reserved for women, their overall earning power will be less than that of men.

38. *Granma Weekly Review*, Dec. 30, 1973, p. 5.

tion and its willingness to single out the repression of women as a problem, not separate from but more complex than the past exploitation of Cubans in general. This is also implicit in the Cuban characterization of the women's movement as "the revolution within the revolution."

As of 1975, women still retained some of the "certain small inequalities" in their favor to which Castro says they are entitled. For example, the Compulsory Military Service Law, while technically applicable to all Cubans, was not used to draft women. The marriage laws permit women to marry two years earlier than men in those cases where parental consent is required (fourteen years for girls as opposed to sixteen years for boys), and give preference to mothers in disputes over custody of children. In addition, some legislation, such as the anti-loafing law of 1971 (adopted to combat the serious absentee and vagrancy problem presented by Cubans unaccustomed to year-round employment), could not realistically be applied equally to women and men; in any case, it is apparently not consistently enforced for women who have no family obligations.

This is all part of the two steps forward, one step backward policy of compromise between political ideals and practical realities. In speaking of the new laws being drafted during the early 1970s, Blas Roca, referring to the idealism of some Cubans, said: "The judicial norm is a reflection of what is, not what might or should be," and quoting Castro, ". . . reality is not what should be adjusted to fit institutions; the institutions are what must be adjusted to fit reality."[39] This thinking is very much in evidence in Castro's Federation speech, which we have relied on so heavily here as the most comprehensive statement of the government's policy on sexual equality in 1974–75. The speech itself is an example of Castro's praising-chiding-cajoling technique of mobilizing mass support for government policy. He praised women's efforts in the Revolution as fundamental to its success; he chided men for their reluctance to hire women, and all Cubans for their anxiety over the Family Code; and he cajoled women to join the Revolution in greater numbers by equating "female virtues"—self-sacrifice and discipline, for example—with those "virtues demanded of the revolutionary militant."

The wide discussion of the Family Code and the Constitution, together with the publicity given to the work of the Federation and preparations for its Second Congress,[40] the activities of International Women's Year, and the preparations for the First Party Congress, held in December, 1975,[41] increasingly focused greater public attention on the

39. *Ibid.*, Oct. 20, 1974, p. 4.
40. Part of the celebration for the Second Congress was a new ballet entitled *Woman*, staged by Cuba's prima ballerina, Alicia Alonso, in collaboration with Vilma Espín.
41. One of the Congress's more than twenty watchwords and slogans was: "Toward the 1st Congress, fighting for the full equality of women." Presumably this was used on billboards and wall posters across the island.

subject of women's rights. In late 1975, for example, Thesis 3 of the First Congress, entitled "On Women's Full Exercise of Equality," was discussed in study groups held by the Party, mass organizations, and work centers across the country. The thesis deals with the history of the oppression of women and the necessary steps to combat the cultural legacy that perpetuates it. Comments and recommendations made during these meetings were collected and forwarded to the Preparatory Committee planning the Party Congress. In addition, other documents and theses to be considered at the Congress dealt with particular problems of women's rights. Out of these discussions is to come a comprehensive policy for achieving equal opportunities for women and men. But the Party is also hoping to improve subjective conditions necessary for enforcement of existing laws. Addressing a Federation anniversary celebration, Raúl Castro said about the First Congress theses: "All this will contribute to the formation of a social awareness which will make it possible to implement the Family Code."[42]

International Women's Year received very substantial press coverage in Cuba during 1975, far surpassing coverage of the year's event in the United States. The Federation and other groups within Cuba sponsored many trips, communications, and meetings to show solidarity with women's movements in other socialist countries. Amidst considerable publicity, Cuba sent delegations to the World Conference on International Women's Year held in Mexico City and to the World Congress of Women held in Berlin in October, 1975.[43] Prior to the Berlin congress, Cuba co-sponsored a regional preparatory seminar on "The Access of Women to Study and Work" for delegates from Central America and the Caribbean. International Women's Year has also been used as a time to publicize the past and present work of women in revolutionary movements, particularly in Latin America and in Indochina.

In addition, the government continues to promote alternative images and life-styles for women, particularly as *miliciana* and guerrilla fighters, blue-collar and farm workers. They have not been as diligent, however (except through the Family Code), in projecting new images for men, although according to Margaret Randall, the Federation has decided that all elementary- and secondary-school children should take both shop and home economics classes.[44]

Perhaps the most intensively publicized new role model for women is that of the construction worker. The women's volunteer construction brigade sent to Vietnam has been especially showered with attention and

42. *Granma Weekly Review,* Sept. 7, 1975, p. 4.
43. Vilma Espín's address to the Mexico City conference appeared in *ibid.,* July 6, 1975, p. 10.
44. "Women's Continuing Struggle for Liberation," *Cuba Review,* Dec., 1974, p. 16.

praise, and newspapers regularly print photographs of women working on construction jobs in Cuba. Castro has predicted that there will be more workers in construction by 1980 than in any other sector except the sugar industry. Woman power is apparently a crucial factor in expansion of the construction industry, and increased construction—especially of homes, schools, and day-care centers—is crucial to the success of the Revolution.

By 1980 the government plans to provide 250,000 additional women with new jobs, which would bring their total representation to one-third of the work force. To this end, the government hopes to expand its day-care center capacity from 50,000 children in 1975 to 200,000 over the next five years, and its boarding-school capacity by an additional 120,000 students.[45] And, perhaps also to this end, the government was beginning to suggest that women have the potential to do the same work as men in every sector of the economy.[46]

In summarizing the progress of the women's movement in Cuba up to 1969–70, and in the five years since, we have tried to describe briefly some of the government's major legal and political actions in behalf of women's rights and some of the economic and cultural limitations to their successful implementation. It should be remembered, however, that government and Party leaders, as well as the administrators who had to implement and enforce their programs, were not of one mind on women's rights, nor were some rank-and-file militants who talked one line in public and practiced another at home. This was especially true in 1969–70, when the field work for this research was done.

II

We believe the autobiographies in this series of three volumes complement the skeletal descriptions of the Revolution's achievements and failures offered, here or elsewhere, by statistical summaries or the itemization of laws and programs. Limited as each informant was by her own experience and understanding, these life stories give, at best, only a partial picture of what was happening to Cuban women and to the nation as a whole. But by illustrating the varied responses of Cubans of different economic and socio-cultural backgrounds to their changing status, the life stories reveal the areas of greatest progress and those most resistant to change.

45. *Granma Weekly Review*, Dec. 8, 1974, pp. 2–3.
46. For example, see the interview with Elsa Simbaco Vilella, a construction worker sent to Vietnam, who said women were as "strong and self-sacrificing as the men" and "capable of doing the same type of work the men did." (*Granma Weekly Review*, Nov. 2, 1975, p. 7.)

The four women in this volume—Mónica Ramos Reyes, Gracia Rivera
Herrera, Pilar López Gonzales, and Inocencia Acosta Felipe[47]—
represent different class origins, occupations, educational levels, political
development, and general outlook. Three of the women are white, one
mulatto, and all but one have been married and separated from their
husbands. Two are mothers and all four have jobs outside their homes.
One was from a small town, one came from a rural background, and two
grew up in poor barrios of Havana. At the time of our study all were
residents of Havana, and three of the four were totally supportive of the
Revolution.

Mónica Ramos Reyes, twenty-four, is the youngest of the four women
and the only one who has been directly or indirectly involved with the
Revolution from early childhood. She is also the only one to have a
university education and to grow up in an economically secure family.
Her father, who died when she was eight, was a postal official, and her
mother, the daughter of a provincial civil servant and justice of the peace,
was a professional educator. Mónica, the youngest of three children, was
raised in Pinar del Río, Cuba's westernmost province. After graduating
from a parochial school in 1957, she and her mother moved to Havana,
where her older sister and brother were attending the University.
   Mónica Ramos was enrolled in an exclusive, North American–run
high school in which the student body was largely pro-Batista. At the
triumph of the Revolution, she helped organize the few revolutionaries
among the students, and when she was fifteen, she spent eight months in
the countryside as a *brigadista,* or student teacher, in Cuba's Literacy
Campaign. She entered the University of Havana in 1962, and that year,
just after her seventeenth birthday, married Francisco (Paco) Solis, a
fellow student. Their first child was born a year later, and their second in
1965, just before Mónica's graduation. During the first four years of her
marriage, Mónica was almost completely preoccupied with her studies
and political activities, and her children were cared for by a
housekeeper-nursemaid and by her mother. After graduation, Mónica
and Paco, a Party member, were both deeply involved in politics, their
careers, and voluntary work. They were frequently apart for long
periods and in 1969 they separated.
   Included in Mónica Ramos's story are excerpts from the autobiographical accounts of her sister Renée Ramos Reyes and her mother,
Beatríz Reyes González. Their voices are intended to give the reader a
greater understanding of Mónica and to complement her portrayal of

---

47. In Cuba (and most Spanish-speaking countries), children take the surnames of both
parents, with the father's name first. The mother's name is sometimes dropped. A woman
does *not* give up her own name when she marries.

some of the important people and events in her life. The excerpts also illuminate the dynamics of the family and are especially helpful in showing generational differences and similarities and the comparative effects of the Revolution upon mother and daughters.

As an educated, independent-minded career woman, Beatríz Reyes was not typical of the Cuban women of her generation. But despite her strong personality and economic independence, she was very traditional in her acceptance of the man's central role in the family, or at least the appearance of it, and she believed strongly in the nuclear family as "the foundation of the state." Committed to keeping the family together at all costs, Señora Reyes ran her home in traditional middle-class fashion and maintained a highly structured family life.

Beatríz Reyes had lived under a succession of dictatorial governments from Menocal to Batista and was almost always sympathetic to the principal opposition party of the period. She was, however, a political appointee, like her father before her, throughout her pre-1959 career as a teacher and school inspector. She and other members of her family became involved in the anti-Batista underground, eventually joining Castro's Twenty-sixth of July Movement, in which her older children were already involved. There is in her story an account of her brother-in-law's torture and murder by Batista's police, and a description of the painful division in the family after 1959.

Señora Reyes had ambitions for her three children and wielded a strong and at times domineering hand in their personal and intellectual development. In her desire for them to excel, she gave them opportunities for education and self-development that were extraordinary for Cuban children at that time. She was particularly eager for her daughters to have careers that would make them economically independent, although she encouraged them in the arts as well. As a pragmatist, she took advantage of available opportunities even when they were against her avowed convictions. For example, she was hostile to the dogma of the Church, but she enrolled her children in Roman Catholic elementary school because she believed the instruction given there was superior.

Although Señora Reyes was determined that her daughters have careers, she also sheltered and overprotected them, and for the conventional reasons kept them under close supervision. Immaturity was one of Mónica Ramos's most striking qualities. When she joined the Literacy Campaign in 1961, for example, she had never been away from home and the emotional shock was very great for her. Her close ties to her family, however, and the strong support and affection she received in her home helped Mónica develop self-confidence and a sense of independence from her peers. But the indulgence she had experienced at home as the baby of the family, and the exceptional amount of attention

given to her education and development led Mónica to believe she was
superior to others. This did not make her a very likely candidate for the
Union of Young Communists (UJC), for which she was selected in 1962.
From the beginning, she was unwilling to subordinate her own opinions
to a party line, or be subjected to the criticisms of members she considered her "inferiors."

Like many young middle-class Cubans in the 1950s and earlier,
Mónica became involved in political activity long before she understood
the nature of the issues at stake. She had a broad moral inclination that
directed her to one political movement as opposed to another, but be-
neath that, no substantive grasp of the individual issues. Mónica's discussion of her involvement in the Young Communists was insensitive to
what was happening in student politics and university reform across the
country. For example, she interpreted her reclassification and demotion
in the UJC during 1965 as a wholly personal attack, while ignoring or
oblivious of the university-wide reorganization of the Youth. She was so
upset by the criticism of her work in the organization that she asked for
her membership to be revoked, and she was, in fact, finally expelled.
Four years later, Mónica regretted her reaction to her demotion but
said, "I can have the same attitude toward life as the militants [Youth
and Party members] and do the same things. I don't need a label."

Mónica's sister Renée also rejected outright the prospect of membership in the Youth or Party. Disenchanted with political organizations
although outspoken proponents of the Revolution, both women hoped
to serve it through their careers and volunteer work. Renée Ramos, eight
years older than Mónica, began her career like her mother, as a teacher,
but temporarily stopped working during the early years of her marriage
to go abroad with her husband, who worked in the Foreign Ministry. At
the time she was interviewed, she was separated from her husband, her
children were in boarding schools, and she held a government position
of considerable administrative and organizational responsibility. For
Renée, as for Mónica, it was work rather than family that dominated her
life.

The relationship between Mónica and Renée was one of deep affection, mutual admiration, and dependence. They considered themselves
allies against their mother, who they believed inflicted her ambitions and
frustrations upon them. They were antagonistic to her as a mother,
rejecting her domineering influence and erratic emotional outbursts, yet
they admired her as a professional woman, and to some extent they
imitated her.

The two sisters differed most markedly from their mother in their
attitudes toward their own homes and families. They gladly left their
children in nursery and boarding schools and accepted long separations
from their husbands, and, in general, subordinated family togetherness

and home life to the needs of their careers, or, as they would say, to the needs of the Revolution. Mónica listed her priorities in the following order: the Revolution, her career, and her children. Neither Mónica nor her sister seemed to regret the breakdown of their old family customs, and in fact seemed relieved to be freed from them.

Gracia Rivera Herrera, twenty-seven, unmarried and living at home with her mother, was working as a secretary at the time of this study. Although her family was poor, Gracia had managed, with moral support from her mother, to graduate from business school. Her father was an alcoholic whose small poultry business had many ups and downs and finally failed. Her mother had been a domestic servant as a girl and assisted her husband in his business for most of her married life. She blamed her husband's business failures on his drinking and often criticized him to her children, building a barrier between them. "Because of her," said Gracia, "I always considered my father a coward and a failure." When Gracia was sixteen her parents separated, and as the eldest child she had to take a job to help support her mother, sister, and two brothers.

Gracia's traumatic home life, which she attributed to her father's drunkenness and unstable personality and to her mother's "lack of initiative," led Gracia to reject her entire family. Her great ambition was to be a "good" person, but that had no deeper meaning than being "successful" and "respectable." Having no acceptable role models in her home, Gracia imitated the most visible symbols of respectability, and tended to become attached to authority figures, who were easily able to guide and dominate her.

Although initially an ardent supporter of the Revolution, Gracia Rivera, a devout Roman Catholic, was recruited into counterrevolutionary activity in 1960 while doing volunteer work in a Catholic hospital. After the arrest of two of her co-workers and the doctor who had recruited her, Gracia joined a religious institute committed to working within the revolutionary system, and eventually she became a nun. She remained in the religious order for seven years, during which time she had a very damaging love affair with the tyrannical, sadistic priest who ran the institute. In 1969, suffering from a nervous breakdown, Gracia left the order and underwent psychotherapy and shock treatments.

Included in Gracia's story are excerpts from the interviews with her father, who was also searching for success and respectability, albeit by a different path than his daughter. Their voices present a counterpoint of different perspectives on the Revolution and on their family life.

Of the four women, Gracia Rivera was the only one who had opposed the Revolution, but she did not have the strength to remain a dissenter once the authority of the Revolution was complete. She was, essentially, a follower of authority who by 1969 was slowly gravitating from the

Church to the Revolution. She was still actively involved in lay Church work but her boyfriend was a Party member. Partly to please him she volunteered for agricultural labor and was beginning to integrate in the Revolution. She tried to resolve the conflict she felt between her religion and her work for the Revolution by emphasizing the parallels between socialist and Christian ideals. Her problem, however, was not so much one of opposing ideals as it was one of competing authorities. Had Gracia's belief been in fundamental Christian principles rather than in the Church as an institution, her conflict might not have been so great. Having made the decision to stay in Cuba and needing to be in harmony with authority, Gracia was aware that her convictions would have to be redefined. This may become easier for her as the new definitions of respectability and success become apparent and widely accepted within the socialist context. As she herself said, "If only I knew some revolutionaries I could look up to, it might help me make up my mind to commit myself to the Revolution."

The third story in this volume is that of Pilar López Gonzales, twenty-eight, a former prostitute who in 1970 was working as a laboratory technician and studying in a pre-university adult-education program at the University of Havana, where she hoped to continue studying after graduation.

Her job and educational opportunities were part of a special educational and rehabilitation program set up for ex-prostitutes in 1961. Pilar López was among the first group of women to attend the rehabilitation school, and from the start she was determined to have a university education. Her adjustment to her new life, however, was not smooth; she suffered two breakdowns and underwent psychotherapy. But she studied diligently and eventually became one of the rehabilitation program's most successful students.

The offspring of an interracial marriage, Pilar was born in Havana in 1942, the second of eight children. Her father, who was white, worked as a bus driver and at a variety of part-time jobs that kept him away from home much of the time. Her mother, a mulatto, was a housewife who had never held an outside job. Although the family was not destitute, Pilar and her brothers and sisters often experienced hunger because of her mother's mismanagement of the family income and her father's inability to cope with the situation. Pilar, particularly, suffered from neglect and physical abuse and described herself as the "punching bag" of the family. Because she was dark-skinned and not a boy, her mother rejected Pilar at birth and openly preferred her brothers and lighter-skinned sisters. Pilar was also rebuffed by her paternal grandmother, who preferred the grandchildren who could "pass" as white.
Pilar was also rejected by her paternal grandmother, who preferred the tary school, but her mother would not permit it. At thirteen Pilar took a

job as a live-in maid and each month sent her 30-*peso* salary home to her mother. At fourteen Pilar married a twenty-eight-year-old laborer who earned 3 *pesos* a day. The marriage was short-lived and ended, at Pilar's insistence, after the birth of their daughter.

Entering prostitution soon thereafter, Pilar again turned over most of her earnings to her mother. During the following two years the young woman suffered almost every form of degradation, and her physical condition deteriorated rapidly from heavy use of alcohol and other drugs, as well as from numerous (illegal) abortions. She appeared completely defeated by a system whose every bad feature—economic oppression, racism, sexism, authoritarianism, and physical abuse—had been reflected in her family, unredeemed by a single good relationship. By 1961, when the revolutionary government started the rehabilitation program, Pilar had made at least two attempts on her life.

During her first nineteen years, Pilar was basically apolitical, indifferent to both the Batista and Castro governments. She was grasping at straws, not pursuing ideals, when she joined the rehabilitation program, but through her own transformation she developed confidence in the Revolution.

After completing rehabilitation school, Pilar was given a furnished house and for the first time was able to provide a home for her daughter. She gave birth to a second daughter as the result of an affair with a married official of the factory where she worked. She broke off this relationship and in 1965 married another man, who divorced her a few years later. In 1970 Pilar was living alone with her daughters, who attended boarding school and came home on weekends.

Having been given an education, economic security, a home, and, more important, a sense of dignity and personal worth, it is not surprising that Pilar López became an ardent revolutionary. In addition to being responsible in her work and studies, she was active in her block Committee, the Federation of Cuban Women, and the student militia. But Pilar was not a blind follower; she had a cynicism that was lacking in the other three women in this volume, probably because she had had so many negative experiences with authority and had been such a constant loser.

Pilar López's grim account reflects the condition of many lower-class women in pre-revolutionary Havana. Her particular problems were so deep and difficult that despite the optimistic undercurrent and the "happy ending," a complete recovery seems almost too good to be true. She had, however, found some stability in her relationship with her children, in her work and voluntary activities, and was making fairly steady progress toward the university career she so badly wanted.

Inocencia Acosta Felipe, a fifty-four-year-old former domestic servant, was the ninth of twelve children. Her mother and father were

Cuban-born of Spanish parentage. After fighting in the War of Independence from Spain, Inocencia's father became a small *colono* or
sugar-cane farmer. The family lived comparatively well and Inocencia
recalls her early childhood with great nostalgia. Like Mónica Ramos, and
in sharp contrast with Gracia Rivera and Pilar López, her early years
were spent in a well-ordered home free from want. Her family followed
strong traditions and maintained strict discipline, but didn't rely on
physical punishment. Inocencia had only happy memories of her childhood, associating her best years with her father, whom she passionately
loved. Sure of her parents' love, she respected her elders and, at least as
a child, had high self-esteem. Throughout her life she had a positive
attitude toward work and did not question her own virtue, intelligence,
or attractiveness.

During the crisis in the sugar industry in the 1920s, Inocencia's family
lost their farm, and a year later, when she was eight, her father died.
Thereafter her life changed sharply for the worse. Her mother, unable
to support the children, sent them to live with relatives. Over the next
decade Inocencia stayed in the homes of her aunt and married sisters,
functioning more or less as a servant. She entered school at age ten and
attended irregularly for three years. At twenty-one she moved to
Havana to take a job as a maid.

Inocencia Acosta spoke of her years of domestic service without serious complaint against her employers, but she felt the humiliation and
frustration of her subordinate, dependent position. At twenty-seven, to
escape her situation and to gain greater security and a home of her own,
she married. But her dream of greater independence and freedom to
express herself went unrealized, for she submitted to her husband and
suppressed her own will. She fantasized about leaving him but could find
no moral support to do it. Unable to ignore the prevailing negative
attitudes toward divorce and with no acceptable means of becoming
self-supporting, Inocencia reluctantly tolerated the marriage for the next
twenty-five years. During that time her greatest satisfactions were in her
job as a saleswoman and in helping the anti-Batista underground. Her
anger against her husband mounted, but it was not until after the Revolution that she gained the economic security and the courage to get a
divorce. Like Pilar López, Inocencia associated the Revolution with her
personal liberation.

Many of Inocencia Acosta's personal traits suit her admirably to life
under the Revolution. In particular, her religious background and ideals
of selflessness, productivity, and service were very compatible with the
Revolution's demand for self-sacrifice and austerity. She spent all her
after-work hours sewing, without charge, for friends and neighbors and
participating in local mass organizations, where her strong sense of integrity helped her to denounce free-loading bureaucrats.

Some of Inocencia Acosta's attitudes, such as her early-acquired, deeply held views on race, religion, and sex roles, were not in agreement with the official revolutionary position. Although she expressed her opinions forcefully and did not always avoid confrontations, she also accommodated in a practical way to political realities. Her racism, her acceptance of male superiority, and her belief in God did not seem to interfere with her integration in the Revolution or cause her any conscious conflict. This was made easier by her genuine concern for people, especially those who measured up to her standards of morality, hard work, and dependability.

Inocencia Acosta Felipe was the most mature and even-mannered of the four women, which is not surprising given her age and her very happy and stable early childhood. Those positive first eight years have undoubtedly helped her to cope successfully with the more difficult times she has had since. One of the most striking features of Inocencia Acosta's life is the lack of excess—the absence of any great new sorrows or joys—after the death of her father. This may be due in part to her compulsion toward convention and moderation in expressing herself, but it is also true that she did not experience the other three women's wide range of emotional problems. Inocencia was decidedly practical, never seeming to take on more or less than she could handle, and, of the four women, she seemed best acquainted with her talents and abilities and the best able to put them to work for herself and for others.

In one way or another and at different stages of their lives, these women had freed themselves from at least some aspects of the traditional female sex role and were searching for broader identities than those of wife and mother. Each of the women had surpassed her mother in education, in economic independence, and in sexual freedom. Collectively they were representative of a trend among Cuban women toward incorporation in the labor force, mass organizations, and continuing-education programs, but they were exceptional among the women interviewed in 1969–70.

In retrospect, it is surprising how small a direct role the organized women's movement played in the lives of these four informants during the first ten years of the Revolution. One woman was privately employed and had never joined the Federation of Cuban Women. The other three were members—it was virtually impossible to be assigned a state job without presenting a Federation membership card or a letter from the local Federation delegation—but only one said anything about its activities or its meaning to her. All three were trying to be good revolutionaries—to be what Fidel wanted them to be—and they assumed that a woman integrated in the Revolution was a liberated woman. None of the four was interested in women's rights as such or in developing a feminist perspective. They were therefore less involved with discussing their rights or with understanding what it meant to be a woman in a male-dominated world than they were with serving the Revolution.

Four Women

24°

Tropic of Cancer

PINAR DEL RÍO   HAVANA   Matanzas Varadero   Sabana Archipelago

Sierra de los   Artemisa   Cárdenas
Organos   Consolación   Güines   Colón   Sagua la Grande
          del Sur   San Cristóbal   Surgidero de   V
Pinar   Los Palacios   Batabanó   Jagüey   Santa
del Río   Ovas   Grande   Clara
                                                        Cienfuegos
22°   Gulf of   Girón
                      Batabanó   Sierra de   Sancti
                  Nueva Gerona   Escambray   Trinidad   Spíritus

                          Isle of
                          Pines

                    Caribbean Sea

20°

Bier

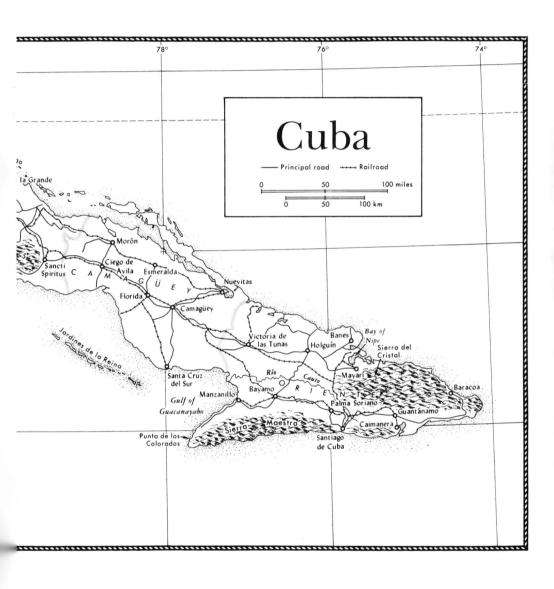

78°   76°   74°

Cuba

—— Principal road   ++++ Railroad

0   50   100 miles

0   50   100 km

la Grande

Morón

Sancti   Ciego de   Esmeralda
Spiritus   Avila
C A M A G Ü E Y
Florida   Nuevitas
Camagüey

Jardines de la Reina
Victoria de   Banes   Bay of
las Tunas   Holguín   Nipe
Sierra del
Cristal
Santa Cruz   Río   Cauto   Mayarí
del Sur   Bayamo   O R I E N T E   Baracoa
Gulf of   Manzanillo   Palma Soriano
Guacanayabo   Guantánamo
Sierra   Maestra   Caimanera
Punta de los
Colorados   Santiago
de Cuba

PART I ✴

Mónica Ramos Reyes

Chapter One

My Family

IF THEY ASKED ME TOMORROW, I'd give my life for the Revolution. I don't see anything strange in that, even if I am middle-class. It seems to me the middle class can very well be incorporated into the Revolution, even if it does keep some traces of its old ways. I know middle-class people who are more revolutionary than people of humble status. I don't know much about the lives of famous revolutionaries, but I would guess that every one of them was middle-class. I have an explanation for that: the middle class, unlike the poor, had the chance to study, and unlike the rich, who had all they wanted, the middle class had the ambition to better themselves. So the young people went to the universities where revolutionary ideals were most fervent. That's what happened to me and my family.

I don't know how or why my love for the Revolution was born. I know that by the time I was ten or eleven I already cared about politics. I listened eagerly when the grownups talked about Batista. I wanted to know everything. When someone was killed, I suffered. I felt the death of some loved one was always imminent. I longed to grow up and fight the tyranny. When my brother and sister went to demonstrations I was in agony because I couldn't go along. I felt useless and it hurt.

The aims of the Revolution are so great that I must give my entire life to attaining them. I cannot give myself wholly to a man and let him become an end in himself. I don't want to feel I couldn't live without him. I refuse to depend on anybody. I will fight that . . . always!

Just now, the focus of my life is the Revolution, which I serve through my work. I feel that as a psychologist I can fulfill myself and at the same time be useful to the Revolution. The new viewpoint here in Cuba—that a psychologist is to serve the community—makes it possible to combine

Mónica Ramos's life history is based on five interviews with her by Oscar Lewis, in addition to three interviews with her mother and two with her sister. An aunt was also interviewed but not included. The account presented here was based upon 598 pages of original transcribed Spanish material.

both kinds of satisfaction. So the Revolution and my work are the two central interests in my life. My third interest is my children. To them and to my grandchildren and the rest of their generation will fall the task of carrying on the struggle in the rest of Latin America.

My parents were middle-class, but they weren't rich. Neither of them owned property, and we lived entirely on their salaries. When they were first married, *papi* worked as a postal official in Consolación del Sur,[1] earning a little over 130 *pesos* a month, and *mami* made almost 300 as a teacher. Between them they earned quite enough to be well off in a small town. So from the day I was born I lived in a good house, wore the best clothes, and was sent to the best schools. As a child I never felt there was anything I could ask for and not get. We always had a laundress and a housemaid, and when my brother and sister were small there was also a nursemaid for them. I remember the Day of the Three Kings as a fantastic event. I always got millions of toys, some ordered specially from Spain. Of course it never occurred to me to question our way of life. It was simply the way we lived.

I was born on November 1, 1945, the youngest in the family. My brother Silvio is nine years older than I, and one year older than my sister Renée. I was born by mistake. I mean, I hadn't been planned for. *Papá* was a diabetic, obsessed with the idea he would die at forty-two, and he didn't want any more children. My parents were much older when I was born, and a baby in the house must have been a great event. I found a great deal more acceptance than Renée ever had. *Mami* says that Renée was a pretty but very difficult child, always whining. My sister was dark, and was jealous of Silvio because he was so much better looking. He was a beautiful boy, blond with pink-and-white skin. But my mother had us all classified: Silvio was the brain, Renée the beauty, and I the most affectionate—so much so that I'd kiss any passerby in the street. The matter was settled for all time so far as my mother was concerned. Somebody once had the bright idea of telling *mamá* I was prettier than Renée, and *mamá* practically had a fit. Still, of the two of us, I'm my mother's favorite, although I don't feel much for her.

Mamá has an extremely labile temperament—pathologically so. She must have had a strong and energetic temperament to begin with. Even when she was a girl she was used to dominating everybody, especially her brothers and sisters. Her stepmother was a meek, downtrodden woman and it was *mamá* who gave the orders in that home. When a situation came up that she couldn't deal with, she fell back on dramatics. She developed that pattern early and has never given it up.

Renée and I suffered from *mamá*'s dramatics. When we did anything

1. In the province of Pinar del Río.

she didn't like, she wept and ranted and said we were killing her. One of her favorite tragic outbursts was, "My children don't love me!" Or else, "I'm going to kill myself!"

It was important to Renée, I suspect, to have a little sister to whom she could be a mother completely different from *mamá*. Besides, a sister would be an ally. So she and Silvio lavished affection on me. I'm sure none of Renée's own children have ever meant as much to her as I did. She thought of me as her daughter and would cry if the maids bathed or fed me instead of letting her do it. It was Renée who taught me to walk at nine months. *Mamá* says I didn't make any effort, and she gives Renée all the credit for it.

It seems that I was a happy and outgoing child and *papá* focused all his love on me. He had ignored Renée but delighted in taking me out. He used to go to bed early and I always ran to lie down beside him. I remember he had a mustache and a very hairy chest. I liked to pull the hairs and cut them off with nail scissors. Sometimes he'd scold me, but I'd go right on hacking away, doing whatever I pleased with him. I spent my days around him and I never tired of lavishing my love on him. We used to kiss and kiss and hug and hug. Then *mami* would come in and say, "Get this child off our bed. You make me tired!" But *papá* would always say, "No, no, let her stay."

He was sweet, very sweet. When I think of him the first thing I remember is his gentleness. He scolded me only once and it still hurts to remember. It was all because of Benito, *mami's* epileptic half-brother who sometimes stayed with us. *Papá* was always careful about the way Benito was treated and wouldn't let anyone bother him. But one day, when I was about seven, I began to tease my uncle and call him names. Benito complained, and *papá,* in his gentle way, said, "How can you do such a thing? I wouldn't have believed such a good little girl could be so mean." I was crushed.

Papá spoke only when he had something pleasant to say. He never raised his voice in anger—in fact, he never raised his voice at all. He spoke so softly you could miss what he said if you didn't pay close attention. The only time I ever saw him act aggressively was when he came home from work one day and found me sitting at the piano crying. *Mamá* had forced me to take piano lessons from the time I was very little. I detested the piano and would have liked to kick ours to pieces but I was terrified of *mamá*. She'd set a clock on top of the piano and tell me, "You must practice two hours." The conflict built up in me until I would weep straight through the practice period. A lot of good it did me! I could have wept tears of blood for all *mami* cared. She said I had to practice two hours, and two hours it was.

Papi knew nothing about it until the day he found me crying there. "What's the matter?" he asked, very upset. "Why are you crying?"

"Because *mami* makes me take piano lessons."

"She what! She *makes* you?"

He called *mami* and said, "Listen well to what I have to say"—all this in a low, controlled voice—"Mónica's piano lessons are going to stop right this minute. If she doesn't want to take piano lessons she will not take them. If I ever find her crying at the piano again I will burn the instrument. And that's that."

Mamá left me in peace for about two weeks. Then one day she said, "You are to begin practicing again. But if your father ever finds you crying about it, I'll kill you!"

So I started all over again and never dared tell *papi*. When I saw him coming, though, I'd get up and walk boldly around. Strong as she was, *mami* respected my father and didn't dare punish me in his presence. If she started one of her tantrums, *papi* would simply walk out of the house for a couple of hours. He never quarreled. But *mamá* was always anxious to have us learn things, so I studied piano for six years, ballet for ten; I was taught to play the mandolin, and at one point I had tennis lessons. If she'd had her way, I would have been doing sixteen things at the same time.

Mamá was particularly concerned about our intellectual development and from our earliest years taught us that our school work was more important than anything else. When I came home from school she'd say, "Change your clothes and get to your studies! Don't go thinking you can run out and play!" I often felt the urge to study, but when I heard that, I'd decide, "The devil with it!"

Mine was a passive resistance. It never occurred to me to play hooky or to stay home from school when I was sick, nor did I disobey *mami* openly and aggressively like Renée. *Mami* would say, "Will you help me do thus-and-so?" and I'd answer, "Yes, right away."

Two hours later she'd say, "Didn't I tell you to do this?"

"Ah, so you did, but I didn't do it." I drove her out of her mind that way!

Papi had a great sense of justice and a deep sympathy for the poor. There was a fellow called Bienvenido who lived in the worst barrio of Consolación del Sur. I remember how scared I was just passing by there. Bienvenido's job was to clean out septic tanks, so he was not only ragged but filthy twenty-four hours a day. You can imagine how people avoided him.

Yet when Bievenido came to our house, *papá* would invite him to sit down on the porch, light his cigarette, and sit there chatting with him as if it were the most natural thing in the world. At first it used to bother me when any of my friends taunted me, "Hey, Mónica, there's Bienvenido on your front porch." But I could do nothing about it, and after a time it didn't bother me and I no longer resented Bienvenido.

It's possible that I idealize *papi* too much and have an inaccurate picture of him. It may be that we would have sunk if *mamá* hadn't been there to keep us on an even keel. For instance, *papi* had no money sense at all. If he was sitting on the porch and a vendor passed by with a cart full of oranges, *papi* would ask, "How long have you been out today?"

"Since 10:00 A.M."

"Well, then, I'll buy a sackful."

That kind of thing made *mami* indignant. "But Guillermo, why?"

"How can I let that poor man push his cart around until maybe 6:00 o'clock?" *papi* would answer. "I can easily afford to buy all his oranges and let him go home."

And if that weren't enough, he loved to play poker, and he usually lost! That was his only real fault. His friends used to come to our house to play secretly, because gambling was illegal. First one would wander in, then after a while another, and so on, and if I saw a policeman in the neighborhood I'd run to warn *mami*.

After the poker game I'd say, *"Papi,* did you win or lose?" If he'd won, I'd ask for ice cream. If he'd lost, it was pointless to ask for anything. I never heard *mami* fuss about his gambling, but now I realize she must have had a hard time budgeting to keep us comfortable.

Papá's ways were so very different from *mamá*'s that I've often wondered how they ever came to marry each other. That's one of the hardest bits of analysis I've ever done. But perhaps between those two extremes of temperament they found some sort of balance.

My father's family was not as well off as my mother's. *Papá*'s father, Alberto Ramos García, was a Catalán, from Spain, and they say he was a very handsome red-bearded man. He was a contractor and traveled all over Cuba before he settled down in Consolación del Sur. My grandmother, Carmen Santiago, came from very humble Cuban and Indian stock, and was an uneducated women. She used to claim that Alberto was an engineer with a university degree. It's not likely, though he did seem to be a man of culture.

My grandfather died in 1913, two years after my father was born, leaving his wife and son utterly destitute. *Papi* was always very close to his mother because they were so alone. There were no other relatives nearby. Carmen took a job as a maid and her employers seem to have been good to her; *papi* had many pleasant memories of them.

I don't think *papi* got as far as the sixth grade in school. He started working as a postal clerk when he was very young and I don't know what happened to him between then and the time he met *mami* in 1927.

Mami's father, Salvador Reyes Rodríguez, was a judge, and her family was much larger and wealthier than *papi*'s. Salvador had married twice and had six children in all. My mother, Beatríz Reyes González, was the daughter of his first wife, and she had four half-brothers, Benito, Bernardo, Ramón, and Gustavo, and a half-sister, Mercedes. But *mami* called them her brothers and her sister and was fond of all of them. We were very close to her family up to the time of the Revolution.

Mamá was teaching school in a small town in Pinar del Río when she met *papá*. When the girls in town heard that a young bachelor was going to settle there they were overjoyed. The newcomer was *papi*. *Mami* tells me he was very good-looking, quiet, and serious-minded, with a sweet disposition. *Mami* thought he was older than she and when she found out it was the other way around she was terribly upset. Even so, they became sweethearts, and when *papi* was transferred to another town, he wrote to her and often came back to see her.

They were engaged for eight years, which seemed strange to me. I once asked, "*Mami,* how could you wait so long?" But she explained that *papi* had to support his mother, and she herself wanted to study and better herself. They were married in 1935, a year after *mamá*'s father died.

My Grandmother Carmen was a big problem; she couldn't resign herself to seeing *papi* married and living with another woman. I assume she was mentally ill—she spent about a year in Mazorra[2]—a woman with a terrific fixation on her son. To a certain extent I understand her. After all, he was the only one she had in this world. But I've heard she was such a mother. . . ! Carmen lived with my parents for some time and it was very tense! *Mami* was pretty difficult herself so the situation was bound to be explosive.

Señora Beatríz Reyes González:

I was born in Los Palacios, in the province of Pinar del Río, the younger daughter of Salvador Reyes Rodríguez and Martha González Galdós. I know little about my mother's family except that most of her brothers and sisters died of tuberculosis. Her father was Spanish and her mother came from the Canary Islands. Islanders aren't exactly famous for their meekness and I guess she had quite a temper. When I used to get angry, *papá* would say, "You're exactly like your grandmother!"

It's my impression that my father's ancestors were very well off indeed. My great-grandfather, who was killed by his slaves, had large coffee holdings, and my grandfather must have been very rich too, because he also owned a hacienda and slaves. I remember hearing how the slaves were punished by being put out in the hot sun all day long, with their hands tied to a stick. People didn't talk much about those things then, but now the Revolution is bringing them to light.

Though my father didn't go to the University, he had a tutor and a good general education. He became a first-rate carpenter and

2. A mental institution in a small suburb of Havana.

cabinetmaker. He was working for a Cuban tobacco company when I was born and we lived on a rented company farm.

Papá married twice. My mother was his first wife and the love of his life, but *papá* lost her when she died of tuberculosis before I was two. He spent over 5,000 *pesos* trying to save her, and he used to say, "It cost me my life." But it was no use. All my mother's family had the lung sickness, the "white plague" as it was called. It wreaked havoc in that family.

And then my adored sister Ana María died of tuberculosis too, when she was only eight. On her deathbed she said her farewells to everyone. It was terribly dramatic. I wept long and often after her death. People kept talking about her goodness and her beauty, and I thought, "If she was so wonderful, why did she have to die? Why couldn't it have been me instead?"

After my mother died, *papá* was the only parent I knew. "*Papá* is my *mamá*," I'd say to people. He was a good father, very good, and I'm so proud of him. He was everything in the world to me.

I was the only child of *papá*'s first marriage to survive, and I must have been pretty spoiled. In that house my word was God's word. "Beatríz doesn't want to," *papá* would say, and that was that. He was a man of character but I guess he was too fond of me or sorry for me or something.

I was about eight when *papá* married his second wife, Fermina. She was a cold, reserved person, the sort that never shows any affection even to her own children. All the same she was good, very self-sacrificing, and for her, *papá* was God.

But she couldn't control me. She managed her own children beautifully but I was too much for her. I suppose there was a bit of natural female jealousy in it, because *papá* so obviously adored me. I realize now that I was stronger and cleverer than she and I had a way with words. She'd threaten me, "Just wait till your father comes home!" But then when he got there she was too kind to say anything to him.

What I longed for most was to have a sister. That was my great dream. I couldn't bear the thought of going through life without one. If one of my schoolmates said, "*Mamá* had a baby sister for me," I'd remember the dead Ana María and I'd think, "*Ay*, if only I had a baby sister!"

Fermina's first two children were boys, and I was eleven years old before Mercedes was born. She was the greatest thing in my life. I felt as if she were my own daughter. In fact, I don't believe the birth of my own children was such a joy to me. You might say I took Mercedes away from her mother—with her mother's consent, naturally. I bathed her, sewed for her, took her wherever I went. Finally, I even got permission to have her sleep in my room.

And as for Mercedes, she too, as she grew up, came to think of me as her mother. If people asked her, "Which do you love best, your *mamá* or Beatríz?," she always answered, "Beatríz!" Of course at bottom she must have loved her mother best, that stands to reason, but it shows how she felt about me. It was Beatríz this and Beatríz that. She even imitated me, and when her friends said, "You're the image of your sister," how that pleased her!

I was enraptured with my brothers, too. There were even times when I thought, "If Fermina dies, they'll all be mine." Gustavo was my favorite, maybe because he was my godchild and I thought of him as my own. Cold and reserved as she was, Fermina had an obvious predilection for Ramón, who really was a charmer and was thought to be very bright. When the boys had some childish fight their mother always sided with Ramón, and I defended Gustavo with cloak and sword.

We children loved one another so dearly that nobody would have guessed we were only half-brothers and -sisters. And yet I remember my childhood as a difficult time. It wasn't that I was ever mistreated, but I couldn't miss the fact that everybody was nicer to me the minute *papá* walked in, so I was always glad when he got home from work.

Papá took great care of my morals. He scarcely allowed me out. There were certain girls he wouldn't let me associate with at all, and I grew up without any friends my own age. I lived on the margin of events. I read a lot—books of poetry, the magazine *Fígaro*—everything I could lay my hands on. But the truth is that even at fifteen I was childish and a bit of a tomboy.

It was from my father that I learned my ideals of womanhood. I had great faith in what he told me. For instance, when bobbed hair came into fashion I wanted to have mine cut. I was already a student at normal school, but I thought, "No, I must ask *papá* first." And when I asked him, he said, "Well, daughter, in my time only a loose woman would wear short hair." So I didn't cut mine.

But in fact *papá* was very modern and after a while he brought it up again himself. "Have your hair bobbed, child. It's the fashion now." He kept right up with the fashions. He was one of the first among the older men to begin wearing undershorts instead of long drawers, and also one of the first to change from boots to low shoes.

Los Palacios was a poor rural town when I lived there. It had one street running right through the middle, two side streets, and a few alleys, that's all. There were only two doctors and two drugstores.

Ah, the life in Los Palacios in my youth . . . how different it was from Havana! We followed the provincial custom of bathing in the afternoon and then dressing up, to pay calls on one another. And I remember the horse-drawn carriages. Every day at noon they would set off to meet the train while everybody sat on their porches to see them go by. When the first automobile appeared in Los Palacios, what a stir that made!

The Jiménez family owned all the land around. It was an enormous hacienda, much of it uncultivated. They lived in Havana and came around only once a year to collect the rent. I remember hearing people remark that they never spent any money on irrigation or improvements. But they charged very little rent so the peasants didn't think of them as exploiters. They even said the Jiménezes were noble-hearted. That's the way a Cuban *guajiro*'s mind works—the one who exploits him least is a hero.

My father was a politician but he seldom talked about it at home. He was a Conservative and I accepted his views. For me the two greatest misfortunes a person could suffer were to be a Liberal or a Negro. You see, when I was a child, Negroes weren't allowed in through the front door, only through the back into the kitchen. It was so depressing to see people treated like that. I used to hear Aunt Tania make remarks like, "The insolence of that Negro! He dared put out his hand as if I should shake it." That kind of thing hurt me so deeply I never, never taught my children any racist attitudes.

In spite of my careful upbringing I rebelled against many things. For instance, my father was a very competent man and it seemed to me he was underpaid. He said, "My child, we must try to be on good terms with everybody."

"No, we mustn't," I'd answer. "We should be on good terms only with people who are on good terms with us!"

After my father remarried, the politicians made him a judge in Los Palacios. At that time it wasn't necessary to be a lawyer in order to be a municipal judge. My father was pleasant and cultured, respected by everyone in town, and even the young girls used to crowd around to hear him talk. He got to be known as "the just judge." All the same, after he'd held that position for many years they passed a law that municipal judges had to be lawyers. He wrote to Judge Baños, who was to replace him, asking to be kept on in some capacity; he was made clerk of the civil registry.

I worked in the courthouse too, when I was only fifteen, and I earned 101.08 *pesos* a month. It was *papá* who got me the job. There were twelve employees in the courthouse and in my opinion that was eight too many. Then Zayas's[3] government came to power, and the judge had to eliminate six of them. He'd given jobs to his own two sons and to *papá* and me, two from each family. *Papá* said I should keep my job and he'd get work somewhere else, but I said no. I wouldn't work

3. Alfredo Zayas, President of Cuba 1921–25.

in a public office unless he worked there too, because I didn't like the kind of thing I saw going on there. Young as I was, I felt it went against my principles. So I said, "If you quit, I quit too. In fact, I'd rather go back to school."

Judge Baños had given my father the power to assign a number of scholarships to a nuns' school, so *papá* said, "Very well, child, I'll give you a scholarship." But I protested, "Oh no, you're not sending me to any nuns' school!" He let me do whatever I wanted because he idolized me, so he didn't insist.

One day about two years later, I said, "*Papá,* I want to study. I'm going to school in Pinar del Río."

"But child, you know I'm in no position to send you. How can I afford it?" He had six children, and studying in Pinar del Río was a very expensive proposition. I insisted and my stepmother sided with me: "*Ay,* Salvador, you have so many cattle. Sell some of them." Well, *papá* sold some cattle and I went to Pinar del Río to attend normal school.

I hadn't yet finished my studies when I got a position as a teacher in an elementary school. By then my sister Mercedes was thirteen and ready to study in normal school herself. I said to *papá,* "Now we'll all move to Pinar del Río so Mercedes can live at home. I don't want her living in a stranger's house as I did." So that's what happened. The whole family moved to Pinar del Río and settled there.

Mercedes counted on me for everything. I paid for her clothing as well as for my own, helped her with her homework, and directed her studies, because I'm an instinctive, natural teacher. I bought her a piano and she took lessons for over two years, but in her third year she gave it up. She was skillful at drawing, too, but she continued to study advanced education through extension courses, just as I did. We both took the courses in Pinar del Río and went to the University in Havana to take the examinations. I also took many, many courses in psychology. I am an educator, but I would have preferred a career as a clinical psychologist.

Mercedes lacked only seven courses to get her degree when she became Jaime's sweetheart. Jaime Pérez was the son of a government official who was quite a big shot in Pinar del Río at that time. Jaime's father opened up a new beach in Punta del Gato and built himself a house there. We built there too, and that's how Jaime and Mercedes met.

When they became sweethearts the first thing Jaime said was, "My wife isn't going to keep on studying." So Mercedes just quit, after we had paid her tuition and everything, and there was no point in it because they had a very long engagement. He earned so little that she was about thirty before they could get married. The same thing happened to me; those were very precarious times in Cuba, economically speaking. After her marriage, Mercedes moved to Ovas and I could feel her drawing away from me little by little, moving closer to her husband and his family. It was only natural, I suppose.

I raised two generations of children, my younger brothers and sister and my own children, as well as my brother Bernardo's daughter Laura, and I've seen to it that they all received an education. Of my three children, not one is a fool. I gave them the best education I possibly could.

My son was a very gifted child, entering the second grade at the age of five and graduating from sixth grade when he was only nine. Renée emulated him. She's only a year younger and she worked hard to keep up with him. She went to high school and normal school at the same time, not that she was so studious by nature, but because of her own pride and the discipline she learned at home. Mónica was a little over eight when her father died, and I always kept her very close to me. He left enough money for her education so I enrolled her in the best schools. She entered high school at eleven and graduated at fifteen.

My children studied the piano, violin, and mandolin, but when I saw none of them was musically gifted, I turned to other arts. I watched them for any sign of artistic talent. The two girls studied ballet, English, typing, Spanish, dance. Whatever I could afford I put within their reach while they were still children. And do you know why? To have a solid foundation on which to build in case one of them should turn out to be especially gifted. I didn't want them to be able to say, "I had the talent but nobody bothered to develop it."

I prepared them well and they made rapid progress in everything they did. I attribute their achievements to my own struggle and direction rather than to any special intelligence on their part.

MÓNICA:
Although neither of my parents was Catholic, I was enrolled at age six in a nuns' school in Consolación del Sur, the same one Renée had gone to. *Papá* had been an altar boy as a child, but he came to detest priests and nuns and the Catholic religion as a whole and became a Mason instead. *Mamá* grew up without ever hearing any talk of religion, pro or con. She doesn't hate Catholicism; she simply knows nothing about it and isn't the least bit interested. My brother went to a nondenominational school, but in those times it was considered very charming for a girl to be a devout Catholic. All the rich girls in the neighborhood went to the convent and my parents wanted me to grow up to be very refined.

Mostly I played with well-brought-up, sheltered little girls whose standard of living was much like mine. When I made one friend who was much poorer than I, *mami* forbade me to play with her, saying she was a little tart with sweethearts all over the place and was bound to be a bad influence. But we lived in the same barrio so it was inevitable that I should play with her, no?

Because my parents were atheists, I found no support at home for my Catholic ideas, and the things the nuns said began to create conflicts in me. For instance, once they started a campaign to get all the girls whose parents weren't married in church to persuade them to remarry according to Catholic rites. I resolved to do it. But first I had to teach my parents to pray. I tried with *papi*, but it was so much wasted effort. I failed completely. Most of the other girls' parents had been married in church in the first place, and, except for mine, the few who hadn't were persuaded to do so. That put me at a disadvantage at school.

Another time, I told my family that the Virgin Mary had ascended to Heaven, body and soul. My brother analyzed my statement, scientifically and in minute detail. "Look, the greatest velocity at which a solid body can travel is such-and-such"—I forget the exact figures. "If the Virgin left the earth one thousand nine hundred and fifty-some years ago, she's been traveling such-and-such a number of days and hours." (I could see he'd spent a lot of time working it out and I was terrifically impressed.) "So, traveling at the greatest possible speed, the Virgin can't be any farther than the orbit of Saturn." Then he added, "If you want to check on it, ask the nuns."

Next day I said to my teacher, "My brother says that at this very moment the Virgin is in the orbit of Saturn. Is that right?"

"My dear child!" the nun exclaimed. "Your brother will go straight to Hell. You must pray for his soul." After that, they marched me off to chapel every single afternoon to pray for my brother.

Another thing that worried me was God. There He was high on a cloud, looking down on everything we did. And I did millions of bad things, like not going to church on Sunday because *mamá* didn't wake me up on time. That made me live in constant fear of the Last Judgment and eternal punishment, tormented by the thought that on that day they'd repeat to me, one by one, all my naughty deeds. I tried hard to be good, but my family was no help at all. What could I do? To my family the nuns were liars; to the nuns, my family were heretics.

In major points of faith the school did influence me, but I rejected some of the more trivial details of doctrine. Thus, I firmly believed in Hell but not in the story of Noah's ark. I knew perfectly well that the account of Eve being formed from Adam's rib was nothing but a childish tale. My brother and sister were both in high school by that time, and they'd jeer, "Don't let them make you swallow those stories. Men are descended from monkeys, not Adam and Eve. As for Noah's ark, how big would a ship have to be to hold a pair of every kind of animal in the world?" Then they'd explain things to me in very simple words, suitable to a child my age. So I knew those stories were big lies. But I never dared mention the subject at school.

I'd often go to my mother saying, "*Mami,* I need 2 *pesos* to buy religious pictures."

"Those nuns are a pack of thieves!" she'd burst out. "Money, money, money, that's all they care about! I will not give you 2 *pesos* to buy that junk; 50 *kilos*[4] is the most I can spare."

So I'd go to my father and say, "Nice, sweet *papito,* I love you very much." Then I'd give him lots of little kisses. I was quite a little flatterer and could wheedle anything out of him.

"What do you want now?"

"Two *pesos.*"

Papi never asked why I wanted money. He'd just put his hand in his pocket and give me 2 *pesos,* and that would make *mami* start in again. "How can you give a little girl all the money she asks for? It's just to buy a lot of little pictures of saints! You're letting the nuns rob her, that's all."

Actually I couldn't bear the nuns at school. I didn't hate the priests, poor guys. They led a sad life. The nuns didn't have the slightest notion how a child's mind works. They were from Spain, very old-fashioned, and I realize now that of all of the nuns in Cuba, they were the most reactionary. Never have I met any others like them.

Papi's death in 1954 brought on my greatest conflict at school. It nearly drove me crazy to think that my father was a Mason and all Masons went to Hell. I would have done anything in the world to get him transferred at least to Purgatory. I got no solace from the nuns, though. *Papá* was eternally condemned to Hell, they told me, and there wasn't anything I could do about it—not even if I became a nun.

So there I was—my father excommunicated and in Hell, my brother headed straight for Hell too, because he was a nonbeliever, and my sister always mocking the nuns. "Why don't you tell them to take God down from the altar and set up a coin instead?" she said. "That's what they *really* worship." I thought, "Surely Renée is excommunicated too, so what's the point of my going to Heaven? What would I *do* there?"

I desperately longed to believe that when I died I would be reunited with my whole family. But as long as I remained a Catholic, my only chance of meeting *papi* again was to be so bad that I'd go to Hell. So I lost interest in Heaven.

It was a great relief to leave the nun's school, to be able to say freely, "I don't believe these things." In a way it was hard on me, because along with my faith went all hope of an afterlife, and there are times when a

4. A *kilo* is equal to a *centavo.*

belief like that can be a great comfort. But at the same time I got rid of so many other trashy things that make life difficult! For the first time I understood what the Catholic religion was and why the nuns created that atmosphere for themselves—setting up a judge to watch over them twenty-four hours a day! That's the whole point of Catholicism.

I've often asked myself, to what extent does a child of eight know what death is? I had a very clear notion of it—it meant that *papi* was gone and I'd never see him again. It meant that other little girls had *papás* and I had none. Whenever I faced trouble I'd think, "If only I could talk this over with *papi!*" Even now, when things are hard for me, I say, "If *papi* were alive, *he* would help."

Renée, too, was deeply affected by *papá*'s death, even though she has some unpleasant memories of him. Sometimes when she talks about *papi* I think she's making up some sort of myth about him, but I don't try to disabuse her of it because I believe the myth does her good. She needs it.

Mami behaved quite normally when *papi* died. She didn't put on one of her tragic performances, which is something I still don't understand. Later, of course, she gave her dramatic instincts free reign because there was no one left to keep her in line.

Renée has suffered more than I from *mamá*'s personality problems and is much sicker emotionally, much more of a product of *mamá,* than I am. It's only logical; I came into the world later and was able to develop better defenses—antibodies, so to speak—against her pathological reactions.

RENÉE RAMOS REYES:

I loved Mónica and often asked *mamá* to give her to me. It's strange that I felt about my little sister Mónica the way *mami* felt about her little sister Mercedes. I felt toward Mónica as I do toward my own daughter, or perhaps more.

Everything about Mónica appealed to me. I'd bathe her, comb her hair, dress her up, take her in my arms and sing her to sleep every night. She came to be almost my own child, and as she was very responsive, she herself got too attached to me. She grew up wanting to be like me and she *is* like me. But I wanted her to be prettier than I was. All my life I considered myself very, very ugly and I knew that nobody loved me.

My mother was very strong-willed, and I could never get close to her unless she cried or showed her vulnerability. Then I felt strong and would seek her out. The stronger I felt, the closer I could get to her. So from the time I could talk, I tried to hurt her. I was always hurling accusations at her. I'd tell her she was a bad mother. I'd say, "You don't love me and never have." Then she'd torture me in return, say she was going to die, that it was my fault my father was sick, that I was incorrigible. I was afraid of her when we fought. She had no compassion at all.

Perhaps the worst time was just before my father died. She had attacks when she would create completely insane scenes. She'd say she was going to die or kill herself, that she hoped my daughter would make me suffer the same way, that she had nothing to live for, that she never wanted to see me again, that I should go away and the farther the better, that she wished I would die, that all of us would die. When she beat me I wouldn't ask her pardon for the world. And that didn't upset her. But when she was carrying on I'd get very nervous and want to change all the things she talked about, so I'd say, "Forgive me. I won't do it anymore. I love you."

I tried to save the situation that way, but she'd reject me and say, "Go away, you don't love anybody. You've never loved anybody from the moment I bore you." Imagine what it was like living with all that hysteria! My father never knew much about it because he was always off playing poker and I don't know what all else. When he happened to witness one of these battles, he'd say, "Don't fight with your mother. She's a very good person. She suffers on your account and she cares for you. She quarrels with you because you talk back. You're too bitter."

Once he told me, "I'm worried about dying. Not because of Silvio—his intelligence will carry him through. And not because of Mónica—she's so affectionate. I'm worried about you. You're such a rebel that nobody can get to love you. You'll be left alone with your mother and I know you don't love each other."

"But I do love my mother," I protested.

"No," he said, "you don't love her. If my mother had done to me what yours has to you, I wouldn't love her either. Even if you want to, you won't be able to love her, you simply won't. So I can't decide whether to leave you with her. It's always going to be the same between you."

"No, no," I told him, "I'm going to change. I'm going to be good to her."

I thought my mother was unjust because she *was* unjust. It's possible that my rebellion and identification with revolutionary action was a reaction against my mother's injustice, since she didn't approve of my attitudes. But I'm sorry *mamá* doesn't have any feeling for me because there are some things about her I admire a lot. For example, there are certain ways in which I know for sure she's much better than my father was. She has great character and extraordinary courage. She was an exceptional woman in her time because of her strong principles and her struggle against the politicians.

Politically my father was very bad, a Liberal, and the Liberal Party was the most reactionary in Cuba. Not that he was really interested in politics at all. He had a very important friend who was a big Liberal and he figured that would cover him in case of need, but he had no concern with social duty. My mother was anti-Liberal and considered herself anti-political, but she believed in Grau and the *Auténtico* Party against all opposition.[5]

The truth is, I wished I weren't my mother's daughter, and I was looking for something that would prove to me that I wasn't. As a child I identified most with my mother's sister, Aunt Mercedes, who was a beautiful woman. At home my father was my model. He wasn't at all dominated by my mother. On the contrary, when he came home, she'd test out his mood and adapt to it. *Papá* was very fair and had a great understanding and respect for other people, although I felt he didn't really love me, and he failed me at the most crucial moments. He wasn't very demonstrative or tender, at least not with me. His affection was always a little cold.

Papá was hermetic. He lived very much for himself and never felt the need to develop his character or sacrifice himself for others. Whatever he wanted in life he took. He gambled and nobody could change that or say anything against it. He spent freely, and whoever happened to be with him was in for a treat.

In those days I spent a lot of time with the maids in our house, and I enjoyed their company. If the maid was black, I liked her even better. I was always in the kitchen, with my mother calling me to come out of there. At the age of seven I knew all about the maids' private lives. I knew that one of them lived with a man, and I knew of their intimacies. When they took little Mónica out, I'd go along and we'd go to their homes. I always felt fine there; in the most miserable shacks I was happy. I realized that if a maid had a child, that child was left alone while the maid worked for us, and I hated it when *mamá* dawdled over dinner. My mother was nasty and nagging with the maids, though she'd help them sometimes. I suffered a lot for them.

One day I told my father I'd like him to play a number in the lottery and give me the ticket. And I asked, in case it should win, how much it would cost to buy a small house and put in plumbing and electricity. I was going to rent out the house, and with the money I made I'd build another house the maids could live in, and then another and another.

---

5. The Liberal Party was the party of Presidents José Miguel Gómez, Alfredo Zayas, and General Gerardo Machado, the latter one of Cuba's most notorious dictators. Dr. Ramón Grau San Martín was a founder of the *Auténticos*, the Authentic Revolutionary Movement, which was opposed to the government installed after Batista's 1933 military coup. As Hugh Thomas has said, the "movement was neither authentic nor revolutionary." (*Cuba: The Pursuit of Freedom* (New York: Harper and Row, 1971), p. 737.) Grau's own presidency, 1944–48, was no exception to the pre-revolutionary rule of corrupt governments.

My father told me my idea wasn't new, that it was called communism, and was on its way already. So I asked, "Why don't you do it then?"

"Because people are corrupt and later on they steal the money." He said they had communism in the Soviet Union, but that wasn't to say there weren't corrupt people there. I said it was a good idea anyway, and that we should do it too. I was sure it was right.

Since my father said this was communism, I began to tell everybody at the parochial school that I didn't believe in God because I was a communist. I was only about eight or ten at the time, but under the circumstances it was true. I was a rebel, all right. Emotionally I was a communist.

Chapter Two

Changes

MÓNICA:
Before *papá* died he agreed to let *mami*'s niece Laura come to live with us. It was typical of his generosity. Laura's father, my Uncle Bernardo, had lived in the United States for twenty years and had married an American. When Laura was fifteen, Bernardo abandoned her and her mother to marry a Mexican girl, and then he returned to Cuba. Shortly afterward Laura's mother died. On her deathbed she begged Laura never to go to Cuba—she must have thought this was a jungle—but when my cousin was about sixteen, she faced up to her North American grandparents and wrote to her father saying she wanted to come. Bernardo was in no position to keep her, so the whole family got together to discuss the matter. None of *mamá*'s other brothers wanted her, and they all tried to fob Laura off on somebody else. Then *papá* got up and said, "Laura will stay at my home! I'm the only person here who is not her blood relation, but Laura will be like a daughter to me." And so she was.

I don't have a distinct memory of Laura's arrival, except that she brought us all little presents. At first she didn't speak any Spanish. She could only say a few things, and with a terrible accent. *Mamá* taught her Spanish so she could enroll in high school as soon as possible. She practically forced Laura through the four years of schooling, yelling at her sometimes—that's *mamá*'s nature—but of course not when *papá* was around.

Laura took me to sleep in her room and from then on everything was different. She taught me to pray in English and heard me say my prayers every night. I felt she loved me dearly, although after I grew up I came to think that Laura didn't love anybody.

We were all very fond of Laura because she was happy, affectionate, and nice in so many little ways. For instance, I used to hate to have my hair shampooed because the soap got in my eyes. I'll never forget the day Laura put me in the bathtub and soaped my hair carefully, singing a children's song in English. The song was about animals and she imitated

the sound of each one in turn. Every time she did that, I had to open my eyes and I didn't cry at all.

That's the kind of memory I have of Laura. She was very sweet. She'd often buy me candy and take me out for a walk. But she was selfish, too. She was quite capable of waking *papi* at midnight and sending him out to get her some candy. She got whatever she wanted. She had even more privileges than Renée, though not more than I because I was the youngest and *papá*'s favorite.

Renée was awfully jealous of Laura. She's always felt so insecure about anybody's affection, and I probably sometimes said I liked Laura better than her. Renée did some pretty incredible things because she hated to see how fond I was of Laura.

One day I asked, "Renée, where's Laura?"

"Dead," Renée said.

"*Chica,* come on, tell me the truth. Where's Laura?"

"Dead, I tell you."

"Renée!"

"She's dead."

"Where's *mami?*"

"Gone to buy the coffin." That suddenly convinced me. I ran crying to our next-door neighbor, "Hilda, Laura is dead!"

"Child, are you crazy?"

"It's true! Renée told me so!"

"She was teasing you."

"No she wasn't! *Mami*'s gone to buy the coffin."

Then she said, "Look, child, there they come, both of them." And there they were, calmly coming down the street. But it had given me such a shock I ran a fever of 39° centigrade that night.

Like any other North American girl, Laura talked to everybody, went everywhere, and had boyfriends all over the place. My parents were so narrow-minded about sex, all that was a shock to them. But they more or less put up with whatever she did until she got involved with a married man much older than she. That was too much for *papi.* He told Bernardo he couldn't be responsible for Laura's behavior any longer.

"Let her stay with you in Havana," *papi* said. "If that man is serious, he'll divorce his wife and marry Laura." So Laura left. It was very painful for me. I was only about eight years old then and I didn't understand why she went until I was much older. That happened only a short time before *papá*'s death.

RENÉE:

The most important things for me during my teens were ballet, politics, and my high school studies. I spent all my time studying. I was twelve when I entered high school, and a few days before school began

I had my first menstrual period. A great change came over me, although I still looked younger than my age. I wasn't one of those girls everybody turns to look at; I didn't even look pretty at my big fifteenth birthday party.

I began to draw away from my mother and father, from everything in my familiar surroundings. I enjoyed other things, like reading books that nobody else read—Tolstoy, for example—and the more serious the book the better. All the girls used to stroll in the park together at night, but my mother wouldn't let me go. However, I wouldn't let *her* forbid me; instead I decided for myself that I wasn't interested. What I wanted was to be alone so I could look into myself and discover everything about me. It wasn't that I was really so different but that I had a need to be different.

High school began at 10:00 A.M. and met only in the mornings. I loved it. I felt I was learning things all intelligent people should know. My mother wanted me to train as a primary teacher because she thought I wasn't clever enough to do anything else. I needed seventh and eighth grades to get into normal school, so in the afternoon I attended a Catholic school run by nuns.[6] I hated that place. Then, at five, I went to a special English class, and later I also took evening classes in painting and modeling at an art school. So I felt I had a very solid background compared to the rest of my schoolmates.

At the art school I got to know Carlos Sosa, who was thirty-one. I'd met him before, at the beach when I was a child. He was a primary-school teacher at that time and understood children so well that all his pupils loved him. You could say he was the "unforgettable character" of my adolescence. But that's all water under the bridge—he means nothing to me now. But he sang beautifully, knew all sorts of stories, was a fine art teacher, and was very gentle and sweet with people, too, a man of extraordinary sensibility. Our relationship was very intense both intellectually and emotionally, but you must understand it was also very innocent.

I was always happy when it was time to go to the art school. It was a public school where the students went to talk of higher things, but not for the wrong reasons. A student there, for example, might be whistling an aria from an opera while he was painting. All that appealed to me.

In the midst of this, my cousin Laura arrived from the United States. She was a tall, stunning-looking girl, very extroverted and affectionate, and also quite self-centered. We soon became very good

6. In the pre-revolutionary educational system, high school was a five-year university-preparatory program (the *bachillerato*) that began after the sixth grade. Entry into the normal, or teacher-training, schools generally followed completion of the eighth grade.

friends. I needed her, you see, but I overestimated her intelligence. Actually, I dominated her and felt I controlled her.

Laura began coming to art school with me. Once when we were studying—I was the one who led in our studies—I noticed that she was flirting with Carlos, but it didn't occur to me that he would take any interest in somebody as superficial as she was. I thought she was making a fool of herself. Besides, he was married, though he didn't have any children.

Then one day Laura told me she was Carlos's sweetheart. It was a terrible blow to me, because this lovely relationship I had with Carlos made me feel very special. I blamed Laura and attacked her morals. I hoped it was only wishful thinking on her part, but one night Carlos told me about his great love for her. In fact, he built up a whole romance around it.

I felt miserable, profoundly miserable. I cried all the time he was talking. His relationship with me had been nothing but a cover and all the things he had ever told me, even on other subjects, were lies too. We'd talked about art and literature, about the Rococo, about Oscar Wilde and other writers, and now it all seemed worthless, as if he'd talked off the top of his head to find a way of being with her. When he said he also had a deep affection for me, I cried and cried and couldn't stop. I was in love with him all right, but he'd never kissed me nor so much as taken my hand. He was my first romantic love.

I persuaded myself that I had to be very sympathetic to Carlos and Laura, and defend their relationship even above my own interests and principles. So from that moment on I lived through the tension of their love along with them. I lived out the feeling I had for him through her, and she grew in my esteem. I assumed that if he loved her there must be something more to her.

Sometimes I tried to influence Laura to act as I might have done in her place. She was a very happy person—all woman, placid and beautiful, and very well-developed sexually, but not particularly dramatic. Their romance was idyllic, very platonic. They liked to get together and talk for hours. We were supposed to be home from school at 11:00 but they'd go on talking until midnight, and when we got home *mamá* would beat me. I couldn't explain why I was so late, even though I knew that the next day I'd be just as late, and the next too, for that matter.

One time my mother came to school. Not that she knew what was going on, but it was already 11:00 and she suspected we might be with men. All she found were Carlos and Laura talking at one table and me talking with somebody at another. She marched us home, shoving me all the way. I put up with this and was even glad of it. It was a point of honor with me to bear this burden, you see.

It must have been about 1950, when I was in the second year of high
school, that I learned about Carlos's best friend, Héctor. He was an
accountant and also a cartoonist for magazines in Pinar del Río and
Havana. One day he dropped around to talk with Carlos. It was only
for a moment, but I saw he had very clear eyes and I was intrigued
even though he hadn't noticed me. Carlos was worried because Héctor
was having an affair with his own ex-wife, who was a bad sort for all
her culture and intellect. After Héctor and she were divorced she
married someone else, but then she and Héctor became lovers. His
attachment to her seems to have been a whole drama. Carlos also said
that Héctor was a bohemian, that all he liked was drawing, drinking,
and reading, that he was indifferent to getting ahead and had no
desire to be an accountant as his father wished. From that time on I
stopped dreaming about Carlos and began to fantasize about Héctor,
about how I might be able to change him.

In about the third year of Carlos and Laura's romance, trouble
broke out at home, and from then on this story becomes rather ugly.
Laura wrote a letter in English to a friend, telling all about her romance, and my mother found the letter. She got my brother to trans-
late it and afterward there was a great to-do. *Papá* sent for Uncle
Bernardo, and then both of them sent for Carlos.

Now Carlos was given to inventing stories about his wife, saying that
she didn't love him, didn't understand him, that she was a very difficult person. It was partly true but he couldn't just walk out on her.
He wanted to wait until he earned enough to help her be economically
independent after they separated.

Then Carlos put on this beautiful performance about how much
Laura meant to him, how he was in love with her and would marry her
and that nothing else had ever occurred to him. He swore he'd never
touched her, that they had done nothing but talk. That was his story,
and *papá* was completely taken in by it because Carlos is a great actor.
It's not really that he's dishonest, but he's not very stable.

Carlos was very sweet, very appealing, asking only that they not send
Laura to her father but keep her with us for a year. He said he
wouldn't see her for six months and would think over what would
make them both happiest. Two weeks later Laura was offered a job as
English teacher in the same school he taught in. And would you believe it? My father said it would be fine.

But the six months passed, then a year, and still not a word from
Carlos about marriage. I was beginning to have my doubts about Carlos. I felt there was something suspicious about him, a sort of weakness, a false generosity, a warmth that wasn't genuine. And by the time
my father died early in 1954, he'd come to agree with me. In fact he'd
told me that Carlos was false, no good, nothing but shit. Later on,

when I met Carlos on the bus, I just stared him down. By then I'd passed judgment on him and couldn't forgive him. All the love I had for him was gone.

This whole affair made a great impression on me. I wasn't going with Héctor yet, in fact we didn't really know each other.

SEÑORA REYES:

We had trouble with Laura. She was a very striking girl with a fine figure. When she was seventeen she fell in love with Carlos—and she wasn't the only one! Renée was just twelve years old at the time and she had such a crush on him! Not that she ever said so, but a mother knows. He was a very attractive, charming boy. He seemed to have fallen in love with Laura and he hung around Renée because she aided and abetted him.

But Carlos was married and his wife's family were very good friends of ours. I have no idea whether Laura and Carlos had an affair, but I found a letter she'd written to a friend, saying they were going to get married and would travel a lot. It was in English and I understood it perfectly.

As soon as I found that letter, I sent for her father and told him, "Laura can be the sweetheart of any man she fancies, but not while she's living in my house. If Carlos wants to divorce his wife and marry Laura, it's none of my business, but I will not have a scandal here when I have young daughters to look after." Bernardo admitted I was right. I said to him, "If you approve of this, take her home to Havana and then receive Carlos as her fiancé."

Bernardo and my husband told Carlos that when school was over he could make the engagement formal. Carlos agreed and even drank on it. But when Laura went to Havana she found that he had indeed divorced his wife—and married another girl!

Laura was so bitterly disappointed that she went right out and married another man, Ivan Valdés. She bore him a child, but left him soon afterward and kept their child, while her husband went North. Later we learned that he'd been in the invasion—as a co-pilot of one of the attacking planes—and had been shot down at Playa Girón.[7]

When Renée met Ivan's stepfather one day, she asked him, "How do you feel about Ivan's being shot down in the invasion?"

"I think it was a good thing," he answered. "He was serving the Americans and might have killed his own child. I'm glad he's dead."

After Playa Girón, Laura left Cuba in great secrecy. She came and offered to sell Renée her son's bed, a beautiful piece of furniture,

7. Girón Beach in southern Las Villas Province, where the Bay of Pigs invasion occurred in April, 1961. In Cuba the invasion is referred to as "Playa Girón" or "Girón."

saying she was going to buy the boy a bigger one. But the next day she got on a plane and left Cuba, without a word to us about her plans. I guess that now she must be living in the United States on a hero's pension. But I'm still very fond of her.

RENÉE:

The day they told me Batista had taken power,[8] I joined the strike at the high school. I was over fourteen at the time, in the third year of high school and the first year of normal school. The coup was a tremendous shock to me, although I wasn't sorry to see Prío ousted. I felt complete contempt for him and all the others like him. I had no faith in anything that was going on in Cuba.

I really expected a big ruckus over Batista's coup, but it didn't turn out that way. My comrades got cold feet and the student president didn't want to support the strike. High school teachers, some of whom were revolutionaries later on, didn't say a word. Even a woman teacher I admired a lot, a lovely person, told me there was no point in striking. I'd expected more from all of them. But I spoke my mind! I said we couldn't allow a thing like this to happen and we should fight it.

The *compañeros* from the normal school were no better. The student president there was a rebel at first, but after a few days I noticed he stopped speaking out against Batista. When they told me he'd been given a *botella*[9] by Batista's government, I couldn't believe it and asked him whether it was true. He said, "Yes, it's true, but all politicians are the same and that's why we're going to hell in a breadbasket." I told him as long as he was part of Batista's regime I didn't want to talk to him or hear his name.

During that period politics was very important to me, but I was able to do little or nothing. It was horribly frustrating. My brother was a year older than I and had more freedom. One day he took me to a meeting of the university students in Pinar del Río, where he was going to be on the rostrum with the main speaker, Armando Hart.[10]

The meeting was at the Milanés, a movie house that used to be a theater. Carlos told me not to go because it was a very dangerous place. There were no emergency exits, and if the police should arrive not a soul would get out alive. The more dangerous the better, I

8. Batista's second coup, March, 1952, in which he ousted President Carlos Prío Socorrás (1948–52).

9. Literally "bottle," used idiomatically to mean a sinecure, usually obtained by political appointment.

10. Armando Hart Dávalos was the first national coordinator of the Twenty-sixth of July Movement, organized by Castro in 1955 to overthrow Batista. The Movement took its name from the date of the attack on the Moncada garrison in Oriente on July 26, 1953, an event which marked the beginning of Castro's armed revolt against Batista (see n. 11). Hart became Minister of Education, and now is a member of the Party's Political Bureau and one of the Revolution's principal ideologues.

thought, and I went. I felt very important to be at such a gathering, especially when I saw I was the only woman there. But nothing happened after all. It was the first time I heard about Fidel and the first time I saw Armando Hart. I was very disappointed because I wanted to talk to Hart and he didn't seem to notice me, even though I was with my brother. He apparently didn't care whether you showed interest or not, and he was a little rude.

Later I was visiting my father's cousin, Ángela Rosa, in Havana when I heard about the attack on the Moncada.[11] I was delighted. But then I saw Batista on television speaking so hatefully, saying, "The whole rebel gang is liquidated now." I had no way of finding out what had really happened. No one I knew would talk about it.

The students in my year at school had no concern for political action, but my brother's class was more intellectual. They'd talk about politics and they read Marx. They took to the streets carrying torches and buried the Constitution as a form of protest. I often took part in their demonstrations. Once, when I was sixteen, we gathered in the school library to protest against Batista. The librarian denounced us and the police came, carrying long, flat knives. They beat people with them and broke the heads of some of the *compañeros*. They were throwing the boys down the stairs while we stood shouting insults at them. One of the police gave me a swipe with his weapon. That was the only time they ever hit me.

My brother had his own circle of friends, and for a time they were very important to me. In fact one of them was my steady. So far as I could see, the group had no concrete plans and no connection with any real action. They just talked about how things should be.

Silvio tried to keep me away from boys as much as he could, but all his friends were involved in my life. They fascinated me. Samuel, who was a lot older than the others, dominated the group. I think he must have been a homosexual. Then there was Rodolfo, who went with one of my girl friends. He owned a clothing store and was fond of material luxuries; I thought him rather effeminate and cowardly. There was David—we campaigned for him as student president of the high school. I cared for him very much, but I loved Ignacio Herrera too, and he was the one I talked to most. I remember how we ran down the Americans. I enjoyed those talks a lot because for me the Revolution

---

11. On July 26, 1953, Fidel Castro led a group of 111 men and 2 women in the attack on the Moncada garrison in Santiago de Cuba, Oriente, with support actions against the Palace of Justice and the Civil Hospital. The latter two attacks, led by Raúl Castro and Abel Santamaría respectively, were successful, but the Rebels were unable to capture the main target, the Moncada garrison. Abel Santamaría was among over sixty Rebels who were killed, most of them after having been captured. Among those imprisoned were Fidel and Raúl Castro, Haydée Santamaría (sister of Abel), and Melba Hernández.

was communism, even though the only idea I had of communism was the explanation my father had given me.

Silvio's friend Alfredo was my steady. He had asked permission to visit the house and had even asked for my hand. I think I picked Alfredo not so much because he appealed to me as because he was safe. I know now he was homosexual. I tended to choose people who wouldn't cause me pain, you see. He broke off our engagement after two years; later he realized that I was really in love with Ignacio and David.

Soon my brother introduced me to some real communists, a shoemaker named Palau—I remember he had a very ugly nasal voice—and Zapata, a professor in the chemistry laboratory. Then I learned in the course of conversation that my Spanish teacher was also a communist. I sympathized with these people, but I didn't converse much with them. I hadn't read about socialism and I didn't care for theory. This mulling over political complexities didn't appeal to me. For me, communism was more a matter of feeling. And besides, they weren't likely to talk it over with me at a time when communism was prohibited, were they?

At home they knew about my brother's circle and their activities but they didn't realize I was involved in it. In my thoughts and feelings I was independent of my family, but in fact I was very tied down. My life was mostly going from the high school to the normal school, from there to the art school, back again to the normal school and then home. I had no friends outside my brother's group, and after he and some of his friends left for Havana, I no longer had even that.

In 1955 I too went to Havana, to study ballet. For years I had wanted to be a professional ballerina. When I arrived I didn't know my way around the city, nor did I have any friends there or know of any political action going on. I felt very lonely, very out of things. I knew my uncles were in politics and my Uncle Ramón was well connected with the *Auténticos,* but quite frankly, I felt a slight disdain for that party. I didn't believe in them. They weren't involved in direct action.

The day I met Mirella Gombal was a very important one for both of us. She says I shouldn't ever forget that day because I was one of the three people in her life who made a deep impression on her from the first meeting. I was just eighteen then and was very poor in my ballet class, but Mirella was even further behind than I was. So when class was over, I stayed to explain the exercises to her. She struck me as very intelligent, much more interesting than the other ballet people. We communicated effortlessly. I felt almost as though I had just met my own self.

She offered to take me home in her car, and on the way I asked her why the motor was exposed and why she didn't get a new car. "It's not mine," she answered. "It's my father's."

"Then why doesn't your father replace it?"

"He's not in Cuba," she said. I didn't know what to think until she confided that he was working with an anti-Batista group in Mexico. That impressed me very much. I saw the possibility of associating with someone who really had something to do with the Revolution. All those *compañeros* of mine had done nothing but hold a demonstration here and pass out leaflets there, nothing real. I hadn't seen any action of which I could say to myself, "Well, at least it's for communism."

Mirella asked me not to repeat what she had told me about her father. At first I didn't feel free to ask her any questions because I was afraid she'd mistrust me. If I acted over-eager she might think I was trying to get information or that I would betray her.

In 1955 bombings were already beginning. When they set off a bomb in the *Selecciones*[12] building, Mirella wanted to go there to investigate. "It will be dangerous because the police will be on hand," she said, "and my car is full of arms." I was overjoyed that I was going to have a real, living experience. The police did stop us but she acted very naturally, saying we were just passing by and were curious. We stayed and watched the entire police operation. From then on I knew she trusted me, and every day I'd say, "Tell me what's going on." She understood I was after action, not information.

At that time very few people were in political contact with each other. One would know a revolutionary here, another there, who might be working in the dark. Some people were doing this, others that. There wasn't any coordination. My ballet teacher, Bartolomé Aguilar, who said he was a communist, used to talk with me about political action and a general strike, but I must admit I never participated in more than minor actions. I felt I should participate only in actions led by groups I admired, but he didn't agree and we never acted on our ideas.

Mirella took part in whatever came up, but not because she belonged to any group or was under special discipline. She would tease Bartolomé. "Hey, when are you guys going to do something? Do you expect to go on discussing things forever?" But the Communist Party itself discouraged militancy, with what seemed to me a very cold attitude.[13] They were against the fight in the Sierra, against the attack on

12. Spanish equivalent of *Reader's Digest.*

13. The present Cuban Communist Party, the PCC (*Partido Comunista de Cuba*), was organized in 1965. Renée refers to the old Party, founded in 1925, which later changed its name to *Partido Socialista Popular* (PSP). The old Party (dissolved in 1961) cooperated with the first Batista government in exchange for official recognition and the right to reorganize the trade-union movement under its control. Support for Batista was part of the Communists' Popular Front policy during World War II, but the PSP continued a policy of coexistence after the war. This included withholding support from student action groups and Castro's Twenty-sixth of July Movement.

the Presidential Palace,[14] against the bombs. Only Fidel's men were known to be militant.

The attack on the Presidential Palace on March 13, 1957, came as a great surprise to us all, even Mirella. Silvio was amazed too. That day he was supposed to study with his friend Ignacio but he got a note saying, "I can't be sure when I'll be there—either today or tomorrow." The next time he saw Ignacio it was to view his dead body.[15]

Before that, Ignacio hadn't taken part in any more action than my brother, but I think he had joined the *Directorio* group and was prepared to die. José Antonio Echeverría, the leader of the *Directorio Revolucionario* and an outstanding university student, was also killed in that attack. Mirella and I went to a demonstration to place flowers on the spot where he died. We began by going to Mass and from there we all marched in a body along Infanta Street to the University. It was very moving.

One day, in the midst of all this, I met Carlos's friend Héctor at the opera and we discovered that we were very much alike. By the time he took me home I already felt we were sweethearts. We both loved music and had the same political attitudes, with identical feelings about the Communist Party; we didn't want membership or anything to do with it. Even now I don't belong to the Party. It doesn't appeal to me and I'd be very unhappy if I belonged. I believe I can be a revolutionary without joining anything. I don't believe in organizations.

Héctor's family owned a lumber mill in Pinar del Río, with a lot of machinery and a lot of land. The mill was really producing and they had the prospect of developing it into something big. But Héctor wasn't interested in any kind of business and during the rebellion he didn't even work. He never had money and was hungry a good deal of the time. He had only one pair of pants and I even would give him his bus fare. Imagine! My family hated him.

MÓNICA:

When Renée joined Silvio in Havana to study, they stayed with a relative, Ángela Rosa Collazo. That was a tradition in our family whenever someone went to Havana to study. In a way, Ángela Rosa was

14. On March 13, 1957, a group of about eighty men attacked the Presidential Palace in Havana in an attempt to assassinate Batista. Most of the attackers were members of the *Directorio Revolucionario,* a university student group organized by José Antonio Echeverría. The rebels were able to penetrate the Palace but could not find their way to Batista's living quarters. In a simultaneous attack, the students took over Havana Radio and Echeverría prematurely broadcast the announcement of Batista's death. Shortly afterward Echeverría was fatally shot by police. An estimated thirty-five rebels and five Batista policemen were killed in the attack. The Castro forces were already involved in the Sierra campaign and were not a part of the *Directorio* action. Castro later criticized the attack as "a useless expenditure of blood." (Thomas, *Cuba: The Pursuit of Freedom,* p. 930. See also pp. 925 ff.)

15. All those killed in the attack on the Palace are considered martyrs of the Revolution and their names are well known. Ignacio Herrera is a pseudonym.

the aristocrat of the family. She had elaborately curled white hair, I remember, and a strong personality, and she was very narrow-minded. I went there once during summer vacation, and when Ángela Rosa saw my bathing suit she was outraged. "My dear, how can you wear such a thing!" she said. "Ah well, I suppose it's up to your mother what she buys for you." I was just a child, but she thought it was indecent to show a bit of bare skin. As for plunging necklines, they were for prostitutes only. I think "prostitute" was her favorite word.

With Renée in Havana, I was left all alone with *mami*. With her dramatic instincts at their highest pitch, she made life a torture for me. I wished classes would never end so I wouldn't have to go home. Life was a constant quarrel. *Mami* would spank me and yell at me for the least little thing. The only thing that kept me going was the hope of having my brother and sister home for a weekend. Oh, that was the greatest joy in the world. Renée sympathized with me and together we built a million castles in the air. We talked of how *mami* would retire and how I would go to Havana to study, and we had fantasies about the house we'd move into. We talked about that dream house for hours on end, planning our own room down to the last detail. I remember it was to have a pink carpet and pink walls because the light reflected from them would flatter us. How I cherished that dream!

At last *mami* and I moved to Havana. What a disappointment! After all my dreams of a beautiful house, *mami* decided to move into a boarding-house first and go house-hunting later. We were to stay in the boarding-house for two or three months, but those months lengthened into a full year, with *mamá*, Renée, and me living in a single room, while Silvio stayed on at Ángela Rosa's.

I was almost eleven and *mami* wanted me to start high school right off. You had to be at least twelve to be admitted, so she went straight to the Ministry of Education and asked for a waiver of the age requirement. She got it, too. I had to take both the sixth-grade final examination and the high school entrance test.

Mami wanted to send me to the most exclusive school in Havana, but Renée and Silvio objected. They wanted me to go to a public high school, as they had, because they felt it would contribute to my development as a revolutionary. I didn't care which school I went to, as long as there weren't any nuns or priests in it. I never wanted to wear a long-sleeved, high-necked white uniform again. *Mami* was quite decided against sending me to a public school, so I finally enrolled at St. Christopher, an American school for the bourgeoisie.

The atmosphere at St. Christopher School was totally foreign to me. At first I was lost there, and I never did completely fit in. The people were always talking about going to the Havana Yacht Club and about the fancy boats their parents owned. Having none of the luxuries they took for granted, I couldn't identify with them. I felt rejected. I made no friends at that school.

My only friend that year was my sister. I was such an ugly girl! Yes, yes, I swear I was! To make matters worse, I couldn't help comparing myself with Renée, who was nineteen, when a girl is at her prettiest. I don't believe that created any conflict in me; I was glad she was so pretty and I was eager to show her off. I wanted my friends to know that not all my relatives were as ugly as I.

Feeling so insecure in school, I was happier in the boardinghouse with Renée, as long as *mami* was away. As a consultant to the Ministry of Education, she often had to go to the provinces, and that was our only relief. When she was home, life was sheer martyrdom. She was absolutely unbearable that year, always throwing tantrums and quarreling and making Renée cry.

One afternoon I came home from school and found Renée red-eyed and puffy. She'd been crying since 3:00 o'clock, because she'd found a note *mamá* had left referring to some little thing Renée had said to her in anger. "On the twenty-third of this month you said thus-and-so to me. I write this merely to remind you of it and I hope you remember it after I'm dead." That's the gruesome kind of thing *mami* was always doing.

Renée and I sat for hours that afternoon analyzing *mami* and confiding our troubles to each other. We identified with each other, especially when *mami* was away. At those times we were happy because we could do as we pleased. If we felt like going downstairs to make toast at night, we were free to do so. Both of us still dreamed about the lovely house we'd have one day and the room we'd share in it, and that dream became our refuge.

Chapter Three

Rebellion and Triumph

MÓNICA:

At home the Revolution was a daily topic of conversation, and my brother and sister would say, "We shall win!" I knew Silvio was involved in politics, though I wasn't sure he was an activist, and my sister often took part in political demonstrations. *Mamá* thought I was too young to go along. There might be clubbing and shooting, and she didn't want me exposed to such risks. But like every adolescent in Cuba under Batista, I wanted to participate. I longed to be a few years older so I could plant bombs or do something else to help. I felt I was nothing, no better than a bit of trash, because I couldn't work for the Revolution.

My brother, my sister, and I have often wondered whether *papá* would have been a revolutionary if he were still alive. He permitted revolutionary propaganda to be organized in our home, but I don't really know what his political position was. He was no fighter, but neither was he apathetic. *Mami* says that when Fidel attacked the Moncada, *papá* commented, "Those people are a bunch of madmen. They're asking for death." The year before *papi* died, when Silvio first went to the University, he had talked with *papá* about the political activities on campus and *papá* had encouraged him to join them, although he did tell Silvio not to do anything foolish.

I'd been warned not to discuss politics because I might get the adults in trouble, but I couldn't help arguing with the blind, narrow-minded people in the St. Christopher School. Most of the students and teachers there were either strong partisans of Batista or else willing to put up with him. They actually condoned Batista's wholesale killings. Nothing was wrong with their world as long as they had a chauffeur to pick them up at 5:00 o'clock!

I was twelve at the time of the 1957 attack on Batista's Palace. At first we weren't aware of anything in my classroom. Then we heard over the intercom that a revolution had started. A number of policemen had been killed.

I jumped up shouting, "I'm glad, I'm glad! I hope they kill them all!"
But I was among people who were pro-Batista and to them he was like a
king. One of the girls, whose father was a police officer, burst into tears.

What a hullabaloo there was in school! They locked us in as a safety
precaution and everybody milled around, talking and crying. Nobody
was allowed to enter, so I was surprised when Renée appeared. She had
evaded the principal and sneaked in through the ground floor. My sister
was teaching school then, and when she heard the news of the attack she
rushed wildly out to get me because *mami* was away that day.

At the boardinghouse a girl told us they'd killed Batista, but later she
came back to say he hadn't been killed after all. While we were at supper
Silvio walked in, looking very upset because his friend Ignacio hadn't
been home to sleep the night before. Silvio went into the bedroom to
telephone again, then he ran out of the house like a madman. That night
he found Ignacio in the morgue. He phoned Renée and I heard her say,
"But tell me . . . tell me, what happened?" Suddenly she dropped the
phone and burst into tears. "They've killed Ignacio!" she said. Later my
brother arrived at the house, half-crazed with grief and cursing Batista.

Ignacio Herrera and my brother had been lifelong friends. In high
school they were part of a group of six or seven who were always together. Ignacio became a labor organizer, and later, in Havana, when he
was studying engineering and Silvio was studying mathematics, they
took some courses together. I suspect Renée was a little in love with him.
So was I—he was the handsomest boy! I used to tease him and tell him
right to his face that I was in love with him. I was only a child when he
died but I was deeply shocked and grieved. Through his death I lived
the political moment intensely and reacted with hatred toward Batista
and all his followers.

It was forbidden to hold any kind of funeral ceremony for the men
Batista had murdered, but in spite of that they buried Ignacio as a hero.
People flocked to the funeral, and the police stood looking on, not dar-
ing to interfere.

Silvio continued his university studies and all that time I was haunted
by the fear that he was taking part in dangerous secret activities. When
the general strike was called on April 9,[16] Silvio went out with some
students. One night just before the strike, my brother came home from a
meeting and asked the time. I said it was 11:00 P.M. Every fifteen minutes or so he would ask again. At 12:00 the lights suddenly went out.

"That's the signal," he said. "That means the general strike has be-

16. The general strike of April 9, 1958, was called by the Twenty-sixth of July Movement
and the Havana Civic Resistance. The Communist Party and the labor unions did not
support the action and the strike failed badly. Thomas estimates that in addition to civilian
and police deaths, perhaps eighty revolutionaries were shot in Havana and another thirty
in Santiago de Cuba, Oriente. (Thomas, *Cuba: The Pursuit of Freedom*, p. 990.)

gun. You, Mónica, can't go to school, and you, Renée, can't go to work. Nobody can do anything."

Mami wasn't in Havana that day, so Silvio drove us to Ángela Rosa's. On the way we saw a traffic light that hadn't been turned off. "Shit!" my brother exclaimed, "it's failed!" The plan was to cut off the electric power in the city, and the traffic light meant that in at least one zone the plan had not been carried out.

The police were looking for the strikers and my brother had to hide out in the boardinghouse with us. *Mami* warned me, "You mustn't mention to *anybody* that your brother is here. If you do, he'll have to leave at once." I had to keep a careful watch on my tongue, but in spite of everything it was divine having him live at home again. What immense joy to wake up at night and see him sleeping beside my bed! Of course I knew he was there only to hide from someone who wanted to kill him. That's the way life was under Batista.

One night I woke up at 4:00 A.M. and found Renée and *mamá* weeping because Silvio hadn't yet returned. We couldn't turn on the light because if the police saw it they might have investigated. We couldn't even talk aloud. So we sat there whispering in the dark, tense and anxious, afraid he'd been killed, until I looked out of the window and saw him. "There, there he is!" I cried.

Worried as she was, *mamá* didn't dare ask why he was so late, nor did she warn him to keep out of politics. She would never have forbidden him to act according to his conscience. The strike was long over before I was allowed to return to school. It was my brother who forbade me to go back with the other students. I piled up a lot of absences that time.

My brother was my joy, and I wanted to feel close to him, to understand him, to confide in him, to discuss all my problems with him as I did with Renée. But it was impossible. He lived in a world of his own. He has a highly intelligent, analytical mind but he's very emotional too, although he tries to hide it. He has a difficult, retiring, introverted temperament.

The most important thing in his life was his studies, and for those he rejected all social activities. He never went to dances and strongly objected to my going. He even disapproved of my listening to popular music. I never wore pants or sandals, knowing how he objected to them. I tried to please him in every way, it was such a delight to have him with us.

We finally moved to a lovely apartment in Nuevo Vedado, where *mamá* still lives. We had no furniture but little by little we bought what we needed. The apartment had three bedrooms, one for *mamá,* one for my brother, and one for Renée and me. It was a beautiful room, with its own bath and balcony, practically independent of the rest. Our dream had come true at last!

By this time my sister had met Héctor, who is now her husband, and *mami* was accusing her of having all sorts of intimacies with him. They quarreled constantly. In *mamá*'s eyes any kind of intimacy before marriage was wrong; sex was dirty, and all mention of it was forbidden. Intelligent as she is, *mami* has a lot of wrong ideas and her rigidity about sex affected both my sister and me. That, and the influence of the nuns at school, made us afraid of men. That was when I needed *papá*. I never felt I could talk over my problems with *mamá*.

The first time I heard my uncles say Héctor was a communist I was horrified. To me a communist was the devil incarnate, the sum total of evil. I remember the nuns at the elementary school once showed us a movie about some horrible people—communists in the Spanish Civil War—tearing a church apart. In those days I thought communists ate live babies. But after Héctor sat down with me and explained communism, I thought it was marvelous. I knew next to nothing about the poor, but I was shaken by movie scenes showing children crying from hunger, and I tried to imagine how life must be for them. It upset me. It really hurt. Something like that should tear anybody's heart out.

I began speaking up at school. "Look," I'd say to one of the girls, "do you think it's fair that your folks send a big car for you every afternoon, when there are people who have nothing to eat?"

"What's that to me? I eat."

"But doesn't it bother you that there are mothers who have no food for their children?"

"Why should I care?"

How I despised those girls! My contempt for them grew as I realized how inferior they were to me.

At home we lived in an atmosphere of secrecy, listening to *Radio Rebelde* and talking in hushed voices about everything Fidel said. When we heard the guerrilla fighters had taken another town, the grownups would say, "We're winning!" followed by the warning, "Don't mention it to anyone."

Renée started having frightful nightmares, often about me. She'd wake up terrified and crawl into my bed, until I began to think she was going crazy. Finally we decided to push our beds together permanently.

One night Renée woke me and said, "No, that noise was no nightmare, I still hear it." She was right. I heard it too. It sounded like dozens of police sirens. *Mami* wasn't home, so we woke up my brother and the three of us sat on the bed listening to the sirens until they finally died down about two hours later. My brother tried to figure it out. "It could be any number of things," he told us. "Perhaps the anti-*Batistianos* have taken over the motorized police. That might mean victory." It turned out that there was a big fire started by revolutionaries in a government building.

For a long time I had suspected that my Uncle Ramón, my Aunt Mercedes, and her husband, Jaime Pérez, were working for the Revolution. I found out for sure in 1958. Whenever I went to their homes they were listening to the underground radio. Uncle Ramón came to our place practically every night to hide from the police. He'd stay until 2:00 or 3:00 in the morning, sitting by a window to watch the street. Once he said, "It's almost over. It can't be long now."

SEÑORA REYES:

The anguish I lived through during Batista's regime! At that time, whenever you saw your son go out, you couldn't be sure he'd return. My son was a student, and they killed so many students during the April 9 strike! They'd drag them barbarously out of their homes. Do you know what that chief of police did? If he saw a group of youths out in the street, he'd tell his men, "Go arrest a bunch of those and if they dare to protest. . . ." And right then and there any of those boys might get killed. It was horrible, horrible!

And the stealing that went on! Under Batista's regime and even before, it was a matter of pride for a man to come into the government poor and leave it rich.

I'm a rebel by nature and circumstance. I was always in favor of the opposition. That was my fate. I saw politics as oppression, bossism, servility, and I couldn't bear it. I became interested in politics when I was an elementary-school teacher. At that time Machado[17] was in power, and all my feelings rose up against him—his abuse of power, his misuse of the Army. Some of the other teachers and I, young girls all of us, were so outspoken about his regime that a lieutenant we knew often begged us, "For God's sake, girls, don't go around talking like that. You don't know how dangerous it is just now." We said some really wild things, but the truth is I never actually did anything but talk.

The only action I ever took was to mobilize and lead a teachers' strike. Guillermo, my sweetheart, was involved in a strike at the time. They won, but the inspector sent several people to my father, asking him to influence me against agitating among the teachers. So my father urged me not to get involved, and I dropped out of the teachers' strike. Things were very different then. Now children do what they think is right and that is as it should be.

I often heard *papá* talk about good politics and low-down politics. When I was appointed school inspector I had to fight hard, really hard, against low politicians. There was a senator who wanted me to assign certain school posts to three representatives who had agreed to vote for him for president of the Chamber of Deputies in exchange

17. General Gerardo Machado, President of Cuba 1925–33.

for the jobs.[18] When I didn't give him the ones he wanted, the senator wrote me a letter saying, "If that's the way things are, be prepared for a fight in the future."

I sent back an insulting answer: "It is not true that I gave the posts I had promised you to someone else. I don't expect you to believe me because you judge others by yourself, and being a politician you are not to be trusted. I am a woman of my word, and even if I were not, you with your power would still get what you wanted. And do not threaten me with a fight in the future. Aren't you ashamed, you who are a lion in power, to threaten me, a mouse? You are a man, I am a woman. You are a senator, I am a poor simple school inspector. With a stroke of your pen, you can have me fired. Do you call that a fight in such unequal circumstances?"

The result was that the senator went to the president of the board of education of Los Palacios and said, "There's the bravest woman I ever saw. Nobody else has dared say such things to me, nor made me blush as she has." But at his request I was called before the Deputy Minister of Education, and when they told me why, I spoke right up, "The senator is the one who should be censured. Why didn't you cite him? Fire me right now if you want to !"

Because of me, the senator later introduced a law making the appointment of teachers a prerogative of the Minister of Education instead of the school inspectors. That's the kind of thing that made me hate politics.

In all my years as an inspector I only attended one political banquet, and that one I organized myself. It was in honor of Aureliano Sánchez Arango,[19] the Minister of Education, who seemed to me to be a man of integrity, as indeed he was, even though now he is a counterrevolutionary.

When Grau was a candidate for the presidency, I wanted to vote for him but my husband forbade me to. Of course I could have voted for

18. Describing the graft-ridden education system in pre-revolutionary Cuba, Rolland G. Paulston writes: "Because Cuban teachers held life tenure as government officials and received full salary whether they taught or not, teacher appointments became a major focus of patronage. Not infrequently, appointments were purchased outright at prices ranging from $500 to $2,000." ("Education," in Mesa-Lago, ed., *Revolutionary Change in Cuba*, pp. 382–83.) Paulston states that this graft reached an all-time high under the Grau presidency (1944–48), when Minister of Education Alemán stole millions of *pesos* from the education budget. This theft of funds caused a decline in the public-school system.

19. A leader of the *Directorio Estudiantil* in the 1920s, Sánchez Arango was a strong opponent of the Machado dictatorship. He was Minister of Education under Prío, and fled Cuba with Prío after Batista's March, 1952, coup. In exile, Sánchez Arango organized the AAA (*Asociación de Amigos de Aureliano*), one of the strongest anti-Batista organizations outside the student factions and the Twenty-sixth of July Movement. As a professor at the University of Havana after Batista's fall, Sánchez Arango joined the anti-Castro underground and fled to the United States, where he remains in exile.

anyone I pleased in the privacy of the voting booth, but I didn't. My husband and I got along very well with each other, very well indeed, and the day he thought one way and I another, it would have meant we were each going our own way. I took great care to preserve the unity of our home, which for me was more important than anything in the world.

I was for Grau when he led the opposition, but when he got in I was for Chibás.[20] Because as soon as the opposition rose to power it was the same old story—the whip, the robbery, the corruption. . . . Chibás was the one who attacked Machado, then Batista. Most of the opposition to Batista came from Chibás's group. At home we were all for him. When he died, the young university student who made the speech at his grave was Fidel Castro.

After Batista's coup of March, 1952, my sister Mercedes, my brother Ramón, and I all came to independent decisions to join a revolutionary group. My son was also involved but he didn't tell me, and I didn't know Mercedes's husband, Jaime, had joined until I went to propose him for membership. As far as I knew, he was dedicated to his friends, to good wine, and to nothing else. But ten days after Batista's coup, Jaime joined Aureliano Sánchez Arango's group without telling any of us about it. That's how secretive he was.

Jaime did a lot of work for the underground. One day Mercedes told me that the group had taken a whole cache of arms to Havana— old arms, all of them. I went to Ramón and said, "Did you know they were old arms? Mercedes told me." Well, he really chewed her out for being so indiscreet. So I said to Mercedes, "I've got an idea Jaime is involved in the Revolution."

"Don't go around saying that, for goodness' sake!" she warned me. "Jaime has nothing to do with it and don't say he does! It might cost him his life."

To frighten me even more she told me about how they had plucked out Abel's eyes in the Moncada jail, put them in a saucer, and showed them to Haydée.[21] Only people deeply involved in the movement knew what was going on. The stories of torture probably came out in the underground newspapers and anyone who got hold of a copy would communicate the news to another revolutionary, and so the

20. Eduardo Chibás, revolutionary son of a wealthy family and treasurer of the *Directorio Estudiantil* that opposed Machado. Chibás supported President Grau's *Auténtico* Party until 1947, when he broke away and formed the more radical *Ortodoxos*. Chibás was widely regarded as a politician sincerely interested in the Cuban people. In August, 1951, he fatally shot himself after signing off his weekly radio broadcast.

21. This is one of the most often repeated stories of the Revolution's martyrs. Abel Santamaría was second in charge of the assault on the Moncada garrison, and his sister Haydée Santamaría was one of the two women who participated in the attack. Both were captured and imprisoned, but Abel was tortured and killed.

story spread by word of mouth. Those things couldn't be talked about freely.

Every time I went to Pinar del Río I would go to Ovas to see Mercedes and Jaime. As time went on I noticed a great tension in the house but I wasn't sure what caused it. Once in a while Jaime would tell Mercedes to dismiss the maid and strange men would come to sleep there. When I visited I always found him busy painting, and I'd say, "Goodness, you people certainly are maniacs for housepainting!"

"Oh, you know that Jaime likes to keep the house looking clean," Mercedes would answer.

Finally she confirmed what I suspected. Jaime was transporting arms for Sánchez Arango from the capital city, Pinar del Río, and hiding them in his house. The house had a peaked roof, which left an empty triangular space just above the bathroom ceiling. When Jaime received arms, he'd clean and oil the guns, break through the ceiling, and store them in the empty space. Then he'd mend the hole with fresh plaster and apply a new coat of paint not only to the ceiling but to the whole room, so that if anybody went to investigate, they wouldn't notice a fresh patch. He did all that in one night, imagine! The empty space was directly above his daughter's room and she didn't even hear him working. He was very handy and could do anything at all. Once the house was searched for arms. Some guns were hidden under the settee where Mercedes sat but the police never thought of telling her to stand up.

Those Rebels really worked for the Revolution and were ready to give their lives. They were just waiting for the final order to go out and fight and they expected it from one minute to the next. My sister would often warn me, "Don't go out tonight, I think there are going to be sharpshooters in the streets." Or she'd send me word from Ovas, "Don't come here this week no matter what. They're going to blow up all the bridges." But none of it ever happened.

We in the province of Pinar del Río heard little about Fidel after he took to the Sierra Maestra in Oriente. Cuba is small but long, and Pinar del Río was far away from the action. It's always been more passive than Oriente. While the fighting was going on I'd say, "Well, let's wait and see if that man works out. If he wins and does well in the government for two or three years, then I'll support him." Things were so completely demoralized at that time—how could one possibly embrace a new government without knowing what it would be like? Fidel was still a question mark.

In the end Jaime and Ramón left Aureliano's organization and joined Fidel's Twenty-sixth of July Movement. Those two revolutionary movements were always in conflict. The Twenty-sixth of July Movement needed arms but Aureliano's organization in Pinar del Río waited until the last possible moment to release them. They were to be sent to the Cordillera de los Organos, which was not a fighting front but only a third front in the mountains of Pinar del Río, established to mobilize troops there. Their only function was to create a diversion while Castro fought on another front.

In 1958, on Christmas Eve, a certain Alano and another man they called El Zurdo went to Jaime's house to collect the arms. Mercedes said, "Jaime, I don't trust that Alano. He's going to betray you."

Jaime pooh-poohed the idea. "Of course he won't."

That same day Ramón meant to fetch Jaime and Mercedes to spend Christmas in Havana, but he decided not to go because Mercedes was in such a state of nerves. On December 25 Jaime told my sister, "I'm going to the Sierra—I'm burned out already." When they said a revolutionary was "burned out," they meant he was being watched or pursued by the police.

"Oh no, Jaime, don't go!" Mercedes pleaded.

"Listen," he said, "I'd be a lot safer in the Sierra than I am here. The only reason I haven't gone yet is that I'm waiting for my new boots."

"Don't go, don't go," she begged.

"Now don't be silly, child," he said teasingly. "You'll make a very pretty little widow. Black's becoming to you, you know." Then he added more seriously, "Don't worry, Mercedes. If I'm killed, the Revolution will take care of you and the girls. And Mercedes, I'm going to ask you one thing. The day they come to arrest me, we won't weep, and that's that. I don't want to leave you in tears."

There Jaime was, making plans for going to the Sierra—they were going to bring his boots the next day, and then he was leaving. Oh well, when something is fated, it happens.

That day Alano and El Zurdo were arrested. Usually, when someone was arrested, especially someone who might be made to talk, the group would go into hiding. Then they'd try to raise the money to get their man out. Batista's government demanded a kind of ransom; for 3,000 or 4,000 *pesos* they'd release the prisoner—after he'd been tortured, of course.

There are people who can stand all sorts of torture and keep their mouths shut, and there are people who can take very little. As Mercedes had suspected, Alano was the kind that talks. It isn't that he was a traitor, but he was weak. He was detained in Havana, and he talked before word of his arrest even got to his group in Pinar del Río. When Ventura[22] asked, "Who gave you the firearms?" Alano told him, "Ricardo Roldán and Jaime Pérez."

---

22. Colonel Esteban Ventura, an intelligence officer in the Havana police, who became Batista's chief of police. Thomas refers to him as "a legendary death-dealer." (*Cuba: The Pursuit of Freedom*, p. 942.) Ventura fled to Miami in late 1958. The U.S. government refused Castro's request for extradition. (*Ibid.*, p. 1077.)

And so that very day, December 26, at 6:00 in the evening, just as Jaime was making his plans to leave, Menocal and his men arrived. The Menocals are relatives of the former President,[23] a very high-ranking family here in Cuba, but this Menocal was a jackal, one of the worst Batista had. He was good-looking, pretty rather than handsome, and carried himself with great elegance. But he was a criminal. The instruments of torture they found at San Cristóbal jail, Menocal's headquarters, were unspeakable! Menocal had a horse he would fill with bisulfate of something and turn on the prisoners to kick them. They even say Menocal sucked the blood of his victims, but I don't know if that's true.

A whole band of policemen with jeeps and searchlights surrounded the block, bringing El Zurdo along to point out Jaime's house. Menocal's men knocked on the door. Jaime saw them and opened it without a word. He was surrounded. Menocal was in front, policemen were in back and on every side.

They searched the whole house for arms, but of course they couldn't find any.

Mercedes was up. The two little girls woke up but stayed in bed, petrified. An armed guard stood at the foot of each bed. Marisela didn't make a sound, but little Mercedes cried and begged, "Don't take my *papá*." Mercedes went right up to the guards and said, "Why do you have to stand there scaring my little girls?" Menocal ordered the men out of the room. It was hellish—armed men in the house, every light on, the dog barking, the child crying. . . .

Jaime was a bit of a dandy; he dressed carefully before leaving. Mercedes gave him some nose drops and a handkerchief. When he reached the front door, he stopped and kissed her, then stood there looking at her without saying a word. "That look said everything," Mercedes told me afterward. "It said, 'I am going to my death. Goodbye.'"

They took him straight to the station and beat him mercilessly. Early in the morning they decided to take Jaime to Guane to confront Roldán, the other man Alano betrayed. Jaime was already in very bad shape. In the car they put a sort of military cap, a *casquito,* on his head, the kind worn by 33-*pesos*-a-month informers.[24] I guess they wanted whoever saw Jaime pass by to believe that he was a *casquito.*

The lieutenant at Guane was a close friend of Roldán, and he interceded in his favor, telling Menocal that Roldán had the lung sickness, so if they were going to torture him, they should only do it from the

23. General Mario García Menocal, President of Cuba 1913–21.

24. This particular type of military headgear was worn by the special forces Batista recruited to fight the Rebels. These men were derogatorily referred to as *casquitos,* literally "little caps."

waist down. Menocal went to see Roldán, taking with him Jaime, the lieutenant, and a squad of men. Along the way they stopped and dragged Jaime down to a dell beside the road—there's a monument to him at that place now—and six men beat him with the kind of whip we call "ox's prick." They beat and beat and beat him. With the butt of their guns they knocked his teeth out, broke his joints, and smashed his leg bones. Supposedly they had no intention of killing him, but he was dying from the prolonged beatings. Miguel, the leader of Menocal's six-man squad and the most brutal, said, "Wait a minute. This man is going to die on us." Miguel wanted a promotion and knew he would get it if they could take all the revolutionaries in Jaime's group.

Menocal looked at Jaime. "Hell, I think we made a mistake. Maybe he's innocent. Oh well . . . put him in the trunk and let him finish dying." So they wedged him into the trunk of the car, still alive.

When Menocal arrived at Roldán's hacienda, Roldán answered the door and his blood ran cold when he saw who it was. He called to his wife, "Here, bring some coffee and cigars for these gentlemen." He gave them coffee, he passed the cigars around, not knowing Jaime was locked up in the car trunk. I don't know whether Jaime was alive or dead at that moment, but he was certainly dying and couldn't talk. That helped Roldán. They had gone too far with Jaime and didn't want to risk killing Roldán too. They wanted whatever information they could get out of him. Also, I suspect the fact that he was a wealthy landowner made it easier for him, because they knew they could get a lot of money out of him. With Jaime still in the car trunk, they took Roldán to San Cristóbal and clapped him in prison.

Meanwhile, Mercedes tells me, she threw herself down on the bed with her daughters to cry. But soon she sat up and told the children, "Stay here, I'm going to get somebody. I'm going to mobilize people." She went to all sorts of people, even government people. One woman told her, "Look for Jaime in Guane, that's where they took him." But Mercedes didn't believe her.

I decided to go to Julio Lázaro's house in Havana. He was a friend of the other jackal, General Eleuterio Pedraza, a grim, horrible man, who had been sent to fight Che in Santa Clara.[25] Pedraza was one of Batista's top men in those last four days. Mercedes didn't want me to go. "Jaime would never accept alms from Batista's government."

"All right," I said, "but I'm going to see Julio's wife, Edita."

Edita was Jaime's second cousin. She had always felt grateful to

25. General José Eleuterio Pedraza, who ruthlessly put down workers' strikes in the 1930s, was recalled from retirement late in 1958 to become Batista's last chief of staff. Pedraza sent an armored train with 400 soldiers to Santa Clara, Las Villas, to pacify the Rebels fighting under Che Guevara. The train was derailed by the Rebels and the soldiers surrendered. Pedraza left Cuba with Batista on January 1, 1959.

Jaime's family, because in her childhood, when her parents had nothing, Jaime's father used to appear at their house loaded down with toys for her. After her marriage she was quite well off, but she never forgot her gratitude to old Pérez and always visited them when she went to Pinar del Río.

Edita and Julio lived in a house like a fort, full of soldiers and guns, but I phoned her and she promised I would be admitted. They showed me and my brother Bernardo into the sitting room, where Edita began chattering about Batista's plans. "Listen, don't let your little girls go out because on the first of the month the blood is going to run in the streets of Havana. You know they tried to blow up Santa Clara. The General is going there now. Fidel isn't the worst by any means; we could reach an agreement with him. It's that foreigner, that Che Guevara, who wants to take over the Republic. Now, I ask you, can we permit that?"

We had to hear the whole oration without saying a word because we were there to plead for Jaime's life. She went on, "Only a few minutes ago we talked with Washington—we have a direct phone to Washington. The movement must be crushed." I thought she'd never stop. It was terrible.

We explained that Jaime had been arrested, and she asked, "Is he involved in something?"

"Well, Edita," I answered, "I don't know. I live in Havana and know nothing about what he's doing. All I know is that Menocal arrested him."

"I'll find out where he is myself," she said. Right there in front of us she phoned Ventura. "Listen, the prisoner Jaime Pérez is my cousin. I want you to spare his life." Ventura called back a little later. Edita listened for a long time, then hung up without saying a word. Then she said, "*Chica,* they tell me that Jaime Pérez asked for permission to use a public toilet on the road to Guane, and when he got out he made for the hills. They couldn't catch him."

We didn't really believe her, but we hoped it might be the truth. "Look," she said, "we'll bribe the police. I'll give them 20,000, 30,000 *pesos*—whatever they demand. Count on it. I myself will get him out of Cuba. I'll send him to a foreign country." That was all very well, but we knew Jaime wouldn't have agreed to leave Cuba.

Ventura was supposed to call Edita back, so we waited. When he did call back he told her, "The man has already been liquidated." But she didn't tell us that.

Menocal gave orders to bury Jaime far away and deep, where his corpse couldn't be found, because Ventura hadn't wanted him killed.

Meanwhile, Mercedes was doing what she could in Pinar del Río. An army officer went to her and said, "Jaime is alive. He was seen at the office in San Cristóbal, watching TV." Since we had his cousin Edita's word that he was alive we believed the story and thought, "Maybe he talked. Maybe now they're treating him better."

Mercedes and all of Jaime's friends went around trying to raise the 3,000 *pesos* Batista's men had asked as ransom. The bloody bastards! They knew Jaime was dead, yet they still asked for money to free him. There were no limits to what they would do.

Then Jaime's brother Natán, who had gone to San Cristóbal to investigate, came back with a different story. He'd been to see a man called Facundo, who knew about all the deaths, and Facundo said, "I understand that he was badly wounded and was sent to the hospital." We didn't know what to believe. But Natán said to me, "Don't get your hopes too high. I have a suspicion that Jaime is dead." I didn't repeat Natán's remark to Mercedes but I no longer shared in the rejoicing.

Six days after Jaime's arrest, on New Year's Day, the Revolution triumphed. We still had no news of Jaime, so very early that day I set out for Ovas to visit Mercedes. Along the way to the bus station, I saw my brother Ramón, who'd been in hiding, and he told me, "Batista has fallen!"

I was the only one on the bus to Ovas who had heard the news. I was simply bursting with it, but there were some soldiers traveling, so I dared not tell the others. The bus had to stop once to be searched and I couldn't help whispering to the woman next to me, "They won't have any more chances to do this. On the way back, this bus won't be searched." We stopped at Artemisa just in time to hear the "Voice of Venezuela" announce Batista's fall.

Then I could tell the others, "I knew about it quite a while ago." The people doubted that the news was true and were afraid of reprisals from the military, so they didn't dare rejoice openly. But by the time we arrived in Ovas, the coup was public knowledge and everybody was shouting, "Batista has fallen! Batista has fallen!"

Poor Mercedes was wild with happiness. Her one thought was, "Now we can find Jaime." She and Ramón went looking through all the local hospitals, while I searched here in Havana. We kept on looking until there was nowhere else to look. Then we still hoped that when the men came down from the hills of the Cordillera de los Organos, Jaime would be among them. We'd been told he escaped and we clung to that lie. But Jaime did not return, Mercedes was getting desperate, and in the end we just lost hope and made up our minds that he must be dead. Still, we had to know where he was so Mercedes would be able to accept her widowhood. She had to know for sure.

My brother and some other revolutionaries went to San Cristóbal prison and got hold of Menocal's henchmen. They worked on them softly to make them talk, promising that whoever told them where

Jaime Pérez was would get off easily. Finally one of them confessed. "He's buried in such-and-such a farm, look for him there."

I was at Mercedes's house. The girls were in the habit of writing a letter to the Three Kings, but Marisela said to me, "Aunt, that's kid stuff. I don't believe in the Three Kings anymore. I'll only ask them to bring back my *papá.*" Ah well, her wish was granted.

That night Ramón came to get Mercedes and me. "We found out where he is. We're going to dig him up now," he announced. We took Jaime's dentist with us to identify him, which he did. Before burying him they had stripped off his new boots and his wristwatch. His body showed clear signs of torture. Naturally we didn't let Mercedes see him.

Later, when the murderers were tried, Miguel, the ringleader, told in complete detail what they had done to Jaime, and Mercedes heard it all. When she was called to the witness stand she said, "I didn't come here to accuse anybody. There are weak men and strong men. My husband is dead because he was a strong man, a man of integrity. He chose to die rather than betray his fellow revolutionaries. But he would be alive now if a weak man hadn't betrayed him."

Alano claimed he had been cruelly tortured and had to speak, but who could believe that? Only a week later he was riding all over Pinar del Río in his car. A ceremony had been planned in his honor, but after Mercedes's speech the ceremony was canceled. "How can we honor the man who's responsible for Jaime Pérez's death?" they said.

I saw Fidel for the first time when he spoke in Columbia[26] about what was going to be done for Cuban children. From that moment on I liked the man. I'd worked for twenty-three years in the field of education and saw so many good minds go to waste for lack of opportunity while a lot of donkeys were sent to study in the United States simply because their parents could afford it. I saw how the Jiménez family, our landlords in Los Palacios, made enough money out of their holdings to vacation in Europe every year while their sharecroppers went hungry.

And I had seen hardship in my own family. My mother's brothers were country people who worked on the land and had very little schooling. My Uncle Herberto was a sharecropper who planted tobacco for the Cuban Land Company. Every year Uncle Herberto would ask me to draw up his accounts for him, and when I was

26. Campo Columbia in Havana had been Cuba's chief military headquarters since 1902. Immediately after the Revolution, on January 8, 1959, Castro made his famous speech there, changing the name of the base to Campo Libertad. In 1961 the buildings on the base were turned over to the Ministry of Education and converted into schools. Thereafter, the base was known as Ciudad Libertad (Liberty City).

through he'd say, almost in tears, "*Bendita,* there's not even enough left over for medicine!" He had worked hard, but all the profits went to the infamous company.

When Fidel expounded on his program I was enchanted, and I waited for him to bring all his beautiful ideas into action. My brother Ramón said, "The trouble with you is, you're turning into a communist."

"It isn't communism I like," I answered, "it's Fidel. Whatever he does is all right with me. If it's communism he wants, so be it."

MÓNICA:

Traditionally, at Christmas the entire family had gathered at the home of one or another of us to celebrate. While *papá* was alive and it was our turn to receive the family, he would go all out for Christmas. It was perfectly lovely. Ill though he was, *papá* loved to eat and he ate a lot. He'd set the best possible food before our relatives and didn't care if it cost 500 *pesos.* He'd even take it out of the rent money and get three months behind in the payments.

In the last years before the Revolution we suspended these fiestas as a gesture of solidarity with the Revolution. In 1958, just before the Triumph, we all had dinner in Ovas with Jaime and Aunt Mercedes. We went back and stayed through Christmas week, because on December 26 Uncle Jaime was arrested. On the 27th Aunt Mercedes came to Havana, trying to get him freed. During the next four days the contradictory news about him kept us in a constant state of anxiety: "Yes, he's alive . . . no, he isn't." My aunt went to pieces. We couldn't celebrate New Year's Eve in those circumstances. Silvio, Renée, and I gathered at *mamá*'s house and talked only of Jaime's arrest. Laura was with us, too. We were on close terms again, and we even convinced ourselves that she was anti-Batista.

The following day we were told that Jaime might be dead. When she heard the news, *mamá* insisted on leaving at daybreak for Ovas so that Aunt Mercedes wouldn't be alone. Silvio got up early to drive her to the bus station, and on the way they passed the house where Uncle Ramón had been hiding. To their surprise, he was standing on the porch, in broad daylight. He yelled to them to come over, and shouted that Batista had sneaked out of Cuba. Things were stirred up, he said, and *mami* couldn't possibly go to Ovas that day.

"What!" said *mami.* "Leave *madrina*"—that's what she always called Aunt Mercedes—"alone when she gets the news that Batista has fallen? Why, that's the very moment we'll find out whether Jaime is dead or alive."

Uncle Ramón insisted it was dangerous but *mami* boarded the bus and left. When Silvio got home it was still only 5:00 o'clock in the morning. We were all sleeping on the same bed, Renée, Laura, and I. He woke us up. "Ladies," he announced, "Batista has fallen! He's gone—run away."

"Oh sure, and just how did *you* get that great news?"

"Ramón told me."

Then we believed him. We all jumped out of bed, wild with joy. In a few minutes we doubted again. "No, no, Silvio, it can't be. Let's wait awhile and see what happens."

Around 9:00 we decided to go over to Laura's house in Vedado. Out in the street all the cars were flying pennants, people sang and whistled, strangers embraced each other, and everybody was shouting, *"Viva Cuba libre!"* I was torn between joy at the triumph of the Revolution and apprehension for my Uncle Jaime.

A 9:00 P.M. curfew had been decreed. Most days we went visiting friends—we couldn't wait to talk over the exciting things that were happening—but we were always home in good time because we didn't want to be caught out after curfew. On the fifth day they told us that Jaime was dead and Silvio would drive us to San Cristóbal, where he was buried. I was frightened. I was only thirteen but they took me along. Why, I can't imagine. When *papi* died, my relatives were careful to keep me from seeing him.

That was one of the most horrible days of my life—a nightmare. When we arrived at San Cristóbal we found a crowd of people milling around. They had all lost relatives in hideous atrocities and were going to question the torturers, who had been arrested during the past four days.

I heard monstrous stories of the crimes Batista and his followers had committed. A man came up to me and asked, "Why are you here? Are you waiting?"

"Yes," I answered. "They killed one of my uncles and buried him here. They're going to dig him up."

"That's nothing compared to what they did to me. They killed my wife by driving twenty nails into her head and buried her with my child, my living child, in her arms."

I was so dazed that everything seemed to be happening someplace far, far away, like the delirium of fever. People talked and talked. I was shocked out of my daze when somebody said, "Bring the dentist." Those words burned into my brain. Jaime was so badly multilated that he could be identified only by his teeth. Then a fellow with a pick and shovel came out of the police station and put the tools in the truck. I asked, "What's that for?" and they told me, "To dig up Jaime." I don't know how I ever lived through that day.

Later, when we went to the wake, I wanted to go to the cemetery because Uncle Jaime was to have a martyr's funeral. But a man walked in and said, "I came to take away the little girls."

"There they are," I said, pointing to Jaime's daughters.

He took them out of the room and returned for me. "I'm not a little girl!" I protested.

"My orders were to take all the little girls somewhere else. You must come with me."

"I tell you, I'm not a little girl!" But he made me go with him anyway.

On the first anniversary of Uncle Jaime's death, there was a memorial ceremony organized by the club where he once worked. I went to the graveyard for the first time and I was deeply moved. *Papi*'s grave was nearby. I had never seen it before. Many wreaths were brought for my uncle's grave and, seeing he had so many and *papi* none, I took two or three for *papi*'s grave.

The triumph of the Revolution made a strong impression on me. Renée used to say, "You'll see how different everything will be once we have freedom here." She was old enough to remember Cuba before Batista, and she'd tell me how people had once been able to say out loud whatever they thought.

"You mean I could have stood out in the street and insulted the government?"

"Yes indeed, yes, you could have!"

It all seemed strange and wonderful to me because I remembered only dictatorship and repression. I could hardly believe there had been a time when a newspaper could oppose the government without reprisals, so when the Revolution triumphed, it was like a grand fiesta that I'd been waiting for. Of course, like so many others my joy was not unmixed; there was my uncle's death to mourn. We Cubans had our tears as well as our freedom.

On the day of Fidel's triumphal entry into Havana, I finally saw the *barbudos,* the bearded, long-haired fighters of the Sierra Maestra I had so longed to see. To me Camilo[27] and the rest of the revolutionaries seemed like legendary heroes. As far as I was concerned, we had already won everything in those early days of 1959. Batista was gone, wasn't he?

At school opinions fluctuated. Like the bourgeois school it was, St. Christopher's had been strongly pro-Batista. But no sooner had he fallen than they cursed his crimes—as, indeed, all of Cuba did—and rejoiced in the triumph of the Revolution. Then, as soon as the revolutionary laws were passed, lowering rents and taking houses away from those who owned more than one, whole groups of students and teachers began turning against the Revolution again.

Those who planned to leave Cuba tried to keep it very secret, especially from the revolutionaries. As a result a rather comical thing began

27. Comandante Camilo Cienfuegos Gorriaran was the only Rebel leader who rivaled Fidel Castro in popularity. Cienfuegos came with Castro from Mexico on the launch *Granma* in 1956 and played an important role in the Sierra Maestra and Santa Clara campaigns. With Che Guevara he led the Army into Havana on January 5, 1959. He was chief of staff when he died in a plane crash at sea on October 29, 1959.

happening in school. When someone is absent you usually assume he is sick, no? Well, in those days a single absence was enough to start the rumors flying! If a student failed to answer roll call, the rest of us would comment, "He must have gone away." Often enough we were right.

We also watched to see who had a fresh vaccination, and we'd ask them, "Oh, so you're leaving?"

There was a boy I knew and liked fairly well even though he wasn't a revolutionary, but we had quarreled about politics and I insulted him, and we hadn't spoken to each other for a while. Then one day we had a long talk and were friends again. The next morning I found out he had left the country. Such cowards, not to say they were going!

Of the 900 students in the school, only about forty of us were revolutionaries, and there were three or four with whom I was very close, especially one girl, Milagros. We were classmates and did our homework together; she often spent the night at my house or I at hers.

We revolutionaries had our share of problems that year. There were arguments every day. Many of the teachers were *gusanos*,[28] and were brazen enough to proclaim it openly in the classroom. When they spoke against the Revolution, one or another of us would stand up and contradict them, and they'd send us to the principal's office, where we found no support either.

When the ship *Le Coubre*[29] blew up, all sorts of rumors about the cause were flying around. I went to school full of fury, ready to eat alive anybody who made the least little remark about it. I knew those people felt nothing for the men who'd died and were quite capable of mocking the tragedy. I was determined not to let them get away with it. I was on edge from the moment I arrived, but nobody dared mention the subject until, in chemistry class, the teacher said there was a law in Cuba forbidding ships to dock. He said that as a security measure, they were supposed to cast anchor a certain distance away and wait for smaller boats to take the cargo ashore.

I stood up like a shot. "I don't know whether you're lying about the law or not, but I would like to know if there's a law in the United States giving them the right to come here and murder eighty Cubans."

"The United States hasn't killed anybody," he said.

"Oh yes they have. Everybody knows the United States is responsible for that explosion."

At that the class exploded like *Le Coubre*. They'd just been waiting for

28. Literally "worms." The term is popularly used in Cuba to refer to anyone opposed to the Revolution, as well as to an active counterrevolutionary.

29. On March 4, 1960, a French munitions ship, *Le Coubre*, exploded in port at Havana, killing eighty-one and wounding more than a hundred. The Cuban government always maintained that the explosion was an act of sabotage by the CIA.

someone to set them off. Of course it ended in the principal's office, with the principal telling me he knew I was a revolutionary, but that I must learn to let other people express their opinions.

The school was owned by North Americans and they backed the counterrevolutionaries, who gradually intensified their propaganda campaign. In response, some of us decided to organize a Committee of Revolutionary Students. I was one of the five directors, and later I was elected leader. I rushed home that day to tell *mami* about it. For me it was a great thing to be chosen leader, even if I led only thirty people.

We had absolutely no experience in politics, so we went to a meeting of the FEU,[30] where they asked us to fight with them by obstructing all counterrevolutionary activity. We began to work actively for our ideas. The counterrevolutionaries at school had dropped leaflets all over the place and pasted up posters with the legend, "This child will grow up to be either a believer or an atheist. It depends on you. Teach him the catechism." Our first move was to paste up identical posters showing the same child, but with the legend, "This child will grow up to be either a patriot or a traitor. It depends on you. Teach him the Revolution."

One day we learned they were going to put up counterrevolutionary posters at 1:00 o'clock, so we put ours up first. The principal came out and insulted us, but we stood up to him: "Leave ours up or we'll take yours down." So they took them all down.

At home we were all in favor of the Revolution but had different ideas about what was going to happen next. *Mamá* was delighted with Fidel. I remember she used to exclaim, "How clearly that man expresses himself! He says exactly what I've thought all my life." And Renée's fiancé, Héctor, would agree. "Those are the ideas I've always believed in. That man is a communist."

But Silvio would protest that Fidel was no communist, rather a great humanitarian. "He talks of cooperatives," Silvio argued. "That means creating many small landowners. In other words, we'll end up with more private-property owners than we have now. It's the very opposite of communism." When I tried to give an opinion they'd shut me up and say I didn't know what I was talking about. But listening to them, I was beginning to learn.

---

30. *Federación Estudiantil Universitaria* (University Student Federation).

Chapter Four

Division in the Family

RENÉE:

The year after the Revolution triumphed, everyone was anticommunist. Even my mother was anticommunist, but only because she believed in God and thought she was defending Him. And the day we received news of the Urban Reform,[31] Silvio said, "Fidel's sure to fall this time. Look what he's done!" I tried to explain the rationale of it, but he answered, "You're crazy, he can't do that. We were getting along just fine without it."

I said, "But he *has* to do it. He can't come right out and declare himself a communist because they might bring him down, but he's taking all the steps that lead to communism."

Mamá said, "Then Fidel's a liar and he's pulling the wool over our eyes."

"No," I answered, "it's just that he *has* to deceive people right now." They broke off the conversation and went away, saying I was an intractable communist.

Communism was an issue of contention among the revolutionaries themselves. I remember that on the day of the Urrutia crisis,[32] after

---

31. On October 14, 1960, the first Urban Reform Law was adopted, nationalizing all urban rental housing. Rent, which was paid to the state, was applied toward the purchase price of the tenant's house or apartment. The period of amortization was determined by length of residency and condition of the housing. The second stage of the law instituted a rent ceiling of 10 percent of household income (effective May, 1961) on all new and vacated housing units.

32. Judge Manuel Urrutia Lleó, first President of the new Republic, was in office from January to July, 1959. As a provincial judge in Oriente, he had refused to sentence 100 Fidelistas accused of insurrection. As early as November, 1957, he had been selected by Fidel Castro as provisional president for the government-in-exile in Miami. Urrutia's short term of office was marked by many clashes with Castro, particularly over the Agrarian Reform Law and the growing influence of communists in the new government. Urrutia offered his resignation for the fourth time after Castro made a speech accusing him of being a traitor. The resignation was accepted and Dr. Osvaldo Dorticós Torrado was immediately chosen to replace him.

Fidel had resigned, we were gathered in the University and everybody wanted to stage protests. The student president met with all of us, and during the meeting a girl cried, "Down with Urrutia!" Almost everybody pointed to her and called her a communist. It wasn't that they were necessarily with Urrutia. Nobody knew too much about what was going on, but Cuban youth were definitely anticommunist. You couldn't even talk communism with them. All that came later.

I myself overestimated the ideas of people who didn't really want anything too new in the country. I didn't see anything that could come up to my image of my native land, so to speak. I was a communist, but I disliked the idea of the Party. I hadn't read about socialism and I still haven't. It wasn't theory that interested me, but the fact of being a communist. But I must admit that most of the communists I met before the Revolution turned out to be uninteresting... cowards, most of them.

Héctor was a communist who spoke and even wrote about his ideas, and he was considering the possibility of converting the family lumber mill into a cooperative. During the early years of the Revolution, the business was floundering because production had been based on sales to the United States. Of course Héctor was delighted because it meant that he wouldn't have to work in it, but I felt rather bad about it.

That year, 1959, after Héctor and I had been engaged two years, *mamá* finally gave her consent and we were married. I was twenty-two and teaching elementary and junior high school in Havana. Héctor was a graduate accountant by then—he hated it but had completed the program to please his father. So it suited him very well when Regulo, a young black schoolmate of his, offered him a post in the Ministry of Foreign Affairs. After that he used to work and work. He worked until 2:00 or 3:00 A.M. every day and would sometimes faint on the job. They'd give him an injection so he could go on because he was doing the work of eight or nine men. Héctor arrived at the wedding after work at about 7:00 in the evening, and our honeymoon was only two days long.

In 1960 Héctor was given an assignment at a foreign embassy. When we left Cuba I was already six months pregnant so my eldest daughter, Nora, was born abroad. I adapted to the new country very well, but Héctor couldn't bear it. Everything people did got on his nerves. He was always talking about "those donkeys" and saying he wouldn't put up with them another minute. I think he actually lost interest in foreign affairs after that visit.

Héctor advanced quickly in the Ministry, at first simply as a result of conditions, but later because of his intelligence and hard work. He was in the foreign service a total of five years and all that time I was no more than his "accompanist," that is, a diplomat's wife. I didn't work but was kept so busy with social duties that I always had to hire a maid to look after the children.

For me life abroad wasn't restricting or confining because I enjoyed the people and was always very open to them, so I wasn't isolated. I really liked traveling, except that it made me sad to be in one country with my friend Mirella in another. It was like being torn in two. Life seems very short when you're away from your native country, and even shorter when you can't be close to the people you care for.

MÓNICA:

When Renée and Héctor got married, I was a bit upset. It had been my dream that our family would be reunited, but after barely two years Renée had to break us up again by getting married. The whole world crashed down about me. At least they moved to an apartment about three or four blocks from ours, so I still had my sister near. I'd have lunch and spend most of my time there. It was tiny, only one room, but they fixed it up very nicely.

Six months after her marriage, Renée became pregnant. I was very, very happy about it. I was sure the baby was going to be a girl, and in a way I felt she would be mine. I thought of her as a kind of doll for me. "Oh Renée," I'd say, "I'll take care of your little girl. I'll give her the bottle."

But one morning when Renée was about four months pregnant, she and Héctor were waiting outside as I passed on my way to school. They stopped me. "Come on up. We have something to tell you."

Héctor had been with MINREX[33] since the early stages of the insurrection and, well, when I went up, Renée told me they were sending her and Héctor abroad. All my dreams about the baby were blown to hell. I wouldn't even be near them when it was born. Happy as I was for Renée's sake, I was miserable for my own. To make matters worse, the following month my brother said he was also going abroad. Now I would be all alone with *mami*. I was terribly depressed about it for a long time.

Living alone with *mami*, I was wretchedly unhappy, and more and more disgusted with her behavior. I began to think she was mentally ill, she did such illogical, dramatic things. At the anniversary of Uncle Jaime's death, we went to Ovas for the Christmas season so that Aunt Mercedes wouldn't be alone at a time so full of bitter memories. I marveled at Aunt Mercedes's self-control. On the night before the Day of the Three Kings she was up till almost daybreak sewing dolls' clothes for her daughters. She understood that she shouldn't sadden her daughters' lives, and during those days I never even saw her weep. I felt deep respect for her attitude, so different from *mamá*'s.

I think it was Christmas Eve when *mami* started to talk of Jaime—it was

33. *Ministerio de Relaciones Extranjeras* (Ministry of Foreign Affairs).

Jaime this and Jaime that and if Jaime were here . . . then she burst into tears. My godmother interrupted her. "Look, Beatríz, I've made a great effort to control myself so my daughters won't see me crying. Please stop."

It was Godmother—that's what I called Mercedes—who was really suffering, but *mamá* who had to make the scene. Instead of trying to help she started quarreling, crying out, "Oh, I know nobody loves me!"

That was only the beginning. She became more and more hysterical, until around midnight she ran out into the street. I was about to go after her but Godmother said, "Stay here. If you give in to her it will only raise her dramatics to the fifth power. I won't have my daughters upset."

I understood *mami* perfectly and was sorry she had caused trouble. So when she came back into the house, sobbing and screaming my father's name, "Oh, Guillermo, if only you were here to see how they treat me!" I could bear it no longer. It was not I but a wild beast who rushed in and shouted, "If you so much as utter my father's name again, I'll walk out and never come back! If *papi* were alive to see you he'd be ashamed."

She tried to answer me but I wouldn't let her. "You have no right to do this! You're the only person in this house who allows herself the luxury of crying. Godmother doesn't even mention her husband's name. Besides, *papi* is sacred to me above everything in the world, and I won't allow you to use his name in your trashy melodramatics." After that she calmed down.

As I grew up, instead of modeling myself after my mother, I tried to be her exact opposite. I tried to be tougher, less melodramatic, and if anybody tried to play the martyr with me, he didn't get anywhere. If somebody tells me that unless I do thus-and-so he'll get sick or die, I answer, "You can go to the devil for all I care."

And now that I have children of my own, I'm careful not to use threats against them. If I have to, I slap their bottoms, but I never tell them I'll die or get a headache. I won't pose as their victim as *mami* did with us.

In those days I dreamed frequently about *papi*. In one dream I met him walking along a street in Havana. "Oh *papi*," I said, "I have so many things to tell you."

"Yes, yes, but I have to go now," he answered.

"But first come home with me," I insisted. "I want you to see *mami*. She's so changed, you'll hardly recognize her."

I took him home and *mami* wanted to talk with him, but I wouldn't let her. "No, no, he's in a hurry. Come, *papi*, I have to talk to you."

"I have to go back," he repeated.

"Oh *papi*, why didn't you come to us right away?"

I always dreamed that *papi* came back for only a very short stay, so I was always tense and eager; I couldn't possibly tell him everything that had happened or show him all the affection I felt in so brief a time.

I dreamed a lot about Renée, too. When she was pregnant I dreamed that she transmitted her pregnancy to me and I bore a daughter, as if it were the most natural thing in the world, and when her daughter was born I had a dream in which I told *papi* he had a granddaughter. I always dream about my father when something affects me deeply.

After a while, Uncle Ramón brought Aunt Mercedes and her daughters to live in Havana. *Mami* says that Rogelio Boza, an old-time politician, had offered Mercedes a house there, but she never got it. The Revolution wasn't made for that kind of cheap politics. People like Rogelio thought the new government was going to be like all the others. Even people who took part in the Revolution expected the same old political deals. So later they were among those who turned against it.

As it was, Uncle Ramón found Aunt Mercedes a very pretty apartment near his own in Vedado, and we began to see as much of them as we had when we lived in Consolación del Sur. So for a while there was a lot of the family nearby, and I wasn't so lonely anymore. Ramón was my god-father, and when I was a child I'd go wild with joy when he and his wife came to see us. They would pick me up in their arms and be sweet in any number of ways. After *papi* died, Ramón was a second father to me. Being my uncle and my godfather gave him a great deal of authority over me. In minor ways *mamá* let him think his opinion mattered a great deal to her, so he really thought he ruled the roost! She'd say, "Your uncle thinks it's immoral for women to wear pants. When you see him coming, change into a skirt." So as soon as I heard Uncle Ramón's car, I'd run and change. And once while we were living at the boardinghouse he told *mami,* "I can't understand why you don't give this child ballet lessons. It's downright immoral not to." *Mami* gave in, as she always did when he pressed for something she fully intended to do in the first place. It was easy for her. So I took ballet lessons until I got bored and quit.

And then, at the approach of my fifteenth birthday, Uncle Ramón got it into his head that I should have the customary bourgeois celebration. So I had quite a big dance at the Havana Hilton, which is now the Habana Libre. Fifteen couples, formal dress—the works. They hired a dance master to train us for the opening waltz, and every time we went to practice we'd end up having a party, dancing the cha-cha-cha and the mambo. That crazy dance master enjoyed it every bit as much as we did. It was at that party that I had my first alcoholic drink. It made me a bit dizzy, but I felt so grown-up ordering a Tom Collins! I wandered into the casino, too, because I wanted to see a roulette wheel.

So as long as I was a child, Uncle Ramón and his wife, Mari, were very affectionate to me. But now that I was growing up, I noticed a change in them, especially in Ramón. He saw how much I missed my brother and sister and that I lived for the letters and photographs they sent. He said it was a good thing they'd gone so far away because they were turning me into a communist. He and his wife often visited us for the sole purpose of mouthing political propaganda. Mari was a bigot, and she began flaunting her prejudices more than ever.

"What's the matter with you?" I'd ask her. "Blacks and whites have the same rights." That's where I started having a hard time, not only with Ramón and Mari, but also with Aunt Mercedes, who began to echo their opinions.

Uncle Ramón made all sorts of complaints about the Revolution and never mentioned Fidel except in a disagreeable tone of voice. He'd say, "Fidel asks all Cubans to unite for the benefit of the Twenty-sixth of July Movement, which conveniently grabs everything for its members."

Fidel had said no such thing. I was furious, I was like a little bantam cock, but Ramón said I was a mere adolescent and that I should listen and learn. But he had nothing to say to a kid like me; he only talked with *mami*. He'd tell her, "The situation is downright dangerous. Everyone is against this government. It'll soon fall."

I couldn't let him get away with that. "Even if worse came to worse, even if your hopes were realized and the Americans invaded, we revolutionaries wouldn't stand by to watch. We'd fight as long as one of us was left alive."

What irritated me most of all was when they said to *mami*, "Don't worry about anything. A relative is a relative, and when we win we'll look after Mónica." They had it all planned. When the invasion came they were going to fetch me and *mami* in Ramón's car, take us to a house where we'd be met by Bernardo's car, and then the whole family would be taken somewhere safe. Oh yes, Ramón would protect us all!

"Thank you so much," I told him. "But I'm not the slightest bit interested in your protection. If that day ever comes, you'll be my enemy, not my protector. I swear, I won't be the one who survives!"

He said I was the limit. He said that was what the Revolution was doing, setting family against family, making a mere child think she could insult her relatives. He called me a sly villian and said I should go crawl under the bed.

"Maybe when the time comes, *you* will crawl under the bed," said I, "but I mean to fight."

"You! You're only a little girl!"

"I'll fight and you'll have to kill me, old man!" I retorted.

When I talked like that, Ramón would get up indignantly and say to *mami*, "It's impossible to come to this house. Your daughter respects no one!"

Mami told me to be more tactful. She was a thorough revolutionary, but it hurt her that I should feel compelled to insult my uncle.

Well, his new attitude hurt *me*. But in spite of those arguments I loved him as much as ever. It didn't occur to me that political differences might affect personal relationships. No matter how mistaken he was about the Revolution, he was still my uncle and he really mattered to me.

The Christmas after Renée and Silvio left, *mami* and I were all alone. The family came one afternoon and left a basket of gifts, saying they weren't going to have their traditional Christmas Eve supper or see in the New Year. Later on I found out the whole family had celebrated without us. Can you imagine? While *papá* was alive the whole bunch of relatives spent Christmas Eve at our house. Now with *papi* dead and Renée and Silvio away, they gave us the cold shoulder. You see, they knew they'd be talking politics and didn't want anybody arguing with them. But it didn't seem right that we should be snubbed for political reasons.

The breach widened between us. It particularly hurt me to see Aunt Mercedes turning counterrevolutionary after the way Batista's stooges had killed her husband. On the second anniversary of Uncle Jaime's death, she didn't even go to his memorial ceremony—none of the family showed up except *mami* and me. When we returned from the cemetery I told my aunt, "You should have been there."

"No," she answered. "This isn't what my husband died for."

"You're wrong," I retorted. "I think this is exactly what he died for. If he were alive now he'd be a revolutionary. How insolent of you to insult his memory by calling him a counterrevolutionary!"

Once she even took me aside and begged me not to indoctrinate her daughters. By that time they were spending most of their time at Mass, and they adored the nuns and priests. It was typical of the *gusanos* that before the Revolution they'd taken their Catholicism very lightly and afterward they suddenly became devout.

My poor aunt had really been in shock since the murder of her husband. She lived in a state of perpetual alert. Every day she'd come to our house and tell *mami,* "Be sure to store a lot of water because the Americans are going to come and save us soon. I'm stocking up on milk and things, because how will I shop for food in the middle of the fight?" The atmosphere in her house was so tense, there were nights I slept there when her small daughter would wake up screaming, "*Mami,* the Americans, the Americans are here!"

At that time Uncle Ramón was working so hard setting up a polyclinic that he lost about 40 pounds. They sent him to carry out a series of special tasks, once to Oriente to settle a hospital strike. He solved the problem by firing a lot of people. It was plain he was not working as a revolutionary!

One day when I arrived home I found *mami* crying; "Ramón is lost," she told me.

"What do you mean, he's lost?"

Apparently, one morning Aunt Mari had found a note from him saying he had to leave for Oriente in a hurry. Two days later the Ministry called and said he'd been absent from work. Just about the time he disappeared, an airplane had been hijacked and the pilot killed, and *mamá,* who is very intelligent but always twists things around, decided that Ramón must have been involved. Poor *mamá* lived through three days of real anguish, fearing he might be caught, jailed, and killed. She cried all the time.

We found out later, from one of Laura's boyfriends, that Ramón had taken asylum in a foreign embassy. Not only that, the whole family knew it except *mamá* and me. They'd invented the story strictly for our benefit, letting *mamá* suffer all that time. It was sheer mental cruelty and I cooled toward them after that. Why didn't they tell us from the start? Once he was in the embassy he couldn't be arrested. In the second place, the State Security men are no fools. I told Mari and Mercedes right to their faces, "You think State Security knows nothing? Why, before you start thinking something up, they know all about it!"

Uncle Ramón never explained why he'd decided to ask for asylum. Later I was arguing about it with a friend of my uncle, and he told me they'd driven Ramón into a corner, demanding things he couldn't do. He said that they'd wanted to fortify the clinic, and Uncle Ramón refused to store firearms or have antiaircraft batteries installed there. He said a clinic was a Red Cross zone, an area respected in all wars.

"How very legalistic of my uncle! How learned he is in archaic law!" I told his friend. "Ramón is an intelligent man, but that's so naive it can't be honest. I'm only fifteen and I know far less about life than he does, but I do know that the Americans have never in all their dirty lives respected the sick or anybody else. Were there no clinics and hospitals in Hiroshima?" It would have served my uncle right if a bomb had fallen on him in the clinic. Then he would have known about the Americans! What do they respect in Vietnam?

It seemed obvious to me that Uncle Ramón was simply splitting hairs to disguise his real ideas. Even so I was dreadfully unhappy to think he was leaving Cuba. The others thought it was a matter of a month or two until they and their kind took over Cuba, but I knew we'd never see each other again.

One day I went with *mami* to visit Uncle Ramón in the embassy, and we met Aunt Mercedes on the bus. She seemed uneasy about us and I said, "There's something strange going on, *mami.* I think she wants to see Ramón alone. If there's going to be trouble I don't want to be involved."

When we got there Godmother confided to *mami* that she wanted to hand Ramón a package. Then she asked me to be on the lookout. "Wait a minute, wait a minute," I told her. "You're of age and may do as you please but don't involve me in it." *Mami* scolded me for being disrespectful but I kept right on saying what I had to say. "If you're a counterrevolutionary, that's none of my business. But if you're going to slip him a package, I'm leaving."

"Watch your tongue, girl!" my aunt said nervously. "Now don't you go accusing me...."

"I won't accuse you because I'm not going to see you do anything illegal. Take care that I don't see you."

It hurt me to see my uncle as I did that day. The embassy was on a corner, surrounded by a high wrought-iron fence and numerous bushes. As we left, my aunt walked away from us to talk to Ramón, who was standing behind the fence. It was a daring thing to do in full view of people who were armed, but she was quite cool about it.

I said to *mami*, "Hurry, let's go another way. If she's arrested, they may be confused as to who's a counterrevolutionary and who isn't!"

But as we hurried along the sidewalk, I turned my head to see Uncle Ramón standing there with Mercedes. I heard her say through the fence, "Chocolate."

I whispered, "What did I tell you? That's a code word for something."

Mami, afraid that I'd accuse them, said, "Oh no, nothing of the kind. She just means there are chocolates in the package."

The next day Havana was bombed, and the day after that they attacked at Playa Girón. That's quite a coincidence, no? Maybe it had nothing to do with the "chocolate," but I'm sure those two were engaged in some sort of subversive activity.

When the invasion was attempted at Playa Girón I was not yet a *miliciana* and had no uniform, but I bought myself a pair of olive-green pants and a light-blue shirt and went out dressed that way. *Mami* was terrified for me. I went to defend the school, but nobody was there except three or four crazy kids who'd had the same idea. There was nothing for me to do there, so I went to Vedado to Aunt Mercedes's.

Now that the Americans had really arrived, my aunt was even more obsessive. In her mind the landing at Playa Girón took on the dimensions of World War II. I found her in a tiny room she'd stocked with big cans of water, powdered milk, and canned milk. "This is war," she told me. "We'll be isolated for months. All communications will be cut. There's going to be fierce fighting."

She called me over to the shortwave radio. "Come listen," she said. "We've already won the war. We took over such-and-such a port and now we're marching down such-and-such a road." According to her program, Fidel had left Cuba.

I said, "Dear heart, where are you getting that news?"

"I'm listening to the 'Voice of America.'"

"And you believe the 'Voice of America'? I believe only the communiqués of the revolutionary government. From the last one I heard, it seems *we* are winning."

"No, no, no!" she insisted. "Come listen."

At first I heard music but in a few minutes there was more news. Raúl Castro, they announced, had committed suicide after declaring that he was not a good communist. They followed with a million more stupidities.

"Did you hear?" Aunt Mercedes said. "Did you hear that?"

I really told her off. "Why do you muck up your mind with such vile junk? Those people came here to kill us—how can you be on their side? Anybody who points a gun at me is my enemy, that's all there is to it!"

I walked out angrily. When I told *mami,* she asked me never to go to my aunt's house again. "I understand why you had to argue with her, but remember that your aunt can't control her nerves. You only make her worse."

On the day of our victory against the invading forces, the papers began to publish interviews with the captured mercenaries. It was a farce. "I came against my will," they pleaded. "They put me on board ship and brought me here. . . . I'm not a counterrevolutionary, I'm willing to work in the country." When they'd spewed their garbage over the radio and TV, I paid Aunt Mercedes a call to needle her, and when I got there I had a sudden impulse to tell the younger girl, Mercy, about American atrocities. I didn't bother with Marisela because she was a mere echo of the counterrevolutionaries in the family. When I said something to her she never answered at once, but repeated it to my aunt and then parroted whatever Mercedes said. Mercy was more apt to think for herself.

Then the TV news program showed a scene of an atom bomb explosion. I'd already thoroughly explained the bomb to Mercy, so when she saw the picture she said, "Look, the Americans kill people with that." My aunt turned to me in a fury. "This is the last straw! How can you teach an innocent child such things?"

I kept telling my relatives that Americans were bloodthirsty killers who had destroyed Hiroshima, but their eyes remained closed to the truth. Foolishly, stupidly, they began to run away from their homeland. In 1961, Ramón, the head of our family, left with his wife, my Uncle Bernardo, my Aunt Mercedes, and her daughters—all of them. Uncle Bernardo had lived in the United States for fifteen years and had a great veneration for Americans and the American dollar. "Bernardo has sold out!" I told *mami.* "All he cares about is money." My Uncle Gustavo left later and Benito and Cuca followed in 1968. All my mother's brothers and her only sister . . . gone.

SEÑORA REYES:

In our family, only my children and I remained loyal to Fidel. Mercedes had sacrificed a husband to the Revolution, so we were shocked when she left Cuba with Ramón. He dragged his brothers with him too, because his opinion carried more weight in the family.

Ramón had been a follower of Aureliano Sánchez Arango and worked secretly for the Twenty-sixth of July Movement, but I don't know whether he did it from his heart. He never did sympathize with communism, and that's why in the end he turned against the Revolution. If Aureliano's group had triumphed, Ramón would have had a high position in the government by now. That's what he had in mind; he never told me so but I'm his sister and I know.

Many people helped the Revolution simply to get on the good side of whoever happened to win. All the fat pro-Batista people sent money to Fidel in the Sierra, playing both sides so that when a new government came to power they would claim to have been in favor of it all along. That way, they expected to sneak in again.

When Fidel won, they found out he was following a completely different line, that he wasn't about to pay back political favors, that he took away everybody's property, no matter what side they'd been on. Then all those slippery characters were disgusted and left.

I don't mean Ramón was one of those people, though. He was a good person, very affectionate, well loved, intelligent, an outstanding man in his profession. He'd had a hard time financing his studies and had to struggle to achieve his goals. *Papá* had seven children and couldn't afford to send any of them to Havana, so although my husband and I certainly didn't have a fortune, we gave Ramón money for his studies and helped him in other ways too, as much as we could. He was so bright and eager!

To think how he struggled, and to see how many poor children from the hills study nowadays with everything paid for—books, classes, food—everything! I think that if Ramón came back and saw how much is being done now for the Cuban children, he'd be moved. He knows what it's like not to have such things come easily. But he loved to live well and by that time he had a fine house, a good car, all the comforts. The Revolution took away those material benefits, and he simply isn't the kind of person who can adapt to hardship. I guess that was at the root of his conflicts.

At the very beginning he tried to integrate with the Revolution, but I noticed many little things which convinced me he was not altogether in favor of it. For instance, he never listened to Fidel's speeches, although he always claimed he heard them over his car radio. He was given a responsible position by the government and did excellent work, but didn't like the change. He began to turn sour on the Revolution and was reported for many things, such as refusing to wear the militia uniform or not cooperating with the Army during a crisis.

Ramón was sent to Oriente to pacify a medical center where workers had rebelled, and he cleaned out the place by firing about thirty counterrevolutionaries. As a result, he enjoyed the complete confidence of the Minister of Health, but that only made his position more difficult. It led him to resign and take asylum in an embassy. From there he made arrangements to leave the country.

My revolutionary tendencies and those of my children annoyed him terribly. Mónica argued with him constantly. One day Ramón said to me, "Your children are spoiled rotten. What does that kid know about the Revolution? What did you do against Batista? Nothing. Not one thing. So how come you're such a revolutionary now?"

"Well," I answered, "Mónica was only thirteen when Batista fell. As for me, my job took up all my time."

"You're always covering up for your children," he said.

When the Revolution triumphed, my son Silvio was appointed attaché to a Cuban embassy abroad. Ramón objected, and eventually we understood why. He was very fond of Silvio, who was his only nephew, and he wanted to win the boy over to his way of thinking. In going abroad, Silvio was escaping his influence. Later on, though, Ramón warned me, "Be glad they're going away. Terrible times are coming. Blood will flow in the streets of Havana. But don't talk about it with your children."

While my brother was in the embassy there were many rumors of invasion, and whenever I heard one I'd run over to Mercedes's house to check on it. She tried to reassure me. "Don't worry, Beatríz, if anything should happen, we'd know about it ahead of time and we'd get you and Mónica at once. Your children have diplomatic passports, don't they? They don't? Well, see to it that they get them. We'll help you at the airport here."

I went to see Bernardo and said, "Look, there's a rumor that something terrible is going to happen here. I don't know what, but that's what people are saying. They know something." But no, he wasn't going to risk telling me anything.

A few days before Playa Girón I realized there was a conspiracy among my relatives. At the embassy there were government people who allowed packages to be passed to the prisoners. One day Mercedes took Ramón a jelly roll with a message in it. I know there was a message because Ramón showed us the bit of string attached to it.

I said, "Look, Mercedes, you've already suffered immense pain over one tragedy. You have two daughters to think of now. Don't go getting involved in anything, much less in plots against the Revolution."

She wouldn't answer that. She only said, "Please don't go to the embassy anymore, Beatríz. Ramón's visiting hours are so few that it's better for his wife to be the one who has the opportunity to visit him." Well, I could see they were up to something but I had no idea what it was. The next day was the attack at Playa Girón.

Sorry as I am not to have them near, I'm glad my sister and all my brothers left. They were better out of Cuba if they were against the Revolution. They'd have been caught sooner or later. They told us they were going to Venezuela but they left for Miami, the same place Ventura and all Batista's men had escaped to. Mercedes did go to Venezuela first but from there she went to Miami. They all left to join Ventura! Imagine! I hate even to think about it.

None of my relatives up North write to me except my niece Laura. I hadn't heard from Ramón since he left, but one day last year I was surprised to receive a letter from my brother himself. Here it is.

Dear Sister Beatríz,

I've been wanting to write you for a long, long time. I did phone you but you were out, so I talked with Silvio.

I'm living in Wisconsin, where I'm studying medicine on a scholarship, and I'll soon be an M.D. specializing in oral surgery. I've been in training three years already and still have one more to go. My life here has been difficult because, aside from the fact that I didn't know English when I arrived, I work hard and have weekly examinations and supervisions, but up to now I've been doing well, having passed all my courses so far. Today I didn't go to class because it's snowing very hard, so I took the opportunity to write you.

I very much wish I could see you. I want you to know I'm still the same. I haven't changed in the least, and each time I pass a course or receive an honor, my thoughts fly to you, who always were and will ever be my inspiration in all my struggles. It was you who awakened my mind and transmitted to me your love of study. You were the one who gave me my very first book, *The Two Brothers*. Do you remember? I've never forgotten. Life changes, the world goes round, and sometimes hatred moves in to replace love . . . but not always. No matter what happens, whether one lives under one creed or another, this depends on a person's capacity to love, and that is something which has never died out in me. Nor has my capacity to understand you.

Mari and I are both well, and she sends greetings. I frequently hear from Mercedes and the girls, who are all well. Mercy is finishing college. She went to New York last year. Tell Renée, Mónica, and Silvio that I love them as always. It's something that can never change. Its roots go deep because they are your children. Perhaps you won't answer this letter but it would make me very happy if you did. Whether you do or not, please see it as an expression of deeply felt longing and of the enduring love I feel for you, sister. Defects we all have, and mine must be great, and when I try to understand and tolerate those of other people I'm simply hoping, as I legitimately may, for understanding and tolerance in return. Whatever wrong I may have done, it never had its roots in malice.

Much love. I hope this letter arrives before Christmas because it carries the unchanging love and remembrance of your brother. With a big hug,

Ramón.

The letter made me weep so much I wasn't able to answer it for months. What courage! Imagine, studying at fifty! It's so very sad. But by now my brother is allowed to practice in all the States. He's won prizes and everything. He's outstanding because he's had an excellent general education.

Ramón would be doing such wonderful work in Cuba if only he had stayed! But there's no chance of his coming back. The Revolution is hard on those who return and keeps a very close watch on them. Because the Revolution must find out whether they returned as spies or in good faith, they must first go to work in the country. Now that Ramón is a doctor he would have to practice in the country for a long time, I guess. He would have to win his right of re-entry.

People are saying that Fidel is going to spread out the welcome banner for every Cuban who wants to return, but that I do not believe. How could he? The housing problem is bad enough without all the emigrés trooping back.

Chapter Five

Growing Up

MÓNICA:

In February, 1961, I volunteered for the Literacy Campaign, which aimed to combat illiteracy in the country.[34] Fidel had been asking for volunteers for several weeks, and I suggested to my friend Milagros that we join. She was reluctant at first but I argued until she agreed. The family made a terrible fuss about my decision but *mami* accepted it. My aunts and uncles, who were still here then, thought it would be a disaster. How could *mami* permit me to go alone to God knows where, to live among God knows who, in the countryside where there was no running water or electricity? Ángela Rosa Collazo practically had a fit! "Beatríz, my child, you must be insane to let Mónica go out to the country!"— adding a phrase that was habitual with her, "The country is for the birds!"

Uncle Bernardo and Aunt Mercedes said to *mamá*, "Well, Beatríz, you know how it is, one goes and two come back." *Mami* was such a stern moralist they thought the fear that I might come back pregnant would be the strongest deterrent. But *mami* is a fighter, especially when people insinuate things like that. She faced right up to them, saying she'd brought me up to be incapable of such a thing.

Mami let us make decisions ourselves, although she had very definite opinions about what we should do with our lives. She wanted us to grow up into independent human beings and often had to stand up against

34. The year 1961, declared by Castro as the Year of Education, saw a massive campaign to stamp out illiteracy in Cuba. Schools were closed in April and 100,000 students from junior high through college level were mobilized as *brigadistas*, trained and sent into rural areas to teach reading and writing. Teachers called *alfabetizadores* taught illiterates in the cities. The Campaign was reported successful in reducing the illiteracy rate from 23 percent to approximately 3 percent. (Lockwood, *Castro's Cuba, Cuba's Fidel*, p. 126.) A Cuban government publication set the illiteracy rate at 3.9 percent in the mid-1960s, stating this figure included 25,000 Haitian residents who did not speak Spanish and people who were mentally retarded or "too old to learn to read and write." This pamphlet estimated the total number of volunteer teachers during the Campaign at 271,000. (*Cuba: A Giant School* (Havana: Ministry of Foreign Affairs, n.d.))

the family to give us children a measure of independence. She herself had more individuality than any of the others in her family. She dared to think for herself and to act on her beliefs. In that sense, she does have self-control and I admire her for it.

For a time I wanted to be a ballerina but I soon gave up the idea, and it's possible that *mami's* opinion of it influenced me. She didn't look upon ballet as my lifework; the thing to do was to have a career. There was a time when Renée wanted to study dramatics, and to Uncle Ramón, that was a monstrous ambition. He said a theatrical environment was rotten and my sister's morals would be perverted. But *mami* stood up to him: "Nonsense. She'll simply have to learn to defend herself against evil influences."

Shortly after I'd decided to join the Literacy Campaign, a letter arrived from Renée saying she was returning to Cuba with her little girl. *Mami* said, "Now you'll have to choose between the Campaign and the niece you've dreamed about so much. You may be sent too far away for Renée to come to you."

It was a hard decision for me, and the family exploited it to the utmost. Every time my aunts saw me they'd say, "After crying so much for your niece, now you care so little!" I told them, "I'll be very unhappy if I can't meet her. Even so, I'm going out to help in the Literacy Campaign."

You see, to me the Campaign was such a great thing, such a historic event. I thought when I was a little old woman I'd be embarrassed to explain to my grandchildren, "No, I didn't join the Literacy Campaign; I was too eager to see my sister again, and meet my niece." It seemed to me that would be downright immoral. Besides, it was a beautiful opportunity to experience perhaps one thousandth of the things Fidel had been through.

I'd get to know the people and be independent of my family for the first time in my life. All those things were important to me. And then, after eight months to return and be able to say, "Seven or eight little old men and women know how to read and write because I taught them."

At last the day came when I was to go to the country. We spent the first week in Varadero,[35] learning how to use the phonetic syllabary to teach people to read. The first few days there was a sort of mild mass hysteria among us. Everybody got sick. We were all young girls who had never been away from home before, and there were so many different rules and regulations to follow. We were strictly segregated from the boys. They lived at Camp Granma and the girls at Kawama.

One day there was an incident. We were all taken to the movies and a net was hung in the auditorium between the boys' side and the girls'!

35. A popular beach and resort in Matanzas Province. (For a broader description of the training program at Varadero and of the Campaign itself, see Fagen, *The Transformation of Political Culture in Cuba*, pp. 33–68.)

That created a lot of tension. Nothing provokes people more than to be forbidden to do something. The boys tore down the net and rushed over to us. Immediately the supervisors gathered the girls together and made us file out, double-time.

The only men at Kawama were some very cute lifeguards, and we girls kept pretending to drown so we'd be pulled out. We'd talk of boys all day long. One of my roommates—she must have come from a lower-class family—startled me with her dirty jokes. It's true that in a convent school you hear more dirty jokes than anywhere in the world, but in Varadero I heard things I never dreamed of. This girl said her brother had relations with heifers. I was terribly shocked. I'd never heard of bestiality. It hadn't ever occurred to me that a human being would do such a thing.

One day *mami* came to visit. We were filling in our requests for the place we preferred to be sent. I wanted to put down the Sierra Maestra in Oriente, which was my dream, but *mami* said no, it was too far for her to visit me and I was too young to be away from home for eight months. Milagros's *mamá* made the same objection. But we didn't want to be too near Havana. What would be the point of leaving home if I was going to have my relatives on top of me as usual? So Milagros and I compromised and put down Las Villas, which was within visiting distance, but far enough away so our families couldn't be there every minute.

We'd been in Varadero only two days when we were taken to Havana in buses for the May Day parade. Arriving in the city I was overcome with emotion, as if I'd been away ten years. Many of us wept. The streets looked so beautiful after our absence!

I phoned *mami* and she rushed over in a hired car, arriving just as we were getting under way again. She got out of the car, I got out of the bus, and we hugged out there in the street. "Ah," she cried, "your sister was supposed to arrive today, but since it's May Day she won't get here till tomorrow."

To think that I'd miss Renée by a matter of hours! Seldom have I felt such anguish. That night in Varadero I couldn't sleep and the next day I could think only of Renée. "Now her plane is landing . . . now she must be getting off . . . she's probably wearing this dress . . . her little girl must know such-and-such words by now." I thought surely they would visit me at Varadero and bring my little niece. There would be so little chance to see me once I was in the country.

Four days went by. I was given my uniform—olive-green pants, boots, the whole works—and I was excited. At last I was a brigadier. That was our rank as campaigners. The day of departure arrived and still no sign of *mami* and Renée. Early in the morning we were told we'd be leaving shortly, and we packed our knapsacks. At 1:00 o'clock the buses arrived and the supervisors began to organize the departure. At 5:00 we were still standing there, and I had hopes that *mami* and my sister might yet arrive before we started.

Around 6:00 we were given the order to board the buses. Suddenly Milagros, who had lived through all my anxious waiting, said, "Mónica! Isn't that your *mamá?*" I looked out the bus window and there she was. The bus was about to start, but I dashed out and threw my arms around her. "Didn't Renée come?" I asked anxiously.

"No," *mami* smiled, "she couldn't make it." Then I turned my head and there was Renée, the baby in her arms!

We embraced, weeping. It's a wonder we didn't smother that child, the way we hugged each other for fifteen minutes. Then I took the baby from her and exclaimed how beautiful she was. I took off her diaper and put it on again. *Mami* says it was the most touching thing she ever saw. There we were, my sister and I, wild with joy, hugging as if we'd never let each other go, standing right by the bus with the driver looking on, the girls all crying and Milagros weeping like Mary Magdalene.

I was so happy to have seen the baby! But I had to leave them and get back on the bus. When I sat down next to Milagros she said, "I cried more than you did."

Our first stop was Santa Clara. Then they took us to Remedios, and from there the commissioner of Remedios took us to a tiny village near Guanabo in Las Villas.

"Is this where we get off?" I asked.

"This is it."

"Oh, but look, I wanted to go to the country—real country, you know what I mean, where there are earthen huts with no electricity. Villages I know; it's the country I want."

"If that's what you want, I can take you. It's no problem."

Milagros, two other brigadiers, and I were driven out into the country in a jeep. First they dropped off the other girls; then they took Milagros and me to houses very near each other.

It was night when I arrived where I was to stay. It felt strange, getting off there and being introduced as "the brigadier who is going to live with you."

"Ah. Very well," the family said.

"Then you're staying?" the commissioner asked.

"Yes." As he drove off in his jeep, I looked at all the people in the house and thought, "Oh, my God!"

There was a little old couple, a girl, Graciela, of about twenty-three, Elías, who was about twenty-one, Pedro, about nineteen, another boy who must have been fifteen or sixteen, a girl of fourteen or so, and a little boy of four or five. It was a fairly good country house, with a porch, a little dining room, and a small parlor with a bedroom on either side, all built of cement. The kitchen had wooden walls and an earthen floor, and was thatched with palm leaves.

It was about bedtime, so I lit my lantern as we had been taught to do. It was a Chinese lantern, something new to me, and when we were first taught to use it I was surprised at the brilliant light it gave, almost like electricity. They told me I was to share a room with the two girls and they showed me my bed. I lay down at once.

That first night was very long. The house was surrounded by cane fields. I'd never heard the rustle of cane at night. It seemed very loud in the stillness of the country. Next morning I woke up with a bad cold and a fever. Sick on my first day in the country! I didn't know what to do. I was awfully far from civilization, too far to expect any doctor to get to me, and worse still, I was among strangers and didn't know how they'd react. *Mami* had warned me never, under any circumstances, to allow myself to be treated with home remedies. Above all, I was not to allow anybody to rub my stomach—that's the standard country treatment for indigestion, and if you happen to have appendicitis it can be very dangerous.

On the other hand, at Varadero I had been told to adapt to country customs. Our aim was to educate the people gradually, not directly oppose any of their beliefs. If the people were not revolutionaries I should try to convert them, but tactfully, without startling them.

I was terrified, which made me sicker, and that's when my asthma started, though I didn't know it was asthma. I'd always been subject to a runny nose and allergic sneezing fits. For three days I ran a high fever and could hardly breathe. Now I realize it was psychosomatic; I was reacting emotionally to my situation.

The lady of the house fed me lots of clear soup. I was afraid she'd doctor me with some strange concoction but she didn't. One day she wanted to put a plaster of sage leaves on the soles of my feet and I agreed. I knew it would do no good, but it obviously could do no harm either. She also put some strange stuff on my chest, but I didn't protest because I dared not contradict her. I was scared though, and finally I asked for a doctor.

"Oh, there's nothing wrong with you," they said, but they called the doctor anyway. He prescribed several things that made me feel a bit better.

One night when my fever was high, Milagros came to see me. I must have been only partly conscious. I remember hearing her voice from very far away but I couldn't make out the words. People seemed to be moving about the room as in a dream, and I was startled to hear someone else call, "Mónica!" It turned out to be the woman in charge of the brigadiers in that zone, and she'd come to tell me, at that late hour, that we'd all been granted permission to spend the following day, Mother's Day, in Havana.

The people in the house protested. "She can't go, she's too sick."

"Sick or not, I'm going."

"You can't take such a risk, you might get worse and die."

"I'm getting up to dress right now," said I.

They gave in and dressed me themselves. I was so weak I could hardly stand. They put layers and layers of garments on me until I looked like a bundle of clothes, then they wrapped me in blankets and put me in a jeep, which drove me to a bus. Later, as the bus rolled into Havana, I found I could breathe freely again, and my temperature went down.

Going home on my first pass was the greatest event of my life. *Mami* kissed me and said, "How are you doing? No, wait, you'd better take a bath first."

"I can't bathe. I've come here with a 40° fever. I've been very sick."

"Tell me all about it later. First the bath."

Mami has never believed you should avoid bathing when you have a fever. She has a number of opinions like that, strange to most Cubans. It was useless to argue so I gave in, and in fact I felt better afterward. Even so, *mami* called the doctor. He said I'd had an acute asthmatic attack, which might indicate the start of a chronic condition or might simply be an isolated episode. It turned out to be chronic—I've been asthmatic ever since. He gave me several prescriptions and I returned to the country with the rest of the group.

As soon as I went back I took a census of illiterates, as we had been instructed. In the barrio assigned to me there were eight or nine illiterates and there was also one little house that nobody told me about. I asked the family I was staying with, "Who lives in that little house?"

"Oh, just some blacks."

"Can they read and write?"

"I don't know, they're blacks."

"Well, I'll just drop in and see if they have illiterates in the house."

"No, no, you can't go there! I tell you, they're blacks."

"All right, I heard you, but I'm going."

They tried to stop me, but seeing my mind was made up, the old man said, "Elías will take you on horseback and wait for you outside."

It was then I realized that country people were a lot more prejudiced than city people. They discriminated brutally against blacks. They never visited them and feared for my safety. They hinted that the black boys might molest me and also said they practiced bestiality. Later I learned that this was true. After a time I realized everybody there practiced it. Frankly I was scared, but I said to myself, "Buck up, kid, be brave," and I went to visit them.

I found that nearly every one of the blacks was illiterate, so I decided to give two classes a day, and, wanting to make people go to the blacks' house, I chose that one for the afternoon classes. My hosts, of course, were shocked.

The most difficult part of the Campaign was living with the old couple and their children. As a family they had more schooling than anybody else in the barrio—they must have gone as far as the sixth grade—and had great natural intelligence besides. But the only person in that house who wasn't hostile to me was the old man. At least he was gentle in his ways, though when I tried to persuade him to join a cooperative, we'd argue and he always came out the winner.

He owned four cows and a jeep, as well as a small plot of land where he planted yucca and beans, and although he planted mainly for family consumption, he hired a farm hand. He was a very kindhearted man, quiet and reserved. The family treated him with respect when he was around but he was hardly ever in the house.

His wife was hard to get along with. At first she made a great show of affection for me, but I could tell it was hypocritical, and she soon showed herself for the harpy she was. It was her fault that the rest of the family was so totally evil, each child more difficult than the next. She was the twin sister of the lady of the house where Milagros was staying, but they had completely opposite temperaments. Milagros's hostess was a good, sweet-tempered woman; she had the same number of children but the two families lived in different worlds. It was so pleasant in Milagros's house, I felt welcome and at ease, and went there for lunch as often as I could. In that house there were no illiterates.

My habit of going to Milagros's house made my family even more unfriendly. They quite often remarked that I liked it better over there. In time I realized that their hostility arose from the fact that they were not revolutionaries but small landowners, afraid of what would happen to them.

At least I learned something living there. Everything I saw was new to me—their family structure, the kind of life they led. I was struck by the way the boys identified with everything Mexican. They listened to Mexican music, saw Mexican pictures—well, of course Mexican movies were the only ones in Spanish. But the strange thing was that they imitated the *charros*.[36]

I never could make friends with the two girls. Graciela, the eldest, was bad-tempered, and the youngest was retarded, almost a moron. Graciela's entire life was organized around her work. She was like a beast of burden. On Monday she washed the clothes for the whole bunch of men, Tuesday she ironed, and so on. Her one great interest was her sweetheart. He'd ride up on horseback every evening at 6:00, dismount, and sit on a stool talking with her while her father sat close by watching.

The atmosphere was already hostile, but I was made even more uncomfortable when some cousins came to stay. Then Graciela and her sister felt they had moral support and no longer made any effort to be pleasant. When I entered a room where the mother and girls were talking, they'd immediately fall silent.

36. Mexican cowboys.

Elías, the elder son, made trouble for me from the moment I arrived. There was a transistor radio in the house, and whenever I listened to music he'd remark contemptuously, "Romantic mush, that's all this girl wants to hear. Let's have some real music," and he'd switch to a Mexican tune.

Luis, his cousin at the other house, was the same age but totally different, a good, kindhearted, shy boy. Milagros claimed he was in love with me. Luis was too shy to mention it but I began to think she might be right, he was so willing to do whatever I wanted. He was unconditionally mine to command. He rode by every day to ask if I wanted anything, and he'd take me everywhere on his horse. That annoyed Elías. When the old man tried to make him take me out on horseback, Elías always refused. He'd say, "Let Luis take you. Milagros is coming with me."

I've never been able to figure out why Elías hated me so much. I never even looked at him, much less asked him any favors. His brothers followed his lead. If he insulted me, they did the same. I confided these things to Milagros and Celia, the girl she lived with. Celia would say, "Never mind those people, they're a pack of savage beasts."

One day when I returned from a visit to Milagros, something happened I've never told anyone, not even *mamá*. It was about 6:00 in the evening. Elías was sitting on the end of a long wooden bench, a hat beside him. I sat on the other end of the bench, very quietly. I hardly dared open my mouth in that house, especially not to Elías.

Somehow, I didn't even notice when it happened, the hat fell to the floor. Like a wild beast, Elías sprang to his feet and roared at me, "Pick it up!"

"No sir, not me," said I calmly.

"Pick it up, I told you!"

"You know you can't talk to me like that. I will not pick it up."

"I said pick it up," he repeated. Quite the he-man, no? But the more he tried to overawe me, the more coolly I answered.

He got madder and madder until finally he began to hit me. I was horrified. He was punching me as if I were a man. If I could, I would have killed him, but I couldn't even hit back because he held me with one hand and hit me with the other. The worst part of all was that his mother, sisters, and brother just sat there looking on as if they were at the circus. Elías hit me till he'd had his fill, then pushed me down on the floor and said, "It wasn't even my hat, it was Pedro's."

Pedro, seeing that Elías had only half killed me, felt that the least he could do was hit me some more. Before I had a chance to get up, *he* started punching me. I sobbed, "Cowards, you're not men. Men don't hit women."

Pedro was smaller than Elías and I tried to hit back, but I wasn't strong enough to hurt him. When he finally let me go I shouted insults at the whole bunch of them. I was on the way to the bedroom, hunched up and crying my heart out, when the father came in. "What's the matter with Mónica?"

"Oh, nothing, the boys were teasing her and she burst into tears," the mother answered.

"You kids should be ashamed, making her cry like that." He had no idea what they'd really done.

Lying there in my bed, weeping bitterly, I could hear them talking gaily in the parlor, laughing over the whole thing. Every now and then Graciela would walk in and out of the room, not giving me a glance. I was overcome by the greatest anguish I've ever felt. I couldn't stay in that house any longer, but I didn't know what to do. If I brought charges against them they'd get into serious trouble for having assaulted a brigadier. I didn't want to do them any harm. But I couldn't go home and tell my mother, "I quit because they beat me up," and let it go at that.

About 8:00 that night Luis came by and asked for me as usual. "She doesn't feel well and went to lie down," they told him. When he asked what ailed me I could hardly speak for crying, but I managed to blurt out, "Go get Milagros. Bring her here—at once!"

About three minutes later he was back with Milagros. I told her the whole tragedy. Milagros was indignant. "They really are animals. I can't believe they'd hit you!" I showed her my bruises. "Pack up your things right away and let's go," she said, and took me to her house.

When Milagros's host, Miguel, heard what had happened, he practically had a fit. "I can't believe they'd do such a thing, Mónica. I'll not have you going back there. You stay here. I can easily feed two brigadiers."

So that night I slept at Milagros's house. Next day I couldn't go out to teach, all covered with bruises as I was. I was too upset and nervous to do anything. I wished the earth would open and swallow me up.

Milagros and I spent the whole day analyzing the situation, and old Miguel said, "I can't let them get away with it. If you don't bring charges against them, I will." I finally convinced him it wouldn't be fair to their poor old father. But I was determined not to go back.

A couple of days later, though, the old man came to ask me to return. His visit was a great event for Miguel's family because he hadn't set foot in their house for fifteen years. I told him part of what had happened—not everything. The old man begged me to come back, saying he loved me like a daughter, and I was so moved that I finally decided to go. He told me the whole family was hoping to see me, that Elías wanted to ask my pardon, that the old lady was very upset. I knew that was a lie because she enjoyed herself tremendously seeing me beaten up.

The return was awful, disgusting. The hypocritical way they begged my forgiveness! The thought of spending two more months with them was agonizing.

About two weeks later something happened that shocked me even more than Elías's violence. The zone I'd been assigned to was almost exclusively populated by relatives of the two families. There were about seventeen brothers and sisters who had settled near each other. Some families had welcomed us, others had not. Of those who had been helpful, the nicest was Eberto, one of Miguel's younger brothers. From the start of the Campaign he'd been especially obliging and among those we most trusted. Milagros and I often asked him to take us places in his jeep, and I was convinced he looked upon me as a daughter because I saw him as a kind of father.

Eberto, who appeared to be in his thirties, was good-looking and agreeable, but was married to a shapeless lump of a woman who looked much older and weighed over 200 pounds. When you saw them together you couldn't help wondering. I was told they'd taken off together when he was young, and then she became pregnant so they settled down together. They'd been living as husband and wife for years, though he was never in love with her. In addition to all her other defects, she was a very jealous woman.

One day I was riding in Eberto's jeep, and as we crossed a cane field he said, "If my wife should see me here alone with you, *muchacha* . . . ! She's horribly jealous of you."

"Then your wife must be crazy!"

"No, she's not crazy. On the contrary, she's too clear-sighted. She knows I'm in love with you."

"What!"

It seems funny to me now but at the time it was traumatic. It never occurred to me that that kind of relationship could exist between us. I was so shocked I couldn't say anything. After a while he said, "If I'd only met you twenty years ago!"

"I wasn't even born then!"

He went on and on, claiming he'd fallen in love with me the very day I arrived, he knew it was absurd, but he had to speak, he couldn't help himself. . . .

"Stop!" I said, "I'm getting off right here."

He stopped and helped me down. Then he got back in the jeep, turned it around, and said, "All right, get in."

"No, I'm walking back."

"Oh Mónica, what will people think if you go back on foot? I haven't touched you—I'm not capable of harming you in any way. Please believe me."

I got back in and he said, "Don't think I had any evil intentions of telling you of my love. I wish now I'd kept it to myself."

When I went home, I felt as if everybody in the house had heard that monstrous declaration. I couldn't eat that night and I hardly slept for the rest of the month, haunted by the fear of running into Eberto. When I heard the noise of a jeep I'd hide in the cane until it passed. After a while he stopped going by.

I didn't tell anybody about it until, about a month after the incident, I blurted out the whole story to Milagros. I wasn't only embarrassed, I was shocked that a married man could court me. I worried that I might have done something to encourage him, but I couldn't think of a single thing. I never stopped to consider that he might really be in love with me. Now I think maybe he was.

By the end of my eight months I had taught almost all the illiterates in my section to read and write. One little lady in her eighties couldn't write because her hand trembled so much, but the others did very well, and the day we finished our work, we hauled up our pink flag, declaring the area free of illiteracy. I often wonder whether our pupils have kept up their reading or forgotten it all by now.

At the end of the Campaign we were called on to do extra work. Apparently a number of girls had wasted all their time with their sweethearts, so there were still many illiterates left in the area, and the program directors planned to concentrate all of them in Guanabo for what the commissioner called "the final push." He wanted us to teach them to read and write in twenty days. We agreed.

But it cost me a lot of suffering and conflict. Renée had arrived from Europe already pregnant with her second child, and I'd promised to be with her in Havana for her second delivery. Her first had been very difficult and I'd decided that no matter what, I'd ask for leave. Well, the final push came up, and since we had to work intensively for twenty days, I made up my mind that I wouldn't go to Havana after all.

Mami wrote frequently, saying that Renée was expected to give birth at any moment. It created an intense conflict in me. The worst of it was that as soon as the baby was born Renée would be going away again. The man in charge heard about my dilemma and he himself got me a ticket to Havana. I returned it with thanks, saying I intended to stay.

He didn't understand. "Look, Mónica, a day or two isn't important. Milagros can do your work while you're away."

I was firm in my refusal but all day long I kept thinking of Renée. I was in class when I received *mami*'s letter saying that Renée had had a beautiful boy named Rubén, and when I read it I left the room at once, not wanting to show my feelings in front of all those people. That night I had my second attack of asthma, worse than the first. Classes were over by the time I got well.

I returned with the last group and arrived in Havana on December 22, 1961. Renée postponed her trip till the 26th so I could see my little nephew. He was every bit as beautiful as *mamá* said.

The day I got home, I noticed a number of foreign knickknacks in the parlor. "Where did those come from?" I hardly dared ask for fear of being disappointed.

"Silvio brought them. He arrived yesterday," *mami* told me.

"Silvio? In Havana? Why isn't he here?"

Mami told me he'd gone to call on Ángela Rosa. I rushed to the phone. When I heard his voice I gasped, "Silvio!"

"You little dope, stop crying and say something," he kidded me. But I couldn't speak. I was overcome by the sound of his voice.

He came home at once and we talked until about 2:00 in the morning. He was awfully sleepy but I wouldn't let him go to bed. It was divine seeing him after a year and a half! Renée and Silvio, home again! So many of my relatives had gone away, but the ones I loved most were with me once more.

Renée, of course, was the great influence of my life. From the time I was ten we were very close, though the closeness wasn't exactly reciprocal. She confided in me about her emotional life but I didn't feel I had the right to tell her my intimate thoughts and feelings. Sometimes we'd be up till 3:00 in the morning talking about what Renée felt, what boy Renée was in love with, what Renée thought and wanted. I would analyze it all for her. Between the ages of ten and fourteen I lived all of Renée's loves intensely. But I didn't dare tell her about the things that happened to me because I was afraid she'd scold me.

Renée was moralistic like *mami* and shared most of her opinions, yet I would obey my sister and pay no attention to my mother. For me, *mami* represented force and Renée reason. After all, *mami* was an old woman who wanted to dominate me, while Renée was always willing to explain things. "There's a proper time and a proper age for everything. Having a sweetheart now would only kill your illusions about love." We agreed that when I had a sweetheart I'd tell her but keep *mamá* in the dark until the day before the wedding. Renée offered to chaperone me when I went out with him. She didn't suggest that I meet him alone, secretly. So in her sweet, reasonable way, my sister won me over to her point of view.

I had actually started falling in love when I was a little girl. At first I had crushes on grown men. It wasn't until I was eight that I began to be interested in boys my own age. Those platonic romances of mine lasted for ages. I could live off one of them for a year or two.

By the end of the Literacy Campaign, I was sixteen and old enough to really fall in love. Neither Milagros nor I had ever had a sweetheart, but we shared what little information we had. Precious little it was! We solemnly promised each other that whoever had a sweetheart first would make her entire experience available to the other.

It was strange the way I met Julio García. Ten days after the end of the Campaign, Milagros, her cousin Sonia, who'd also been a brigadier, and I went to the rally of January 2.[37] During the mass meeting I suddenly

37. Anniversary of the triumph of the Revolution.

noticed Julio among a group of boys in military uniform. He's one of the few men I've ever been attracted to at first sight. He was a dream. Milagros and Sonia agreed.

Sonia was jumping up trying to get a glimpse of Fidel over the heads of the crowd. One of the boys with Julio offered to link his hands together for her to climb on. When she got down, he introduced himself and his friends, and Milagros immediately reminded Julio that they'd once met casually, on a bus.

We were neatly divided into couples from the first, Milagros with Julio, Jacobo with Sonia, and I with some guy whose name I didn't even take the trouble to find out. He tried to talk to me, but I wasn't the least bit interested and answered only in monosyllables. Poor boy, what a boring afternoon he spent with me! When the rally was over, one of the boys said he could get a jeep and offered to drive us home.

Milagros was all for it, but I told her, "Listen, if I drive up to my house in a jeep full of soldiers, my family will kill me."

Milagros said, "I'm willing to risk it. I don't care if they scold me." Naturally she didn't care; she was with Julio. But what had I to gain? I suffered agonies, knowing *mami* had been watching the rally on TV and would be wondering where I was at that hour. The boys finally showed up in the jeep and said they had to stop awhile at Jacobo's house. I was scared to death but I said, "All right, let's go."

When we got there neither Milagros nor I dared get out of the car. At last they persuaded us to go in, and I was greatly relieved to be introduced to Jacobo's mother. An older man, also in military uniform, asked us, "What are you girls so jittery about?" We explained, and he said, "Don't worry. I'll go and introduce myself to your *mamás*. I'll tell them I was the one who spoke to you."

"That's perfect. If you go, there's no problem."

All that afternoon I didn't exchange one single word with Julio, though when I sat at the piano and played "Blue Moon" he began to sing along with me. He sang beautifully, which impressed me even more. Later, I learned that he had studied in a seminary, and sang so well because he'd been trained for the choir. He didn't stay long in the seminary because he realized that a priest's life wasn't for him. He left to join the Army, and when I met him he was attending a military boarding school.

Mami disliked Julio from the very first, and she imagined I'd lose all interest in him knowing he once wanted to be a priest, but in fact, the only thing I didn't like about Julio was his age. He was as young as I, and at that time it seemed important to fall in love with a man at least ten years older.

Four days after our first meeting, on the Day of the Three Kings, Julio phoned long-distance to ask if he could call on me. He said he'd been granted special leave—usually they give a student leave only to visit his parents. I said yes, and called Milagros at once. "Julio just phoned. He's coming here to my house."

She hurried right over, but that night it was clear that Julio was interested in me, not her. Later Milagros said, "I do think he's attractive, but I'm not in love with him, so there's no problem." From that moment on, a purely platonic love sprang up between Julio and me.

Julio was a very shy boy with acute emotional conflicts. One day an older man accompanied him when he called on me, and told *mami* Julio's whole story. It seems his parents were divorced. He hated his mother and had generalized his feeling into a hatred of all women. I decided I was the one to cure him, to straighten out his life and compensate for the family he no longer had.

I became obsessed with Julio, though our romance was very innocent. He never said he loved me or tried to kiss me, but I lived many imaginary experiences with him. Being in a boarding school, he could visit me only on weekends, but he'd phone during the week, and I hardly stirred from home for fear he might call while I was out. I'd lie awake at night listening for the phone. Normally I'm frank and outgoing, but when I was with him my personality was completely nullified. I could barely speak; he affected me too strongly. We talked together no more than two or three times, and then it was in a superficial way. I was tongue-tied and he was shy. That's what I called "being in love."

Then, suddenly, he simply disappeared from my life. He stopped calling, I heard no news of him. I wept and moped, building the whole thing into a tragedy. I simply could not understand why he should drop me without an explanation. Milagros tried to talk me out of it. "Look, he obviously didn't care for you in the least. You simply have to forget him."

But Julio had become too important for me to forget him just like that. I had planned in detail the whole of my future life with him, convinced that one day we would marry and have beautiful blue-eyed children. Julio had the loveliest blue eyes!

Having completed the fifth year of high school, I was ready to enter the University. There had been a great deal of talk about the need for engineers and technicians, and women, they said, were as capable in those areas as men. So I decided to study engineering and I took the entrance examinations for the School of Technology, but I failed. I found out I should have specialized in science in high school. I had majored in literature!

I tried to enroll in the science program at high school but was told they were not admitting anyone new because they were starting a new system of pre-university studies. I argued with them. "Can't you see what a mechanical rule that is? It means that somebody who already has a high school degree has no chance of specializing in science!"

When I told *mami* she asked, "But aren't you going to study something?"

"No," I said furiously, "those people are a bunch of squares!"

Milagros, who had taken her fifth year in science, was excused from the entrance examination and admitted to the School of Technology. She asked me to go with her when she enrolled. That was the day I met Paco, the man who was to be my husband.

Like almost everything else that's ever happened to me, my meeting with Paco seemed accidental. He was a third-year student at the School of Technology and head of the orientation committee. At that time there were no industrial engineers in Cuba and they were badly needed, but most students, left to themselves, chose the conventional courses. So it was decided to orient them to industrial engineering when they came to enroll.

I was introduced to Paco and he asked, "What courses are you planning to take?"

"None."

Off he went into his spiel. "Why not industrial engineering? It's a fine profession. . . ." I just let him talk, and he went on for about an hour.

Finally I said, "You're wasting your time. I can't enroll." And I told him the whole story.

"All right," said he, "so you can't study engineering. Surely you're going to study *something*? What are you interested in?"

"Well, psychology."

"Fine. I'll take you over there."

So Paco and I rushed over to the School of Psychology. He stole my papers out of the School of Technology file, stayed with me in line until 5:00 o'clock, and got me enrolled. It was quite a show!

One day I helped to prepare a party at the School of Technology, and Paco asked me what time I was planning to go. I said I didn't go to parties or even to the movies. You see, I was being absolutely faithful to Julio, just as if I were a mature woman of thirty.

"But you must go!" Paco exclaimed.

"Oh no, she won't," Milagros said. "She's a nun now that she's become a widow."

"What does that mean?" Paco asked, and Milagros told him about Julio.

"The boy's obviously a neurotic," Paco said. "This is absurd, Mónica, you can't waste your life like this." He tried to convince me that I didn't love Julio at all, that I had only a schoolgirl crush on him.

Paco and I became fast friends, which Julio and I had never been. Paco was the first real boyfriend I'd ever had. He fell in love with me, though it was months before he told me so, and courted me in spite of my insistence that I cared only for Julio, Julio, Julio.

I felt confused in a million ways. It seemed absurd that I should be in love with a figment of my imagination. Oh yes, I knew I idealized Julio. I'd been strongly attracted to him, and the anxiety he aroused in me, the impatience I felt when he phoned and said he was coming over—these were intense emotions. But maybe Paco was right, maybe that was only a schoolgirl crush. For one thing, I didn't know what it was like to be really in love. My affection for Paco grew very slowly and it was much calmer, not in the least like being in love. Yet I liked being with Paco and talking to him, and had complete trust in him. Also, he was an adult. It was the first time a man had fallen in love with me and I was flattered.

It took me a whole month to accept Paco's invitation to go out at night, but finally I decided I'd be quite safe with him, and I was right. He didn't make a single pass at me and that gave me a great feeling of security. We just went for walks in the park because I still didn't feel it was right to go dancing or to the movies.

I'd almost convinced myself I didn't love Julio when he reappeared. He explained that his school had been sent on military maneuvers to a distant and very secret place, and that's why he'd left without a word. Now, he said, he thought he would be stationed in Havana.

Seeing him, I was overcome with emotion—a thing that never happened with Paco. It was agreeable—divine to be with Paco, but he didn't stir my emotions. Now which of the two reactions was I to define as "being in love"? It was very difficult.

The day the Welfare building burned down, Julio and I went together to see the fire, and on the way home he told me a soldier's life was hard, and asked if I would be willing to share it. How could I say no? To me it would be heaven!

That evening there was something going on at the University and I went there to see Paco. He began chatting, but I interrupted, "I came here because I must talk to you. Julio is back."

"He is? What's happened?"

"Simply that I've agreed to be his sweetheart."

The news hurt Paco deeply. He told me he thought I was unsure of myself and didn't know what I really wanted. "I know what *I* want, though," he added. "And this is no child's play for me."

I understood it was hard, and to make it easier, I asked him if we couldn't be friends.

"No," he said. "Either I'm your sweetheart or I'm nothing to you." Then, very stiffly, he said goodbye. That night I lay awake a long time with a million fantasies going through my head. Doubtful as I was, I decided to become Julio's sweetheart, and secretly considered myself his fiancée.

Next morning I received a letter from Julio that I'll never forget. He hadn't been assigned to Havana but to Matanzas. "I can't even tell you the name of the place," he wrote, "and I don't know when I'll be able to see you again. But I love you." I wept bitterly. I kept that letter until less than a year ago.

The following weekend he came to visit me at the dormitory. "I'm in a great hurry," he said once we were out of the building. "They only gave me a few hours."

I had so many things to tell him, yet we hardly talked at all that night. I wanted to tell him what I felt for him and how I had suffered during those four months, but I couldn't. I couldn't talk to him. Julio was turning out to be very disappointing.

There was no way to avoid seeing Paco. We were involved in so many activities together, but sometimes when I said hello to him he wouldn't even answer. When he asked if I were still Julio's sweetheart I always said yes.

The day before May Day there was a rally at the University. Paco and I were separated by quite a number of people but all my girl friends, who knew the whole drama, hated Julio and were on Paco's side. They started changing seats until Paco and I found ourselves side by side. We chatted awhile, then he asked me the same old question, "Are you still Julio's sweetheart?"

"Yes, I am."

"But you don't love him. You know you don't love him."

"Yes, I do."

At the end of the day Paco saw me home and asked, "Will we be together at the demonstration tomorrow?" I said yes. The May Day rally was beautiful. It seemed wrong to be with Paco while I was Julio's sweetheart, but all the same it was a delight. What a problem! On our way back to the dormitory we stopped at a very pretty place near my house, and Paco said, "I can't stand it anymore, *chica*. You'd better go now." His words scared me and I hurried off.

That week every time we met he'd ask me, "Are you sure you love Julio?" And I'd always answer, "Yes, I'm sure." Paco's friends told me he couldn't eat or sleep and his grades were going down.

The following Saturday Julio came to Havana again, and we went for a walk along the Malecón. We tried to talk but we simply didn't speak the same language. I couldn't explain to him what I did in the University or tell him about my daily life. I would have liked him to tell me about what it was like being in military school, but he didn't talk about that; the things he did tell me simply didn't interest me.

That night I thought, "I can't be in love with Julio. Love should be more than just physical attraction." I needed to be with Paco more than with Julio, and I began to think Paco must be the man I really loved.

One night we met, and Paco took a photo of me out of my purse. It had become a regular ritual: he would take the photo, look at it, and I would take it back. But that night I said, "Keep it."

"Do you mean it?"

"Yes, yes."

"Now I really don't understand you."

I explained I wasn't in love with Julio and that night Paco and I became sweethearts. It was the first time he had kissed me. If I were to describe that kiss, all I could say is that it was odd. I felt no trace of physical passion. Julio never tried to kiss me, so I have no idea how I would have reacted with him. I've always been shy enough about that kind of thing but Julio was ten times shyer.

Later I arranged to meet Julio, to tell him I was breaking with him, but he didn't show up and I didn't see him for quite a while. Every three days he'd send a telegram: "I love you. Julio." I still have one of them put away. Those telegrams sickened me, and Paco got mad as the devil every time I showed them to him. He'd say, "Give me his address—I'm going to tell him what's what."

In August, when Paco went away for fifteen days of military training, I missed him a great deal, and I thought that must mean I really loved him.

One day I was told a boy was waiting to see me, and I rushed downstairs expecting to meet Paco. It was Julio. He'd been transferred to a base outside Havana. That day he looked happy, quite different from his usual self, and as he spoke he held my hand—something he had never even thought of doing before. "Now we can really be sweethearts," he said. "We can even get married."

"It's impossible," I told him. "I'm Paco's sweetheart. Look, Julio, I'm sure you never loved me. How could you, when we saw so little of each other?"

Then for the first time Julio told me a little about his feelings. He said he'd always had a low opinion of women, and never completely trusted one before he met me. "Usually," he said, "I don't confide in anybody about my personal life, yet every man in my unit knows your name. They even know exactly when I came to see you, because I'd exchange passes with them. Those were the only times I felt human." He really screwed up my life with his explanations!

He said he'd still go on loving me, and that if I ever felt like phoning him I could reach him at the base. But I never saw him again. The harm I did to Julio hurts me more than anything in my life. After I married Paco, I heard that Julio had been discharged as a psychotic. I'm sure it had nothing to do with me, but I can't help thinking that I might have been a factor in his breakdown. The memory of Julio haunts me like a ghost.

Paco returned from military training the next day and was overjoyed to learn I'd broken with Julio. I think he'd been brooding about it. He used to tease me, saying it was Julio's blue eyes I had fallen in love with and he was going to get some blue contact lenses so he could compete. Many times, especially when we first became sweethearts, I told Paco I loved him madly. But that upset him tremendously because he could feel it wasn't true. He believed from the very first that I agreed to be his sweetheart as a concession, and he often said that I loved him but wasn't *in* love with him. For many months our relationship proceeded on that basis. So as long as Julio had been in the picture, Paco had been insecure. I couldn't blame him. When he asked, "Do you love me?" I always answered, "Well, yes, I think so." With my scant experience of life, I couldn't give a name to what I felt, and with Renée away from Cuba I had nobody to talk it over with.

Little by little I began to believe I did love Paco, but I never once had any overwhelming impulse to express it. He was the one who took the initiative. He had to know what I was doing every moment of the day. The slightest change in my schedule disturbed him. If I told him I'd be in the lab at 5:00 o'clock and when he got there he didn't find me, he'd feel sick about it. I couldn't understand his reaction at all. I'd tell him, "I can't make a rigid schedule and stick to it. I might suddenly feel like doing something else."

And the idea of sex was difficult for me. I was so ignorant. For me, there was the kiss, and there was the sex act. The sex act belonged to marriage and the kiss to courtship. To be introduced to any sexual activity during the engagement seemed downright traumatic.

I first learned such things went on from one of the older girls in the dormitory. She's rather morbid, in fact, and she still shocks me even though I look upon sex quite differently now. One day at the table she announced she was going to break up with her Bolivian boyfriend. He didn't know how to do things, she said, and proceeded to describe in minute detail just what he did wrong. I couldn't stand it. I left the table and sped up to my room. My roommate, Mirta, who was twenty-eight or twenty-nine and treated me almost like a kid sister, could see I was upset.

When I told her why, she burst out laughing and said, "You're the most innocent creature I've ever come across." From her I learned what went on between sweethearts in Cuba. To protect the girl's virginity they didn't have intercourse, but they performed all sorts of things just short of it. Mirta admitted that she, a person for whom I had the greatest respect, had done even more intimate things than those. There was so much I didn't understand. When the other girls said things like, "Yesterday I came with my boyfriend," they never explained what they meant by "came."

Apparently it was quite normal for a sweetheart to ask for more than a kiss. It's just as well I found out in time. I might have thought Paco was horrible and I might have broken with him. My conversation with Mirta helped me to accept these things as something everyone did when they were engaged, a duty to my sweetheart. But it still shocked me, and only toward the end of our engagement did I begin to like it.

This period was insecure for Paco and me, and one day he told me that instead of feeling more sure of me as time went by, he felt less sure. I thought we were about to break up. But he'd face the situation one day, then back out the next and avoid the subject for a long time.

The night of the missile crisis, Paco left. There was a feeling of war in the air—the rain, the army trucks, many of them Soviet trucks, the boys carrying arms, the trenches we were beginning to dig. It was very exciting, but in the midst of all the activity the only thing I wanted was to see Paco. "I must be in love with him," I told myself.

At one point he came back to Havana and phoned me. He was only five or six blocks away but had come on army business and had to leave immediately. After he hung up I burst into tears. I couldn't accept that we could be only a few blocks apart and yet unable to see each other. One or both of us might be dead before we had another chance.

But we had another chance. Two or three days later, he phoned and told me to meet him at Cárdenas Plaza. I found him dressed in his olive greens, carrying a tommy gun and a hand grenade. Perhaps I wasn't madly in love with Paco, but as we embraced I wished that moment might never end.

I told him that the night before, Fidel had come to the University and warned us that the Americans were going to invade Cuba. "Yes," Paco said. "This may be the last time for us."

We spent most of the afternoon together. I told him what I was doing, how I had joined the women's militia and how we planned to defend the University. After a while Paco said, "If we get out of this alive, let's get married."

That was exactly what I wanted. "Yes, yes," I said. "You'll have to fight of course, but you'll be fighting for me and for our children."

It was so beautiful and the emotional pressure of the situation was so great that all of my doubts vanished. We agreed we'd be married the same day he returned to Havana. We'd go to the nearest place, wearing whatever clothes we happened to have on at the time, and pick up passersby as witnesses. I thought we should be married with no fuss. It didn't seem right to have a beautiful wedding in the midst of a crisis.

Throughout those weeks I thought constantly of Paco and all the things I wanted to tell him. I was beginning to feel the need to say, "I love you." But when the crisis ended they demobilized everybody except him. As his friends returned, I asked, "And Paco? Where's Paco?"

"His group is in such a super-strategic place they aren't demobilized," I was told.

It was November. I was still in training with the militia. We reported at 5:00 A.M. and remained until afternoon. Then, at night, I gave the same training to the platoon I headed.

One day as I returned from duty, all muddy from crawling along the ground, my friend Olga said, "Say, look, about two blocks in front of us... there's Paco!"

"Oh no, it can't be!" I said. Then I realized it was. There, in the middle of the street, we ran into each other's arms. A circle of people gathered to see, it was such a spectacular reunion.

Paco's first words were, "Come on, let's get married." I said, "Wait till I go up and change." I couldn't stand all that dirt and such ugly clothes. I changed into a dress I knew he loved and went back down.

"Well, when do we get married?" he asked. I explained that I still had two exams to take, the second on the morning of December 22. "Then let's get married the very next day," he suggested, and I agreed. It was only a little over a month away.

Next day, out of the blue, Paco told *mami*, "Mónica and I are getting married on December 23."

"Impossible! Just like that? You two are crazy!"

"Make me some pretty clothes," I told her. I was right in the middle of examinations and couldn't take the time to choose a trousseau. Anyway, I'd been to weddings where it was quite normal for both bride and groom to wear military uniforms.

I didn't want a traditional wedding but I did want a bit of gaiety. Paco didn't. "No, no, no, I don't want a fancy wedding with all those people and dancing. Let's get married by a notary with nobody there except the two of us, your *mamá* and one more witness."

I didn't like his plan, and the girls I worked with didn't like it either. Mine was the first wedding on our dormitory floor and to them it was the event of the century. So we began to work on Paco, to persuade him to have the wedding in one of the lovely patios at the University.

"Well, all right, but there'll be none of that cutting of the cake; in fact, there'll be no cake."

I agreed, but the day before the wedding I got sentimental and wanted something traditional. I said, "Oh, Paco, I'd like to have a cake."

"Fine time to tell me!" said he. "I'll see where I can get one. Do you really want it?"

"Yes... no... I mean, it isn't a matter of life and death, but it would be nice."

So Paco went all over Havana looking for a cake.

Meanwhile, *mami* had been sewing nightgowns for me. There was a scarcity of fancy lingerie, especially the traditional bridal nightgown and transparent negligée. Anyway I didn't want such an enormous thing, so I got what I liked—a short, loose, white-lace nightgown with a matching short coat. I let Renée take care of getting me some underclothes in Europe and they arrived the afternoon before the wedding. That's the way everything was—crazy!

On December 23, 1962, after being engaged for seven months, Paco and I were married. My brother rode with me in the car. At the University the whole patio was beautifully decorated—a surprise from *mami* and the girls on my floor. There was a cake, and *mami* had hired a professional photographer to take pictures. It was a lovely wedding. Paco's parents and most of his relatives came. If only Renée and *papi* could have been there!

We had a very gay time with all our schoolmates, but Paco wouldn't let me stay long. He's always been impatient, and that day he was downright desperate to get away. As soon as we'd signed the register he said, "Hurry up and change so we can go."

"Can't we stay a little longer? I'm enjoying myself."

"No, we're leaving right now." That's Paco all over.

We spent our wedding night at Bacuranao Beach. The next day I decided that Paco and I must have midnight supper with *mami*. It was Christmas Eve and my brother was to go to Las Villas or Cienfuegos and Renée was in Europe, so *mami* would be all alone.

Mami liked Paco a lot and the supper went off very well, but afterward I couldn't force myself to get up and go into the bedroom with Paco, with *mami* right there. The fact that he was my husband didn't make the slightest difference. I was horribly embarrassed because I'd lived there all my life.

"Then what do you plan to do?" he asked me.

"I can't move from this room until *mami* goes to bed—you couldn't drive me with a stick."

Paco kept saying, "This is really the height of absurdity!" And finally I got up the nerve to go to bed with him.

Señora Reyes:

When Mónica came back from the Literacy Campaign she said, "I want to study at the University on a scholarship next year, *mami*."

"And why not this year?" I asked.

"Because I don't want to leave you all alone."

I told her, "Go to the University now. I know that's what you want." So she went and I stayed here all by myself.

She was only sixteen and hadn't been long at the University when she and Paco fell in love. He was her first sweetheart, the only man she'd known well, so when she told me they were engaged I said, "Make it a long engagement, Mónica. Give yourself a chance to find out whether you're really in love with this boy." But then came the October crisis and Paco insisted on getting married right away. I reasoned with him: "Paco, Mónica is a child, not only in years, but emotionally too."

Mónica complained, "You're so negative, *mamá*. Instead of pushing for the marriage, you push against it."

I answered, "Look, child, I don't have any stale goods on hand, you hear? My daughters are not one-eyed or blind or lame or stupid. Why should I run after a man for you? I haven't the slightest interest in your getting married so soon, but if that's what you two want, go ahead, get married."

Some of my friends advised me not to give my consent because Mónica was only seventeen. But I answered, "Yes, I will. Suppose I don't and she never gets married, or suppose she marries another man and isn't happy with him—she'd never stop blaming me. I can just see her saying, 'If only you had let me marry Paco, I'd be happy now.'"

Well, as it is, if she's unhappy she can't blame me. Mónica made her own choice. Nobody forced Paco on her. And I warned him, "Mónica doesn't know anything about housekeeping."

"That's all right," he answered. "She can learn by doing." Well, she did learn to cook, but she only cooks when she feels like it. Renée is the same way. Both of them can cook if they want to. The trouble is they never want to.

At home we always had a cook, a laundress, and maids, until the Revolution did away with all that. How could I prepare the meals when I left for work early in the morning and didn't get home till 1:00 or 2:00 in the afternoon? But even so, when the cook quit or when we stayed out at the beach, I cooked and served my children's meals. If they don't want to cook now, it's not my fault.

I worked for thirty-two years but I never neglected my children on that account. I know many women who were housewives and might have spent a great deal of time with their children, but instead they left them in the care of servants while they went out to play canasta. But not I. I directed them until they were old enough to understand things for themselves, at twelve or fourteen. Then I left them completely free. Whether I like what my daughters do or not, I don't interfere.

MÓNICA:

I had firmly decided long before I married that I wasn't going to be a housewife. It was very clear to me that I didn't need to be one because *mami* had never been one either. In fact, she rather despised women who gave up their lives to homemaking. I never saw her do any housework except when we were temporarily without a maid and she was desperate. If she didn't have a cook, she couldn't eat. With that example, it never occurred to me to want to be a typical housewife, cook meals, take care of children and all that stuff. I married quite decided not to follow that pattern and Paco knew it.

Even if socialism hadn't come to Cuba, it would never have occurred to me to marry simply for the sake of being somebody's wife. My mother felt that way too. She has always been a person with her own life to lead, sometimes even to a greater extent than *papi*. I identified with her and admired the freedom of action she had in relation to the very constricted social norms of her time. She took pride in never depending on a man, economically or in any other way, so I learned that attitude early.

When Paco and I got married we went to live in a dormitory for married students where my chief activity was studying. I had no house-wifely duties. Paco knew that when the time came I would have a very hard time adapting to the role of housewife; that was something he had to accept.

When we'd been married three months, Paco and I discussed a sexual problem of mine that we'd already talked about during our engagement. I believe my problem was due to a sexual experience I had at the age of fourteen. It was so traumatic that I've only talked about it twice. It still shocks me. I had no idea of its negative results until later. I thought that after I married and got rid of a whole series of inhibitions partly caused by that experience, I would be rid of the problem.

I decided to tell Paco only because he suffered a great deal from my attitude during our engagement. It was quite logical that he should be upset, and I wanted him to know that I loved him and that he had no reason to feel inadequate since my coldness was due to a problem of my own. If he had been Paul Newman or Marlon Brando, I would still have reacted the same. Several times I was on the point of telling Paco but I couldn't get up enough courage. One night when he was terribly upset—really suffering—I finally explained the whole thing to him. I don't know whether he cared or not—he claimed he did. He said he understood but he loved me and needed more than I could give him. We didn't come to any conclusions or decisions—we simply discussed the matter. A long time passed and neither of us ever mentioned it again.

It was shortly after that confession that I got pregnant for the first time. It was a mistake, I guess, but the idea of having a baby delighted me, and in any case, at that time I wouldn't have done anything to prevent a pregnancy. When Cristina was born a year after our marriage I felt very content.

It's quite possible that I wasn't really in love with Paco when I married him. I was going through a difficult stage then and I felt very unsure whether I had made the right decision. But Paco's immense affection made me will myself to love him. During our first few years of marriage, we gradually built up our relationship on a new basis. I told Paco everything, repeated to him the slightest conversation I'd had during the day and kept him up to date on all my activities. I got used to . . . well . . . the dailiness of our life together and began to need him more and more.

Chapter Six

The University and Politics

MÓNICA:

I'd finished high school at fifteen with no political experience except the Committee of Revolutionary Students, which wasn't much. But at the University's School of Psychology I very soon became intimately involved in student politics and revolutionary activities. The university elections hadn't been held yet, and we hardly knew one another, but one month after the term started, a group of us formed an unofficial committee to look after different aspects of student life. I was elected *responsable* for the Teaching Front.[38] It was my job to look into disputes between teachers and students over examinations. Other *responsables* were appointed for cultural activities, sports, and so forth. The University was administered by what you might call "co-government," in which administrators, faculty, and students were all represented.[39] One student representative attended all meetings of the directors of the School, so we had some power.

When the official FEU elections were held six or seven months later, I was elected secretary-general of the Association of Psychology Students,[40] and shortly afterward my friend Olga became president.

38. The term used to designate the various areas of responsibility with which an organization concerns itself. "Front," as opposed to "committee," for instance, suggests militant action, as in its meaning: "line of battle."

39. *Co-gobierno* was a system whereby students and professors shared administrative responsibility within the University. Each university faculty (a faculty is roughly comparable to a college in a North American university) was governed by a *junta de gobierno* (governing council), headed by the dean of the faculty with the participation of three professors and two student representatives. *Co-gobierno* provided an outlet for student grievances as well as a way for students to monitor the political attitudes of professors. (Jaime Sucklicki, *University Students and Revolution in Cuba, 1920–1968* (Coral Gables: University of Miami Press, 1969), pp. 114–15.)

40. The University Student Federation (FEU) was for years an important although highly fractionated political action organization for university students in Cuba. In 1962 the FEU, along with all other youth and student groups, was incorporated into the *Unión de Jóvenes Comunistas,* Union of Communist Youth (UJC). Because of its prominence, the FEU was allowed to maintain a separate structure and leadership until 1967, but it was subordi-

After that, I became very involved in the political life of the School. I
spent my days in class and my nights in committee meetings. The School
of Psychology was a hotbed of conflicts. One of them concerned Isidro
del Pino, who'd been a revolutionary in the thirties and a professor at the
University for many years. He was a man with a chip on his shoulder, a
real paranoiac. His lectures were a constant outpouring of poison against
the Revolution. He was against the director, as well as the head of every
department in the School. He built up an image of himself as a victim of
persecution, and posed as one who had the courage of his convictions.
He was able to get the support of some of the students. I myself was at
first one of his followers. I was in a special position with him because he
thought only brilliant students should be admitted to the University. He
gave us a series of intelligence tests and divided the class into quartiles.
We, as members of the Student Association, opposed that business of
excluding average students from the University. I discussed it with
Isidro one day in his office and told him, "Look, I just can't accept that
idea."

"Don't worry, my child, you're in the superior quartile," he said.

My active opposition to him began at that moment. "That's not the
point. I didn't ask what my IQ is. I'm against the plan whether it affects
me or not."

Later I found out that half the things he said were lies. For example,
he'd walk into the classroom and slap down a textbook by Smirnov,[41]
saying, "Look at it, there it is. We are *required* to teach from a Soviet
Russian textbook." Then one fine day the director of the School told me,
"I wouldn't dream of dictating what Isidro del Pino teaches. He chose
the textbook himself."

A number of students, led by Olga and me, aligned themselves against
del Pino. Two girls, Elisa and Aida, who were also members of the
Student Association, were for him. In committee meetings we were divided into two groups: one, led by Elisa and Aida, thought Isidro had
acted in good faith; the other, led by Olga and me, believed he hadn't.
Elisa and Aida had been good friends of mine, but after clashing over
Isidro we were like the Montagues and Capulets. Whenever I proposed
something, however absurd, Olga and the rest of my band would automatically side with me. Elisa and Aida, no matter how sensible a thing I
proposed, automatically took their stand against it. The matter was settled when Olga and I sent a long account of Isidro's offenses to the
rector. An investigating commission was formed and all the psychology
students were questioned one by one in the rector's office.

---

nated to UJC authority. Nominations to positions in the student associations (which existed
at the school, faculty, and university levels) were largely, although not completely, controlled by the UJC, so that an officer in the FEU was invariably a member of the UJC. (*Ibid.*,
pp. 87–135.)

41. Russian psychologist Anatolii Aleksandrovich Smirnov.

While the investigation was going on I hardly took time off to eat or sleep. We all *lived* on the steps of the rector's office, Olga and I on one side and Elisa and Aida on the other. Each time one of our people came out, Olga and I would stop him. "What did they ask you? What did you say?" We wouldn't even look at Elisa and Aida nor they at us. We got terribly melodramatic about it. The end of the story is that Isidro left the school but our political groups remained divided on every issue.

For a full year we'd been demanding each other's heads and insulting one another. One day Rubellón, the president of the FEU,[42] said to us, "Look, we're going to stay here until you've told one another everything you want to say and gotten it out of your systems. After that, what we need is unity." So we had many long meetings, some lasting the whole day, entirely given over to expressing our hostilities. Mostly the arguments ran: "You said such-and-such a thing in regard to Isidro." It was Isidro, Isidro, Isidro, all day long.

Later, Elisa quit school to go abroad with her husband, who was a diplomat. When she returned, she tried to re-enroll in the School. I was president of the Student Association then and I completely opposed her re-entry. "If the director takes you back, that's his business," I told her. "But if he asks me, I'll tell him I'm against it."

The director refused her request without consulting me, but later Elisa went around telling everybody I was to blame. That shows you what a low opinion she had of the director. After all, why should he be influenced by what I might say?

In spite of such time-consuming activities, we studied. I was usually an average student but when examination time came, I'd stay up most of the night and always passed with fairly good marks. That year they were the best ever. I was living in Vedado then, near the University, so I usually went home to eat. I had a woman who took care of the house and the baby. I paid her 50 *pesos* a month. I tried to get a job then but Paco didn't want me to. He was more interested in having me finish studying for my career. We don't pay to go to the University but Paco supported me all that time. I've always told everyone that it was he who gave me a four-year scholarship.

I wasn't serious or methodical about my studies, however. I think I was negatively influenced by *mami* in that; it was one way I resisted her authority. But now I'm a lot like *mamá* in my working habits, not quite as conscientious as she, and not excessively hard-working, but well disciplined. I regret missing a day's work even when my children are sick, but I don't remember a single day that *mami* stayed home, even when she herself was sick. Such an attitude was rare indeed, because in those days administrators stayed home whenever they felt like it.

42. José Rubellón, an engineering student who was president of the FEU from 1962 to 1965. In 1960 he led an attack by students against "counterrevolutionary" professors at the University of Havana.

Mamá was an energetic, hard-working professional. She made many decisions on her job, solved problems, and was always active. It is she all three of us have to thank for stimulating us to grow as persons.

Just before I joined the UJC, there was a meeting to determine who was qualified to be a militant, who first had to go through three months as an aspirant, and who was unacceptable even as an aspirant.[43] I was classified as an aspirant and so was Olga. At the meeting every case was analyzed. The decisions were made by students on a level superior to ours.[44]

When my turn came, I experienced the first crushing blow of my life. I was told that there had been flaws in my work and that I lacked experience. Well, I was the youngest in the political group and, naturally, I'd committed about seven hundred errors precisely because I was inexperienced. Some of the comrades pointed out that they'd called my errors to Olga's attention, but she hadn't told me because she was my friend. They said I looked down upon Olga, that I felt superior to her because I had better grades. Olga is a mulatto and has a complex about it; she chooses to consider herself white. A mulatto's life is a difficult one. They're very unfortunate people. Olga has suffered a great deal and has a lot of personality conflicts.

The criticism of my work didn't bother me so much. What upset me was the way they attacked me as a person. They said I was too immature to be a militant. I don't quite know what they meant by "immature." Nobody bothered to define it. They seemed to mean that I was so gay and talked with everybody, that I ran upstairs instead of walked. Maybe the fact that I worked rather erratically had something to do with it . . . things like that. Perhaps it was my age, maybe I really was immature, I don't know. It's a word I've come to hate, the weapon with which I was always attacked.

The assault on my personality was terribly destructive. I felt they'd rejected me as a person. At that time this was the method used to form people. I don't know whether it's good or bad, but for me it was a shattering blow. I went home crying. Paco said, "What's the trouble?" When I was a bit calmer, I told him the whole story and we had a long discussion about it. Paco had personality problems of his own and had once been in exactly the same situation, so he was in a position to give me advice. He helped a lot.

43. A militant is a full member of the Communist Party or the Communist Youth; an aspirant is a candidate for membership. In 1962, the year Mónica entered the University, the UJC was organized as a successor to the *Juventud Rebelde* (Rebel Youth). She was among the first group of students recruited when the UJC began organizing in the University.
44. A higher level of authority within the organization than that of the School, that is, the decisions were made by the faculty-level or university-level UJC committee.

I remained an aspirant in the UJC for eight months. I never felt at ease as a member of that group. Instead of discussing the good and the bad things people did, they harped on their errors. I felt that from the very first meeting I attended they had been too aggressive with me. Aggressive is not the right word . . . perhaps I'm being too subjective, but I did feel attacked. They never tried to help me improve my work. Instead, I felt they were on the lookout, watching for mistakes, always ready to pursue the slightest provocation.

They kept running me down on a purely personal basis and that made me feel kind of up in the air. I felt terribly inhibited, afraid to open my mouth because I might say something "immature." That label stuck with me for a long time. I thought, "At eighty I'll still be immature. This isn't a problem of age but of personality."

During the eight months I was an aspirant, the committee neither discussed whether I should be admitted to militant status nor asked me to leave the organization. I couldn't understand it. If after three months of probation I still didn't qualify, well, ladies and gentlemen, health and success to you, but it's only fair to tell me that I don't fit in and ought to get out.

At last it was decided that I did have the qualities of a militant. They admitted it was an error not to have discussed it earlier and apologized for having been remiss. They said I had been too severely criticized, that nobody had mentioned my many good qualities—that I'd done well in my courses, for example, and that I'd always faced problems with a very good attitude.

So I became a militant. I was a militant for about a year and a half and during that time I worked very hard. My life was the University, going from one meeting to the next. I don't know whether I liked it or not. I never thought about it that way. It was the hub of my existence, and it never occurred to me to do anything else. Paco and I were very close to each other in those things; we both devoted a lot of time to politics and went to the University together. At night we waited for each other so we could go home together. Sometimes we'd say, "Tonight we must stay with the baby. She needs us." And we'd stay at home.

Three months before the university elections were held, I was appointed president of the Association of Psychology Students to substitute for Olga, who'd been appointed to the University Bureau.[45] By then, I was told, I was more than qualified for the post.

Those three months were my time of triumph. Olga praised my work highly, and I did work hard, often spending the whole day at the Uni-

---

45. The UJC committee responsible for political education and organization within the University. The FEU maintained (nominally) its own bureau until 1967, when a single bureau under UJC control was created. (Sucklicki, *University Students and Revolution in Cuba*, p. 101.)

versity. Some of my methods were wrong. For instance, I didn't delegate enough duties, or give the leaders of the fronts an opportunity to participate. I was unofficially criticized for that, but my actions weren't entirely unjustified, because most of the front leaders failed to carry out their tasks while I almost always did mine.

At the end of the three months they discussed who should be the candidates in the elections. It was suggested that I be promoted to the Executive Committee of the Science Faculty's Student Association, and put in charge of the Public Relations Front.[46] I was highly praised at the assembly. They said I'd been politically active since my first year at the School, that I had done wonders and was a very unselfish, self-sacrificing person. No one mentioned my errors as president. So I became the *responsable* for the Public Relations Front. I worked really hard at the job for about three months; then I became pregnant with Alegría.

I'm always very ill during the first three months of pregnancy—I can't walk, I get dizzy all the time, and I vomit. If I could, I'd spend those first three months in bed. As Public Relations *responsable,* part of my work involved visiting all seven schools in our Faculty.[47] I'd get so sick and dizzy under that burning sun, I couldn't complete the rounds. Olga knew what a strain it was for me.

Except for the Public Relations Front, the Science Faculty's Student Association was in a bad way. It was a disaster! One day Olga called a meeting to which I didn't go—either my daughter was sick or my belly was giving me a hard time—but I knew what was on the agenda. It was decided to restructure various fronts, including Public Relations, so they appointed a new *responsable.*

Next day I said to Olga, "So they kicked me out, eh?"

"No, no, don't take it that way," she answered. "I told them how hard you've been working. But we all understand that your pregnancy makes it too hard for you to keep up with the work, and it isn't fair to let the Front decline because of that."

"Well, I don't look at it that way," I told her frankly. "I think if they kick me out of the Front they should go all the way and kick me out of the UJC too."

"Look, Mónica, we haven't kicked you out of anything. We just think you should step down until your baby is born. After that, you can come back."

---

46. Each faculty had an executive committee composed of the officers of its students associations, plus the *responsables* of the various fronts. Mónica was nominated to her office by the UJC. Election slates offered only one candidate for each position, although candidates could be written in. Competition took place mainly during the meetings or assemblies for nominating candidates.

47. In addition to Psychology, the six other schools were: Mathematics, Physics, Chemistry, Biological Sciences, Pharmaceutical Biochemistry, and Geography.

I wasn't satisfied. I phoned the secretary-general of the UJC and told her, "I'm surprised that at the meeting they didn't deprive me of my militant status after kicking me out of the Student Association. I feel very uncomfortable in the UJC and I'm fed up with all the quarrels and problems and personal conflicts. All these upsets are making my pregnancy worse. I want to get out. I'm as much of a revolutionary as ever and I'll work for the Revolution, but I refuse to attend any more meetings where you people do nothing but criticize one another."

"Forget it, Mónica, wait until the baby is born," she said.

I retired from politics and concentrated on Cristina, Paco, and my belly. I felt terribly sick. In my sixth month I developed severe anemia and practically had to live on Cola drops to keep going. It was difficult even to study, so I was in no condition to be politically active.

My second daughter, Alegría, was born in January, 1965, and for a time I devoted myself entirely to her. When I returned to school I was told I was no longer a militant.

"You don't say!"

They explained that there had been a fight in the UJC between the school- and faculty-level committees. Our committee had sent a letter to the university committee and that was disapproved of by the intermediary level. Such a fuss was made over it that the faculty UJC declared a crisis in our base committee and abolished everyone's militant status. The question of who was to remain a militant and who would be eliminated from the UJC was declared open. I never did grasp all the details because there had been so many problems and quarrels I wasn't sure what had happened.[48]

When the meeting to analyze individual cases took place they discussed everybody's record from the time they first enrolled in the School, again dwelling upon their errors and personality traits. When they discussed me they said I had committed some errors—and here they trotted out my infamous "immaturity"—but had improved in many ways. Although my record was uneven, they said, there had been times when I displayed a magnificent attitude toward my work and made many sacrifices, and they pointed out that my slack times coincided with my two pregnancies. They finally decided that I should be demoted to aspirant for three or four months before being received as a militant again. At that, I stood up and said I wanted to resign. I said no one was more conscious of my errors than I, and that I realized I didn't have the

---

48. We did not learn the details of the dispute Mónica refers to, but a general reorganization of the UJC took place in 1965, after a UJC candidate for president of the Technology Faculty's Student Association lost to a non-member of the UJC. Many UJC members were denounced and expelled from the organization. At the same time, the UJC undertook a recruitment drive to broaden its base in the University. This was also the year the present Communist Party was founded, and it was beginning to organize cells (i.e., base committees) in the University.

qualities of a militant. I said I preferred to sink back into the mass of students, but if in the future I improved enough to qualify, I would join up again.

That provoked a discussion. They claimed it was absurd to make such a statement when I was so intimately involved in the history of the School. I insisted. Somebody else requested the floor and said I should stay. And there the matter stood.

When I got home I told Paco I was going to ask again to be released. He disagreed. I wasn't sure I was right, and I wanted to discuss it in depth with somebody. But for some reason Paco never took the trouble to discuss that particular problem thoroughly. He just said, "I don't think you should do it. Period." There was nobody else with whom I felt free to talk—certainly not with Olga.

The great day came when we were to be told who was to stay and who was to go. First they read the list of people who had been dismissed, then those who had been demoted to aspirants—me and two others.

I stood up and said it was incomprehensible to me that someone who had asked to be released hadn't been. The following month I insisted again, though I now believe I was acting emotionally rather than rationally. But I don't see why you have to belong to an organization in order to be politically active. I can have the same attitude toward life as the militants have and do the same things. I don't need a label. In my last year at the University, as punishment for having insisted on being released, I was finally dismissed from the UJC.

Renée's return to Cuba a year after the October crisis was a great event for me. I talked of nothing but my great longing to see her, and I couldn't sleep at night I was so excited. She had been away for three years. I was still a child when she left and we'd never had a chance to establish an adult relationship. All the same, we remained very close. Paco had an inkling of how I felt and looked upon Renée as someone who could steal some portion of my love from him as soon as she returned to Cuba.

While Paco and I were engaged, Renée, who was in Europe and pregnant again, had fallen downstairs and miscarried. I cried and cried, and Paco couldn't understand why I made so much of it.

"She had so many dreams about that baby," I explained. "Besides, imagine how she must be feeling in a foreign country full of such odd, unfeeling people."

Paco said my strong reactions were symptoms of a pathological love for my sister. The idea had never occurred to me. It seemed a very coldhearted way of analyzing the situation. He was more jealous of her and of Silvio than of other men. He once asked me, "Whom do you love most, me or your brother?" It was a cruelly difficult question to answer. I adore my brother, I can't bear to have him hurt in any way, and I was never too sure I loved Paco. With my brother I shared my childhood, my whole history, and a great many things I could never erase from my mind and heart. Had I answered Paco with complete honesty, I'd have admitted that I loved Silvio more. I never did, but Paco noticed how I hesitated.

It annoyed me that he should ask such a question. It seemed illogical to compare what I felt for him and what I felt for my brother and sister. They were completely different kinds of love. And he's wrong to say my love for them is pathological. Silvio, Renée, and I are so close because ever since *papi* died, *mami*. . . . Anyhow, what's wrong with my loving them and Paco too?

After Renée's return, Paco and I had our first serious quarrel—only it was with Renée he quarreled, not me, and that cut me to the quick. Paco and I were living in *mami*'s house and Renée and Héctor came to visit us there.

Renée had been home a couple of days when she came to our room for a chat and started talking about the Soviet Union. She'd acquired a number of new ideas in her travels, among them the idea of the "pure man." Comparing Soviet and European communism with ours, she said ours was much purer. It was simply her opinion, but Paco reacted violently. At that point he was dedicated to the idea of the "new man," and to him the "new man" was to be found in the Soviet Union.

I agreed with Paco, but when someone brings up a new idea it's a good thing to listen, no? Afterward I can reach my own conclusions, but why should I automatically reject an idea propounded by someone who isn't telling me any lies?

Renée wasn't in the least aggressive. She just ignored Paco's outburst and went on talking. Then, at one point in the discussion I argued in favor of one of her ideas. Paco turned to me angrily, "You agree with everything she says!"

"I'm not agreeing or disagreeing," I said. "But I don't close my ears to what people have to say."

"Very well. I'm going to report this conversation to your UJC base committee." He could make that threat because I was a militant then, you see. "We'll discuss it at the committee level."

That was like a slap in the face. For the first time I got really angry with him. I said, "Don't bother with the base committee, take the case right up to the Central Committee! We'll discuss it with Fidel himself. I'll listen to what I damn well please and neither Fidel nor anyone else can stop me. If you don't want to listen, that's *your* problem!"

That made him twice as hostile toward Renée. He ordered her out of our room and she left. She didn't pay much attention to it, no more than I'd pay to an argument with Héctor. I don't care a hoot for anything he might say to me. He's merely my brother-in-law, but Renée is my sister. Héctor could say terrible things to me and I'd just answer, "Look, you're nothing but a shit-eater. Unfortunately my sister married you, so I'll have to get along with you as best I can." Renée would never have rejected me either, not even if I'd married a murderer, and she wouldn't have bothered to quarrel with him. She'd simply think, "My sister married a beast, but she's still my sister."

I was furious with Paco, not so much because of his dogmatic attitude, but because it was so mean of him, knowing how I feel about my sister, to provoke a fight only two days after her return. I saw that as an act of aggression toward me. Never before had I felt so angry with anybody. I could have chopped him up in little pieces! Intellectually, I could understand Paco's emotional outburst, but I didn't like it. I'm not a machine, I react emotionally too. I went to bed and fell asleep without saying a word to him. Next morning he got up as cheerful as if nothing had happened. He can have a terrific argument with me, and half an hour later, without having settled anything, he will be oh so terribly affectionate! I ignored him. That went on for two days. When I quarrel with somebody, I can't express any affection until it's been cleared up. I can't feel aggressive and affectionate at the same time. It just isn't in me.

In spite of everything it was easily resolved—one day we talked it over, and things went back to normal. But all during Renée's stay we had our little encounters. Héctor wasn't exactly best friends with us and didn't much like staying at *mami*'s house. Renée and I were both unhappy about the situation, and one day we sat down to discuss it.

I put it frankly. "Héctor hates to visit us and Paco hates to visit you. So what of it? We're sisters and our relationship has nothing to do with them. It was purely accidental we met them at all. We don't have to have them around to see each other."

After the quarrel between Paco and Renée, my feeling about discussing things with Paco changed a great deal. We had been very much alike in our reactions to politics and everything else, but gradually that unity between us collapsed, and now there are many things we simply do not discuss.

Paco is a Party member and I am not, and our reactions to political questions are sometimes very different. He considers me a bit of a liberal and that provokes confrontations between us. He's much more dogmatic than I and finds it harder to accept anything that deviates in the slightest from the Party line. When he disagrees with me, he scolds and I feel he is acting like a judge. I can't help taking inflexibility as a sign of lower intelligence. I absolutely reject it in any form. I'm much more tolerant and understanding than Paco.

RENÉE:
  Once we were back in Cuba, I wanted to work again. Thinking that we were to be sent abroad in a short time, I didn't apply for a teaching

post but took an office job in the Cuban division of UNESCO. Mirella was still at the Ministry of Foreign Affairs, and it was good to be home and near her again. We spent a lot of time together.

Héctor was no longer interested in the diplomatic corps. He joined UNEAC,[49] the artists' and writers' union, and taught drawing in the Cubanacan Art School. He's basically an artist, after all. But he had some trouble in the School and was transferred to the Museum. Then he left UNEAC for a while because he had difficulties in connection with the writer Padilla.[50]

I know a lot about that, because from the first Héctor always talked Padilla, Padilla, Padilla, defending him; Héctor doesn't think Padilla's poetry is antirevolutionary. That isn't Padilla's problem. He's had communist ideas from the start, but he places himself above politics and is a trifle aloof from social problems. He has a mild disdain for Fidel. Héctor says that Padilla wants to look beyond the historical moment and that's certainly true.

In my opinion Padilla's book has been badly misinterpreted. The poetic mentality, the poetic stance, is never the same as the political. When he says, "Oh, people, people," he isn't referring to the Revolution but to history.

I think he's very brilliant, one of the most brilliant people around, and he has a great gift for language. If he isn't an absolutely first-rate poet it's for lack of passion. He has a kind of profound bitterness and holds a sort of mordantly critical attitude toward life and people, but I don't find anything really passionate in his recent poetry. His childhood and education may account for that.

There are people who don't like Padilla personally but still stand up for him. I myself could easily feel contempt for him, but see him as a person troubled by conflicts. He's very cultured, very studious and sophisticated, and cynical, even with himself. He's very hard on himself. Right now he may be having a session with his own conscience.

He's too self-centered to be a good person; he wants to see the

49. *Unión Nacional de Escritores y Artistas Cubanos* (National Union of Cuban Writers and Artists).

50. Herberto Padilla was awarded the annual poetry prize by an international panel of judges in the 1968 writers' contest sponsored by the Casa de las Américas. Some of the members of UNEAC, the writers' and artists' union, strongly opposed the selection of Padilla on the grounds that his work was not sufficiently revolutionary. As a result Padilla was fired from his job, though after an appeal to Castro, he was given a post in the University of Havana. Renée discusses only the 1968 incident; it was after these interviews were completed that Padilla became a cause célèbre in some noncommunist countries. In 1971 he was imprisoned for alleged counterrevolutionary activities, contact with foreign agents, and for not fulfilling civic duties. An open letter from a group of foreign writers asking clarification of the charges was sent to Castro, who denounced them all. Padilla was released from jail about one month after his arrest, following issuance of a statement of self-criticism which he later read before the writers' union.

whole world intellectually under his feet. In order to like people, he must first crush them intellectually, as though they were flies. Yet he needs a chorus of followers to listen and to admire him. His trouble is that he gets into arguments wherever he goes. He *creates* conflict. All the same he's developed his talent extraordinarily. He'll never leave Cuba, no matter what happens to him. Such things aren't important to him! What he wants is to be part of history.

Here in Cuba we talk a great deal about the importance of the "new man," that is, one who is physically, intellectually, and emotionally well developed. El Che embodied all those qualities. He had the capacity to love not only his immediate family and closest friends, but also mankind in general. There are many stories describing his warmth during chance encounters with perfect strangers. Like Lenin, he felt a common humanity with people he had never known, and that is partly why the Revolution adopted him as the prototype of the "new man."

El Che is our model for endurance, courage, and selflessness. From his early years he had acute asthma, but he never let it interfere with what he set out to do. He suffered a lot when he was fighting in the Sierra. What seems incredible is that he should have been able to live and fight with his guerrillas in Bolivia.

Now there is much discussion as to how we are to develop the "new man," and whether heredity or environment are the basic factors in his development. It seems to me that if heredity is the determining factor, we would have to kill off all the ugly, stupid, and bad people, which is clearly impracticable. Conversely, if we brought up twenty children in the same environment as Fidel or El Che, I doubt we could produce twenty Castros or twenty Guevaras.

To me, the most logical theory accounts for both heredity *and* environment. Some people are born potentially tall or short but their environment will determine whether that potential is fulfilled. The same holds true for emotional and intellectual qualities. I believe that environment encourages or else frustrates and stunts the development of a hereditary trait. So it seems to me that what we must do is create an environment, especially in the schools, that accommodates only favorable hereditary traits. Then we may see the "new man" emerge in our society.

MÓNICA:
The year I graduated from the University, Fidel asked the students from Cuba's three universities to make a trip to the Sierra Maestra. It was decided that we would hike all the way from the Sierra Maestra to

the Sierra del Cristal, where the Second Front had been.[51] The trip was organized and we went by train to Santiago de Cuba. At Santiago we boarded trucks that took us as far as San Lorenzo. From there on, we walked. There must have been about 800 to 1,000 university students participating. The trip lasted twelve days.

That first stage of the hike was very difficult for me. I'm not physically strong and have flat feet and I could hardly carry myself uphill, much less my knapsack. Two or three times on the way I had to give my knapsack to one of the boys. I hated to show such weakness because it was a point of honor to carry one's own knapsack. I arrived at the first camp exhausted.

The camps consisted of rows of poles between which we slung our hammocks. We camped more or less by platoons because that was the way we were organized, in brigades and platoons according to our school and faculties. I was in a platoon with the rest of the psychology students. We hung up our hammocks, ate, slept, and set out before daybreak the following morning, but it wasn't long before we were struggling uphill under a burning sun. Many people were exhausted after a few hours. There were times when I felt I couldn't lift my feet to take one more step. I was convinced by then that I couldn't possibly bear the physical strain for long and wouldn't be able to stay with the hike until the end. That first stage was horrible.

We continued walking to a camp called La Gloria, then to a camp called El Paraíso. And I must say, never were two places less appropriately named; there was nothing of heaven or paradise about them! Those three stages were the longest and most difficult. All we did was walk, walk, walk. When we got to camp we'd rest in the afternoon and go to bed early at night.

I don't remember how long it took the Rebels to cover that same ground but I know they did it in a fraction of the time, only about a day and a half, I think. Of course they didn't stop every afternoon and rest in camp until the following morning, as we did. Their rest breaks were often only ten or fifteen minutes long. The situation for them was different in every way. We were well clothed, well fed, and had nothing to carry except our knapsacks; they were ragged, hungry, weighted down by their arms, utensils, and what few supplies they had. It seemed beyond human strength to have covered so much mountainous ground so fast and under such unfavorable conditions.

Fidel met us one day, almost at the end of the trip. By then my feet were covered with blisters and hurting terribly so I had slipped some

51. The Rebel Army's First Front, under Fidel Castro, fought in Oriente Province's Sierra Maestra. The Second Front, under Raúl Castro, fought to the east and north in the Sierra del Cristal.

cotton supports inside my shoes to relieve my arches. A large group of us had fallen behind the rest—in fact, I wouldn't be surprised if more people hadn't fallen behind than had kept up. We walked along kidding each other and cracking jokes about how we were the lame, the halt, and the blind.

When we were about halfway to the next camp, a truck came to pick us up. "Why?" we asked. "Are we that far behind?"

"Oh no," they answered. "We're taking everybody to see Fidel." Oh, we were so excited! As the truck neared the place, Fidel came walking up with two or three others and stopped and asked, "What happened to you kids?"

"Oh, Fidel, we are the halt, the lame, and the blind," we answered laughing. "We just couldn't keep up with the rest!"

I asked him, using the familiar *tú*, "Say, Fidel, where are you going?"

"I'm going to a melon field near here, to show it to the kids, but you go on where you were bound because they're passing out refreshments." Like the undisciplined kid I was, instead of going on as he had told us to, I jumped off the truck, landed right beside Fidel, and stuck close to him the rest of the time. I said to him, "I don't want any refreshments, I want to go along with you."

As we walked along, Fidel explained to us that the zone was especially interesting because it was on a mesa and had its own micro-climate. It was something very special because the only thing that grew there naturally was . . . I have a lousy memory, but I think it was pine trees. I believe the place was near the Pinares de Mayarí. The farmers had never cultivated that region until one of them—or maybe Fidel himself because he pokes around everywhere and gets interested in all sorts of things—discovered that the place had a micro-climate and was suitable for melon plants, which would yield several harvests of beautiful big fruit every year. That land was good for about three different things but what Fidel wanted there was melons. So he had them planted, but then the Mineral Resources people told him there were mines in that place and the plants should be pulled up.

Well, Fidel felt insulted. "How can you ask me to pull up my melons?" he said. "You people simply lay waste to the land—after you get through with a place it looks horrible." I don't know all the details, but there was an argument about it.

When we got to the melon field, every time we were near a plant Fidel would push us aside and say, "Careful, don't step on my melons!"

Fidel was having one of his good days, when he was in a pleasant, joking mood and teasing people. They brought us ice cream and it so happened that the boys were served first. Fidel said in a tone of annoyance, "What's this, bringing ice cream to the men and not to these girls? That's not right!" Then he began to feed us girls by turns, giving us ice cream with his own spoon. It was a lot of fun.

He kidded us too. First he asked if the boys helped us. We said, "Oh yes, Fidel, they're real nice. Sometimes they even ask to carry our knapsacks."

"Don't trust them, kids," he told us. "Maybe that's just their technique. Remember that cavemen used to grab the women by the hair and drag them to their caves."

Then he told us that our pullover sweaters were very becoming to us, and he kept teasing like that. We were with him a long time. He told us the whole history of the melon field. Fidel had lived near there as a child and he told us that at the age of seven or eight he went there for the first time and climbed up to the mesa, and liked it a lot. He talked on and on, telling us all sorts of anecdotes.

Then it was decided to have all the students on the hike gather at the melon field, where Fidel would talk to them. They arrived marching in a beautiful, disciplined way, like an army. They stood where Fidel put them, at a distance on three sides of the melon field. Meanwhile, our little group was close to him. He turned to us and said, "You see? You're a bunch of undisciplined kids. Just see how beautifully the rest of them marched here and deployed themselves as they were told to."

"Yes, yes," we agreed, "but we're going to stay here with you." So we stayed there, chatting with him. Just us, out of all those thousands! It was a really pleasant experience.

In his speech, Fidel more or less repeated what he had told us and gave the history of the zone. Then they picked melons and cut them and passed around slices. I hate melon but I had to eat it like crazy that day. Fidel would ask me, "Good, isn't it?"

And I'd gush, "Oh, it's divine, simply divine!"

"Here, have some more," he'd say, and I accepted it because I couldn't just up and say I didn't like melon.

When we camped for the night, it began to pour down rain before we could even hang up our hammocks. It was a terrific rainstorm. We were all wet and up to our ankles in mud and our equipment got soaked. Everybody was tense, and some were so upset they cried when they found themselves all wet and with no place to sleep.

All of a sudden in the midst of the rain, Raúl came riding into camp. His horse almost ran over me because it was too dark to see. "Well, what are you going to do about this?" he asked us. "It's your problem, so let's see how you solve it." Then he said, "As soon as the storm's over, you should build a campfire." So we made a campfire to dry our clothes, but it wasn't much help. We slept as best we could. I found shelter in the house of some country people.

Next morning the place was more than muddy and our knapsacks weighed three times as much because everything in them was heavy with water. We had to go up a slope slippery with mud and we had to tie ourselves in lines with ropes so we could negotiate it. That night was one of our worst experiences on the hike.

Raúl showed us around, telling us, for example, where the Almeida command was.[52] "Did the police come up this far?" we asked him. "Oh no, not they! None of Batista's people ever came here." He told us a lot of details about the war, and it was really awe-inspiring to find oneself in the places where the revolutionary heroes had been and to hear details of the life they had lived there.

That hike was a great experience for us because it gave us some slight idea of how hard life must have been in the Sierra Maestra. I learned to appreciate what the guerrillas must have suffered. It was very impressive.

52. Comandante Juan Almeida Bosque, a veteran of the Moncada attack, was head of the Rebel Army's Third Front in Santiago de Cuba. Almeida is now a member of the Political Bureau of the Party's Central Committee and First Secretary of Oriente Province's Central Committee.

Chapter Seven

New Developments

MÓNICA:

I often wonder whether it's heredity, environment, or upbringing that makes Renée and me so alike. Our histories and our marital relations are very much the same. I find it easy to confide in her and I always feel sure she'll understand. It helps a lot.

Renée went to a psychiatrist for a while, though I don't think she has any faith in them. I don't either. I've never gone to a psychiatrist and have no intention of doing so. I haven't met one I trust enough to talk to frankly, and even if I did, I doubt he could do anything to help me. Some of our problems are so old . . . so fossilized. I know enough psychology myself to understand what's bothering me, yet I can't get rid of it. I guess there are many factors I haven't been able to dredge up. At first I thought time would cure my problem, but I worry about it now.

I was so very, very ignorant about sex! I realize my husband must have been made to feel insecure because of it, but he's never felt he was to blame, and I certainly haven't either. Paco has seen it all as part of my upbringing. Knowing that the same thing happens to my sister, he sees it as a family problem. I don't believe I've hurt his male pride at all. But I do realize he suffers from the situation and I'd give anything to change it.

One day after we'd been married for years, the subject came up. He was horrified that I wanted to talk about it, and he said, "I'd rather not discuss that. I don't want to hurt you."

"You won't hurt me," I assured him. "I want to hear your point of view. I don't think it's fair to sacrifice you because of my problems." He said I hadn't even tried to solve the problem. I answered it was true, I hadn't, and what's more I didn't mean to.

In spite of everything, it never crossed my mind that I might ever be interested in another man. I was so used to Paco. I believed then that there were two types of married women: those who could fall in love with another man and those for whom such a thing was impossible. I was convinced I belonged to the second group. Renée had been as rigidly conventional as I, if not more so, but when she returned to Cuba, I found she'd changed. I was amazed at the casual way she mentioned extramarital relations—not hers, but other people's. I told her, "Those things don't happen in my group."

I had lots of male friends because most FEU leaders were men, but my relationship with them was relaxed, casual, and sexless. I'd say, "Hi, Skinny, how's everything?" If any of the boys got even slightly out of line, the rest would jump on him: "Hey, stop kidding around with Mónica or I'll tell Paco." I felt completely secure with them. Now I realize that no men approached me because I set up barriers against it. I couldn't so much as accept a compliment. It seemed like an offense against Paco, disagreeable and improper.

Then when Paco was in Poland for three months and Cristina was about a year old, I ran into one of Paco's close friends at a university function. I was tremendously fond of him. We'd lived in the same house one year and I'd always consulted him when I had a problem. We talked until midnight and he offered to see me home. When we got there he asked if I wouldn't invite him in for a beer. I said I'd be delighted. It all seemed very normal to me, quite aboveboard. But once inside he displayed his talons. He gave me an odd look and asked, "Do you miss Paco a lot?"

"I miss Paco terribly," I answered quickly. Then I started praising Paco and talking about him until our friend got up, said goodnight, and left. I couldn't feel the same way about him for a long time after that.

Paco was still in Poland when I met a Czech at a dance. I don't think he had the faintest interest in me, but he had the bright idea of inviting me to dance, and I accepted. He was the first man I'd danced with since my marriage. Nobody enjoyed dancing more than I did, and when I was single I had danced a lot. After I married I wouldn't have dreamed of dancing with anyone but Paco, and since he didn't dance, I didn't either. That night I got home at midnight. I immediately sat down to write Paco, telling him I had danced with the Czech and that it was all Paco's fault.

I'd been married four years before I realized I could be attracted to another man, and it wasn't easy for me to admit it to myself. It happened to be a very superficial attraction and it came to nothing. I didn't even know the man, but every time I saw him I'd feel a thrill. That upset me terribly. Even when I was driving with Paco and saw a car that looked like his, I'd get excited. It seemed wrong to feel that way with my husband sitting right there beside me. I couldn't stand it, and deep inside I rejected it. I was relieved when the attraction for the stranger gradually subsided.

At the Ministry of Education, where I was working, the head of my department was a Brazilian psychologist, a dark Indian type, tall and muscular. When I first saw him I wasn't at all attracted to him—I was sure he was an ogre—but his personality was in great contrast to his appearance. He impressed everybody, not only me, with his self-confidence, his calm, his poise. As our boss, he was very permissive with everyone in the department. He'd *suggest* that we do this or that; he never once said, "You *must* do this." Such a sweet man . . . just like *papi!*

When we began to work together, I was the one he singled out, I don't know why, and as I got to know him I realized he was capable of the utmost tenderness and trustfulness. He began to discuss departmental affairs with me. That was the beginning of a great friendship.

After work, we'd stay on in the office talking about thousands of things—the work we were doing, life in general. There were very few people with whom I could talk so freely or feel so completely secure and self-confident. By approaching me in a fatherly way, he overcame my defenses. I couldn't have yielded to any other kind of attraction in a man who was not my husband.

The psychologist was much older than I—in his forties—married and the father of two children. He reminded me of *papi* in many ways; he had a heart condition similar to the one that killed my father. I was aware that after *papi*'s death, I tended to look for a father figure. I always thought that my rather introverted brother could attract any woman, so my image of the ideal man was a somewhat reserved, dignified type—exactly the opposite of my husband, and very much like the Brazilian psychologist.

Not that I analyzed it then; one doesn't feel the need to dissect pleasant things. Besides, analysis is so destructive. Had I forced my feelings into my consciousness, it would have been my duty to struggle against them, and I hadn't the slightest wish to do that. As my relationship with him became more intense I began to need him, never feeling physically attracted, but drawn to him as a person with whom I could communicate. The great difference in our ages kept me from thinking he might be attracted to me as a woman, but gradually it began to dawn on me that our relationship went beyond friendship. It was a surprise—an agreeable one—to realize that I had the capacity to love other men and feel wonderful when I was with them.

One Saturday morning the director of our department told us we were to leave on the following day for three weeks of productive labor, and he was giving us the day off to get ready. I couldn't understand why agricultural labor was compulsory all of a sudden when it had always been voluntary before. It seemed to me the most absurd thing in the world and I argued about it. I thought it was a mere whim. I asked, "Why must we go now? Usually you leave us free to decide."

I phoned Paco and he said he'd meet me around noon at my mother's house. My friend invited me to El Carmelo for chocolate. There he told me the whole story of his life, ending by saying he had to leave Cuba, but that first he had some emotional ties to break. It was all very ambiguous. When it was almost noon I asked him to take me home. He protested. "At this moment nobody needs you as much as I do," he said. "I must talk to someone, and you're the only person I really trust." But he took me home all the same.

The next day, on our way to productive labor, we rode in the same car, and he asked what I'd done after he left me. He seemed to have an insatiable need to know everything I'd done and said and thought.

He said, "I had a terrible day. Every single minute I was wondering where you were, who was with you—life is so cruel." That was pretty direct. Still, I tried to find a million different explanations for it. I told myself, "He's very inhibited and simply needs someone to talk to."

During our period of productive labor, I saw him only once. He was very happy to see me and we talked awhile. When the three weeks were almost up, I heard he'd had a heart attack and was in a hospital in Havana.

Paco had sent for me so he could see me before he left for Camaguey for six weeks of productive labor, and I returned to Havana two days early. I went to see my friend in the hospital and found him a changed person. Instead of being quiet and depressed, he was talkative and laughed frequently. He refused to let me go and I stayed about five hours. I could see it did him good to be with me. It did me good too, seeing the effect I had on him.

I went back to see him every day. I was so happy to be with him, to reach for the things he needed, to give them to him! Each minute of my life was important to him, and I loved telling him everything he wanted to hear. He didn't make any passes at me. I think he must have understood me better than I did him, and he didn't want to scare me away.

I didn't try to conceal the fact that I went to see him so often. When anybody asked, "Are you going to see the psychologist today?" I always answered, "Of course, I go every day." I never imagined that our relationship could turn into anything serious, but it had become a very intimate one without our ever putting a name to it.

By the time he left the hospital, people were gossiping about us. It's the woman who gets the worst of it in those situations, but I didn't care. I was living so intensely and it was such a great thing for me, I wouldn't have cared if the most important person in the world had called me to account. I would have admitted my feelings to anybody, and I certainly wasn't going to hide them merely for social considerations.

My friend left the hospital on a Saturday, and the following Monday morning he was back at work, though he felt very ill. "Why did you come?" I asked him. "Are you trying to kill yourself?"

"Don't worry about me, I have to talk with you. I must see you tomorrow at 5:00."

The next day at 5:00 he stopped by. "Will you go for a ride with me?" he asked. By then I would have done anything for him. I loved him to the point of idolatry. We were together all afternoon, and only when it began to get dark did I ask him to take me home.

"Why should I, when we both feel so happy?" he objected. Paco was still away, cutting cane, and the children were with *mami*. Nobody was expecting me. But I didn't like to be away from home after dark, so he drove me home. From then on he came to pick me up every day after work, and sometimes he visited my home and saw the children.

One night he kissed me. I reacted as I'd never done before. It awakened something in me I hadn't known existed. I was shocked that I could feel so much more than I believed possible. I really didn't want to know it. I was horrified . . . I felt ill. But after that, I became acutely aware of the most insignificant details. It was so beautiful, so sweet. . . .

Renée was all for my relationship with the psychologist, although she was troubled by his resemblance to *papi*. All the same, she thought he was right for me and even encouraged me to have sexual relations with him. But I couldn't go that far.

With every day that passed, my feelings became more intense. I wanted to do things he liked simply because it gave me pleasure. Never have I felt such joy in giving. Normally, I allow no one to interfere with personal things, the way I dress or do my hair, but with him it was different. He suggested a certain way of doing my hair and I wore it that way for a long time. I still do, now and then.

One day we went to El Patio for coffee and he asked me to describe how I acted at home, so he could compare reality with the image he had of me. In his mind, he said, he pictured himself married to me, living with me and our children. I'd never known anyone could create such a detailed fantasy world to live in, that it was possible to have such a spacious, beautiful inner world. Not that he idealized me. He'd tell me frankly, "You have your faults, but I don't care—I find them charming." And sometimes he said, "I know I love you better than you love me." I don't believe it, I don't believe it! I loved him deeply and I needed him, really needed him. Every day I felt it more.

During that year Paco and I were seldom together. A great many things came up to keep us apart. I would go to do productive labor, and a few days after I returned Paco would leave to cut cane or to go on a job assignment in the interior. Then he went abroad for a month. When Paco was due to return I told my friend I couldn't go on. He said, "I can't stop being in love with you. But I accept your decision. I'll even help you act on it."

And he did. It was almost impossible for us not to see each other, we had established so many links between our work. So he encouraged me to let another man in the department drive me home after work. The two men knew each other well and often talked together. I've never understood my friend's attitude but I agreed to go home with the other man.

And still we were finding it impossible to break up our relationship. We couldn't pretend indifference for more than two days. When he kissed me a second time I felt ready to surrender to him completely. That terrified me.

The following day we tried to be very distant with each other and talked of nothing but work. That afternoon I was waiting for the other man to pick me up as usual when my friend asked to drive me home. I didn't know what to do and I hesitated. What a fool I was! My friend said, "Are you going with me or waiting for him?"

"I'll wait for him," I answered, and then realized that his question carried a much deeper meaning. He took my answer as a definite farewell.

He looked at me so sadly. "Are you *sure?*" he asked.

"Yes," I said. Nothing I have ever done has hurt as much as forcing out that word. Even as I spoke, I wanted to take it back.

That was the end of our relationship. It had been very brief, and I couldn't stand the strain of it, but I've always regretted the cruel way I ended it. I'd have given anything to undo what I'd done. After we broke up he stayed in Cuba for another year, and during that time our contact was completely impersonal. Finally he broke his ties with the department and we didn't see each other at all.

One day it was formally announced at a meeting that he was returning to Brazil. I was very upset. I wanted to talk to him, to erase the impression of that last day. I had to tell him what a great part he had played in my life. I didn't want him to go away thinking I didn't return his love.

I found my opportunity when I learned that he was in the hospital again. Nobody was visiting him because he had committed some grave error—I had no idea what—and was in disgrace. I knew I might be called to account for it but I didn't care, I decided to go see him. I felt sure he'd confide in me, and I wanted to hear from his own lips what he'd done. I couldn't bear to be told by others, by people who judged him harshly. But when I visited him and we talked about his plans for the future, he said not one word about his trouble.

The following day when the other man was driving me home, he told me that my friend had written a letter to the United Nations asking for a job in their Pan American Department. It was bitter to hear it from him. The case was never made clear to me, but the action was considered treasonable, and the other man called my friend a traitor. "Stop the car," I said. "I'm getting out." I wouldn't hear my friend insulted, least of all by that man.

Next day I went to the hospital again and asked my friend what he planned to do. Still he didn't mention applying for a UN job. I was terribly hurt, not by what he'd done but because he didn't tell me about it. I could see he no longer trusted me.

I went to see him the day before he left Cuba, to say goodbye, and when we parted I felt he loved me as much as I loved him. I know he's recently been very ill again because he writes to a close friend who knew something of our relationship. He wrote a long letter without even mentioning me, and then at the end he asked after "the singular Mónica." I had to laugh... I said, "He couldn't have chosen a more ambiguous word than 'singular.' What does he mean? Singularly good? Singularly bad?"

"He considers you unique," his friend replied. "That's what he means."

I remember my Brazilian friend with deep affection. It was a brief experience but it opened up a whole new world and I began to look at life differently. I never slept with him because I couldn't bear the thought of keeping it from Paco, and even now, though it's conceivable that sometime I might have an affair, it would be difficult for me. Intellectually, I understand perfectly. I can imagine loving two men at the same time, but emotionally it would be too much for me. I can analyze it a thousand ways and convince myself there's nothing wrong with it. But I just can't stand it.

I was tempted to tell Paco the whole story, but we had very different approaches to life. He never was one to discuss such things; he prefers not to know what I think and feel, to blind himself to reality. It's easier for him. I don't see anything wrong with having an extramarital relationship as long as I tell my husband all about it. With mutual understanding, an affair need not be considered an infidelity. But Paco would simply reject the possibility of my loving another man. He would see it as a betrayal and that would *make* it a betrayal. I believe if Paco ever told me something like that had happened to him, I could understand it and sit down with him to analyze it.

I see the ideal marriage as one in which husband and wife are good comrades. Aside from being revolutionaries, the two of them must fit together perfectly in their opinions, tastes, interests, and of course in their sexual life. Sex is basic. And they should see each other as friends and companions, free to discuss any event in their lives and to talk about all their feelings. They should feel there's nobody with whom they can better discuss things than with each other. The fundamental thing is that they should respect each other as human beings who have a right to lead their own lives.

At this stage in my life it's very difficult to have an ideal marriage because we live too intensely. So little time is left over for two people to become really united, to develop common interests... although I don't really think it's the fact that people work twenty hours a day and are separated so much. It's an obstacle, a grand excuse, but it's not a sufficient reason for their not developing a good relationship. The busy, hurried life we lead is not the true cause for the absence of a good marital relationship. I believe it depends on the couple's attitude and adjustment to marriage.

I've never known an ideal marriage. My own marriage was nearly ideal but not quite. In the sexual aspect we're maladjusted so there's no hope of a solution. I suspect it's caused by my deficiency and is bound to exist forever, with anybody, under any circumstances.

The trouble is that men are so much more quickly aroused and satisfied than women. Paco doesn't need any stimulus at all to get sexually excited. I can't understand such rapidity. It makes me lose interest. It seems impossible that after seven years of marriage he should be particularly excited by me. He doesn't need any foreplay at all, but I do. I need a lot. When he does it simply to please me, I'm not interested. I only enjoy it when both of us spontaneously engage in it, and I can always tell when it's that way.

I never refuse Paco when he needs me, but there have been times when I've found ways for avoiding sex without directly refusing him. I only refuse him outright when I'm very, very upset. There are times when I want Paco to take the initiative, but mostly I don't need sex at all. I have two alternatives when Paco is excited: I either find a way to prevent him from asking me or I give in. Sometimes I even get really enthusiastic after we begin.

Lately I've read a little of *Human Sexual Response* by two North American researchers,[53] and I'm convinced a man's sex drive is no stronger than a woman's, despite men's fuller sex lives. The fact that a man can procreate for more years than a woman is not, it seems to me, valid proof that at twenty he has a stronger sex drive than she does. I don't believe the goal of human sexual activity is procreation. The differences between men and women are, for the most part, culturally determined. From the day of his birth, a boy is told he must act like a *macho,* a he-man. If he cries, he's shut up at once and told that men don't cry, and he's taught that to be a real *macho* he must have hundreds of mistresses. This is especially true in Cuba, where *machismo* is carried to extremes.

On the other hand, people keep harping on a girl's modesty and decorum. "You must not take off your panties... girls don't sprawl, they sit with their legs close together... girls walk this way... girls never look

53. William H. Masters and Virginia E. Johnson (Boston: Little, Brown & Co., 1966).

at boys . . . girls must preserve their virginity until they can give it to some saintly man at the age of twenty or so. . . ." I was brought up that way myself, and I never questioned why I should preserve my virginity until marriage.

There was a time when *mami* talked freely to me about sex and it annoyed me. I didn't like to have my own mother talking to me about such things and I rejected her. Now I permit her to talk to me about sex but I take a stand and freely express my own opinions. I tell her lots of things I don't really mean: for example, I tell her I'm going to bring up my daughters to believe in free love and do as they please. She always answers, "Well, they're *your* daughters. I already brought mine up. You raise yours any way you like." I sometimes hint that she used very erroneous criteria in bringing me up, but I don't really want to hurt her. Basically she's a good person.

I've tried to teach my daughters to think of sex as a normal activity. I haven't ever talked to them about it, because so far they haven't asked me and I'm not going to force any information on them prematurely. When they're old enough to start asking questions I plan to give them answers they can understand.

When my daughters are ten or eleven years old, I want them to have normal relationships with little boys. I mean to encourage friendships. I'll tell them to invite the boys home to listen to records, and when they have little sweethearts, I'd like to know about it, though of course I don't expect to be their pal and confidante. Still, I hope they'll want me to be a real comrade to them.

I'd rather my daughters didn't have sexual relations as adolescents, but I wouldn't forbid them to. If they have them, they have them. I don't think it would be immoral. I just don't believe it would be good for them at that period of adjustment. I expect them to indulge in sex play during their engagements and I hope they'll have sexual relations before marriage. I think they probably will.

I'll tell them they must be sure they're in love with a man and that he loves them before going to bed with him. Also they must know that he thoroughly understands and approves of a woman's having premarital relations, and that he looks upon sex as they do—as the highest expression of love. If both agree, to wait until marriage would be a mistake.

Everywhere in Cuba women have had to adjust their attitudes to marriage, because now they're committed to working along with men for the success and continuance of the Revolution. The state has the right to expect, even to command and force, a woman to spend forty-five days a year in agricultural work, and it's just as likely that she'll be sent to one place and her husband to another. In the old days husbands wouldn't have permitted such a thing. Now, to object would be to oppose the Revolution.

I think that many men, deep inside, would rather their wives stayed at home, but they know that a good revolutionary doesn't take such a stand. It's a rare man who feels that his wife is a person in her own right, and should have the opportunity to find fulfillment in her work. At the moment it's the social pressure that activates the majority of men into living up to the ideal of the Revolution, but this will eventually work a change in their basic attitudes.

Even so, there are a few revolutionaries, and good ones too, who don't hesitate to boast, "*My* wife is no working woman." I've argued with some of them, "You don't have the moral right to ask me to hammer a nail in the wall if you forbid your own wife to work. My husband is made of flesh and blood just like you. He'd like to have me waiting for him when he comes home, but he lets me work all the same."

Paco and I were separated this year. On the whole I've felt better since, and I believe our separation was a step in the right direction. Oh, I have my ups and downs. There are moments when I'm depressed and want to go back to him, especially when I'm under pressure, but that's to be expected. When I actually came out and told Paco that we couldn't go on living together he was panic-stricken. He wouldn't even acknowledge the possibility that our marriage might break up, and I was truly afraid it would affect his entire life.

It's painful to admit, but I think Paco loved me more deeply than I loved him. He treated me a little *too* carefully, like a fragile object he was afraid to touch. He was so frightened of hurting me he put up with all my faults. What he should have done was tell me, "Look, I don't like this particular trait of yours, or it bothers me when you do that."

After we separated, Paco told me, "If you think it's important and can help us out of this mess, I'll go to a psychiatrist." And he did, to save our marriage.

One Sunday morning when he came to visit me—how terribly difficult those visits are!—he told me he had gone to a Soviet psychiatrist. The psychiatrist told him he was a bit depressed but otherwise all right. At first I told him he shouldn't talk to me about his treatment, but he did anyway, and the truth is, I *was* curious. We didn't go into detail though, because Paco was restless and hurt and it was difficult to talk.

I wouldn't call myself a good wife or a bad one. I do admit that I lack a great many qualities that make a traditionally good wife—one who would take scrupulous care of her husband's clothes, cook his meals, raise his children, and clean his house. But I don't think that was crucial in my marriage. I saw myself more as my husband's comrade and friend, a woman with whom he could discuss things.

I'd never let myself care so much about a man that I couldn't live without him, and Paco knew it. To a man I'll give what's mine to give—a mother's tenderness, a wife's tenderness ... not anything specifically sexual, but all the rest. Perhaps if I were capable of responding totally as a woman it would make me a bit more dependent on a man and I don't want to be dependent on anybody.

I know love is necessary, and I know it's a fault in me that I can't love. But love is hard to find, and even if you find it, it shouldn't be the focus of your life. No, it can't, and it shouldn't be an *aim*. There have always been people who could love, even in the old society, but it's always been a mess, a tragedy, and very difficult. I don't think much about it. It's something I kind of keep away in a drawer and never touch.

I think love should just happen, it shouldn't be sought. All the same, I don't think I want it to happen to me. That's not where happiness is for me. I'm happy in brief moments, when I'm listening to music, looking at one of my children, above all when I feel useful, doing a piece of work. When you have ends in mind, when you have goals to attain, you're too tense to concentrate on pleasures along the way. That's why I don't have any *personal* goals.

Mami was very upset when Paco and I separated. She's retired from her job and now that she's old and has nothing to do, she leads a rather lonely, empty life. She wishes we'd go see her, talk with her, listen to her, but it isn't in us to understand the problems of her old age and help her bear them or even to sit and listen to her talk. She's sixty-five now, and it's only fair that in whatever time is left her, I should be considerate and remember to visit her. I really do make a conscious effort to act like a loving daughter because I've analyzed all the things she did and now I understand why. I even kiss her when I arrive, but I can't bring myself to caress her. If she caresses me, it feels odd.

When she asks, "Why didn't you phone me?" I start thinking up some excuse, "Well, old lady, you see ... ," but with *mami* you can't say the slightest thing without having her complain that her children no longer respect her. Perhaps this is the moment when we should give her moral support, draw closer to her, try to understand her. But that's not the way it is; we haven't done any of that since we've married. My brother and sister have pulled away even more than I. *Mami* says that I'm the best of the lot, that none of us pays enough attention to her, and I think she's right. We've rejected her somewhat.

But she's a very difficult person to get along with. When you try to get close to her, her personality jars against you. She's frightfully domineering and still tries to rule our lives. I can't bear that. When she visits me on a Sunday, she tries to change my house around, and she interferes in important matters too, criticizing the woman who takes care of my children. *Mami* knows perfectly well that whether my children are at home or in an institution, whoever takes care of them is going to be human and have human defects. But she also knows that my children mean a lot to me and I'm not going to turn them over to just anybody. I say, "Look, *mami,* whoever looks after my children is entitled to privileges in my home." But that doesn't stop her. She nags and nags. "None of you loves me anymore. I'm nothing but a burden to my daughters." The best solution is to stay away from her. I've been more or less a good daughter, according to what was expected—one who studies, who marries a man of whom her parents approve, who devotes herself to her home and to providing her parents with grandchildren. Actually I don't think there is such a thing as a good daughter. We're simply individuals who respond to certain situations. I believe I responded pretty well, considering my temperament and environment.

SEÑORA REYES:

Let me tell you it was a blow to me when Mónica separated from her husband. Why, she'd studied psychology and was always criticizing parents who got divorced and caused problems for their children! She did try to make a happy home at first, but she couldn't keep it up. The trouble was, she married far too young.

Paco is a good boy and he and Mónica used to get along very well indeed. But you see, Mónica was spoiled at home, and after she got married Paco went right on spoiling her. He was so much in love with her he did whatever she wanted, and she can get what she wants in her soft, easygoing way without exerting any pressure. Oh well, for all her slowness, she was the only one of my children who completed her university studies. The other two quit before they graduated.

Mónica was in her first year at the University when she married. I said to Paco, "I want her to finish studying for her career."

"Don't worry," he told me. "I'll see to it that she does." And Mónica did complete her studies because of him, as if she had been his daughter. She wasn't quite eighteen years old when her first child was born, and her second daughter came very soon after. Paco helped take care of the children to leave her time for study. As long as she was a student, at home, or with her husband, even when she had children of her own, Mónica was still a child. Paco faced all the difficulties and resolved all the problems to enable her to have a career.

Then what happened? She got her degree, began working, met this man and that one, and suddenly she matured. She was a wife and mother at an age when other girls are just beginning to think seriously of marriage. Now that she's twenty-four, her children are no longer babies. She has a Negro woman to take care of them during the day, and when she gets home they're ready for bed—or rather, they should be. They're apt to act up when their *mamá* gets home.

Paco, who is a young man of great integrity, joined the Party, and went to meetings and more meetings. Mónica would get home and Paco wouldn't be there. What interest could she have in going home? There was no one there to talk to. So she was bored with home, husband, and motherhood.

When gasoline rationing began, instead of her husband driving her to work every day, her sister began to do it. Sometimes when I asked about Paco she'd answer, "How should I know? I haven't seen him for the past three days." So he neglected her, partly because of his interest in politics and partly because he was so confident their relationship couldn't deteriorate, and when she told him how she felt about all those things he was amazed.

At one point I myself thought Paco didn't love Mónica. But he does, he worships her. He praises her to the skies. He said to me, "It's my fault. I forgot I had a very childlike and romantic wife, who likes to be made much of and spoiled."

The way I see it, Mónica arrived at a new stage in her development just at the time her husband stopped paying much attention to her. Then, too, she's surrounded by bad examples. Nowadays a woman's friends tell her, "Don't be a fool. Get a divorce!"

In my time, when a married woman talked over such problems with a friend, her friend would say, "But stop and think, *chica,* what about the children? What would your family say? How would your parents feel about it?" So you gave up the idea of divorce. But now...! It's a time of libertinism. Women say, "Why put up with anything? No! If I don't like the way things are, I'll get out." That's the kind of environment Mónica is in now.

Paco is a good man, a good father to his children, whom he adores, and Mónica is a very good mother, but her environment doesn't allow her to be one—the excessive work, meetings at all sorts of inappropriate hours. I know the Party isn't the whole problem. If it had been only that, she'd simply have talked it over with Paco. No outsider ever knows what's really going on in a marriage. It pained her to make the decision she made. She isn't indifferent to him. Plenty of tears were shed by both of them.

Mónica has behaved very intelligently since. She wants Paco to keep on going to the house until they get divorced or whatever they decide to do. He often goes to visit her on Sundays and they talk and laugh like friends. He finds subjects that interest her and makes jokes, because he hasn't given up yet.

I think there's still a chance they might be reconciled. He certainly wants to be. Mónica is experimenting. She thinks things over a long time and reasons them out before doing anything. But when she reaches a decision, nobody can change it.

I think it's disastrous that married couples and families should not be united, and that homes are being destroyed. The home is the foundation of the state. Each individual home is a little piece of the Republic, no? In my youth families sat down to meals at the same time every day. This was no burden on anybody, as offices and schools closed at 11:30 or 12:00 for the noon break, so every family could set their own hour and tell their cook, "We dine at 12:30."

At home all the members of my family would get together at mealtimes. It was very rare for anyone to skip a meal at home. We never sat down at the table until *papá* had taken his place, and we'd talk as we ate, lingering after dessert for more talk. After that, everybody would go back to work or school and be home punctually for supper.

When I had my own family I had to travel quite a distance from work, but I'd practically kill myself to get home in time to dine with my children. I still try to keep it up, but I don't insist because I think people should make their own choices. Now that I have one of my granddaughters staying with me, I don't go to the movies or anywhere else during the day so I'll be sure to be home when she gets here.

Our custom in Cuba is to have three meals a day and a mid-morning and mid-afternoon snack. But really there are no customary mealtimes anymore. After the triumph of the Revolution, school lunchrooms and workers' lunchrooms were established. Then came the gasoline shortage, and deficiencies in transportation when people's private cars wore out and couldn't be repaired or replaced. My son, who had always eaten at home, decided to have lunch where he works, and that's what most people do now. The husband eats in one place, the wife in another, and the children in yet another. So families see each other only at night, and sometimes they no longer even have that because there are so many meetings to attend. The husband has to go to one meeting, his wife to another. It's my impression that people go to so many meetings not because they have to but because they want to get away from home.

I know numbers of young engaged couples who don't get married anymore, housing or no housing. Following the Spanish custom, a Cuban wife used to be her husband's chattel. Now that she's been freed from domestic obligations, she isn't about to return to them of her own free will, which is a good thing.

I'm not entirely happy with everything happening in Cuba, but I'm not criticizing our government or socialism as such when I say that. I'm no counterrevolutionary. I'm decidedly a revolutionary but not blindly so. In the privacy of my home I have the right to say what I think.

Things have changed so much! If the emigrés were to come back they'd find life here very different. It's become terribly difficult. I get depressed and ashamed sometimes, seeing a chair broken and no way to replace or even repair it. The *consolidado*[54] doesn't help a bit. Now and then I've managed to get a carpenter to come and do a job for me on the sly. But even if you can find one willing to break the law and do a private job, where is he to get the materials, the nails and all that? When you find a plumber or a carpenter or somebody who does a job of his own, you may be sure he stole the materials from his place of work. There's no ration for them, you see.

There used to be cobblers who went from house to house repairing shoes. They'd get a small ration of material from the government, but when small businesses were closed down[55] this ration was rescinded. Of course there was a reason for it. Cobblers didn't always confine themselves to working with the materials the government assigned them. They had friends at the *consolidado* who stole bits of leather and other materials. So you see, even the measures that sound strangest make sense when you find out what's behind them.

I'm positive that Fidel wishes the best for all of us. I don't believe he has a single idea that could be criticized as an idea. However, not all those who work with him are able or intelligent, and others are negligent. Fidel says one thing, the extremists do the other. There are always those who'll play political tricks to get what they want. For instance, some people will do anything to get a good house. The mother of a certain *comandante* lives near a distant cousin of mine, who isn't in favor of the present government but stays because she lives very well. The *comandante,* a very militant revolutionary, has gone to see my relative several times and sent about twenty emissaries besides, to tell her he'll make it easy for her to leave the country. And do you know why? Because he wants her house, so he can live near his mother. There are many like him, ready to weave any kind of a web around you so they can get your job or your house.

There are a thousand details to be seen to if things are to be done right, and Fidel can't be expected to attend to all of them personally. So what's the result? Things don't go as smoothly as we'd like. But I've found that his government is honest in every way. It has dealt forthrightly with so many ill-gotten fortunes, with so much oppression that the Cuban people suffered previously.

If the government sends somebody to jail as a counterrevolutionary, you may be sure they have conclusive evidence that he is one. They're

54. A general term of reference for any consolidated enterprise. Here it is an abbreviated way of referring to the state-operated repair-service centers.

55. In March, 1968, approximately 55,000 small businesses, largely family-owned and -operated, were "intervened" and closed down by the government as part of a new "revolutionary offensive."

very fair and really investigate all such cases carefully. And that's not all. They've freed a number of known counterrevolutionaries because they have heart disease. People with a record of subversive activities, even some who have worked for the CIA, have been released and allowed to go scot free!

I remain in favor of the Revolution even if I myself lost a few possessions in the process—not much, but my house and so on. I owned three houses, including one on the beach. I sold two and they took the remaining one.[56] I asked no compensation because I figured the Revolution had given me more than it took away—it gave me peace of mind.

I've always liked Fidel a lot, but I'm no hero worshipper. I'm simply an admirer of his achievements and I think he's doing a fine job in spite of all the inconveniences of communism. Of course, Cuban politics don't depend exclusively on Fidel.

I believe the Revolution has matured sufficiently to go ahead even if we should lose our leader. We speak of Fidel because he's our greatest figure, our rampart, but the men under him have plenty of good ideas too. The Party gets together and makes decisions, naturally, but the idol of the people is Fidel. Fidel is unique. The affection we feel for him, we couldn't feel for anybody else.

It isn't only here in Cuba that Fidel has followers. I'm told that in foreign countries they admire him too, admire him passionately, just as those who hate him, hate him passionately. And why? Because they realize what a great man he is, that's why.

MÓNICA:

Since I graduated from the University I've been working as a psychologist. Most of the psychology students in my class stayed on in Havana to work in different organizations. One group is working in the sugar industry; they concentrate mainly on social psychology and industrial psychology. Another group is in the Ministry of the Interior, and a larger group, including myself, is in the Ministry of Education. A number of my classmates became teachers in the School of Psychology, and still others were accepted as trainees in the School of Public Health, where they were taught epidemiology, hygiene, and social sciences, all of which were considered essential for cadres in the public-health program.

The School of Psychology where I studied didn't restrict itself to any one school of thought—behaviorism, gestalt, conditioned reflex psychology, or psychoanalysis. We were taught about all the different schools and were even assigned some North American works to read.

56. Under the Urban Reform Law of 1960, Cubans were generally allowed to retain ownership only of the house or apartment in which they lived. The one remaining house Señora Reyes owned was in Pinar del Río and not used as a personal residence.

Freud's theories weren't taught in depth, only the rudiments, but perhaps now the School of Psychology is more open-minded. In fact, we didn't study any psychological theory in depth. We were never told, "This is the best theory" or "This is the school we believe in." Instead we were taught what the different schools had to say about the theory of learning, for example. They didn't teach us clinical psychology, preventive mental-health practices, or the role of the psychologist in the community. But after I graduated, the degree program in psychology was extended to five years, and the great majority of students participated in clinical work. But then most of the new graduates who came to work in my department wanted to be assistants to psychiatrists instead of community psychologists. We really had to work on them.

We've developed a new point of view about the role of the psychologist here in Cuba. It's the concept of the psychologist *in* the community and *for* the community, rather than for the individual patient. We see the psychologist as an integral part of a whole and want to train him to work at the community level. The psychologist would be placed in a polyclinic and be responsible for the psycho-social health of that whole public-health area.[57] It would be his job to meet the families, visit their homes, educate pregnant women, deal with social problems as well as industrial psychology problems in factories, and help couples who have marital problems. He'd be trained in educational psychology because it would also be his responsibility to see to it that the schools in his area function properly. But the psychologist wouldn't do the work alone. He'd train as many people as possible, nurses and all other employees of the polyclinic who have direct dealings with the community, and utilize all available resources. To do that, the psychologist himself must undergo special training. We've set ourselves a terrifically ambitious task.

We are, in a way, self-educated in community psychology. For example, psychologists working in public health aren't supposed to just sit around talking to patients, but do research on their own and report their findings. And they're being taught to incorporate in their work some of the new viewpoints of medicine. They're hoping to begin a program whereby the psychologist in a public-health area would get together with

57. Cuba has a massive public-health program founded on the principle that health care is a biological right and should be extended to everyone at no direct cost. The country is divided into thirty-eight health regions which are subdivided into public-health areas, each having at least one polyclinic. Greater Havana had over fifty polyclinics in 1970. Urban polyclinics are designed for out-patient treatment and are required to have on duty a gynecologist, dentist, pediatrician, epidemiologist, internist, and nurses. Health workers are assigned to polyclinics to teach local communities basic hygiene practices. Rural polyclinics also offer in-patient treatment. (Richard Leyva, "Health and Revolution in Cuba," in Rolando E. Bonachea and Nelson P. Valdés, eds., *Cuba in Revolution* (New York: Anchor Books, 1972), pp. 476–77.)

groups of pregnant women and give them a bit of instruction and a bit of psychotherapy. Actually, psychologists here don't have much experience in that area, but they'll do whatever they can.

At the moment there are six psychologists in three different poly-clinics, two in each, and they're already setting up the work. This is a very small start, we know that. The problem now is that the plans have to be reviewed and perhaps the aims redefined. For instance, some people maintain that the psychologists should be placed not at the area level but at the regional level, where they would have a great deal more personnel at their disposal. That would mean that the psychologist himself couldn't work directly with the community. Rather, he'd concentrate on training doctors, nurses, nurses' aides, and so on. That is, he'd develop well-rounded personnel who could do psychological as well as medical work.

I don't know which plan would work better. The program has barely begun. With time and experience we shall find out. At present, I see one insurmountable obstacle to setting up the program on an area basis: Cuba simply doesn't train nearly enough psychologists to serve the whole country that way.

Years and years will pass before we can even hope to have enough psychologists to fill the area posts. Meanwhile, it's better that each region have one psychologist who can start introducing minimal community programs. Otherwise, a few polyclinics would have psychologists doing intensive community work but the rest of the country would be left without any program at all. These problems will have to be discussed a lot more than they have been so far.

It seems to me that doctors and other medical personnel who deal with patients and with the community are totally ignorant of the psychologi-cal aspects of their work. It has been our privilege to initiate programs to improve matters in that respect, and we have great possibilities of doing really constructive work. However, experience has shown us we need some knowledge of the other social sciences. For community work I think we should have teams of psychologists, sociologists, and an-thropologists. So far, though, we are graduating only psychologists be-cause we don't have schools of sociology or anthropology. That forces us to go in for a bit of self-education by reading sociology. We do our best, but the logical thing would be to have teams.

At the moment, the outlook for our work is magnificent. We are in a privileged position. Right after graduation, very few professionals have the opportunities we have. At this stage of development we're beginning something completely new. Just now things are going rather slowly, but I have a hunch sometime soon they'll really get under way.

My aim is to serve the Revolution through my work. My life is a pathway toward a socialist society. Sometime in the 1970s we'll undoubt-edly enter a period of great economic progress; we'll be far ahead of where we are today. Not that it will be the end of the fight. As long as the Americans are screwing the whole world this thing won't end. The time will come when we have to confront North America. I don't know when, but it will come. The Revolution can't rest just because we've achieved a certain measure of progress. We can't really build a communist society or live in abundance as long as the rest of South America is in such a pitiful state. Just now we can't hope for the success of guerrilla warfare, but new conditions will arise. Then the Revolution will triumph everywhere.

PART II

Gracia Rivera Herrera

Chapter One

Getting Ahead

AT FIRST I WAS EXCITED by the changes in Cuba. When my friends claimed that the new government was going communist, I paid no attention. I could see the good that was coming out of the Revolution; it fought for the oppressed and was dedicated to justice and dignity for all people. Before, only the fortunate few had jobs; now there was plenty of work for everyone, even if it was only cutting cane.

Thanks to the Revolution I got a good job when I graduated from business school, and my two brothers were educated for free. Like most people who remained in Cuba, my family is living better now. Our only problem is the shortage of food, which has turned many against the government. But they're the kind who reason with their bellies. It wasn't the food shortage that changed *my* mind about the Revolution, it was the deliberate spiritual starvation of the Cuban people.

The government is careful to give the impression that there is complete religious freedom here in Cuba, but it's a lie. It didn't take me long to see the oppression all around me. For one thing, we Catholics were no longer permitted to teach religion outside the church. We had to wait for the children to come to us, and the government kept them so busy with revolutionary activities that they had no time for spiritual things. We tried to enlist the aid of parents, but there weren't many devout families left in Cuba.

Little by little, our nuns and priests began leaving the country too, and one church after another had to close its doors. It was for that reason I began to do counterrevolutionary work with a group of Catholics. Eventually the group was broken up and the leaders arrested. Luckily I wasn't implicated—I'll never know why—but I, too, thought of leaving Cuba.

Then I met a group of nuns who introduced me to their director,

This autobiography is based upon sixteen interviews with Gracia Rivera, fifteen by Oscar Lewis and one by Ruth M. Lewis. Four interviews with her father and one each with her great-aunt, her mother, and a friend brought the total number of transcribed interview pages to 841. An additional 123 pages on assigned topics were written by Gracia herself.

Padre Torres. He was a man with very progressive ideas about religion and one of the founders of an institute that was trying to prove religion had a place in a socialist society. "This is what I want to do," I said to myself. "I want to show everyone that Christians can contribute to socialism."

I joined the institute and became a nun. My family opposed it, and I had to make the very painful decision to leave them. It was especially hard to leave my *mamá*, but I knew what I had to do. For once in my life I had no doubts about my decision.

When I first entered the institute I told the padre about my counterrevolutionary activities. I planned to continue them, but he advised me not to. "You're not here to make counterrevolution," he said. "You're here to lead a religious life for the glory of God." So I was; the religious ideal had always meant more to me than the political ideal. I let myself be guided by the padre.

Padre Torres was an amazing and powerful man, and at first was the only person I trusted completely. He saw I was determined to study and better myself, and when I told him my father was a drunkard and a failure, and I was ashamed of my family, he helped me accept them as they were. "I am the father you never had," he said. But after a while I found I had put myself in the hands of a man impelled by earthly ambitions, who wanted to rise in the eyes of other men, and who exploited the institute for his own personal ends.

I was a nun for seven years. When I finally left the institute, my adjustment to the outside world was very difficult. I still live to serve mankind, but I realize now that the only way I can give myself to others is by becoming a revolutionary and a communist. But communists are atheists, and if I were to give up my religion my life wouldn't be worth living. That is my conflict; I feel as though I'm fighting a battle for my soul.

I was born on January 27, 1943, in the single room where *papá* and *mamá* lived after they were married. My *papá*, Moisés Rivera Morales, was a clerk in a poultry market in Marianao. The owners were Spanish and were good to him because he was a hard worker. He earned 45 *pesos* a month—not much, but the rent was only 3 *pesos* a month. *Mamá* was careful and they managed quite well. Their room was large and had a little yard in front that *papá* enclosed with wood panels and fixed up as an extra room with a table and chair. They bought a few other pieces of furniture, good-quality pieces; *papá* said he wanted them to last a long time. *Mamá* had made the sheets and linen with her own hands. That's the custom here—it's called *habilitación*—the way every bride prepares for marriage.

I, Gracia Rivera Herrera, was the eldest child, my brother Diego was born a year later, and my sister Aurora two years after that. Gabriel, my youngest brother, wasn't born until I was ten.

I was closer to Diego than to Aurora and he was the one I played with. When I was about three years old I almost killed the poor kid. I saw a man go by our house pulling a pig at the end of a rope, and my little girl friend and I decided to tie a rope around my brother's neck too, and we dragged him along until suddenly he started turning black. I screamed with fright, "*Mima,* Diego can't speak . . . Diego can't speak!" Luckily *mamá* cut the rope in time to save him, but they had to take him to the hospital.

Papá gave me a beating, accusing me of being a selfish child who didn't want a brother or sister. I ran to a neighbor's house but he caught me and beat me with a belt until it was torn to shreds.

My *papá* didn't coddle me the way he did my sister Aurora. She was his pet and she got away with murder, probably because she was sickly and a cry-baby, and also the youngest for so long. I wasn't jealous because my *mamá* seemed to favor Diego and me, though she's not the least bit affectionate. She never encouraged us to show her any love, and not once has she kissed any of us spontaneously or shown the slightest gesture of tenderness.

I don't know why, but I always had the impression that my parents considered me superior. I was never one for playing games; the noisy ones bored me and I didn't like playing "house" or "school" unless I was the mother or the teacher. Or if it was "lottery" we played, I had to be the one who wrote down the bets. When we had company or went to visit somebody, my brother and sister always played outside, but I liked to hang around listening to the conversation of the adults. They'd scold me and say I was only interested in gossip, but it was just that I wanted to learn things.

I loved going to church and school. Aurora and Diego never went to church unless I put pressure on them, and Diego had to be beaten almost every morning to make him go to school. I started kindergarten at age five and attended Winburn Academy, a good private school. I loved it from the very first day and walked off with all kinds of prizes and presents. Then the girl next door got a piano and began to take music lessons. I dreamed of getting one too, and *papá* said, "I'll buy you a piano if you get promoted." That was all I needed. I really put my heart into my school work, and at the end of the year I was not only promoted but skipped to second grade. I came home covered with medals and eager to show them to my *papá.* But he never bought me the piano and I never studied music.

Papá had nothing when he began because he came from a poor family of twelve children. *Papá's* mother, Aurora Morales, was born in Spain and came to Cuba when she was fifteen. Her brothers were well-established storekeepers here but she married a Mexican and her family washed their hands of her. The Mexican was a heavy drinker and one day he hit her so hard he smashed the bridge of her nose and caused her to lose an eye. She left him and then married my grandfather.

My grandfather was also from Spain and was a barber, a very capable man who could draw and write well, although he drank a lot. Grandmother Aurora ordered everyone about, including her husband, and once when he was drunk she locked him in a room for two days to sober up. She watched every move he made and didn't let him touch a drop. He did the cleaning and shopping in that family, but had to hide money to buy himself cigarettes and drinks.

When I was five *papá* was doing well. He practically had his own business, which is what he'd always wanted. He didn't own the shop itself, he rented it, but the profits were all his and he bought his own supplies. Financially it was his best time. We moved to a much larger house that had two bedrooms, a living room, and lots of furniture. *Papá* paid 40 *pesos* a month rent for it. The landlord, Benito, was a friend of ours.

My most pleasant childhood memories are of the years when we lived in Benito's house. *Papá* and *mamá* were very happy there. They often kissed and I liked the way *mamá* used to put her arm around *papá*'s shoulders. He'd laugh and say that she was the one who had to do the embracing because she was taller than he. Every day *mamá* would take us kids to *papá*'s poultry market after school. We'd stay until the shop was closed at 7:00, then we'd go home together.

Mealtimes were special. The table was always properly laid for each meal and no one ate until we could all sit down together. It was then that we'd talk everything over, the problems as well as the good things that had happened. After dinner *papá* would lean back in his chair, tipping it against the wall, and sing songs that were popular when he and *mamá* were sweethearts. How I loved those songs! *Papá* had a fine voice, too.

My parents always shared their household problems. Every payday *papá* turned over his whole salary to *mamá*, but he was extremely fussy about how the money was spent. *Mamá* never did anything without talking it over with him first. It was very difficult for her to save money for a Father's Day gift without his finding out because they never had any secrets from each other.

Almost every Saturday my parents would leave us at home and go out to dance in a nightclub with their friends. They'd always bring home some goodies for us—fritters, ice cream, candies. Sometimes on Saturday *mamá* and *papá* would invite people to our house for a party. Those parties were fun, though we had to keep watch, because things got stolen. One Sunday morning after a party we found our three piggy banks out in the yard with the pigs' heads broken off and the money gone. We must have had about 20 *pesos* in each bank.

On Sundays *papá* would take us to the amusement park and put us on the merry-go-round. One day he bought us bathing suits and a beach ball and took us to the beach at Varadero. I really enjoyed it, but when we got home he said it was immoral and he'd never allow us to go there again. After that, we'd put on our bathing suits and splash around in our big bathtub, then go out in the yard soaking wet so people would think we'd been to the beach.

When it came to the holidays, *papá* went all out. Christmas was a big event in our house. As early as December 18 we'd start setting up the artificial tree and the Nativity scene, and hanging the decorations we'd bought at the ten-cent store. Here in Cuba, Christmas Day itself was a pagan holiday, not a sacred one, so practicing Christians held their celebrations on Christmas Eve. It was the custom for families to get together at the grandparents' house, but in our family we always celebrated Christmas Eve at our house, with my Aunt Victoria, my Uncle Joaquín, and their children, Simón and Margarita. When my mother's brother Daniel was a bachelor, he'd have dinner with us too. Looking back to the time we lived in Benito's house, *mamá* still sometimes says proudly, "At midnight that Christmas Eve there were twenty-four people around the table."

Christmas Day itself had some religious significance for us, of course, because it was the birthday of Our Lord, but it was more an occasion for outings, parties, and dances in the Silvestre nightclub. New Year's Eve was another day for parties and dancing. At midnight the bells would begin to ring and everybody would eat grapes, apples, and pears. Couples would go into the streets with hats and noisemakers, and there would be a big hullabaloo.

My parents made birthdays happy occasions too. It's the same to this day. The night before my birthday I'd have all kinds of exciting dreams, and then, the next morning, what a beautiful day it would be! I'd get a present, everybody would congratulate me, and my sister and brothers would kiss me. When things were going well for *papá* we'd have a party for all our friends and classmates. There would be a cake, candies, soft drinks, paper hats, and all kinds of favors. When we were not so well off, there would always be at least a new dress or a pair of shoes. My *mamá* would begin saving two or three months earlier so she could buy us something new.

We children had our big day on January 6, the Day of the Three Kings. No matter how bad things were, *papá* dug up the money somehow—I know he didn't steal it—and we'd get lots of gifts. The night before, on the 5th, we'd be so excited we could hardly sleep. We had to go to bed early, but first *mamá* would write our letter to the Kings for us, giving us more or less an idea of what they were going to bring. We'd put the letter in a shoe, and outside our house we always left some water and grass for the Kings' camels. The next day we'd find the gifts the Three Kings had brought us on behalf of our relatives.

Papá was doing so well in Marianao, he wanted to open another poultry market. *Mamá* was against it and kept saying *papá* was going to ruin himself by trying to do too much. She was angry because he'd never stay home from work, not even when there was a bad storm. Once he was on his way home from the market in a hurricane when a falling roof-tank cover almost killed him, and all *mamá* said was, "That's what you get for going to work."

Sure enough, *mamá* was right about *papá* going to ruin. In those days poultry dealers always cheated a little on the weight to make more money per pound. *Papá* was as bad as the rest and got into a lot of trouble when an inspector caught him short-weighting an order by 1 ounce. At that time *papá* was involved in politics, and when he received a closure order he went to his political friends for help. A man named Eladio, who was a political organizer in Marianao and the secretary to a local *político*, had used *papá* to go around with a loudspeaker asking people to vote for Prío,[1] but when *papá* needed him, Eladio didn't lift a finger to help.

Papá owed money to the dealers who sold poultry wholesale, and as he himself put it, he was in debt to "eleven thousand virgins." The business began to flounder and his dream of opening a second market was shattered. Eventually he lost everything. He had to give up his market and look for a job. Times were hard for us then. *Papá* couldn't pay the rent so we were dispossessed. That happened more than once. There was no end to the degradation we suffered. We were never actually thrown out on the street with our furniture, but only because we moved just in time.

We moved to Los Pozitos, a bad neighborhood where knifings were common, and I was always afraid. Our tiny house rented for only 27 *pesos*. It had a porch but we couldn't use it because the neighborhood was so dangerous. Whenever both *mamá* and *papá* went out, they'd lock us in.

I remember so much death from those days. In Los Pozitos people were poor and ignorant. Just about everybody there believed in witchcraft. They fought all the time and parents didn't care what happened to their children. One of our neighbors was a little orphan boy who lived with relatives. I became very fond of him. One day he was walking barefoot in a ditch filled with dirty water and he stepped on glass and cut two tendons. He was supposed to be given an injection at the hospital the next day but that stupid family of his didn't care! They didn't take him until the following week, and he died of tetanus.

There were a lot of blacks in that area and I had colored girl friends.

1. Dr. Carlos Prío Socorrás, who was elected President in 1948. (See Mónica, n. 8.)

Mamá did too. They were like members of the family and would come to our house for dinner, but my parents showed their prejudice when they talked about them. They'd refer to a certain *solar*[2] as "the one with those brawling Negroes in it." Or they'd say, "Only a black would kick up such a row." Marriage with a black was definitely out. In one breath my parents would say, "Me, I get along fine with Negroes," and the next minute they'd be saying, "I saw a so-and-so of a black with a white woman. . . ."

That prejudice was inculcated in me. There have been times when I've been attracted to a Negro, but I'd say to myself, "I could never marry him, not for anything in the world. It would be humiliating." Not so long ago I danced with a black fellow and that made me wonder whether I could possibly change. At home that night I said, "I had a wonderful time. I even danced with a Negro." You should have seen the look that came over *mamá*'s face. It was awful. Racism is a social blight.

I started public school in Los Pozitos and they made me repeat the second grade because we moved in the middle of the year. Going to a public school was a whole new experience for me. I was used to a private school with a better class of students. Public school was very noisy, and those tough black girls were real fighters. I was timid and from the time I entered that school I had to give away my lunch. If I didn't they'd say, "Just wait till we meet you outside," which meant they were going to knock me down and give me a bloody nose. My parents could afford to give me only enough to buy a cracker and some guava for lunch, and it was hard to give that up every day.

One day I rebelled. When the biggest, toughest girl asked for my lunch, I refused. "Be ready," she said. I stayed inside the building after school. My brother Diego was with me, but he was young and couldn't help much. The girl waited for me, followed me all the way home, and complained about me to my *mamá,* who turned and slapped me. I've always held that against her. Years later I told her, "You really got me in the guts that day, *mamá.*"

At public school each room was crowded with a lot of pupils, and all of them had lice. When a girl got lice, somehow everybody knew and would tease her. I'll never forget the day it happened to me. I went out to recess and they began shouting "Lousy!" at me. I went back inside and cried. The teacher ran her hand through my hair and said, "No, my dear, you don't have lice." But she was just being nice. I did have lice and I brought them home to *papá* and *mamá.* We had to go to a doctor to get rid of them.

I was a good student, always at the head of my class. My teachers told

2. A *solar* is a low-rent multiple-family structure, usually one story high, with one or more rows of single rooms or small apartments opening onto a central patio.

me I should study English in night school, so I went with a neighbor, and I was the youngest in the class. The teacher took a liking to me—he said I reminded him of his daughter—and he'd pick me up and carry me around. I liked him, too, until one day he began to feel my behind. I was afraid of him after that and dropped the English course.

We kids were growing up and wanted to have a little money of our own, but *papá* had none to give us. I made a few cents helping a man sell confetti at carnivals, and I helped a seamstress next door take off buttons from clothes she was redesigning. For that I'd usually get a *medio*,[3] enough to go to the movies.

Some of our sadness in those days was the result of *mamá*'s lack of initiative, especially when it came to serving food. Instead of looking for new ways to serve the same old food, she fed us nothing but soup for a whole year. I've hated soup, any kind of soup, ever since. But one thing I have to give *mamá* credit for is the way she took care of our clothes. We didn't have fancy clothes, but we always had smocks that *mamá* made from remnants she picked up for 25 *centavos*. And no matter how badly off we were, our school uniforms were always spotless and we never left our house with torn shoes.

In Los Pozitos *papá* tried hard to start over again. He used our living room as a poultry market and we lived in the back rooms. He bought chickens wholesale, cut them up on our kitchen table, and sold them to customers who came in on the sly. But he could never make a go of it.

As I look back now, I can see that *papá*'s sense of personal failure began with losing his market. He was incapable of facing up to trouble. Rather than admitting he was unable to support his family, he looked for a way out, an escape, and started the drinking that took away everything we had. I'll never forget the day *mamá* and we children came home from the park to find *papá* lying drunk in the hall outside our door because he'd lost his key. I'm still not over the terrible shame I felt seeing him there. It was the worst experience in my life.

Much as he made me suffer, I feel very sorry for *papá* now. People who drink almost always do it because of their sense of impotence. *Mamá* couldn't accept that; she saw it the other way around and blamed all his business problems on his drinking, which only made him feel worse. She had a blind spot about that.

I guess I get my drive for self-improvement from *papá*. That's why I can understand why he tried so hard to succeed in business. We're so alike, we even watched the same television programs! If *mamá* hadn't built a barrier between him and me, I think we would have been good friends. Because of her I always considered my father a coward and a failure. I was too young to realize how tragic he was.

3. Five *centavos*.

SEÑOR MOISÉS RIVERA:

Lots of people said I didn't prosper because I was a drunk. But when a man is going to fail in business he fails, drunk or sober. I've seen so many drunks and woman-chasers who got ahead. There was no bigger drunkard in all of Cuba than Rogelio Lorca, yet he became a millionaire.

The truth is, my poultry business failed because I had a set-to with a policeman. He came in and tried to carry off a chicken, just like that, without paying. I said if he wanted the chicken he had to pay for it. So he took the cage outside and then I was fined for not keeping the cage inside the premises. After that, the cops would drop in every five minutes to fine me for something, like not having a chamber pot in the shop. Seeing that the police persecuted me, people were scared to buy from me. I had to give up the market because it became impossible for me to make a living there.

There I was, out of a job and broke. Digna didn't complain. She was always contented with what we had, little or much. She was a good wife that way. But I felt frustrated and angry and I began to drink. I'd lose my temper and want to take it out on Digna. Many times I controlled myself and held back the blows. I used to hang out at a gambling joint and sleep in the poolroom, because I was boiling inside and knew I'd get rough with my wife if I saw her.

Finally I became an alcoholic. I'd wake up in the morning and drink whatever was handy. After the first drink I had to keep on. That was the worst time, when I was the most broke and couldn't get my head above water.

My *papá* liked drink and women, just as I do. He had one woman after another until one day the old lady got mad and hit him. She really wanted to kill him; he had to jump over a fence to get away.

Papá got violent when he was drunk. He quarreled with *mamá*, smashed pictures, furniture, his barbershop equipment. But I was always very attached to him. Sometimes he'd take me on the ferry, and when the whistle blew I'd be so scared I'd wrap my arms around him. I must have been about eight years old then. I'd go wherever *papá* went. When he got home, drunk, there I'd be right beside him.

I was my father's first child by his second wife. I was born in 1920; my sisters and brother, Teresa, Luisa, and Gabriel, came later. My *mamá* had been married before too, and had four children—Rolando, Modesto, Juan Carlos, and Tina—by her first husband. My *papá* also had four children by his first marriage, but they didn't live with us.

We were very poor and lived in an apartment behind *papá*'s barbershop. Actually it was only one room, but it was so large that *papá* put up a dividing wall and we lived in back while he worked in front. *Papá* made hammocks out of sacks and strung them between the window and a pole, so we didn't have to sleep on the floor.

We all hustled to earn our food and never had to ask anybody for anything. My brother Rolando stole milk off the doorsteps of rich houses, not just once or twice but lots of times. We boys sold newspapers and candy and homemade molasses taffy. I also sold lottery tickets and collected tin cans that I sold to gardeners. I always liked being free and active, with a *peso* or two in my pocket.

I and my brothers had very little schooling, and what we had we fought for. I learned to read at home with the help of my father and my half-brothers, but when I started school they put me into first grade because I couldn't write. I sold newspapers every morning with my brothers Rolando, Modesto, and Juan Carlos, and went to school in the afternoon. I enjoyed school very much but didn't spend much time there. As soon as a boy began to show a bit of growth, a bit of strength, they put him to work. My father took me out of school when I was in the third grade so I could help him.

Things were very bad in the thirties, Machado's time,[4] and people were going hungry. The political situation got worse day by day. A lot of students came to *papá*'s shop to get their hair cut and somebody would call the police station and say they were plotting a revolt or a bombing. It was all a lie, they weren't doing any such thing, but the police would come and arrest *papá* and everybody else in the shop. When they raided the place, all they found was *papá* peacefully cutting somebody's hair. That was around the time that two men were killed by a bomb near our house. I remember seeing an arm with a gold rosette on the sleeve hanging from an electric wire. Just the arm! In those days people killed as easily as they drank water.

Business was bad and days went by without a soul stepping into my *papá*'s barbershop. He had a bunch of kids to feed so he decided to take to the street. He'd stand on a corner shouting, "Barber, barber," as though he were selling mangoes. He'd take whatever he could get for a haircut—a *real*, a *peseta*.[5] I carried his barber's satchel for him and he made me yell "Barber, barber" too. There were days when he took in 40 *centavos*, other days, 30. Sometimes he'd give a haircut in exchange for a chicken. Once he barbered a whole family and brought home forty eggs. The thing was to bring something back home. We'd cover hundreds of blocks, then walk all the way home to save carfare.

When I was ten, I was walking along the street with *papá* one day when a grocer approached him and said, "If you let me, I'll train that

4. See Mónica, nn. 5, 17.
5. A *real* is 10 *centavos;* a *peseta,* 20 *centavos.*

kid in the grocery business and help him grow up to be a man." *Papá*
agreed, so the grocer took me on as an apprentice with wages of 60
centavos a week.

My job was to go out, get orders, and deliver them. To get orders
you had to go around on a bicycle blowing a bugle because there
weren't many telephones. I'd go to all the rich people's houses and
take down their orders in my scrawl, one letter at a time, then I'd go
get the things they asked for. I talked easily and was wide-awake so I
did very well, but I wasn't learning the grocery business. My boss was
Spanish and he looked down on Cubans. Well, I was one little Cuban
who didn't enjoy being treated like a dog.

A Chinese lived in the grocery store down the street, and one day he
stopped me and said, "Look, Moisitos, your boss is exploiting you,"
and he hired me for 7 *pesos* a month. Seven *pesos* a month! I felt like a
rich man, but I did the same work for him and I still wasn't learning
how to be a shopkeeper. I've always had a good head though, and I
sure learned a lot of tricks on that job. When I made a delivery I'd do
other chores for the customers, like clean up the garden, wash their
cars, or scrub the vestibule. That way I would make 20 or 30 extra
centavos. When I got back I'd tell El Chino that the bicycle got a flat.
He'd answer, "Say, you get a flat every Monday!"

When I was thirteen I went to work for another Spaniard, César,
who owned a saloon. I slept in a little clerk's room in the back and
was paid 45 *pesos* a month. I was now not just rich—I was a millionaire!
The saloon opened at 5:00 in the morning to pick up business from
people on their way to work. Often the owner would tell me, "Even if
so-and-so doesn't come in for a drink, you mark him down anyway."
And on Saturday, when the customer came in to pay up, he'd protest,
"I didn't have anything on Wednesday." But there it was written down
and he'd have to pay. The saloon closed at 10:00 or 11:00 at night and
by that time I'd be dead tired. The next morning, at 5:00, I'd be up
and at work again.

I was the only one in our family who earned a steady wage, and
though I worked my head off I never saw the money. My brothers had
their ups and downs; Juan Carlos was a delivery boy in those days,
Modesto worked for a flower vendor, Rolando sold newspapers. At
home they'd say to me, "Ask for a *peso* advance, Moisitos, won't you?
Ask for 2, 3." At the end of the month I couldn't even buy myself a
pair of shoes. I was earning 45 *pesos* and my family had already taken
55 or 60 on my wages. The boss would say, "Hey, Moisés, hold up. The
wagon is ahead of the oxen."

Once a month I got an afternoon and night off. We started being
men when we were still children, so on my one night off I went to the
Academia dance hall, where mothers would take their daughters to
dance. Those girls gave the impression of being respectable, but I

found out that the *mamás* were really procuresses. If you wanted to dance, 2 *centavos* went to your partner and 3 *centavos* to the house. Some of the girls did business on the side but that cost 5 *pesos*. What could I do with my 1 *peso*?

My *papá* cut the hair of a Spaniard name Lorca who had six coal wagons, two poultry markets, and a long list of good customers. Lorca got the idea I was stealing his customers for a friend of mine who had a poultry market. I *was* stealing his customers but not for free, of course. I'd say, "Listen, lady, there's a good poultry market on such-and-such a street. If I can't deliver your order myself, I'll send somebody from there."

Lorca checked up and found out how I worked, and as he liked to steal good clerks away from other stores, he hired me for one of his poultry markets. He offered me 100 *pesos* a month.

I felt I owned the world! Three days after I began, I was plucking, cleaning, and dressing chickens, turkeys, ducks, and geese. Like the saloons, poultry markets opened very early, at 3:00 or 4:00 in the morning. You broke your balls on that job from early morning till 10:00 at night. There were no refrigerators or machinery then, either. Left-over poultry had to be packed in layers of ice and paper to keep till the following day.

To be a clerk in a poultry market you also had to be a thief. You started by making love to the servants or cooks in the rich homes, so that it wouldn't matter if the poultry wasn't fresh or tender.

One day I was singing in the poultry market when Ruperto Montés, the head of the Montés Quintet, happened to be there. "*Chico*," he said, "with that voice, you shouldn't be pedaling a bicycle for a living!" He took me to audition at station CMCW and I was a success. After that, I sang regularly on the radio, but instead of paying me with hard cash, they gave me some *Aguila de Oro* cigars, a tie, and a small jar of brilliantine. Now I'm a man who's always liked money, so I said to them, "No sir, I can make 100 *pesos* working in a poultry market. Why should I sing and stay up till all hours for nothing? Thank you, but I'll go back to selling chickens." After that I sang now and then at dances, not professionally but just to amuse myself.

I was a grown man, eighteen years old, and getting fed up with my family because they took every *centavo* I earned. My brother Gabriel wanted to better himself—he was the youngest and the favorite—and when he told me he wanted to go to business school, I encouraged him. Rolando felt the same—between the two of us, we paid for Gabriel's education. And then, when he graduated and started going up in the world, he wouldn't even look at us. How's that for thanks!

Finally I decided to stop trying to provide for my relatives and make my own way in life. Someday I'd have a wife and children and I didn't want them to go without shoes or beg for food the way I did. And they'd give me all the love I didn't get at home. My own future family was what I had to start thinking of.

I met my wife at a dance. We fell in love, and when I wanted to ask for her hand it was hard to know who to address, as she had no mother or father. Her Aunt Constancia disapproved of me because I spent most of my time singing and dancing.

I went to *papá* and told him I wanted to marry Digna Herrera Ferrán. She was the first woman I had really been in love with. I told *papá* where Digna lived and he said, "I know that girl. Don't go thinking you can treat her like all the others. She's a fine girl." He went to talk to her aunt and we got engaged. Finally, on January 19, 1942, we were married. I was very young, barely beginning to be a man, and I was very much in love. We had a fine wedding, with liquor to spare. The fiesta lasted until midnight, but there was no honeymoon as I had to be at work at 4:00 A.M., just like any other day.

From the first I wanted to better myself and have the best of everything in my home—a radio, a car—the very best! It was natural to want a nice place to live in; people practically drove one to be that way. Anyway, I was willing to work for it. Meanwhile, I had what was most important to me, a family and a home of my own.

GRACIA:

I don't recall *mamá* working on a regular job, because *papá* didn't want her to. *Mamá* was satisfied with the little *papá* was able to give her because she had come from a very poor family and always had to work terribly hard. From way back, *mamá*'s family had to struggle just to stay alive. My Great-aunt Matilde told me quite a lot about my mother's side of the family.

Matilde was my Grandmother Gracia's sister. There were eight children and they lived with their mother and father in one room of an apartment they shared with two other families. Matilde's father, who was my great-grandfather, used to drive a horse-drawn carriage and was paid very little. My great-grandmother took in washing; she did all her work at night so she could take care of her children during the day. They were so poor the children didn't have shoes and wore cloth slippers instead. Their clothes were hand-me-downs from the well-to-do families their mother worked for. She ripped up old clothes to make things and unraveled piles of old stockings to knit sweaters from the yarn. She'd sell the sweaters to buy food for her children.

Those were very hard times, when Cubans were awfully hungry. The Americans first came here then and Matilde remembers the tins of American food they handed out when Estrada Palma[6] was in power.

6. Tomás Estrada Palma was elected first President of the Republic of Cuba, without opposition, on December 31, 1901. He was re-elected without opposition in 1905, and he resigned from office September 28, 1906, under pressure from the Liberals.

That was the only food the poor could get, and it was worse out in the country, where people were dying of hunger. They'd come to Havana from all over looking for something to eat. They were skinny and diseased and crawling with vermin—lots of them died.

"*Ay*, my child, life was bitter in the old days," Matilde told me. "Even to bear a child was difficult." When her mother was about to go into labor, she was too poor to call in a midwife. She simply spread newspapers on her bed and placed clean clothes for herself and the baby nearby. Then she set a washtub filled with water underneath the bed. When the baby was born, she wrapped the afterbirth in newspaper and someone buried it out in the yard. The next day she was up and about again.

Matilde said it was hard to be born in those times, and it was hard to die, too. They didn't even have enough money to bury their dead. My great-aunt remembers a little Negro girl who died and there was no money to bury her, so my great-grandmother wrapped her in a sheet and laid her out on the floor. Then a big black car—"the Owl" they called it—came and took her away. When Matilde's mother died, "the Owl" came and got her too.

Matilde told me that my Grandmother Gracia was pretty and could read and write. She had some sort of lung trouble, asthma I think. The man she married, Diego Herrera, came from a very rich family in Matanzas, but he'd been cheated out of his inheritance by his half-brother, and at the time of the marriage he was working as a helper on a beer truck in Havana. Grandmother Gracia bore three children: my mother, Digna, my Aunt Victoria, and my Uncle Daniel. During the great hurricane of 1926 my grandmother had an attack of asthma, and in that terrible storm my grandfather went riding around on his horse looking for medicine. While he was crossing the flooded Almendares River, the horse slipped and my grandfather fell and drowned. His raincoat was found later, hanging from a branch.

One day not long afterward my grandmother found 20 *pesos* in the doorway of her house, and the excitement brought on another attack. She died, with her three little children at her bedside. The orphans were distributed among their relatives: Aunt Victoria went to live with her Aunt Matilde, *mamá* with her Aunt Clara, and Uncle Daniel took turns staying with each of them.

Of the three, my *mamá* lived the best. Her Aunt Clara was a widow who supported her six children by taking in washing. She was sorry for *mamá* and was too busy to be strict, so *mamá* had a rather free childhood, playing ball with the boys and being a tomboy.

Clara allowed *mamá* to go to school through the sixth grade, which was more of an education than her own children had. They could read and write, but that's all. Her son Omar, who was never quite right in the head, went around with a pushcart selling brooms and feather dusters;

Héctor and the other children peddled vegetables and candy from house to house. The important thing was for each of them to bring something, anything, into the house. Hard as they all tried, they often went hungry. Things were especially bad in 1933, after the Machado administration ended. *Mamá* remembers going out at night with her cousins Pedro and Raúl, each with a tin can, to knock on the doors of rich homes and beg for food. Finally, Clara decided that *mamá* would be better off at her Aunt Matilde's house.

Mamá was much happier at Clara's than at Matilde's; no one who lived with Matilde liked her. She was domineering and methodical, just the opposite of Clara. Everything in her house had to be just so. You had to leave some food on your plate because it was considered bad manners to eat everything. Imagine teaching that to a young girl who didn't know where her next mouthful was coming from!

Matilde only cared for her widowed daughter, Eusebia, and worked to support her, yet Eusebia refused to lift a finger to help in the house. But my *mamá* and Aunt Victoria had to work as domestic servants, and Uncle Daniel worked as a delivery boy. *Mamá* worked long hours for only 3 *pesos* a month and wanted desperately to run away. But being *mamá,* she didn't.

Mamá was fifteen when she began keeping company with my *papá.* Whenever he came to see her, one of Eusebia's daughters had to sit with them in the living room. One day my *papá* tried to get the girl to leave so he could be alone with *mamá,* and there was a fight. Matilde went after *mamá* with a knife and cut one of her fingers. Thinking she'd be better off with *papá, mamá* agreed to marry him. He was earning a living and she wouldn't have to work anymore. But I think there was more to it than that; I think *mamá* really loved *papá* then.

Chapter Two

Mamá and *Papá*

GRACIA:

My *mamá* hated people who drank and I became just like her. We looked upon my father as some kind of monster. He lay in bed and drank while *mamá* tried to keep things going. He'd drink beer when he could afford it, but most of the time he drank *anís,* the cheapest liquor around. If I wouldn't go buy it for him he'd beat me. When he ran out of money, my brother and I had to go and borrow some. He made life impossible for us.

Papá was difficult even before he took to drinking heavily. He was always self-indulgent. He wanted *mamá* to do everything for him, and she did. I can't honestly say she seemed unhappy about it as long as he was sober and had a job. He used to come home at noon for lunch and sleep for an hour. His siestas were sacred, so no one made a sound. We couldn't clear the table or wash the dishes; not even a fly dared to buzz! When *papá* woke up ahead of time, poor *mamá!* She bore the brunt of his anger. He'd leave the house in a rage, and come home at night still angry.

He had a lot of peculiarities. He would eat only cold food. At home we cooked once for the whole day. If we were to have rice, black beans, and meat, we prepared it in the morning to eat for dinner and supper. The only food prepared in the afternoon was the salad, or banana fritters when we had them. At supper the food went straight from the cold pot to the plates. That's the way *papá* wanted it; the rest of us had to force it down, like it or not.

Papá wanted the house spic and span all the time but he wasn't one to help out, not even when he was out of work, never. *Mamá* had a temporary job in a dressmaking shop once, and we kids did what we could at home. After school I prepared dinner, standing on a bench to reach the stove; I also did the washing, the ironing, and looked after my brothers and sister. *Papá* didn't lift a finger except once, when we children went to my Aunt Victoria's, leaving a huge pile of clothes for me to iron later. When we returned home, there was *papá* ironing! It looked so funny! He was trying to press starched clothes without dampening them. "*Pipo*, how can you iron dry clothes?" I said.

"Oh, this is the old-fashioned way to do it. My *mamá* taught me."

I've never forgotten that. But usually *papá* was careless and dirty; he knew nothing about hygiene. He accused me of being finicky because I didn't like to use another person's towel. My family couldn't afford more than two towels, one for my parents and one for us kids. Once I was going to take a bath right after *papá* had bathed and his towel was soaking wet. I asked *mami*, "Change the towel for me. This one is soaked." We had company that day and my father put on a terrific act in front of them, scolding me for wanting a towel all to myself. "Where do you get such elegant ideas?" he asked. Then he slapped my face. He was so ignorant!

Papá was the one who messed up the house. He smoked continually and never once did I see him drop the ashes anywhere but on the floor. Nor did he ever wipe his shoes before coming in out of the rain. One day, Aura had just finished scrubbing the floor and asked him in the most polite way, "*Pipo*, please wait until the floor is dry."

"Nobody gives me orders!" *papá* roared, and he went out to the yard, deliberately muddied his shoes, walked back into the house, and scraped the mud off onto the floor.

He had this explosive nature, and when he was drunk we were all very scared of him. The slightest thing would make him fly into a drunken rage and beat us until we screamed "Enough!" My brother Diego got the worst of it. He was only a child, but *papá* insisted on taking him to work as his helper. They made the worst possible team, always at each other's throats. Diego was young and wanted to play with the other children, but *papá* would beat him if he caught him idle. Then he claimed that when Diego worked in the poultry market, nobody bought anything. He blamed his business failure on him. He said Diego was unlucky. Later, when *papá* worked as a salesman for a food wholesaler, he'd take Diego along with him on his motorcycle and they'd go from store to store showing their samples and taking orders. *Papá* worked on a commission basis, and if a day went by without a single order, he'd accuse my poor brother of bringing him bad luck and would beat him. I felt like beating *papá* myself when I saw the way he treated my brother. When one of the blacks in the *solar* teased Diego, *papá* said, "You must fight him," and my brother did. I've never been able to bear seeing people fight, and I yelled, "*Papá*, stop them! Separate them!"

"No, Diego has to learn to be *macho*. That kid is turning out to be a sissy."

SEÑOR RIVERA:

I never, never took one single *peso* from my children to pay for my drinks. Their needs came first, my beer second. When we were badly off, I didn't touch liquor. I'd say to myself, "I won't drink anymore," and I could go for six months, one year, two years, without taking a drop. Then something would start me off again.

But now, more than ever, I realize how my drinking affected my children. I remember when I was a child my *papá* came home drunk and *mamá* would say, "Drunk again! So that's what you went out for." Right away *papá* would burst into a string of curses, "I shit on God, I shit on the Virgin. . . ." And grabbing a chair or whatever happened to be nearest, *bam!* he'd smash it. He would tear off its legs or throw it at a mirror while we children huddled together in fear.

I never made a scene or smashed furniture, no matter how drunk I was, and no policeman ever had to pick me up off the sidewalk. No, when I was drunk I went peacefully to sleep, or else I'd cry and say silly things—at least so they tell me. I was never violent. I never hit my children when I was drunk. If I was hard on them it was because I was a strict father. My son Diego used to complain that I was always hitting him over the head. Now he says he's grateful for the way I brought him up.

Gracia agrees, though she'd have preferred me to treat her more gently. She says it's better to bring up children with love than with blows. That's where she's wrong. That wouldn't have worked. When my children found themselves alone, fatherless one might say— because what kind of father was I, drunk in a ditch half the time?— what would have happened to them if they hadn't had a strict upbring- ing? As it is, none of my children has ever stepped out of line. Take a look at their cousins or the kids they grew up with. What are they now? They could have been like my children. But are they? No. And why not? They were given too much freedom, that's why.

When I was a kid, boys got whipped for any little thing. One time my father ran after me with a machete, and I wasn't the only boy that happened to. It was my ambition to become a soccer player, but as a kid I had to play with a ball made of rags or a crumpled-up wad of paper. And after a game I'd get licked with a switch—a special leather strap with five tails—because running made the soles of my shoes come off.

I felt that nothing was too much for my kids, because when *I* was young, when did we celebrate the Day of the Three Kings? When did we have toys? My godfather once gave me a bicycle to ride, but it was only for one afternoon. What memories of childhood can a boy have when he never owned a bicycle or a ball? So I worked hard to give my children a bicycle on Three Kings Day. It was a rare thing at that time.

My children should remember what else I did besides taking the stick to them. I gave them plenty of food and clothes to wear. When I was having a good time, driving around in my car, I paid a woman 10 *pesos* to take them out riding somewhere, too. Once I even put on a show in a cabaret at the beach to amuse my kids. Bad times, sure. But what about the good times? They should remember those too.

GRACIA:

Mamá was afraid of *papá,* but that didn't stop her from fighting. She didn't have enough sense to be quiet and she flared up at the least provocation. That's the way *mamá* is, even if it makes matters worse. Diego and Aura got out of the house when *mamá* and *papá* had arguments, but I'd stay to try to stop them. If *papá* saw me tugging at *mamá's* skirt, he'd turn his fury on me. Once he broke a fishing rod over my head.

We children were defenseless against *papá's* rages and grew closer to *mamá.* She couldn't help us much when *papá* beat us, though we could tell from the look in her eyes she was on our side. Even Aura, *papá's* pet, began to ally herself with *mamá.* When he got drunk and wanted my sister to rub his forehead with ice and bring him black coffee, she'd refuse and go out to play. Then I ended up doing it for him—I was too scared to refuse.

Papá was not affectionate himself, but he expected us to run and kiss him the minute he came home from work. If we forgot, he'd get upset and say, "These kids don't love me anymore." When he was drinking we hardly ever felt like kissing him. *Mamá* made me greet him anyway. *Papá* knew we rejected him and I guess he must have felt very lonely at that time. He needed some kind of refuge, an ally, and he found one when my youngest brother, Gabriel Moisés, was born. That was in 1952, the year of Batista's coup. *Mamá* was happy then. She thought a lot of Batista, I'll never know why. I remember her watching him on television as he arrived at the Palace, saying, "There's a man. He's the one!"

Papá stopped drinking when *mamá* got pregnant. We had some peace at home for a while so she went ahead and had the baby. Sometimes when she was pregnant she'd have an abortion, not that she told me in so many words, but I remember times when she was ill and I put two and two together.

I was ten years old and just beginning to feel self-conscious about sex when *mamá* became pregnant with Gabriel. Her big belly embarrassed me terribly. She'd take me with her to see the doctor and everybody seemed to stare at us.

For some reason I began to worry that the baby might not be born normal, and just to be on the safe side, I made a vow to dress in white for three weeks. I didn't keep the vow and felt guilty about that, but thank heaven the baby was born perfectly normal. Though my family was not religious in other ways, they were great ones for vows. *Mamá* often made vows to the Virgin Mary so *papá* would stop drinking. She still dresses in white on the 24th of every month, though I'm not sure why, now that she and *papá* are separated.

Mamá's pregnancies were not difficult. She went to the maternity hospital, and when the baby was born we children were sent to my Great-aunt Matilde's, where we spent three unhappy days. We were so glad when *papá* came in a car to take us to the hospital to get *mamá* and our new little brother. What a fuss we made over that kid! I began to feel like his *mamá,* proud because he was chubby and blond. But later on I was pretty annoyed when I had to wash the diapers and do all the housework.

The birth of my younger brother made a big change in our lives. I was going on eleven, Diego was nine, and Aurora was seven, so there was quite an age gap between us and the baby. They didn't share my feelings for Gabi, especially Aura, who wasn't fond of him at all because he took her place as *papá's* pet. One day Aura sucked the baby's bottle and *papá* gave her a terrible licking. I can still see poor little Aura huddled in a corner, crying her eyes out. That was the first of many similar scenes.

I remember when I finished the fifth grade and came home loaded with diplomas and medals. It had been my best year in school and all the teachers were talking about the good marks I got. All *papá* did was take a sideways glance at my report card, and then said, "Go take care of your brother." Throwing my diplomas on the bed, I picked up the baby. As I stood there holding him, I suddenly felt *papá's* heavy hand coming down on me from behind because he thought I had thrown my things down in anger.

Papá's obvious preference for Gabi caused more of a division in the family. Then *papá* began drinking again and accusing *mamá* of having an affair with a neighbor. I'm sure *mamá* was innocent, but *papá,* who was a woman-chaser himself, was a bitterly jealous man, and one day he went to strike *mamá,* screaming, "You're a degenerate and a whore!" Aura, Diego, and I jumped on him, beating at him and tearing his shirt, while *mamá* defended herself with a chair. A week went by without them speaking to each other. *Mamá* would set the table and serve our meals but refused to sit down to eat with us. That shook us; our meals were a ritual and we felt family unity giving way.

Mamá said and did many little things to set us against *papá.* My father could be as generous as he was brutal, though his most lavish gifts often followed on the heels of his worst drunken rages. Being children, we liked to get gifts, but *mamá* always took care to let us know that they were just to make up for his drunkenness. She'd tell us that *papá* didn't care about us, but that was a lie. He loved us but just couldn't show it in a way children could understand. He claimed he worked only for us and he backed up his words with deeds. Now that I look back, I can see we meant a lot to him.

It must have hurt *papá* to know that *mamá* was always harping on his defects. I sometimes wonder whether his cruelty and his intolerance of normal childhood behavior weren't simply a desperate attempt to assert his authority. He *was* the final authority in our family, but right up to the day they separated, *mamá* was continually undermining him.

SEÑOR RIVERA:

My children despise me. I blame Digna for that. She kept running me down because she hated my drinking, and she turned them against me. She had always been domineering but she turned completely against me when I began to drink. If I said, "I'm going to run over to the corner for a beer," she'd say, "Oh, all right, go ahead, but I bet you get drunk." Now that's no way for a woman to talk to her husband, especially in front of the children.

I remember once I was yelling at Digna when Gracia said to me, "*Pipo*, I'm fed up with you," and she would have hit me if my sister Tina hadn't been there and grabbed her. Those are things a man can't forget. I thought, "Time solves everything. They'll be sorry," but a man gets tired of waiting for someone to give him a little love.

I'm a man who needs affection, lots of it. But from the very beginning, Digna never showed me any. Oh, she had an itch, she still has, but demonstratively affectionate she was not. She was always brusque, very brusque. I'm dry and tongue-tied but she's worse. If I touched her bottom while she was in the kitchen, she'd snap at me, "Quit it! Don't annoy me!" The lovelessness between us came from that. That's why I began to have affairs with other women.

After three or four years of marriage, I had women all over the place, like a free man. Digna didn't know a thing about it until I left her and went to live with Candita. Not that I loved Candita, but I said to myself, "Well, let's see if this one will love me. One thing's for sure, my wife doesn't." A young man's error, that's all it amounted to. I always kept after Digna though, and never stopped giving her things and seeing my children. Then we made up and got together again.

I had no reason to doubt that Digna was faithful to me, but I'm a jealous man and I loved my wife so much I often saw phantoms, and among the phantoms I saw something true—that she was very nice and kind to everyone but me. That's what happened when my brother Rolando stayed with us, and then again with Ismael, who lived next door. She paid them more attention than she paid me.

I got suspicious of Ismael because he was the kind who didn't respect even his own wife. I may have had twenty mistresses, but no woman slept in my house except my wife and my daughters. But Ismael brought another woman into the house when his wife was away working in the country. Not only that, he kept talking and boasting about all the women he had. He did us some favors, yes, but he was fresh. I complained to my wife and she said, "You disgust me." That was the last straw. I knew then that she didn't love me.

I never got any affection, not from my *mamá*, my *papá*, or my brothers. My brother Gabriel was always my mother's favorite. He's the one who got all the breaks, and all the affection too.

GRACIA:

I've always thought that *papá*'s terrible inferiority complex was made worse by his brother Gabriel's success. Uncle Gabriel was the only one in *papá*'s family who made any effort to get ahead. Before the Revolution, he studied and got himself a wonderful job with Westinghouse, then kept on taking courses at school. His wife also had a job and worked very hard. Out of the whole family those two were the only ones with a stable place in society, but they earned whatever they had, so I say more power to them!

Gabriel broke his family ties completely; the only time he set foot in our house was when my grandmother died. I often heard *papá* and my Uncle Rolando remark that even though they had worked to help Gabriel complete his education, he would have nothing to do with them.

One way Gabriel and *papá* were alike was that they were the only two in their family to marry legally. But Gabriel went *papá* one better and got married in a church, which in those days was a luxury very few people could afford. *Papá* was the only one in his family who went to the wedding, and it was too bad he did because Gabriel behaved badly toward him. I've heard *papá* tell of it often, always making nasty remarks about Gabriel and his "society" wife. Actually she's the daughter of a newspaperman but she's well educated, so perhaps that did put her in a slightly higher social status.

Nobody in *papá*'s family got along. On Mother's Day they'd all gather at my grandmother's house. How I hated those family get-togethers; they were always so quarrelsome! I think it may have been my grandmother's fault—she had to be the center of attention. If by chance Uncle Gabriel and his "society" wife happened to show up, my grandmother would get very nervous and try to shut *papá* up. That would create such a scene we'd have to leave in a hurry. My grandmother openly despised *papá*. She called him "a drunk" and I remember her saying to my mother, "I can't see why you put up with so much from Moisés. I'd have kicked him out long ago."

When *papá* was down and out, not one of his brothers lifted a finger to help him, and they were all well able to do so. Juan Carlos, my father's eldest half-brother, owned a tobacco business and was the wealthiest. He gave *papá* a job for a while but they had a falling-out. Anyway, *papá* repaid Juan Carlos by taking in his two sons when Juan Carlos abandoned them and their mother.

His two sons, Ceferino and Juan Marcos, worked for *papá* in the poultry market and lived with us for a long time. I remember Ceferino—his nickname is Cefe—especially, because it was with him that I first experienced sex. He was about seventeen at the time; I was no more than four. We happened to be alone in the house while *mamá* was at the shop, and Cefe took off all my clothes and pulled me into the bathroom. He sat on the toilet bowl and I remember feeling him push his organ into me from behind. Then I was naked and he put me on the bed and it's possible he did things to me that I don't remember. It's all very dim. Anyway, after that I hated Cefe and was terrified of him. *Papá* fought with everybody sooner or later and relatives were no exception, so Cefe and his brother finally quit their jobs and left our house.

I told *mamá* about it much later, after I was grown up, and she said, "If your father ever finds out, he'll beat Cefe to death."

Of all his brothers and sisters, *papá* got along best with Rolando, the poorest in the family. He was an adventurer, a real rolling stone, who worked as a circus roustabout and got us into the circus for free. A lion bit off his left hand so he quit the circus and started working at the racetrack.

At one time Rolando had an infectious kidney disease and came to stay with us. People always spoke well of *papá* for that, but there was some trouble at home because *papá* got very jealous. He thought *mamá* was in love with his brother, but I'm sure she was just taking good care of him so he'd recover.

I myself later had an unpleasant experience with my Uncle Rolando. When we were living in Los Pinos, he and his wife Julia lived just across the street from us. Julia was a very dark Negro and I was terribly fond of her. I used to clean her house and sometimes I spent the night with her while my uncle was traveling with the circus. If Rolando came home unexpectedly and found me sleeping there he'd climb into bed with Julia and me. That was all right until one night he began pulling my pants down. I was only eleven then, but if he behaved like that with me, God only knows what he may have tried with my *mamá*.

My Uncle Modesto, another of *papá*'s half-brothers, had a little refreshment stand in front of the cemetery, which was a good business location, but to look at the way he lived you wouldn't think he had a *peseta*. He was practically illiterate and always poorly dressed. He lived with his wife and three children in one room of a *solar* with no bathroom or anything. Modesto sent his children to a school for the extremely poor.

Most of Modesto's money went for women; he supported his wife and two mistresses at the same time. He used to ask my sister and me to write letters to his women for him. Yolanda was the one he was with for the longest time, and his wife knew all about her. He'd sleep with his wife some nights and with Yolanda others. My family thought she was a fool to put up with it, and I guess she was because Modesto doesn't even go to visit her anymore.

My father's sister Teresa married an engraver and she worked too. They had plenty of money, a lovely home, a good social position, and they gave their children a fine education. But Teresa had a nervous breakdown when her last child was born and for the past fifteen years she hasn't stirred from the house or seen anyone. She continually washes her hands in her own private bathroom that nobody else may use. It's a pity; she's really neurotic.

Luisa, *papá's* youngest sister, claims to have been a dancer, but actually she's always been a woman of the streets. Very refined, to be sure, but a prostitute nevertheless. She was a numbers runner on the side, though she's so ignorant she couldn't even write the figures properly. But she really made it big financially and had the most luxurious home of anyone I knew. She and her first husband began to take trips to Miami—to buy a car, she'd say. Before long they had several cars, and one day we found out they were stealing cars there and selling them here. They were almost millionaires! It was then that, according to *papá,* my grandmother suddenly became awfully fond of her daughter. During that time Luisa dressed very elegantly and her two children were well looked after. How I used to envy them! One time Luisa gave my sister and me two smocks each, the prettiest ones I'd ever seen. That was one of the few gifts I ever got from my father's side of the family.

The only one who didn't have money was *papá's* half-sister Cristina— Tina, we call her. She was a slave in the homes of her relatives, when they'd have her. They'd keep her by turns and throw her out whenever they wanted to. They made fun of her, partly because she's such a dope and partly because she had a limp and a speech impediment from a childhood attack of polio. My Uncle Modesto was the only one who ever helped her.

Everyone in *papá's* family went their separate ways. Some got rich and some got poorer, and the differences in their lives only increased the jealousy they felt toward each other. As for *papá,* he had cut himself off completely from them and it made him feel all the more isolated.

Mamá's relationship with her family was quite different. She and her sister Victoria and her brother Daniel were always very close. I think the loneliness they suffered when they were separated as children accounts for the strong bond between them.

Mamá grew up with her Aunt Clara's children and they too were like sisters and brothers. *Papá* hated them because they took her side against him. He'd say the most offensive things about them, that this one was living with a whore and that one was a fallen woman. The one *papá* disliked most was Raúl, Aunt Clara's son by her married lover. For a while I cleaned house for Raúl on Saturdays, until *papá* forbade me to visit there anymore because he found out that Raúl walked around the house in his undershorts. What a fuss *papá* made! In our house appearances were strictly observed. We children never saw our parents or even each other in underclothes.

The only ones in *mamá*'s family whom *papá* got along with were Victoria and Daniel. Before Daniel got married he'd spend every Sunday with us. My *papá* was a big newspaper reader, and on that day we bought all the papers and saved them for Uncle Daniel, who'd read the comics to us. He worked in a drugstore and would give us free samples or let us have medicines at a reduced rate. He's my godfather, and on my birthday or the Day of the Three Kings the best presents always came from him. He was wonderful to us.

The relationship with my Uncle Daniel was broken when he married and went to the United States. I felt the loss keenly; I missed his visits and his gifts—he doesn't even answer my letters—so I might as well have no godfather at all.

My Aunt Victoria has been our closest relative over the years. After her husband committed suicide, she earned her living by doing laundry. Although she was poor she helped us most when we needed it. On the Day of the Three Kings, which we always celebrated at her house, she'd have gifts for all of us. My parents were godparents to Victoria's children and were good to them too. *Papá* made a point of taking my cousins along with us to carnivals and inviting them to spend weekends with us so they'd feel like part of our family. He was on top financially then.

Chapter Three

Starting Over

GRACIA:

Whenever *papá* got a new job he moved to a new house. It gave him a feeling of starting life over. I think he actually enjoyed moving. So long as he was going up in the world it wasn't so bad, but when he was going down, every move was another step down in the social scale.

In 1955, when I was twelve, the Spaniards *papá* had once worked for said they'd help him set up another market—in Marianao. *Papá* had always wanted to return to Marianao, where his first business had flourished, so we moved once again.

Mamá was excited. She loved Marianao, and her sister Victoria lived there. But *papá*'s moves were always taking me away from my friends, making me miss school. To this day I cannot bear moving from one house to another. It messes up my whole life. I don't make friends quickly and it's painful to have to end relationships just after they get started. Also, when you move to a new house it takes at least three days before you can put things in order, and I hate that kind of mess. Whenever I visit friends who've spent eight or ten years in the same house, I wish my life had been like that.

I'll never forget the day we moved back to Marianao. I cried and cried. I had to go to the store for old newspapers to wrap things in, and I went back and forth with the tears running down my face. I was the most careful so I got the job of wrapping the cups and plates and packing them in *mamá*'s big zinc tubs. We tied up the bedclothes in sheets, *papá* took apart the beds, the wardrobes, and the dish closet he had made of codfish cases, and then we looked for a mover's truck. Marianao was a long way off and the move cost 13 *pesos*.

Papá was actually an alcoholic then, but he had a lot of willpower if he wanted to use it. When he opened his new market he said, "I'm through," and he didn't touch a drop for a whole year, not even beer. We began to come up in the world again. *Papá* started to take an interest in our home and bought things for it on credit: a living-room set, a kerosene stove, and for the first time an electric refrigerator.

We'd always had a radio and an electric iron but no other appliances. We were too poor, and besides, my mother and father didn't seem to want them.

Television had come in a few years earlier and *papá* liked it so much he'd take us to watch it at the local bars. It became very easy to buy one after a while, 10 *pesos* down and 10 *pesos* a month, and we got our own, though we were never able to meet the payments. But *papá* had a plan: he'd pay 10 *pesos* down and the first month's installment, then he'd keep the set for a few more months without paying until finally they'd take it away. As soon as *papá* managed to get another 10 *pesos* together, he'd make another down payment and the whole thing would start over again. We must have had about twenty television sets before we were finally able to pay for one.

The best thing about the house in Marianao was that for the first time in my life I had a room to myself. I was overwhelmed.

Papá even bought a car, something we'd never had before, and then a second car. He set up a coop in the yard and raised his own chickens, then he went all out and bought an electric chicken plucker.

Papá's business flourished for about a year, and again he got the idea of opening a second market. But he opened it in a bad neighborhood and it didn't bring in enough money to cover his expenses. Pretty soon he owed his suppliers, and when he saw he wasn't going to be able to pay, he began to drink again. That finished everything. He spent every cent on liquor and before long he was out of work, hopelessly behind on all his payments, including rent, until we had to sell all those lovely things and leave the house I loved so much.

For nine months *papá* was out of work. He had a lot of friends in Batista's police force, and one of them told *papá* he had a job for him. How sad *papá* looked the day he came home after talking to that captain. It seems he had offered *papá* a job as an informer, and for only 33 *pesos* a month! My *papá* told the man he would never do that kind of work—he even got into a fistfight over it!—so that's something to his credit.

SEÑOR RIVERA:

After I lost my second market, there I was, out of a job and broke! One day I remembered a former customer of mine, Captain Alberto Flores, who used to buy at my market. I always gave him the best in the shop and he acted as if we were great friends. I thought he might help me find a job, so I went to see him. It cost me a lot of trouble to get in, and when I did, he said to me, "If it's a job you want, Moisés, I can get you one. You could be a plainclothesman and wouldn't have to wear a uniform." He wanted me to be an informer. Some friend!

A few days later they were going to put my furniture out in the street because I couldn't afford to keep up the payments. That was around 1956 or 1957, when it got harder by the day to go out and earn a *peso*. I couldn't find a job in my own trade or out of it. I would have taken practically anything; I've never been afraid of hard work. So I went to see Captain Alberto again. I thought he could make the furniture people hold off two or three days until I had a chance to resolve that problem. When he saw me he said, "What do you want now, Moisitos?"

"Look, Captain, tomorrow they're going to throw my furniture out in the street."

"Say, didn't you tell me you were a chauffeur?"

"Sure," I answered.

"Would you like to drive a bus?" That was at the time of the April 9 strike.[7] I caught on at once and answered, "Oh, no, no, no, I already have a job. I'm just waiting till they notify me when I can start. Besides, I've never driven a bus." He was asking me to go in as a strike breaker, and I wanted no part of that.

GRACIA:

What really broke my heart about moving so often was the haphazard way I went to school. With every move, I found myself a little behind the new class. I, who loved to study!

Papá was strange. He wanted me to get an education—you could see that—and in his way he seemed to be proud of my good grades. But at the same time there was something about my love of school that bothered him, perhaps because he hadn't been able to go to school, or maybe I reminded him of his brother Gabriel. One of the worst things he'd do was punish me by keeping me home from school, making me miss examinations and other things. Once, when I was in the sixth grade, he took me out of school for a whole week. "You're through with school!" he said. I lived in misery until he let me go back.

When we moved to Marianao, I was so far behind in my studies the school didn't want to let me enroll. What a fight we put up! *Mamá* promised to help me, and they finally agreed to consider me if I got a note from my former teacher saying I was a good student and able to do the work.

I'll never forget that year. At 1:00 o'clock in the morning I'd still be copying topics and studying, with *mamá* helping. *Mamá*, dear *mamá!* I couldn't have made it through sixth grade without her. She was good to us children that way, genuinely interested in our school work, insisting we do our homework before going out to play, even helping us review our lessons. But *papá* was drinking heavily again and we were in serious financial trouble.

To graduate, I had to take exams in a regional school as well as in my own. I exhausted myself studying. Our diet was so poor then, I wasn't getting enough energy. *Mamá* would buy cans of juice and give them to

7. See Mónica, n. 16.

me behind *papá*'s back. I can still taste them, they were so good. My grades that year averaged only 80 or 90, the worst I'd ever had, but at least I was able to graduate. Because of all the time I lost going from one school to another, I was thirteen when I finished sixth grade. Otherwise I would have finished three years before.

I lived for the day of the graduation ceremony, which was to be held at the Rex Theater in Marianao. Of my two great ambitions, to be an actress or to be a teacher, the first was partially fulfilled when I was chosen to recite a Spanish poem in the graduation program. How I loved those rehearsals, the thrill of being backstage as one of the performers, practicing our entrance to the music of the "Graduates' March"! It was very much like being in the theater. It was also a good way to make friends, because I met a lot of students graduating from other schools. Everybody there felt so united!

Another reason for my excitement was my first real crush on a boy. He was graduating from the eighth grade and lived only two blocks from us. All the girls were crazy about him—he was very good-looking—so I had no reason to hope he would notice me. I was such a skinny kid, in spite of all the vitamins *mamá* fed me. But I had such dreams about that boy! Not that he ever gave me any encouragement or even said a word to me. But he'd *have* to notice me reciting my poem on the stage, and in my dream I imagined him applauding me, along with the audience.

My graduation dress caused quite a problem for my family. I finally got one only because my Godfather Daniel gave me the cloth as a gift. He was very generous that way. His wife bought me a pair of shoes, my Aunt Victoria bought me my first pair of long stockings, and *mamá* gave me a permanent.

Graduation was a fabulous occasion, but for me there were disappointments. The only one in my family who attended was *mamá*. *Papá* didn't like to go to anything like that, and my brothers and sisters were too little. Then, after reciting my poem, I looked around for the boy I idolized and couldn't find him.

The next year and a half I didn't go to school at all and during that time I looked upon myself as a failure. I had hoped to go to secondary school and on to normal school to become a teacher, but we couldn't afford the required books and uniforms. We couldn't even afford to pay the 40 *pesos'* rent for our home.

Despite this, I was determined not to become a servant. There had to be something better in life for me, so for only 3 *pesos* a month I took a course in shorthand and typing. I did it just to keep alive my dream of studying. For eighteen months I earned the money by doing housecleaning for some of my relatives. Then I applied to business school, figuring I could become a secretary and maybe get a decent job. It was probably because of Uncle Gabriel that *papá* consented to my entering the business school. It was the very place *papá* had sent his brother to, and now he wanted me to have the same advantages. In his own perverse way he really wanted to see me get ahead. I entered business school six months before my fifteenth birthday.

That birthday was a sad one. I'd been especially looking forward to it because it's an important year in a girl's life, but my grandmother had died a few weeks earlier and we were in mourning. It so happened that my *mamá,* after saving for weeks, had bought my first grown-up dress, a lovely, elegant one. But because I was in mourning, she wouldn't let me try it on. Even on my birthday she made me wear a black skirt and white blouse to school. Naturally I didn't have a party.

I remember saying to *mamá,* "I'm not going to wear mourning anymore. Not that I've forgotten my grandmother already, but after two months I just don't feel the sadness of her death." From then on I began doing things more my own way, though I've never been able to flaunt tradition by not wearing mourning when someone dies. I wish I could.

I was the only one in my family who fought to get an education and who had ambition to live on a higher social level. Diego hated school and quit in the sixth grade. Aura quit too, while I struggled on in spite of our financial difficulties. My younger brother Gabi studied, but he was helped by the Revolution.

I was fond of little Gabi because he was a baby and couldn't get in my way socially, but I was ashamed of Diego and Aura in those years and didn't want to be seen with them. I remember having terrific quarrels with Diego. He'd accuse me of being the family pet and take sly digs at me, purely out of envy. I guess compared to the things he suffered I seemed to get special treatment. Once he was so angry he flung the electric iron at my head—I ducked and it missed.

Papá made me take *mamá* and my sister to parties, but oh how I hated to. Poor Aura! I remember one party I took her to—I was fifteen, she thirteen—and I didn't introduce her to a soul but left her sitting beside *mamá* while I danced and enjoyed myself. I treated her as if she didn't exist. And do you know, my sister's so good she never said a word about it! She'd rather explode than complain.

I hate to admit this, but my alienation from Diego and Aura lasted until about five years ago, and we're still not as close as people think. The adolescent shame I felt for them was like an illness. Even now I have just the slightest trace of it. I can't seem to help it. I've always been too concerned with what people thought of me.

The truth is I rejected my entire family, especially my father. I hated him even more when he told me, "Look, Gracia, you can't continue business school." I was heartbroken. There was very little chance of my ever starting again. When I explained my situation to the director, she said, "No, we can't let you leave. You have a splendid record. We'll give you a scholarship." And they let me earn my way by working as an assistant to one of the teachers.

Papá finally found work in a gambling casino. Being a poultry dealer was bad enough, but now he was an ordinary employee—and in a gambling room! When people asked me what *papá* did for a living I still told them he was a poultry dealer.

At school there were other girls like me, working on scholarships as teachers' assistants, but I made no friends among them. I associated with girls on a higher social level, children of army officers and government officials. They were the ones who became my friends, but I felt very inferior to them because they were well-to-do and lived in beautiful houses. I began to cut myself off from my family as much as I could; I was living in two different worlds.

Strangely, all my friends have been very domineering. At school I became quite friendly with a girl named Mariana, whose father was a well-to-do doctor. Her parents would invite me to their house and to their farm in Matanzas, and her *papá* took us out in his sailboat in Miramar. Her mother was a country woman from a much lower social level, and her husband wasn't at all nice to her, though he was very nice to me.

Mariana was allowed a lot of freedom, and she led me around by the nose. I'm easily influenced, but one thing she could never get me to do was go to the movies without first asking my parents. I was too scared of my papá. As for parties, I still wasn't allowed to go unless *mamá* went with me, and I couldn't bear that.

The boys were all after Mariana and that made me more aware that I hadn't yet had even one boyfriend. Being poor was a special drawback, and there were too many other things against me. I was just beginning to be aware of myself as a woman. I'd never heard about girls menstruating, at least not from *mamá,* because anything that had to do with sex was taboo in our house. All I knew I learned in the street. But then one day there I was—a señorita. It frightened me. I called *mamá* and said, "Look what's happening to me, *mami!*"

She said, "Here, wear this cloth. From now on you're a woman, and you must be careful, especially when you go out with a boy. I'm going to pass on some advice my grandmother gave me: 'Keep your eyes and ears open and your legs closed!' " That was *mamá's* way of explaining the facts of life!

I wasn't very attractive. I weighed only 90 pounds and one of the boys nicknamed me "Popeye," after Popeye's skinny wife. I wanted to die every time he shouted that at me in the bus! *Papá,* too, had ideas about my condition, and for my sixteenth birthday he gave me a brassiere with foam-rubber cups. "Wear this," he said, "so you'll look as if you had something there."

To improve my chances, I took a course in beauty care and grooming and the proper way to stand and walk. But that proved humiliating too. One day the teacher said, "Stand up, Gracia, and let's see if your belly sticks out." So there I stood in my old worn dress, for all to see. I'll never forget it.

Oh, the things I had to wear to school! I had four or five dresses and a couple of pairs of shoes, almost all hand-me-downs. *Mamá* did what she could with the dresses, but I was never satisfied. I couldn't afford to take them to a real dressmaker, so clothes were another of my complexes. I felt particularly self-conscious when I was in charge of the class at school. I looked so bad the teacher would give me clothes now and then; in fact, she gave me my first garter belt, and did that feel good!

Papá was fussy and old-fashioned about the way we girls dressed. For example, he didn't allow us to wear slacks or to cut our hair. *Mamá* once took me for a permanent wave and *papá* raised the roof. The permanent left my hair kinky and he infuriated me by calling me *negrita*. He really put his foot down about keeping my sister's hair long, because hers was blond and lovely.

With all my handicaps I was convinced I'd never get married. When I met a boy, I felt so unattractive I'd blush and put him off. *Papá* was very difficult too. He laid down a rule that I must bring my boyfriends home to meet my parents, but he'd be furious if I went out walking with them.

I got my romance from cheap novels, particularly the ones written by a woman named Corín Tellado.[8] I could never read enough of them. I identified with the heroines, and my ideal was a man much older than I, someone who would cherish me and treat me like a little girl, teaching me the ways of life and love and passion. In school they were always trying to improve our taste in reading but they didn't succeed with me. I even did my book reports on romantic novels, because as a teacher's assistant I knew nobody read the reports. After the Revolution books like that were said to be too gushy, but that was why I liked them.

When I was almost sixteen I fell in love with Emilio Aguero Flores, a student at the school. He was nineteen, and the moment I saw him I said to myself, "What a handsome boy!" I began to daydream about him instead of my imaginary heroes, and when I was the substitute teacher, I'd look for some pretext to talk to him about his work. People thought I was easily infatuated, but really it was just that my ego needed bolstering. I always had an awful inferiority complex.

I never got as far as a love affair with Emilio, although it was obvious he liked me a lot. There were dances at school on Saturdays and he'd

---

8. A popular writer of approximately 500 short sentimental romances published weekly in inexpensive pocket-book form, with titles such as *You Are a Sinner, Seeds of Hatred,* and *Your Betrayal and My Destiny.* Published in Spain, these novels were widely read throughout the Spanish-speaking world.

seek me out to dance with him, but we danced in a small hallway instead of the main ballroom. He said he didn't like crowds. But he acted as if he were trying to hide or run away from something.

Emilio used to go to the gambling casino where *papá* worked, and *papá*, knowing I was in love, would tell me whenever he came in. *Papá* also noticed Emilio's sudden appearances and disappearances and said to *mamá*, "That's a very strange boy." I should have suspected it had something to do with the Revolution, but we never discussed politics. My mind was on more romantic things.

A lot of policemen would hang around the casino, and I saw some terrible things happen. Little by little I began to hate Batista because of what his police did, and I began to love the Revolution, although I knew very little about it. At school we didn't discuss such things, probably because so many students had parents who worked for the government. My brother, on the other hand, was studying at night school and he was very enthusiastic about the Revolution and wrote Twenty-sixth of July slogans in his books. One night a policeman came to our house and advised *papá* to take Diego out of school before he got into serious trouble.

The only time anything revolutionary happened at school was the day Batista held his mock elections.[9] Emilio came by at noon. He was wearing a suit and I said, "Where are you going, all dressed up?"

"Just around," he answered. It was the last I ever saw of him.

That night some people in the gambling casino said to *papá*, "Say, did you hear? They killed that boy, Emilio!" They said Batista's police killed him while he was drinking with some friends. They say Calviño[10] himself was the one who shot him.

When I learned what had happened I was numb. On Fridays I always watched the wrestling matches on TV until after midnight. I found myself automatically doing the same thing that night. Then, slowly it dawned on me that Emilio was gone. He had loved me, he told his friends I was the woman he wanted, and now he was gone. I started to scream until people came running in from outside. My grief was terrible.

Not long afterward, I learned from Emilio's friends that he'd been involved in sabotage. I understood, then, why Emilio had always seemed to be hiding and why he'd told others instead of me that he loved me. His friends said he was afraid because *papá* had the reputation of being an

9. On November 3, 1958, Batista held a presidential election so fraudulent that ballots had been marked and distributed in advance. The great majority of the electorate stayed away from the "polls."

10. Ramón Calviño was a gunman for Batista and was said to have assassinated at least twenty revolutionaries. He fled Cuba in 1959 but was captured when he took part in the Bay of Pigs invasion. He was one of three prisoners, all Batista henchmen, whom Castro refused to ransom to the United States. All three were shot. (Thomas, *Cuba: The Pursuit of Freedom*, pp. 1360, 1371.)

informer and there were always so many policemen hanging around the gambling casino.

After Emilio's death I thought about becoming a nun, but I gave it up because my parents detested the idea. We were very hard up at that time—*papá* earned only 80 *pesos* a month and we were costing him more and more money. Again he began to come home drunk and quarrelsome. That New Year's Eve *papá* made a scene and refused to eat, so for the first time there was no celebration in our house at midnight. We were all in bed by 10:00 o'clock.

The next day, January 1, 1959, I was plucking a chicken when I heard *mamá* say, "Did you hear? The man left! Batista took off with his people!"

I was so happy! At last the time of terror was coming to an end. There were lots of revolutionaries in my neighborhood and soon they came out dressed in red and black. I put on my red skirt and black blouse and went out to watch. "How do you like that!" people were saying, "Batista is gone, finally!" Emilio's family were wild with excitement and came to my house. It was a wonderful day, except for *papá*. They closed the gambling room that afternoon, so he was out of a job. As you might expect, he got drunk.

I saw Fidel in person on January 8, the day he entered Havana. He was going to pass by 41st Avenue, so I went to tell my cousins, who were ardent revolutionaries. We got there early and stood watching the tanks and the *barbudos* go by. We screamed and yelled at them and asked for rosaries, souvenirs, and autographs.

At about 6:00 o'clock, along came a tank with Fidel and Camilo Cienfuegos[11] sitting on top of it. Fidel was wearing glasses and reading a newspaper. It thrilled me to see him; that man was something wonderful! I'd taken down every one of his radio speeches—that's how I used to practice my shorthand. For three hours I'd sit, writing furiously, yet if my life depended on it I couldn't tell you now what he said. I didn't think deeply about things then.

I adored Camilo Cienfuegos too, although I knew very little about him. But he had such an open, friendly disposition I was actually half in love with him. He was always at Fidel's side; anybody could see they were good friends. When Camilo's plane disappeared later that year, I suffered.

It was a strange time in my life. In many ways I was enthusiastic about the Revolution. The boy I loved had died for the Revolution, and I hated Batista for killing him. Also I loved my country, and the Revolution brought hope for a better way of life for all Cubans. And it seemed to me then that the Revolution had the same goal as Christianity.

11. See Mónica, n. 27.

Those first six months of 1959 were the saddest in my entire life; the Revolution was overshadowed by the breaking up of my parents' marriage. My father was out of work at a very critical stage of his life and he seemed to go to pieces before our eyes. The end for my family began on January 16. I remember the date because I got up early, about 4:00 A.M., to study for an examination. At 5:00 *mamá* made *papá*'s coffee, and that's when he started to quarrel. I was at the table and he was still in bed. He said—and I'll never forget his words as long as I live—"You and your mother are exactly alike. I don't know which I hate the most."

Then he locked the door, saying, "You're not going to school." He had the house key and refused to let any of us out, even to get food. He was like a crazy man, insulting and tormenting us. *Mamá* came right back at him, and the things they said to each other were horrible. *Papá* accused her of not being a virgin when he married her. I didn't believe him for a minute. My *mamá* had an absolutely flawless character.

For six days *papá* kept us prisoner in our house. We ran out of food and had nothing to cook; all we could do was watch television. The Sosa Blanco[12] trial was being shown and we followed it closely, day and night, for three days. So many hideous things came to light. A real thunderstorm! Sosa Blanco denied he had killed all those people in Minas, but then the peasants began arriving to name names and accuse him to his face. The man was a hateful tyrant and I thought it very dramatic and wonderful that Fidel had brought all the bad people to justice.

On the other hand, I pitied Sosa Blanco because I learned that his family were Protestants, so he must have been a religious man. If there's any good thing about a person, no matter how bad he may be, I sympathize with him. I read in the papers how Sosa Blanco's daughter came to see him the day before he died and I wished they hadn't shot him. Killing is against my religion.

My *papá* was watching the trial too, and one day at about 3:00 o'clock in the morning he suddenly said, "Look what they're doing to him! That one's a tyrant, just like me. They ought to put me up there! Watch, watch! You'll see my own tyranny on trial. You're going to witness what happens to a man like me!" His identification with Sosa Blanco impressed me deeply. I don't know whether there really was any comparison, but I realized that if I could feel sympathy for Sosa Blanco, a perfect stranger, I could feel a little sorry for my *papá*. And I did, for a while.

One day *mamá* got out of the house and went to Aunt Victoria's, but she came back in a few hours because she was worried about us. The next morning Victoria's daughter, my cousin Margarita, came to see us, but *papá* hurled insults at her too. "Your father was a drunk and a

12. Major Jesús Sosa Blanco, an officer in Batista's army accused of crimes against the people of Oriente Province. He was tried in the first public war trial in Havana and was executed in January, 1959.

degenerate!" he shouted. Poor Margarita, who adored her father, began to cry. Before long we were all crying with her.

I was afraid of being expelled from school and losing my job. I escaped from the house by jumping over the backyard wall, and I phoned the school to tell them I was going to continue attending. "*Ay*, Miss, you must help me! My *papá* has locked me in and won't let me go to school." The woman I spoke to said, "Don't worry about your classes, but you'll have to do your job here."

Much as I hated to, I returned to the house. *Papá* was getting worse, continually drunk and becoming more incoherent. Finally *mamá* could stand it no longer. "Look," she said to us kids, "I've put up with this for you, but now I'm going to leave your father. If you ask me to stay with him I'll do it, but you can see how things are."

We told her, "Don't worry, *mamá*. If you leave, we leave too."

She told my *papá* to leave the house, but he answered, "Not me. You're the ones who have to go."

On March 1, just as Cuba was beginning a whole new life, we moved again, this time not to be near *papá* but to get away from him. I was sixteen, Diego fifteen, Aurora nearly fourteen, and Gabi five.

Poor little Gabi hadn't the slightest idea what was going on. He hadn't actually lived through most of the drunkenness and quarrels, and besides, *papá* kept Gabi for himself, took him places, spoiled him in all sorts of ways, and even threatened to keep the boy when we left. But small as Gabi was, he refused to stay. *Papá* wouldn't allow us to take anything with us. We had no money, no hope. I felt lost. Not that *papá* had ever given me any real security or support, but something that I'd had was gone.

The truth is, when my parents separated the whole world came to an end for me. *Mamá* felt it even more. She said that although *papá*'s goings-on were hard to bear, she loved him in spite of everything, and I believe her. She still feels the same way. Not long ago I overheard her talking to Aura, who was having some trouble with her husband. *Mamá* said, "I know how painful this separation from Felipe must be, child. I left your father after seventeen years of marriage, yet no matter how much he made me suffer, I couldn't forget that he was my first sweetheart, and I still love him."

SEÑOR RIVERA:

Digna hadn't the remotest idea how much I loved her. If I'd been a violent man, the kind who doesn't care whether he lives or dies, I'd have killed her when we separated. After all, it's easy to kill. All you need is a knife in your hand or the strength in your fingers to choke someone. But I always stopped to think, "If I kill her, they'll take me to jail. Do I want to be a prisoner, suffering all my life?" Also, if I'd killed

Digna I'd have had to kill the four children too, for none of them ever cared for me.

After the separation, I was in the hospital with bleeding hemorrhoids and no one came to see me. I had an operation and the anesthesia gave me a kind of desperate sensation, as if my life were ebbing away. I was sure I was going to die without a soul to comfort me. Every time I remember that, it cuts me to the very soul. If there's one virtue I've had all my life it's being humane, but I can't say that for my family.

Even after I got out of the hospital I felt so abandoned I almost drank myself to death. Once when Gabi was spending the day with me I drank and drank and drank until he couldn't stand it and went away. I don't know what got into me then, but I went to the drugstore and told them I needed a bottle of lye to clean the toilet. I went home and drank every last drop. I was very sick then and some of my vomit fell on a coat of *papá*'s I was wearing and burned a hole in it. That's how lethal the lye was! It ate away the enamel of my teeth—they all had to be pulled out later. I was at death's door but no one cared enough to visit me.

I had a neighbor who came by once when I was sick. He wanted to phone my family. "*Chico,*" he said, "send for one of your daughters. They'll mix some medicine for you. Let me call them."

When he called, the only reply he got was, "Oh, he claims he's sick, but he's only drunk."

That's a hurt I'll carry to my grave.

Chapter Four

Surviving

GRACIA:

After *mamá* left *papá,* our first problem was survival. We needed a home and food, and I wanted to finish school if I possibly could. I had only one more year to go.

Mamá sent my brother Diego and me to stay with my Aunt Victoria, while she, Aurora, and Gabi went to my Uncle Raúl's house. Knowing how *papá* felt about Raúl, that must have been humiliating for him. Still, it was a natural thing for *mamá* to do because Raúl was like a big brother to her.

My Aunt Victoria lived in one little room and I was so miserable I lost 12 pounds and cried myself to sleep every night. Not that my aunt wasn't kind to us, but we knew we were in the way and didn't have a *centavo* to give her. She was spending a fortune to send her son Simón to a good private school in Vedado. To ease her burden a little, on Saturdays and Sundays I'd stay at the home of one of my schoolmates.

I must say, people were awfully nice to me at that time. I tried to avoid my friends, but they and my teachers all comforted me. When I returned to school that first day after my parents' separation, I burst into tears and was sent to the principal's office to calm down. Everyone was afraid of her, but to me she was always understanding and helpful. I'll never forget how kind she was, stroking my hair, asking, "My child, why are you crying? Somebody's going to think we've half killed you." It was no use, I cried on and on.

After the separation I never tried to get in touch with *papá,* though I knew he was hungry and homeless and bumming around the streets. I was so ashamed of being his daughter I didn't want people to see me with him. My brother and I would sometimes come upon him dead drunk in the street, and sometimes he'd come to my aunt's house and stand out in front, yelling so everybody could hear, "Your mother is a low-down, good-for-nothing whore!"

One Sunday *papá* showed up at Raúl's roaring drunk. There was a terrible argument, with *papá* begging *mamá* to come back to him and *mamá* refusing. *Papá* got abusive, *mamá* and the children began to cry, and Aunt Clara was so upset she got sick. Finally *papá* left, but when Raúl returned and saw the state his mother was in, he was furious. He said to *mamá*, "Digna, if anything happens to *mamá*, I swear I'm going to kill Moisés!"

When I found out about it, I was so worried I couldn't keep my mind on my studies. I knew *papá* was desperate. I could never be sure what he'd do next. One day, at 4:00 in the afternoon, the prinicipal's office sent me a message: "Gracia, you're wanted on the phone." *Mamá* was at the police station, where *papá* had filed charges against her in an attempt to take us away from her. Fortunately he didn't succeed. But that day my legs trembled so I couldn't go to the police station, and it was Diego who had to go and straighten out the situation.

Mamá began looking for a place for us to live. Much as her relatives were willing to help her, she realized she had to begin looking out for herself. As the eldest child, I had to take on the greatest responsibility, a burden I didn't want but couldn't refuse.

To rent an apartment I needed money. At school all I earned was the cost of my tuition. I spoke to the director about my financial plight and said I'd have to leave school unless some better arrangement could be made. They immediately put me on a salary of 50 *pesos* a month, which more than covered the 24 *pesos* for my fourth-year tuition. The balance, 26 *pesos,* I received in cash. They also gave me a monthly allowance for textbooks and bus fare. We needed the money so badly, I often gave the bus money to *mamá* and, when nobody was looking, walked the forty blocks to school.

With the help of the nuns at the church I attended, *mamá* got a job as a housemaid for an American family, earning 25 *pesos* a month. My brother Diego got a job selling candy in a movie house. He got a commission on what he sold, but all he brought home after a day's work was 30 or 40 *centavos.* Poor boy, it broke my heart.

With all our earnings we had a total monthly income of about 65 *pesos.* At last we were able to live together. On March 1, 1959, we moved into the *solar* where *mamá* and I still live. There were twenty apartments there; ours had a tiny living-dining room, bedroom, bathroom, kitchen, and small patio. The rent was 25 *pesos* a month. It was unfurnished, and we had nothing to put in it. We slept on the floor, and when I saw my brothers and sister undergoing such hardships, I couldn't keep back the tears. The first night my Aunt Victoria showed up with her daughter they burst into tears too.

My Godfather Daniel later gave us an old mattress, and *papá* finally gave us the sofa-bed, the television set, a few kitchen utensils, and about five dinner plates. Then he sent us a bed frame for our one mattress. He had sold almost everything else and then drank away half the proceeds. He used the rest to buy us rings and other trinkets to win back our affections. He gave me the first wristwatch I ever owned and I still have the mantilla he bought me.

After he got a regular job, *papá* didn't give us money because relations between us were so strained. We remained stubbornly independent, hard up but never going hungry. We spent very little for food in those days. Lunch at school was no problem for me; *pasteles*[13] were 5 *centavos* apiece, and when I couldn't pay cash they gave me credit. Besides, the teacher for whom I worked often paid for my lunch and gave me occasional gifts of 5 *pesos*.

Once, in his campaign for peace, *papá* gave us some help with our food. He had a part-time job driving one of the trucks carrying food for the people who came in from the country to attend the Twenty-sixth of July rallies in the Plaza. *Papá* was given some of the leftovers and he brought us whole sacks of beans, cans of meat, tomato sauce, and coffee.

In spite of the separation, Gabi was closer to *papá* than ever and sometimes spent a few days with him. It was annoying because my brother would tell *papá* everything he saw or heard at home, and the first chance *papá* had, he'd repeat it to us. Then *mamá* would slap Gabriel. Occasionally *papá* bought Gabi clothes and gave him money, and even bought shoes for Aura and me. That was a real help to us, but nothing he could buy would have won us back.

For a long time *papá* showed up every single day, standing out in the street, weeping and drunk, yelling, and sometimes bursting into our apartment to fight. I'll never forget one night when he came to *mamá* and fell at her feet, clinging to her legs and weeping, "Let me stay here! Please let me stay here!" But she wouldn't relent; her hatred for him was simply terrible.

When he found himself rejected so completely, *papá* became violent. One day he went at *mamá* intending to hit her. I started to scream at the top of my lungs—bloodcurdling screams—and they did the trick. *Papá* got scared and left at once. But I'd lost control of myself and couldn't stop screaming. The noise attracted everybody in the barrio, and a soldier came and fired a shot at the house. It was a nightmare. After that incident, I was obsessed with the fear that any day I'd get a call from the police station, informing me that *papá* had killed *mamá*.

Señor Rivera:

My wife and the children might have come back if it hadn't been for Digna's relatives. Her family had never liked me and thought I was worthless, but underneath they envied me.

13. Small pastries, usually deep-fried.

I've never liked Aunt Clara or Raúl or Mario or any member of that family, not since the time Gracia spent a few days with them and I went there and found Raúl in his underpants with his *pito* out. I told Raúl it wasn't proper to go around like that when there was a señorita in the house. I always had disputes with those people. What I can't forgive them for was that they hid my own children from me when Digna went to live there. The kids got sick and I didn't know it. After I'd been such a good father to them! I'm sure her family put Digna up to it because she's never been mean at heart—strong-minded and strict, but never mean.

I went to the nuns, the ones who'd indoctrinated Gracia, and told them I wanted my wife and children back, but it seems Digna had told them I was a drunken good-for-nothing and they said, "You don't deserve your wife. She's too good for a degenerate like you."

Well, it's easy to call people names, but those nuns never had to feed any of my children. And what did they do to help? Why, right away they got Digna a job as a servant. As long as she was with me, my wife never worked. Once, when I was very hard up, she took a job as a maid, but at the end of the first morning she returned home, saying, "I can't be a servant to so many people. Who do they think they are anyway?" And she never again worked while she lived with me.

So thanks to those nuns, my wife was back to where she was when I met her, working as a maid. I knew then that I'd never get her and the children back.

After they found an apartment I was able to see more of Digna and the kids, but in time I began to catch on to the way I was despised there. I have plenty of sad memories about my children. They could see how I ran after them, and yet . . . they took it all wrong.

How can a son treat his father the way Diego treated me? He went to the police and told them I was disturbing the peace. He led them to me, and there I was, in Digna's apartment, peacefully lying back in an armchair! I hadn't even gotten into an argument with anybody, but Diego thought I'd come back to stay. He said to his mother, "If *pipo* comes to live here, I go."

I remember one day Gracia enraged me by saying, "*Pipo*, don't come here again. Every time you come it means trouble." I thought, "Damn it, even my children tell me to get out!"

Gracia:

We had to adjust to many changes in our way of life. *Mamá* was now the head of our family, although she always consulted with us about everything. Aurora was still going to school and kept house for us. With three of us working, we had to give up our family tradition of sitting down to dinner together. I came home after the others had already had their meal, but I remember with pleasure that *mamá* would warm my food and sit down to talk with me while I ate. That's when I'd tell her everything that had happened at work and school.

With all our efforts, we were still living from hand to mouth. I decided I'd have to make more money than the school could pay me, so I began to look for a real job. Not that I planned to leave school—I'd study at night or in the afternoon. I wrote to some government agencies, explaining my situation and asking for work, and also registered at the employment bureau at the school. I took examinations at Firestone and an import company and passed them both, but at that time it was still illegal to employ anybody under the age of eighteen, and I wasn't quite seventeen. As soon as they asked my age, it was all over for me.

Finally I learned that the director of the business school knew the director of the University Library. I wrote him explaining my situation, and he hired me in spite of my age. I began working in September, 1959, in the University Library, but when the director's secretary left, he offered me her job—on a probational basis, as they had no permanent jobs to offer at that time.

I had quit working at the school to take the library job, so for two months I had no income whatsoever. That meant we had only what *mamá* and Diego earned. On top of that, I had to take a bus from the office to the school at night. It was hard, but when I finally received my two-months' check from the library, it was a large one. That day we rushed right over to the pawnshop near my aunt's house and bought a dining-room set we'd fallen in love with. Then we bought a lot of other furniture on credit, paying so much a month—a bedroom set, a living-room set, a new television set, and a living-room lamp. We even bought dress materials on credit, enough to make dresses for my sister, my cousin, and me.

The same day I received my big check it was rumored that Camilo Cienfuegos had been found. Somehow I put the two together in my mind, and I felt that the Revolution was working for the good of mankind. It seemed to mark a new beginning.

Then Diego got a better job through *papá*, who had been hired as a garbage-truck driver. He got my brother a job at the garbage dump and the pay was 79 *pesos* a month, which was a lot more than he got selling candy.

My sister had refused to go on studying after she finished the sixth grade, but we insisted that she get some kind of training for a job. She was interested in being a hairdresser, so Diego and I paid for a 55-*peso* course for her, after which she began helping out at a nearby hairdressing shop. She wasn't paid a salary, but she earned about 2 or 3 *pesos* a day in tips. By doing our neighbors' hair on weekends she earned an additional 9 or 10 *pesos*.

My take-home pay was 79 *pesos* a month after deductions of 4 percent for Cuba's industrialization program[14] plus a small percentage for maternity and retirement benefits. That, combined with Diego's salary and Aurora's tips, gave us a combined income of about 170 *pesos* a month.

With my brother, my sister, and me working, we decided that *mamá* should quit her job and stay home to look after the house. We had more money than we had ever had, but our expenses were larger than our combined income, so one month *mamá* would pay the installment on the TV but not on the bedroom set, the following month she'd pay on the bedroom set but not on the TV, and so on.

That year we learned to stand on our own feet and we saw the material benefits of the Revolution beginning to take shape. At first *mamá* was not an ardent supporter of the Revolution, but we made a revolutionary out of her by pointing out the good it had done. Everything that Fidel had promised was like a wonderful dream coming true. I could see it with my own eyes.

The Urban Reform Law[15] meant so much to us personally because we had suffered from having to move so many times when *papá* couldn't pay the rent. Under the new law you couldn't be evicted if you didn't pay your rent on time, so when we were short of money *mamá* could fall behind on the rent. After some time they began deducting the rent from Diego's wages, but then our rent was cut in half, from 25 *pesos* to 12.50, which was a great relief.

I was all for the Agrarian Reform Law[16] too. I didn't know anything about the country, but equitable distribution to the people in the countryside sounded like a good idea. Another thing that made me enthusiastic about the Revolution was the way they opened up the schools so more people could get an education.

At the end of 1959 we were quite prosperous, because both Diego

14. The Four Percent Voluntary Contribution for Industrialization was enacted into law on March 18, 1960. This amount was withheld from the wages and salaries of workers who did not refuse, in writing, to participate. According to the Cuban Economic Research Project: "The contribution was considered a loan or an investment on the part of the worker," and at the end of each year he or she was to receive a "People's Saving Certificate." (*A Study on Cuba* (Coral Gables: University of Miami Press, 1965), pp. 688–89.) In reality, of course, the deduction was the same as a tax on earnings.

15. See Mónica, n. 31.

16. The first Agrarian Reform Law, adopted May 17, 1959, prohibited private farms larger than 400 hectares (approximately 988 acres). The expropriated lands were to be distributed among former tenant farmers and sharecroppers, but during 1961 and 1962 most of the land was organized into state farms. The second reform law, enacted in October, 1963, prohibited private farms larger than 67 hectares (about 5 *caballerías*, or 167 acres). The remaining privately owned farms were incorporated into the National Association of Small Farmers (*Asociación Nacional de Agricultores Pequeños,* or ANAP) under the National Institute of Agrarian Reform (*Instituto Nacional de Reforma Agraria,* or INRA). INRA has been responsible for all major agricultural and marketing functions since its establishment in 1959. (Carmelo Mesa-Lago, "Economic Policies and Growth," in Mesa-Lago, ed., *Revolutionary Change in Cuba,* pp. 282–83.)

and I got a Christmas bonus, my sister earned extra money at the hair-dresser's, and *papá* showed up loaded with gifts. But we had to spend money, too, because we always gave presents to my Aunt Victoria, my two cousins, and to each other. We also bought something for *papá* and for my brother's sweetheart. At the library the employees exchanged gifts, so that was an added expense.

After starting that year so pitifully, we had made a lot of progress. When I thought of it, my gratitude simply flowed out to both God and the Revolution. I'm a fanatic by nature; I didn't think about what the Revolution was—I just loved it. It had been good for me and my family, so I thought it was good for all Cubans. When someone complained that the Revolution had done them harm, I paid no attention. I'd point to those clean-cut boys in the new Army—so unlike the old one—and say, "Those young men fought for the Revolution, so how could they harm anybody?"

SEÑOR RIVERA:

If it hadn't been for the Revolution, I'd never have pieced my life together again. In January, 1959, I was out of a job because they'd closed all the gambling casinos. I was drinking heavily and living from day to day, scrounging food from my family and sleeping on park benches. Then a guy approached me one day.

"What are you doing, old boy?"

"Selling everything I own, piece by piece," I told him.

"You can drive, can't you?"

"Sure I can," I lied. All I knew was how to drive a car, but I've never been afraid of anything. Right away I got a job driving a garbage truck. I'd never in my life been in such a big truck, but I drove it and learned to operate the garbage hatch.

Being very competitive, I worked harder than any of the other drivers. If one of them was absent when I finished my shift at 5:00 A.M., I'd take over his truck. I was always ready to take another truck and work day and night, night and day. I even slept in the trucks. That way I doubled my wages, because for every extra shift I took, I got an extra day's pay. I netted around 250 *pesos* a month.

Many of the men I worked with were ex-convicts. Some were low-class but others were very good guys. At the beginning of the Revolution the garbage men used to get gifts from all the shopkeepers—bread from the grocer, coffee from the warehouse, shots of rum at the bars. I would drive along drunk as a grape, and all the comrades riding on the back would urge me on: "Faster, drive faster." I came to the end of my route without ever knowing how I'd done it. The streets in Old Havana are so narrow, if you're an inch off turning a corner you can drive right into a house; it's a mystery I never had a smash-up. I was just lucky all along the line.

After I quit my job as garbage collector I went to work at MINED,[17] and there I've been ever since.

I drive all kinds of cars for MINED, as well as trucks. I'm the pinch-hitter chauffeur there. If something has to be fetched or carried and the person who should have done it doesn't feel like it or forgets, right away they call me. "Moisés, take the station wagon and go to such-and-such a place."

My workday is supposed to be from 7:00 to 3:00, but I've never worked less than ten or twelve hours a day. Until recently I was paid for working overtime. Now I get a standard wage each month, but I still work as many hours as I'm needed.

I used to be ambitious; I wanted to be a success. To me that meant having plenty of money to spend, and I drove myself to get it. Now I drive myself just as hard, but it's to support my family, to keep my job, and to contribute to the Revolution. I give to the maximum of my ability. Seeing what the Revolution is doing for the poor, I'd be ashamed to walk down the street and have someone say, "Look at that lazy bum!" It's the urge to do something for the Revolution that keeps me going. Nowadays I work all the time; I say, let's do all we can.

I'm in the militia and stand guard when it's my turn. And I've worked in the sugar-cane harvest too. I no longer want to get rich. And I don't even want to be designated Vanguard Worker. That's a step toward becoming a Communist Party member and I don't want to be singled out for honors.[18]

GRACIA:

Once my family's economic needs were taken care of, I was able to pay more attention to my spiritual needs. More than anything I wanted to become a truly good person, and the way to goodness was through a deeper knowledge and experience of God. That was almost impossible for me when we were living with *papá* because he hated the Church and anything connected with it. He'd never allowed *mamá* to go to Mass, but she'd seen to it that we children had a good religious upbringing and went to Catholic schools.

In Sunday school we learned about Communion, the devil, tempta-tion, and all the things we shouldn't do. I was an outstanding student in

17. *Ministerio de Educación* (Ministry of Education).
18. The Vanguard Worker program was part of a new system of union organization introduced in 1965–66, following the founding of the present Communist Party and the establishment of Party cells in all work centers. Requirements for Vanguard Worker status were similar to those for Party membership, so these workers provided a reservoir of potential Party candidates. In fact, membership in the Union of Young Communists was often awarded conjointly with Vanguard Worker status. (The Vanguard Worker program is discussed by Lionel Martin in the *Guardian* in a series of six articles beginning in the issue of May 10, 1969, and ending on July 5, 1969.) After 1970, this merger of Party and union functions for Party membership selection was abandoned, but the Vanguard Worker status was retained.

catechism and was allowed to make my First Communion at the age of six instead of seven. I prepared myself with such fanatical devotion, trying to become absolutely pure in heart, that on the day of my First Communion I got sick to my stomach and vomited.

As a child I worried a lot about my sins. I went to confession often because I had a bad habit of talking back to my parents, and sometimes I used bad words, like *coño* and "I shit on your mother," but never really low words like *maricón*,[19] which was forbidden in our house. My parents never used them except when they quarreled. In my own way I tried to lead a very pious life. Besides going to Confession regularly, I prayed every night and wore modest clothes.

I didn't eat meat on Friday and that really annoyed *papá*. I realize now the proper thing for me as a good Christian would have been to eat the meat and avoid crossing my father. Christians today are taught to use a little judgment in matters of conscience, but in those days eating meat would have been considered a sin.

After my parents separated I was free to practice my religion. I attended Mass at the Church of San Pedro, sang in the choir, and taught catechism in Sunday school. Both *mamá* and *papá* were afraid I'd become a nun because I was very friendly with the North American nuns in the church. They were trained nurses and social workers and ran a dispensary for poor children. Three doctors worked there and gave the children marvelous care.

I began to help out in the dispensary. One of the doctors, a very kind man and a good Christian, taught me how to take blood pressure and give treatment to asthmatics. He believed the Revolution was made to help the poor and was inspired by Christian feeling. He often said, "I don't understand why more Christians aren't revolutionaries." He encouraged my enthusiasm for the Revolution; in short, that doctor was like a god to me. He had a wife and seven children and went to Communion daily, yet one day he slipped me a folded note that read, "I must see you alone somewhere."

I was frightened. I was seventeen years old and knew what he was after, but it was my first encounter of that kind. I stopped going to the dispensary for about a month. Then a woman doctor who worked there told me, "Look, Gracia, you don't have to stay away from here. Simply stop working with that doctor. He's a fresh guy anyway." I took her advice.

The apostolic mission of the nuns was to visit the poor, and after a while I began to work with them in my free time. We'd visit the blacks, the poor, and the sick, in the slums of Buena Vista. It was work I came to love. I couldn't do enough for the nuns. I'd sweep, scrub floors, type— anything.

19. Slang term for homosexual.

Being North American, the nuns were, of course, against the Revolution. Only two months after the Triumph they told me that Cuba had become a communist country. I was so indignant I refused to speak to them. Not that they had any great desire to talk to me, either; they were afraid I was turning into a revolutionary. I knew nothing about communism except that communists were atheists, which to me was shocking.

My cousin Simón had a strong influence over me at that time. He'd been a revolutionary and was also a practicing Catholic. Thanks to the Revolution, when he finished school he got a good job at the Ministry of Education earning 200 *pesos* a month, so he had reason to be grateful. After a while he turned against the Revolution and attended the Church of San Pedro. His sister Margarita and he began telling me that communism was an atheistic movement and I began to believe them. Gradually my religion became a powerful force that pulled me away from the Revolution.

It was Fidel himself who helped to quench my revolutionary fervor. In 1960, on the day after the explosion and burning of the ship *Le Coubre*,[20] there was a funeral for the accident victims. I saw the tears of the mothers and wives of those workingmen, and wept with them. But Fidel didn't take a moment to pay his respects to their anguish. Instead, speaking over the dead bodies, he accused the Americans of having provoked the fire. I wondered how anybody could be so hardhearted as to talk of politics at a time like that. "Stop! Stop!" I thought. "Talk about the sorrow of these women." Then I thought, "This man's a liar. Are we supposed to believe that within twenty-four hours they were able to prove that the CIA placed bombs in *Le Coubre?*" I felt I couldn't believe a word Fidel said.

For the first time I began to see many aspects of the Revolution I didn't like. It was very wrong, for example, to be forced to stand guard or to defend something you didn't believe in. I spoke my mind to the boy who was head of the union at the library. "How can you ask me to stand guard here? I don't love the Revolution. It's against what's most important to me, being a Christian and believing in God."

I was confused about many things at that time. At the dispensary I was deeply involved with the director, Doctor Velasco. I think I was actually falling in love with him, and that upset me because he was a practicing Catholic and a married man with children. We had many talks together and finally he told me he was doing counterrevolutionary work. He asked if I would like to help and I accepted.

My reasons were very superficial. It seemed an appropriate thing for a Catholic to do and it made me feel important. Since I could type, I was assigned the task of addressing propaganda materials—newsletters,

20. See Mónica, n. 29.

pamphlets, and such. I never read the stuff, so I only remember some of the points that were made most frequently—that the Cuban government was communist and atheist, that there was no real freedom, only a temporary semblance of it that would soon be revoked. None of it made much of an impression on me, but I was a very enthusiastic worker.

I got everybody in my family to help me, even *mamá*, who was a confirmed revolutionary by then. "You kids are crazy!" she complained. "First you talk me into believing in the Revolution, and now, after I see how much good it has done, you want to turn me against it."

The group loaned me a typewriter that I pounded like crazy every night until 2:00 A.M. Sometimes I mailed the material myself, sometimes I gave it to *mamá* to mail. To play safe, we mailed small batches from different sections of the city, which kept me running all over Havana. I really went through hell and high water. *Ay, mi madre!* If I'd been caught, they would have pulled my head off!

I'm by no means a brave woman. On the contrary, I scare easily. But when I get really excited about something I become quite daring. The way I looked at it, I was leading an adventurous life and I was part of a great romantic epic.

Doctor Velasco did a lot more than I did; he worked with several three-man cells. I belonged to one of those cells and knew only the doctor and the two other members of my cell, the man who delivered the propaganda material and his daughter. We worked that way to avoid problems. In December, 1960, the doctor and his wife were arrested, as well as the two other members of my cell, but nobody ever suspected me, I'll never know why.

It's a terrible thing to say, but I've always thanked God they arrested Doctor Velasco. I was too close to falling in love with him. I just didn't want to do to any woman what I would hate to have done to me. As it worked out, the doctor and his wife spent two years in jail, and when they were released they left Cuba. I was safe then. By a stroke of good luck I got to keep their typewriter.

At home, since I was the first one to become disillusioned with the Revolution, we had our share of arguments. Then, little by little, my family began coming over to my side, all except Diego. I think that was because his sweetheart, who is now his wife, was an active revolutionary. She had more influence over him than I did.

At the time of the invasion of Playa Girón, Diego told me he was against the Revolution and almost had me convinced. We were asleep when the bombing started and the noise woke us. Our apartment was only a few blocks from some barracks and there was a lot of activity going on there. From our window we could see the bombs falling.[21] There had

21. On April 15, 1961, two days before the invasion at Playa Girón, Cuban-marked American planes bombed the airport of the Revolutionary Armed Forces on the outskirts of Havana.

been very little instruction about what to do in such an emergency, but we remembered that the safest place to be when bombs were falling was the corner of a room. All five of us crept into a corner and started to say the rosary. That was the first time in my life I ever said the rosary with my family.

As soon as we could, we went to my Aunt Victoria's house, which was safer. Diego was in the militia and had to report for duty, but before leaving he said, "Gracia, you're the only person who will understand what I'm going to say. If I should die, remember that I'm against the Revolution." I was moved; we had never shared a moment of such intimacy.

The next few days were sheer torture for us because we got all kinds of conflicting reports about my brother. First we were told that he'd been killed. Then a friend of his told us that a grenade had exploded in Diego's hand, burning him badly. *Mamá* went from hospital to hospital looking for him, and *papá* spent all his time sitting in the Plaza de la Revolución, looking up at the planes carrying the returning troops. We couldn't find a trace of my brother. His name was not even on the list of the dead or wounded. We could only assume that he was missing. I thought to myself, "Which side was he fighting on?"

About ten days after Playa Girón my brother returned, skinny and terribly broken up. He told us he'd eaten only Russian canned meat and drunk water with mosquito larvae in it. One whole week at the front and that was all the nourishment he'd had. War—how I hate it!

My brother was in Fidel's favorite regiment and Fidel personally led the men into battle. He was out in front of them all. Even a counter-revolutionary like me couldn't help admiring the man's courage. It must have inspired my brother as well, because from that time on Diego has been a dedicated revolutionary; he even joined the Communist Youth.

My feelings, however, didn't change; I was actually hoping the Americans would win. That may seem strange, considering that the revolutionaries were my fellow Cubans, but if my country was drifting into communism I felt we were already sunk. The Americans wanted to help but we couldn't count on them. They didn't back up the invasion—all they wanted was to make their country the most powerful in the world. Their politics are as dirty as anybody else's. If we're ever to get ahead, we'll have to do it on our own.

I wanted to be useful somehow. Although I was against the Revolution, the Literacy Campaign was a good thing and I wanted to participate in it. It was my opportunity to do some good for the people. I wanted to go to Las Lomas but *mamá* wouldn't hear of it. "What, go to that place where there are men and women together?" That worried me a little too, because I've always been preoccupied about morals. All of us had a great respect for my mother; besides, she'd suffered so much that I didn't like to do anything to add to her unhappiness. On the other hand, I was already earning my own living and it was my responsibility to help in the alphabetization campaign. In that dilemma, I decided the best solution was a compromise. So I stayed home and worked for the Campaign in Havana. I taught two illiterate ladies who lived on the ground floor of our building, and some of the cleaning women who worked in the library.

After the invasion I looked for another job, because we really needed more money at home and I couldn't get a raise at the library. Dr. Padín, a friend of the director's, asked me if I'd take on some extra work transcribing tape-recorded lectures delivered before UNESCO by some foreigner. It meant a little more money for me, so I agreed. Well, the lectures turned out to be totally atheistic and materialistic, which was a shock to me. This sign of communist influence on our government was too close for comfort. I worked all week on those lectures and then on Saturday I visited the nuns at San Pedro. I told them, "I'm so sad, I believe I've just done my first piece of communist work." Their eyes filled with tears and one of them burst out, "What a shameless wretch!"

The following Monday when my cousin and I went to Mass, we found that all the nuns had left for America. "Who's left to spread religion now?" I asked myself. During 1960 one convent after another closed its doors. Now it wasn't my *papá* who kept me from practicing my religion, it was my own government. It was becoming more and more difficult for me to be a good Christian in Cuba. I decided to go where I was free to love and to serve God. I had no choice. I got in touch with a friend who was thinking of leaving the country and we began to make preparations to go together.

During 1960–61 I waited for my permit to leave Cuba. All my ties with the Church were broken, yet I drew still further away from my family, retreating into a world of my own, gradually freeing myself from my mother's authority. I set my own standards of dress, of friends, of where I went. I spent more and more nights at a girl friend's house, and I'd stay out late without telling *mamá* where I had been. It was then that the "pagan" period of my life began. I went to a nightclub for the first time and many times after that, never telling *mamá*.

I've always been fond of dancing and I'm good at it, though for a long time when I went to parties I'd hide in a corner watching the others. One night I went out with a boy I knew in school. We started to dance but he pressed me close and kissed me. It was terrible. I had to struggle to pry myself loose from him. I was really shocked. I couldn't understand how just seeing me could drive a man to kiss me. Another time I went dancing, my date's hands began to stray all over me. "What's this?" I said to myself. "He isn't my sweetheart and I'm not even interested in him, yet what he's doing excites me. I can't let this go any further. The only way out is to get so drunk that I can't dance."

So I got drunk for the first and only time in my life. I did it not only to escape his passes, but also to see how *papá* felt when he was drunk. I got sick to my stomach and had to be taken home. Drunk as I was, I know nothing wrong happened that night.

I've always been a little uncomfortable about sex and afraid of my own impulses. It seems to me that if I lost control over them, that would be the end. I liked the abstract idea of love but was anxious about physical love. I was what people called a "puritan." I believed I had to keep myself pure and never allow any man to touch me except my sweetheart, the one who would one day be my husband.

Whenever I had a negative sex experience, I'd rush to the confessional, feeling the lowest of sinners. Years ago, just after my First Communion, something happened that I was too embarrassed to confess. I had a playmate who was several years older than I—about eleven. One day we were playing house—my girl friend was the *papá* and I the *mamá*—and she began to hug and kiss me. I'm embarrassed even to remember it. There was something odd about her but I didn't know she was a lesbian until I ran into her again when I was about seventeen. This girl also taught me to masturbate, which I continued to do until I was about thirteen.

When I was young I yearned for a home of my own and especially children. I'd say to myself, "I want a home that's better than my *mamá*'s. I don't want my husband to be like my *papá*." It was my obsession that my husband shouldn't drink. But I never dwelt much on sexual relations in marriage.

In 1961 I met a boy named León Alvaro who had just graduated from the University. He used to phone me every single day and meet me at night after class, and not until we became sweethearts did he kiss me. I was enchanted with him. I could tell him everything I felt. In spite of the fact that he wasn't a practicing Catholic, we understood each other perfectly.

I was eighteen, and *mamá* didn't approve of my going out alone with a boy. She chaperoned my sister even to the corner drugstore and had every intention of doing the same to me. I didn't want to upset her, not only out of respect, but because she'd suffered so much with *papá*. Why should I add to her troubles? So one night, as León was walking me home, I said to him, "León, I don't want you to wait for me after class anymore. *Mamá* doesn't approve."

He didn't say another word until we got to the door of my house. Then he told me, "When you grow up, let me know."

That was the last I ever saw of him. His indifference made me feel like an utter failure. Had he really cared, he would have kept on meeting me, no matter what I said. I was so hurt I didn't have any more boyfriends after that.

Chapter Five

I Become a Nun

GRACIA:

At the end of 1960, I met the nuns who showed me that it was still possible for a Christian to work in Cuba. The Church in Cuba was divided on the question of the Revolution. One faction rejected it completely—that was a great error because there was an exodus of practicing Catholics. The more progressive faction encouraged Catholics to stay and work within the Revolution. That's what I chose to do. When I finally received my permit to leave Cuba, I renounced it.

After the Revolution the Church had established a secular institute to carry out its apostolic mission and to answer Cuba's present needs. The nuns at the institute were instructed to be open-minded, to integrate with the community and be willing to talk with people. Some of them spent as long as three months working in the countryside. They didn't wear nuns' habits because they wanted to live the Christian life without any trappings to separate them from laymen. At first they bought their clothes at a special store for nuns, but I guess when the government noticed they wore the same clothes as everybody else they said, "All right, let them buy where everybody else does!" So they began to buy with their ration books in regular stores.

Father Vicente Torres was the director of the institute, and like many priests in Cuba he had progressive ideas about cooperating with the government and tried to establish a dialogue with them. Even so, they gave him trouble because he worked hard to spread Catholicism. Once, when he started a campaign to celebrate Catechism Day, posters were put up with the slogan, "This child will grow up to be a believer or an atheist . . . it depends on you." The government had all those posters pulled down and substituted with others saying, "This child will grow up to be a patriot or a traitor . . . it depends on you." After that, it was impossible to carry on the campaign.

I began to work intensively with the nuns every weekend. I went with them to Luyanó, a very poor barrio where I visited people in their homes and tried to persuade them to go to church. I gave lessons, taught catechism, and prepared couples for marriage. I was fascinated with the idea of teaching religion to the children, helping them to see that he who has God has peace.

My ideal had always been to serve others through religion, so I said to myself, "I'd better become a nun." That decision was not the climax of a great personal crisis, nor did it seem to be an outstanding event in my life. I simply saw the need for people willing to work for religion and I responded to it.

There were two types of nuns at the institute, the "known" and the "unknown." The second type weren't known even by their closest relatives. They didn't live in the institute. I had no choice but to enter as an "unknown" because, being a minor, I needed my mother's approval. I joined in January, 1962, with María, a friend of mine, but she joined openly. How jealous I was of her because she could enjoy the religious life to the full.

I struggled to become independent. When I'd go to the institute, I'd lie to *mamá*. I'd tell her I was going somewhere else. Those lies were pardonable, but they were a burden because I've always been truthful. As a nun I could no longer go to parties, and when I turned down invitations my family thought it strange. I began to keep silent about the invitations I declined. Members of the institute were also forbidden to go to the beach. That had been my favorite pastime, so I had to make up all sorts of excuses not to go. I also stopped wearing pants or sleeveless dresses, and as bare legs were forbidden, I wore nylon stockings, even to do the housecleaning.

Mamá knew something was up and eventually discovered I had joined. I tried to make her understand. "What I want to do is good," I argued. "I want to help people. I want Christ to reign over their souls, to have people love one another and live in truth." Somehow I was constantly hurting my mother, making her cry. "How can I initiate my service to others by sowing discord in my own family?" I thought.

Mamá had been in the habit of bringing me a cup of coffee when she woke me in the morning. It was an affectionate gesture that she began when I started to work for a living. She stopped doing it when I went to work with the nuns. I was hurt because it had meant a lot to me. I was also very hurt one day when my little brother Gabriel said, "Gracia, I'll never go to church again, because when you go, *mamá* cries." Diego also grew more and more distant from me. Every day there were terrific quarrels at home. Whatever I did annoyed my family and whatever they said cut me to the quick.

I still worked at the library from 8:00 A.M. to 1:00 P.M., but nobody there knew I was a nun. Many of the sisters living in the institute held outside jobs to help support the institute, whose mainstay was the contributions from the churches where we worked. That was the point of our vocation, to give others a real testimony of the spirit of Christianity through work and cooperation. It seemed to me that the best way to attract people to God was to go out and do good. So I tried to be the best worker of all.

Most days I went home to lunch to keep *mamá* happy. It upset her that I was out of the house so much and she'd scold me for it. I usually got home at 3:00 in the afternoon and left again for the institute at 6:00. There I'd carry out my tasks of praying and studying.

Because I was one of the few typists in the institute, Padre Torres requested me as his secretary. He had a great deal of work. Not only was he director of the institute but he also helped organize programs for religious instruction on the diocesan level. He subscribed to many foreign reviews and ordered lots of religious books. He also had many North American friends, and I'd type his letters to them in English. Some days I'd spend the whole afternoon in his office. I was happy to help him with his work, but it seemed odd to be working alone with him in that office. He had a bed in it, you see.

That bed made a terribly bad impression on me. There it was, along with his desk, his files, the closet where he kept his clothes, the table with a big radio on top of it, and the record player. The bed was the first thing you noticed when you entered. When I learned that he slept at the institute I was frightfully shocked. God, was I shocked! I told my friend María, "A man of thirty shouldn't sleep in the same house as girls of sixteen and seventeen. I can't see why they allow it."

"I don't like it either," María agreed.

Not that his superiors didn't speak to him about it. The padre just did as he pleased. Priests in Cuba were granted permission to stop wearing the cassock, but Padre Torres kept on wearing his. Only in the house did he wear a shirt and trousers.

From the first, Padre Torres was interested in me and began to work on my "vocation." I noticed this when I went on the monthly institute outing in December. We went to Matanzas and drove in three automobiles. Halfway there, the padre said we should change places. Well, he changed us all around until there were only myself and Aleja in his car and all the others crowded into the other two.

The padre was driving and Aleja sat in front beside him. I was alone in the back. Both of us sang in the choir, and at the padre's request we sang his favorite songs. He and this girl, Aleja, had a relationship that I didn't like one bit. She had a blister on one hand and I saw the padre take her hand and say something, but I couldn't make out what it was. I was shocked. "Lover's talk!" I thought.

We had a good time that day. On the return trip five other girls and I were with the padre, who was driving. We sang happily as we went. I had

dozed off when I heard one of the tires blow out. The next moment the
car overturned, the back of it smashing against a tree. The impact threw
all of us forward except a nun who had changed places with me during
the ride. She fell backward and was crushed to death when the roof
smashed in. Only a few minutes earlier I had been sitting right where she
sat! It was God's mercy I wasn't killed instead.

We were taken to the hospital, where they prescribed one week of
complete rest for me. One of my eyes was slightly injured. Two days
later, Padre Torres gave me Communion at home. After he left *mamá*
said to me, "I don't like the way that man looks at you." That kind of
remark puts ideas in a woman's head.

Two days later they held a Mass for the girl who had died. She was
only nineteen and, as it happens, was the first person to whom I had
spoken about my wish to become a nun.

Remembering that, I was very sad at the Mass and afterward I burst
into tears. Padre Torres put his arms around me, hugging me tight. I felt
a shock of surprise, but then I thought, "He does it only to comfort me."

When I recovered from the accident I returned to my daily tasks. I
had to work, study, take examinations—my whole life was work, work,
work. There was no time left for anything else. I was always exhausted.
Other members who were living at home were asked to move into the
institute, and I wanted to, not only because of my home situation but also
because it seemed to me that the girls who lived there had gone through
more stages of religious growth than I. My friend María, for example,
had made great progress, and it made me feel unhappy and inferior to
see how she'd outstripped me.

My mother's reaction was terrible. She cried all the time and complained that I was making her suffer even more than my father. "Only
two years ago we separated, and now you, of all my children, are the one
who hurts me most!"

Everybody was against me except my sister. Even the neighbors interfered. They told me I should remember how much *mamá* had gone
through and how unhappy my being a Catholic made her. Aura gave me
moral support when I needed it. She's been everything a sister should
be. "This is your ideal," she said, "so you must do everything in your
power to attain it. I'll help you as much as I can." When I finally moved
to the institute she brought me what I needed from home. It was then
that I began to really love her. She comforted *mamá* but defended me all
the same.

Aura has a lot more character than I do. She's the one who knows best
how to get along with *mamá*, not setting herself against her, never talking
back, and always taking into account *mamá*'s tendency to explode. I was
just the opposite. I'd quarrel with *mamá* about the most trivial differences. I think I felt she was my inferior. With others, especially my

superiors, I was tongue-tied and cowardly; with *mamá,* I gave vent to all the hostility inside me. In the end, I did what I wanted but at the cost of some horrifying outbursts. My sister often got her way too, but much more peacefully.

Just before I moved, I quarreled again with *mamá,* and for the first time in years she struck me. I went weeping to the padre and he comforted me. He took my hands in his, which frightened me, but he backed up my efforts to free myself from my family. He said I should move over to the institute as soon as possible, and I vowed to the Virgin Mary that I would. The Virgin Mary was the saint I'd prayed to ever since I was a little girl, and for years I was a member of the Daughters of Mary, a religious association for girls with a special devotion to the Virgin.

The break with my mother was unbearably painful. On July 9, after a fierce argument, I told her I was definitely leaving the next day. She cried and cried, but the next morning she silently brought me my coffee in bed; she didn't even say good morning. I got up, packed three dresses in a straw bag, and waited for someone from the institute to fetch me. *Mamá* didn't say one word; she just went out to the yard and started doing the wash. Later my sister told me that *mamá* had a tremendous nervous attack after I left. But, well . . . I went away feeling I was doing something noble. In fact, for a coward like me, entering the institute was just short of heroic.

I was still a minor and I needed the written permission of one parent to join the order. *Mamá* was threatening to go to court to get me out of the institute and I was terrified that she might do it—the fear of scandal has always been very strong in me—so I decided to ask my father for his consent.

I didn't dare visit him alone so María went with me. She was free of prejudices toward the lower class and I knew that my father's inferior position wouldn't bother her. We found him lying on a filthy cot in a hall, in a pigpen of a place. I asked him to sign a statement I'd typed beforehand, granting me permission to enter the institute. *Papá* agreed, and after signing it he said, "Don't think I do this because I like the idea—I don't. I do it simply to displease your mother."

I'd counted on that. That was the one time in my life when I acted as a complete opportunist. I still consider it a stain upon my integrity.

SEÑOR RIVERA:

I only wish I could have kept my daughter Gracia away from the Church. It was her mother's fault. "Let the child go to church, let her!" Digna would nag. And when Gracia was a bit older, and would fast, my wife would say, "Oh, leave the child alone. Today is a Retreat."

How I hated that! I remember one year I sacrificed myself to make Christmas Eve a special occasion, bringing a pig, roast chicken,

Christmas sweets, and all sorts of delicacies. Then, when we sat down to eat, Gracia said, "Oh, I can't eat today, I'm fasting. I'll sit at the table with you and have a few spoonfuls of broth but I can't eat." I felt like blowing up. For whose sake did I spend so much money on Christmas Eve supper? I'd think, as I did so often, "Nobody loves me."

Church and school were all Gracia cared about, but church more than school. I told Digna, "This girl will grow up to be a nun, I know she will." But Digna paid no attention, so when Gracia wanted to enter the institute and came to me I gave her my consent. I remember her sitting on the stoop crying, "Oh *pipo,* what an unhappy life I lead." So I said, "All right, I give my consent. I'll sign your papers, but I disapprove." I suppose it was my duty to sign, but I did it mostly to get back at my wife. I knocked Digna on the head with it.

GRACIA:

Once I was installed at the institute I was so overcome by happiness that I lost my appetite. That first afternoon the padre called me in to congratulate me, then he took me with him to make the rounds of the churches. His parish had asked him to prepare the chronicles, which were long daily accounts of everything that happened in the apostolate. He told me that now, with me living in the house, he'd be able to get it done a little faster. I began to work on the chronicles right away, making a great effort to keep them up to date, never falling behind by so much as one single page. I was exhausted by the long hours, but I enjoyed showing off and was delighted to be called "the padre's confidential secretary and assistant." Working on the chronicles as I did, I once came to an entry under the date I'd first met him. He had written, "Met Gracia and María today—friends—good kids both, and likely material to develop a vocation."

Life at the institute was beautiful. The more I learned about it, the more I loved it and wanted to give myself completely to others. Love was our aim and our slogan. Our prayers always began, "This is my command; that ye love one another as I have loved ye."

Our days were full. We arose at 5:00 A.M. and had fifteen minutes to dress. This included all personal care, putting away our nightclothes, and making our beds neatly. At 5:15 we all gathered in the chapel. We beginners, postulants as we were called, said our morning prayers together with the novices. They were lovely prayers, invoking the Lord with a series of psalms, asking him to bless our daily activities, whether at work, rest, or study, to protect us against sin, and to make us grow in the image of Christ and Mary. After that we said the institutional prayer, which we called "The Link." This was supposed to unite us with every other member of the institute, even those doing missionary work in different parts of the world.

My favorite part of the morning service was the *Oratorio,* taken from the Apostle Paul's Epistle to the Corinthians. I've never forgotten it and often repeat it to myself: "Charity suffereth long and is kind; charity envieth not; charity vaunteth not itself, is not puffed up, doth not behave itself unseemly, seeketh not its own, is not easily provoked, thinketh no evil; rejoiceth not in iniquity, but rejoiceth in the truth. . . ." Charity was our watchword.

After morning prayers we had half an hour of meditation on a theme determined by the padre. Usually it was a biblical text illustrating one aspect of Christian life. Meditation was one of the most difficult duties for me. Little given to reflection, I made a tremendous effort to concentrate, but it was torture for me. I often fell asleep and had to be awakened; other times, I'd soon be looking out the window at the sunrise, listening to the roar of the ocean, or watching the Russians across the street set off for work at 6:00 A.M.

At the end of the meditation period, we said the prayer "Under Your Protection" to the Virgin. The reader would say after each prayer, "This is my command." And the rest of us would answer, "That ye love one another as I have loved ye." The thoughtful repetition of this prayer was supposed to keep us loving the rest of mankind.

After leaving the chapel we had to maintain absolute silence. I confess that was also very difficult for me. At the slightest opportunity I'd start a conversation, especially if by any chance I had to go into the padre's office. He and the Superior were the only ones with whom we were allowed to talk during "the great silence."

At 7:30 we had breakfast. Breakfast was a hearty meal prepared by the two sisters assigned to the kitchen that month. On Sundays we ate eggs given to us by the many friends of the institute. We were able to get all kinds of food—vegetables, fish, and meat—because of special privileges. We also kept chickens until chicken feed was rationed. After that, a group of us would rise at 4:00 A.M. and each go to stand in line at a different store to buy chicken. As the food administrator, I often had to wait in line to buy things for the institute.

We said grace before every meal, and while we ate one of the sisters would read aloud to us for ten minutes. We'd read about the lives of saints or exemplary nuns or priests, or else we'd read articles from Catholic magazines, which were still received here at that time. Because I had to hurry off to my job at the library, I heard only the readings at dinner.

While those of us with outside jobs were away, the rest of the sisters performed their morning duties, cleaning the house, caring for the garden, and washing their clothes. Then they studied and prepared for their apostolic activities, arranging lectures for groups of young people and calling on parishioners.

Those of us with outside jobs had a lighter load of housework at the institute. I had to clean the hall at the main entrance, a little bit of a place that I scrubbed and polished to perfection. Two or three times a week I also cleaned the classroom. On my afternoon off I tended to my personal things. I did my household tasks when I returned from work, unless the padre needed me right away. I had fifteen minutes of assigned spiritual reading in the chapel. Then I bathed and had supper.

At supper we said grace, recited the *Angelus,* and read from the New Testament continuously until dessert was served. The reading was begun by the Superior, then taken up by any sister who had finished her soup, and so on by turns. Somebody, usually the padre, tinkled a small bell whenever a sister made a mistake. She'd have to read the sentence or paragraph all over again, explaining what she'd read up to that moment. I loved to read aloud and I did it well, but I was scared to death of that little bell, although it didn't ring often for me. I was afraid I might be asked to interpret what I'd read; most of the time I merely read to hear how well I sounded, without paying much attention to the meaning of the words.

I felt especially reluctant to explain anything because so many of the nuns were teachers, professionals, and intellectually superior to me. They had university degrees while all I had was a secretarial course in Spanish and English. It seemed to me that I had nothing to contribute to a serious conversation. I can be quite open about my opinions when I'm at home or among friends, but around the people who work with me, I always feel sure I'll offend someone or sound foolish. I hate to admit it, but I'm like *mamá* in this. She becomes frightened among strangers. She can't even ask questions if she needs something.

Another thing that made me uneasy at first was eating my meals with the rest of the group. Strict attention was paid to the rules of etiquette, which I had never learned. We were expected to eat everything that was served, and this was difficult for I was a picky eater. I'm very glad now, though, that I learned to eat all sorts of food. We had to know how to use each piece of silver and how to help ourselves to our portions, then wait until the Superior served herself before we took a single bite. I often forgot that after cutting a piece of meat I was supposed to shift my fork to my right hand. I'd be terribly embarrassed when I made a mistake like that. Not that they ever called my attention to it in public. In fact, most of the time it would have gone unnoticed if my embarrassment hadn't made me conspicuous. I got so depressed by my ignorance that they gave me a book on etiquette. It taught me table manners, how to behave in groups, what to say when I was introduced to somebody, how to walk, and so on.

There was a rule of silence after dinner, although that's when everybody feels like chatting. Four of us took turns washing the dishes; in fifteen minutes we had to wash, dry, count, and put away all the tableware used by twelve people and mop the floor. Even with four of us it was difficult to get it done in time. I'd been used to living in a small household where table settings were much simpler. It was even harder for some of the other sisters because they'd never had to wash dishes at home.

This rigid schedule was to teach us to organize our work efficiently. It was a good thing but the way they punished us disturbed me. When the fifteen minutes were up, we had to drop whatever we were doing and leave it for the sisters assigned to the kitchen the following day. Imagine! The poor things had to finish up our work besides doing the cooking, for which they were also only allowed a short time.

After supper came recreation period; we played table games, checkers, parcheesi, dominoes, Monopoly, crossword puzzles, and cards. Sometimes we played games like baseball or basketball, in which we could run. I've never liked exercise and didn't enjoy those games. Every evening we had one or two study periods or seminars to prepare us in the ways of a nun. A few days each week, this time was used for evaluation meetings to assess how much we'd learned. We also discussed profound religious subjects, or else something serious we'd read in the paper.

I tried to read every magazine that came into the institute, from popular ones like *Bohemia* to the numerous religious reviews, but when the sisters started talking about a subject of current interest, I couldn't follow the discussion. I'd forget everything I had read because I didn't read for my own interest but merely to keep up with the rest.

What with my job at the library and studying the Bible, techniques of catechizing, liturgy and dogma, singing rehearsals, and all my other duties, I always felt tired and harassed. The sisters were allowed one hour a day for a siesta, but I couldn't take advantage of that because I worked outside. Only on Saturday afternoons did I get an hour to rest, and time to wash and iron my clothes. I was excused from apostolic duties to tidy up my shelves and drawers, and to catch up with any task in which I might have fallen behind.

I looked forward to Sunday all week long. We got up an hour later, said our prayers as on weekdays, but there was no reading at meals, and we talked as much as we liked. It was pleasant to relax a little after working so hard. I also felt happy being able to celebrate the Day of Our Lord, something I'd never been allowed to do properly at home. After Sunday breakfast we all went out in pairs to do our apostolic activities. I worked at a church under the pastoral supervision of Padre Torres. My job was to see that all things used during the Mass were ready and in their proper place before Mass began. I also organized the singing and rehearsed the choir.

At noon the institute sent someone to pick us up and drive us back to have communal dinner at the house. In the afternoon we were allowed a longer rest period, and we could also talk while doing the dishes. In the evening we had a meeting dealing with matters of the apostolate, then there'd be a long recess, and we retired early.

Once a month we went on an excursion, but since these had to take place on weekdays, those of us with outside jobs were unable to go. We longed for those excursions, but our anticipation was always mixed with anxiety. For some reason the padre got upset on those days, and when he was upset everybody was upset. We all tried to behave perfectly, but he would quarrel over every little thing. If one of the girls sat carelessly, showing too much leg, he'd scold her, then be cold with the rest of us. We'd worry and say, "*Ay*, what can be the matter with the padre!" I was always afraid I'd make a mistake. We were very tied to him; he was more our master than our superior.

No matter where we went, we had to comment on the natural surroundings, saying whether they moved us to humility in the face of God's greatness or to gratitude for the beautiful manifestation of His power. If we went to the beach, each sister in turn had to tell the Lord out loud what the marvelous spectacle of the sea meant to her. I mention the sea especially because it has always brought me very near to God, impelling me to meditation and the contemplation of beauty.

But our shared meditation was just another source of anxiety for me. It was with great trepidation that I waited for my turn to speak. I forgot that I was praying and worried only about making my little speech sound pretty. My most sincere prayer to God at those times was that He overlook my vanity.

Every night before going to bed, the padre had us write an analysis of our weaknesses and achievements that day and of our efforts to attain the ideals of Christ. I hate to display my errors and at times I felt very rebellious indeed while I wrote this report, but it was helpful, too, enabling me to start each day afresh.

In many ways, being at the institute helped me to look at myself in a new light. I came to realize that my wish to emulate this or that girl arose simply from envy. The sisters pointed out that everybody was fond of me and admired my hard work and my spirited efforts, but that wasn't enough for me. I wanted to do everything and do it perfectly. I was always struggling to attain something beyond my powers and this prevented me from developing my real abilities. It seems I didn't want to be myself.

There were two years of training before we could make our first vows of poverty, chastity, and obedience. We were still training at the time of the October missile crisis and were in Retreat, keeping silent all day long, praying, and reading. That night, when Retreat was over, the padre called us together. He announced that Cuba had been ordered to remove the missiles, that the United States had taken a very aggressive stand on that situation, and that we faced the possibility of going to war. "In such circumstances," he asked us, "what do you prefer to do, stay here or go home to your families? None of you has made her vows yet. You are not absolutely bound to the institute and I have no right to order you to stay. Anyone who wants to leave is free to do so."

I've always been a coward and I volunteered to stay. I thought, "I don't want to spend this crisis at home." Some of the others left, mostly those whose families were alone.

When the missiles were taken away I was glad. I was against it simply because I was a Christian. It made me angry to think that the Russians wanted to exploit Cuba by using it as a base in the eventuality of a third world war. I remember thinking, "They didn't put those missiles here to help Cuba. They did it because it's to their advantage. As for the Americans, they're doing exactly what they did at Playa Girón; they do what they please. They got the missiles out, but what good did that do us? We're still as screwed up as ever with communism."

Yet, by then I was a far less ardent counterrevolutionary. Most of us at the institute had been pretty reactionary to begin with, but the padre gradually transformed us. I, for one, have always been weak-willed, and the padre took advantage of that to make me more positive. If I'd had a strong-willed person like him to push me into defiance of *mamá* at the time of the Literacy Campaign, I'd have gone into the hills to teach the illiterates. As it was, if it hadn't been for the padre, I'd never have been able to break with my family and join the institute.

Chapter Six

Battle for My Soul

GRACIA:
When I started working for the padre his attitude toward me was very fatherly. One day he asked me, "Is there nothing else you care for but your religion?" I'll never forget that moment.

"No, there's nothing else in my life."

"Don't you ever feel attracted to another human being?"

I really didn't, not at that time. I thought only of Christ and I told the padre so.

He didn't insist on his line of questioning, but from then on he'd call on me at all hours to take dictation. I became his favorite secretary. He had several girls helping him but he overloaded me with work till I thought I'd go crazy. I'd leave his office with twenty thousand different things to do. It was too much for me. I'd say to him, "I can't handle my job at the library and all this work here too." But I kept on just the same, telling myself, "This is for the good of human souls." To give as much time as possible to the padre, I didn't go out to work in the parish.

One day he stopped in the middle of dictation and said, "You have a lot of pimples on your chest. Why don't you squeeze them out?"

"Because I'm too busy. I don't have the time."

"Would you like me to do it for you?" he asked. It was such a strange offer . . . but I assumed he was being fatherly. After that he always squeezed the pimples on my chest.

One night the padre tried to kiss me. First he asked me to take off my blouse so he could squeeze the pimples. Fool that I was! Anybody who hears this must think, "What a stupid girl!" He pressed out the pimples, then he kissed me. I thought, "Oh no, what am I doing? Here I am with this man, when I plan to make vows of chastity." I burst into tears.

That kiss was one of the greatest shocks of my life. I pushed the padre back and struggled . . . it was a terrible, terrible thing. "I'm going to leave the institute," I told him. "This is wrong. I'd better go."

He argued until midnight, trying to persuade me to stay.

"No, no, I can't," I insisted. "How can I stay if I'm in love with you? I entered the religious life renouncing a husband, a home of my own and children, intending to give my life entirely to God and to save human souls. If it hadn't been for that, I'd be married by now, because once there was a boy who loved me."

I didn't choose the religious life because I wasn't interested in men. There may be some who do it for that reason or because they're afraid of marriage. I was not one of those. I liked men, but I truly wanted to belong to Christ.

Aleja, the girl I'd seen flirting with the padre on our tragic December outing, had received a permit from the government to visit her ailing brother in Miami and was due to leave the next day. So I said to the padre, "You're bad. I know you've done this to Aleja and I'll not allow you to do it to me. All you want is a substitute until she gets back from Miami."

He was taken aback, but he recovered and said, "Forgive me, it was a momentary weakness. What you've said isn't true. I was overcome just as you were. But now let us kneel together and beseech the Virgin to help us."

Well, I'm a pushover. I thought, "He really is a good man; I was weak too." So we knelt and said the *Ave María*, asking the Virgin to forgive us and give us the strength to resist temptation. Never in my life have I prayed so fervently.

"We must keep on asking the Virgin's aid," the padre told me.

Instead of helping me overcome temptation, his words made me love him more. "What a fine man he is!" I thought. So I went on working with him and he kept on trying to win my trust. He was simply getting ready for action. He began by giving me more and more work. I became more and more excited by him until I lost what fortitude I had. The next time he kissed me, I couldn't draw back. I'd found someone who understood me, who knew me through and through . . . my soul was naked before him. By then I was in love. I felt very guilty but he excused us both, saying, "These things round out your development as a woman; you still have too many complexes." He said I needed to go to bed with a man in order to lose my inhibitions, and it's true that with him I began to feel like a woman for the first time. I was not yet twenty when I became the padre's mistress. That was the tragedy of my life.

The padre exercised an extraordinary influence on men and women alike. As a person he was fascinating; as a man he was overwhelmingly attractive. The physical type that most attracts me is tall, dark, and slender. I'm attracted even more by a man who is quiet, thoughtful, a great reader. The padre was none of these things; he was short and stocky, and he had red hair. He would confide in me about his work—a technique he used with every girl—knowing that would give me a sense of fulfillment. I fell more deeply in love with him every day.

The padre did a lot of work outside the institute so we hardly saw each other during the day. Being out so much gave him a fine excuse to be alone with one or another of his secretaries at night. I'd wait until he returned. Sometimes I prepared his dinner and after he ate I'd go to his office. He'd lock the door before we began; the office was air-conditioned so no explanation was needed for the closed door and windows. Afterward I'd comb my hair and leave as coolly as if nothing had happened. Nobody ever entered his office without knocking, even when the door wasn't locked; that way he protected his privacy and prevented anyone from catching him in a compromising situation. Because I was his secretary, it caused no comment when I spent such long hours with him.

At first the padre treated me with great delicacy and respect, realizing how very young I was—infantile, I should say. I was ignorant rather than innocent. All I knew about sex was what I'd learned from romantic novels.

For a time he only touched and kissed me. I refused to take off all my clothes, but I was weak and later on he could do what he pleased with me. He'd kiss my breasts and excite me in other ways. Everything that happened between the padre and me shocked me to the depths of my soul, but in spite of my fears and conflicts, I enjoyed it. There was a crucifix hanging on the wall opposite the foot of his bed and I couldn't keep my eyes off it while we were together. It isn't that I thought the image could see me, but it reminded me I was doing all those things in the presence of God. When I got especially excited, my eyes would fly to the crucifix and I'd burst into tears. We reached our climaxes separately; he never waited for me, and I was never fully satisfied. Sometimes, after we had been together in the afternoon, he'd refuse his dinner at night. "I won't eat today," he'd tell me. "I'm doing penance." Such acts filled me with illusions, and I would do penance too, for the sin we'd both committed.

I don't believe he ever loved me, but in the beginning he was affectionate and understanding even though I refused to go all the way. I'd close my legs to prevent him from penetrating me, and sometimes when my excitement became unbearable I'd get up and leave. I couldn't, I simply couldn't go on. It was panic, fear of getting pregnant, that drove me away. It was stronger than my desire for him. He never offered to use a condom and I didn't suggest it because I'd never heard of contraceptives. Technically I was still a virgin, though that didn't make me feel less despicable.

Because I wouldn't go all the way, the padre's manner toward me changed. He was interested only in going to bed, and he always ended up angry. To get even, he'd mistreat me, making me stick to the typewriter while others were sent out to give talks and do the big things. He persecuted me by ignoring me, sometimes for weeks on end. Everybody remarked, "*Ay,* the padre really has it in for you!"

And I'd think, "If they only knew!"

One time a large supply of sweet potatoes and beet greens spoiled, and because I was in charge of food he blamed me. He made me eat nothing but rotten sweet potatoes and beet greens for a whole week. If I burned the food, I had to eat every scrap of it. If I had nothing but boiled tubers ready at 12:00 sharp for dinner, that was all my sisters got to eat. This was worse torment for me than if I myself had had to go hungry.

I wasn't the only one he tortured; he did it to all of us in every way he could think of. One of his favorite punishments was to isolate a girl completely, virtually keeping her a prisoner. Two girls were punished that way while I was at the house simply because of some minor misbehavior. They couldn't say a word to anybody and the rest of us were not allowed to say even good morning to them. It was practically medieval, just like the time of St. Theresa. He himself told us that St. Theresa was once locked up in a cell because her ideas were considered too advanced.

Sometimes the padre would remove someone from an assigned task in the most humiliating way possible, discussing her deficiencies in public. Whenever it was my turn to speak in chapel, the padre would interrupt me. "Stop! You're doing it all wrong," and in front of all the others he'd tear me apart. In the evaluation meetings he took great joy in analyzing our limitations, particularly mine. Knowing I had a complex about not being as bright as the other girls, he announced everybody's IQ in public. I felt totally humiliated. That man was cruel and sick; he lacked even the smallest grain of charity.

We put up with his behavior because he was our superior and we were bound to obey him. He dominated us completely; he was the very center of our lives. Looking back, I can see he was an effeminate type, although he hated effeminacy so much he wouldn't allow us to put pink sheets on his bed or even a vase of flowers in his office. He said only women and faggots used them. He displayed such an intense hatred of anything like that . . . and yet, you should have seen his mincing walk! He came to my home one day, and after he left, the lady next door asked, "Who was that faggot?"

I often wondered if he wasn't partially impotent, but, no . . . he couldn't have been. He was like a wild beast in bed! The way he asked me to do things was brutal. He'd come right out and say, "Do this to me, do that. . . ." He wanted me to masturbate him, which really repelled me; it wasn't normal. One time he was angry with me—I don't know why—and for three days he didn't speak to me or even pass the serving dish to me at the table. Finally, to put him in a good humor again, I masturbated him. It was the worst thing I ever did with him. That day I felt like the lowest reptile crawling in the dust.

I never took the initiative in having relations with him—I had too many inhibitions to dare. Once, and once only, did I ask him, and he refused. I felt terrible. And yet I still wanted him. I reacted to him not as a nun toward her spiritual guide, but as a woman to a man. I couldn't resist him, and he, being ambitious and ruthless, took whatever he wanted, no matter whom he destroyed in the process.

Sometimes he'd call me to his office when everyone else had gone to bed. There was a study room connected by intercom to the padre's office, and he didn't hesitate to call "Gracia!" at 12:00 or 1:00 or even 4:00 in the morning.

When I heard his voice my heart trembled. I couldn't refuse. I knew I was going to sin, that I'd give in and be humiliated. I knew I was being destroyed but I lacked the strength to resist him. One time when he called me I went down dressed in my pajama top with nothing but a blouse and skirt over it. I knew why he was calling me and I was too excited to wait. In the institute we were required to wear lots of underclothes, a chemise over the brassiere and so forth, yet I went down that way! As I went I pleaded, "Dear God, why don't you prevent me from going? Why should he have such power over me?" But I had to go.

I remember one terrible time when he called "Gracia!" over the intercom with such desperation: "Gracia!"

The others asked me, "What's the matter with that man?"

That time I was angry, really angry. "What do you want?" I asked coldly, when I went to him.

"Didn't you say you wished to talk with me?"

So I had, about a week before. I had some personal problems to discuss. When he said that, I could no longer contain myself and rushed over to him. By then I no longer loved him but was driven by my sexual appetite. I felt like a prostitute. But worse than that, I didn't give my body for money but for prestige. Deep inside, I wanted to show off as his favorite. My inferiority complex even lurked at the bottom of that miserable affair. I was proud to be called at all hours, in the hearing of the other sisters. I imagined the other girls thinking, "What long hours he works with her! She's his favorite," and I gloried in it.

The padre knew how I yearned for affection, for recognition, for admiration, and he exploited my weakness. My vanity was stronger than my ideals, much stronger than my fear of sin, stronger than my self-control. Sometimes I wonder if it wasn't even stronger than my sexual desire.

I suffered keenly. I realized how low I'd sunk and I wanted to leave the institute. The padre persuaded me that I still had a true religious calling but I knew my religious life was trash, just plain trash!

"How can I have the calling if I'm in love with you? How can I save anyone's soul when my own is soiled with sin?" I would object.

"That's only human. We're weak and fall into temptation."

In the midst of those crises of conscience, I never dared face him and say right out, "I'm going. I won't sleep with you anymore." Sometimes when I was angry I stayed away from him for as long as three months, but my determination didn't last. I would yield just a little, then I'd get so excited I had to go further. We usually had relations every two weeks.

I suffered tortures being the mistress of a man I respected so highly, a man who was almost sacred to me. I remember one time I caressed his ands, then suddenly ran out of the room overcome by horror, thinking, Dear God, those hands are consecrated to You and I'm defiling them!" n Mass, when he lifted up the Host, I'd think, "Those are the hands he oiled so shamefully." I developed a terrific guilt complex. Many times I left his bed in tears and lay awake all night long. My great conflict was that I was betraying Christ and deceiving everybody. I, who was so soon to take a vow of chastity, was sinning against it.

I felt I couldn't go on as I was. Even in Confession I wasn't able to tell the whole truth. At first I used to confess to the padre right after we had relations, and he'd give me absolution. But later I found out that it wasn't valid because he was a partner in my sin, so I went to another priest. But the padre would give me detailed instructions about what I could say. For instance, he forbade me to tell the priest that I was a member of a religious order, and I was so completely under his thumb I did as he said.

One day he told me that what he and I were doing was not a sin. "Look it up in the Bible," he said, picking up a Bible and opening it. "It doesn't mention this anywhere. Adultery is forbidden, but we're not committing adultery."

Oh, fool, fool that I was! Of course we were sinning. He'd made vows of chastity just as I was to do. But what did I know? When I entered the institute I was completely ignorant of religion.

From the very first, I realized I was not the only one. I suspect there were many others, including two mulatto girls. We didn't discuss those things with one another, but I had eyes. I'm sure the other sisters did too. We watched one another, we knew how many girls he called in, and it caused a lot of trouble among us. I'd think, "The same thing that happens to me happened to her." One of his habits always betrayed him. After spending the night with a girl, he'd refuse to officiate at Mass the next morning. He had some scruples, I suppose, but that meant we had to go out to Mass and fall behind in the rest of our duties.

My jealousy made me miserable. Aleja, the girl I was most jealous of, was one of my four roommates. She was prettier than I and knew better how to exploit the situation. I always came out of the padre's office loaded down with folders, but when Aleja came out, she didn't have one little sheet of paper in her hand. Once I asked her, "How come you don't have anything to do when I burn up all my energy trying to keep up with the work he gives me?"

"Oh, my child, I don't do that kind of work. The padre and I were discussing plans," she said airily.

"Well, maybe it's a good thing I'm here to carry them out!" I retorted.

At that time the padre was angry with me and we weren't having relations, thank God. Still, I couldn't go to sleep as long as Aleja was out of the bedroom. I begged the padre, "Please let me sleep in the infirmary or I'll go crazy. Remember I have to get up at 5:00 A.M." He said no, it was good for me to learn what jealousy was. He seemed to get a morbid pleasure out of watching me suffer. I was angry and I slammed the door when I left his office. He called me back. "Go kneel in the yard!" So at 11:00 at night I had to go kneel for an hour.

I especially dreaded the meetings where we had to tell one another's defects. "Padre, don't make me talk in public about Aleja's defects! I'm too jealous of her," I pleaded.

And like an executioner he'd say, "It'll be good for you."

"At least let me tell you in private, and when you repeat them don't mention who told you," I said.

Then, at the meeting, he'd say, "Gracia said such-and-such about Aleja."

One evening he said, "Tomorrow get up at 4:00 A.M. and come to my office. Don't knock, just walk in; I'll be asleep."

I followed his instructions. When I went in, there was Aleja in bed with him. I didn't see them doing anything, but what a shock! The next day I kept thinking, "He knew he was going to be in bed with that girl. He just enjoyed seeing me suffer."

When I went to his office I burst into tears. "I'm going crazy," I said to him. "I have to leave the institute. You've done me terrible harm and I've seen . . . things." I always used the formal *usted* when addressing him, even when we were having relations. But more ridiculous, I always called him *padre*. Even in bed!

I lashed out at him. "We come here to serve an ideal, but you betray the Church and the soul of every one of the girls who enters the institute. You know we can't resist you and you exploit us. You've done it to me, and now I understand! You're a pervert!" When I said that he slapped me. "Now I'm really going," I said. "You aren't much of a man if you can hit a woman. A man who hits a woman is only proving that he can't make her do what he wants. He's impotent, that's all!"

I thought he'd burst. That really cut him to the quick. He slapped me a second time. I got up. I didn't have as much as 1 *kilo* to my name so I picked up a *peseta* from the change he always had on his table and walked out. It was midnight.

"Gracia," he yelled. "Gracia, come back!"

I had always caved in when he scolded or screamed.

"Gracia, you must come back! This is no time to leave."

When I left the house I saw Aleja waiting in the sitting room. He sent her to catch up with me and ask me to return.

"Go to hell!" I told her.

I had to wait a whole hour for a bus. I cried and didn't even have a handkerchief. The people at the bus stop stared at me. "What will these people think of me?" I worried, but I couldn't stop crying.

It was 1:00 o'clock in the morning when I got home. "What's the trouble? What are doing here at this hour?" *mamá* asked.

"I quarreled with the people at the institute and I'm quitting," I answered.

The next day the phone calls from the institute began, but I refused to go to the phone. I was afraid they'd talk me into going back if I did. Then I set up a test for God. I was especially fond of the Superior at the institute. Her name was Asunción. She was a woman of extraordinary character who had given herself to Christ in every possible way. I prayed, "Dear God, you know I want to be a nun. Help me. Show me the way. I'll answer the phone next time it rings. If it's Asunción I'll interpret that as a sign from You to go back to the institute. If it's someone else, I'll send my sister to get my clothes."

It was a real test of God's will. When the phone rang I answered it and it *was* Asunción. I told her the padre had slapped me and I couldn't stand working with him anymore. But she urged me to stay, so I packed my things and went back to the institute.

I guess the padre was scared to death that once I got out I'd talk, and so I would have. I'd made up my mind to go to the archbishop and tell him everything. "He *must* know what's going on," I thought. "Other girls have left and must have talked. How can he permit the padre to go on living at the institute?" About half of the girls at the institute had left, but the padre maneuvered things in such a way that his superiors could do nothing. He'd tell them he wasn't sleeping at the institute anymore, then he'd sleep two nights in his parish and three nights in ours. Since they couldn't watch his every step or check up on where he slept each night, the only way to solve the problem was to remove him from the institute altogether, but they lacked the courage to take such a firm stand because the padre was quarrelsome and devious and had extraordinary power.

When I returned to the institute I decided, "I'll save my vocation, no matter what it costs me. The important thing is for me to be a nun." One day everyone went out to Mass because the padre wasn't officiating, so I stayed behind. I waited till the others had left, then went to the padre. I said, "Do you really want me to be a nun?"

"Yes," he said.

"Then I must ask you to stay away from me. If there's any good left in you, please do this for my sake."

At that time the institute was getting ready to open a new house outside Havana. Everybody knew that the Superior would be assigned to go there, and we all thought Aleja, the padre's favorite, was going too. Nobody thought I'd be among those chosen, because the padre had always said I wasn't good enough for anything like that. But that day I asked him, "If you want to save me, let me go to the new parish."

"I'll keep you in mind," he said. That was the one and only time I saw him look sincerely repentant, even guilty, like someone who had broken a glass object. His eyes almost filled with tears. It was a moment of truth. I felt there was a chance he'd let me go, and that would be my salvation.

A few days later, at dinnertime, he announced, "I'm going to read the names of those assigned to the new parish." My name wasn't on the list! What noise, what gaiety! Everybody congratulated those who were going. I was so bitterly disappointed, I began to cry right there at the table.

He explained to me privately that for the first time he was trusting me with something important. "I've made you the Superior of the new house in Havana," he said.

"I don't want to be the Superior. I only want to get away from you, and that means leaving Havana."

"I couldn't send you. You'd never make it there, you're not good enough. Not with all those complexes."

What a lie! I knew I'd be good enough. What could be simpler than working among country people?

Later the padre called me into his office. "I guess you've been assigned to the new parish after all," he said. "The Havana job is too big for you. You couldn't possibly handle it."

I told him, "I know you're deliberately humiliating me, but I don't care. I want to leave this place."

Because I had tried so hard to do well in my studies, I'd surpassed the other girls and was one of the first to make my vows and be consecrated. I was to take my vows on June 13, and on the same day we were to go to the new parish. I wanted to purify myself, because a nun can't take her vows until her religious formation is complete. Wonderful religious formation *I* was getting! But now I was going away. I'd make a clean break with the padre. It was marvelous; I felt like the girl I had been when I first entered the institute.

How full of illusions I was. When I went to the padre's office to get our final orders, he made a play for me. The very day after taking my vows, we made love once more. What a terrible blow! I was so sad, so very sad. I took a sheet of paper and wrote to him: "I've failed again. Why does this have to happen to me? I can't keep on this way or I'll go crazy. Why don't you help me? You know that all you have to do is look at me in a certain way and I fall in love with you all over again."

That night the padre sent me word from his parish that I was to stay up till he came because he had to talk to me. He was in a rage. He blamed me because Aleja had read my note. He told me that once again I'd acted like a stupid fool. He used terrible words, dirty words, even calling me shit-eater. It was the worst scolding he'd ever given me, but thank God, he didn't hit me again.

"Haven't I told you, time and again, not to leave your conscience reports on my table?"

"Very well, so you have," I admitted. "But the one who deserves a scolding is the one who reads them. And let me tell you, that's the last conscience report you'll get from me."

So ended my intimacy with the padre.

The time I spent in the rural parish was the most wonderful period of my religious life, the beginning of my salvation. My dream had always been to do the kind of work we did there. I was among simple country people and they loved me. I felt free to open my heart and speak without fear.

The parish was made up of one church in town, two churches in sugar-mill settlements, and another church in a village. Asunción was the Superior and she and I were the only nuns there. We tended the church, gave talks about religion, made house visits—everything except say Mass, which was done by the priest, of course.

The government had taken over the church house in 1961, and during the first eight months Sister Asunción and I lived and ate our meals at the bishopric of the nearest city. We went to see the official in charge of church matters, and he promised we'd get the house back, but we never did. We were well looked after at the bishopric; we didn't have to stand in line to buy food but simply turned over our ration books to the cook and he bought the food. We had no complaints, though I would have preferred to live within the parish itself.

Once a month we went back to the institute in Havana. There the padre talked to Asunción and never said a word to me. He didn't even receive me in his office, though I was in charge of writing up the reports on our apostolic work. Instead he always sent back a list of the errors he found in them.

At the bishopric each morning, Asunción and I studied religion, sociology, and a smattering of psychology. Then we planned our work for the day, and at 2:00 in the afternoon we took the bus to the country, where we visited families in their homes.

We found a marvelous girl who introduced us to the Catholic families. It was forbidden to make visits for purposes of religious propaganda, so we were very careful not to go to people who might create problems for the Church. We didn't talk about religion at first but waited until the people spontaneously opened up to us. Our purpose was not to invite them to church, but simply to make friends.

I began to understand the mentality of village people. They were hardworking and conscientious, but they lived merely to eat, sleep, and have children. They were very family-centered and the father was looked upon with extraordinary respect. They were apathetic as a community, so we had to work really hard to interest them in church functions. According to the priest, not one of the local political leaders came from a village or small town.

The villagers were very unsophisticated. They followed city fashions but carried them to extremes. If miniskirts were in fashion, country girls would wear them a couple of inches shorter; when fishnet stockings came in, the village girls would knit them in black to make them more conspicuous. They considered a walk in the park at night an outing. If we asked people to go to church on Sunday afternoon, they'd say, "No, we can't miss our walk. How are we going to get married if we don't go to the park?" That's all they lived for.

They go to school more than they used to. Most of the girls go as far as secondary school, but they still marry at the age of fourteen or fifteen. When a girl marries, she leaves her job, if she has one, and stops going to church, to the movies, and for walks in the park.

Practically nobody in the country gets married in church, but during the two years I was there we had fourteen church weddings. Of course, those who got married in church did so mainly to put on a big show. We eliminated all that—the wedding march, the maids of honor . . . the excessive display. We even went so far as to have the bride wear a short dress and no veil. A church wedding was a religious commitment, not a fiesta.

The Cuban people baptize their children, but mainly out of ignorance. In the countryside they say baptism "takes the Jew out of a child." It's a common superstition. Sometimes when a child is naughty they'll say, "He's like that because he's unbaptized." They practice mass baptism, and those children hardly ever see the inside of a church again.

The Church realizes we're baptizing those children purely as a matter of form; in all probability they'll grow up to be communists. But there are cases where communists, even members of the militia, have accepted invitations to be godparents to please a friend and to have a *compadre*,[22] which shows how deep-seated the custom is.

For a Catholic, baptism is only a first step toward leading a Christian life. If the parents don't look at it that way, what's the point of baptizing the child? So one of the things the Church is considering today is the elimination of mass baptisms, and instead, giving better religious instruction to parents. As we can no longer approach people directly, parents

22. *Comadre* and *compadre* are terms used by a child's parents and godparents in addressing or referring to each other.

who come to baptize their children are asked if they're willing to "form a Christian." If so, they're promptly offered a course in religious instruction.

At first, people in the parish called us socialist nuns. For one thing, we didn't wear a habit; for another, we tried to clear away all sorts of irrelevant details. Many Catholics keep seventeen thousand saints' images in their homes and don't believe in any of them. They keep them because they were gifts. They adopt a saint as an intermediary to God—some even begin to think of their saints as God—but we tried to persuade the villagers to give up the saints and we took down the images in the country churches. People complained we were turning into Protestants, but we explained that Christ should be the center of a Christian's life and that Christianity and its principles must be lived.

Everybody is surprised that we never had any difficulties with the government. In other towns catechizers were jailed for teaching or making home visits but nothing like that ever happened to us, probably because we were so restrained. We'd planned to set up catechism centers in several homes but the government forbade it, so we held classes only in church.

A Social Circle[23] was next door to one of the churches in the parish, and whenever we gave a talk or held a meeting, the young people would turn the radio on full blast so we couldn't hear ourselves. There was never anything like a direct confrontation, though. The only time we had to talk to government officials face to face was when a young fellow—they say he was drunk—went into the bell loft and rang the bells. They asked us to testify at the police station, but there was no hostility against us.

I can't say that the number of churchgoers in the parish increased as a result of our work, but at least we created a more positive outlook both among Christians and the rest of the community. My two years there passed quickly and happily. In 1965 they again made Asunción the Superior of the institute in Havana, and I was promoted to Superior of our parish house. Asunción and I had planned the work for the next two or three years, so everything was organized before she left.

I don't know why it was, but soon after that I developed a fear of the solitude of life in the country. I became very nervous and got a gallbladder infection. I lost 30 pounds and after six months had to come back to Havana, where they made me Superior of another large house set up for apostolic work.

My new appointment was a mark of achievement, but it brought on an acute spiritual conflict. I was afraid of my new responsibilities. Besides directing five sisters, I was put in charge of missionary activities in sev-

23. An organized community recreation center.

eral districts in Havana and had to attend to all our publications. We published two monthly reviews, one for priests and the other for laymen, several thousand copies of which were to be sold all over the island. Frankly, I didn't feel qualified for all that work.

I'd been terribly worried about returning to Havana. In the country I had become a real person. I was really appreciated there and was chosen for all kinds of work, but as soon as I returned to Havana my torment returned. I thought, "Now I'll fall into sin again."

But by that time Padre Torres's past was catching up with him, and he was busy trying to beat an orderly retreat. It seems the Church was keeping an eye on him at long last. He had smashed his car, been ticketed for speeding and running a red light, and as a result the Church stripped him of all his posts except the one at the institute.

Shortly after I returned to Havana he left Cuba for Venezuela on a temporary leave, but I believe he never intended to come back. He had no further connection with the institute as far as the church hierarchy was concerned, but to the sisters he was still director. He'd send scolding letters from Venezuela and in his devious way even interfered in the running of the institute.

One day the institute government council, of which I was a member, met to discuss the dismissal of a girl because of her obvious lack of vocation. The council unanimously decided to dismiss her and wrote to the padre, informing him of the decision. The day he received the letter he phoned me long-distance from Venezuela: "That girl must be recalled to the institute immediately!" he said.

"But how can she return when she doesn't meet the requirements?" I asked him.

"She must be reinstated, and that's that!"

I slammed the phone down. Then I sent him a letter. "What can be the reason for your great interest in this girl staying?" I wrote. "Can it be that she had the same painful experience some of us have had?" When he received my letter he phoned again, ordering that I be demoted. I was no longer to be Superior because I'd been disrespectful to him! It was a long struggle but finally the institute broke with him. We asked the sisters to stop writing to him and that ended his power over us.

I didn't realize it at the time, but the strain of the past few years was beginning to show. I was so depressed I couldn't carry out my duties. I didn't study or work. I've always walked with a slight shuffle but I began dragging my feet as if I had neither the desire nor the energy to go anywhere. I was sure I'd never get ahead anyway and I was desperate to leave the institute. I didn't pray—I couldn't. In chapel I'd fall asleep! I lacked the will to live. My lethargy was setting a very bad example for the other sisters. The only thing I felt like doing was going to the movies. I never thought of suicide: I'm too much of a coward.

The Superior, knowing that some of us had been emotionally battered by the padre, went to see a Catholic psychiatrist on our behalf. She told him that we had problems and would like to see him. The institute offered to pay for the treatment. I was the first to go. If Padre Torres had still been there I'd never have done it, nor would he have allowed it. Many times I had asked for permission to see a psychiatrist, but he had told me that would be an act of treason on my part. Now, with the monster out of the way, I was free to go.

The psychiatrist was an outstanding man. The very first time I saw him, I explained to him frankly what had happened to me. He heard me out, then said, "Come back next week for an amytol injection."

Under the influence of amytol I wrote 145 pages, putting down whatever came to mind—it all came out bad, completely negative. I didn't mention one good thing, only what had hurt me—my unhappy childhood, problems with *papá* and *mamá,* my relationship with my brothers and sister, the troubles I had getting an education, the blows, punishments, and scoldings I had suffered, my pain when Emilio Aguero died, and finally, my whole problem with the padre, and my shame and remorse at having betrayed Christ.

The psychiatrist told me that even a hasty reading showed I was suffering a deep depression. He said I needed electroshock treatments before I'd be ready for psychotherapy. It took him a month to persuade me to submit to them, and I begged the Superior to accompany me.

When I went for a shock treatment, a male nurse gave me a shot of anaesthetic so I wouldn't feel anything. In spite of that I was terrified. I never missed a treatment, though. That's the way I am. When I have to do something, I do it.

What frightened me most was losing consciousness. I dreamed a lot about death and one day I told the psychiatrist, "I'm much better, Doctor, but when I go to bed I'm overcome by a fear of death."

He explained, "Your fear of death is an expression of your fear of losing your self-control, which is what brought on this hurtful situation. Your fear of anaesthesia comes from the same source." He said it may have had some root in my childhood, but what specifically brought it on was the fact that I lost control with the padre. That fear is so great I still don't even take sedatives for a headache.

I was in treatment for a year and a half. At first I went weekly, then every fifteen days, and finally once a month. I didn't tell anybody about it because some people don't understand such things. Later on, I did tell the nuns and they all commented, "But Gracia, I never would have imagined you needed electric shocks!"

I did need them though, and it's because of them that I started to live again. I realized I was mistaken to have renounced so much to become a nun. I hadn't been able to consecrate my life to religion because there was still too much that was human in me—my complexes, my conflicts, and my weakness for a man who knew my defects. If the institute had given applicants a test, as they later did, to determine their psychological fitness for the life there, they might not have admitted me at all.

The Church wanted to send the institute another priest as director, but we were dead set against having another man on the premises, so the Church left us alone, to see what would happen. I realize now what a grave mistake that was on our part. We did the best we could, but we had been hurt, our religious growth had been stunted, and alone we couldn't survive. We had no clear idea of what was involved in the religious life. Our concepts of poverty, chastity, and obedience were equivocal, and our religious formation was essentially negative. Finally, we came to understand that the Church, with its centuries-old wisdom, wanted to prove to us that we couldn't go ahead without a priest.

Facing reality, the Superior consulted the rest of us about the desirability of dissolving the institute. "We've been the instruments of a madman," she said. "Perhaps some of us are able to go on but others are not. Each of you knows which is your own case. As for me, I propose that we dissolve the institute." The council voted unanimously in favor of her motion.

Our vows were not meant to be binding forever, but only for a length of time determined by the institute. That was one of the great advantages of that kind of secular institute. Under the old rules, if we'd wanted to leave the Order we'd have had to request a release from the Pope himself. Now every year we could simply renew our vows; those who didn't wish to were free to go.

We officially dissolved the institute; it was the best thing to do. If those who still had the calling wanted to found a similar organization in Cuba or elsewhere, they were free to do so. But all the sisters were at loose ends. A group of them went to see the papal representative and asked him to get them special permission to leave Cuba immediately. If they left through the usual channels it would entail a wait of two years, and what would they do during that time? They didn't even have a place to stay. Apparently the papal representative in Cuba had very good relations with the government, and within two months he was able to get those girls a special permit to leave. Call it public relations, propaganda, or what you will, it was essentially a good thing the government did.

One of the conditions for our having been admitted to the institute was the promise not to leave the country. It had been our aim to give our testimony for Christ right here in the new Cuba. But being freed, the girls left; some went to Spain, some to the United States.

SEÑOR RIVERA:
    It was Digna who phoned to tell me that Gracia had quit the convent.

That was the happiest day of my life. I almost felt like crying. If they were to tell me that Gracia was to be married, it wouldn't make me so happy.

I've never trusted nuns, and I've hated priests and the Church ever since I was a boy of fourteen, when I used to deliver meat to a certain house every morning, and I'd see the parish priest sitting on a bed with a young lady. Since then I've had nothing to do with the Church. Now I hope to see the day when Gracia will say to me, "*Pipo,* you were right about priests and nuns."

And I'm right about the Revolution, too.

Chapter Seven

Back to the Family

GRACIA:

While I was away I'd almost lost touch with my family, but during the last three years of my life as a nun, my sister Aurora came to see me every Sunday—visiting day—and from what she told me, I couldn't escape the fact that my entering the institute had caused my family economic hardship. When I lived at home I'd given *mamá* my whole monthly salary, 126 *pesos,* and after joining the institute I gave her only 80. In 1963 I had to reduce my contribution further because the institute forced me to quit my job at the library and gave me only 50 *pesos* for my family.

When I was transferred to the country parish, the institute told me I could no longer send money home because my sister was old enough to work for a living. As if Aura had been idle all that time! That brought on a crisis in my religious vocation. I had entered the institute with the understanding that I'd be allowed to continue helping my family— otherwise I'd never have become a nun—and I was hurt by the way they tried to wean me away from them. I wanted my independence, but I also had a sense of responsibility. In spite of my protests, my family was deprived of my aid. Now and then I'd get 5 or 10 *pesos* as a gift, and with the permission of my Superior I'd send it to *mamá.*

That period was especially hard for *mamá* because my brother Diego was saving for his marriage and gave her only half his wages. Later, when he got married, he sent her a mere 13.50 *pesos* a month. With all those time payments to make, it wasn't easy for *mamá.* Luckily the only large expense we had during that time was her set of false teeth, for which she borrowed 45 *pesos.* When that was paid off, she borrowed 75 *pesos* from Uncle Modesto to repair the TV set. Once *papá* gave her 400 *pesos* to keep for him, telling her to use what she needed and to pay him back later, but *mamá* never paid back 1 *centavo* of it.

Aura tried to earn money by stringing beads and making artificial flowers at home. The beads came from rosaries given us by the nuns of

San Pedro when they left Cuba. Both *mamá* and Aura sewed for friends
and neighbors, but unfortunately they allowed the customers to set their
own prices and earned very little. For a while Aura gave haircuts to
women prisoners who were being rehabilitated, but dropped out because she was afraid of the place. She earned a little extra money giving
permanents to friends in the neighborhood, but it was becoming difficult for a free-lancer to obtain hairdressing products and she couldn't
continue. At the end of 1963, during the holiday months, Aura got a
temporary job as a salesgirl. Then she and *mamá* began to wash and iron
for the neighbors, earning 15 or 20 *pesos* a month.

I thought Aura should be learning something so I encouraged her to
take basic secondary-school courses at night. It cost only 7 or 8 *pesos* a
year for textbooks and notebooks, but with bus fare and snacks it was
one more strain on the family income.

At that time my youngest brother also began to study the basic
secondary-school course, which meant added expense. One day when I
went home for a visit, Gabi called me aside and told me a secret: *mamá*
gave him 20 *centavos* for the bus almost every day, and he'd managed to
save some of it by using discarded transfers or by sneaking on the bus
through the back door. He was keeping the coins he saved and was
planning to give them to *mamá* at the end of the month. I felt shocked
and guilty about the whole thing.

At about that time my sister began to work as a teacher while still going
to school herself. She taught one course at several Workers' Education
Schools.[24] After a few months she was teaching at four different schools,
earning a total of 100 *pesos* a month. With my sister's steady income, the
family's economic situation improved somewhat.

By the end of the 1965–66 school year, my sister had a sweetheart and
quit teaching. She began to knit sweaters, which were just then coming
into fashion, and earned from 60 to 70 *pesos* a month. Then Diego had a
fight with his in-laws and he and his wife moved in, giving *mamá* 50 *pesos*
a month for expenses. They lived together for about nine months, until
they quarreled with *mamá* and left.

I continued to worry about my family, and when I was appointed
Superior of the house in Havana in 1966, I got my sister a job at 50 *pesos*

24. *Educación Obrera-Campesina* (EOC), or Worker-Peasant Education, offered three
courses of study: grades one through three; grades four through six; and secondary school
(equivalent to the first year of basic secondary). Classes were held in factories, farms, and
offices, usually in the evenings. Graduates of the secondary program were eligible for
vocational schools or for the Worker-Peasant university-preparatory program. Due to the
rapid expansion of the educational system and the consequent shortage of trained personnel, most of the teachers in the EOC's primary grades were, like Gracia's sister, not professionals. (*Cuba: El Movimiento Educativo, 1967–68* (Havana: Ministry of Education, 1968),
pp. 15, 102–3. Also see Nelson P. Valdés, "The Radical Transformation of Cuban Education," in Bonachea and Valdés, eds., *Cuba in Revolution*, pp. 429–31.)

a month in the archbishop's office, where we worked on our little publication.

When Gabriel was fifteen he received a scholarship to study chemical engineering and explosives at a military school. He was given 7 *pesos* pocket money, out of which he'd give *mamá* 2 *pesos* every two weeks. As part of his training, Gabi was sent to the Isle of Pines to work on land clearance and the construction of a reservoir. He was away twenty days a month, but *mamá* kept his ration book and was able to buy more food.[25]

That same year my sister got married, and she and her husband stayed in *mamá*'s apartment for three or four months. Aura's husband had a job and contributed 50 *pesos* for expenses, until they too quarreled with *mamá* and moved out. With only herself to support, *mamá* got along on what she earned taking in laundry.

I returned home to live with *mamá* in the summer of 1969, happy to be reunited with her. My sister and my older brother were both living in their own apartments and were estranged from *mamá*. On Mother's Day I was able to reunite them, and *mamá* was very happy to have all her children around her again.

We were on better terms with *papá* too. He had stopped drinking and had a steady job at MINED. Sometimes, when I went to the Ministry on institute business, I'd see him there, and I visited him at his home, too. He was living with a woman named Araceli and appeared to be contented with her. Now that I'm home again, *papá* phones us every day to see how we are.

SEÑOR RIVERA:

After I separated from Digna I had a thousand women, one after another, like a mule looking for new pastures. Araceli was the only one who manged to settle me down and give me a home. I've been living with her for six or seven years now.

Araceli is good to me in the very ways that Digna failed me. When I first met Araceli I still had occasional bouts of drinking. One day I said to her, "Gosh, I really feel like a beer!" Without a word she grabbed a shopping basket and came back lugging a case of twenty-four cans of beer!

After a while I drank less, and now I hardly drink at all. True, there's no drink to be had, but it seems to me that I finally quit drinking because Araceli never tried to dominate me and prevent me from doing it. Digna had tried a million ways and none of them worked.

25. Children and adults who regularly ate meals away from home, whether at boarding schools, work centers, or work camps, remained registered in the family ration book, and their rations could be purchased in their absence for use at home. Thus a large number of families received full rations for household members who ate only one or two meals at home each day and, in some cases, for those who ate only a few meals per month at home.

Araceli pleases me in every way and gives me the kind of affection I never had in my first marriage. Her family makes a fuss over me too. When we visited my in-laws, Araceli's *mamá* came running to meet us with all her other children behind her, kicking up a cloud of dust.

The old lady hugged me and from the moment we arrived we were feasted and fussed over. Her old man said, "Let's butcher a pig" and then stuffed cigarettes in my pockets, while every five minutes her *mamá* said, "Give Moisitos another cup of coffee." That night we were given the best bed, the best sheets, and the best mosquito net in the house.

Araceli will do anything for me. If anyone deserves my love it's that woman, but I'm a monster to her. When I can afford to take her to eat in a restaurant I do, but when I have a chance to take another woman, I take her instead. In the past, whenever I've made a pass at a woman and she's been willing, I've gone to bed with her. As long as I'm capable I'll go on having women, because where the ox falls, there I beat him.

In a way, I'm simply playing it safe by having a lot of women. Araceli is much younger than I and one day she may find herself another man. I don't think I'll be the one to leave her; after all, she bore me a son.

Another reason I wouldn't leave her is that she has very bad asthma and can get an attack any time. One day I came home and found her on the floor, hardly able to breathe. I had to take her to the hospital.

Araceli is an honest woman and a homebody, not the kind who's always wanting to go to fiestas. She works hard to please me and I love her. It took me a long time, but I've finally found the affection I've needed. Digna never showed such love for me; even so, I can't feel for Araceli the love I felt for my first wife.

Gracia:

Thanks to my years at the institute, I'm no longer afraid of *mamá,* nor does she try to exert so much authority over me. "You're a woman of twenty-seven," she says, "and far be it from me to tell you what to do. After all, if you could spend seven years away from home why shouldn't you keep on doing as you please? Why should I count for anything with you?" But she really still treats me like a child.

For the first few months after my return home, we got along very well. I tried to be the very soul of peace and always showed a smiling face. *Mamá* tried hard too. She tried to understand me and gave me lots of advice. At first I was very helpful around the house, washing my own clothes and getting up early on Saturdays to clean—all those habits I'd acquired at the institute. Pretty soon, though, *mamá* got me accustomed to my comfortable old way of life again. She does all the housework and cleans so thoroughly during the week that there's nothing for me to do except the cooking. Usually I prepare our dinner because I like to cook; besides, *mamá* says I have the knack of making a tasty dish out of thin air. With food as scarce as it is, you have to use your imagination to stretch it. Give *mamá* a few eggs and she'll fry them, but I hard-boil them and dress them up with cream sauce to give some variety to our menus.

Through my old boss at the library, I got a job typing for people in the University. When I come home from work *mamá* talks with me as I eat dinner in the parlor. Afterward I study while she knits and sews. It's good to be home, and just to see *mamá* happy makes me glad.

The only problem, at least for me, is our lack of privacy. A young girl in the building usually stops in each day to gossip, then there's another neighbor who's always in and out of our house. That's not so bad, but because we have a telephone the neighbors receive calls there, and then they stay and chat, making it a public place.

The neighbors insist on talking to me because I was away for so long, and I just can't say, "Excuse me, I'm going to the bedroom to read." I accept the situation, but I escape sometimes and spend the night at my friend Elisa's house. That upsets *mamá* and then I get upset too.

Things were more difficult when my sister came to stay with us. She was far along in her pregnancy and the doctor advised her not to walk up the long flights of stairs in her building. Everything went well at first; Aura is very industrious and sewed several dresses for me, fixed up the house with the curtains and tablecloths I'd been given when the institute broke up, and helped *mamá* do the housework. I came to feel very close to Aura. She and *mamá* and I gathered in the parlor at night to talk as we used to, but my sister has many friends and the house filled up more than ever at night.

It was even worse when my sister's husband, Felipe, arrived on the scene. He's very antisocial, and when the house was full of people he'd pass through without so much as a good evening. He disliked having neighbors use our phone and would stick his head into the hall and scream out their messages. He often yelled at Aura to show what a he-man he was, and because he didn't want the baby.

I used to think I could help civilize Felipe or at least polish him up a bit, so I'd jokingly point out his defects, especially criticizing his attitude toward the Revolution. He's a reactionary and doesn't want to work for the government, because he sees nothing but its faults. But the real reason he complains is just the scarcity of food and clothes. I was bored to death at the endless arguments between him and a revolutionary friend of his. I'd be in such a state of angry tension I couldn't read, much less study.

Naturally my brother-in-law didn't feel at home with us, although we did our best to avoid problems. He's a strange guy, very contradictory.

He has some noble sentiments, but he had an unhappy childhood and is very bitter. He thinks people are no good and that everybody has it in for him. To avoid arguments I tried to stay away from home as much as possible. And at last Aura returned home with her husband and baby daughter.

I thought my life would go back to normal, but it hasn't been that way at all. Lately everything *mamá* does annoys me. When we go out to dinner or to the theater she embarrasses me without intending to and manages to stir up all my complexes. For instance, she doesn't know how to behave in good company; in the restaurant she sits with her arms folded across her stomach. I can't just say to her, "Don't fold your arms like that, *mamá*; it isn't done." I wouldn't hurt her feelings for the world, but at the time I wish the earth would open up and swallow me. It's sheer torture for me. Without Aura and Gabi, to whom I could confide my deepest thoughts, I feel more and more alienated from *mamá*. She's never really forgiven me for having left her. It hurts to realize that my religious vocation has opened a chasm between us that can never be healed. Only God can smooth things out between us.

My brother Gabi graduated from school and began working the same month I returned home from the institute. He earns 118 *pesos* a month, plus 60 *pesos* for expenses because he works out in the country. He also receives a rent-free place to stay wherever he's sent, and when he returns to the city on a pass, he's given twenty certificates worth 3 *pesos* each to buy his meals. Gabi comes home on a pass on the 21st of each month and then he always gives *mamá* 100 *pesos* for household expenses. He also gives my sister 10 *pesos*.

I earn 100 *pesos* a month working four hours a day; in the afternoons I go to school to study French. I give *mamá* 60 *pesos* a month, save some, and keep the rest for my expenses, such as bus fare, snacks, movies, etc. I started my savings with 600 *pesos* the institute gave me when it was dissolved, and now I have about 800 in a box I keep at home. I'm saving up to buy a refrigerator. Gabi is saving money too; he says he has 60 *pesos* but he doesn't know what to spend them on. As for me, if I get a chance to buy something, I buy it; if I get a turn to eat, I take it; and if I get a chance to take a trip, I accept it.

The combined monthly income from both our jobs is 278 *pesos*, but our regular expenses don't amount to much. We've been living in the same place for ten years and we no longer have to pay rent. We've owned the apartment since October, 1969. We don't make installment payments either because everything we bought on credit was paid for years ago. We spend 5 to 6 *pesos* for electricity because of the extra current used by the electric hot plate and sewing machine. Our telephone bill is about 6 *pesos*, but it will increase to 8 or 9 *pesos* because my brother has started to call home every month.

Other expenditures include those for repairs. It cost 95 *pesos* to have our record player fixed. I asked a friend who still takes on private jobs. But our TV set has been out of order for the past two years and I haven't been able to find a mechanic who will fix it. We sent the set to the *consolidado* twice and each time it worked for about a month. Now the waiting list at the *consolidado* is so long I can't get a turn for two or three years. Anyway, a friend told me the *consolidado* isn't fixing TVs any more because it's out of spare parts. I also hired a plumber who charged me 30 *pesos* for labor and parts to fix our toilet, and another man who does private jobs to fix our spring mattress. He charged 75 *pesos* but now it's like new.

Anything anyone is willing to sell me for about 15 or 20 *pesos* I buy, whether for myself, for *mamá*, or for my brother. I recently bought a pair of long pants for 30 *pesos;* a belt and a pair of gold-colored earrings for 45; a pair of dressy sandals for 30; a pair of dressy shoes for 15; three pairs of everyday sandals for 45; and three pairs of arts-and-crafts earrings made by private individuals for 25.

Other personal expenditures include a trip to Cruces that cost 39 *pesos*, and a weekend at the beach where I spent 30-odd *pesos* for food. Some friends paid the rent on a beach house as a gift. My other expenses are carfare and going to the theater, sometimes with my friends or with *mamá*. When I'm the one who first hears about a new show, I invite the others and pay for everybody's tickets. I do that at least once or twice a month. I spend a total of about 5 *pesos*. I also indulge myself in a meal at La Cocinita at least once every two weeks. I always invite my friend Elisa along because until recently she didn't have a job. Whenever I go to La Cocinita I buy something to take home and cook, to vary our meals a little, so it usually costs about 4 *pesos* altogether.

As far as food goes, we were better off before the Revolution. During the times when *papá* was unemployed and we didn't have 1 *kilo* of income, it was always possible to get something to eat. We'd borrow one day, sell something the next, anything to survive. Nowadays we're given a fixed quota of food that is simply too little.

Fortunately, under the plan for workers in dangerous vocations, my kid brother, who works with dynamite, receives a lot of extra food. Every twenty days Gabi brings home fifteen cans of milk, 5 pounds of spiced ham, and five boxes of codfish. Ham and codfish are not usually available. Of course our family helps my sister and she helps us. During her pregnancy we gave her my meat ration and a piece of a 2-pound slab of bacon we received from a lady who had slaughtered a hog. In exchange we gave the woman half a yard of cloth. When we're running out of rice my sister gives us some, so we all manage one way or another.

Recently I started eating lunch at work, so now *mamá* just makes a snack for herself at noon and saves the best food to share at supper. Sometimes when I eat dinner in a restaurant, *mamá* warms over my dinner for her lunch the next day. I don't go to fancy places; most of the time I'll stand in line for an hour or more to get a measly hot dog at a snack bar.

Actually nobody is starving. People buy on the black market or barter coffee or rice for milk or something else. Some go to the country and exchange clothing for beans or tubers. Neighbors help one another; ours give us things in exchange for the use of our telephone. *Mamá* is able to get at least fifteen or twenty extra eggs a month from a neighbor who is often away in the Army, and from another who has eight children. Sometimes *mamá* gives her coffee, though this isn't a regular arrangement.

At our home none of us smokes, and we have a neighbor who does. Every fifteen days when we each get our ration of two packs of *suaves*,[26] we exchange them for our neighbor's 3 ounces of coffee. Another neighbor has planted leeks, wild hot peppers, and garlic, and twice a week she gives us some.

Although nobody starves here in Cuba, hunger is the state's worst enemy. I'm sure the only reason there hasn't been a counterrevolution is because you can be clapped into jail for anything. The people aren't happy with the present state of affairs. How can they be? They're hungry! Most families eat only one big meal a day, and they don't have enough education to appreciate the government's efforts to solve this problem. They're still pulling in their belts, so they feel betrayed. They didn't fight in the Revolution for ideals; they were simply hoping to find a way out of their misery. The government doesn't know how to win back the people's confidence. For instance, it has forbidden any kind of celebration this Christmas Eve.[27] If the masses want to eat roast pork at that time, the government should let them eat roast pork and keep them happy. That's mass psychology, no?

Perhaps one basic error of our government was to shut itself off so completely from the United States. Of course the United States shut *us* off when it saw Cuba turning slightly pink. As long as we're blockaded and there's a scarcity of American dollars, we'll have to go on being hungry, because what money do we have for trade? I don't know what help Russia or any other country is giving us, but as I see it, when two great powers fight, it's the small countries that suffer. Cuba is suffering because it's caught up in the cold war between America and Russia. Vietnam suffers even more.

My only hope for Cuba is the rumor that at high government levels we're trying to get on better terms with the United States. A policy of peaceful coexistence could help us. But the United States does such

---

26. Mild cigarettes, popular in Cuba and less available than *fuertes*, strong ones.

27. Celebration of Christmas, 1969, was officially deferred to July, 1970, at which time it was expected that the harvest goal of 10 million tons of sugar would be achieved.

foolish things. Imagine, sending that capitalist Rockefeller to Latin America! His very name is enough to set the people against him.

Another thing I find very wrong here is that there haven't been any elections.[28] Without them what we have is a form of dictatorship. Of course I wouldn't go back to the horrible fake elections we had before. Poor people had no faith in those elections, and the middle class just didn't care because they were more or less well off. They thought, "I'll look after myself and the devil take the hindmost." The great problem of mankind is this kind of selfishness.

During Batista's regime a great deal was made of the fact that there was no freedom of the press, but we still don't have it, nor do we have freedom of speech here, or a chance to learn how other people think. The government permits only the communist dogma; the state is the center of everything.

Of course, there are good things the Revolution is doing. Among my own neighbors there are many who have improved their situation, although often they're the worst complainers. One old couple has eight children. They're country people and have had a hard life. One of their sons, who was only eight when we met them, used to shine shoes and would still be a bootblack under the capitalist system. Now, at eighteen, he's a high school graduate and in the Army. Naturally he's an ardent revolutionary. Another son is a sergeant, another a lieutenant, and both are studying to rise even higher. The daughter worked as a housemaid from the time she was a mere child, but now she's studying to be a nurse. The whole family dresses better and is trying to improve the atmosphere in their building by stopping the quarreling that goes on in the hall, something they'd never have bothered to do if there had been no Revolution.

My own relatives are better off than before. Most of my uncles and cousins who used to sell stuff from a pushcart now have steady jobs. Modesto sold flowers in the street; now he works at the Hotel Nacional and is well off, though he's not integrated in the Revolution. Uncle Rolando, who used to sell newspapers in front of a shoe store, got a job in that very same store and now has risen to become head of the warehouse there. And both his children have scholarships. No wonder he loves the Revolution!

28. Cuba's first elections in fifteen years were held in Matanzas Province in 1974, as the preliminary stage in implementing *Poder Popular* (People's Power), a new system of administrative-legislative assemblies. (See Inocencia, n. 51, for a description of the earlier system.) All citizens sixteen years and older, with the exception of prisoners, applicants for emigration, and candidates in the 1958 elections, were eligible to vote. One candidate for the post of delegate to district-level representative assemblies was nominated in meetings held in each base areas or neighborhood of an electoral district. In Matanzas, 1,079 delegates were elected by secret ballot from among 4,712 candidates. (*Cuba Review*, Dec., 1974, pp. 10–15.) Before *Poder Popular* was instituted on a national basis in 1976, the island was divided into new politico-administrative units. See *Granma Weekly Review*, Nov. 14, 1976, p. 6.

The best example of a changed life is that of Tina, *papá*'s crippled half-sister. Before the Revolution Tina was practically a homeless beggar, scrounging a meal from one relative or another, turned against even by her own mother. After the Revolution Aunt Tina was still a housemaid, but she got a job with a revolutionary family who treated her very well. Instead of working for room and board and hand-me-down clothes, she was just like any state employee, and she worked only from 7:00 A.M. to 3:00 P.M. Tina looked very happy while she was with them. She felt that finally justice had been done to her.

Then, a few months ago, at the age of fifty-seven, Tina got married to a fisherman. He earns good wages so he wouldn't allow his wife to work. Tina admits she's better off than ever before, and if she doesn't like the Revolution I'm sure it's because no one has ever taken the trouble to explain it to her.

My mother's cousin Raúl is the most revolutionary member of my family. I haven't seen him in years but someone told me, "Raúl has aged a lot. He's burned out by the tremendous effort he's been making for the Revolution." Quite possibly Raúl earned more as a waiter before the Revolution than he earns now as an electrical engineer in MINCON,[29] but the Revolution stimulated him to study.

My cousin Simón is against the Revolution but he's a good kind of *gusano*. He refuses to work for this government, not out of self-interest but because of his ideals. What he rejects is the lack of freedom, which is a real and legitimate objection. Simón is highly intelligent, but he's a rebel without a cause. He's so pro-American he tries to explain away the bombing of Hiroshima. He'll calmly insist that radioactivity is harmless. He spends his days shut up in his house and doesn't make the slightest effort to support his two daughters. I'm afraid he's losing his mind. My Aunt Victoria lives in fear that he'll carry out his threat to hang himself as his *papá* did.

Of all my relatives, the only ones who have left Cuba are my Uncle Gabriel, my Godfather Daniel, and *papá*'s sister Luisa. Aunt Luisa and her husband said they were doing fine under capitalism, so in 1960 they both left for Miami. I've heard that they've gone into drug-trafficking.

In my immediate family we're divided in our attitudes toward the Revolution. At the moment *mamá* is a *gusana* because of the food shortages. But the other day she said, "I can't say I've actually gone hungry these past few years. I've been worse off lots of times before the Revolution." She doesn't have a completely closed mind, and she's the first to admit that the Revolution made it possible for us to live decently and for my kid brother Gabi to study.

It's hard to tell what my sister thinks. Felipe, her husband, does all the

29. *Ministerio de Construcción* (Ministry of Construction).

talking and he's a *gusano*. Before they got married my sister told him, "Don't work for the government if you don't want to, but you'll have to earn a living somehow because I'm not going to marry you unless you can support me." For a while he did a little gardening for foreign families, but recently he's started gardening for the government. He earns about 155 *pesos* a month, so he and my sister are doing quite well.

My brother Diego, who was against the Revolution, is now in favor of it. He had quit school earlier than the rest of us and yet the Revolution inspired him to finish the sixth grade and secondary school. He's now a bus driver. Gabi, of course, is completely integrated. But of us all, the most ardent supporter of the Revolution is my *papá*.

SEÑOR RIVERA:

I, who have always favored the Revolution and hated *gusanos*, had the bad luck to find myself living in the midst of them after I separated from my wife. I was staying with my sister Tina and my brothers Modesto and Rolando and I began to notice some very strange goings-on. There was a lot of whispering around the house and conversations abruptly stopped when I appeared. I praised the Revolution and Fidel and finally Tina kicked me out of the house. Now she's changed her tune and is all for Fidel, and my brother Modesto, who was involved in their conspiracy, has joined the militia.

There are no true counterrevolutionaries or *gusanos* in Cuba anymore. All I see are hordes of *panzistas*, people who think with their bellies. Why, the minute the government gives such men a few beans and a bit of rice, they become more revolutionary than I am. To me a real *gusano* is a man who sets bombs, a man who would have the courage to walk up to Fidel and shoot him. Immediately after the Revolution triumphed, a bomb went off every five minutes. Then Fidel said, "If we catch anyone planting bombs anywhere, I'll tear his head off," and the bombings stopped. Some counterrevolutionaries!

Those *gusanos* forget the miserable poverty in Machado's time. People were starving to death; some even ate the soles of their shoes. I remember how the people in my neighborhood used to live when Prío was in power. Sometimes they didn't get even one meal a day. A man would come into my poultry market and ask for a half-*centavo*'s worth of necks and wings for soup. When I meet those very same people today, they tell me they used to live in luxury. That's just talk, not fact. Well, Cubans have poor memories.

People are not as hungry now as before the Revolution. We may not be living in abundance but we aren't sunk in misery like before. There's enough for everybody if it's distributed right. Every single day Araceli prepares both lunch and supper. I don't know how she manages, but at the very least we have yellow rice, soup, and watercress salad, which is a pretty good meal. We're always short of coffee but Araceli stretches it with burnt sugar. In Batista's time . . . but forget it! It would take too long to tell the things that went on then.

In the old days the country seemed to belong to those who were in power. The people had no freedom, even the elections were rigged, and you could win the Palace for a bottle of cognac. I have proof of that. A guy once came into my market trying to buy my vote. He said, "Hey you, *gallego*,[30] you who like drink so much, do you know what we have here? Two hundred boxes of liquor!"

I told him, "That means nothing to me, brother. I'm not interested," but that's how elections were won then.

Before the Revolution I was mainly interested in having more and better things. And why not? Appearances counted for everything and there was so much envy then. If I got a really good pair of shoes, I'd glory in them, thinking, "I have these fine shoes and so-and-so doesn't." I felt, "If so-and-so has a TV set, why shouldn't I?" I wanted all the things other people had because I didn't want to be inferior. But now I see men who earn a lot more than I, and they don't have TVs either. People aren't interested in acquisitions anymore, so why should I worry?

People complain that there's no freedom of speech in Cuba but that's untrue. Before the Revolution people were arrested just for talking. Nowadays, if they were to arrest people for talking. . . ! Why, you hear the *gusanos* talk everywhere. Those big-mouths say what they damn well please in the grocery store, in front of everybody, but nobody stops them. If only Fidel would promise to tear out the tongue of anyone who spoke against him! Then you wouldn't hear a single complaint in the whole of Cuba, because the *gusanos* are cowards. All they're good for is talk.

People complain we're not free because we have no elections and are under Fidel's dictatorship. But there's more freedom now in every way. And it was Fidel who gave the country back to the people! I feel patriotic for the first time, because now Cuba is *our* country.

I'm fifty and already too old to get the maximum good out of the Revolution. If only I had been twenty when the Revolution triumphed! I'd have stayed in school and gone on to the University. I'd be a lawyer now, or a doctor maybe. I missed out on that. But even if I were to die tomorrow, I'd die content. With each day that passes, I see our children doing better and better. They've all grown up and studied, they can look after themselves now. I see such equality and humaneness in all this. I've always tried to be humanitarian. To me, the Revolution means love of humanity.

---

30. A person from Galicia, Spain; often used in the vernacular to refer to light-skinned people whether or not they are of Spanish descent.

GRACIA:

Analyzing the effect of the Revolution on my life and that of my relatives, my feelings have always been rather ambivalent. The truth is that deep inside I'm grateful to the Revolution. Thanks to it I was able to get a fairly decent job after my parents separated; my brothers were able to study and work; our rent, which had been too high for our income, was reduced; and for the first time in my life I could afford to go to the public beaches near Havana.

On the other hand, I think—selfishly perhaps—that I would also have gotten ahead under any other system. After finishing my secretarial course I would have been able to get a good job, and after my brothers grew up they would have gotten jobs too. Then the whole family would have been able to rise to the place I had always desired on the social scale. I would have been an office worker, as now, but I would have had a house with all the comforts proper to that station in life, such as TV, refrigerator, living-room set, bedroom set, electric or gas stove, sewing machine, electric mixer, and so on. That was what I had always aspired to, although I don't believe I would ever have attained the social position I wanted—to be a member of exclusive clubs like the Yacht Club and Club Casino and such; they would have been too expensive for me. I couldn't have afforded to go to the University either. That's why I say that my feelings about the Revolution are so contradictory.

I liked to study, but at that time I didn't feel the urge to grow as a person or to contribute to scientific and human progress. The urge I now feel—to learn, to study, to help mankind—would never have been born in me without the Revolution. I'd say that my aspiration then was to attain the kind of standard of living North American women have.

I do know, though, that if I had never entered the religious life, I would be completely integrated in the Revolution. In spite of my resistance to excessive communist propaganda, to statements that have been proved to be lies, to the shortages from which I suffer, I'd have been able to know better its really positive factors—above all, what the Revolution had done for the really poor, for the dispossessed.

I especially resent the movement to starve religion out of Cuba by involving people so deeply in this new society's activities that they lack even one moment in which to grow and develop in the knowledge of God. It's practically impossible for them to find the time for religious contemplation. But you see, I might never have perceived all these negative aspects of the Revolution if I hadn't isolated myself from the real life of my country by entering a religious institution and becoming a nun.

Chapter Eight

Bearing Witness

GRACIA:

Recently I've been frightened to find myself leaning more and more toward the Revolution. It seems that the only way I can bear witness to Christianity is by integrating in the Revolution, even though it goes against my religion. I want to do good, to give myself to others. If I have money and someone else needs it, I give it to them. But my friends and the people around me are all busy looking out for themselves. They tell me, "Why do you go around doing so many favors for people? Don't be a fool, give only to those who can give you something in return."

If only I knew some revolutionaries I could look up to, it might help me make up my mind to commit myself to the Revolution. My friend Temilda Álvaro, a fifty-year-old woman with a Ph.D. in chemistry, was an auxiliary member of the institute and knew of my troubles with the padre. I admire Temilda, though she's a bit bourgeois and likes her comfort, always traveling in a car and paying other people to stand in line for her. I don't hold those things against her, because that's what she's been used to all her life. She's a devout practicing Catholic and a counter-revolutionary, but she pointed out to me the good things about the Revolution.

When I was offered my present job typing for university people, I went to her and said, "Ay, Temilda, help me. What shall I do? Do you believe that I, as a Christian, should accept this job working for revolutionaries?"

"Yes, yes, do become fully integrated. You're one of the few who can stay here and bear testimony for Christianity. I was raised in bourgeois circles and I'm too old to adapt myself to new situations, but you can choose one side or the other. Take the plunge, be a revolutionary or be a counterrevolutionary, whichever you prefer, but stop straddling the fence."

I followed her advice and took the job, but I was in conflict about it. I'd stayed in Cuba because I wanted to bear witness here, in this society. In the institute I had felt I was living an easy life, cut off from the people. We talked a lot about doing things but never did them. That was one thing I disliked about it. I wanted to live with the people, to work, to go out to the country and share in the hard times others were having, because then I'd know what made some people revolutionaries and antagonized others. I wanted to find out what was good and what bad about the Revolution, why some people loved religion and some hated it, what were the defects of my religion and what the virtues.

"If I take this job now, pounding a typewriter, I won't be bearing witness. How can I, while I'm holding a bourgeois kind of job and living well?" My friends' example influenced my decision, I know. They all have bourgeois jobs in foreign embassies, and so on. So I stay in my comfortable rut because I don't have the courage to break away. Everybody likes to have nice things to wear, women especially. I don't mind being short of food but I *would* mind not being able to fix myself up nicely. And since my friends are the kind they are, until I break with them I won't be able to do anything else.

Since I plan to stay in Cuba, I wouldn't mind working for the state if I could. I'd feel I'd be working for a system that's trying to elevate the masses and I'd give my best. Even when I worked directly for the state before, I was the first to get to the office and the first to finish my work. My friends tell me there's no point in working so hard. "Just do what's assigned to you and take your pay." But I'm not like that. I can't look upon my work as something outside of me; it's my whole life. The more I give to it, the more satisfied I am because I'm bearing witness to Christianity.

Not so long ago the language professors at my school offered an intensive course lasting six months. I've always wanted to teach, so I said, "I'll take the course and quit the job I have." But then I thought, "After all, I'm learning on my job, too. I'll stay for the time being." I'm always rationalizing. I feel chained to my home and my work and I'm tired. My family discourages me, especially *mamá*, who's a thoroughgoing conformist, incapable of striking out for herself. It's no wonder she seems so dried up and stagnant. Perhaps that's why I can't feel really close to her.

The result of all this is that I don't take the plunge. It isn't that I'm afraid to or that I dislike the idea of taking part in the work; those things don't bother me a bit. No matter what it costs me, I don't care. After all, that's the reason I stayed in Cuba instead of going to Spain or the United States with the rest of the sisters.

Maybe what holds me back is that it's just more comfortable to keep on as I am. It's true that I never went out to work in the country because I couldn't see how that would solve the problem of production. But I don't deny that I also hold back because it's uncomfortable to go to work in the country every Sunday. I don't like to use a latrine instead of a toilet—and sometimes there isn't even a latrine available. I once had to live that way and I hated it. I don't deny that shows a lack of the spirit of sacrifice in me, but I make other sacrifices. Right now I'm working for the Church and have no time I can call my own. I teach the catechism to two different groups and spend up to three hours preparing each class so it will be worthwhile. Otherwise, I'd just have to keep repeating the same things and that would be plain trash.

Another thing that keeps me from plunging in is that somehow I've come to regard revolutionaries as being on a lower level than my own circle of friends. That's the influence of the group on me. They're always saying, "Only the rabble are revolutionaries." I argue a lot with my friends, but to simply reject them would mean tearing myself to pieces.

My two best friends at the moment are Elisa and Leonor, both very different. Elisa is an all-out *gusana,* a woman whose family was pro-Batista. Her father, who is a mulatto, is one of the few doctors in Cuba still allowed a private practice. And yet he and his children are against the Revolution and criticize it continually.

Elisa is twenty-eight and still single. I've known her ever since we were students in business school. From the first I was struck by her elegance. Even now she's still a very, very elegant little *mulata.* But I never think of her as colored, because you don't expect a mulatto to have such a knack for dressing and using makeup. I really believe her love of good clothes is one of the reasons she's a *gusana.*

Life is so strange! At first Elisa was surly and kept to herself. She may have a bit of a complex about her race. It took all my Christian charity to be nice to her. When she looked crossly at me I couldn't even speak to her. Then I'd feel guilty and beg her pardon—I flattered her a lot—but it took all my willpower to do it. Yet now Elisa and I are practically as close as sisters. She loves to be helpful and runs errands for me; we talk on the phone every day, though I still can't have a conversation with her about social problems or books or anything like that. But she knows all the rules of etiquette and has helped me a lot that way. She learned all that on her own, because of her deep wish for self-improvement. But she has no ideals, no spirituality. We have nothing in common.

Elisa and I go everywhere together, to dances, movies, the opera—we even go to clubs like the Tropicana, the Caribe, and the Habana. I try to help her, but men don't seem to like her much; in fact, they seem to like me more. She lives such a narrow, lonely life—a constant round of standing in line, finding out when the hot dogs arrive at La Cocinita, going to get a reservation for supper at the Sudaika restaurant, fetching and carrying for her family. She won't work for the government and is supported by her *papá,* so she feels obliged to do all the work at home. It's such a sad, boring way to live.

Yet Elisa is intelligent. She was in her third year of psychology when she left the University. She quit because she didn't approve of the changes. It would be very difficult for her to go back. Anyone who isn't integrated has a hard time at the University. Elisa could never adapt to the present system so I advise her to leave Cuba. "Why stay?" I ask her. "It simply makes you unhappy and in the end it will drive you crazy." But she says she can't leave her father and brother alone.

I feel much closer to Leonor, my other girl friend, whom I met when I was a nun. She's no longer a practicing Catholic, though she studied in a nun's school. Leonor is twenty-three and comes from a rich, distinguished family. They live in Old Havana, in a typical Spanish colonial house three stories high. It has one whole room lined from top to bottom with books. At present her father is teaching in a dental school and seems to be ideologically sympathetic to the Revolution.

Leonor fell in love with a boy on a much lower social and cultural level. He's a factory worker and all he talks about are nuts and bolts. Her parents were against him and Leonor would often run to me for advice. I pointed out how incompatible they were. I'd rather be single all my life than marry a man on a lower social level—but Leonor married him anyway. It was one of those crazy marriages, without a trousseau or anything. She already regrets it. She can't relate to her husband at all; they're not close to each other in any way, not even in bed.

I couldn't marry a man without knowing whether I responded to him physically. I have a sweetheart now and when he arouses me, I confess it to the priest. Do you know what the priest tells me? He says sweethearts are only permitted to hold hands! If I told my boyfriend that, he'd leave me!

One day I told Leonor that although Christian morality forbids it—I wouldn't dare say this to a devout Christian—I'm in favor of premarital relations because it keeps people from making mistaken marriages. She said, "If I had gone to bed with my sweetheart, I'd never have married him."

Leonor is neither a revolutionary nor a communist, but she's motivated by the ideal of helping the masses. She works hard as a teacher in a workers' self-improvement school. She also belongs to the Women's Federation, but only because of her job. Yet her husband and in-laws are *gusanos* of the worst kind. His parents have already left Cuba. In fact, Leonor's marriage will face a crisis when her husband is twenty-seven because then he can get out of Cuba legally, and he's bound to ask to go.[31] They have no children, thank God.

If it weren't for her husband, Leonor would be a great deal more integrated than she is. He isn't the only reason, though. Being an only

31. Men of peak draft age, sixteen to twenty-seven, were not permitted to emigrate from Cuba.

child, she's been spoiled all her life. To be integrated in the Revolution you have to make sacrifices, and Leonor doesn't want to. But she's the only friend I feel free to talk with about social problems, and, like me, she loves to think and study and investigate.

I try to get together with people who think the way I do, but there are so few of them. Most of the Christians I work with are materialists, every one of them—*gusanos,* simply because of the lack of food or clothing. Anyone who tries that kind of an approach with me is on the wrong track. The counterrevolutionaries I know seem to have lost all hope of overthrowing the present regime and depend on a counterrevolutionary movement in Miami which, in fact, doesn't exist. It seems pointless to involve myself in a counter-reaction that's virtually ineffective. But if I become revolutionary, I'm conspiring against my religion, and I want Christianity to grow and flourish. Yet there's no way I can commit myself to my religion without working for the Revolution.

Sometimes I feel I'm going crazy. When I try to explain how I really feel, the first thing I know, people are twisting around what I say. I'm completely closed off from any meaningful discussion. Even at home, when I point out something good that the Revolution has done, my family says I'm turning into a communist and losing my religious faith. On the other hand, if I tried to discuss my doubts with a communist, I'd probably be met by an equal display of fanaticism. We Cubans are like that—fanatical—about anything we believe in.

My psychiatrist had warned me, "In time, I want to talk with you again because you're going to feel terrible when you try to adjust to the outside world." He was right. The conflict I found myself caught in became worse. While I had to admit that the Revolution wasn't all bad, I also began to see that the Church wasn't all good, and it brought on a tremendous crisis. I was so upset I was on the point of going back for psychiatric treatment.

The Church has made errors in the past and now we're paying for them. One of the worst mistakes was that the Church didn't develop the spiritual life of its members. If Cuban parents had been real Christians, they'd now be teaching religion to their own children. But the Christian mentality, especially in my parents' generation, was completely hypocritical. For instance, the most devout Catholics in Cuba were the rich, but they'd put 20 *pesos* in the collection plate at Mass, then go home and bully their servants. That's not being a Christian. And many people will admit, "Oh, I went to catechism when I was a kid because they gave us candy." It's wrong to bribe our children to come to church; when the sweets are gone, we lose the children. They'll never go to church again.

I believe in the ideals of primitive Christianity, which is a Christianity of witness. This emphasizes acting out one's faith rather than paying it lip service. About a year ago I gave a talk in a church and told my audience that as Christians the important things are not rituals, structures, or anything external, but to love God, to love mankind, to help the needy, and to cooperate with others. I said that according to the new Pope, we had to change our old-fashioned Christian mentality if we were to communicate with other people and transmit Christ's message to them. What kind of Catholics were we, I asked, if our servants were miserably poor and we didn't even bother to ask whether their children had anything to eat?

A man in the audience, an old bourgeois who stayed in Cuba to maintain property rights over his house, later told someone, "That girl has a rather pink mentality, criticizing old-fashioned Catholics like that." I liked what he said.

We've changed our methods of teaching religion and catechism. In 1959 the catechistic board wrote a new catechism which replaced the old one introduced by Pius XI. The new one was pedagogically very sound, but its critics say it's just a bit short on religion. Nonetheless it was a great stride forward and was used all over Cuba.

In the old catechism, children memorized stock answers to set questions. Prayers were learned by rote without any idea of what they meant. Now I'm teaching my classes differently. Because the catechism contains the essence of Christian education, we kept it and modified it. Instead of rote learning, we teach the children how to put Christianity into practice. I use a new system, developed in France, by which the children learn to observe and love nature. We talk about plants, fruits, flowers, animals, the sun, and the sea. I find a very positive value in this practical approach to religion in the modern world.

The new catechism teaches us from early childhood to stop and think and pray. There's a moment in every class when the children are asked to meditate on what they've been taught that day. After the meditation period, the children are asked questions—without questions there could be no learning—but under the new method we don't make them the most important part of a class.

My work includes getting acquainted with the children's parents. Cubans who send their children to church these days are hardly ever revolutionaries. Mostly they're people who plan to leave the country as soon as they can. They may even feel that being against the Revolution makes them better than other people. That distresses me. But usually the parents of my students do have some religious feeling, and now that the Church is changing, many of these people have become real, practicing Catholics. I hope their number will increase.

Catechizing the parents is especially important because we have so little access to the children. Every day the government closes more doors to us. They're waging a devious campaign to keep the children busy, filling Saturdays and Sundays with the activities of the Pioneers.[32] The Street Plan[33] programs always coincide precisely with our working hours. The street the church is on is closed on Sundays to allow children to play there. They stretch a rope right in front of the church door so people can't enter without going under it. They offer the children what we can't—games, candy, ice cream—so most of the kids stay out in the street to play. Often not one single pupil shows up. We had expected some Party opposition but we didn't expect our field of action to be so drastically limited.

We may teach religion only in the church and are forbidden to conduct study groups in private homes, or even to go to people's homes to pick up the children. Neither can the Protestants, so it's not only the Catholics who are restricted. There's simply no freedom of religion. In any basic secondary school you'll find only one child in five is a Christian. The rest are against us. Being a minority, the Christian kids find it difficult to carry on. They get to the point where simply being told they shouldn't be religious is enough to make them give up.

Once when I was still a nun, another sister and I got into a conversation with the thirteen-year-old daughter of a family we visited. We began to talk about movies. Naturally we try to teach children to avoid immoral pictures. The girl said to us, "You just don't understand me. You live in your world and I in mine. My world in secondary school is gradually absorbing me. It isn't that I'm a revolutionary, but the modern world is materialistic, and I'm a part of it. Out of ten pupils there, I'm the only Christian, the only 'puritan,' as they say. I can't just up and say to the other kids, 'Hey, let's go see this picture—it doesn't have any immoral anti-Christian propaganda.' If I did, they'd say, 'You're a dope. You're a reactionary,' without my even having touched on politics. And let me tell you this—I'll probably wind up being a communist. Morally speaking, it's a lot more comfortable—free love is permitted and a lot of other things. You nuns don't realize that. Offer us something new!"

I was so disturbed when I left that house! "Dear God," I thought, "what can we do to help these poor children?"

32. *Unión de Pioneros* is an adjunct of the UJC open to all children seven to fourteen years of age. Many Pioneer activities are incorporated into school curricula although there are also extracurricular activities, including productive labor.

33. *Plan de la Calle*, a recreational program for school children developed by the National Institute of Sports, Physical Education, and Recreation in cooperation with the CDRs, the Women's Federation, the Young Communists, the Pioneers, and school faculties, all of whom assist in its implementation. The *Plan* is initiated at the regional level, then passed down to the sectional or (in rural areas) the *municipio* level, where it is adapted for the local school. The recreational programs (e.g., parties, games, and parades) are not designed for individual schools but rather for groups of schools which employ the grounds, facilities, and neighboring streets of one centrally located school. (*Cuba: El Movimiento Educativo*, 1967–68, pp. 89–90.)

More and more Cubans are becoming communists. They're trained in school, in meetings, in study circles. But Catholics have no way of training people, no means of communicating with them. The Party feels that Catholicism is in direct conflict with communism. Spiritism and *santería*, the African cult, are unimpeded by the Revolution. They're not dangerous because they have no religious ideology which might set them against the government. In his book *Los Negros Brujos*, Fernando Ortíz[34] says that the Christian religion is the great enemy of African religion in Cuba because the Spanish forced Catholicism on the Africans. So what happened? African religion became anti-Catholic and anti-clerical, but it's very mixed with Christian ideas.

I like the Afro-Cuban cults, not that I know much about them, but they're so much a part of our folklore, I feel they're a part of me too. Besides, I respect them as an expression of religious feeling. But they'd just as soon pray to their gods for a curse against someone as pray to remove an evil influence. As a Christian, I couldn't ask God to do that or to cure an illness or transform one thing into another thing. I could only pray to be enlightened, so I myself could find a solution to a problem or a practical way of curing an illness. To me, this difference is a manifestation of their ignorance. But their faith is as strong as mine.

It's more and more difficult for Catholics to integrate in the new society. A poor factory worker who goes to Mass every Sunday has no chance of being considered a Vanguard Worker. And I have Catholic friends who were students in the University and had to quit because there you must be revolutionary. So a religious person is free to study or work, but he can't ever get ahead, unless he believes in spiritism or one of the cultist religions, which are no barriers to becoming an exemplary socialist.[35]

Yet I believe there's enough common ground for Christians to integrate easily in our communist society. A good revolutionary policy toward the Church would seek out the things we can agree on and leave the rest to the conscience of the individual. Nowadays people talk a lot about freedom of the individual conscience and I firmly believe in it. It

34. *El Hampa Afrocubano: Los Negros Brujos (apuntes para un estudio de etnología criminal)* [*The Afro-Cuban Underworld: The Negro Sorcerers (notes for a study of criminal ethnology)*] (Madrid: F. Fe, 1906). Dr. Fernando Ortíz, a well-known Cuban scholar of Afro-Cuban culture and other aspects of Cuban society, died in Havana in 1969. Other important works include *Contrapunteo Cubano del Tabaco y el Azúcar* (Havana, 1940), and *El Engaño de las Razas* (Havana, 1946).

35. Religious practitioners, including those who practiced *santería,* the Yoruban religious cult, or other Afro-Cuban cults, could not become members of the Cuban Communist Party. The Afro-Cuban religious cults were officially viewed as "folklore" and were studied by the National Institute of Ethnology and Folklore in the Academy of Sciences and by the National Council of Culture. (David K. Booth, "Neighbourhood Committees and Popular Courts in the Social Transformation of Cuba" (unpublished Ph.D. thesis, University of Surrey, 1973), pp. 259–61.)

was God Himself who granted men free will, and it's only if we exercise that freedom and bring about a revolution in the Church that we'll be able to accommodate to the socialist revolution in Cuba.

The Catholic Church has not yet taken the necessary steps to join in the revolutionary process. I don't mean just the Catholic Church in Cuba, because I realize this revolutionary process is one step in universal social evolution. This is not merely a Cuban form of government. I believe eventually every country in the world will do away with capitalism and begin building a new social system.

Christianity and communism have many points of similarity and our ideals are the same: both have a deep faith in man and his ability to overcome obstacles, and we share the belief that work dignifies man. Among the few young Catholics we have, many do productive labor. It means spending four months without going to Mass, but we advise them to be good citizens and go work in agriculture. In the institute the nuns who studied or worked outside all did productive labor.

There's a group of young seminarians who spend a month doing agricultural work at the end of the school year. Many Catholics criticize that and say it's the fault of Padre Carlos Manuel de Céspedes, a terrifically vanguardist priest, who they claim is being used by the communists as a propaganda tool to make people think there's freedom of religion in Cuba. There may be a grain of truth in that, but Padre de Céspedes and the other revolutionary priests are living realistically, integrating with the rest of the Cuban people. Those priests are really aware.

It seems to me that since the whole world is in the process of revolution, it was bound to come to the Church too. And it *has* come, in the debate on priestly celibacy and birth control. Some radicals have gone so far that the Pope has had to re-emphasize certain points of Catholic dogma. During his visit to Colombia, the Pope said that in Latin America, where overpopulation is most acute, they should find some other means than contraceptives to solve the problem. When the bishop repeated those words to us I thought, "Sure. And if they can't figure out any other means, what are they going to do? Starve?"

I understand the attitude of the priests who favor birth control and I understand the Pope, too. Why I've seen cases right here in Cuba where professionals with good jobs, good houses, and secure futures obtained their priest's permission to use contraceptives although they had only two children. Imagine! I think that's wrong.

My approach to religion has always been simple and spontaneous— primitive, the communists would say. I still believe in all the Catholic concepts, and whatever I do, I do because I feel I'm in God's presence and have His help. He is my constant companion, invisible, but I feel Him and His Providence. When I'm suffering most, I especially feel His nearness. I'm the sort of person who thinks God will even perform a miracle by making the bus come a bit sooner for me.

My model for living is Jesus Christ, and in my nightly examination of my conscience, I ask myself whether I've really tried to do good that day. Some evenings I'm so tired I drop off to sleep before I get around to the answer, but I never omit saying three *Ave Marías*. What a strong hold childhood habits have on us! When I was very small I heard the story about a girl who went into the easy life and died in an accident at the age of eighteen. In spite of her sins she didn't go to Hell. The Virgin saved her soul because the girl had said three *Ave Marías* every night since she was a child. I believe in the life eternal and my aim is to save my soul and get to Heaven, so even if I'm dying of fatigue and even if I've been drinking, I'm never too tired to say three *Ave Marías* at night.

There are still many points of incompatibility between communism and the religious way of life. Communism doesn't accept our rites because it considers them superfluous. They say it's not true that there exists a God whose flesh can be eaten. And we *do* believe in this. I can't be against it, nor is it bad, because it brings me closer to God. I think a little ritual is natural and has a valid purpose, though I'm opposed to the formal, hierarchical Church.

Any common ground that might exist between Catholics and communists is undermined by issues such as these. I don't yet believe the Revolution will solve the problems that seem important to me. So, though I now see the Church's defects, I can't just transfer my commitment from the Church to the Revolution. It's not that simple.

When I finally met a revolutionary who might have given me some guidance, he was too stupid to do it. What a shame! He's my boyfriend, Arturo, whom I met at a dance. He's studying electrical engineering, not because it particularly interests him, but because it's his duty as a revolutionary.

Arturo has blind faith in the Revolution, and I can't bear people who close their eyes to reality. For instance, once I remarked, "There really aren't enough houses in Cuba. Construction of homes has practically been at a standstill for the past ten years."

"That's a lie!" he said. "They've built in East Havana."

True, but that was in 1961 and they didn't build nearly enough. "What a fool he is," I thought.

All in all, I feel superior to him. He has no intellectual curiosity; he never bothers to analyze things or to read. It's impossible to have a conversation with him. If I ask him, "Have you read this or that book?" he always answers, "No, I haven't." When Arturo and I talk about anything—anything at all—I'm the one who talks. Yet there's nothing I'm really interested in discussing with him. That kind of thing is disillusioning to me. I want a man who can teach me things, an intellectual from whom I can continually learn something new.

Arturo and I simply are not compatible. Physically I'm very attracted to him—he's tall, dark, and a bit stout, though I don't think he's as good-looking as people say. I love him physically, but when passion is over, what's left?

He's the first man with whom I've had what I consider to be a normal relationship for sweethearts. A girl who knows him told me he's the kind who, three days after he's met a woman, asks her to go to a hotel, so I made it clear to him that he couldn't make such propositions to me. I told him, "You should know I won't be your woman unless you marry me first. I don't mean it has to be today or tomorrow; on the contrary, I think we should get to know each other well first."

The problem is that Arturo, who is thirty years old, doesn't seem to be the marrying type. In fact, he's told me frankly he has no intention of getting married. I don't mind too much. I know that when I get married I'll be as tied down as when I was a nun. That's the Cuban mentality, no? When a woman gets married she's as good as dead. Those seven years I spent as a nun, cut off from the world, I didn't really live. So I think it's natural for me to make up for it now. I have friends who are always inviting me to go out, but as long as I remain single, I'm denied the full sexual expression I need as a woman. That's what prevents me from breaking off with Arturo. Also, my friends consider being an old maid a disgrace.

Although we talk on the phone every single day, I can't count on going out with Arturo. He's the production manager in a factory and those people have an extraordinary work load, with meetings to attend at any hour, night or day. He's full of other excuses too. If his corns don't hurt, he has a headache; when he feels all right, he has a sick uncle; and when he can't think up an excuse he calmly tells me, "Oh no, not today. I don't feel like going anywhere."

It seems to me that when a man is attracted to a woman, he should make every effort to be with her and talk with her. Arturo's weekends— except Saturday evenings, when we always go out together—belong to his two army pals. He took me out on weekends when he was first courting me, but now he's sure of me and doesn't bother. Yet he has a high opinion of me. He never gets angry and he says he trusts me completely. But I need more than that. I want a man who's strong, but not one who acts like an executioner. A really manly man can be gentle and understanding with a woman, dominating her without treating her like a slave, or a mistress. No, no, I don't mean that. I'd like to have my husband look on me as his mistress as well as his wife.

A while ago I got fed up, and for a week I didn't call Arturo. Then he began phoning me and I always answered very coolly. One day he phoned and I'd gone to the theater without telling him. That was enough to make *him* feel like the victim for a change. He complained to a friend of mine that I went to parties without him.

"But you've often gone out with your friends and stood up Gracia," my friend told him.

Arturo's not young and already has had one unhappy experience. He'd been in love with a girl for four years but he told me—I remember how he hid his face in his hands as he said it—"That girl tortured me with her jealousy."

I said, "I don't want to torment you as your former sweetheart did, but when a woman has a boyfriend, she expects to go with him to parties, the theater, the movies. I'd like to be able to count on you; as it is, I have to go alone. If you don't want to be my sweetheart anymore, that's all right. We can be friends." Without a word he began to caress me. "Don't!" I said. "I'm annoyed with you. Until this situation is resolved, I don't want you to touch me, because when you do, I give in and nothing's settled."

The following Saturday I didn't hear from him. I finally phoned to ask, "Well, Arturo, are we going somewhere or not?"

"Call me back at 6:30, *chica.*"

At 6:30 I phoned again. He was out, without leaving word where he'd gone. On Sunday I had no word from him all day long. On Monday I called him at 11:00 at night because I thought it was high time to pin him down. "You've simply cast me aside, the way you neglect me," I told him.

"Oh, but you see, yesterday I went out with Willy."

I thought, "I can't go on this way."

Mamá doesn't like my sweetheart. She says Arturo doesn't treat me with the devotion a woman expects from a man who loves her. I quite agree with her, annoying as it is to hear her criticize him.

I finally decided I had to try to integrate in the Revolution. I couldn't go on standing on the sidelines without contributing anything. I love my country, no matter how difficult the situation is here, and I don't think it can be wrong to help it be more productive. If I do agricultural work it doesn't mean I've stopped being a good Catholic. I keep saying to myself, "I'm going to do my bit and it's nothing to feel guilty about."

When I told Arturo about it he shouted with joy. "That's great! I promise you'll like it. You'll feel wonderful." My decision meant a great deal to him. What a difference it made in his attitude! He became very affectionate, and I was filled with joy to know he was pleased with me. He kept saying that someday I'd be a fine revolutionary.

Once I made up my mind to do it, I had no anxieties. In fact I was enthusiastic. I went on a Sunday, getting up earlier than necessary. I was the first to arrive at the appointed place, at around 6:15 A.M. Being alone gave me time to think about what I was going to do. Every Sunday I try to read a little of the Bible and meditate upon it, so I took the opportunity to do it then. I put myself in God's hands: "Well, Lord, You know I'm doing a good thing, so here I go."

I was on a team with people from the library. They began to arrive, and we waited together for a truck which was to take us to the country. The truck was a closed one, like the old laundry trucks. They also had open trucks, fenced in with boards, but only men ride in those. There were both men and women in our truck.

The people had a wonderful spirit. We were piled one on top of the other, but nobody complained. What a difference from the crowded buses where there are always people who protest loudly. We were singing and joking all the way.

We started out at 7:10 and were taken to a camp in *El Cordón*.[36] The camp was quite large and planted in coffee. It was a nice place, with music coming through loudspeakers.

The men were going to spade, and went off in a truck. The women were told to pile grass around the coffee plants. Some protested, "One week we pick up straw, and the next week we put it back where we found it. I guess they have to figure out some way to keep us busy." At first I couldn't see the good of it either, but I hated to hear them mocking the work. Another girl who felt the same way I did went with me to a farmer and asked him, "Why are we doing this?" He explained that when the grass is wet, it keeps the coffee plants damp. We understood then, but unfortunately the others didn't.

One of the two farmers leading our group seemed very bored and careless. He just stood there watching us, remarking in a loud voice, "Look at that! This is no work for women. If I ever get married again, I won't let my wife do farm work." The other farmer was working hard and making every effort to get things done well. He encouraged us, saying, "See how much you've done already? Why you're practically through!"

As usual, I wanted to do a good day's work, but I was shocked by the attitude of some of the people there. For instance, some didn't cover up their plants properly. One woman who noticed said, "I'll leave it as it is. I'm not going to do their work for them." What difference does it make who does what? The point was to get the work done and get it done well. The work was light and went very fast.

The teams were organized into competing brigades. A goal was set and a count made: "Such-and-such a brigade completed three rows." Later at the office, the work of each brigade was figured out and the winner declared. There was a lot of good fellowship; when we took a break, everybody shared their snacks in a friendly manner. I felt happy, truly happy, and it was wonderful to be where there was no racial prejudice or class division. It was so different from my friends!

All sorts of people worked together—office workers, administrators, janitors, and charwomen. The difference between them wasn't all that

36. *Cordón de la Habana*, the cultivated greenbelt that encircled Havana.

obvious—everybody wore old, torn, soiled clothes for agricultural work—it's something about the person. There was an elderly woman, poor thing, who worked harder than anybody else, and it was obvious that she was a charwoman. I knew it because her clothes looked poor and shabby even compared to the rest of our outfits. Yet it was clear that she was integrated, as much of a comrade as anyone else, and people paid the same attention to her as they did to the office workers. I don't believe anyone noticed the difference except me. I'm still awfully class-conscious.

We Christians are prejudiced against the lower classes, no matter how loudly we deny it. I've been told there are class distinctions among the revolutionaries also, but I don't know whether that's true. I saw no such thing when I did productive labor. I can't help classifying people according to status myself. For example, I and other Christians I know look down upon a waiter in a pizzeria. Even at the institute, if we talked about the cook, or invited her to participate in one of our activities, it was in a patronizing way. This is something we must overcome.

I don't intend to do productive labor every Sunday because I teach a catechism class at 8:30 Sunday mornings. I told my pupils all about my experience but not my friends—I can't talk as freely with them. They already think I'm turning into a communist, so I keep my mouth shut. I always worry a lot about what people say, and I'm so unsure of myself I wouldn't know how to explain to them that the change in me doesn't mean I've lost my faith.

After I came home that Sunday, I phoned a friend and she said, "Well, well, how's the little comrade? So we lost you, eh?" I know she meant it as a joke, but in a way she really believes it. Later that afternoon, two women who teach in my Sunday school phoned me. Honestly, they sounded as if they were offering their condolences! "Are you terribly tired?" they asked pityingly. I don't try to explain my feelings to such people, they'd only be horrified.

The process of change that began when I stopped being a nun is still going on, and I don't know where it will lead. For the present, I feel as maladjusted as ever. For example, if I have children, I don't intend to rear them in Cuba. I hope I can leave before that. But if they were to live in Cuba, my children would study on scholarships and be integrated so they could live a normal life, though I'd see to it that they were Christians.

The other day when I went to Mass I prayed, "Listen, Christ, You know I want to imitate You. No matter where I am, I want to be good. If this new life that's awakening in me is going to draw me away from You, try to put an end to it. But if it's going to develop into something good, then make it develop fully."

So far I haven't had the courage to be a revolutionary, though sometimes I think I have it in me. I'm too afraid of becoming an atheist; I feel held back by my religion. If I stay, I'm not going to be like most of my friends with their bourgeois jobs in the midst of a socialist society. They simply don't adapt. If I ever do, I'll go all the way.

PART III

Pilar López Gonzales

Chapter One

It Was All *Mamá*'s Fault

IT WAS ALL SO DIFFERENT before the Revolution! A girl like me, from a poor family with never enough to eat, well, she had only two ways to go, the brothel or domestic service. I went to the brothel; there was more money in it. But how I detested it! And detested myself even more! Believe me, if it hadn't been for the triumph of the Revolution I'd be dead by now. It was my salvation.

Now, thanks to a government that cares for all the people, no matter what they've done or what color they are or how much money they've got, now I can be anything I want. All I have to do is work hard and I can have a career. Anybody can; the opportunity is there for the taking. I know what I'm talking about because I was one of the first to be rehabilitated. The Revolution found me in a brothel, and today my daughters and I live in our own house and I'm studying in a great university.

Don't think it's been easy adapting to society. Some women have been prostitutes for so long they can't change, but I was lucky—I did it for only a couple of years. Even so, for a long time I felt tense with people. At first I thought I'd never get rid of the stain of it. If anybody looked at me, I'd shrivel up inside and think, "He knows, he knows I was a whore." Now I'd rather come right out with it, no matter how it hurts, no matter what anybody thinks of me.

When I first started working at the textile factory I used to overhear a lot of bigots making remarks. Like the day I moved into the new house the Ministry gave me and went shopping at the Minimax.[1] This man was talking to one of the girls there, and he said, "What are you doing clerking here, kid? You'd be a lot better off at the factory; why don't you apply?"

Pilar López Gonzales was interviewed fourteen times, twice by Oscar Lewis and twelve times by Maida Donate, a Cuban assistant. Pilar's elder sister was also interviewed but her account is not included; a lengthy interview with Pilar's first husband was confiscated (see *Four Men*, Foreword). There were 779 pages transcribed from Pilar's original taped interviews.

1. The name of a former food-store chain; it is used synonymously with "supermarket."

Another man who was shopping there spoke up: "What kind of advice are you handing her? Don't you know that place is full of whores? Trash, that's all they hire."

It made me sick. I said, "Look, comrade, don't be so quick to pass judgment on something you don't know anything about. Sure, they've got rehabilitated prostitutes there, but there are a lot of other kinds of women too." Oh, I faced right up to him, but I didn't have the nerve to say which sort I was. If something like that happened now I'd come out with the whole thing.

Another time some tools were missing at the factory and a neighbor of mine said, "It must be one of *those* women, you can count on it. I can't see why the Revolution bothers with that riffraff. They ought to line 'em up against a wall and shoot 'em." He knew perfectly well I was one of "those" women.

Well, they caught the thief that very afternoon. I went straight back over to his house and said, "You see, it wasn't any kind of woman, it was a man, covering his tracks by pretending to be a revolutionary."

I never had any trouble with anybody in the factory itself, but I did have a serious run-in with a comrade from the FMC.[2] When I applied for membership you'd have thought I was trying to get into the Party itself. This comrade knew about an affair I'd had, and even though I'd left the man as soon as I found out he was married, she wanted me to repent, and she acted as if bearing him a daughter was a sin. I was furious. I told her to go to hell, that if I had to drag my private life into it, I couldn't care less about joining the Federation. "I live as I damn well please," I said. But I know I have a debt to society and I won't be satisfied until I pay it back. The day I attain my ultimate goal, to graduate from the University and go out to have a career, that'll be the happiest day of my life.

If there were any pleasant moments in my childhood they've been completely erased from my memory. Everything engraved in my brain is painful.

I was a slave at home from the time I was seven. It was taken for granted that all the housework would fall to me. My big sister Francisca was hardly ever home, and when she was I had to do it all anyway. My little sister Susana tried to help me but she was too small to be much use. *Mamá* knew I was the most reliable of the lot, and when she told me to do something I could never turn her down.

Mamá would lie in bed every afternoon while I cleaned the house and washed the clothes, standing on a box to reach the washtub. The neighbors told *mamá* it wasn't fair, such a little girl doing the laundry, but

2. The Federation of Cuban Women. See Introduction, n. 4.

what did she care? She made me wash the dishes, she sent me on errands, she even sent me to borrow money for her—from my Uncle Arnaldo, from the landlord, from the grocer. When she told Francisca to go ask for money, my sister flatly refused because it embarrassed her. She was selfish and spoiled and *mamá* didn't press her. She just told me to do it. I'd be dying of embarrassment too, but I'd have felt even worse refusing.

I was scared to death of *mamá* because she was always hitting us and swearing at us. When we wanted to go to a birthday party or a movie or if I wanted to practice volleyball, she'd say, "That's just a way of going whoring." She used to tell me I was born wrong-headed and had whoring in my blood.

When she hit you she didn't care where the blow landed—on your face, your head, anywhere. If she was washing dishes she'd hit you with the dishpan. If she was sweeping she'd throw the broom at you. She liked to carry a whip or a belt, but when she was in a hurry she'd just hit you with her hand. Sometimes she left my body black and blue.

I don't know why I was the punching bag of the family; my sisters were more docile. I helped *mamá* as much as I could, but all the same she had it in for me. She said I was domineering, awkward, and stupid. If I talked back to her she'd hit me and say, "I won't stop until you cry." Afterward she'd just let me go on crying and not give me a glance. But sometimes I refused to cry. I'd keep talking back, and eventually she'd have to stop because she was worn out.

When I did cry it was as much from rage as pain. What a monster she was! How I wished I could return blow for blow! But I didn't have the nerve to raise my hand. Mind you, if I had hit her I wouldn't have regretted it. That's how I am. When I see injustice done by anyone, even my own mother or father, I tell them what I think of them. And I've never been sorry for it either.

I remember one time I rebelled. *Papá* had just finished dinner and *mamá* put his dishes in the sink and told me to wash them. For once I got the nerve to say, "I haven't had anything to eat all day. Why should I wash somebody else's dishes?" *Mamá* hadn't cooked for us kids and she was afraid *papá* would hear. She didn't want me to repeat it, so she grabbed me and knocked me against the sink again and again. When she let me go I screamed, "Why did you bring me into the world? To work hard and go hungry? I didn't ask to be born!"

My mother hated me, all right. Once she told me I was born by accident, and according to *papá*, she'd taken many things to abort me. When I was about eight years old, I overheard a conversation between my parents. "Why do you hate Pila so?" *papá* asked. "You've hated her ever since she was born. When she was a baby and threw up on the bed, what made you spank her?" Now that was news to me!

"Pila was a mistake," *mamá* answered. "I wanted a boy."

Now that I stop to think of it, maybe I bear a grudge against *mamá* for never having wanted me. She often said she wished she'd had more boys. People used to look down on women who bore mostly girls, and my father's mother often made remarks about *mamá* being an *hembrera*, a bearer of females, which made *mamá* furious.

She had big ideas for her male children, though she had hopes for my sister Niurkita too, because she was such a darling baby—chubby, blond, and very white. When someone remarked how pretty she was, *mamá* lapped it up. She must have nursed Niurkita for three years, and the boys too, of course, because she favored them so much.

My brother Aurelio was named after *papá* and was his favorite. Aurelio would mess around with the photos in *papá*'s darkroom and break things and *papá* would scold him, but *mamá* never allowed *papá* to spank him. *Papá* would tell her, "You've got to untie the apron strings or that boy will turn out a real sissy." Yet when *papá* spoiled Francisca, *mamá* would get furious.

I think my brother must have been half crazy. At school when the boys called him "sissy" he'd pretend he hadn't heard, and when they started beating him up he'd get scared and just let them. Then I'd have to stick up for him. It bothered me. I used to tell him, "You've got to get wise. If you'd let those boys have it just once they wouldn't call you any more names." But he didn't do it so I had to stand and fight. Poor little guy!

When we were little we lived in the barrio Palatino, in a single room in a *solar*. In those days *mamá* would get dressed up and go out almost every afternoon, padlocking the door on the outside so we couldn't go out. She'd tell us she was going to see *papá* and I thought she meant she was going to take a ride on the bus he drove. I noticed they never arrived home together but I thought that was because *papá* worked so late. It never crossed my mind *mamá* wasn't telling the truth, until years later I found out she used to go around with a bus driver on Route 4. I don't know for sure what was going on between them but I hear he was in love with her. Sometimes she'd get on his bus or she'd wave to him when he passed by, but I never saw him come to our house—he wasn't one of *papá*'s friends.

My Grandma Bella often asked us whether *mamá* left a candle burning when she went out. "Yes," we'd tell her, "in front of her little altar."

"*Ay,* she must be crazy," *mima* Bella would say. "What if the house catches fire!" Even the neighbors warned her, "Bárbara, don't padlock the door when you go out. If anything happened we'd have to break it down." But *mamá* didn't care.

She never took us on those little outings of hers and we hardly ever went out with both my parents because they couldn't get together on anything. Even if *papá* asked her to the beach she'd tell him to go on alone. Sometimes he took us and once in a while *mamá* did. Usually, if we went anywhere it was to *mima* Bella's. Once when I was about six or seven *mamá* took us to see a Shirley Temple movie, but that was unusual, a real fluke.

Later, when we went to live in barrio Jesús María, *mamá* stopped going out and didn't bother about how she looked. And yet that was when *papá* was better off than ever before. I was about eight years old then and *papá*'s *mamá,* my Grandmother Nicolasa, left us her apartment. Then we had two bedrooms—we used one as a dining room—and a living room and a kitchen. The furniture was really shoddy and there were only two beds, one for my parents and one for all of us kids.

In our house we hardly had any visitors except now and then my *mima* Bella and *mamá*'s sisters. I remember one Christmas Eve at Palatino, though, when *mima* Bella did the cooking and Grandfather Arnaldo brought lots of nuts and filberts. It was splendid! I had the mumps, but sick as I was, I ate and ate and never got tired. When I was older, our family got together for Easter now and then, but it wasn't a custom with us.

Papá's friends never visited him at home except on his birthday. That day we always ate. *Papá* would buy beer, snacks, and a cake, and *mamá* sometimes even made a custard dessert. She took part in the celebration but she was her usual dry, bitter self. On our birthdays, if we could afford it, my parents would buy a cake and some soft drinks and we'd have a little party. But there was no birthday dinner.

When I was still too young to notice the troubles at home, the Day of the Three Kings was a happy one for me because I always got a new doll. But once when I was about ten years old I overheard *mamá* and *papá* arguing because there was no money to buy us anything. *Mamá* was making her usual demands and *papá* was defending himself as he always did. "Remember last year?" he said. "The driver and I got together and took 3 or 4 *pesos* out of the fares. I'll just have to do it again."

It was a sad blow to learn that the only way we could celebrate the Day of the Three Kings was for my *papá* to steal.

The fact is, my parents didn't get along and I almost never saw them happy. *Mamá* snarled at everybody—why should *papá* be an exception? She'd call him a faggot, a good-for-nothing, degenerate son-of-a-whore. She couldn't open her mouth without losing her temper. She even quarreled with the neighbors, though she got along with strangers all right. She really hated a woman named Concha because *mamá* claimed *papá* was having an affair with her. *Mamá* kept going on about how Concha was a low-class flirt and moved like a bitch in heat. Poor Concha! She was sweet to all of us, but I'm sure she had no special interest in *papá*.

Mamá always said she worked bitterly hard but that *papá* was so stingy he wouldn't give her anything she needed. I believed her then and pited her, so I protected her. It was only later that my eyes were opened to the lies she told. After all, he didn't keep her so badly. She dressed a lot better than we did. She bought things for herself first and us kids afterward so we hardly had a decent set of clothes. About once a year she'd buy us a nightgown, a pair or two of underwear, and some shoes and socks. That's about all. She had pretty dresses and went out in high-heeled shoes. Perfume, too. Honeysuckle was her favorite scent. She didn't pencil her eyebrows but she used eyeshadow and a lot of rouge and lipstick, and she'd wear flowers and butterflies in her hair. She was crazy about those butterfly ornaments! Her hair really was lovely then, long and black, and I have to admit that when she dressed up to go out she looked pretty good.

My father worked so hard he had to go without sleep a lot of the time. Once he had four jobs at the same time: he was a bus driver, a photographer, he sold jewelry, and he worked for Public Works. Even I could see how, to please *mamá*, he tried hard to find work, but it seemed like the minute he felt secure in a job, he'd get laid off. Then we had nothing, not even enough for food. And sometimes when *papá* did have a job, he didn't get paid because the boss claimed there was no money in the cash box.

Papá was always working or job-hunting; he'd go to the bus route and stay there all day long in case there was a chance to work, so he was out of the house most of the time and that meant *mamá* was the boss. *Papá* didn't know what was going on. If she said, "I have to buy myself a dress," he didn't object. Somehow he just couldn't put his foot down. It was as if he was blindfolded.

Sometimes, though, he'd come home and wake up to things, and then the trouble would start. For instance, if he'd left money for food and came home to find nothing cooked, or if he'd had a good spell and left enough to buy us clothes and she'd squandered it, he'd ask her what she'd done with the money. Then she'd flare up and say he was always prying and asking questions. "I don't feel like telling you about every measly *centavo* I spend!" She was like that every day. Any little thing would set her off with a bang. But every time *papá* quarreled with her, he was right. Every single time.

Only once did he hit her. As usual, he'd left money for food and she hadn't bought any. They argued and shouted until *papá* lost patience and hit her, not a hard blow, more like a push. He controlled himself at once but *mamá* screamed her head off. When we got to the kitchen she was cowering back in a corner. As soon as he saw us, *papá* went out.

Mamá wanted more and more money, but it was mostly for witchcraft and trash like that. If she had 2 *pesos* she'd buy a lottery ticket, even though there was nothing for lunch. She spent 6 or 7 *pesos* a week that way, and then she'd tell us, "Blame your *papá* if you have to go hungry.

He doesn't work, yet he goes out and throws his money around." Poor *papá*, such lies! He never had other women and took only one holiday a year—his birthday, which he always celebrated at home. It's true he liked to play the lottery, but he played it less than *mamá* did. They both always played no. 217, and after years and years they finally won a prize, but by that time they'd probably spent ten times as much as they won.

Another time when they won 200 or 300 *pesos* they bought each of us girls a cheap dress and a pair of shoes, and *papá* handed over the rest to *mamá* to pay the rent. Imagine giving her the rent money! Well, that's exactly what he'd been doing for seven or eight months, and naturally *mamá* had been spending the money for other things.

Finally the landlord asked *papá* to please make an effort to pay before the debt grew too big. "I don't owe you a thing," *papá* told him. "You're a brazen liar, trying to charge me twice!"

Papá told *mamá* about it and said, "Get the receipts so I can show him." She pretended to look everywhere, then she said, "I can't find them, I guess they got lost."

"*Papá* won't believe that," I thought. "It's the end of the world! He'll kill her for sure!"

But he swallowed it! That was when I realized *papá* loved *mamá* like a fool. I thought, "There's no doubt about it, he's an idiot. Love has blinded him." I didn't say anything because I was sorry for *mamá* and afraid of what he'd do to her.

When *papá* was a jewelry salesman he gave us lots of gifts—a ring, a bracelet, a chain, earrings. So if *mamá* wanted money she'd pawn a piece of jewelry. Her bracelet went to the grocer for 10 *pesos,* and when *papá* asked her about it she said, "Oh, I lost it."

"*Ay,* why don't you take better care of your things?" That was as near as he came to reproaching her.

Pretty soon all *mamá*'s jewelry was gone and she began to pawn ours. Then she'd tell *papá* we'd lost it. When he asked, "Did you really lose those earrings?" I always answered yes, even if it meant I'd get a spanking. I wouldn't have told the truth for anything in the world.

I always knew when there was going to be trouble because it was me *mamá* sent to borrow money. When she "lost" the bracelet I thought, "The catastrophe is at hand." When she took the rent money, I thought the same thing. When she pawned the ring and my sister's chain—a beautiful one with a religious medal that had four diamonds on it—I thought, "Now everything is going to blow up!" She must have been apprehensive too, because her temper was worse than ever. By that time *papá* was beginning to argue with her a lot, but he never took a stick and beat her for being such a liar.

Mamá believed in God and no matter where we lived she kept a picture of Him on a little altar, with flowers in front of it sometimes. Still, that doesn't make her a fanatical believer, does it? She believes in a little of everything. Her parents thought of themselves as Christians but they weren't the kind who went to church every Sunday. I wouldn't say they were Catholics exactly. If you talked to *mima* Bella about spiritism, she believed in it; if you talked about God, she believed in that too. Not in *santeros*[3] though—there's never been a *santero* in our family.

Well, *mamá*'s like that. She'd just as soon spend what little she had on sorcery as on flowers for the saints. She'd go to spiritists every couple of weeks, not on fixed dates, only when something was tormenting her. They'd tell her to buy lots of flowers and set out glasses of water and dry wine. After saying some words she'd drop egg white in water and clean the house with the mixture. Or she'd get ice or perfume and clean the house with that, or sometimes the spiritists would demand that she buy a hen or a rooster. Those things cost money, money we needed at home, and instead it went to people who made a living by exploiting fools. *Mamá* didn't understand that.

When *mamá* got married, it wasn't in a church. All her children were baptized, but only my sister Susana—and maybe Xiomara, too—made First Communion. As for me, I've never confessed, gone to Communion, or even to Mass. *Mamá* would take us to church during Holy Week but not for Mass. Good Friday at home was like any other day. We celebrated Christmas Eve, and on the Day of the *Virgen de la Merced,* *mamá* would put flowers on the altar. That was all.

Although *mamá* talked about God all the time, it was usually to tell us we were being punished by Him, and I came to think of God as a monster. When I was about nine I remember thinking, "Why should we suffer so cruelly when other children live so well? If God exists and this is His punishment, *He* must be the bad one, not us."

Whenever *mamá* was pregnant, she prepared the layette grudgingly, as a necessity. She'd buy the diapers, and her sister Eleonila, who was very handy with a needle, would embroider them and make little kimonos. As fast as one baby outgrew them, they'd be passed on to the next newborn.

Mamá never bought baby bottles. As far as she was concerned, the most convenient and economical thing was a beer bottle with a nipple on top. She never carried her children around the house either, but then there were so many of them she never had time to pick them up. She'd only carry a baby when she had to go out; the rest of the time she'd put him in the cradle and let him cry. In that way I guess we sort of raised ourselves.

Mamá never cared whether we were in school or wandering around in the street, and she didn't give a damn how hungry we were. She'd fix rice and beans or a bit of cornmeal mush once a day, about 4:00 in the

---

3. Priest-practitioners of the Yoruban *santería* cult; also called *babalorishas.*

afternoon, and not very well cooked at that. Two or three times a week she'd decide not to cook at all. Those days we'd get a glass of milk in the morning and, if we were lucky, a piece of bread at night. That's what I call going hungry.

Food just didn't matter to *mamá*. But she always took care of her own comfort. She'd make *café con leche,* or else she'd go out and buy herself a dish of ice cream, and if she shared anything with us it was an accident. I can remember her sitting down to her coffee, telling us there was nothing to eat. "Anyway, you kids don't need to eat the way I do because I work so hard."

Mamá liked to have the house clean and pretty, but you can't make much headway where there are so many small children. *Papá* never helped in the house but he did the shopping sometimes. Now and then he'd try buying a month's supply at one time, other times he'd buy it daily. He loved lobster or shrimp enchiladas and he'd often get the ingredients and make them himself. In fact, when a meal was actually cooked at home it was bound to be *papá*'s idea, not *mamá*'s. *He* liked to have us eat well, and if he had a lot of money for some reason, he'd go to the butcher shop and buy us a big supply of beef.

It was *papá* who gave us baths, too. The shower was outside and he'd say, "I'm going to take a shower, who wants to go with me?" We'd form a line and he'd bathe us one by one, and take his own shower later.

Mamá wasn't the kind to go to a doctor. When we were little she never showed the slightest concern if we were sick or hurt. Whether it was a pimple or a broken head, she treated everything with home remedies, and she didn't even make those herself, she sent for *mima* Bella. If one of my brothers cracked his head open all *mamá* did was put a mixture of mercurochrome and brown sugar on it. When my brother Aurelio had appendicitis, she sent for a woman to massage his belly and he almost died because it got infected. Of course it's true that at the time, during Batista's rule, there were no hospital beds available, and my father had to talk with a politician he'd voted for before he could get my brother into the Calixto García Hospital. If they'd waited a bit longer they wouldn't have needed to bother—he'd have been dead.

Then there was the time my sister Xiomara was about six years old and I was about twelve; she was sitting on the floor playing jacks while I ran back and forth from the front porch to the back porch. In passing, I hit her hard on the head with my knee and knocked her out. I thought I'd killed her. I went crazy with fear. "*Ay,* what a stupid shit-eater I am!" I yelled. "If I've killed my sister I'll jump off the porch and kill myself!"

Mamá was taking a nap when I ran in crying, "Run, *mami,* run, you'll have to take Xiomara to the doctor. I think I killed her. Oh hurry, I've killed Xiomara!" I said it all in one breath. "*Mami,* get up!"

Not her! Instead she snapped, "That's what happens when you play. God is punishing you."

I ran to a neighbor and told her what had happened. We rubbed a little alcohol on Xiomara's head and she fell asleep, with a big bump rising where I'd hit her. When *mamá* finally got up I said, "Look, *mami*, please let's take her to the doctor, maybe she broke something inside."

"It's nothing, it'll go away," she said, but the blow did affect my sister; it made her deaf in one ear. I feel guilty myself but I blame *mamá* more. After all, she was responsible for us, no?

We never complained about those things to *papá* because she threatened to beat us if we did, and besides, she always painted him as mean, so we didn't go any closer to him then we would have gone to a cockroach.

Mamá tells me she married my father for love. Well, that may be, because I have some photos of him as a young man and he was a prime example of male beauty: young, tall, strong, and very handsome. Later on he deteriorated a lot, especially after his illness, but all the same he was very *simpático*, full of charm, attractive. But *mamá* says after the children started coming she lost interest in him and only stayed with him for our sake. What good was that to us? I don't remember her ever being in the mood for a kiss, a loving word, a bit of praise. It was always "Go away, leave me alone all of you, quit the smooching!"

Papá wasn't exactly affectionate either, and never asked us for a kiss, though we'd kiss him in the morning when he left for work. None of us ever sat on his lap except Francisca. She'd go to him and he'd lift her up and chat with her. I never did that. If you're told somebody is a no-good, you keep out of his way as much as possible.

Now I realize there are fathers who really are concerned about whether their children eat. There was no such thing in my childhood. If *papá* brought bread home he'd give us a slice, but he never asked what else we'd had, or whether we'd cleaned our plates—that sort of thing.

Still, he was a lot easier to get along with than *mamá;* he never let loose with a stream of dirty words the way she did. To us he'd say, "You kids be quiet or I'll hit you with my belt," but really, we had to be pretty naughty before he actually used it.

So far as I remember, *papá* hit me twice. The first time was when he found something broken in his darkroom. He was furious. He gathered us all together and said, "That's expensive equipment. I work hard to pay for it and then you kids mess around in there all the time. Now tell me, who was in there?"

We all knew it was Francisca but nobody tattled. "It must have been you, Pila," *papá* said, and *prácata!* he hit me on the head with the handle of a hacksaw. He didn't break my head or anything, but I was so scared I wet my pants.

The second time he hit me because of a letter. I was about twelve years old at the time, and I had a school friend named Elsa who used to write

letters for the rest of us to send to our sweethearts. One day I said to her,
"I have a sweetheart."

"Ah, then I'll write a letter for you." It said horrible things that I only
half understood. I was reading it on my way home when I happened to
meet *papá,* and he took it from me. I almost died of fright watching him
read it. Then he took off his belt and started hitting me.

As soon as he gave me a chance I explained, and when he looked at the
letter again he realized it wasn't my handwriting. Besides, he must have
seen in my face that I'd never even thought about such filthy things. It was
like a woman's letter, not a girl's, and contained every dirty word in the
language. To me, who thought even marriage was a sin, it was shocking.

If it hadn't been for *papá* I believe we'd never have gone to school.
Mamá provided us with clean clothes and made us take a bath on school
days, but we didn't have toothbrushes or anything like that because she
never thought they were necessary for children. I had to clean the house
in the morning—I went to school in the afternoons—and after school I
washed the dishes. I never studied much. I just wasn't interested in
learning, as my bad grades clearly showed. All I was interested in was
fooling around, and I was constantly worrying about my brother getting
into a fight at recess.

I loved to give the teacher a hard time and was proud of my reputation
as the main troublemaker. Sometimes they even had to call in my
mother. She'd never have bothered about what happened at school but
they made her go. They told her I was always causing trouble, didn't pay
attention, that I had no respect whatsoever for the teachers. She'd give
me a good beating when I came home and make sure *papá* never found
out about it.

The Palatino teachers used to make deals with each other, and I'll
never forget the time I overheard one of them saying, "You'll have to
pass Pilar; you'll never get anything more out of her. When the year is
over, go on and promote her to the sixth grade." But when we moved
from Palatino to Jesús María we had to change schools, so they gave us a
test and I fell back to the second grade.

The barrio of Jesús María was an obscene place, full of marijuana
smokers, pimps, and all sorts of delinquents. Hardly any decent people
lived there. On my way home from school I'd see couples going into
brothels, or a policeman chasing a whore—scenes like that were so familiar that my sisters and I often played at being prostitutes.

My mother didn't know about our game because she spent most of her
time asleep. She'd take a long siesta every afternoon and go to bed early
at night. Then we were as good as alone. We'd pretend we were streetwalkers and my brother was a policeman chasing us. We'd put something
under our arm like a prostitute's purse, and stand around until we saw

Aurelio coming down the street, then we'd run away and stand some-place else until he caught us again. I knew nothing about sex then. I knew that prostitutes sold themselves to men, but I thought all they did together was talk.

Once I passed a handsome man and I thought he looked very nice, so when he said he wanted to talk with me I followed him to the hall stairs of a house. He asked me how old I was. "Twelve," I said.

"Only twelve? Well, when you get to be fourteen, there's something you and I will have to talk about," he said. That's all that happened, but a neighbor saw us and told *papá*. *Papá* explained to me that the man led a wicked life and had not one wife but two or three women, none of whom he loved. I didn't know what he was driving at and thought he just meant I was too young to be thinking of men.

Only once did I get a real scare, not from a pimp but from a thief and marijuana peddler. I was thirteen or fourteen then and he said he had to talk to me in the plaza. When we got there we went up several flights of stairs with steps missing; it was really a struggle climbing them. At the top he started kissing me and tried to take off my panties. I was in a panic. I knew I'd kill myself if I tried to run down those broken steps—so I screamed. That scared him and he turned me loose. "Go on, beat it," he said. "I won't hurt you."

The whole thing really terrified me. I swore I'd never follow a stranger again. And I never did.

As a girl I was very outgoing and had many friends—mostly girls because I preferred their company—and they told me what went on between men and women. One day the girl who'd written the letter *papá* found told me how she and her sweetheart kissed and touched each other. I thought she had a dirty mind but I didn't stop liking her.

When I had my first period, at the age of twelve, I didn't tell *mamá* because I'd confide in anybody but her. Instead I went to a neighbor, who reassured me it was the most natural thing in the world and ex-plained what I had to do. At home they didn't bother about cotton or Kotex, so I'd use a rag, wash it, and use it again. That's what *mamá* did too, but she didn't trouble to wash them; she'd let them accumulate under her mattress. I used to see them when I stooped to clean under the bed. My sisters must have seen them too because children get down on the floor to play and crawl under beds. Oh, how I hate to think about that!

Later on *mamá* noticed me doing the necessary things when I got my period, but even then she didn't give me any instructions. I didn't pay any attention to old wives' tales and I lived my normal life, shampooing my hair, bathing, walking barefoot—whatever I always did.

When I was very little I planned to have a lot of children, but later on I swore I'd never get married because I got the idea that if I did, *mamá* would be angry. She made me think men were brutes and a wife was nothing but a drudge. I got the feeling that marriage was not the kind of thing a decent woman should think about, that a single woman led a better life.

As I grew older and began to understand the situation at home, I changed my mind. Marriage would be a lifesaver for me because it was the only way to get out of that house. And when I thought of having children, I planned to be the exact opposite of *mamá,* to be everything to my children that she'd never been to me.

The truth is, *mamá* didn't like kids. When she was pregnant she was always out of sorts. And still she had eight children because she had no means of preventing them. Grandmother Nicolasa detested women who brought so many children into the world only to let them go hungry. "Poverty has an ugly face," she'd say.

Who knows how many abortions *mamá* had? She'd take all sorts of things to provoke one, any kind of a mess—boiled cinnamon water, senna leaves boiled in beer—she'd even stick yellow laundry soap up her uterus. Anything she was told would work she'd try. If it didn't work, she'd go to someone who'd do it for her. She never came right out and told me she was going to have an abortion, but she never tried to hide it from me either. I remember especially three abortions she had when I was little. The first was when we lived in Palatino, but that time I didn't see the fetus, all I saw was the blood that flowed down her legs when she stood up. I didn't know what it was about and was afraid to ask.

The second time I remember was when she stuck a twig of parsley, or maybe it was some sort of root, inside her uterus and practically died because of it. Nothing could stop her vomiting and hemorrhaging! Every time she tried to get up she'd begin to bleed big clots of blood. It was horrible. I don't know how they finally stopped it.

The third was the worst. *Mamá* must have been about seven months along, so the fetus was big by then, and she'd provoked the abortion herself. Usually when she was in labor, she sent for her mother so we wouldn't see anything, but that time—I was about nine—she needed my help. It seems the baby was feet first and *mamá* couldn't expel it. We were living at Jesús María then and *mamá* already had five children. She was alone in the house with us, and as I was the eldest at home, she called me. "Forgive me, Pila, for the harm I'm doing you, but please help me. Pull out the fetus."

That's the only time I remember *mamá* opening her mouth to ask my forgiveness. Her moans, her prayers to the saints and to the *Virgen de la Caridad del Cobre*[4] made a deep impression on me. And then asking my pardon! Never had I seen her look so defeated.

Step by step *mamá* told me what I must do. First she asked me to try to

4. The "compassionate Virgin" and patron saint of Cuba, enshrined in Cobre, a mining town near Santiago de Cuba.

put my hands inside her. "I'm straining as hard as I can," she said. "Help me, Pila, or I'll die!" I put my hands in and felt around. Then she said, "The first thing you'll find is the baby's head."

"*Mamá*," I said, "the only things I can find are its feet."

"Never mind—just pull!" I did and the baby came out, but the umbilical cord broke and the placenta was left inside. Not that I had any idea what those things were! *Mamá* said, "There's something still inside. Help me! Press down on my belly." It took me about two hours to get the placenta out. I'd sent my brother to fetch *mima* Bella, and when she got there I'd already put the fetus in a tub. It was a girl, with hair and everything. Grandma was bitter about it. "This baby could have been born alive. You've committed a crime," she told her. "If you'd done it earlier, when you were one or two months pregnant . . . but now!"

Up to that moment I'd thought of abortion as a perfectly normal routine; there were so many of us already, it seemed fair enough that no more children should be allowed to come. But that baby was such a fantastic sight I couldn't take my eyes off it. I thought of it as my little sister, and like my grandmother, I felt *mamá* had committed a crime.

Papá didn't know anything about these goings-on. He loved children and said he wouldn't stop till he had a full dozen, so of course *mamá* did all that behind his back. Then she'd tell him she was in bed because she'd fallen down or something. Most of the time he didn't even know she was pregnant. That time he did, because she had such a big belly, but when he came home she told him she'd had a miscarriage. *Papá* was brokenhearted, but I didn't tell him the truth. I felt sorry for *mamá* and wanted to protect her.

Years later, when I was on my own, I began to think about why my mother wasn't a normal person. Because that's what she was, abnormal. Poor woman, she's still the same way. If I suggest a psychiatrist she flares up and screams that there's nothing wrong with her. If only she'd gone for treatment years ago! She might have been a different kind of mother and I might have grown up loving her. But the poor didn't go to psychiatrists then the way they do now, and people had to put up with their relatives' strange ways.

I think *mamá* must have suffered a great deal in her childhood. Her father, Arnaldo, was a career soldier, an old-fashioned dictator with a terrible temper, who ruled his home with an iron hand right up to his last breath. Only *his* orders were carried out and *his* whims were sacred. *Mima* Bella, *mamá*, and both aunts were terrified of him. Grandma was black; he was white and dominated her completely, and she was too noble-hearted to defend herself. He insulted his daughters all the time, calling them whores and degenerates. Of course *mamá* was a bit offensive herself, but the other daughters weren't.

And, in fact, my grandfather didn't mistreat *mamá* as much as he did the others precisely because he and *mamá* were so much alike. What with their violent tempers, they got along fine. When he wasn't home he delegated his authority to *mamá*, so she was the one who gave the orders and went out to do the errands. *Mima* Bella never complained—that's the way her husband wanted it.

Mamá was the one who went to market and that's how she met *papá*, who was a driver on Route 2. He wasn't stuck-up like the rest of his family and he fell in love with her even though she's colored. He especially liked her hair. She was pretty then, but I'd better not say too much about that because people tell me I'm her living portrait, and it would sound like boasting.

My parents became sweethearts in secret because *mamá* was very young, only fifteen I think, and didn't dare tell her father. Then somebody else spilled it to him and he tried to make her break with *papá*, but she refused and brought him to the house instead. Grandfather gave in then, and some time later they got married. *Mamá*'s mother wasn't consulted at all, but she always agreed to everything anyway.

Mamá's family was much poorer than *papá*'s. There were four children and none of them worked, so naturally there wasn't much food, mostly rice and beans. At *papá*'s house they served meat every day!

For a long, long time *mamá*'s family lived in La Víbora, in a house that Grandfather built himself with the help of some friends. It was a medium-sized place with two bedrooms, but it was uncomfortable because it had no bathroom, just a latrine at the back of the yard, and no running water. They had to get their water from a well. But at least the house was made of cement, not wood.

My Grandfather Arnaldo was a first lieutenant—he'd gone through a school for cadets. He didn't want his children to study, though; he said he couldn't afford the textbooks or bus fares or lunches. *Mamá* claims she graduated from the sixth grade but that's just another one of her lies. I don't believe she went as far as the third—at least her handwriting is illegible and she can only count on her fingers.

Mima Bella was so meek it never occurred to her she could contradict Arnaldo. If he said something was green, it was green for her, even if it was plainly yellow. I was very fond of her and talked to her a lot after I grew up, but it always annoyed me that she was such a dope. When I'd ask her why she let her husband push her around, she'd answer, "When one marries, that's the way it must be. What would life be like if a wife refused to obey her husband?"

I remember Grandma protesting only once—when Grandfather was having an affair with their next-door neighbor. Sometimes my unpredictable grandfather would close the house in La Víbora and rent another for a few months in El Cerro. People said it was so he could be closer to his mistress. I was born in that house in El Cerro—on January 2, 1942.

I was just a little girl, but I'll never forget when my grandmother went to her neighbor's window to call her—whether she suspected something and did it on purpose, I don't know—and caught them in the act. What a scene she made! I remember her shouting, "You don't earn enough for your own family! What right have you got to squander it on that woman?" Apparently he'd bought his mistress a lot of presents. "She's a slut," my grandmother told him, "and I won't stand by while you have an affair right under my nose. Why don't you look after your own family a little better?"

Grandfather beat her and even pulled out his pistol, but I threw my arms around her so he couldn't shoot, and then my aunts, hearing all the noise, rushed out of the house and intervened. In the end, though, Grandma had to shut up. I remember the incident vividly because I was so astonished to see her show a bit of spirit. I never saw it again.

The reason I spent so much time at their house when I was small was that I was sickly and *mima* Bella asked *mamá* to send me to her. Sometimes Grandfather would sit with me and tell me stories about his military career, but it didn't keep me from being scared of him. When my brother and sisters came, which was very seldom, he acted as if he hated children. We had to obey him down to the last detail or he'd grab a slipper and beat us. He really liked to use that slipper!

Mima Bella used to suffer when she saw *mamá* spank us. Grandma would burst into tears and beg her to stop, but *mamá* would keep right on. When I complained to *mima* Bella about the times we had nothing to eat, she'd lament that she had such a daughter. "Poor little things," she'd say.

Papá got along very well with Grandma. As much as he loved his own mother, he saw qualities in *mima* Bella that his mother didn't have. She was understanding, loving, charitable, and she never worried about the color of anybody's skin. Besides, like my aunts she always sided with him against *mamá*, so he'd go to see her after he'd had a fight at home.

Grandfather Arnaldo never worried about our problems, never interfered or criticized *mamá*. When she went to the house she'd sit on the terrace with him the whole time, shaving him, cutting his calluses, telling him stories, lighting his cigarettes, bringing him coffee. She hardly said two words to my grandmother.

Mamá was always complaining about her sisters, but only behind their backs, and my aunts did the same to her. Eleonila, my godmother, would say *mamá* was tough and stupid and she couldn't understand what was the matter with her. Eleonila visited us a lot so she saw how things were.

Eleonila took very good care of me when I stayed with her, and if I got sick she'd massage me and kiss me. But when I wanted to cuddle up next to her, she'd recoil if I brushed against her breasts. Apart from that she was always loving, and after I started school she encouraged me to study and helped me with my school work. On my fifteenth birthday she gave me a dress, a purse, and a pair of shoes, but that's the only time I remember getting a present from her. In fact my mother's family could seldom afford presents, but I feel much closer to them than to my father's family because they never played favorites among us children.

Aunt Paula is exactly like *mima* Bella. Out of obedience to her father she never married. It was Grandfather's fault, too, that Eleonila's first marriage failed. He was always interfering in her life, and when Eleonila tried to obey him she got in trouble with her husband. Even after they moved to an apartment of their own she spent more time at her father's house than her own, and finally her husband found himself another woman and divorced Eleonila.

Aunt Caridad was the liveliest and prettiest of the sisters, and the only one with a happy disposition. I used to be crazy about her. She took off with a sweetheart one night, but she came back out of fear of her father. When he found out she was pregnant he wanted to kick her out of the house, but his other daughters persuaded him that nobody would know if they were careful. So for nine months Grandfather kept Caridad at home, letting her out only to see the doctor. The whole barrio knew all about it, but Grandfather convinced himself the secret had been well kept and he registered the baby as his son. That boy, Nelson, has been brought up as a brother to Aunt Caridad but everybody knows he's her son.

Grandfather Arnaldo's death aroused no feelings in us except gaiety. He was such an ogre! What a relief to my poor grandmother. If he had lived, she'd still be struggling along and suffering, because she's such an idiot it would never have occurred to her to leave him. His death was the only solution.

When I arrived at the wake I burst out, "Oh Aunt Paula, at last!" Then I apologized. "*Ay*, what have I said!"

That night the whole family got together to tell jokes and bring one another up to date on what had been happening. We talked about everything except my dead grandfather. *Ay*, what things some people do to make their families feel like that! When *mamá* dies I have a hunch all her children will sit around telling jokes.

Papá's family was so different from *mamá*'s. There were only his parents, my *papá*, and his sister Gertrudis. Grandfather Raimundo and Grandmother Nicolasa were teachers and held sixth-grade classes in their home. She taught Spanish and he mathematics, until he got a job as a night watchman for Public Works.

I don't know whether my father finished high school, but he was pretty well educated and had good manners, and he became a photographer. Aunt Gertrudis was a schoolteacher even before the Revolution, so she must have passed the eighth grade. In those times it was really hard to find a teaching job, but since she was able to speak English, a friend of hers, an army captain, got her a job in the ten-cent store. The salary was good and Aunt Gertrudis always lived better than my mother's sisters, dressed better, and had more social poise, more polished manners. She used to go to the beach and other places to amuse herself. My mother's sisters never went anywhere.

The only nice one in *papá*'s family was Grandfather Raimundo. Nicolasa and Gertrudis were mean, hard women. Nicolasa had always opposed *papá*'s marriage, claiming that he had lowered himself by marrying a *mulata*. My grandmother helped us out a bit by sending food and things, but she was a selfish snob who hated my mother and never stopped reproaching *papá* for marrying her. So whenever *papá* visited his mother, there'd be a fight at home.

Nicolasa and Gertrudis favored Francisca, my eldest sister, who spent as much time at their house as I spent at *mima* Bella's, and even when we were both there I noticed that if visitors came, Grandmother would introduce Francisca but not me. I never complained, but it gave me intolerable pain. My sister had a higher position than the rest of us in all sorts of ways—she always, always, had plenty to eat, and she even had a Banker's Club credit card that Grandmother had bought her so she could go to the beach. My grandmother came right out and said that she took Francisca with her because my sister could pass for white and colored people weren't allowed in the places she went. My brother Aurelio was also on the light side, but Susana, Xiomara, and I were dark-skinned and she was embarrassed to be seen in public with us. Little Susana was even darker than I, and Grandmother used to call her "the monkey of the family."

So there was always some tension between the rest of us and the "white" girl of the family. If Nicolasa gave Francisca oranges she'd say, "Don't go giving your sisters any. They eat enough and you don't." Francisca had more clothes than we did because Aunt Gertrudis kept buying them for her, but Francisca would never lend them to the rest of us. She was very selfish about everything. Naturally we were a bit jealous.

Francisca had the kind of style that wins people over. I didn't—I was too dry and serious. She was proud and vain and I was quarrelsome and dominating, so we often fought, though when we were little we played together a lot, too. I'd get pretty mad at Francisca when they took her to parties or the beach, but I think I may also have been scared of her because she used to threaten me with her fingernails. We'd start fighting and then *mamá* would spank us both.

My paternal grandparents lived in the barrio Los Pinos in an apartment that Aunt Gertrudis got through a friend of hers. They had a corner apartment with two bedrooms, a living room, dining room, kitchen, bathroom, and terrace. After the Revolution Aunt Gertrudis found a better place and left that one to *mamá*.

Often on Saturdays Gertrudis would send for me to spend the day. That meant they were going to clean the house. I was the one who had experience, my aunt said, and Francisca didn't—meaning Francisca wouldn't lift a finger. Oh, my aunt was willing to use me when she needed me, but she never showed me any affection, nor did I ever get anything from her but cast-off clothes.

Grandfather Raimundo was different. He was very sweet to me and didn't pay much attention to Francisca, because, as he used to say, "She gets more than enough affection." He'd often argue with Grandmother about us, poor man! He'd say, "They're all your grandchildren. You should love every one of them. You shouldn't play favorites!" And it wasn't just words on his part. That's why he took me with him to buy the groceries. He used to buy me bananas because my sister was always getting special treats at mealtimes.

Papá never, never caught on to the situation. Oh, he knew his family liked Francisca best but he thought it was because she was the eldest and had spent the most time with them. Grandmother never said anything about skin color in front of him.

Papá adored his mother, and she respected him, even if she was always criticizing him and trying to run his life. She'd tell him he should come over more often because she was worried about his getting enough to eat, and she was always after him not to have any more children. He had to work hard enough as it was, and even so he couldn't support us all. How could he think of having more?

Papá didn't listen. He'd tell her, "I'm going to have at least a dozen and you needn't worry about what doesn't concern you." They were always arguing about that, but on the whole they were very loving with one another. My Aunt Gertrudis was forever complaining that Grandmother favored *papá*. "I'm the one who does everything for you. *I* make the sacrifices, and you thank me by paying more attention to Aurelio." Grandmother Nicolasa wasn't any model mother; she was self-centered and cared only about her own comfort, but at least there wasn't any violence in her home and nobody used foul language.

My grandmother made a slave of her husband. The problem was, he lost his job, and since he was home most of the time he did the woman's work—the cooking, the cleaning, the shopping. A cousin of Grandmother's lived with them too, an invalid in a wheelchair, and it was Grandfather who had to carry her and bathe her, even clean her and change the bed because she couldn't go to the toilet. Poor henpecked guy! And though he tried hard, Grandfather didn't really know how to give the house a good cleaning.

My aunt treated her father as if he were her servant, or even a woman.

They all slept in the same room, my grandparents in one bed and my aunt in the other, and in the morning Gertrudis would get up in nothing but a transparent nightgown and go into the bathroom. She never took a bath, she just washed and used a lot of cream to keep herself from looking old. She always had a peculiar smell about her . . . I mean, it was horrible. Then she'd come out of the bathroom stark naked and say, "Hand me a bar of soap," or "*Papá,* get me my panties." I thought it was revolting.

I'd never seen my father or my brother naked. My sisters slept in the same things they wore during the day and changed in the bathroom, *papá* slept in his underwear but always covered himself, and *mamá* slept in a dress. My brother Aurelio never saw *mamá* without her clothes on. But Aunt Gertrudis wasn't ashamed for her *papá* to see her like that.

The first time Gertrudis got married, the groom brought her back home the day after the wedding. My aunt claimed it was because he wasn't a real man, but I heard a neighbor say, "What a brazen lie! Everybody knows why he brought her back—she's not a virgin." I also heard someone say that the only way she got her job at the ten-cent store was by giving herself to that captain. I don't know if it's true, but I don't suppose Grandmother cared what her daughter did as long as she herself was comfortable.

Aunt Gertrudis believes children should sacrifice themselves for their parents and that's what she's done all her life. Grandmother died a short time ago and now Raimundo lives with Gertrudis—he's ninety-two years old and a real nuisance. I don't mean he's bad, he's just troublesome because he's so old. Still, if my aunt really loved him she'd have taken his side when her mother was treating him so badly. As it was, he didn't dare open his mouth because every time he did, *boom!* they'd both jump all over him.

What with one thing and another, I never saw a happy marriage in my family. Not one! When it comes to that, I never saw one outside my family either.

Chapter Two

I Had No Choice

I BEGAN TO REALIZE what school was all about when I got to the sixth grade again. I wanted to go on, but the money situation at home was very strained and *mamá* told me they couldn't afford to keep me there. My sister Francisca had gone as far as the eighth grade. So I said, "When Francisca was in school you could afford it."

"Now it's different," *mamá* told me. "Besides, what's the use of more studying? It isn't worth so many sacrifices." She said it was high time I got a job. *Mamá* never cared about her children having a career. *Papá* did, and he would have liked to let me go on studying, but as always, he gave in to *mamá*. It hurt to leave school, and I had an unsatisfied feeling for a long time after that.

I was thirteen when I got a sleep-in job in Almendares as a housemaid at 30 *pesos* a month. Pretty soon all my sisters started working as domestics too. We all applied without telling *papá* beforehand, because he didn't want his daughters to be servants. *Papá* didn't let *mamá* work precisely because a servant's job was the only kind she could have gotten. She had never held a job in her life.

When I started to work I was embarrassed to say I was a housemaid, so I told everybody I was going to live with one of my aunts. In a way the job made me feel liberated; it got me out of the house and away from all those abnormal goings-on, but I also felt humiliated and cried a great deal. The difference between me and my employers was made clear from the very start. I was given a uniform and had to address the lady of the house and her mother-in-law as *señora* and the man as *caballero*. When her brother came to live with them, I had to call him *señorito*, though he was as old as the devil and looked kind of effeminate. The lady of the house was the type who can be very despotic with her servants one day and the next day she'll be chattering with them about her intimate problems. It was hard to keep watch over my tongue; sometimes her first name slipped out and then she'd say, "To you I am *señora*."

My job was to take care of a month-old baby and do the laundry and all the housecleaning. All of it! In the morning I'd change the baby's crib and her diaper, give her the bottle, bathe her, and then start to clean the house, or wash or iron the clothes. Whatever else I was doing, I was supposed to be taking care of the baby at the same time, and I had to stop and heat a bottle to give her every three hours. When she cried I'd practically go out of my mind because I couldn't do everything at once. A two-story house to clean! And what a big wash I had to do! Sheets, clothes, the baby's diapers—everything. *Ay, mi madre!* Then the lady would pass her fingertips over the furniture and say to me, "These are dusty, Pilar, you haven't cleaned here." The one thing she did for the baby was to check the diapers every day to make sure I'd washed and ironed them to suit her. I was going crazy with so many demands.

The only thing I didn't have to do was cook, because the food was prepared in the mother-in-law's home and sent over by car. I'd set the table and wait in the kitchen until they were through eating so I could wash the dishes. They ate well in that house but I only got what the señora decided I should eat, usually rice, beans, and leftovers. She never gave me meat. I wasn't allowed to take even a soft drink or a bit of anything from the refrigerator without asking permission. Yet from 7:00 in the morning until 10:00 at night, when I gave the baby her last bottle, I couldn't stop for a minute.

And then the baby wouldn't let me sleep. Her mother slept in another room and didn't bother about her in the least. One night I was so tired of that kid's constant bawling I decided to put a stop to it. I soaked a piece of cotton with 90-proof alcohol and held it to her nose, thinking the smell would shut her up. Well, I almost killed her! The kid's face got purple. I was so scared, I never tried that again.

The husband was a bum who didn't like to work for a living; it was his mother who supported them. The house, the servants, the car—all of it belonged to his mother. And she was the only one who showed any concern for the baby. Her daughter-in-law, the lady of the house, was no model of virtue; she was hardly ever at home and she often came back with presents from a man who owned a hardware store. She called him her "friend," but it's pretty clear they were lovers.

There were times when I felt contented in that house. I enjoyed taking care of the baby and liked the responsibility. But that was the only part I enjoyed—the rest I detested. The lady would stay out late every night, and I was left alone with that kid, frightened to death in that big house, wondering what I'd do if something happened to the child.

I stuck it out there for two years. When I got fed up I went back home. Nothing had changed there, and I started worrying about my family's problems again. I couldn't bear to see my sisters going hungry and having to put up with my mother on top of that. I still thought of her as a good woman but I never felt any affection for her; I was just sorry for her. I thought she was what you might call a victim of circumstances.

I didn't want to let my parents support me, so I decided to get married. What did it matter to me if I wasn't in love? I couldn't afford to wait, I was having too hard a time at home. Even now I don't regret my decision. I had no choice, and if I found myself in the same circumstances I'd do it all over again.

I'd met Eleodoro in Jesús María when I was thirteen and he was twenty-nine. He worked at the plaza, carrying heavy crates, loading and unloading trucks, and on my way home from school I'd stop and chat with him. He wasn't well off but he did have steady work with regular wages, so I decided he was the man for me, even though he wasn't my age. At least he was a chance for my family to have enough to eat. Besides, I thought I'd like to get married, have children, and be happy.

As a man, Eleodoro wasn't disagreeable to me. He was fair-skinned, tall, with very black straight hair. His face wasn't too awfully handsome but he had a good physique. None of that mattered particularly because I saw him as a refuge. Now I realize our relationship was never normal.

It really started as a friendship, but when time passed and Eleodoro said nothing, I decided to take the initiative and we became sweethearts. We kept it a secret for over two years, and even during that time Eleodoro's gifts helped with the food shortage at home. If he had to haul a load of mangoes, he'd bring us a box; when he carried meat, he gave us enough for the whole family. The plaza was a real labyrinth, with all sorts of places where we could meet safely—on a staircase, at a cafeteria. . . .

We never slept together while we were sweethearts; Eleodoro told me that he controlled himself for my family's sake. We often went to his home after the movies but we never did anything except kiss and pet. I enjoyed it all right but I never felt the sensation of well-being you have with a man you really desire. He'd touch and press me through my clothes and it didn't repel me, but it didn't bring me joy either. Once he took off my blouse and put his hand inside my brassiere. He tried to kiss my breasts, but I pushed him away and said I was leaving at once. Sometimes when we were petting, he'd have to get up and change because his pants got stained.

My brother and sisters sometimes saw us together and then they'd go tell *mamá,* who greeted me with blows when I got home. She'd tell me that Eleodoro was a nobody and that I was a loose woman. I'd answer right back that whatever I might be, I was a product of her upbringing. Then she'd be all hurt and insulted.

When I asked her for permission to go to my aunts' house or someplace, she'd say, "No, you can't go anywhere." I'd shout, "I want to go and I will!" And I did. But she'd get even with me by throwing away the few clothes I had, and my shoes, too, so I couldn't go out again. I didn't let that get me down, though. I'd just go help Aunt Gertrudis clean house in return for one of her old dresses.

Papá opposed my marriage to the very last. He said Eleodoro was much too old for me and it wouldn't work out. Grandmother Nicolasa was against it too, but her reason was that Eleodoro was nothing but a poor laborer. "You should be practical. Look around for a man who can keep you comfortably. This is sheer madness, following in your mother's footsteps by marrying at fifteen. Well, if you insist on getting married, at least don't have any children. You'll only be adding to your troubles if you do.

"Look at your father," she went on. "He wouldn't listen to me, and where is he now? Working harder and harder with nothing to show for it. To have children is to court destitution."

One evening Eleodoro and I went to the movies, and I said I wanted to go home with him that night. We didn't do anything because I had my period, but the next day *papá* came and begged me to go back home with him so people wouldn't talk. I didn't argue because after what I did *papá* didn't have any choice, and he finally gave his consent to the marriage.

Eleodoro and I got married at a notary's office in Old Havana, with just a few friends and relatives present. Eleodoro's mother was there, his sister, and his brother-in-law—I can't say any of them seemed to be happy about it. Uncle Julian and my Godmother Eleonila were there too; the others were waiting at home. I wore a very pretty white dress, gloves, and a small hat. All my clothes were new and Eleodoro had bought everything, even my panties.

From the notary's office we went to my house for the reception, which was nothing special; it was rather like *papá*'s birthday parties. Although *papá* had objected to the marriage, he did nothing to embitter the occasion for me. He was the one who invited all the family and bought the beer, the cake, the sandwiches, and the soft drinks. He took the wedding photographs, too. *Mamá,* naturally, did everything she could to spoil the party. She refused to be photographed, and she wore her very worst clothes, as if she were going to clean house instead of celebrate her daughter's wedding.

I'd always heard that honeymoons were spent in lovely places, a hotel beside the beach or someplace like that, so I was bitterly disappointed when the hired car drove us to a shabby, ugly little old hotel that turned out to be a brothel. Beautifully dressed as I was, I walked into that place and there I spent my wedding night. It's true Eleodoro was a poor man—he earned 3 *pesos* a day—but he might have shown a little more interest in our honeymoon. He didn't volunteer any explanation as to why he'd taken me to such a place, and I was ashamed to ask.

Everything that happened that night was horrible. I realize the poor guy was crude and uneducated, coming from a childhood of poverty and hard work. Besides, he wasn't intelligent. But that night he didn't even bother with preliminaries. He undressed as soon as we were alone in the room, without even turning out the light. Then he looked at me and said, "Go on, take off your clothes."

I went into the bathroom and came back wearing my panties and brassiere. "Take those things off!" he said, without a kiss or a single word of affection. He got into bed, and when he saw I hadn't taken off my panties, he reached over and jerked them down. If only he'd turned off the light! I wanted him to take off my panties, but not like that, not so abruptly. He could have kissed me and caressed me while he was doing it, to sort of disguise what he was doing. A man should be tender at such times; he should say lovely, sweet things first. But no, off they came, *rán, rán, rán.*

I can't stand a man who says dirty words. You don't have to call things by name, you don't have to come right out and ask for anything. A man should turn the act of coitus into a nest of love. But for Eleodoro there was only one way he could tell me things—by their filthy names. I was only fifteen and a virgin, yet that first night he asked me to . . . to suck his prick! I didn't want to and he forced me. When I tried to pull back, he came right in my face. I was so disgusted I kept vomiting all night long. Afterward he tried to start all over again. I told him he'd done enough already and I wanted to be left alone, but he entered me, and the pain was unbearable.

He was so harsh, so crude, so completely unlike the Eleodoro I had known. He'd respected me so much that although we'd often lain in bed together, he'd never pressed me to go further than I was willing to go. And then to use such filthy language! He was bestial; he treated me like a whore he'd picked up. I'd married just to get away from home, and the monstrous first night made me realize one pays a price for everything one gets in life.

Afterward our sexual relations settled down into something more normal, and Eleodoro was so good to me in other ways that I didn't feel I could ever reject him. Besides, I was sorry for him. So I did as he asked, though in a whole year I felt pleasure only once.

We were to live in my mother-in-law's house, and she and her husband had gone to their daughter's for a few days to give us some privacy, so the morning after the wedding we went there. It was a small modern house with a living room, dining room, kitchen, and one bedroom. Eleodoro's mother had bought him a bedroom set on the installment plan. It was made of yellowish wood varnished a caramel color. My mother-in-law slept in a single bed in the bedroom and my father-in-law slept in the dining room, so we put Eleodoro's bedroom set in the living room and slept there. His parents put up a curtain so as not to bother us in the mornings.

I'd met Eleodoro's mother only a few times but she'd always been nice to me. After we were married she insisted on doing the cooking and all the housework, even cleaning our room and making the bed. All I did was sit by the open door watching people pass in the street. It made her angry to see me sitting down, but what could I do? When Eleodoro came home she'd say to him, "What kind of a woman have you married? She doesn't do anything except sit and look out all day."

"But you don't let me help you," I'd object. "What else is there for me to do?"

One day when I was sitting on the front stoop to watch the kids out playing in the street she began to grumble that I shouldn't have gotten married, that I was still a child with no sense.

"What do you expect me to do?" I answered. "Lock myself up in the house? Whenever I go near you, you look grim. At least I want something to look at."

She came at me with a stick then, but I tore it out of her hand and hit her across the back with it. When Eleodoro came home, we each told him our version of the story and he took my side. He himself had noticed the dirty looks she gave me, but she'd made light of it and said there'd be no trouble between us if only I would do my share of housework.

During the week it was my mother-in-law who managed the money and did the shopping, though if I needed 10 or 15 *pesos* I only had to ask Eleodoro for it. My mother-in-law spent Saturdays and Sundays at her daughter's home, so Eleodoro gave me the money to buy whatever we needed for the weekend, and I would buy the food and take it to *mamá*. I didn't give her the money because she'd have spent it on anything but food. My mother-in-law saw that I exploited her son and that upset her badly.

"Do you think Eleodoro works just to support your family?" she'd say angrily. "What kind of a life is that for him?"

From time to time Eleodoro himself protested that my duty now was to take care of myself and my own home. Sometimes when he brought food home I'd just cart the whole lot over to *mamá*. Then when he went to get something to eat, he'd ask, "Where's the food?"

"I took it to my family."

"All of it?"

"I don't care what you say, they need it more than we do," I'd answer. And then we'd quarrel.

Practically from the first day of our marriage, Eleodoro kept asking if I'd menstruated or had any signs of pregnancy, and it took only a month for me to get pregnant. I suspected it right away because I was so tired, and kept getting dizzy spells and vomiting. I went to the Workers' Maternity Hospital as soon as I missed my period and the doctor told me I was about a month and a half along.

Eleodoro was very happy with the news and so was my mother-in-law. *Papá* was glad too, and my sisters were delighted to think they were going to be aunts. Only *mamá* remained indifferent.

I had a "bad belly" and felt so sick that I spent most of the nine months in bed. My mother-in-law didn't say much about it, so on the whole things calmed down.

During my pregnancy Eleodoro behaved very well. He never made me get out of bed or do any kind of work at all, and he was always trying to please me. He'd go right out and buy whatever I wanted to eat or tell his *mamá* to prepare it for me. He also bought baby clothes and a crib. I don't mean he went into ecstasies over the idea of having a firstborn, but he wasn't indifferent. He'd always wanted a child. Not that I cared what he thought. I was happy because I'd always wanted to know how it felt to be a mother, to have a little girl to bathe, suckle, and carry in my arms. For me, expecting a child was the greatest event in the world.

Ana Bárbara was born in 1958. She weighed 7 pounds, and had a pretty face and a lot of very black hair. Eleodoro had a lot of work just then and couldn't visit the hospital right away, so the first person to see the baby was my *papá*. He was very happy and came to see me every single day. *Mamá* didn't visit me there; my baby was no great event as far as she was concerned, but the day I left she came with Eleodoro to take me home. I'm sure she didn't go of her own free will. She acted very cold. She didn't take the baby in her arms, and only looked at her because I showed her to everybody. She said, "Oh, how pretty she is," but in such an indifferent tone of voice!

I think Eleodoro must have been broke because we took a bus home, although it was raining. That was just like him! The things he did were so unsuitable, they just didn't fit the occasion. He was so tactless, so . . . so stupid! I know he didn't *mean* to do things wrong, but oh, what a disappointment.

My mother-in-law had only one other grandchild, a little girl who'd been crippled by polio, so she was overjoyed when Ana Bárbara was born. How she bustled around cleaning the house and scrubbing the floors all day! "If you weren't such a slut, you'd do this yourself!" she used to tell me. "It's a good thing I'm here to wash the floors. The baby would catch her death of cold in all that dust!" All I did was wash the diapers.

I couldn't have cared less about having Ana Bárbara baptized, and Eleodoro wasn't much interested either, but in those days baptism was taken for granted and people still swallowed all that bilge about what a great honor it was to be a godparent. *Papá* was anxious to have the ceremony, then Francisca asked to be godmother, and *mamá*'s father wanted to be godfather because Ana Bárbara was his first great-grandchild.

So when she was four or five months old, just to keep everybody happy, we went off to La Caridad Church near my home. We didn't have a party or get a special christening gown or any of that, though my sister did give her a receiving blanket. Grandfather Arnaldo, even though he was godfather, attended in shirt-sleeves.

I'd never given much thought to the future, but I did take it for granted that I'd live out my days as Eleodoro's wife. Then one day, right in the middle of an argument, he told me I must change. "We can't keep on living like this," he said. "You'll have to get a job."

I couldn't understand why I should go to work when he was earning 3 *pesos* a day and had been well able to support me up to then. I felt trapped in the same old problems I'd always had—having to get a job, with a baby and a home to take care of. I began to reject him in bed. "You're right," I told him. "We can't keep on this way. I don't feel the same with you anymore."

I had a talk with a friend of mine who was a domestic, and once again I got a job as a servant. The day I started to work was the day I decided to put an end to my marriage, and I moved back to *mamá*'s house. There I found the same old problems—no money, no food, no this, no that . . . I hated being there.

Up to the time Ana Bárbara was five months old, I was the only one who took care of her. After I went back to work I think my daughter spent as much time with her grandmothers as with me. My mother-in-law was very affectionate and I felt the child was safer with her than with my own family, but my mother-in-law kept on nagging at me, so in the end I had to take the baby and leave her with *mamá*. It was hard to do.

By the time I left Eleodoro I was pregnant again, and I had an abortion. I didn't want to but things were too difficult between Eleodoro and me. I knew a doctor *mamá* had often gone to, so I went to see him. He charged 40 *pesos* and did the job very fast because there were about twenty more women waiting. It was a monstrous experience. When the fetus is big a curettage won't do, so they give an injection in the navel to kill it and a miscarriage follows. Four days later I felt the first symptoms, and I was very ill. I went back to the doctor, spent the night there, and by morning I'd aborted. I was alone at the moment and was curious to see the fetus. It was a boy. Afterward I hated myself for having killed my son. Eleodoro wanted to have children so I hadn't breathed a word about it to him. When he learned about it he told me it was very wrong, and I had to agree. Abortion is a criminal act even if it's performed five days after conception. After all, the child is already beginning to take human form.

I was sixteen years old when I started on my second job—not a sleep-in job this time. For 15 *pesos* a month I had to clean the house and do the laundry for a lady and gentleman who were constantly humiliating me. I hated it. The señora's brother-in-law was an older man, about forty-eight I think, and one day as I was going home from work, he came by in his car and stopped beside me. "Get in," he said, and I did.

Then he said I should leave my job. "I'll give you 100 *pesos* a month if you'll just go out with me two or three nights a week," he said. A hundred *pesos* a month! I agreed at once. It was as if I'd known what he was going to say before he opened his mouth. Even he was taken aback and said, "I honestly didn't expect you to react this way."

Yes, I thought, here I am earning 15 *pesos* for being an honest woman and I can get 100 for doing something wrong with a married man. But I didn't care. It seemed like a good exchange.

It was a Saturday, and that very day he took me to Marianao Beach for a few drinks and afterward to a hotel. But he made no demands on me. He was very affectionate and asked only that I kiss him, though later on he began complaining that I didn't love him because I was so much younger than he.

It's true I didn't like being with him, and we quarreled a lot. He gave me fine presents and took me to cabarets and clubs to show me off to his friends. Maybe he was in love with me, maybe it was only vanity. When he'd start to annoy me by trying to kiss me in public, I'd remind him that I was with him for money, not for love. I really enjoyed saying that!

With him I learned the worst. He drank too much and wasn't any too potent to begin with, so he couldn't do much in bed. He couldn't have an erection and I had to work awfully hard to satisfy him, kiss him all over his body, horrible things. I think he was sick in the head. I'm ashamed to admit it, but sometimes he'd say I was his husband and ask me to caress him the way a man caresses a woman. Oh, he was absolutely odious! It was martyrdom to be with him.

Not that he ever mistreated me; on the contrary, he treated me very well and solved all my financial problems. It was a job, that's all, but I hated to think he was buying me. I always handed my 100 *pesos* to *mamá*. I explained exactly where it came from and she didn't say a word. In fact, my mother looked on the whole thing with complete approval.

Rich men have their whims and expect others to put up with them. If I said, "Tonight I feel like staying home," he'd say, "Oh no, tonight we're going out," even if I had my period. He took me to hotels, never to anybody's house. Sometimes we'd go to a bar on the corner of the block where he lived, and twice his wife saw us there.

Then one day he took me to the beach when his wife, son, and sister-in-law were also there. He'd spend a bit of time with me on one part of the beach and then go to his wife on another part. His son, who was twelve or thirteen years old, must have heard his mother talk about me, because when he saw me he came over and begged me to stop seeing his father. "I love *papá* and *mamá* both," he said. "I don't want them to separate." He spoke like a grown man and it was obvious that he adored his parents.

"That depends on your *papá*," I answered. "Talk to him about it, not to me."

But when the old man heard about it, he took his son away and told me to pay no attention.

Our relationship lasted only a few months, then I couldn't stand him anymore. *Mamá* said I must be crazy. "You should be practical," she told me. "What difference does it make if you find him odious? How can you say he's disgusting when he gives you so much money? You're the disgusting one!"

When I got home from the beach that evening, no sooner had I shut the door than there was a knock. I opened it again and there was Eleodoro. He'd found out about the old man and came over to make a scene. He socked me, beat me up, split my lip. After he was through with me he went for Ana Bárbara's crib. I struggled with him, screaming, "You can't take the baby, you can't!" But he pushed me and I fell against the medicine cabinet. He snatched her and shouted he wasn't going to leave her with a whore!

We made a lot of noise, but it was a long house and my folks slept at the other end of it. Nobody heard a thing. Eleodoro was already leaving with the baby when *mamá* woke up and asked, "What happened?" I told her. Then *papá* took me to the doctor for my cuts and bruises and from there straight to the police station to file a complaint against Eleodoro. When the lieutenant in charge heard my story he said, "Don't you worry, we'll give him a taste of the "ox's prick."

But when they did arrest him, it turned out they were old friends! The lieutenant embraced him and they both turned on me and accused me of being immoral and unfaithful. Then they let Eleodoro go and I went back home.

A few days later Eleodoro came to see me, very ashamed of his outburst and remorseful about what he'd done. Finally he told me that if I wanted the baby, I could have her. I did, so he brought her back to me.

I had no money and somehow I had to feed and clothe my daughter. I began to think there must be an easier way of earning a living. Then I ran into a girl I'd met when I was a domestic. She knew I was separated from my husband and couldn't stand my lover and she advised me to try a brothel. She claimed that a prostitute doesn't have to put up with so much from a man; she doesn't have to pretend to love him. "It's all over in a minute. You get paid and that's that."

I never wanted to be a prostitute. It's much more pleasant to do honest work and take on a man only when you feel like it. As we Cubans say, "It isn't the same and it's spelled differently!" But as a servant I couldn't earn enough to keep us and there was no other kind of job for a woman. I had no alternative; if I tried to stay honest, I'd starve to death.

None of my sisters had the courage to take such a drastic step. Besides, to them it seemed perfectly normal to go without everything, including food. But I'd never been willing to accept that situation and I felt I must sacrifice myself, not only for my daughter's sake, but also for my younger brothers and sisters.

I don't blame my mother. It wasn't her fault the government exploited people and didn't bother to provide schools or jobs. My decision was a result of the times we lived in and my desperate eagerness to get away from the old man and from Eleodoro.

So I went with my friend, just telling my folks I was spending a few days in the country. They accepted without question since I often spent nights out with the old man. My friend was working in the province of Pinar del Río, at a bar in Candelaria. At the beginning she didn't say it was a whorehouse, she only told me, "If you want to earn more money, come and work at the bar with me." She was almost certainly paid for taking me there—that's what they always did, and it's only natural, though I never tried to talk anybody into becoming a prostitute.

When I got to the bar I saw right away it was a brothel and I didn't like the looks of it. It was a run-down old house where all kinds of men were allowed. The parlor was cramped, the six or seven bedrooms were tiny, the dining room and kitchen were small, and the furniture was old and shabby. The women were sitting in the parlor, fully dressed, and the men would go in, pick one out, then go to a room with her.

Most of the brothel owners were women or perverts; I never knew a real man to own one. My friend introduced me to the madam. "Here's a girl who wants a job."

"Delighted," said the madam. "Please consider this your home. As for work, there's plenty of it."

She explained that I was expected to talk with the men and be pleasant. Then when a man asked me to go to a room with him, I must accept and charge 1.50 *pesos,* half of which I could keep and the other half turn over to her. Every brothel owner gave a cut of his profits to the police so they'd look the other way.

"Here I'll have a place to live and plenty of food," I thought, "and I'll earn a lot more money to boot." How wrong I was! I managed to earn enough so my folks could eat, but that was all, and even for that I had to work hard.

I started the very day I arrived. I changed my name to Mercy, thinking it would be easier for me. At first I was terribly depressed and just sat without saying a word to anybody, but the madam soon saw to it that I had customers. When the first man asked me to go with him I went at once, but when we were alone in the room I was paralyzed. "Are you going to stand there?" he said roughly. "I didn't come here to look at your dress, I came to fuck." That horrible, filthy word! I wanted to run away—to vanish—but I obediently took off my clothes and did it.

Afterward I told the madam how I felt. "It's that way with everybody the first day," she said reassuringly. "It'll pass. Besides, where else are you going to get a job?" There was no answer to that, and I thought maybe I'd get over my revulsion. But that night was almost as bad as my wedding night. Most of my customers were like Eleodoro, rough and crude, and it wasn't a matter of education—a lot of cultured men went there. I think they had a morbid desire to humiliate a woman.

I slept, ate, and lived in that house, attending my clients in my bedroom. We closed at 3:00 or 4:00 in the morning and opened again for business sometime around noon. In between we slept. From the moment I became a prostitute I began to drink. I had to. I couldn't stand the men and suffered bitterly from shame. Unless I had a few drinks first, I didn't feel capable of going into that room.

After I became more or less adjusted to the style of life, though, it didn't seem so bad. At least my daughter had enough to eat and so did my brothers and sisters. I'd gone to Pinar del Río feeling sure that my family would never hear about it, but afterward I stopped caring whether they knew or not. After all, *mamá* more or less suspected what I was up to, and all she cared about was the money. She was the only one I visited; I always chose a time when I knew nobody else would be home. I just handed over the money, asked her how everybody was getting along, and left after ten minutes or so.

Finally one day I met *papá*. He thought I was still seeing the old man and even that upset him. "Come back home with us," he said. "We may be poor but at least we're decent. How can you stain your family's name like that?"

I told him that honor and decency no longer meant anything to me; all I cared about was that the kids didn't go hungry.

Another time I ran into *papá* near a brothel in Havana, and he said, "I've been watching you. If I ever again so much ʑ s see you near one of those places, I'll set the police onto you." I didn'ʾ even bother to answer him. After all, if he'd gone there looking for me, it meant that he knew. I don't know who told him, maybe Francisca.

One morning when I went home I overheard one of my brothers saying that Xiomara had two sweethearts at the same time. "*Ay,* what's going on here?" I thought. When I saw my sister I said, "Look, Xiomara, I'm no model of virtue but I have a right to talk to you about this because I've had a very rough time. What are you doing with two boyfriends? Either you like one better than the other or else you love neither. That's all wrong for a señorita. You have a right to have one sweetheart, no more, so just choose the one you like best."

Mamá overheard me and burst in like a fury, screaming, "What right have you to talk? You're nothing but a whore!"

I answered calmly, "And why am I a whore? To earn money for you. When you phone and say, 'Pilar, hurry over, I'm broke,' you don't call me whore. But when I try to give my little sister decent advice, *then* I'm a whore."

That only made her madder. All she could say was, "Get out of here!"

What a cruel experience that was! All my life my mother had asked me for money and nothing but money. She knew perfectly well how I earned it—by long, exhausting nights. She knew I'd stumble out the next morning, dead tired, thinking of all the things I couldn't afford because I gave nearly everything to her.

When Eleodoro found out I was a prostitute, he called me and begged me to think of my daughter. As if I wasn't thinking of her! "You can't solve my problems," I told him. "So I have to solve them the best way I can."

Three times, though, I asked Eleodoro to help me when things were too much for me, like going to jail and coming out crushed and penniless. I wanted to break with it all and begin a new life. So I went to ask for his help, and he was always ready to give it. He'd take me home as his legal wife or give me money. I never gave him money; he wasn't a pimp. Every bit I earned went to my family.

Eleodoro's mother accepted me into their home when I stayed there, of course, because he forced her to, but she wouldn't so much as say good morning. I was uneasy there anyway, because I wasn't earning money. My family would start running short of food again and I'd think, "How can I be so selfish?" And back to the whorehouse I'd go, alone, on my own two feet, of my own free will. I'd walk out of Eleodoro's house without even saying goodbye, leaving his mother to tell him, "Oh, Pilar just packed up her things and left."

I stuck it out in Pinar del Río for two months, then I went with one of the women to a house in barrio Colón, where a homosexual told us of still another in barrio La Victoria where the atmosphere was much more pleasant. He took us to a place run by a madam called Gladys. I stayed there a few days, then I went to a house run by a man named Orlando, and after a while I began to live in a hotel, always moving from one to another.

I never had a pimp. Usually it was the streetwalkers who did. A pimp taught his woman the tricks of the trade and she could make a lot more money than girls in a house, but the pimps took most of it so those women's families went hungry. Once I met a pimp who was bent on taking me to Venezuela. He threatened to cut my face and mark me for life if I refused. I stood right up to him. "You're welcome to try. I'm in this life for my family, not to support some lazy man. I only ask one thing, don't sneak up behind my back. Come at me face to face and I'll do my best to defend myself."

I knew a pregnant girl who had trouble with that same guy. He kicked her and she miscarried. And the girl really wanted to have her child! She lay between life and death, yet no sooner was the pimp taken to the police station than he was freed. The girl went any number of places trying to press charges against him but he bought everyone off. That's the kind of justice we used to have. On sale to the highest bidder.

To a girl like me who was not yet seventeen, being a prostitute was terrible, and I drank more all the time. I noticed the other women taking benzedrine and Aktedrom pills with their liquor, so I began taking them too. With pills and drink, I was able to face the night. When I was high, though, I'd get into arguments with the men. Any little thing would make me angry. One day a young queer who cleaned the house used some of my new makeup. "You don't need it," he said. "It looks better on me." I struggled with him, and when I saw I couldn't take it away, I burned my bed and three new dresses. That's the way I let off steam—I'd burn my clothes. I did it about twice a month, sometimes once a week.

Some of the men thought they could do anything they wanted for the measly 3 *pesos* they paid. I fought with them all the time, especially when they wanted anal coitus, and with the ones who were a bit effeminate or who'd had too much to drink and tried to bite me. When I fought and screamed at them, the police would come and arrest me. Now and then men came in drunk and made a scene just for the fun of it, and when that happened, the madam called the police.

Many, many times—about ten or twelve—I was taken to the police station and had to pay 100 *pesos'* bail. There were bondsmen who'd guarantee bail for a fee of 20 percent. I spent a lot of money on that, as well as on my personal appearance. Clothes were a big expense, especially underclothes, because I made a point of replacing them before they got shabby. I liked dainty, lacy things. I've never cared about jewelry or makeup, but I love perfumes—not that I ever used good French ones, just ordinary stuff.

After a while I got so depressed I'd take a day off whenever I'd earned enough. The madam didn't make a fuss about it, but I had to tell her I didn't feel well. We weren't forced to work when we were menstruating, but all the other women did, so I did too.

One day I was drinking with some friends at a bar near the brothel when a policeman came in. He knew me because I'd already been arrested two or three times, and he accused me of having been involved in a street fight.

"Oh no, I haven't been in any fights," I said, grabbing his tie, "but if that's what you want, I'm ready for it right now." And fight I did. They had to call the patrol car and haul me to the station. When we got there I turned around at the top of the steps and said, "I'm not going in there for such a little thing. No sir, not me!"

I struggled with him again until we both rolled downstairs. I fought him like a wild beast, as if I were another man. They locked me in a tiny cell where the men were, and I wasn't the only woman there by any means. The government considered it perfectly normal to lock men and women up together. In times like those what woman wouldn't be aggressive?

Once I was drinking and the police lieutenant on patrol told me women weren't allowed to drink on street corners. He said if I didn't go out with him he'd arrest me. I said, "Go ahead then, because the answer is no." Well, he put me under arrest and I didn't have time to sock him, but I managed to scream out at the top of my voice, "You pig. Is this what you call morality? You proposition me and then you arrest me for saying no? Is this the kind of law we have?"

That's all I said but it was plenty. They charged me with contempt of duly constituted authority. The lieutenant wasn't at my trial but his written accusation was enough to get me fined. I didn't have the money and nobody knew I was on trial that day, so they sent me to jail for about seven days.

Every single day in a brothel was a day of anguish. Once I started at 1:00 P.M. and worked straight through till 5:00 A.M. the following day. I laid about twenty-five men, one after the other, twenty-five to thirty minutes apart. Drink and pep pills kept me going.

The longest I ever stayed with any client was a whole night, for which I'd get 15 or 20 *pesos*. But I had to need the money pretty desperately to do it. If you agreed to spend the night with one man, you had to put yourself out to please him, even if you'd never met him before. Having several clients a night wasn't such hard work because you didn't have to pretend so much. I hated to pretend.

Lots of men, especially Americans, liked to watch two women lie together. When women agreed to that kind of act they chose their partner if the client let them. But he paid his 30 *pesos* and was free to take his pick. He didn't necessarily choose two who got along.

Actually I never went to bed with a real lesbian. We knew all the things lesbians did, so we could put on a good show, but it was fake. None of us enjoyed it. It was a bitter cup but I drained it because I had to—the two-woman act was the best-paid job in the brothel.

One time there was a Puerto Rican who took two of us out to a *posada*[5] because he wanted a place where there were no other people around and we could have a few drinks. But he didn't go to bed with either of us, he just looked on, and after we were through he sent for a faggot. We were there only a short while and he paid us each 30 *pesos,* so I got out early enough to attend to several other men. All in all I made 98 *pesos* that night, but half went to the madam.

I never went to any of the gambling casinos they had before the

5. A lodging house where rooms are rented by the hour.

Revolution, but I went to all the big hotels—the Riviera, the Capri, the Sevilla, the Hilton, the Deauville. Prostitutes weren't supposed to be allowed in places like that, but with money you could buy your way in anywhere.

Once I went to the Hotel Sevilla with an American, but they called up from the desk and told him he could only take a woman to his room if she'd checked in as his wife. "Very well, then," he said. "Bring down my luggage. I'm checking out." Then he took me to the Habana Libre—it was still the Hilton then—and signed me in as his wife. That was the only time I ever got into a big hotel legally, without having to hide.

I was wearing a flowered dress with a plunging neckline and a very tight skirt and I looked every inch a prostitute. The man at the desk gave me a look as if to say, "Some wife!" Of course he couldn't come right out and say anything, but what a look!

On the whole, my memories of Americans are ugly. Oh sure, they'd take me to places like the Hilton, but it was as if they did it to humiliate me. And there were some who'd threaten you with a bottle if you refused to comply with their whims. Most of our American clients brought drugs along with them. They'd arrive in Cuba loaded with cocaine and marijuana, and they'd pay you extra to take it with them. They'd put cocaine up their noses and sniff it, take it in their mouths, and some of them would rub it on their private parts. I tried not to take drugs but I couldn't avoid it. To refuse was asking for trouble.

As long as I was a prostitute, I hated the guts of every man I went to bed with. I never let a customer hang around afterward—no friendly farewells for him! If he didn't get up right away I'd say, "You got what you paid for. You're through. Beat it!" I loved to flaunt that in a man's face! I always got my money in advance, of course, so I could say whatever I pleased.

I had to be pretty worn out before I'd get any pleasure from sex with a client. The few times I was weak enough to react like a woman, I felt so soiled and degraded afterward that I wanted to die. Not all prostitutes feel that way. I've heard others say nothing is more normal than getting pleasure in bed, even if you don't care for the man. My reaction depended on the man; some are gentle, others are brutes. In a brothel you get maybe a couple of nice men to every ninety-eight brutes.

We got—oh so rarely!—a man who, having paid his money, would say, "You don't have to go to bed with me unless you want to. I won't force you. If you don't like me that way, we can sit and talk for a while." With consideration so rare, how could you help but respond? When I had a customer like that, I'd never have thought of taking advantage of his offer. On the contrary, I was all the more eager to please him because he didn't feel he'd bought me.

Some of the men, after being with me several times, acted like old friends and really seemed to like me. It wasn't love, far from it! But they made me feel good now and then. Never to the extent that I wouldn't charge them, though. Oh no! Some girls did that, but not me. Money was the first consideration.

Prostitutes get lots of marriage proposals, but I never accepted any. I had a romance with one man but I never really fell in love. I couldn't stand submitting to a man's will. I always had it in mind to get out of that life and live normally, but I couldn't have said to a husband, as I did to my clients, "I only lie with you for money." The marriage would have ended in disaster for sure!

I often got pregnant. I've never been able to wear a diaphragm because my uterus is out of place. I was never tempted to carry one of those pregnancies to term. How could I, not even knowing who the father was? So I had an abortion about every two or three months. I never tried home remedies; I always went to the same doctor and always alone. No sooner did I get rid of one child than I'd have another in my belly. My folks never knew anything about it, only the madam and the other women. After an abortion, I'd rest three or four days, then work as usual until I got pregnant again.

I dreamed of getting out of the brothel and working at a decent job. I wanted to study. I wanted to be somebody. But that was before the Revolution and there was no hope of any such thing. One time I went to enroll in a school, but the first person I met was a man I'd slept with. I turned around and left.

Another time when I was about seventeen I made a vow to *La Caridad* to dress in yellow gingham. I kept my vow faithfully but the Virgin didn't help me. Finally in my desperation I went to a spiritist. Not that I believe in them. I think once you're dead and the worms eat you, there's nothing left. But I thought, "What can I lose?"

It was a farce. Like a psychologist, a spiritist knows that if you go there you must have some problem. So first she tries to draw you out to see what's worrying you. The things that woman read in my cards she'd practically dragged out of me first. When she was through I said, "None of this is news to me; after all, I told it to you."

If it hadn't been for the Revolution, I'd either have killed myself or gone to the dogs. Once, near the end of the dictatorship, I did try to kill myself. Burning my clothes was no longer enough. I was so overwhelmed with disgust for the life I led that I wanted to end it at once. I went to the hotel where I was living, lay down on the bed, and began to cut myself almost mechanically with a knife—my thighs, my arms. . . . I didn't actually cut my veins but I made myself bleed more and more. Then, as the blood poured out my mood changed, and I began to think of my little daughter and my brothers and sisters. After living such a life of sacrifice for them, how could I abandon them? What would become of them?

Nobody ever found out what I'd done. One day my sisters saw the scars on my thighs and asked how I got them. I told them I'd been on drugs one night and it had given me pleasure to cut myself. Xiomara said, "What a lie! You couldn't possibly have done that to yourself. It must have been a man." The others didn't believe me either. They still think a man did it.

Trying to kill myself wasn't the impulse of the moment. I'd been brooding a long time, from the very first day I entered a brothel. The contempt people had for prostitutes was only the drop that made the glass overflow. But the Revolution came in time to save me.

Chapter Three

Saved

AT THE TIME OF the Triumph, I was seventeen and still a prostitute. I didn't know what the Revolution was all about. I was stupid, living just to stay alive, filled with nothing but my worries and my unflagging struggle to keep my family fed. I never stopped to think about what was happening in Cuba, much less to figure out why or whose fault it was. Now and then I'd take up a newspaper and read something like, "A number of merciless and impious men were killed at such-and-such a place," but I never paid any attention.

I'd gone out twice with one of Batista's lieutenants. Damn it, it was against my will, but the owner of the house made me go. I never liked Batista's men. I saw the things they did. I knew a nice guy, maybe twenty-five years old, who often came to the house to visit one of the girls. They were in love, I guess. One day I saw him in the street with all his teeth smashed. He told me, "I had a run-in with the police. They did this with the butt of a gun." He didn't say anything about the Revolution or joining the Rebels, he just said he had to get out of Havana and needed 60 *centavos* for carfare. I gave it to him. I had no way of finding out what became of him. Sometimes I look to see if I can recognize his face among the martyrs of the Revolution, but I never have.

On December 31, the eve of the triumph of the Revolution, there was a *Batistiano* soldier who'd been drinking a lot and wanted to spend the whole night with me. He'd been with a woman who worked in the same house and his doings were no secret to me. He was a pimp and a homosexual whore, a really low character. I'd had a few drinks myself, so I told him he was a dirty fag and I wouldn't get in his bed for 1,000 *pesos*. "Don't think you can impress me with your uniform," I said.

He was vicious. He said the way to cure my temper was to take me where they'd apply a bit of torture; *that* would show me some respect! Then other people intervened, and the owner of the house took me away to another hotel. "You're looking for trouble for both of us," he told me. "That soldier is capable of anything." He told me never to come back. "I'm fond of you," he said. "I've kept you on in spite of everything, but you know you can't drink without getting into fights. Just don't come back to the house, that's all."

Next day the Revolution was triumphant and I was too high on pills to know what had happened. But when I heard such enthusiastic crowds out in the street, I got excited too. I thought, "The Revolution can't be so bad when so many people are happy about it." But it was confusing. Madams and pimps spread rumours that the new government would be ruthless with prostitutes. They made a great deal of that kind of propaganda. They said prostitutes would be jailed if they were lucky enough to escape the firing squad. But others thought it was no more than a change of corrupt officials and life would go on in the same old way. Never did I imagine everything would be so different!

Life in the brothel changed at once. Lots of the owners ran away, and exploitation by those who remained was stopped. We girls started working for ourselves—if I earned 10 *pesos* they were all mine. Of course we had to make a contribution toward the upkeep of the house, servants' wages and so on, but it wasn't anything like half the take.

Three months, more or less, after the triumph of the Revolution, the police went to each brothel and told the owner that all the women were expected at the station at 5:00 the next evening. Our madam hired a car to take us there, and the police photographed us full face and profile and took our fingerprints. Then they told us we were required to have periodic medical examinations—a general checkup, a blood test, and a vaginal smear—and carry a kind of health certificate. We had to show our card to the police every week, and if it wasn't up to date we wouldn't be allowed to work.

Some of the prostitutes resented the new rules and had a lot to say about being photographed, too, but like it or not, we all had to do it. The pimps had said we'd be shot, or jailed, or sent somewhere to pick tomatoes, and it all seemed possible.

Homosexuals who owned brothels or worked in them were also rounded up. Practically every brothel had homosexuals to do the cooking and cleaning and sometimes to go to bed with clients. I'm sorry for queers and always got along well with them. There's no excuse for what they are, but at least they're better than lesbians.

It seemed perfectly fair to me to throw brothel owners in jail. They were exploiters, one and all. When you brought them a lot of money they were all smiles, but when you had to fight to defend yourself they didn't stand by you—a scandal in the house was too inconvenient for them.

In my opinion the revolutionary government was taking some very necessary measures to make brothels less disgusting. They put an end to the selling of drinks, they required us to meet the customers fully dressed, and a madam who didn't make sure her girls complied with the medical rule would have had to shut the house down. They made drugs illegal, too, so I hardly ever smoked marijuana or sniffed cocaine anymore. At first some men continued to bring a little, but they were scared to death.

Abortions were more difficult to arrange after the Revolution. To get one you had to go to the doctor accompanied by a friend of his, or he wouldn't have dared take the risk. In 1961 I had an abortion that cost 150 *pesos!*

There had been a time, near the end of the dictatorship, when hardly anybody came to the brothels, and it was a bad time for us. But right after the Revolution business picked up. Not that lines formed at the door, but everyone earned more and the men began to come back. Of course with our working hours shortened, we could attend to fewer men in a day. We worked from 8:00 to 12:00 at night; we had a heavy work load on Fridays and weekends, but the rest of the time there weren't many clients, and some days I didn't earn a thing.

I still had problems with the police now and again, but they treated me very differently from the way Batista's force did. If I got into a fight they'd ask me to go to the police station, but they wouldn't sentence me or ask for bail, they'd just tell me it wasn't right to make such scenes and let me go.

Toward the end of 1959, at the time of Camilo Cienfuegos's disappearance,[6] I had a bit of trouble at La Victoria. There was a rumour that Camilo had reappeared, and everybody was out in the streets celebrating. I went out drinking with somebody, and when we got to the hotel I suddenly couldn't bear the thought of his touch. When he came toward me I grabbed a highball glass and flung it at him. He began to bleed and I got scared. I rushed out in nothing but my panties and shoes and locked myself in an empty room down the hall. The man left, taking my clothes with him, and the hotel owner called the police.

When the policeman saw me he exclaimed, "*Ay!* What's this! Here, at least wrap a sheet around you. I'm as embarrassed as if you were my mother or sister! Poor kid, wait here, I'll go find you some clothes." He came back with a blouse and skirt. Well, he fell in love with me and courted me in the most respectable manner, taking me to meet his folks and everything. For about a month we saw each other twice a week; he couldn't afford to take me out any oftener. One time when he was broke I offered to pay for us both, but he absolutely refused. "Don't ever offer me money. I'd rather wait until I can afford to take you somewhere." I

6. See Mónica, n. 27.

wouldn't have minded giving him money; I could see that wasn't what he was after. But maybe if he'd accepted it that night I would have been disillusioned with him.

In time I fell in love with him. He was so decent, so unselfish, and he offered to take me out of that life. But he wanted to marry me on the condition that I'd live with his *mamá,* and I knew all too well what it was to live with a mother-in-law. I thought we could go on as we were and maybe later on things would change, but when I said I wouldn't live with his mother, he said, "Very well. Then it's all over."

I suggested we could be lovers, because I liked him, but he said I was completely mistaken. "I'll have to forget you, that's all. I have my self-respect. What kind of man would I be if I kept on with you while you're living in a brothel?"

By then my strongest desire was to be independent. I wasn't really independent in the brothel, but at least it was a different kind of dependence. I had my own money to spend as I liked. I didn't want to live in a home that wasn't mine, to be bossed or forbidden to work. Marrying him would have got me out of the brothel, yes, but how could I take my daughter to live in the same house as his family? No, I decided I'd depend on myself.

I kept getting into quarrels, and eventually the police told me I had to get out of La Victoria, so I went to Colón, an altogether dirtier, lower, more depraved barrio. Any brothel is depraved, but La Victoria was refined by comparison. In Colón the houses were worse and the women ugly, old, and very dirty. In La Victoria we were all young, and you could choose whether you wanted to be with a man. In Colón you had to accept anybody who asked you, even a black, and if you said no, the man could get you kicked out of the house. For me, black or white, it was all the same. In either case, it was depraved to strip naked and do whatever they wanted because they paid for it.

By 1961 there were no brothel owners left. In Colón, when the madam left, my friend Margarita offered to take charge. Margarita didn't feel the way I did about being a prostitute and had adapted very well to that kind of life. She had a pimp, but she was sober and responsible, never quarreled with anybody, never drank or made a scene.

Since I could keep everything I earned, I worked only enough to cover my needs. With 10 *pesos* a day I was satisfied. But even though conditions were improving, I was in a horrible state of mind. One night, full of pep pills and drink, I went to the kitchen and poured a whole bottle of alcohol over me. I had just picked up the matches when Margarita came in and said, "No! I forbid you!" She struggled with me and called the other girls. They got the matches away and gave me a bath to get rid of the alcohol. That's the reason I always say that if it hadn't been for the Revolution, I wouldn't be alive to tell of it.

At the end of 1961, comrades from the ministry in charge of the rehabilitation plan began visiting the brothels, one by one, to offer us a fresh start. They told us the Revolution had decided to put an end to the horrible life we were leading. We were to spend some time at a rehabilitation school, and if we needed it, we'd be trained and given a job. They said if we were willing to study and work, our debt to society would be wiped out.[7]

I couldn't believe it. I thought, "A chance to study? They'll support my daughter while I go to school? Give me money without my earning it? These promises can't be true!"

Of course the pimps campaigned strongly against it. They said the revolutionary government was a monster of hypocrisy—no ministry could possibly be so generous. When had we ever known any government to help anybody? There must be a catch to it. "When they put you to forced labor you'll be sorry!" That was what the pimps said.[8] But to my way of seeing it I had nothing to lose. Anything was better than a brothel.

7. In May, 1970, Oscar Lewis had two interviews with Armando Torres, former secretary-general of the Superior Council for Social Defense, who was instrumental in establishing the rehabilitation program for prostitutes. Torres estimated there were 10,000 prostitutes in Havana and 30,000 to 40,000 on the island as a whole in 1959. The campaign to eliminate prostitution began in 1961 and lasted five or six years.

Torres said, "At the beginning, we didn't have any definite plans as to how to undertake this work . . . everything came into being spontaneously. It occurred to one of us to go to the brothels and talk to the prostitutes and see whether we could persuade them to abandon their way of life . . . we were a trifle romantic about it.

"It was essentially a matter of persuasion. That is, the state let them know that their way of life wouldn't be tolerated, and that everyone would be given work. Some were afraid and said they would go for that reason. . . ."

Torres said that all of the school's first students were volunteers, but that later some women were "detained" and sent to the schools.

"The initial treatment was philanthropic in nature. It wasn't a planned piece of social work but rather a matter of forming groups and talking things over. . . ." The Revolution was explained to the women, as were the social conditions that led to their becoming prostitutes, and they were asked if they didn't want to change along with everything else. More and more women volunteered to go, and after several months classes were organized, beauty parlors were set up to teach the women to dress and fix their hair in ways which were not "over-ornate," and all the women "were briefed on table manners and helped to break other habits."

Jobs were found in nearby factories, although it took the help of the mass organizations to break down the hostility of the other workers. With the cooperation of the Ministry of Industry, a garment factory was established at one of the schools. Torres said, "The effort was primarily to direct them into production, into a trade." Unlike Pilar López, most of these women did not continue their schooling beyond the elementary grades.

8. Pimps were subjected to a different kind of rehabilitation program. According to Torres, "We were hardly going to call on them and ask them to stop being pimps. Trying persuasion on pimps would take more romanticism than even we had. You can't re-educate pimps that way. More forcible means are required." In fact, after a lengthy process of identifying men who worked as pimps, hundreds were arrested and sent to work farms. Their families were supported by a state pension of 50–200 *pesos* a month, depending on family size.

One day Portilla, the comrade from the ministry, asked if we had any ideas about how the school should be set up. Should it be voluntary? What should be done about the comrades who didn't volunteer? Should they be forced to go? Prostitutes themselves stood up then to say that anybody who didn't understand what the Revolution was all about at that late date should be forced to go, because eventually they'd be grateful. I approved of the voluntary system, but all the same I think any woman sent to that school, even if she had to be dragged there, would have benefited from it.

In fact the government decided on a completely voluntary rehabilitation system. Those who didn't choose to go were just told they'd better be very careful not to disturb the peace, because at the first sign of a street fight they'd be given another chance to participate in the rehabilitation plan. My friend Margarita was jailed for flatly refusing to be rehabilitated and for non-cooperation. When she got out she left for Venezuela, and from there she went to the United States.

I was finally convinced that the Revolution was different from what I'd expected. Here was help, with no strings attached! It was a great thing. I told them yes, I wanted to go, that very night if possible. They said arrangements were not quite completed, but in view of my eagerness, they'd see if I could go to the school before it officially opened. Lieutenant Alvarez, the comrade in charge of the rehabilitation center, was away on her honeymoon at the moment, but they phoned her and she gave authorization for me to go to the school at once. The following morning they came to get me.

My daughter was no problem. I told *mamá*, "The ministry will pay you a monthly allowance for her support, and when I'm through with the school, I'll get a job!"

"All right," *mamá* said. She showed no emotion at my news, neither anger nor joy. She just said flatly, "You're doing the right thing."

I'd never known what it was to call my life my own. I'd done whatever I had to in order to survive. But now everything had changed. I had a chance to start over again.

The school I was sent to had been a rich man's home and was not really suitable for a school building. The ministry planned to remodel it, but so many women were anxious to quit prostitution, it was decided to start school at once and fix it up little by little, so at first there were no workshops, machine shops, or schoolrooms—those things came later.

The school was only for former prostitutes. When I arrived there were very few women there, but after a couple of weeks there were 50, and by the time I graduated seven months later there were about 300. All who wanted to attend were admitted.

From the very first day I realized that all the things I'd heard against the revolutionary government were lies. Everyone, from the director to the most humble employee, treated us kindly. They were concerned about our children's welfare, they wanted us to have enough clothes and good, well-balanced meals. And we had excellent medical care from a doctor on call and a full-time nurse. When we first enrolled we were given a medical checkup to see if any of us had syphilis. The only thing they found wrong with me was the way my uterus was tipped, so they sent me to another doctor for treatment. They gave me vitamins, too.

One of the girls was found to have the lung sickness. Measures were immediately taken to protect the rest of us. The poor girl was so afraid we'd be repelled by her illness she wouldn't talk to anyone, but in time she was cured and lived a normal life.

Three other girls and I had completed the sixth grade, so we were excused from classes and housework and given the first jobs, at a textile factory. We rose at 5:00 in the morning, made our beds, and went to breakfast. Some days we did exercises and marched around before starting to work. The factory was quite a distance away, so we were taken in a school car and our lunch was brought to us. Sometimes the lieutenant in charge of us came to fetch us in her own car, and we'd sing all the way home.

We had two different uniforms: blue slacks and pink blouses for school, gray skirts and pink blouses for street wear. The director thought the uniforms set us apart too much from the other comrades at the factory, but I didn't mind. If you go to school, you wear a uniform. That's only proper.

School was a wonderland! The director was a kind, affectionate woman, and our group was so small at first that we could eat out together sometimes, or go to the movies. That was something new to me! For the first time, too, I was free from family worries, and I began to take more of an interest in things, and to read.

Naturally a certain amount of discipline had to be maintained; you couldn't just take off whenever you felt like it. Saturdays and Sundays were our days off, and occasionally we got a weekday pass as a reward for good behavior. If you overslept, came late to the workshop or class, or were disrespectful to a teacher, you lost your pass, but I never broke a rule so I never lost mine.

Lots of the women didn't like getting up early, or going to classes and workshops. One said, "This is all very well, but I can't bear studying."

"Well, then, don't study," I told her. "Tell them you'd rather be assigned to a workshop."

"Oh no! I don't want anybody ordering me around. I want to earn money my own way. Besides, I hate to be shut in here all the time. I need to be out in the street."

Finally, a few of the girls said they wanted to leave. They were perfectly free to go, but first they were asked to talk it over with the rest of us, and we persuaded them to stay. Thanks to that they're now happy women.

All the same, there were some who sneaked out at night to avoid our talks, and some, influenced by pimps, went to the United States, where they're still prostitutes. I know because they write to people here.

Those of us who worked in the factory had a few encounters with the women there. To them we were whores, rehabilitated or not, and they didn't want to fraternize, until some comrades from the ministry called a conference to explain why they shouldn't ostracize us. The director told them how lucky they were that they'd never had to become prostitutes, and she said they should admire us for wanting to find a better life. The women were very moved and most of them cried. After that we had no more trouble. In other factories where I've worked, I've never run into that kind of problem, though it's among working people that I come up against the worst prejudice.

Productive labor was a new experience for all of us. It was completely voluntary but everybody wanted to go. I'd never worked on a farm before and I liked it. We went first to the sugar-cane fields, where they'd burned the cane to make it easier to cut. We arrived about 10:00 A.M. and they gave us our machetes. We watched to see how it was done and then started right in cutting cane. We weren't actually expected to do much that first day, just learn what it was like.

It didn't seem hard because the group was so gay and happy. From the moment we got into the truck, we started singing revolutionary songs like "Nikita has the key/and he will only give it/to a Socialist countree." Another one went like this:

> ¿Quién viene ahí?
> pregunta la gente.
> Y nosotros como prudentes
> les vamos a contestar,
> somos becadas por Fidel
> y Marxistas-Leninistas. [9]

I get awfully sentimental remembering some of the things we did. It was like a picnic. I still have the knapsack I used that day, with a sailcloth sheet, a canteen, and a tin plate, all gifts from *papá*. He'd had them when he served in the Army. I'm very fond of them.

9. Who goes there?
   People ask.
   And we, being discreet,
   Shall answer them:
   Fidel gave us scholarships
   And we are Marxist-Leninists.

Another time we went to a nearby citrus farm to pick lemons, oranges, and grapefruit. It was easier and cleaner than cutting cane. The farm was prettier and we had a definite goal. In a cane field we'd just heap up the cane and leave it, but on the citrus farm we emptied our baskets into sacks, so at the end of the day we could see what we'd accomplished. We also raced each other to see who could pick more fruit. It was great fun.

We did productive labor once every two weeks, but later on, instead of going to the country, I went to the factory to help put the storeroom in order.

I've been a militiawoman since 1962, the year I became a permanent employee at the factory. We were given a note to buy our uniforms and I got two sets of shirts and slacks at only 8 *pesos* a set. The olive-green belt and three pairs of olive-green socks were gifts from *papá,* and the school gave us boots. When I stood guard at the factory once or twice a month, I sometimes wore my uniform, but not always. It wasn't a rigid requirement.

On May 1, a month and a half before graduating, I went to a mass meeting at the Plaza de la Revolución with others from the rehabilitation school. Ah, it was an impressive spectacle, so many people gathered there! Afterward, as we marched in the parade, we passed in front of the speakers' platform to get a close look at Fidel. He was exactly like his pictures in the papers, perfectly natural, just like any other man.

I had quite a problem with *mamá.* She brought Ana Bárbara to visit me several times, and one day I noticed the child had bad breath. "What did she eat today?" I demanded.

"Well, actually, she hasn't had anything to eat for two days," *mamá* confessed. I was disgusted! I'd been giving her every *centavo* I earned. My starting salary at the factory had been 30 *pesos* a month, but by then they'd raised it to 110, and even before that the ministry had sent her 60 *pesos* a month for my daughter's support. *Papá* was working as a truck repairman for the Army in Oriente, so he sent her 120 *pesos* a month. Then too, one of my sisters and her husband stayed with *mamá* and they gave her 85. And with all that money, she had the nerve to bring my child to see me hungry! It just didn't make sense. I told her to get out of my sight. I told her it would have been better not to have come at all. It made me desperate to have a home of my own, where I could be with my daughter and not have to depend on anybody. But I didn't have any money. I'd given it all to my mother.

I began to brood over everything *mamá* had done to me and I felt terrible. One day I began to cry. The director was alone in the recreation room, playing the piano, and as I walked by she called to me. "You don't have to tell me anything," she said. "Just sit down and I'll play you some music."

In all my time at school, I cried only that once. When I told the director I was homesick for my daughter she gave me kind advice and I was able to go to sleep peacefully.

The final days of June, 1962, were happy ones for me. Nothing could touch me. The school director, who had exquisite taste, personally chose my graduation dress and shoes, and that pleased and flattered me. The graduation fiesta was delightful, with cake and soft drinks, and we were given corsages made of flowers from the school garden. But I invited nobody. I didn't want *mamá* or anyone else there.

The comrades from the ministry told us our graduation meant that we no longer owed anyone a debt. From that moment on, they said, we were just like everybody else; we had earned a place in society. But they told us we could count on their help any time we needed it, for as long as we lived. Without a doubt, the happiest period of my life began that day. Since then I've had no financial problems of any kind.

About fifty comrades graduated with me, and like me they kept on working at the factory. But I never gave up my dream of studying. In my early school days, my teachers had passed me from grade to grade just to get rid of me, and I couldn't feel much satisfaction about having graduated from elementary school. That's why while I worked in the factory I began to study at night. There I earned my EOC certificate. I repeated the course so I could qualify for the Workers' Secondary School, where you can complete four years of secondary school in one year.[10] From that day to this, I've never stopped studying.

When I learned that rehabilitated women were to be given homes, I was so happy! I'd lived in brothels or hotels, sleeping on sheets that didn't belong to me, eating out because I couldn't cook in my room, evicted if I couldn't pay. Never had I had a house to decorate and manage by myself. Never had I been able to sleep with my daughter beside me. Now I would have everything—my job, my house, and my daughter.

The director herself brought me to the house where I live now and handed me the key. I was enchanted with it from the very first moment. It was big, with a living room, dining room, three bedrooms, a kitchen, two bathrooms, all completely furnished. There was a garden, a hall, a patio, and a garage. The houses I'd always known were old and ugly, with uncomfortable dirty bathrooms. Here the door opened into a clean, airy room flooded with sunlight. Never had I seen such a house as this, and it filled me with hope. It even made me want to have more children!

The electricity hadn't been connected yet, but I was so happy I insisted

10. Pilar's first course covered grades one through three, and the second course, grades four through six. This qualified her for the Workers' Secondary School, a course equivalent to the first year of basic secondary school. The remaining three years of the basic secondary course were offered by the Worker-Peasant Colleges within Cuba's three universities. (See n. 16.)

on staying. The director said, "Good! If that's what you want, move in today. I'll bring your dinner tomorrow." So she brought my meals from the school until the electricity was connected three days later. In the meantime the school loaned me Chinese lanterns.

The house had once belonged to a Señor Martínez, an employee of the electric company, who'd taken off for the United States. The beds were neatly made and the cabinet was full of food, as if somebody was still living there. In fact, the house had barely been given to the ministry before they turned it over to me. The only thing I didn't like was in the back bedroom: a coconut with a face painted on it, surrounded by glasses of water and liquor, the sort of things people used for witchcraft. Probably the owner had put them there to scare away anyone who took over his house. I had a good laugh. After I threw the stuff away, I gave the room a thorough cleaning and changed all the furniture around.

The house was only a short walk from the factory, which suited me fine. If I'd had any objections to it, I wouldn't have been forced to keep it. Some comrades preferred to be near their relatives rather than their job and the government tried to accommodate them, only sometimes they had to wait a little longer.

I had to sign a contract for my house and I was more than pleased to do it. My rent came to 10 percent of my salary, 9.50 *pesos*, plus 5.45 for the furniture.[11]

I went to OFICODA[12] and explained that I'd never been issued a ration book because I was in school when rationing began. The comrade said, "Oh, a scholarship student! It'll be my pleasure to make one out for you right now." And so for the first time I found myself in the Minimax, shopping with my basket, ration book in hand, buying food to cook in my own kitchen just like other women. It was a strange and wonderful feeling.

Shortly after I moved in, some comrades came around inviting everybody to a meeting of a committee to coordinate neighborhood activities. I joined the CDR[13] right away, which I consider an obligation, like

11. Pilar's rent (in fact an amortization payment) was regulated by the 10-percent-of-household-income rent ceiling provided for under the Urban Reform Law.

12. *Oficina de Control para la Distribución de Alimentos* (Office for Control of Food Distribution).

13. The *Comités de Defensa de la Revolución* (Committees for Defense of the Revolution) were founded September 28, 1960, and are active in a broad range of programs including public health, education, political education, urban reform, sports and recreation, local administration, as well as in surveillance work against counterrevolutionary activities. The Committees' activities (organized as *frentes*, or fronts) include recruiting volunteers to work in agriculture, standing guard duty to prevent neighborhood vandalism as well as sabotage, administering vaccines and other injections, encouraging adult education, organizing study groups, and calling meetings to deal with problems that arise at the block level (e.g., noisy or disorderly conduct by residents, neighborhood clean-up, school attendance, organizing support for national campaigns, etc.). Membership in the CDR is open to all Cubans fourteen and older who are "willing to defend the Revolution."

joining the militia. Both are ways of looking out for our people's interests. If any counterrevolutionary movement starts, the CDR knows it
immediately. The CDR president asked if any of us wanted to volunteer
to stand guard, and I said yes. I thought it only fair. I'm not the kind who
can go to sleep and let others do all the work, watching out for my safety.

Ana Bárbara moved in with me the second week. She was almost six
years old and all her life she'd lived either with *mamá* or with my
mother-in-law. Still, bad as her situation was, my daughter was better off
than I'd been as a child. At least she had food, and if she got sick I'd take
her to the doctor and buy her medicines. As for affection, or rather the
lack of it, she was just as badly off as I'd been because my folks quarreled
as much as ever. And she suffered deeply over my separation from
Eleodoro. Whenever I went to see her she'd ask, *"Mami,* why don't you
go back to my *papá?"*

Ana Bárbara takes after her father's family a bit more than mine. She's
tall and slender like Eleodoro's sister, light-skinned, with straight black
hair, big black eyes, and lips not quite as full as mine. But really she
doesn't look like either Eleodoro or me. She's rather introverted, ca-
pricious, and when she was younger she was quarrelsome and always
having tantrums. Sometimes I'd let her tire herself out, other times I'd
lose my temper and give her a couple of slaps on the bottom.

Ana Bárbara had started going to nursery school when she was five,
along with my two little brothers, Eugenio and Victor, who were born to
mamá after I left home. When my little girl moved in with me she
changed schools and had to be there from 8:00 in the morning until 6:00
in the evening. I started work at the factory at 7:00 A.M. and was through
at 3:00. Then at 8:00 at night I'd go out again to the Workers' School, so
I needed a babysitter. Carmelina, a girl from the rehabilitation school,
shared the house with me, but I couldn't count on her because she
worked at the factory too. Finally one of her sisters brought her daughter and came to live with us, to do the housework and take care of the
two children.

It was in the factory that I met Tomás Alonso Ordónez. He was an
executive and had studied in the Party schools and traveled to the socialist countries. He was deeply involved in the Revolution but never
attained the status of militant in the Communist Party because he's a
repatriate, and they're never completely trusted.

When I saw him my very first day at the factory, I gave a start, as if I'd
been frightened. He was a big man, about 6 feet tall, a bit stout, well
dressed, dark-skinned—only a little lighter than I—with large eyes and
straight black hair. Well, I fell in love with him.

Of course I told nobody, least of all him. I was still being rehabilitated
and I thought it wouldn't be right for me to get involved. Besides, as far

as he knew I was still a prostitute, and I didn't know what he'd think of me.

So we chatted as comrades two or three times; then he started courting me. I told him everything about my past but he never threw it up to me. One time when I was on guard duty he came and told me he was married but wasn't living with his wife. I checked up on his story and it was true. His wife, Coralía Diéguez, was a housewife with no outside job, and they had two children, Coralía, eight, and Tomás, seven.

Apparently Tomás and his wife couldn't get along. He explained that for the moment he didn't want to get a divorce, for family reasons. I didn't really understand what he meant by that, but when I was given my house I agreed to let him come and live with me. I met his family only two or three times and his mother treated me very formally, as if I were a stranger. She didn't even kiss me. When I asked Tomás whether she approved of our relationship, he just said she never interfered in his private life.

We were very happy. I was in love with Tomás, as I had never been with my first husband, and it was a delight to go to bed with him. But the union lasted only about three months. He had a peculiarity that worried me, though I never rejected him because of it. Now and then when we were in bed he'd ask me to pretend that I was the husband and he the wife. I'm sure he must have been to bed with a man at some time. In fact, I think he may have been a homosexual, but I loved him anyway.

Sometimes we quarreled, because Tomás was a womanizer and was always giving one of the girls a lift in his car. That hurt my feelings. "What did you do that for?" I'd ask, but he'd only laugh. He didn't take my objections seriously and that mortified me even more.

Tomás would also tell me I was too independent. He didn't like me to go out without telling him, but I didn't see why I owed an explanation to anybody. If I ran into a woman comrade who said, "Come on home with me," it never occurred to me to say, "Oh no, I have to get home early." Whatever I do, my conscience is my only judge. I don't need anybody else's opinion of it. Tomás didn't like that attitude.

Then one day he told me he was going back to his wife. After all, he said, she was the mother of his children, and he realized that we couldn't get along with each other, although he still loved me very much. He asked me to be his mistress, but for me our love had been too pure to degrade. I preferred to live on memories. "I approve of your going back to your legal wife, but I certainly won't be your mistress," I told him. And I added, "You're leaving me a great reminder of your love. I'm going to bear you a child."

He went back to his wife, leaving me pregnant and alone. I suffered terribly. Still, I rejected him. He came to see me almost daily but I told Carmelina to say I wasn't home. She resented what Tomás had done to me, so she was quite hard on him, not bothering to answer his questions and never opening the door to him. Hiding, I heard everything but I kept still because I knew if I ever talked to him face to face I might give in.

I began to get uncomfortable at the factory when I realized that a lot of the people there, including the executives, disapproved of my affair with Tomás. As I got bigger, I kept thinking my comrades were giving me dirty looks, and I developed all sorts of complexes. I was sick, too, because of the pregnancy, so when I was about six months along I took time off at half-salary.

When Ludmila was born, on June 9, 1963, I didn't tell anybody, not even my family, but Tomás went to my house and must have figured out I was at the hospital. The nurse said, "Someone called to ask how you were doing and whether the baby was a boy or a girl."

"Did he leave his name?" I asked.

"Tomás Ordóñez."

He was waiting for me when I arrived home. I hadn't meant to let him see the baby, but since he was there I couldn't very well refuse. Ludmila was plump and pretty, dark like her *papá,* and she had a little mole on one of her ears just like his other children. He insisted that we register Ludmila's birth, and he began coming to see her every day. He bought her a crib, a mattress, and her whole layette. I hadn't bought anything but diapers for her, I don't know why. Because I felt so betrayed, I guess. I was seeing a psychiatrist by then.

When my daughter was about two weeks old, Aunt Caridad came by one day and saw the baby lying on the bed. "Of all things, Pilar!" she exclaimed. "Why in the world didn't you tell us? I'll never forgive you, never!" Then she gave the news to the rest of the family, and after a while they began coming to see Ludmila.

Ludmila was a healthy baby, not sickly or difficult as Ana Bárbara had been. She's an amazing child. She sat on her little potty chair when she was only half a year old, and never wet the crib after about nine months. She could walk all around her crib at eight months and pretty soon she was walking without holding on to anything. At the age of seven she was nearly as tall as her sister. Ana Bárbara wasn't very strong and she did everything later. Even now, at thirteen, she sometimes wets the bed, and then excuses herself by claiming she was too cold to get up.

Carmelina, the woman who was living with me, married, and both she and her sister left, so I had nobody to look after the girls. Luckily I ran into Celia, who used to live in Jesús María. She'd been married and divorced but she kept on living with her mother-in-law because her ex-husband went to the United States. Her house wasn't far from mine, so Celia stayed with my children while I was working, and after a while I asked her whether she'd be willing to move in with me. She said yes, she'd be glad to get out of that place. She lived with me for about three years while her own daughters stayed on with her mother-in-law. I never paid her a salary or offered her one, but every payday I'd make her a gift of 20 or 25 *pesos*.

After Ludmila was born I had some trouble with my ovaries and had to go every month for a pretty painful treatment. The doctor had known me in rehabilitation school and was interested in how I was getting along. I told him it was pretty rough adjusting and that I was anxious and depressed a lot. He said I should go see a psychiatrist, and he sat right down and wrote me an introduction to Dr. Evidio Gómez at the Fajardo Hospital, so I went over the same day.

They say you never forget your first interview with a psychiatrist. *Ay*, the things they ask! And every time he came out with a question, he expected me to give him a whole life history. I resisted, but after a few sessions I thought, "What the hell, if I want to get better I'll have to tell him everything." Not that I came out with it all at once, and I never got to the point of really confiding in him. See, for me he was a man, not a scientist; it embarrassed me talking about sex with him. He asked me how I felt about women and if I liked doing it with them. I don't know, maybe he thought I was queer. Then he wanted me to tell him all the things I like to do with men, but I refused. I know he was being scientific about it and all, but I just don't like to talk about such intimate things. I think it's disgusting.

Dr. Gómez's mother was a social worker in the psychiatric ward of the hospital, and one day he told me he thought she'd be very interested in my case, so I started going to see her too. She was an older woman, very warm and pleasant, and it was easier to trust her and confide in her. She helped me a lot. She said at least I was clear about what I'd done, but if I started examining the lives of so-called virtuous women I'd be in for a lot of surprises. She said, "You've got about twenty failures to account for; some people have seven hundred. I admire you because you did what you did out of need. I know some who do worse by choice, because they like it. You're as good as any woman alive, Pilar, and don't you forget it."

When I started treatment at the hospital I stayed there the whole day, then later just twice a week. I'd been going to night school ever since I got out of rehabilitation, and it was hard keeping my grades up. But I did. I graduated from Workers' Secondary School in the spring of 1965. I was eligible to apply for permission to continue studying full-time under the plan for outstanding students. They gave me a scholarship for excellence and full-time leave to study. I continued to receive my regular 123 *pesos* a month. I was the happiest woman alive. Getting out of that textile factory was like waking up from a nightmare. I could never relax there because all the comrades knew which women had been prostitutes.

I felt so good I thought I could do without the therapy sessions. The doctor never said the treatment was over; I just cut down to going once a week, then once a month, and then I stopped going altogether.

I began attending a special branch of the Workers' College run by the factory. At first the school was held in a building where there's a department store now. About a month later the school was moved to a factory near Rancho Boyeros, and from there to two other buildings, then to the School of Commerce in Havana and also to the Normal School on Infanta. All of that in the course of my first year!

While I was a student I had my first experience as a *permanente* in agriculture.[14] It was very different from the productive labor I'd been doing, because we had to live on a farm for thirty to forty-five days at a time. The camp we were sent to was a thing of beauty, a chalet with cement floors and stucco walls, and baths with running water quite near. However, the chalet was already full when we arrived because many more women had come than they'd expected, so we had no choice but to move into a wooden shelter with a dirt floor and a thatched-palm roof. We slept on sackcloth hammocks and kept our clothes in knapsacks hanging from pegs. We were pretty disgruntled because we'd been told what excellent condition the camp was in. We adapted though.

Everything there was whitewashed and very clean, and we found it extremely well organized. There were plenty of cement bathtubs and lots of running water, so we never had to stand in line for a bath. Two or three comrades stayed behind every day to clean the bathrooms and straighten up the shelter. Later we were told there was room for us in the chalet, but by then we preferred the shelter. We'd made it quite pretty with bunches of wild flowers in glass jars.

Reveille was really a punishment. When they said, "On your feet!" at 5:30 A.M. I felt as if I'd just lain down to sleep. I detested getting up early, but once I was up and the chatter began, I felt fine. I'd go out in the fields wide-awake and happy. Camp life was very gay. When we finished our work in the afternoon, we'd sit around and tell stories, and sometimes a few of the comrades would dress up and act them out. The best part of it is that in a camp you forget your problems. During the day you simply don't think; you work and joke with your comrades and it keeps your mind off whatever you left behind in Havana.

At night it's different. When the lights are turned off and you go to bed, you start remembering. Then I missed my little girls and I'd be anxious for the period to end. Fortunately the camp wasn't far from Havana, so I didn't have to go the whole month without seeing them. My daughters always begged me to stay home, but when I explained to them why I went to the country they understood perfectly.

The farm work wasn't very hard, but picking tomatoes crouching down

14. A long-term volunteer for productive labor.

all the time tired me out, and I couldn't bear cutting with a machete. Hoeing is more comfortable because you do it standing up. Besides, it's the kind of work I've done most and I'm used to it by now. I have a good feeling about productive labor. In the old days the only people to work on the land were those who had the bad luck to be born there. Now, under the Revolution, everybody shares the good and the bad.

Tomás still followed me everywhere. He'd been transferred to another factory, but every day he showed up at my house, begging me to return to him, swearing he truly loved me. But of course it was still impossible for him to leave his wife!

I admitted that I loved him dearly, but I flatly refused to be his mistress. "I want you all to myself," I said. "You went back to your wife. Fine! I quite approve, only don't bother me, that's all."

Finally I agreed to meet him on a certain day, at a certain hour, at such-and-such a place, but instead of going there I waited till he must have left home, and then went to see his wife. I told her that I'd had Tomás's daughter, but that I was through with him and wanted her to help me convince him.

"I've been waiting for this visit a long time," she said. "I knew about the child."

"You and he were separated when we met," I explained. "When he wanted to return to you I agreed it was the right thing to do, only I refused to have anything further to do with him."

"You were a fool. It makes no difference where he lived," she said. "In the eyes of society, I was always his legal wife and you nothing more than his mistress."

There was no quarrel between us. We talked in a perfectly natural and friendly manner, and she even agreed to come and visit me someday, but she never did.

I thought Tomás would stop chasing after me, but my visit made no difference. He didn't care. One evening when I was alone at home studying, he showed up and offered to drive me to school, which he'd never done before. I refused. Then he told me he wanted me to bear him a son. "Ay! Isn't it enough that I've got your daughter and you've gone back to your wife?" I burst out. "I never heard such gall!" I was so outraged I couldn't think straight. I went to my room, changed my clothes, and went out blindly, not knowing where I was going. I got on the bus and then thought of the El Gato Club, where I often used to go when I double-dated with Carmelina. "I guess I'll go there and have a drink."

At El Gato I sat at the bar and ordered. The bartender, Gustavo Hevia Soto, recognized me and said, "How strange to see you here all by yourself. Do you mind if I sit down? I just got off work."

"All right," I said, and we had a drink together. Then we danced.

Gustavo told me he was divorced and claimed he'd been interested in me for months, ever since I first started coming to the club. It's true I used to see him looking at me, and I looked back because he was a very attractive man, a lot like Tomás. He dressed well too, and was taller than I, slender, dark-eyed, but light-skinned. Unmistakably white.

After four or five drinks Gustavo said he'd fallen in love with me and asked me to marry him. "You're alone and so am I," was the way he put it, "so why don't we get married?"

When he said that, the thought came to my mind, "If I get married, Tomás can never bother me again." So I said yes to a man I hardly knew.

We went to a hotel and spent the night there. I told Gustavo what my life had been. "It doesn't matter," he said. "The past means nothing to me, it's the future I care about."

When I told Tomás, he warned me to think it over. "You know you're not marrying for love." That made me mad and I told him it was none of his business.

Before that, Tomás had been very loving toward Ludmila, and so generous that on her second birthday he gave her several little dresses, but from that day to this he's never tried to see her again.

Gustavo and I got married six weeks after we met, on July 2, 1965. It would have been even sooner, but I had appendicitis and they had to operate. I left the hospital only a few days before the wedding and didn't feel up to bustling about making preparations, so Gustavo took charge of everything, from my dress and shoes down to the photographs and the notary.

My wedding day was an unhappy one for me. I knew I was marrying to forget Tomás, and even the fiesta couldn't cheer me up. But Gustavo looked downright joyful. We were married at home and planned to honeymoon at the seaside, but since I was recuperating we decided not to go.

Gustavo loved me the way *papá* loved *mamá*, so crazy about me he couldn't see my faults. He overwhelmed me with attention and caresses. He did the housecleaning, looked after my daughters, ran errands, washed the dishes. Wherever I wanted to go, he took me. Necklaces, bracelets—he got them. He catered to all my whims. He even put up with my children's rudeness, and that's something without parallel in history!

I don't like a husband like *papá*—a man more concerned for his wife than his children. That's not right. To make a marriage grow, there should be some kind of balance—"a measure of sand to a measure of lime," as we say. Otherwise a man just makes a fool of himself.

Imagine! Such flattery, such efforts to please me, and I didn't even love him! In fact I was really mean. When *papá* came to see us, he and Gustavo would argue about politics because Gustavo wasn't yet a revolutionary, and I'd take *papá*'s side just to put Gustavo on the spot. I didn't hesitate to tell him, thousands of times, "You own nothing in this house but your clothes. Take them and go wherever you please. I don't love you!" Then he'd beg me not to leave him, and I would despise him, because never once was he man enough even to make a gesture of leaving. If he ever had, maybe it would have opened my eyes. Our differences were mostly about silly little things. When we quarreled, poor Gustavo always went and lay down. As for me, I'd do what I did in the brothel—destroy my clothes.

We didn't always fight and I wasn't mean to him all the time. Sometimes I was sorry for the poor guy. When we went out together, I was proud to be seen with such a handsome, well-dressed man. Isn't that strange? It was nothing more than vanity.

But this is even stranger: we harmonized marvelously in bed. I was completely satisfied and I'm sure Gustavo was too. In fact, there are only two men I've ever really enjoyed in bed, Tomás and Gustavo, and Gustavo more than Tomás!

Gustavo had no children and wanted me to have one. With two different fathers, I didn't want another with yet a third surname. What would my daughters think? When I lived with Tomás, Ana Bárbara had said, "But *mami*, you left my *papá*—do you think you should marry again?" When I married Gustavo, she said, "Aren't you ashamed to marry so often?" I got pregnant by him once, only once, but I didn't tell him. I just went and had an abortion.

Today a woman can go to the hospital and have it done, but at that time, early 1966, abortions were still illegal.[15] I consulted a friend who knew a doctor who'd do it for 200 *pesos*. The penalties for practicing abortion were harsh. I went to his house alone to be less conspicuous. I was given no anesthesia and the pain was terrible. It was brutal. Afterward I felt very ill but said nothing because I didn't want to arouse any suspicions at home.

I knew from the very first that our marriage couldn't last. Gustavo didn't want me to work, and he objected to my going to night school or doing guard duty; if I got home late, he tried to question me. When I volunteered to do farm work as a *permanente,* he argued that a month was too long for us to be apart. But I asked him if he knew of any other kind of government that had rehabilitated prostitutes. I said that after all, I'd been on leave to study for a long time, yet they'd never docked a single *centavo* from my wages. How could I refuse when they needed my services? "It's a matter of principle," I told him. He gave in with good grace then and wrote me very nice letters while I was away.

I pressed Gustavo to quit his job at the club. I liked to see a man work in production. "You're young enough to go into training and learn to be

15. See Introduction, pp. xxiv–xv.

a technician," I told him. Little by little—partly because of me and partly because he could see all the achievements with his own two eyes, Gustavo began to understand the Revolution and finally became integrated into the revolutionary process. He joined the militia, gave up his job at the club, and started to work in a factory. After a while they sent him to study, then he joined the Communist Youth and was picked from a hundred-odd students for a brigade that builds factories in different parts of the country.

I used to help Gustavo with his homework, and studying together, we understood each other better. He'd changed a great deal, and I was so pleased to see him become a revolutionary that I began to love him, truly love him. He'd become the man I'd dreamed of marrying. But just as I was beginning to realize this, I lost him.

It was too late. I'd offended him too much with my destructive, fault-finding ways. I've always looked out for myself and had to face the most difficult situations alone, so I couldn't stand any man calling me to account. I don't know, maybe I didn't want to depend on anybody. But that attitude didn't help my marriage, and in the end he really got back at me. We'd been married two years and I'd finally gotten over Tomás when Gustavo left me.

If only he'd talked to me and made me face facts, maybe our marriage could have been saved. We'd discussed our problems two or three times and I'd admitted I was difficult to get along with, and promised I'd change. But the fault wasn't all mine. Gustavo has a lot of complexes and trouble with his nerves. He's the kind of person who, once he decides to do something, goes ahead and does it no matter who suffers.

And there was another thing. After Gustavo left me, he took up with a woman who people said had been pregnant by him when we got married. He never mentioned her when he left me. In fact, he stayed with his family for several months before going to live with her.

Whenever I ran into him he always asked, "How are you getting along in school?" I told him, "I'm quitting, that's how." I was still attending classes then, but paying no attention to what was said. I really had lost the will to go on.

"Oh, don't do that," Gustavo said. "Think of the beautiful thing you've done for me. Think how you awoke in me the desire to study. Pilar, you can't lag behind now." Very fine, but he wouldn't come back to me.

I had lots of clothes then, pretty ones too. I'd look at them and think, "What do I want these for, when Gustavo's up and left me?" And *rip, rip, rácata!* I tore them up. I dropped the pieces into a big can and threw a lighted match on them. I didn't want even a scrap left to remind me of our life together.

Chapter Four

The Workers' College

WE STUDENTS WERE TOLD that those of us revolutionaries who met certain prerequisites and who never had any problems at their work center could apply for one of the Workers' Colleges at the University.[16] I sent in my application, but they didn't even bother to answer.

When I realized all the applicants had been notified except me, I thought there must have been some mistake. I went to the comrade in charge and asked him what had happened.

"Look, Pilar, I'm embarrassed to have to tell you this. You were the last person I expected to get an unfavorable report. . . ." Well, it all boiled down to the fact that I was considered morally unfit to enter college because I'd lived with Tomás. That affair kept messing up my life.

I wrote a letter to the Bureau of the College[17] that very afternoon. I came right out and admitted I'd lived with a married man, but I told them it was long over, and from the time I'd been in the school for outstanding students, no one could criticize my behavior. In spite of the fact that I'd completed the sixth grade long before, I repeated that grade

16. *Facultad Obrera y Campesina*, established at the University of Havana in 1963–64, is a three-year university-preparatory program that "prepares workers and peasants for enrollment in specific university divisions and for positions in industrial and agricultural enterprises." While the curriculum includes social science courses and Marxist-Leninist studies, special emphasis is given to training workers "in technical and scientific studies on a level higher than or equal to secondary education." Applicants are limited to workers or peasants at least eighteen years of age who have passed an examination and whose revolutionary qualities are certified by the Central Organization of Cuban Trade Unions (CTC). Over 8,000 students were enrolled in Havana University's branch of the Worker-Peasant College in 1968, and 1,400 had graduated and gone on to university studies. (Sucklicki, *University Students and Revolution in Cuba*, pp. 129–30, 163 n. 57. Also see Valdés, "The Radical Transformation of Cuban Education," pp. 429–31.) Branches of the Worker-Peasant College were established in cities and towns whose residents did not have access to branches at the universities in Havana, Santa Clara (Las Villas), and Santiago de Cuba (Oriente). Pilar had been enrolled in a factory branch and was trying to transfer to the university campus.

17. The University Bureau of the Young Communists and the University Student Federation, which was responsible for political education and organization within the University.

at night school and then went on to evening secondary school, because I was anxious to improve myself. I was a militiawoman, I did productive labor, and my attitude toward defense and study had always been excellent. I said I couldn't understand why I was considered unfit to enter the College, and I was ready to argue my case with anybody.

Apparently a lot of people had the same kind of problem, so the Bureau held a series of hearings. When I was called before them they didn't make any charges or offer any explanations; they just asked why I disagreed with their report.

I am explosive, and when I believe in something I fight for it. I told them that in the first place I no longer had anything to do with Tomás, and even if I did, I couldn't see why that should keep me out of the University. "It may not be the conventional thing," I told them, "but what counts is a person's attitude toward study—and, of course, toward work. Right?"

They called me in for a second interview, and after that they accepted me, so in the spring of 1966 I entered the Workers' College at the University.

Once more I found myself in a wonderland. I feel at home there because I'm among people without prejudice, and with the true collective spirit. If you have a problem, even a personal one, everyone is ready to help. They really care about you, because if you look a bit glum they'll ask, "What's the matter? Come on, tell me what's wrong" or "How is your little girl today?" When I had some difficulty with chemistry, a monitor helped me out, and I didn't even know her well. She's very sweet. Sometimes I don't dress up much to go to school and she'll tell me I should always try to look pretty, if only to keep up my spirits.

This school was organized for adults who lack the formal education to get into the University. When it opened I thought, "It surely won't be as good as the rest of the University." But no, I was wrong. One college is no different from another here; ours is as good as any other school in the University. The courses are more elementary but more intensive.

There used to be only one Workers' College in Havana, now there are many branches, sometimes with seventy students to a class. Everybody wants an education and everybody has a right to it. That makes for a few difficulties, like the short supply of textbooks, but obstacles are quickly overcome by the spirit of comradeship.

Gradually I've become integrated into the revolutionary life at the Workers' College, and I attend the Communist Youth meetings whenever I can. I'm also a member of the Red Brigade, which has very strict requirements. You must maintain 100 percent class attendance and a grade average of at least 80 percent, be a member of the militia, and participate in productive labor.

For military training I attended the combat-preparation school of the university militia. That's a marvelous thing! Military discipline is very hard, but it toughens you and prepares you for anything. I really learned what war is like. Why, they even teach you how to build a shelter in case of attack!

They showed us films demonstrating how to stand guard, how to dress, and how a sentinel should behave. For instance, they warn you that if a comrade should ask for directions, you must never turn your back to point the way or he could bash you on the head. You're also taught not to do anything to pass the time, not to get into a conversation with anybody, and not to smoke. At the factory you sit by the door when you're on guard. At the University you must stand up the whole time, and if you're caught sitting down you get a demerit.

In military school we practiced everything out in the field—taking the offensive . . . the works. Sometimes they gave a combat alarm at 3:00 A.M., which meant the Yankees had landed. What a sight we were— rushing out in that early-morning cold, crawling through the wet grass, simulating combat with Roman candles!

We were divided into two companies. In one exercise, Company 5 had to hide, and my company, 6, had to look for them. When we caught anyone, we took her rifle away and made her walk with her hands in the air. We'd hurl the most horrible insults at our prisoners, things like "You pig of a Yankee!" and "I shit on your mother!"

Before we took the course we couldn't have done much to defend ourselves if the Americans came. I had no experience with firearms and I was terribly jittery the first time they gave me a Mauser. It has more of a kick than other guns, and the noise is deafening. When they gave me a target test, I passed the 200-meter shot, but I got nervous and failed the 400-meter shot because I was so anxious to get through. It was exciting to run up to the target to see how many points you scored.

The hardest thing about military training was the discipline. To us the officers seemed like monsters. For instance, in the dining room you weren't allowed to cross your legs, and when an officer entered you had to stand at attention. That irritated some of the women, and the officers finally relaxed the rule a bit. Every afternoon they'd inspect our quarters. You had to stand beside your cot, and when the officer passed you had to make a turn, take a step forward, turn back again, and then stand at attention until he was through. I was awkward making that turn, but I practiced it until I did it perfectly.

It was a serious offense to lay down your rifle for any reason, and when we had classes on military theory we had to keep our rifles leaning against our shoulders. We couldn't even put them across our laps. And if the guns weren't clean, we'd be reported.

I vowed I wouldn't do anything to be reported, but once when it was my turn to stand guard at 6:oo in the morning, I woke up and went straight to the bathroom to wash. When I got back, the chief of the company told me to relieve the sentry right away. Of course I went. But according to the rules you had to make your bed *before* going to wash, and I'd neglected to do that. So I was reported.

Another time I was reported for wearing an "unauthorized object." I had a pen in my pocket and that was against the rules, though I didn't know it at the time. We weren't required to dress in full uniform since not all the women could afford it right away, but we were required to have our shoelaces tied and all our buttons buttoned.

Ay, what a sorrowful day when I had to appear before the court! How I dreaded it! You had to make the turn perfectly, salute correctly, and stand at attention without lowering your salute until the chief of the court lowered his. All this while you were dying of fear. You could go into the court with a single report against you and come out with a whole list of them.

When they asked, "Do you plead guilty to the charges?" I answered yes. I was lucky—they only made me stand guard duty twice as punishment.

I had both my girls at home but then Celia moved away and I needed someone to take care of them. My sister Susana and her husband and children were living with *mamá* at the time, in the apartment in Los Pinos that Aunt Gertrudis had turned over to her. Susana and my brother-in-law were having trouble with *mamá* so I suggested they move in with me.

Susana has an ideal marriage because everything her husband does is right in her eyes, although he drinks too much. He got to the point where he didn't even keep himself clean, and the rest of us would say to Susana, "*Ay,* how can you stand to live with him?" But she doesn't like anybody to point out his flaws and always swore he didn't drink. He's changed a lot now though—the liquor shortage has been a godsend to him. He's put on weight, he's always neat and clean, and he's even become revolutionary.

Susana won't use contraceptives. We tell her, "Don't have any more babies. You can get a job and get scholarships for your kids." But she says no, she'll welcome any babies that might come.

Susana was still with me when the ministry told me that since I had such a big house, I could easily share it with another woman from the rehabilitation school. I agreed, and Gabina moved in. In the beginning she helped me just as Carmelina and Celia had.

But there were problems. One day Susana's baby wet Gabina's bed and the two of them started quarreling. Then once *mamá* was planning to get rid of a litter of puppies by turning them loose somewhere and I decided to take them to El Bando de la Piedad[18] instead. Meanwhile I took them home, even though I detest animals and hate to clean up their messes. Well, Gabina claimed the puppies didn't let her sleep and she went to the police station and filed charges against me!

Gabina's room had its own outside door, so she locked the connecting door between her room and the rest of the house and after that she could come and go without having anything to do with us. That's all very well, but it cut us off from one of our bathrooms. Then after a time she told me she wanted another room. It seemed to me one was enough, but when we went to court over it, it was decided in her favor. The government built a brick wall between her section of the house and mine, and a cement walk from her door to the street. Then they remodeled the garage to make another room for me. Actually there are two houses now instead of one, and Gabina's electricity is no longer put on my bill, so we get along much better.

The government gave Susana a house too, but it's a very poor one with a dirt floor. She's the worst off of any of us, yet she's the only one of my sisters who married for love and claims to be happy with her husband. The rest of us married just to get out of that house.

My brother Aurelio's first wife was very much in love with him, but she was so sluttish he finally couldn't stand it and left. My brother's no lamb himself, let me tell you. He's very domineering. He remarried but he's no happier in his second marriage than in his first, and he told me he was getting another divorce.

My eldest sister, Francisca, took off with her sweetheart, and only a few days later he went to study in Poland, leaving her pregnant. The baby was already born by the time he came back and married her. That was about eight years ago. Now Francisca tells me she only stays with him because she doesn't want to give her children a stepfather.

Xiomara says the same thing, that she feels no love for her husband and stays with him for her daughter's sake. And in fact, her little girl has a serious problem. Xiomara works in a school, and one Saturday afternoon when she had to attend a meeting she took along her daughter, who was about seven then. A fifteen-year-old boy was there, the son of one of Xiomara's co-workers, and when the meeting was over they found the girl lying unconscious on a blood-soaked cushion, a handkerchief stuffed in her mouth. She was immediately operated on in the Children's Hospital. The boy was sentenced to about seven years for rape.

My younger sister, Niurkita, took off with her sweetheart when she was thirteen years old. I think it was because one night she saw *mamá* in bed with a man. The girl was so disillusioned!

For five years *papá* was in the Army in Oriente and came home once a

18. The humane society.

month on his five-day pass, and all that time my mother was taking his money and carrying on with a bus driver! When *papá* was transferred back to Havana *mamá* told him, "For the past five years I've loved another man." If I'd been my father I think I'd have shot her, but he did nothing.

I can understand how *mamá* could fall in love with another man, but to say nothing to *papá* until he returned, full of illusions and longing to be with her—that I don't understand. *Papá* was completely destroyed by it. We couldn't get him to talk of anything else. It's her fault he had a lonely old age and I'll never forgive her.

For a while *papá* lived with me, but then he moved back to his own house. At the time I had no one to look after the children so I phoned *mamá* and said, "I know you don't feel at ease with *papá* in the house. Why don't you move in with me? You can look after the children, which would be a big help to me and a good thing for you too. I have plenty of food, and when you want a new dress, I'll buy you one."

Mamá agreed, and she and my two little brothers, Eugenio and Victor, moved in. I might have known: from the time she arrived, our whole life was quarrels and vexation. Not only did she not cook, she sold our food. The food shortage provided her with the best of business opportunities!

At first I said nothing, but finally I couldn't bear it. "Look, *mamá,* I've told you that any time you need 20 *pesos* I'll let you have them. Why should you sell our food? These children must eat!"

She didn't understand. If she served them eggs and bread for lunch, she felt she'd done her share and didn't cook any dinner. An adult can fast for three days a week and no harm done, but children can't! Besides, there was no need for anyone to go hungry. There was money enough—not to stuff ourselves, but at least to eat every day.

The very fact that *mamá* hasn't changed since the Revolution proves there's something wrong with her. Now there are so many opportunities to learn that nobody can resist them. Before 1959 I was a fool. I never read and nothing interested me. Now I'm completely different. But *mamá* simply lives locked up in herself. She's not the least bit interested in the Revolution. I don't even try to talk to her about it. Now and then she'll say she's going to the United States to live with her brother Arnaldo, who she claims left because the Revolution put an end to his career. The truth is he left because he's too selfish to be a communist. He was one of those Playa Girón invaders we later exchanged for American baby food.[19] Need I say more?

To get away from *mamá,* I went to stay with Eleodoro's *papá* while he

19. In December, 1962, an agreement was concluded between Cuba and the United States for the release of 1,113 prisoners captured during the Playa Girón invasion in April, 1961. The United States agreed to send to Cuba $23,000,000 in drugs, $14,000,000 in baby foods, $9,000,000 in powdered milk, and $7,000,000 in surgical, dental and veterinary

was ill. He was alone because my mother-in-law had died in 1967, of a bad heart. I'd become very close to Eleodoro's parents since I graduated from rehabilitation school. They'd sent a letter saying there were no grudges between us and begging me not to put any distance between myself and them. They adored Ana Bárbara. "But even above that," they said, "is the fact that we love you. Please count on us whenever you need us." Maybe knowing I'd gotten out of that brothel made my mother-in-law, Ana, change so much toward me. When I went to her house, she always made me feel at home. It was after her death that I went to see a psychiatrist for a second time.

I never loved my father-in-law as I had the old woman, but he was very fond of me and I felt sorry for him because he was so alone, with his daughter up North and his son so indifferent. When I moved in with him I left my ration book with *mamá* for the children.

After a time I returned home, and it was a horrible sight; even the walls were filthy. *Mamá* had brought a dog and a cat with her and always kept them inside, knowing perfectly well how I hated animals. We had so many fights she finally up and moved to Susana's, taking all my sheets and towels and my good iron. The last thing she did was go to the police station and accuse me of throwing her out and stealing a pair of her stockings! Can you believe it?

When I heard what she'd done, I marched straight over to my sister's. Susana was ironing my sheets with my iron. As soon as she saw me, she said, "Oh Pilar, I know these are your things. Take them if you want, I won't say anything."

"No, my child," I answered. "All these things I can replace; the stores have them. The one thing I can't buy is a good mother."

With my mother-in-law dead and *mamá* so unreliable and unpleasant, I didn't know what to do. I discussed my difficulties with a comrade at the College, and she suggested I get scholarships for the girls. That way I'd have some peace of mind.

I explained my problem to the university authorities and took advantage of the occasion to let them know that my two younger brothers needed scholarships too. Those two boys spent their lives out in the street. All four children were granted places in boarding school, but I had a terrible struggle getting *mamá* to sign the authorization. She said she couldn't bear to have her children so far away from her—my mother, who never paid the slightest attention to any of us! One thing's for sure, they were a lot better off in boarding school.

I myself suffered a great deal the day I said goodbye to my girls in the

---

instruments, plus $2,900,000 in cash as ransom for prisoners released by Castro in the spring of 1961. (*Time*, Jan. 4, 1963, p. 14.) Castro has maintained that the United States never completely fulfilled its part of the agreement. (See Lockwood, *Castro's Cuba, Cuba's Fidel*, p. 232.)

school director's office. Ana Bárbara was nine and Ludmila only four; she'd never been to school at all. They both reacted very well and went off to lunch with the assistant director looking perfectly happy, but as for me, I thought I'd die. That night I dreamed Ludmila was drowning in a river and I couldn't save her.

When I went to get them the next Friday, the director told me Ludmila had cried a lot because she hadn't expected to be separated from her sister. The director had let Ana Bárbara walk Ludmila over to her dormitory and stay with her awhile until she calmed down. I felt very bad about sending my children away, but I have them home every single weekend and it's just fine.

Eleodoro's *papá* finally died of tuberculosis. I never suspected he had tuberculosis and neither did Eleodoro, but my mother-in-law must have known because she'd always kept his dishes separate. I guess she was afraid I wouldn't let Ana Bárbara stay there if I knew. It was unforgivable not to tell us. Because of their secrecy, my daughters had to go through horrible treatment, and have frequent X-rays and blood tests. All the adult members of the family had to be examined for infection, too, and the health authorities even fumigated the house.

For some time my own father had suffered frequent stomach upsets and diarrhea, and a few months after my father-in-law's death, *papá* woke up one morning with his legs badly swollen. He went to a doctor and found out he had cirrhosis of the liver.

Papá was in the hospital about two months, and after he was discharged he followed a salt-free diet of skim milk, chicken, and meat. He got awfully demanding about little things during his illness. From the hospital he went to Niurkita's house in Los Pinos but complained that she didn't look after him properly. What did he expect? Imagine, Niurkita was a child of fourteen and already had a daughter. How could she look after an invalid? Francisca cooked his meals, but then her frigidaire broke down, so he went to stay with Aunt Gertrudis.

That year Francisca and I rented a place at Santa María del Mar Beach and *papá* asked to go with us. He'd been sick for several days but said it was only diarrhea. One night he was in a deplorable state and the doctor sent him to the Calixto García Hospital. I stayed there all day. *Papá* looked very bad to me and I asked Xiomara to phone the rest of the family. He didn't realize he was dying and insisted that they let him go back to the beach. He kept on like that until he died, at 10:00 that night.

Xiomara, Aurelio, Aurelio's wife, and I were at his bedside. I threw myself on his body and clung to him so they couldn't pull me away. In the months before he died *papá* and I had become close friends. He was more spontaneous with me and would confide his intimate thoughts and feelings. I couldn't resign myself to my loss. Aurelio also, though calmer than my sisters and I, felt his death deeply. *Papá* was only fifty-three.

Funerals were free by then. Aurelio made all the arrangements, but I was the one who dressed *papá* and laid him out. That was the last time I would see him and I didn't want anyone else to do it.

It's *mamá* who killed him. How often he clamored for her, especially on that last day of his life! Yet when my brother went to get her, she refused to go. Nor would she come to the wake or let my little brothers go. But Victor, the youngest, stood right up to her and said he was going. "If he wants to go, he shall go," Aurelio told her. "I'll take him myself." And so he did.

My mother was raising those two boys to be monsters. She'd taught them to hate *papá* and call him a faggot and all sorts of names. One time Eugenio even threw an iron bar at him. And I remember how *mamá* would try to drag Ludmila from him. The child would beg, "Let me go kiss Granddaddy!" and she'd struggle until *mamá* had to let her go. My little brothers never even wanted to kiss him.

I have a hard time getting along with my family, but sometimes I think I'd feel better if I saw more of them, in spite of all their flaws. I tell myself, "What the heck, nobody's perfect—life is like that." And Ana Bárbara says, "Grandmother has her faults, and maybe you have a few yourself. That's no reason a mother and daughter can't be on friendly terms."

That was how I felt one day not long ago when *mamá* came to visit a friend in my neighborhood. Ludmila saw her and ran up to kiss her. Suddenly I wanted to see her myself and I told Ludmila, "Go ask your grandmother to come here when she's through." But *mamá* didn't come. Ludmila tried to excuse her. "She must have forgotten, *mima*."

She didn't forget. Not her. She had my little brothers with her and they're old enough to carry a message. She could have said, "Eugenio, run over and ask Pila if she really wants to see me or if Ludmila made it up." All she did was kiss Ludmila and give her some candy. Anyone could do that. Ludmila is so sweet that anybody who wouldn't give her a kiss and a handful of candy must have a heart of stone.

I didn't notice when *mamá* left, but even if I'd seen her, I wouldn't have called to her. Lower myself like that? Not me! She's the one who should come humbly to me, not I to her.

A girl once told me an old saying: "Though she be like vinegar, a mother is always a mother."

"I don't agree," I said. "There are women who bear a child and then give it away. How can you compare such a woman with a mother who brings her children home from boarding school every weekend and is always thinking about them?"

Oh well. I've tried to make friends with *mamá*, but inside I detest her.

Why should I forgive her just because I'm her daughter? Why? If she
doesn't know how to act like a mother, that's her problem, not mine. I'll
hate her as long as I live.

I was under psychiatric treatment when *papá* died, because another
terrible depression had hit me. I started losing interest in my studies
and I cried all the time. When I thought about my past life I was so
low I could have drowned in a teaspoon of water. But tears help a lot,
and usually after a good cry I'd cheer up again. I thought I must be sick,
because sometimes in the middle of class I'd get a violent headache or a
pain in the chest, so I went to the hospital for a checkup. They gave me
an electrocardiogram and X-rayed my heart, and the doctor said there
was nothing wrong, it was just nerves. And what did he recommend? A
psychiatrist!

Then examination time came, and I was in pretty bad shape. When I
was taking my math exam, all of a sudden I panicked. I thought, "I can't
turn this in. I can't. There's nothing on it but a bunch of stupid mistakes."
So I tore it up and walked out of the room and got on the elevator.
When I reached the ground floor the professor was there to meet me.
He said, "What's the matter, Pilar? I glanced at your paper two or three
times. You were doing all right. Why walk out? It makes your professor
look bad, you know. It's selfish. Come on, Pilar, for my sake, go on back
and take that exam."

He couldn't talk me into it. I felt really bad for him, but I left anyway.
All the rest of my exams were disastrous too, and I had to take the whole
year over. I was lucky at that. The coordinator told me that if a
scholarship student wanted to repeat a year, the Union of Young Communists had to meet and discuss it, and they'd only allow it if they were
convinced the student had done his best.

I think my math professor must have talked to them, because before
the term was over he told me, "Look, Pilar, we've studied your case and
we think you should be given another chance. But I must tell you that I
and several of your other professors agree you're very introverted. It
isn't normal. You must have some kind of problem." And he finally
convinced me I'd have to have some more psychiatric help if I was going
to straighten myself out.

I went back to Fajardo Hospital, to a doctor named María Puerta.
When *papá* died, it hit me so hard I told Dr. Puerta I wanted to drop out
of school for the rest of the semester. I didn't think I could pass. She
said, "You can't let me down, Pilar. You must pass all your subjects."

But I just wasn't up to it. I was letting her down all right, dropping out
like that, so I told her, "I know I've disappointed you and I won't ask you

for any more help. I'll come back to see you when I've graduated, not before."

Well, I'll graduate from the Workers' College next year, and then I'll go back and visit her as I said. I owe it to her. She helped me enough, now it's up to me to handle the rest of my problems.

Chapter Five

No Reason to Worry

I'M NOT VERY OLD but I already feel middle-aged. Eleodoro is separated from his second wife, and not long ago he asked me to marry him again. Although he's a strange kind of person, he's changed and improved a lot. He does all kinds of things for me, I don't know why. He takes care of the garden, he visits me on weekdays, if I don't go to work he phones my sister to find out what's the matter. That's his way. I don't understand him. I never have. But I've come to believe that he's always been in love with me. Imagine, asking me to marry him again at this late date!

I was very lonely with the girls away at boarding school, and Ana Bárbara dearly loves her *papá*. She's always wanted to see us together again, so . . . well, I accepted. It's true I never loved Eleodoro, but nothing in life is ever complete. If sex was a trial with him, what does it matter? Maybe that's changed, and even if it hasn't, I've reached a point where I don't need a man that way. I can spend the rest of my life very happily without sex, and as for love, I don't think about it anymore.

So I accepted, and then, later, it was Eleodoro who drew back, saying it was better to keep on as we are now. But I don't want to live alone. I hate being alone! Yet at my age, I can't consider somebody new. When one's children are grown it's no longer possible to look for love. What would my daughters think of me if I should marry again? The same thing as I'd think of myself: that the age of marriage is over for me.

It was my sad fate to live it before the Revolution, and now I must take my happiness from seeing my daughters have what I never had. I'm at the stage in life of bringing them up in the best way I can, making them happy. I don't have to worry about money for their education, I don't have to buy them school books or medicine. What more can I wish for, when I have everything?

As a member of this society I have a duty to educate myself and contribute toward our common goal. That's why I want to get rid of the little complexes I still have—like my dreams, for instance. I've never had a pleasant dream in my life; they're all nightmares. One I've had many times is that I'm falling into an abyss. And ever since *papá* died, I've dreamed that I'm in bed with him. I wake up in a dog's mood. Lately I've been having dreams about my comrades at work, and even about my last husband, Gustavo. The dreams always end in bed with the man. One night I dreamed I was riding a horse, or a sort of jitney cab, across a bridge, then a man tried to get on and I was falling off. What odd dreams!

One thing that upsets me is to run into any of my old friends from the brothel, especially when they call me Mercy, the name I used in those days. Not long ago one of those girls came to see me. Of course I prepared coffee for her—after all we were once very close—but all I could think about was getting her to leave. Ana Bárbara was dusting nearby and I'm sure she heard the girl call me Mercy. My daughter's so bright she must know all about my past anyway. She lived with *mamá* for a time while I was in the brothel, and she probably heard my relatives talking. Maybe she's even overheard remarks in the *reparto*,[20] but I've never, never dared bring up the subject, though naturally, when I talk about the Revolution, I always point out that it helped rehabilitate criminals and others who had once taken a wrong turn.

Perhaps my past is known in the University too, but I've had no problems with anybody there. Once I got into an argument with a classmate, but he's the kind who quarrels with everybody. We were reviewing the work in class and he kept butting in. All I said was, "Oh comrade, stop interrupting!"

After class he stopped me and said, "You acted like a woman of the streets."

I thought, "He knows I was a prostitute," but maybe he didn't mean that. Later he apologized but I refused to accept. I have such a bad temper!

The only friend I have from the past is Arnulfo, who used to sew for some of us girls in the brothel. When I drank a lot and tore up my clothes, I'd go to Arnulfo and ask him to make me a new dress that same day. "Don't you have a coat to wear?" he'd ask. And if I didn't, he'd lend me one. Then he'd advise me not to drink so much because it was bad for my health.

Arnulfo was so happy to learn I'd graduated from rehabilitation school, and he asked me to let him keep on sewing for me, which I did. In a way he's my best psychiatrist. Sometimes I've gone to him, overcome by boredom and depression, and he's tried to cheer me up by talking about the opportunities the future offers, and why a woman has no reason to worry nowadays. He reminded me of Lilia, who entered a brothel at thirteen. "You don't have that problem now. Nobody can

20. A suburb or subdivision of a city.

deceive your daughters, because they go to school and learn a lot. Who'd be able to trick them into a brothel? And remember that kid Miladis, who ran away from home because her stepfather tried to rape her? Such things don't happen anymore. So what have you got to worry about?

"Have you forgotten you almost committed suicide? Why, you might still be a whore and ashamed to face any young man who came courting your daughter! But you're not; you have a place in society and can face up to anybody. Right now you're alone—that's what's getting you down. But things change, Pila, and someday you'll be happy."

When I was most stable, during my marriages to Tomás and Gustavo, I tended to stay away from Arnulfo. Now I visit him at least twice a week. He's like home folks to me. If I'm there at dinnertime, he won't let me leave till I've eaten. He knows how much I like coffee and always makes me some. He's a very sweet guy and looks after me like a brother.

True, Arnulfo is no man, although with me he behaves like one. He never mentions his intimacies with men or anything like that, but he says he hates being the way he is and that it saddens him to think of growing old without having fathered a child.

I try to be with my girls as much as I can. When they're home on weekends, I make some special dessert. If they get sick, I keep them at home and take them to the doctor myself. I tell them, "Don't worry if I have to miss a few days at the University, I'll make it up later." It isn't that I distrust the school doctor, it's just that I want to be with them and look after them lovingly. I make every effort to be the kind of mother *mamá* never was. My daughters didn't ask to be born, I brought them into the world, so I want to offer them whatever I can to make them happy. Sometimes things weigh on my mind, but if my daughters run up to me wanting me to play when I'm sad, I make an effort to be affectionate.

I feel especially loving toward Ludmila, because she gets no love from her father. I heard there's a new scholarship plan that would permit her to have lunch and dinner at school but come home to sleep. I'm sure she'd prefer that to boarding school and so would I. I talked it over with Ana Bárbara. "Look, you're a big girl now. Why don't I take you both out of boarding school and you can look after your little sister at night while I'm at school?" She roundly refused to do any such thing. She told me she liked her school and wanted to stay where she was. If that's what she wants to do, let her.

The fact is, I give my daughters more affection than I get from them. Ana Bárbara is very withdrawn; sometimes I think she doesn't love anybody. I notice that she doesn't kiss me, the way I never dared to kiss my mother, so I make a point of kissing and caressing her, especially when I pick her up at school and when I take her back.

The other day I asked her, "Do you plan to marry young?"

"No," she said. "I don't plan to marry at all."

Ludmila is my joy and comfort, the best I have in the world, the most affectionate, attentive child. She notices every little thing, whereas Ana Bárbara is all wrapped up in herself. The other day I woke up thinking about Tomás. "That shameless good-for-nothing doesn't care about his child!" But then Ludmila did something that made me think, "I should bless that man every day of my life for giving me such a daughter!"

Ludmila still asks about her *papi*. I say to her, "*Mi vida,* he's working in the cane fields and isn't allowed to go anywhere. He works there so that all children may be happy."

"But *mami,* everybody is given leave from work in the cane fields."

"Ah, but he's in the vanguard," I tell her. "He uses his free days to do more work."

"Well, all right. I'll tell you what—as soon as I learn to write, my first letter will be to *papi.*" And we leave it at that.

There's no reason to worry about my daughters' future, and there's plenty of cause to rejoice. Ana Bárbara is studious, intelligent, and alert; she really cares about being a good student and I'm always finding her reading my university textbooks. "Don't read those books," I scold her. "You'll just get confused. Ask me what you want to know, maybe I can explain it." On Sundays she talks to me about mathematics and such, and I listen eagerly when she tells me what she's learned.

Ludmila is quite the opposite. I try to set her straight but she doesn't like me to teach her. She's a terrible chatterbox. When someone told her babies were brought by the stork, she piped up, "No they aren't. They come out of their mothers' bellies."

I asked her, "And how many children are you going to have?"

"As many as want to come out of my big belly," she answered.

Once she asked me if the mother's belly has to be cut open to get the baby out. I said, "Yes, almost always." I didn't know what else to say. Then she said, "It must hurt, *mima,* because if they cut it open they have to sew it shut again."

Ludmila loves to try on my dresses and high-heeled shoes, and when she especially likes something of mine she tells me I must keep it until she's fifteen so she can wear it.

With the other girls at school, Ludmila is very quick, very alert. They don't dare hit her because she's found out how to hit back. "Look, *mami,* I have a technique. If you slap a girl's hand or her bottom, she can keep on hitting. But if you punch somebody smack in the stomach it hurts so much they can't hit you back."

Ludmila can be quite a little pest sometimes, and then I have to slap her because she drives me out of my mind. The other day I was very nervous and she was acting up. I called her several times and she didn't come right away, so I lost my temper and slapped her face. I was terribly sorry afterward, although I didn't want her to know because she's so hard to handle. I didn't speak to her all day, but later, when I was washing the dishes, she came and said, "*Mami,* I won't misbehave anymore, because when you get nervous you hit awfully hard." She drew up a chair to stand on. "I'm going to help you with the dishes."

Ana Bárbara doesn't seem to return my love as Ludmila does, which makes it hard for me to be nice to her. Sometimes I even have to pretend, because I know it's my duty as a mother to make life pleasant for her, and I don't want her to suffer the injustices I suffered. Even though I tell her I'm her best friend, she doesn't confide in me and I have to drag every bit of information out of her. She answers my questions, but I can tell she only wants to run out and play with her little friends. Sometimes, to keep her by me a little while, I try to think up a subject of conversation that will interest her.

Ludmila is like Francisca, a real charmer, while Ana Bárbara is dry, like me. The two girls don't get along at all well, but I suppose that's just the difference in ages. Ana Bárbara complains that her sister is a spoiled brat. When she goes out with friends and Ludmila wants to tag along, Ana Bárbara says, "Beat it, I don't want you." Still, I know the two girls love each other, because when Ana Bárbara's weekend pass was rescinded for the first time, Ludmila cried and cried. We went to Ana Bárbara's dormitory and the two of them clung to each other and wept. But no sooner did Ana Bárbara come home than they started to quarrel again.

Ana Bárbara did productive labor on weekends when she was in the sixth grade, but this year she did her first two-month stretch. She said the girls were looking forward to being in the country, but one had told her, "I'm going to play and have a good time. I hate work."

Ana Bárbara was disgusted. "Imagine, going there just to waste your time," she said. "It's expensive to send us to the country and we're not sent there to play."

Ana Bárbara's letters from the country were a great deal more expressive than she normally is. Really, they were moving. She regards farm work as a necessary aid to the Revolution, and in one letter she said, "I'm in a hurry because I must go and do my bit for the 10-million-ton harvest."

In Ludmila I see none of the traits of the "new man" that I see in her sister, though she understands what she's told and often compares modern children with those of the past. If she sees a naughty child she remarks, "*Mami,* that kid shouldn't be in this country. He stole a pencil from me. Only bad children who live in other countries do that."

If she only practiced what she preaches! Whenever she sees something pretty, she wants it for herself. I've seen children of six and even younger who aren't so grabby. She isn't obedient like Ana Bárbara, and she still creeps into my bed almost every night she sleeps at home.

Sometimes I tell Ludmila how, when I was a little girl, there were lots of things in the stores that we couldn't afford to buy. Nowadays, I explain, things are scarce but everybody can get some of whatever there is. Then she'll ask, "And how did the Revolution make it that way? With guns?"

Sometimes I marvel at her. For instance, if she sees anything that isn't right somewhere, she'll say, "That kind of thing is going to end just as it did in Cuba, by people taking up arms. That's the only way for everybody to have the same things."

My daughters are not in the least bothered by the shortages because they don't lack anything, and they're not interested in money. Ana Bárbara comes home from school alone on Saturdays, and I tell her she should always carry enough money to hire a car, just in case. I gave her the prettiest red purse to keep it in.

"But I don't need money," she objected. She hated the purse and wouldn't use it. She got so tired of my insisting that she finally threw it away.

The other day I had an argument with Eleodoro about some shoes with a bit of a heel that I bought for Ana Bárbara. She wore them to see if they fit and they were tight, but maybe it's only because they were new. Eleodoro gave me a whole song and dance about it. He wants me to be terribly strict with the girls. Hell, I can't. It's not like me. I said, "Listen, don't come around bothering me. These shoes have been used and can't be returned, so what's the good of getting upset about it? When I get my next ration coupon, I'll give it to Ana Bárbara so she can buy another pair."

It's funny, but all the while I was in prostitution Eleodoro never bothered about his daughter. He got closer to her when I entered rehabilitation school, precisely when she least needed him because the ministry was sending the allowance. Now he's always coming to see her and does everything to please her. Well, I guess I ought to be glad.

Eleodoro treats Ludmila with affection too, and sometimes when Ana Bárbara calls her father *papi*, Ludmila will do the same, and kiss and caress him just like her sister. Eleodoro never says "my daughter" but talks of both girls together. When he brings candy it's for both of them, and for Three Kings he always says, "What presents shall we get the girls this year?"

Now that Ana Bárbara is old enough to take an interest in boys, Eleodoro's chief fear is that she might fall in love with a black. I told him *I* certainly wasn't going to make her think that was wrong. After all, he married me, a *mulata*. "Let her decide who she loves," I said. "She can pick the man she likes, and if she isn't happy with him, she can get another one. I'm not going to tell her she should stay with one man all her life."

Eleodoro keeps bringing up the same fears. Not that he talks about these things with the child. When Ana Bárbara came back from productive labor, I found a letter in the pocket of her blouse. It was from a boy—just a comradely letter, the sort boys and girls write each other from their camps telling of their experiences. There was no sign of anything else. I asked her about it. "Oh, that's a letter from a boy in school," she answered. "He's a swell kid."

"What's he like?" I asked.

"He's the cutest boy. Black and very slender." I told Eleodoro and he said, "Don't tell her I know. I'll watch her."

Eleodoro's mother never called me a *negra*. I don't know why he has to take such a stand all of a sudden. It's just nonsense. He says he disapproves of mixed couples. I tell him, "Black skin isn't contagious; it doesn't rub off on you."

Francisca has a serious prejudice problem with her husband's family, but they've got to be kidding. There's no trace of negroid features in her daughter Zoraya. She's a brunette, but she's white. It's mainly Francisca herself who worries about her daughter's color; she has a complex about it because of Grandma Nicolasa. When we were kids we were always picking on Susana, and I guess Francisca just chose one of her children to badger. She can't do it to her son Luisito because he's blond as a Russian, so she picks on Zoraya.

Ludmila is dark-skinned and has straight black hair. Her eyes are large, with very long lashes, and her mouth is small. Ana Bárbara sometimes calls her *mulata*—not in a rude way, but affectionately. Ludmila knows what her color is—I taught her—and if you say she's white, she'll correct you: "I am *mulatica!*"

My dearest hope for my daughters is that they won't be disappointed in their husbands. I mean, a man and a woman should do everything before they get married, so they know what they're getting into. Lots of people have criticized my attitude, but if a man and a woman are attracted to each other, why shouldn't they go to bed together? Some of my friends object: "But if you're going to be with one man today and another man tomorrow. . . ."

Well, why not? I think free love—I mean real love, not doing it for money—is a good thing. If you like a man, have an affair for a while and feel good with him. If the time comes when you no longer hit it off, isn't it better to find out before you're tied to each other? That way you go into marriage with your eyes open. Frankly, sex is one of the determining factors in marriage. It's basic. The only thing is, the girl should use a ring, so as not to get pregnant.

Young as she is, Ana Bárbara knows a lot about contraceptives and understands the facts of life because I've talked about such things in front of her. Not that I've told her outright, "Look, Ana Bárbara, a man and a woman do thus-and-so together." I've simply found opportunities to discuss sex and childbirth in a conversational way.

If she'd give me more of a chance to talk to her, it would be easy. As it is, I have to use a different technique. For instance, I tell her off-color stories so she'll pick up a few facts, and I encourage her to tell me one in return. Of course her stories are very mild, but then I let go with something really spicy. That way I'm trying to get her to confide in me.

At Ana Bárbara's school the girls are allowed to have sweethearts, though they must have some rules about hugging and kissing. I wouldn't like Ana Bárbara to get pregnant while she's still on scholarship. It would look bad in school. But the thought of my daughters getting married doesn't worry me in the least.

I'd worry terribly if there were any risk of Ana Bárbara going with a man for money. But she has no financial troubles and so no reason in the world to end up a prostitute. Since the Revolution you don't see any of the things I went through; nobody has to commit the crimes I was driven to commit. When the police arrested 300 young delinquents on La Rampa in El Vedado and Fidel gave his speech about them, I was really shocked. He said those kids were stealing, throwing orgies, taking drugs, and some of the young girls were trading their bodies to strangers for merchandise.[21] I'd been so sure that nothing like that happened in Cuba anymore!

Some companions are a bad influence. I tell my Ana Bárbara, "When you see a comrade acting rude to the teacher, speak up. It's up to you to tell them their attitude is wrong. Then, if they don't improve, leave them alone. Don't get involved with them."

It's the parents who are to blame, not the kids. It all comes from not knowing just how much your daughter may be longing for a bottle of perfume or a pack of cigarettes. Or maybe she's even hungry because you don't feed her well. If you don't give your daughters what they need, what can they do except go out and get it any way they can? Still, a girl like that has to be downright shameless because there are plenty of jobs in Cuba. Anybody looking for work will find every door open and plenty of choice.

21. In a radio speech on September 29, 1968, Fidel Castro reported the arrest of a group of young people who had broken into a high school, destroyed television sets used in the classrooms, and torn down pictures of Che Guevara. The arrest came during a period of concern over young people whom, according to José Yglesias, "Cubans characterized as hippies; unshaven, unwashed, uninterested in work, outlandishly dressed by Cuban standards, they were given to hanging around La Rampa, a street that [was] the nighttime hub of the Vedado section of Havana." ("Cuban Report: Their Hippies and Their Squares," *New York Times Magazine*, Jan. 12, 1969, p. 43. Also see Sutherland, *The Youngest Revolution*, pp. 42–45.)

At school the girls have sewing and knitting workshops, and are taught to make artificial flowers and also to wash and iron, so they get good training as housewives. The only thing they aren't taught, so far as I know, is cooking. Not that housework is such a problem nowadays; a husband and wife should share the responsibility and both of them should work to support their home.[22] There's no inequality between men and women. If a wife and husband hit it off, they help each other in everything. If they don't, they separate and that's that.

Gustavo and I have been separated for two years and eight months, but the divorce decree only came through on August 26, 1969. Xiomara tells me that Gustavo has visited her lately and claims he's never forgotten me, that he loves me still, and that he's separated from the woman he was living with.

I said, "Look, if he comes to see you again, tell him I'm quite ready to go back to him. I love him too." But he hasn't been back.

One day we happened to get on the same bus and he hurried off at the next stop as if he'd seen the plague. I got off too. I spoke right up and said, "Gustavo, are you in a great hurry?"

"Yes, yes, I am," he said nervously. "I'm due at a meeting right now, and tonight I leave for Oriente." That was all. No "I'll see you later" or "Another day we can talk." He didn't even say "So long" before he turned and left me standing there. Oh well, it's no wonder, I've changed so much. I've gotten so ugly and fat, so odd-looking.

Afterward he told Xiomara he hadn't snubbed me at all and insisted it was true about the meeting and leaving town. Besides, he said, his *papá* had died in an accident and he was in an awful state about it.

What nonsense! You can take it from me his father's death didn't affect him in the least. He adores his *mamá* and never forgave his *papá* for gambling his money away on the horse races. Why, Gustavo was always urging his *mamá* to leave home. How can he expect anyone to believe he was so upset? I'll bet he was glad.

No, I haven't much hope of getting him back, much as I'd like to. I'd even like to have another child, if only it were Gustavo's. At least I think I would. One thing I'm sure of, though—under no circumstances would I stop studying or working. To me that means independence, freedom in every way. There's no greater delight than getting things through your own efforts. Me, sit and wait for someone to bring me what I need? Never!

One night I dreamed that Gustavo and I got together again, but he said we could marry only if we left Cuba, because he didn't like this

22. The new Family Code that went into effect in March, 1975, lists housework and household management among the joint responsibilities of marriage. (See Chap. II, sec. 1 of the code in *Granma Weekly Review*, Mar. 16, 1975.)

system. Well, if Gustavo really made any such conditions, I'd tell him roundly, "No! We'll have to set aside our love, for I'll never leave my homeland." Indeed not! I'm much too happy as I am.

There was a time when I thought of having a career in mathematics because that's the easiest subject for me. I always get 86 or 90 points in the examinations, and the only reason I don't get 100s is that I never pick up a book. I take the examination with nothing to go on but the professor's lectures. But I could no longer be satisfied with being a mathematics teacher. I'm working part-time in a laboratory in the CUJAE,[23] but I don't want to be just a technician either. I don't mean to run them down—they have a very important function—but I want a university career.

Right now I'm thinking of taking up industrial engineering. Nobody used to know what an industrial engineer was, but recently a number of professors have given talks explaining industrial, civil, and all the other branches of engineering. Industrial engineering appeals to me, and very few students choose it so they need me there. It means five extra years of study, but after I get my degree I mean to apply for a scholarship to do graduate work.

I got my technician's job through the Workers' College, where the great majority of students were on scholarships. We were allowed to choose the job that most appealed to us since it's considered part of our training. Now, if for any reason I can't keep on studying after I get my degree, at least I'll be a trained laboratory technician.

My days are very busy. I work at the laboratory from 8:00 to 12:00. From noon to 1:00 I study. Then I have my lunch at the students' dining hall, and go straight to Havana from CUJAE. I review assignments in the college library until my first class begins at 4:30 P.M. Occasionally after class I go to Coppelia for ice cream or to a pizzeria, but usually when I get home around 9:00, I only have a glass of milk because I've eaten a hearty lunch at the students' dining hall.

I never stand in line at the grocery store, but I manage to get all my rations just like everybody else. Coffee is distributed to the stores on Monday, so I wait until Tuesday to get it, when there's no line. On Saturday the meat comes in and I get mine, but if I find people in line ahead of me I turn in my card and walk around for a while. When I come back, it's packed and ready. Since the grocery store is too far for me to lug my parcels on foot, I go home on a bus or hire a car for 1 *peso*.

I'm very fastidious about my clothes. It would be more convenient to send them to the laundry, but I don't like the idea of having my clothes dumped in with everybody else's, so I wash and iron them myself.

23. *Ciudad Universitaria José Antonio Echeverría* (José Antonio Echeverría University City), named for one of Cuba's most famous student martyrs.

On Sundays I iron and cook lunch and dinner for the girls. I give them the whole week's meat ration to make sure they eat well when they're with me. In my opinion, there's more than enough food to go around and everybody earns enough to buy it. Take me. My children and I eat a whole lot better than I did as a child.

When they cut the rice ration down to 3 pounds a month per person, it was plenty for me. I don't like rice anyway. When they put it back to 4 pounds I had loads of it left over, so you can imagine what it's like now that they're giving 6 pounds a month per person. When my daughters were at home with me, the lard and oil ration was enough, and now that they're away at school I have more than I need. The same goes for milk. I buy a liter a day and save it up for when Ludmila, my youngest, comes home for the weekend. I have more eggs than I know what to do with, too, because I don't like them much. Now meat I *do* like, and I get enough of that.

The way I see it, the most important goal for Cuba today is to eliminate underdevelopment. We've had no great industries, no progress, nothing of our own for years and years. Everything we had was made outside Cuba. Now we're making radios, and we're beginning to get some machinery for our agriculture. It's not going to be easy. The only way we can do it is with hard work.

We still import our buses and the replacement parts for them, and if there's not enough cash we have to pay for them with *malanga*.[24] That means less to eat, but we must have the buses. Our agricultural products are all we have to trade so we've got no choice. Sure there are shortages, but what's the good of having plenty to eat if there's no bus to take you to work?

You see, work is the only way out for Cuba, because there's no point in trying for an understanding with the United States. I agree heartily with our supreme leader: peaceful coexistence with the capitalists is no good. We have a saying, "Better no health at all than a little health." Maybe the Russians can manage to be for and against something at the same time, but we Cubans aren't like that. If we aren't for something, we're against it. I feel a lot friendlier toward the Chinese because I've heard they're more like us. Not that I really understand such a difficult subject, but it seems to me that Chinese policy is more open and clear-cut, like Fidel's, not hypocritical like the Russians'.

It's only lately I've been reading a bit more and taking an interest in world problems. Frankly, it just isn't in me. I live in a different world. All I can do is say what I think, based on the little I understand of the situation. For example, I think it's quite possible that I or my daughters may have to fight as guerrillas in Latin America some day. To tell you

24. A root vegetable that is a favorite among Cubans.

the truth, I wouldn't want to. But it would be very selfish of me to stand aside just because I'm well off while others suffered the trials we Cubans once went through. It would be hard, bitterly hard, to leave my daughters, but I don't know how I could refuse.

What I can't figure out is why there aren't more guerrilla groups to deal more blows to imperialism. If everybody would only get together and "create more Vietnams," as Che Guevara used to say, our common enemy would be divided and easier to finish off. I've always been impressed by the guerrillas. It's inspiring to know that in spite of their lack of schooling, the poor can decide to take up arms and fight for their freedom.

The man I admire most in the whole world is Ernesto Guevara. I've never idolized a man because he was good-looking or had beautiful eyes, or that sort of thing. It's a man's attitude toward life that counts, but even so I couldn't single one out on that basis alone. To me, Che is head and shoulders above them all because he was so selfless, so just. He never thought of himself, always of others. *El Che!* Imagine a man in his situation, a doctor, well off as all Cubans are now, who left his wife and children and gave up a comfortable life to go and fight in Bolivia! There will never be another like him.

Oh, I admire Fidel Castro very much, but I don't like to worship anyone who's still alive. I like the way he takes hold of a problem and goes about solving it, but my greatest admiration is reserved for a man like Che who dies in defense of a just cause. And when I say Che, I include all the comrades who were with him in his last days. I looked up to Camilo too, but he didn't die as Che did.

When Che died, I was in the country doing productive labor. We got the newspapers there and every one had a different story about the way it happened. A lot of the comrades at the camp said, "Ah, that's a lie for sure. Those people are always killing off Che Guevara. Don't believe a word of it. Why, they wouldn't risk such a valuable man at the battlefront, now would they?" Meanwhile, *Granma* hadn't published a word about it, but when it was announced that Fidel would make a speech, then we started to believe.[25]

After the speech I felt horrible, horrible. The thought that a man of Che's stature should die at the hands of such beasts and then be buried like that—Che, who had given up all for the sake of the Revolution!

I mean, I love the Revolution as much as he did, but who am I? A nobody. And I have plenty of personal motives for being a revolutionary. But there are others who have been hurt, like my psychiatrist's *mamá,* who lost her husband and whose son left for Spain—yet she says

25. *Granma* is the official newspaper of the Communist Party. It takes its name from the launch that carried Castro and his followers from Mexico to Cuba in 1956.

that the achievements of the Revolution compensate for everything. Now there's a woman you really have to admire!

The other day I got this letter from my Aunt Caridad in the United States:

February 23, 1970

Dear Niece:

I hope this finds you well. We are all well, thank God. Pilar, don't go thinking that we've forgotten you. We could never forget the days we spent together at your house. But we didn't have your address and had to wait to write until it was sent to us.

My dear niece, it's very pretty here, and as peaceful as the place where you live. The climate is cool but it never snows. The houses are wood, prettily painted, and they all have glass windows with curtains. It makes a lovely picture.

Well, Pilar, we're renting a furnished house with a living room, a kitchen, two bedrooms, and at the back what they call a "family room," which is used for washing, ironing, sewing, or anything you like. We have a wonderful view. At night the lights are reflected in the sea and it looks just lovely. Let me tell you that your adored uncle is already working as a carpenter at a TV station. I wouldn't be surprised if he were in a show one of these days! As I write, it's already evening and he's painting the frame of a picture and fooling around. He's saying, "Tell that Cuban girl to come up here any time she likes. I miss her a lot. Say I'll cool some beer for her." The same goes for Eleodoro.

I hardly dare tell you about the abundance of things here . . . beautiful things for your girls. And you, who like to cook so much, how I wish you were here.

Please give our best regards to Ana Bárbara and a big hug to Ludmila.

Pilar, send us snapshots of you and the kids. With all our affection for you and the girls,

Caridad

That letter makes me mad! Maybe they have all those pretty things up there, but I know for certain there are a lot of lies in that letter because it's not even two months since Caridad left Cuba. We used to have pretty things here too, but I couldn't afford them, so what good was it to me? When all is said and done, I'm quite content with what I have now—it's enough and more than enough. I feel like telling Caridad that the only thing I regret is that they won't be here to celebrate Christmas in July with us. That's going to be a spectacular event! I'll have beer all right, free too, icy cold the way I like it. And I'll have it here, in my own country. I do like to cook, but what I like to cook is Cuban food, and I never heard Caridad complain about the meals I served her, so I don't know why she has to say I'd eat so well *there*.

When I got that letter I wished she hadn't bothered. As far as I'm concerned, anyone who abandons his country is no relative of mine. I'd feel the same if it were my mother—even one of my daughters. That's the kind of answer she has coming and that's what she's going to get.

If she can get so many lovely things in the United States, how come she could never afford them in Cuba before the Revolution? Here she was a nobody, a starveling. They were dirt-poor and she dressed shabbily; buying a pair of earrings meant a real sacrifice. She never got beyond the sixth grade in school and went out to work as a domestic, but after the triumph of the Revolution she got a job at a polyclinic.[26] Well, let's see if she has better luck there!

I'm not saying there are no mistakes committed here. I've heard about some administrative errors. There are always people around with bad intentions or without much brains, who manage to make themselves pretty comfortable. They've got contacts so they know nobody's going to kick them out, and they just don't bother to go to work most of the time. Absenteeism is a carry-over from the past and it's true that there's more of it now than there was before. A lot of people here just never got used to working. Well, myself for instance—when I started in the factory, it was a completely new experience for me.

I love living in a socialist country. I've lived under capitalism and I can see the difference. Maybe I haven't read about it, not even the *Communist Manifesto,* but to me socialism means there's real equality. We've got no social classes in Cuba now. We're all equal here. There's no private property, in the sense of big landholdings; everything belongs to the state and whatever is produced is for everybody. The rents have gone down and there's no prostitution. I suppose capitalism has its advantages too, but I don't know what they are.

For me the Revolution is the most humane thing in the world, the perfect kind of life. It's so beautiful it can inspire nothing but love. How could it cause people to do anything bad? It encompasses all human welfare, the solution to all economic problems, the abolition of all social evils. You're no better than I—we're equals with the same right to self-improvement and the same assured future. That's why what I live for, what I work for, what I struggle for, is the Revolution that has given me so much. So very much!

26. See Mónica, n. 57.

PART IV

Inocencia Acosta Felipe

Chapter One

Paradise

BEFORE THE REVOLUTION, a servant was like a dog—at the bottom. That's what I was, a servant, and even my family looked down upon me. At our reunions I always felt inferior. Their clothes were good, mine were not, and I could never afford to go to beaches or on outings as they did. But what else could I work at? I wasn't trained for anything. Out in the country we couldn't go to school because it was a long ride on horseback. Later, when we lived in a town, I got through only the first few grades. I loved to study but it wasn't until after the Revolution that I went to high school.

I'm a servant again, but working for the revolutionary government is a different matter. I'm no poorer than anyone else and I'm not treated like an inferior. I feel the same as if I were a clerk in a store.

Before the Revolution women didn't have the opportunities we have today. No matter how intelligent a woman was, if she weren't pretty or well connected, she couldn't get along on her ability alone. Nowadays you work at what you're fitted for, and above all, at what's in keeping with your dignity. I wouldn't have suffered so much in the past if there hadn't been such prejudice. I'd have had a different kind of job, and a pension. . . . I might even have remarried and had children instead of having to put up with a husband who didn't give me a single pleasant memory in twenty-three years. That's why I'm interested in women's liberation. I was reading a book—I can't remember the name of it—a lovely book that tells when Lenin first began to see that women didn't need to go on being merely dishwashers.

When I became engaged to Reinaldo Serrano, I was very hopeful. I,

Inocencia Acosta Felipe's story is based upon 627 pages transcribed from eighteen interviews, fourteen by Ruth M. Lewis, two by Oscar Lewis, and two by both investigators. An additional 100 pages were gathered in three interviews by Oscar Lewis with Inocencia's sister, cousin, and nephew Efrén, a Jehovah's Witness, who gave an account of his personal conflict with the government because of his religion. These interviews have not been included in Inocencia's story.

who'd been a slave all my life, thought that at last I'd be able to say and do what I wanted. But Reinaldo killed all my dreams; the only difference marriage made was to give me an even tougher boss. His nature was very different from mine. I tried to fight it, but it was like banging my head against the wall.

Reinaldo thought of no one but himself. I, on the other hand, was brought up to feel I had to sacrifice myself for others. I've made it my aim in life never to ask anything of anybody; helping others makes me happy. And I've never consciously done anything bad.

Even though I'm for the Revolution, I believe in God. Fidel never said that if you believe in one you can't believe in the other. He doesn't interfere in religion. But I don't go to church anymore because I'm not sure how the Revolution would look at it. It seems to me that the principles of the Revolution are the same as those of religion: to share all one's possessions, to love one another as brothers, to become as one. That way there's solidarity, unity, like in a family. It would be a fine thing if everybody assimilated these principles, yet one doesn't necessarily have to be a revolutionary to be good. I don't judge people by their political position but by their feelings.

If you really feel the Revolution inside as I do, you make the necessary sacrifices and stay with it. I know we Cubans are going to be all right, because when I'm with a group of revolutionaries I can feel something that joins us to each other. It used to be faith in God and in the organized Church that kept us united; now it's a political policy. The Revolution is like that religious faith.

My earliest memories are marvelous. As long as I had my father, I was happy. Of all that has happened to me since, the misery and misfortune and the good things too, I only remember what was good about those first eight years with my father. My life consists of the present moment and of my memories of those early days. It's like reading a fine book that you never forget no matter how many others you've read and forgotten afterward. Someday I'd like to ask a psychiatrist why this is.

I remember the house in Matanzas where I, Inocencia Acosta Felipe, was born fifty-four years ago. I still see it clearly. To me it was paradise. A road of white earth wound round and round the hill leading up to the top, where our house stood. It was a large house, built of *guano*[1] wood with a palm-thatch roof and a porch all around it. An enormous oak tree shaded the entrance and cast its magnificent shadow over the whole patio and part of the flower garden. Wherever we lived we had a flower garden filled with roses, because *mamá* loved them more than any other flower. In back of the house was a pasture with a stream and a little

---

1. A type of palm.

waterfall. Flat stone slabs formed a swimming pool where we used to bathe because the water was so nice and clear.

To one side but quite near the house was our kitchen garden, where we grew cabbage, lettuce, radishes, tomatoes, hot peppers, and lots of other things. Farther off were the fields of yucca, corn, sweet potatoes, plantains, and other vegetables; beyond were the sugar-cane fields. The vegetables grew in such abundance we even had enough to sell. There was always something fresh and good; each month had its own particular crop. The only vegetables we stored for year-round use were onions and garlic hung on strings in the kitchen. We always ate well because that was *papá*'s main concern. If my married sisters had a poor crop and were short of food, *papá* would send them a sackful of beans or potatoes, whatever was in season. He was especially generous with my sister Gabriela, whose husband was unable to work. *Papá* was very protective toward her.

Papá was a *colono*,[2] and all *colonos* were well off in those days. *Papá* rented the farm from the owners of a sugar mill, but a tenant was secure and could do as he liked as long as he paid the rent on time. It was paid in cash once a year at the end of the sugar-cane harvest. What money was left over *papá* used for household expenses and to buy us clothes. My parents were very economical, but they never thought of saving up to buy the farm because they believed they could rent it forever. Besides, the rich people who owned the land wouldn't sell all that easily. Renting out those farms gave them an income for life. If they sold a farm, they'd get money for it only once.

The Zayas family owned the mill and all the land around. I think they were Basques. They lived in the capital city of Matanzas, but once a year they'd spend a month in the country to take a look at their land. Their country house was very well furnished and had a full staff of servants, just as if it had been a house in the city. They also had a house in Havana.

As a child I used to see Señorita Zayas playing the piano. She was pretty and elegant with curly blond hair, and sitting at that piano she looked like a great lady, a legendary character. I told my parents I was going to be a piano teacher and they said, "Sure, sure, when you grow up." I really thought they meant it, too. What an imagination kids have!

The Zayas family was very proper, agreeable, and easy to get along with. They weren't nosy as long as a tenant paid the rent. They never asked why he made a path here or why he didn't plant more cane or anything. When they made the rounds on horseback, they treated their tenants well.

The sugar mill made life easier for its *colonos* by selling them almost everything they needed—cattle and other livestock, seeds, shade trees,

2. Sugar-cane farmer; refers to all cane growers whether they owned or rented their farms.

and different vegetables, fruit, and foods. We'd buy big boxes of codfish from them, and huge sacks of sugar, rice, and dried horsemeat. All we ever had to buy in town were salt, coffee, and kerosene, which *papá* bought in large quantities. Our storage shed looked like a grocery store.

There were three roads near our farm; one led to my godfather Nicolás Santiágo's house, another to the Córdobas' house, and a third, down a steep slope to a footbridge that crossed the creek, led to the Carrils' and to the Estébans', the family my sister Felicia married into. These were our next-door neighbors, but they each lived about a mile away. Then there was *comadre* Paula's, the little old woman who was our godmother of baptism. She was also *mamá*'s midwife and would come to help after each birth until *mamá* was up and around again. The relationship between *compadres* was a very sacred one. For my parents, their *compadres* were like something holy. *Comadre* Doña Paula was well loved all over the neighborhood. When she came to our house, it was as if God had arrived.

Our neighbors were all kind, decent people. They were almost all *compadres* to each other and they looked after us children as if we were their own. In the country, people who live on farms bordering on yours are treated like relatives. This group of families helped one another in every way. When we needed meat at home we killed two pigs, one for us, the other to distribute among the neighbors. We borrowed from one another, got together for the plowing, and shared every fiesta.

Not only did we celebrate together, but when one of the neighbors was sick or sad, we all worried, and when someone died, everybody mourned. For nine days we didn't have parties, and we didn't laugh or sing gay tunes. The relatives, of course, kept full mourning; the women dressed in black from head to foot for one year, and in black and white, or all white, purple, or lavender, for another year of half-mourning. The men kept mourning by wearing a black band on their sleeves or ties.

All the relatives of the deceased would gather at the wake and weep desperately. Everybody wept, even the men. It was the custom for two or three neighbor women to spend several days helping the bereaved family and keeping them from getting too downhearted. This visit was called *novedad*.

It was a good life the small farmers in our zone led, and in 1959 there weren't many revolutionaries among them. Later, at the time of what we call "the clean-up in Matanzas," almost the whole zone was counter-revolutionary. I know two members of the Carril family who were clapped in jail.

Nowadays you find only two political factions in Cuba, the revolutionaries and the non-revolutionaries. In *papá*'s time it was rather like that except that the factions were Liberals and Conservatives. I guess the Liberals were democrats and the Conservatives were moneyed people like the Menocal family.[3] My father was a Liberal, and on election day he and the other older men would mount their horses and go to vote in Quintana. The women never voted and neither did the young men.

Quintana, the nearest town, was a tiny community with a church, a courthouse, a pharmacy, and four or five badly kept streets. It was on the road that went from the city of Matanzas south to Santa Clara. A number of villages stretched out along this road—Quintana, Perico, Colón, and Los Arabos.

Our *colonia*[4] was called Maravilla. It was fairly large, about 5 *caballerías.*[5] We had a houseboy and four or five farmhands who lived in a large thatched shed called a *bohío*[6] that was also used for storing crops and tools and as a shelter against hurricanes. The *colonia* had about fifteen paddocks, some for horses and some for cattle. *Papá* owned three or four saddle horses, fifty or sixty head of cattle, oxen for plowing, and ten or twelve dairy cows. *Papá* or the farmhands sold two cans of milk and kept one can for the house. We kept a gray cow called Guarina for our own use. She gave us plenty of good milk to drink and we had enough left over for cheese and milk pudding.

Papá had a large flock of laying hens—at least 300 or 400. When the corn was scattered they settled down on it like a cloud. There were many hogs too, about fifteen or twenty, fattened on *palmiche*[7] and corn in a small corral, because a pig without much room to exercise gets fat and gives good lard.

We also had a lot of farm tools and three or four Spanish and American-made plows. *Papá* had saws, hammers, a hoe, machetes of different sorts—the broad-bladed ones and the large "mountain" blades. He had bought these things himself, and he took good care of them.

There was no electricity on our farm, but the kerosene lamps gave a very bright light. Once a week water was brought to the house from a well in a big barrel drawn on an oxcart. I loved to go riding on the cart while my brother urged the oxen on. That was a marvelous outing.

Our house had two bedrooms and a large parlor that we used as a dining room. Everybody ate there, the family and the farmhands too. We had a long table, with many Spanish-style hide-covered wooden stools. We didn't have a sofa then. There was a china cabinet with wooden doors and storage space at the bottom, and many shelves for glassware and cups.

Books were also kept in this cabinet. We younger children couldn't

3. The family of General Mario Menocal, leader of the Conservative Party and President of Cuba 1913–21.
4. Sugar-cane farm; some were independently owned, others were company-owned but operated by tenant farmers.
5. Approximately 167 acres.
6. Rural dwelling with thatched roof and dirt floor.
7. The fruit of the royal palm.

read, but when my married sisters, Gabriela and Felicia, came to visit, they'd read to us from the history books and other textbooks. Gabriela and Felicia had learned from teachers who came to the farm, but they read very poorly. Our brothers-in-law also taught us a bit.

Our parents could neither read nor write. They couldn't even sign their names, nor could any of the neighbors. Uncle Simón did know how to read, and when we went to visit him we'd often see him reading. In fact, I think he read every single night.

As I remember, our house had an earthen floor. In the country they sprinkle ashes on the earth to make it shiny, then pour water over it and sweep it, as we did, leaving it smooth and as hard as concrete.

The kitchen was separate from the house, in a lean-to where the cattle and pigs were slaughtered. Enormous cans of lard and pig cracklings made by *mamá* were always there. We cooked on a wood-burning stove, but for roasting and smoking meats we used a charcoal brazier. The firewood for the stove was gathered in the woods or along the edge of the stream where everything was allowed to grow wild. There the dry branches were easy to break off. *Mamá* usually gathered the firewood because it wasn't far from the house, but sometimes *papá* did too.

My parents were Honorio Acosta and Adriana Felipe, Cubans both, but children of Spaniards. The only one of my grandparents I ever saw was *mamá*'s *mamá*. She bore fifteen children to her husband, Miguel Felipe. They lived in Las Villas, where *mamá* was born.

Papá was born in Matanzas. His and *mamá*'s folks were all country people who lived by the labor of their hands, but *papá*'s family was better off. They owned their farms and had an easier life. *Mamá*'s family had to rent their land. *Papá* was rather old when he married—twenty-five or twenty-six, but *mamá* was sixteen. I know nothing about how they met or about their courtship.

Papá was a *mambí*, a volunteer soldier who fought in the hills in the War of Independence against Spain from 1895 until it ended in 1900. He was very young then and I doubt that his younger brothers Boris and Lelo fought in that war. But *mamá* had two sisters and twelve brothers, and they were all *mambises*. Eleven uncles of mine died in the war, killed in the Limones Massacre. The Spaniards practically wiped out the Cubans then. It was a sort of ambush, I think, and almost all the men of the district died in it. My Uncle Ignacio, whom we call Uncle Nacho, the eldest of my mother's brothers, escaped because he was in a different band. He's a bit of a poet, and when he came to visit us he'd bring his guitar and sing many *décimas*[8]—he still does, old as he is—but I don't remember ever hearing him sing or speak of the battle.

8. A Spanish stanza of ten octosyllabic lines.

Papá's family was very large; there were fourteen children. His two brothers, Uncle Boris and Uncle Lelo, loved to sing *décimas* and make up verses. When I was little, they'd come to visit dressed like my father in *guayaveras*,[9] with long machetes dangling from their belts, and they'd sing for us. Their visits were like fiestas.

My eldest sister, Felicia, was born in 1895, during the war. *Papá* was away fighting until she was five years old. She was raised in my grandmother's house, so she got a lot more petting than we did. She was our grandparents' favorite. People were different because of the war; they prized their children more. Maybe that's why my parents allowed her more privileges than the rest of us, or perhaps it was because she was the eldest. Maybe that's why she's so different. Anyway, by the time I was born she was already married.

At the end of the war *papá* rented the farm, and there my mother bore eleven more children, five girls and six boys. Gabriela, the second child, was born in 1902. Then *mamá* had three more, who died before I was born. Two of them, boys, died in an influenza epidemic. The little girl, Sofía, died of meningitis. Luis Heberto was born next, then Alicia, then Adolfo, then I, the ninth, then Honoria, who was sickly. After that *mamá* had two more boys, Teodoro and César.

When I was born *mamá* had a congestion and high fever, so I was the only one of all the children who was given canned milk instead of the breast. I remember lying on the floor on a small sack, sucking my milk from a beer bottle with a rubber nipple. Up to the time I was four or five, they gave me a bottle at night to help me go to sleep. I used to put it under my pillow and at midnight I'd wake up and suck it.

I used a pacifier until I was about seven years old. I liked to have ten or twelve pacifiers on hand. Anyone who went to town had to bring me back a new one, and all day long I'd go around sucking one of them or holding it. Many's the outing they took me on in return for my promise to give up the pacifier. I'd throw it away, and when I got back home I'd look for it again. *Papá* kept telling me that sucking it looked ugly and would give me blubber lips like a black. I grew ashamed to have anybody see me at it and that's why I gradually quit.

We children got our first taste of coffee when we were forty days old, and I've never since failed to drink my coffee each day. Coffee is a great purifier of the system and strengthener of the blood; I give coffee the credit for my strong, healthy constitution. *Mamá* told me that in the old times babies were given teaspoonfuls of pennyroyal to form their palate. "Well," *mamá* said, "instead of pennyroyal I'll give them coffee to form their stomachs." At every meal, but especially at breakfast, *mamá* would give us each a teaspoonful of coffee. When we were old enough to sit at

9. A pleated shirt-jacket popular among Cuban men.

the table, she made us weak coffee with sugar; she and *papá* took theirs strong and bitter, with no sugar in it.

My sister Honoria was born when I was one year old. She suffered from asthma like *papá,* and *mamá* took better care of her than of the rest of us. Honoria was always with *mamá* and I was always with *papá.* I was his favorite. Honoria and I were the family favorites; we dressed like twins, and we had better clothes than our brothers. But the boys weren't jealous, because *papá* had them under his spell too. He had a special art of winning and pleasing each of us.

Papá was crazy about me. He used to call me *"mi madre."* That's right, he said I was his *mamá.* I knew I was his favorite because he gave me more privileges and showed me preference. For instance, he gave each of us animals as presents, but to me he gave all the chicks that turned out white. None of the white chickens were ever killed because they were mine. "That one belongs to *mare*"; he'd say *mare* for *madre,* see? He once gave me a wonderful little bull calf I named Bayamo. His mother was Guarina, our gray cow, and he grew into the loveliest young bull in the herd. I think he must have been purebred.

Papá was a short man, about 5 feet 6 inches tall, and not too stout. He weighed about 140 pounds, and was white with black hair and mustache and black eyes. His skin was very tanned by the sun, and his arms were very hairy. He dressed simply, usually in work clothes, except when he went to town or to a party, when he wore a white *guayavera* and a straw hat. I never saw him wear a suit.

Papá was affectionate and attentive to everyone. When he arrived home we'd all be waiting to kiss him and talk to him. He kissed us every morning before he went to work, every night before he went to bed, and at any hour of the day for no special reason. *Mamá* wasn't at all like *papá.* She was very strict, dry, and rarely smiled. She kissed us only on special occasions.

Papá was easygoing; if he saw us break the rules, all he'd say was, "Take care your *mamá* doesn't see you do that!" *Mamá* was the one who scolded us. She was always the boss with us kids, the one who gave orders. She wasn't the kind who threatens, "Just wait until your father comes home and I'll tell him!" No, not she. Nor did she spank us. When she opened her eyes wide and looked at us severely, it was warning enough. She demanded respect and got it. At times she'd grab a slipper to threaten us but she never actually spanked us. *Papá* didn't allow it. Sometimes when *mamá* scolded us we'd run to him and he'd take our side.

That's not to say *papá* was a weakling. He was a man of character. He had a quick temper when anyone offended him, but he got over it quickly. We children were his one real weakness. He was very good, very tender, with all of us. He'd put us to sleep every night when we were small, first praying, then singing if we asked for a song. He'd sit on one of the leather-bottomed stools—we had no rocking chair—and sing us to sleep one by one, starting with the youngest.

Papá sang a lot, mostly *décimas* and old-fashioned songs because that's what country people sang in those days. One of them went like this:

> *Hermosa vanidad no llores*
> *ni de tu amor pongas quejas,*
> *pues sabes que las abejas*
> *viven en todas las flores.*[10]

We had no other music at home. That was in 1922, when there was still no radio in the country.

Mamá was very slender, blond, and blue-eyed, with skin so fair it got blotchy and red whenever she was in the sun. Her hair was straight and twisted back into a tight bun. She never went out bareheaded; even to visit a neighbor, she wore a shawl over her head. She had a lovely figure and stood very erect. Her clothes were no different in style from my grandmother's and she dressed that way all her life. Her dresses were of percale, always in a small flower print, with a full skirt that went down to her ankles; nobody ever saw her bare legs because she always wore stockings—brown ones—and laced shoes. Her blouse was made of the same material as the skirt and modestly cut with a high neckline and elbow-length sleeves trimmed with little ruffles. Underneath she wore a camisole and a voluminous petticoat with eyelet-embroidered ruffles. For going out, *mamá* had only one good dress, white with lace on it. Neither she nor *papá* owned a single ornament. After *papá* died, *mamá* dressed all in black.

Mamá was a serious, self-denying woman and a good mother. She did all the proper things for us but she was not understanding or affectionate. She pitied and petted only Honoria, who was sickly. With the rest of us *mamá* was very detached. But all children need to be pampered and petted! I can't recall that *mamá* ever explained things to us the way *papá* did. Many mothers tell their daughters about life, but mine never warned us about anything or explained how we should act. Her way was to wait until we did something wrong, then scold us for it.

I never saw her show any affection for *papá* either, although she was always attentive to his needs. I was so small when *papá* died, maybe that's the reason I don't remember. But I never saw them sit close together or anything like that.

None of us children looked like *mamá*. I haven't inherited a single one

10. Vain beauty, don't cry
   Or complain of your lover,
   For you know that the bee
   Goes from flower to flower.

of her traits. Most of us take after *papá*. The only ones like *mamá* in temperament are Adolfo and Felicia. They're also very withdrawn. It isn't that they dislike outsiders; they like people, but in their own way.

I was normally a respectful, obedient child and was seldom punished or even scolded. I'd play for hours with any little thing I picked up. Even *mamá* said I was good. She'd say, "If all children were like this one, it would be easy to raise twenty."

We children were controlled not by punishment but by scary stories of the bogeyman and witches, and especially of blacks. We were told that blacks kidnapped children, and whenever we saw one climbing the hill to our house, we'd disappear while *mamá* opened the door and talked with him. The adults would tell us, "Don't go to that place where the blacks are. Never go near a black or accept anything to eat from him." They told us those things to protect us from danger, not to threaten us. In that region everybody adored children.

At home we children usually ate before the grownups did. If *papá* was at home the adults ate first, but when he was working in the fields he'd come home late and the children would be served first. A custom at home that we still keep, even the great-grandchildren, is that nobody starts eating until one of the parents sits down at the table, and everyone remains seated until one parent or the other leaves. My sister in Camaguey has raised her children the way we were brought up, not the way people do nowadays, with everyone coming to eat when they feel like it.

In our house the dining table was sacred. We weren't allowed to sit on it and we never ate a meal without a tablecloth, no matter how old and worn. Before we sat down we had to comb our hair and wash our hands, then sit straight and keep still. Our parents talked a little while eating, but not much. If we wanted to talk we had to ask *mamá*'s permission first. Otherwise, we were only permitted to ask for our food. We were never allowed to drink water until we'd finished eating. The discipline was very strict, just like at a school run by priests or nuns. Later, when I worked as a housemaid, people asked me if I'd been educated in a convent. Imagine! To this day, no matter how angry I am, I never make an abrupt or grotesque gesture or slam a door, and I never talk during meals.

Our home was well ordered. Each of us had his own mug, nobody drank from anybody else's, and each had his own toothbrush and towel. In the kitchen *mamá* would hang up two cloths to use as towels, one for hands and one for the dishes. I still do the same thing. *Mamá* cut them from flour-bag cloth and sewed them herself, pulling out threads at the edges to make a fringe.

Because my elder sisters were married, *mamá* did all the housework by herself, looking after the dairy, the kitchen garden, the orchards, and sewing all the children's clothes by hand. She even cut the men's hair.

Mamá was the first one to get up in the morning. The hired man chopped the wood and arranged it in the stove so that all *mamá* had to do was light it. She'd make the coffee, strain it, and serve it to *papá* in bed. Then he'd get up, and he and *mamá* would have their breakfast together. *Mamá* would bring a cup of coffee to each of us children as soon as she heard us stir. My sisters still keep that custom of serving their families morning coffee in bed.

After coffee we'd get up and dress, then eat breakfast, hot milk with a pinch of salt to make it more digestible, and bread, if the bread man had come. If not, *mamá* would bake delicious flat cassava cakes, or she'd sometimes bake cornbread.

When we got up we'd wash our faces in the washbowl and comb our hair. We had two combs, one with large teeth for the women and another with fine teeth for the men. We didn't use hairbrushes, nor did we use toothpaste. Instead we'd rub the toothbrush on the soap. Later in the day, we children were bathed in lukewarm water in a large tub set in a corner of the room. I remember being bathed and dressed by *mamá* until I was quite a big girl.

In the country everyone old enough to do farm work gets up at cockcrow—4:00 in the morning. The hired hand, Ruperto, would milk the cows, then he and *papá* would go off to work in the fields. Most days *papá* would already be gone by the time we children ate breakfast at 7:00 or 8:00.

After breakfast *mamá* would dress us, wash and peel the vegetables, wash clothes, sweep . . . well, do all the housework. She was the one who cleaned the latrine, which was off to one side in a wooden outhouse. She never asked us children to help her with that task, or the hired hand either.

At about 10:00 in the morning *mamá* gave us milk again or else we'd pick ourselves some fruit. You can always get something to eat in the country. We had an early lunch, and supper as soon as it got dark. We'd eat things like rice, beans, vegetables, fried eggs, fresh or jerked meat or codfish. Mostly we ate stuff that didn't spoil because there were no refrigerators. We ate a lot of chicken too. I don't mean that we had meat or chicken every day of our lives, but we had one or the other pretty often. We did have sweets every day after lunch, because *mamá* loved to make desserts—orange or grapefruit peel in syrup, guavas in syrup or paste, bitter orange paste, also corn pudding or fritters, which I've always loved.

At 3:00 in the afternoon *mamá* always prepared a snack for us of corn fritters, cheese, or milk dessert.[11] It was a tradition in our home to make fresh coffee at this time of the day, no matter how hard up we were. I

11. Milk soured with lemon juice and boiled with sugar to form dry, sticky curds or a smooth paste.

still always feel a need for it at 3:00 o'clock. By the time I was an adult I drank fourteen or fifteen small cups of coffee a day, with sugar. I prefer it freshly made, not reheated. After I was married I'd always make it fresh no matter how many times a day I drank it. I'd go to the store where they roasted the beans and buy the 2 pounds a week I used at home. I always served coffee to visitors, too. I still do, even now that coffee is rationed—*"Teniendo café, tenemos la vida por delante."*[12]

My parents were very thrifty. *Papá* took care to provide us with all the comforts, yet no money was ever squandered. Both *papá* and *mamá* always saved money, he in the bank, she in a trunk. Some of it *mamá* kept in old tin cans buried in the ground or hidden behind the boards in the wall near the roof. I don't know why she did it like that; it couldn't have been for fear of thieves because there weren't any. She'd hide the money with all of us kids looking on. I saw big rolls of bills, but I have no idea how much money she had. I guess she saved it for the rent or perhaps to buy farm animals; they did add to the herds every now and then.

Mamá never kept aside any spending money for herself. She had no need to. She managed the house, but *papá* handled the money. Whenever *mamá* had to buy something, she'd tell *papá* and he'd bring it home from town. She never went because it was so far you had to go on horseback. *Papá* even bought her clothes and shoes, and he made sure we had plenty of sheets, towels, tableclothes, pots and pans, and whatever was needed in the house.

Every week Don Roberto Santella rode up on his horse, bringing in his large saddlebags everything the *guajiros* needed—kerosene, yard goods, bread, candy. He also must have brought all the news to our neighborhood, because I never saw a newspaper in our home. Letters were addressed to the sugar mill and were sent with Don Roberto from there to the homes of the *colonos.*

If anybody was sick, Don Roberto was asked to notify the doctor or fetch medicine—usually bicarbonate of soda, the *guajiros'* favorite remedy. *Mamá* always kept special bedclothes and towels ready "in case the doctor comes," but I don't ever remember a doctor being called for any of us children. I guess they must have charged a lot to come all the way from town. Besides, not every doctor was willing to go out to the country. *Comadre* Doña Paula, the midwife, took care of the sick in our neighborhood, mostly with her infusions for colds, sore throats, and other minor ailments.

One time the doctor did come, when my youngest brother, César, was born. He weighed 12½ pounds at birth. I don't know exactly what happened but it seems *mamá* had a hemorrhage. I remember seeing the bed

12. "So long as we have coffee, we can get along."

and the floor of the room all bloody, then *papá* went on horseback to fetch the doctor because cars couldn't go up the hill.

At home I had nothing to do but play. I loved to search for hens' nests and I'd bring home an apron full of eggs. The chickens would lay under the bushes or anywhere, and every day we'd fill baskets of eggs from the new nests we found. I gathered fruit, chili peppers, and vegetables with *mamá,* because that was all the amusement there was. Nobody said I had to do it but I loved to. It was like an outing.

The hired hand, Ruperto, was very good to us children. He'd let us watch the cows being milked and carry the milk pails. We rode horses a lot, too. I rode in front with *papá* or with one of the bigger children. I had no fear of horses or oxen, or bats or snakes, or any living thing except scorpions and black widow spiders. Wherever there's roof thatching you have to be careful because the leaves tend to rot and scorpions and spiders hide underneath.

I swept and cleaned when I was only five or six because I liked seeing the house and yard looking nice. I'd pick up the shoes and clothes after breakfast, then my sisters and I would make the beds. Afterward *mamá* would make the rounds, smoothing a sheet here, pulling a mattress straight there, because our work wasn't all that perfect. Sometimes I washed dishes, too, but we weren't allowed to work in the kitchen at that early age for fear we'd get burned or upset a kettle.

By the time I was eight or nine my main chores were to sweep the floors and burn the trash every day. We girls washed our own clothes, the smaller pieces at any rate, and I had to get up on a stool to reach the high wooden tubs. *Mamá* washed most of the clothes, and we tended the fire in the stove when she boiled them.

I liked all kinds of games when I was small, especially boys' games! I loved to play ball and climb trees. I had no nieces then, only nephews, and I had no girls to play with. The neighbors' children would come to our house only on fiesta days or for a baptism. My brother Adolfo was my favorite playmate because Teodoro was too little and Honoria would get out of breath. Many games were too strenuous for her, and she couldn't get wet either. She usually stayed in the house with *mamá.* Adolfo, however, was strong as an oak, and I was his devoted follower.

With Teodoro and Honoria, I was the leader. I always played the role of their mother, which meant I was the boss. I got along very well with Honoria; she was very dear to me. I saw her as something fragile, like glass or a precious bit of porcelain. She came first, before anything else in the world. She was a beautiful girl with marvelous eyes, black hair, and smooth skin—pretty as a doll. I was good-looking too. When I was small I was very plump. They dressed me in short, pretty dresses and always kept me looking nice with my dark-brown hair cut in bangs.

Whenever I was not out playing with Adolfo or away visiting my elder sisters, Honoria and I would laugh and play together. We were always talking and making plans for our future. When we got older, a favorite game of ours was to plan the meals we'd serve each other after we were married and had homes of our own.

Papá loved Honoria, and nicknamed her "Amarilla" because of a yellow dress she had. *Papá* had nicknames for all of us. I was never jealous of my sister but I was a bit jealous of Teodoro, because he was the youngest and *papá* was very fond of him. I wanted *papá* to love me the most. If he took Teodoro in his lap, I'd sit beside him and pull at his pants until he picked me up too. And if he sang to Teodoro, he had to sing the same songs to me.

I always slept with *papá* and so did Teodoro. I'd lie at his feet crosswise with my little pillow, and Teodoro would lie lengthwise at the head of the bed. The cot wasn't very wide and the three of us wouldn't fit if we all slept the long way. God, it makes me cry to remember. One doesn't usually talk about these things.

Papá always said I guarded his feet at night so the blacks wouldn't steal them, and he told us that if we saw a black when we were getting ready to go to bed, we should hide. I was absolutely terrified of blacks. They use blood in their religious rites, and when I was little they stole children in Matanzas for that purpose. I remember they once killed a little girl as a sacrifice to St. Barbara. All the country people lived in mortal fear of that. They told us the black sorcerers would suck blood from our veins, but I don't believe that anymore. What they probably do is kill you and then let the blood drip into a basin or something. At least, I know that's what they do when they sacrifice a fowl, a calf, or a goat. They cut its throat, then hang it up by the hind legs over a pail.

When it was known the blacks were going to have a celebration in honor of a saint, or when they seemed restless, the grownups would warn us to be on the alert. Fear was in the air, like when there's been a wave of robberies and everyone makes sure to fasten the doors and windows, or when there's a hurricane warning and people start making things safe

My big fear was of black men. At night I covered my head with the bedsheets in fear, and I often had bad dreams. I'd dream I was flying, with the blacks flying behind me, almost near enough to grab my feet. Once I dreamed I saw a black man crouching at the open window. I was so frightened I tore up the mosquito netting on my bed. But after I got to the city here and lived alongside black people, I began to get used to them and the dreams stopped.

It was because of that fear that I asked to sleep in *papá*'s bed. I was about two then, I think, because that was when my sister Gabriela got married. Gabriela slept with me before she was married, but then I slept with *papá* until I was about five or six. After that I slept with Honoria in *mamá*'s bed. Luis Heberto and Adolfo slept in the other room, each on his own cot.

Mamá had an iron bedstead, the old-fashioned kind with curlicues. The bed was covered with cowhides and we girls used to love to sleep in it. All the other members of the family slept on folding cots. They were like army cots, made with flour-sacking stretched across a rectangular frame. Each of us had a mosquito net, a mattress, and blankets, and we all had pillows stuffed with a woolly plant called ceiba. When the pods fell off, we gathered them and separated the fine cotton from the seeds and used the clean fluff for the pillows.

When my sisters were having babies I began to ask where babies came from. I must have been ten or twelve years old by then. Our parents lied to us, saying the stork brought babies, and I believed them. It was some time later, when we took in a little female puppy, that we found out how animals were born. We saw other animals giving birth, but never did we see a woman having a baby. I've never in my life been present while my sisters were in labor, nor have I seen one of them naked. When one of them was about to give birth, I'd take her children to the park or to the movies, and when we got back, the midwife would already have the baby dressed and lying beside its mother.

Neither did I ever see *mamá* or *papá* or my brothers naked, nor did I ever see my parents in bed together. Even my brother Teodoro, who was the youngest, was never allowed to run around without any clothes on. I saw him naked as a child only when he was bathed or dressed. When we children bathed outdoors, or splashed in the puddles after the rain, it was always with our clothes on. At bedtime *mamá* would undress Honoria and me and put on our long-sleeved nightgowns, then lay our clothes beside the bed ready to be put on in the morning.

When I noticed the first few hairs growing under my arms and elsewhere, I was frightened to death. "Something terrible is happening to me!" I thought. I told my sister and she said, "Oh, that happens to everybody when they start to grow up. It's nothing to worry about."

The same thing happened when my breasts began to grow. I must have been about thirteen or fourteen at the time. When I saw the two swellings on my chest, I thought it was some sort of illness. It was awful. I think that's the worst part of growing up. They hurt me terribly, and I didn't want to tell *mamá*. I had to lie on my back because everything irritated me. I never wore a bra until I was an adult.

My period didn't come until I was sixteen. My younger sister got it before I did; I don't know why, because I was big and strong. When Honoria got her monthly, she told *mamá*, then she came and told me, "Look what happened to me, and *mamá* says it's for this and that reason." Before that nobody had ever talked to me about such things, not *mamá* or anybody else. She didn't tell me to be careful with boys, not even after I started to menstruate. But she really didn't have to, because we grew up with no friends, alone and isolated, away from civilization. All our contacts were with relatives or neighbors, never with strangers. We never saw anybody who went out with boys, and even when we went to school we had no contact with boys other than our brothers and nephews.

My parents were very clean-minded. They brought us up with blinders on, very remote from things, so we had childish mentalities. People didn't talk the way they do now, about abortions and mistresses, the sorts of things that are shown on television. They didn't talk in front of children about a girl's having her period and not being able to bathe or wash her hair. Never did I hear such conversation at home; it was absolutely unknown. I don't even remember noticing a big belly on a pregnant woman, that's how ignorant I was about such things.

We children would play house in plain sight of everybody. The boys would play the part of *compadre* or priest or *papá* to the girls' dolls. We didn't think of sex. We'd baptize our dolls, make fiestas for them, and gather the seeds of the wild amaranth for "rice" for their dinners. I sewed their dresses and knitted coverlets for their beds until I was ten or eleven. It wasn't until I was thirteen that I began to catch on about sex.

Never did I hear stories about bad women or about a stepfather having relations with a stepdaughter, or brothers with sisters, or cousins with cousins, not until I was practically an old woman. To us our cousins were sacred. No member of our family ever married a cousin. We little ones never even saw our cousins because they lived a full day's journey from us. It was a tradition in our family that the eldest of the cousins visit their uncles and aunts, so my older brothers and sisters would go. I remember Gabriela riding off on a special woman's sidesaddle, a very elegant embroidered one, taking with her as gifts the best of everything we had at home. My family got along wonderfully with those cousins.

All the couples I knew as a child were married in church. People simply weren't allowed to live together without first getting married. In those times no woman ever took another woman's husband from her, or lived with somebody else's husband or sweetheart. Never! And there were no divorces or separations either. We had no homicide, no instances of one person killing another while drunk or anything of the kind.

The same families are still there, but I don't know how their children behave now. Maybe their children now get divorced or separated, but the ones I knew died of old age still living with their first wife or husband. It was a very proper, good life. I remember that one of the Córdobas' sons fell in love with his sister-in-law's sister and his parents refused to let him marry her. I don't know why. As a result, the girl became a nun. Yes, the Córdobas are very proper people, and so are the del Valles and the Fríases.

I heard that Silvia, the daughter of the Carrils, had borne a child out of wedlock, but we weren't living there by then. When something like that happened to a girl, she had to isolate herself. She'd committed a mortal sin and there was no more to be said about it. It's probably different now that all the children go to school and many are brought to Havana as scholarship students. Life has completely changed.

At home we were devout Catholics, *papá* even more than *mamá*. That's not to say that *mamá* was lukewarm. No, she had absolute faith in God. If she met with a difficulty she'd lay it calmly in God's hands, certain He would solve whatever problem was brought to Him. When she rose in the morning, she'd open the doors and windows and say, "May the grace of God enter this house and protect us all." It impressed me deeply; I still go through the same daily ritual.

We prayed each night before going to bed and said grace before lunch and dinner. *Mamá* prayed in a low voice; we closed our eyes and repeated together, "God bless this bread and bless us, His servants." And sometimes we'd say after *mamá,* "So says the Lord" or "Thanks be to God." I said grace aloud every day of my life until I married. I have by no means given up praying, but now I don't make a display of it. I pray no matter where I am—silently.

On Sundays no work was done at the farm—no plowing, no cutting sugar cane, nothing. The hired man had the day off, beginning in the morning. No housework was done either. On Sundays *mamá* would cook only our midday dinner and receive guests. We all wore our best clothes that day and sometimes we'd visit the neighbors.

In my parents' bedroom there was an altar for the *Virgen de la Caridad del Cobre,* with an image of Jesus Christ and one of the Virgin Mary. Those were the only saints we had. Once a week—I forget whether it was Tuesday or Thursday, but it was a very holy day—*mamá* would light candles for the saints. She always had candles at home.

Mamá never lost her deep faith in God, not even after *papá* died and we were very poor. Whenever we lacked coffee or food or something, *mamá* would say, "I trust God will give me what I need." She'd say to me, "Don't worry, daughter, I'll just light a fire in the stove and put the water on to boil. The coffee will appear, you'll see!" And it always happened that some friend or relative would come, sometimes from a long way off, bringing coffee. Little things like that built in me the same faith in God *mamá* had. She prayed like that a lot during the Machado regime, when we lacked so many things.

At night, while *mamá* was doing the dishes or putting away things or feeding the pigs, *papá* would make us say our prayers. He was the one who taught us to pray the *Credo, Ave María, Pater Noster,* and this other prayer, "Four posts has my bed, may four little angels guard me: St. John, St. Peter, St. Vincent, and St. Matthew." Then he'd tell us, one by one, "Go to bed, Inocencia, and don't be afraid; go to bed, Teodoro, and don't be afraid," and so on until he'd named us all.

As soon as the planting was done, *papá* would bless it with these words: "May God bless this field, that it may yield a good harvest." *Mamá* would say it too, out in the fields with *papá*. On St. Isidore's Day, the day of blessing for the animals and the planting, everybody would gather in the fields to pray. We'd repeat after my parents, "Send blessings on this field, for the peppers and the tomatoes," and we'd also sing, "St. Isidore take away the rain and bring in the sun."

Recently I blessed a kitchen garden belonging to Leida, a friend of mine. Her neighbor also had a garden there but he didn't bless his. It was the same land, the same kinds of seeds, nothing but a fence divided the two pieces of land. The man who plowed my friend's plot also plowed the other exactly the same way. Both gardens were watered every single day. Well, Leida's tomatoes and onions and lettuce flourished but the ones next door were tiny. They didn't grow big the way Leida's did, which just goes to show you.

Mamá was deeply religious to the day of her death. It was important to her to get all her babies baptized before the forty days were up. All my brothers and sisters were confirmed, and all were married in church. Nobody forced them to but they themselves felt it was important. That's the way they'd been brought up.

I don't remember ever having gone to church before I was nine years old, not as long as we lived on the farm. When the priest came to call, we always kissed his hand and asked for his blessing. After moving to town, we did go to church on Sunday morning. It was at that time we were confirmed.

I thought of God as a saint, dressed more or less like Jesus Christ, a man with a beard but not old, and with a pretty face, as becomes the Father of Christ. We learned that bad people who told lies or harmed others were carried off by the devil and were boiled alive in big cauldrons of oil. We were afraid to tell lies. When something was missing, *papá* would say, "Whoever has the hottest ears took it." The one who'd taken it would automatically touch his ears and give himself away. It was really funny! And it never failed.

I wasn't afraid of Hell because I believed in God, and I could see no reason why the devil should snatch me away. I felt perfectly sure that I'd go to Heaven and be an angel with wings. But I had a burning curiosity about Heaven; I wished I could open up the sky to see what was behind it. Now I know that Heaven and Hell are right here on earth, because it's here that you reap your rewards and punishments.

We always celebrated the religious holidays. I recall Palm Sunday in Holy Week, when *papá* went to church to get the blessed palm leaves to protect the house from thunder and lightning. When we lived in town, it was moving and exciting for us to go to church ourselves and get the palm leaves.

On Good Friday we children were very quiet. The other days of Holy Week, Saturday of Glory and Resurrection Sunday, were fiesta days when everybody was happy, but Good Friday was a day of mourning. We children didn't run around or play or sing or even laugh. We kept absolute silence and prayed from early morning on. On that day it's the custom to put away the scissors and the knives; I've honored it all my life—I never sew or cut or iron anything on Good Friday, nor even sweep. If I have to go to work on my job now, I go because that's not for me to decide.

Mamá never failed to gather medicinal herbs on Good Friday, because on that day they're especially blessed. We'd go out before sunup and gather them to dry in small bags for use the rest of the year. Some plants, such as lime and peppermint, were used while still green and fresh.

At home, no matter how poor we were, we always celebrated Christmas Eve. There'd always be a small Christmas tree, a pine branch set in a corner that we'd help *mamá* decorate with flowers and ribbons. And when *papá* was alive we had new clothes to wear and *mamá* would make supper for everybody. Four or five days ahead of time, the larger pigs would be slaughtered for lard, and later a couple of suckling pigs would be killed and roasted.

The whole family would gather together at our house the night before Christmas—uncles, aunts, cousins, nephews, nieces. We'd greet each other with an affectionate hug and a kiss on the cheek—that has always been our custom—then we'd all talk about what we'd been doing, what difficulties had arisen since we last met, who was sick—all the family news. There'd be about fifty guests for Christmas Eve supper, and according to country custom, anyone else who happened to pass by would be invited in. We'd all sit down at two tables made of sawhorses and planks, one for the grownups and another for the children. We were considered children until we were about fourteen.

The food would be black beans, rice, yucca, roast suckling pig, and sweet-potato pudding. *Mamá*'s sweet-potato pudding was baked in an earthenware pan with glowing coals on top to make it golden and delicious. For dessert we had nougats, walnuts, filberts, and figs that came from Spain in a pretty little wicker basket. I'd get the basket for my sewing things, because even when I was little I liked needlework and embroidering.

Whenever we had a fiesta, my sister Felicia would bring her phonograph and someone would play the guitar while others danced. I love music and enjoy seeing ballet and old-fashioned dances, but I've never danced myself, or sung. At parties I had a good time just watching others and chatting with everybody. *Papá* loved to make us drunk and sleepy on red wine on Christmas Eve. That was all we ever drank; rum I never heard of until many years later.

Our relatives stayed overnight with us—women sleeping with women and men with men, lying across the beds, which was the only way everybody could fit in—then we all had lunch together on December 25. New Year's Day was also a time for family get-togethers, sometimes again at our house, other times at one of my sisters' homes. That was the day we wore our new clothes.

For the Day of the Three Kings we children always received toys, even if only rag dolls made by our elder sisters. They were very pretty rag dolls, beautifully dressed. Our brothers-in-law made us wooden doll houses and furniture, and we ourselves learned to make little rocking chairs out of cardboard.

Birthdays have always been sacred to us—they were special days with special foods and we'd give presents if possible; if not, we'd at the very least go and kiss the person and wish him a happy birthday. My married sisters, even those who lived far away, came to visit; they'd also come on Mother's Day. On my birthday there would be a party to which all my friends and neighbors were invited. If we had no money I was taken to the movies, or perhaps on a picnic with my nieces and nephews and brothers and sisters. We've forgotten those customs somewhat since the Revolution. Now if we can't visit we send a telegram.

The other fiestas I remember were weddings and baptisms, both ours and the neighbors'. Many baptisms took place at our house, with the priest and all the neighbors attending as though it were a church. Afterward there'd be a great fiesta, with dinner for everyone.

In 1920 the country's economy was slow and we were on the way down. I didn't realize it then but the farm was producing less, or maybe the price of sugar had dropped, and we were very short of money.[13] There wasn't even enough to pay the rent, which must have been pretty steep then—I think it was 200 or 300 *pesos* a year—because *papá* had so much trouble paying it.

By that time *papá*'s asthma was really bad. Actually, he had cardiac

---

13. The decade of the 1920s was disastrous for the sugar industry, beginning with a period known as the "dance of the millions," when the world sugar price fluctuated rapidly. The world market price fell from 22.5 cents per pound in May, 1920, to 3.75 cents by December, 1920. As supply exceeded demand, prices rose and fell throughout the decade, to as low as 1.72 cents per pound in 1929. Many persons in the sugar industry were financially ruined. (Thomas, *Cuba: The Pursuit of Freedom,* pp. 536 ff.)

asthma as a young man, because of the tough time he'd had fighting in the War of Independence, and later because he worked so hard. His heart became worse and he was very sick for three or four years. When he had to go to bed with an asthma attack he'd be terribly upset because he couldn't work. He'd try to get up and do a bit of light work, but he'd get out of breath and have to go back to the house. Usually he was all right if he didn't exert himself or get agitated.

Little by little, *papá* had to sell the cattle. When they were all gone he started selling the pigs, then the chickens, until he had very little of anything. I didn't know what was happening as my parents never discussed their troubles in front of us. One evening, as I made the rounds with *papá* to watch him separate the calves so the cows would have plenty of milk in the morning, I couldn't find my calf, Bayamo.

"*Papá*, somebody stole Bayamo!" I cried. He said the calf might have gotten lost, and for many years I believed he'd been stolen. I felt a great sense of loss. Now I realize he must have been sold.

That was the first time that *papá* ever caused me pain. I was about eight, old enough to have understood if *papá* had told me it was necessary to sell Bayamo. I know he was trying to spare me suffering, but even if he'd been honest with me, I couldn't possibly have understood about being poor. At that age what did I care about poverty? I didn't even know what it was.

After *papá* had sold most of the farm animals, he became a peddler because that wasn't as strenuous as farm work. He'd ride his horse from house to house selling cigarettes, coffee, and matches. It was the last work he ever did. Every evening when he returned home, Honoria, Teodoro, and I would run out to meet him. There wasn't any greater joy for me than seeing *papá* come home. And no matter how badly things were going, when we ran out to meet him the world seemed to become a happy place for him again. He'd divide the loose change among us, and we'd put the coins in jars for safekeeping. Then he'd go into the dining room and chat with us there until supper was ready. Those last three years when *papá* was sick were difficult for him but not for me. I was as happy as I could be.

But I did notice how sad *papá* looked, how little he talked, how even his tone of voice was different. I thought it was because of his illness, but he must have been worrying about the lack of money. Now I believe he felt worse in his mind than in his body.

The death of César, our youngest brother, undermined *papá*'s health even more. He'd sit in a corner brooding, and he often cried. The other children had died as infants, but César was nine months old and already taking his first steps and saying *papá* and *mamá*. He was a plump, pretty baby, but he caught bronchial pneumonia because he touched some starch *mamá* had prepared and laid out on a cot to dry. He had a cold and it seems that the starch, which is cold while it's drying, brought on the illness. At least that's the way *mamá* explained it.

César died in 1922. *Papá* spent a lot of money to cure the baby, and in 1923 we had to give up the farm. We moved to Felicidad, a hamlet about 20 kilometers from our house. To get there, our wagons had to pass through the whole sugar-mill community. We had two or three wagons and it looked like a covered-wagon train in a Western movie, with us children riding on a platform in the back of the last wagon. Of our animals, we took only Guarina, the cow, and two horses, and what was left of the farm tools. There was also our furniture, and food for the trip.

It was a horrible journey, wet and dangerous, with thunder and lightning all the way. We had to descend a hill along a precipice and I was terrified the whole trip. When we got to Felicidad everything was soaked, the furniture and all, because there wasn't any canvas and the rain had gone through the sacking.

Felicidad was smaller than Quintana, but this was where the big landowners had their homes. It had a school, a medical clinic, a general store with clothing and hardware, a large grocery store, and a train stop. We lived nearby in a *batey*[14] with the other tenants. The houses were a lot closer to each other, although our new house was very nice and had a plot of land planted with fruit and vegetables. But it was not nearly as big as the farm.

Being a child, I was very enthusiastic about moving to a place where there were a lot more people. We children didn't realize that the move meant we were much worse off than we'd ever been before. For us life hadn't changed much. If we missed anything about our former home, it was the greater space and freedom. We could no longer say, "Let's go to the river" or "Let's go pick fruit." Everything was more restricted, but there was enough room for us to play in.

Papá still took such good care of us that we didn't lack anything. He often had to go to town on horseback to buy the merchandise he sold, and he'd always bring us back candy, bread, and whatever we needed. He also bought condensed milk for me because I didn't like fresh milk. I used to say that when I grew up I'd marry a grocer so I'd have plenty of condensed milk to drink.

In Felicidad we went to school for the first time. I started the first grade at the age of eight. That year all we had to do was draw and cut pictures out of books. I loved school and talked enthusiastically about it at home. My first teacher was very pretty and always wore a hat to school. She'd set us to drawing things and many's the time her hat was the model for our drawings. I was chosen as the best pupil, and on that occasion she

14. Sugar-cane workers' settlement on company-owned land.

gave me a small box of Coty powder with a puff in it. I felt she'd given me a treasure. I was her favorite and the favorite of every other teacher I ever had. You see, I respected them all and was also fond of them. Every time they went home to Havana or Matanzas they'd bring me a gift when they returned.

We'd been in Felicidad about a year when *papá* died. He wasn't an old man—he died in 1924 at the age of about fifty-six. He faced the certainty of his death with resignation. He never blasphemed or complained. Never did I hear him curse God as people do nowadays. He accepted his destiny passively, tragic though it was.

Papá didn't suffer much pain during his illness, but he was always tense and restless. Lying down made him choke and he'd be up most of the time. He'd sit gasping for breath, with his hands pressed down hard on the edge of the stool, and *mamá* would give him medicine or fan him or stroke his back. He had several wine-flavored medicines that I liked the taste of, so he'd always let me have a spoonful too.

The day *papá* died, I was out in the yard with my sister Alicia, hanging the laundry to dry. When *mamá* screamed, we ran in and found *papá* already in his death agony.

His wake began that night and all the neighbors were there. He looked so peaceful and natural, as if he'd fallen asleep. It was horrible when they took him out of the house. I wasn't even allowed to go to the graveyard with him. In the country the corpse is taken away in a horse-drawn cart, followed by men on horseback. The women aren't allowed to go because the graveyard is always far from town. I was desperate, desperate . . . it was cruelly hard. We cried—we couldn't believe he could die and leave us, that they could take him away like that. Oh, we knew that he was seriously ill, but children never think their *papá* can die. When they buried him, I was wild with grief.

Chapter Two

Painful Memories

AFTER *papá*'s DEATH *mamá* was always sad. The house in Felicidad had painful memories and none of us wanted to stay in it anymore, so in a month or two we moved. *Mamá* couldn't afford to pay the rent and would have had to leave the place in any case. We left with nothing but a few pieces of furniture and some hens; everything else was taken by the landlord as payment for the rent. He himself set the prices, saying, "This is worth so much and that is worth so much," until he made up the amount we owed. We were horrendously poor—there was no money to be earned out in the country except a few miserable *centavos*—and our economic losses added a great deal to *mamá*'s suffering.

Our new house was not far from Felicidad in a town called Retamal, which had a sugar mill and sugar-cane farms. We called our place "the lost house" because it was poor and run-down and was on a hill surrounded by woods. It was the only one available, and besides, the owner of the big farm on which it was located had promised to give my brothers—Luis Heberto, who was about eighteen, and Adolfo, who was a mere child—jobs all year round.

That landlord exploited my brothers, that's what he did. They worked in the cane field, hoeing, planting, and cutting cane at 1 *centavo* a row, earning only 30 to 40 *centavos* a day. At mid-morning Honoria, Teodoro, and I would bring them coffee and fruit and we'd hoe for them awhile, or we'd pile up the cut cane in heaps to make it easier to load it onto the cart. We made a game of it and it gave my brothers a chance to rest.

At "the lost house" our only close neighbor was an old Negro, one of those very dark blacks, who would come by at night. We'd never before lived near Negroes and I was scared to death of him. I thought he was going to kill us and use us for witchcraft; we were so terrified we couldn't sleep or anything.

I'd suffered terribly when my *papá* died, more than the others, so when the old black man came to the house and sat right in our midst, my nerves began to be affected. I imagined I saw great yellow cats underneath the table and I'd stay awake crying. Finally they had to take me to the doctor, who prescribed injections and other medicines that they gave me for about two years.

The doctor must have told my mother to take me away from there, because I went to live at Aunt Teresa's for a while. Maybe it was because we were so terribly poor, because at the same time Teodoro was sent to my Aunt Josefa, who lived near our farm. *Mamá* was left with only Honoria and the two brothers who worked.

The first day I arrived at my Aunt Teresa's I was very frightened because the house was tucked in among a lot of trees and it seemed to me like the end of the world. But being with my cousins and going to school must have helped because my illness left me. I loved my cousins and we had a wonderful time playing together.

The only bad thing at Aunt Teresa's was that my Uncle Simón was a communist who had come over from Spain, and night after night we had to sit in the living room listening to him read communist propaganda. Aunt Teresa was a communist too, and now their children are revolutionary in their ideas, although they're not real communists like their parents. Anyway, we didn't understand a word of what Uncle Simón read. It went in one ear and out the other. By the time he got through, we were dying to be turned loose so we could play.

Uncle Simón worked as a track inspector for the railroad. They lived just outside the city of Máximo Gómez near the tracks, in a rent-free house that belonged to the railroad company. Later *mamá* moved close by; then all we had to do to reach my uncle's place was to follow the tracks from our house. We could go there alone and that came to be our favorite outing. My grandmother lived in Máximo Gómez, and *mamá* was able to visit her often. I began to see her once or twice a week, too.

Máximo Gómez was the first city I ever saw. It was like an unknown world to me, all lighted up and full of pretty things. It was a kind of paradise. I'd never imagined there could be so much beauty in the world.

My grandmother was poor and illiterate but honest, and a devout Roman Catholic. She was a widow who'd had to bring up her children alone from the time they were little. She'd worked for many years as washerwoman for the Zacosta family, who owned a sugar mill. Grandmother had a small apartment in their house, a cozy place with a bedroom, living room, kitchen, and little bath, and she lived there for a long time without paying rent. But she was so poor she hadn't been able to visit us on the farm more than once every five years or so.

Grandma was like *mamá*, unsmiling, a bit harsh, and lacking an affectionate temperament. She was very orderly, ceremonious in her bearing, and would never put up with any sauciness from her grandchildren. She was always scolding, claiming we were spoiled and disrespectful. *Mamá* didn't allow her to hit us, but even so, I don't have any pleasant memories of my grandmother.

My brother Luis Heberto worked in the cane fields of a sugar mill outside the city, and we children looked after the fruit trees in our orchard and grew our own vegetables and fruit. We had to haul water in buckets to water the trees and the chili pepper and tomato patches. Nobody made me work, because I was still little, but I helped *mamá* wash the clothes, and we children managed to earn money by gathering crabs and selling them in Máximo Gómez. We didn't make much, but everything was so cheap in those days we could buy a lot with 1 *peso*.

I had a large patch of creole bananas, the kind you fry, and we sold every last bunch. We saved the banana money to buy furniture, because by then we were old enough to want our home to look pretty. All our friends had chairs and armchairs in their houses and we had only stools. So for about 30 *pesos* we bought a living room set—two armchairs, four smaller chairs, and a small table—from a neighbor of ours who was to be married but who had quarreled with his sweetheart and let us have the furniture cheap.

When Luis Heberto was about twenty years old he got typhoid, and the doctor prescribed a terribly expensive medicine costing 15 *pesos*. *Mamá* nearly went crazy. One way or another she had to get that medicine, so she went to the mayor, and he gave her the money to buy it. But when the prescription had to be repeated, she was ashamed to go back to him. Instead, she took the prescription from house to house and everyone gave something, not only money, but sweets, oranges, apples, all sorts of things. At that time only people who were in great need begged for alms, not like later, when all sorts of bums went around begging and people stopped giving. *Mamá* kept this up, going from place to place asking for alms, until Luis Heberto was well. That was the first and last time any of us had to beg.

I was about ten when I went to live with my sister Gabriela and her husband, Lorenzo, who's dead now. They were still living at the sugar mill near Quintana. Lorenzo was a maintenance man there. Gabriela had a hard life, because from the time they married, Lorenzo had gallbladder trouble and often couldn't work. *Papá* had helped them out when he was alive, and after he died my sister had to go out and hoe and cut cane to buy the children's clothing and house supplies for the year.

Gabriela's family lived in dire poverty in an ordinary three-room wooden hut with a thatched roof, but the house was always very clean, a pleasure to see. There was only one daughter and seven sons—the boys slept three or four to a bed—and all were very hardworking and honest, the poor things.

I was happy with Gabriela because she's affectionate. She showed no preference among the children, and Lorenzo was a good man who loved me as if I were his own daughter. They're a very close family. Gabriela is always on the go helping her children. If somebody gets sick, or has a birthday, or a child is born, there she is at the house. When Gabriela herself gave birth, they'd send for me to look after the children. Felicia, my eldest sister, who lived in Colón in the province of Matanzas, had nine children and I looked after them too. So I was the one who actually managed both families. I spent my youth taking care of my nieces and nephews, playing with them and going to school together. I was very happy with them.

At Gabriela's I went to an elementary school, and every day before and after school I'd do the housework, run errands, wash and iron my sister's and the children's clothes. I never refused to do anything. Gabriela's daughter didn't come along until the youngest son was thirteen, and with so many boys I had to help out. Being males, my nephews dirtied a lot of clothing, didn't take care of their things, and never did any housework.

When I went to school I felt poverty-stricken for the first time. Before this I'd led an easy life. I had no problems. Everything I wore was of good quality. My boots were of fine leather with small buttons; my dresses were nice too. But I was humiliated at school because I wore no stockings and couldn't even afford to bring a snack to eat at recess.

I was promoted immediately because I already knew how to read, write, and do sums, as well as other things my brother-in-law Lorenzo had taught me, and I caught up with my nephews in third grade. In those days, in addition to the regular subjects, boys were taught the elements of carpentry and girls learned the basics of sewing—making buttonholes, sewing on buttons, mending, knitting, embroidery, and all sorts of fine work—we even had to bring a torn sock to mend in school.

The teachers liked me very much and would give me the keys to their houses to get things for them. We loved them all, but my favorite was Nilsa, the judge's wife, who devoted a lot of attention to me—because I was an orphan, I suppose. She lived across the street from my sister and saw how hard I worked. Whenever she went to the city of Matanzas she'd bring me handkerchiefs or a box of powder.

I was living at Gabriela's house at the time of the cyclone of 1926. I was young then but I remember it clearly. I wasn't afraid of big cyclones, only of the little "banana-tree flatteners," as we call the whirlwinds. Those used to terrify me. Now I'm more terrified of thunder and lightning. My face turns green and yellow and becomes so disfigured with fear that I look like someone else. This fear began in my childhood when the roof of Gabriela's house was struck by lightning, killing a chicken roosting there and burning everyone in the family. Since then I've always been afraid of being struck by lightning. *Mamá* taught me to cross myself and pray, "Oh, great Power, calm your rage," but I also disconnect all the electric appliances and sit with my feet raised up so the electric current from a thunderbolt won't run up into me through the floor.

When I was thirteen and in the fifth grade, *mamá* fell ill and I had to leave school and go live on a farm with her. They gave me books, paper, and pencils so I could keep up my studies until I was able to go back, but the years went by and I never again attended school.

We were living on this farm in 1933 when my grandmother died. *Mamá* was terribly upset at not being able to attend the funeral and she cried and cried. Grandmother had worked almost up to the time of her death, though she'd been very ill with heart disease. Her granddaughter Yolanda had supported her by doing sewing, embroidering, and knitting, and Uncle Ignacio, in Camaguey, sent them a little money almost every month, but he didn't visit very often because of lack of transportation. Besides, he couldn't very well leave his job; someone else would have come along and taken it.

I met my first boyfriend, Ramón Pérez, at my girl friend's home when I was only fourteen or fifteen, and we fell in love right off. We courted only by writing letters and poetry, because *mamá* wouldn't stand for boyfriends. She brought us up differently from other girls and I was very much afraid of her. Nowadays girls get married at fourteen, but at that age Honoria and I were still playing with dolls. Besides, *mamá* didn't like Ramón. He had pimples on his face and she said he was sickly.

Ramón and I would send our letters with the help of the barber. Sometimes Ramón and I would look at each other from a distance, or he'd ride by on his horse and sing me songs. Later he was allowed to visit me about once a month. We'd sit on the sofa and kiss a little on the sly, because somebody was always sitting nearby. In those days couples didn't go out alone. We were very much in love and were to be married in 1937. But Ramón was anxious to be a soldier and went off to the Isle of Pines to join up. He wrote me regularly and sent money every month to buy things for our future home.

The year 1936 was very hard for me. My brothers went off to Camaguey, and *mamá*, Honoria, and I moved to my sister Felicia's house in Colón. Felicia and her husband, Emigdio, were lower middle class and Emigdio earned quite a lot of money as a produce wholesaler. Later, business in Cuba started going downhill and only people in politics prospered. When his business failed, Emigdio went to Havana and ran a flower stand that did quite well.

I hadn't really known my sister Felicia until she was a grown woman, but I think she was always the same selfish person she is now, the kind who looks out for her own. For instance, my sister Alicia was raised at Felicia's house because Felicia claimed she was sick. She's a sharp one, Felicia. Sick indeed! Well true, she'd sometimes get paralytic attacks and become unconscious—that's why *mamá* sent Alicia there—but with that excuse Felicia used her to take care of the children until Alicia was married.

Felicia didn't treat us well, because we were in need. I was a big eater, and though I worked hard in her house and was always ordered about, she served me very small portions and gave large portions to her own children. I didn't complain—to whom could I complain?—but at night I cried. Honoria wasn't used to being scolded, and she and I wanted *mamá* to let us get a house of our own and work for wealthy families in town, although Honoria wasn't allowed to wet her hands or work hard. But Felicia wouldn't hear of it. It was to her advantage to have us there working for her, so she said, "What would people say if you became servants!" and "IIow could you go off and live by yourselves with me having such a big house?" She was very domineering and *mamá* didn't contradict her.

There seemed to be no possibility of our getting out of Felicia's house and that's why Honoria killed herself. I'd gone to the post office to pick up some letters, and by the time I returned Honoria had taken poison, something called *Rompe Roca* that Emigdio kept for spraying the cattle against ticks. When Honoria saw me, she started to cry and said, "Cencia, I'm sorry on account of you and *mamá*," and squeezed my hand and asked me for water. Then she died. By the time the doctor got there it was too late. I was carried away by grief.

Mamá took it badly. My brothers didn't say anything but everyone knew it was Felicia's fault. Yet she wasn't affected in the slightest. She went to town to see the judge about getting the autopsy waived—an autopsy was such a botched-up business at that time—and she succeeded on the grounds that the doctor had already reported the cause of death.

Had my little sister died in an accident I might have accepted it better, but this way was so senseless. Honoria had no reason to take her life. Everybody has troubles but one should struggle and overcome them. I felt God could have prevented it and at that moment I almost lost my faith. I had serious doubts, but even in my desperation I didn't curse or blaspheme. I cried out, "My God, why have You done this senseless thing?" It filled me with despair to think that it could have been avoided if only *mamá* had agreed to leave Felicia's house. Then the priest told me that true Christians were formed through such tests. "It's a harsh trial," he said, "but those who overcome such trials are the true believers." His words comforted me.

My doubts were over but not my sorrow. I never really doubted because I saw that it is we human beings who create problems for ourselves. God wouldn't hurt anyone; He watches over us to protect us. It is we who are responsible for what we do. If one deliberately puts his hand in a fire, whose fault is it if he gets burned?

To me, suicide is a sin. I've heard that the soul of someone who's taken his own life is in pain until the hour comes when he was really meant to die. Many times I've asked the souls out beyond that if they can really communicate with the living, to have Honoria send me some message. I'm not afraid, for I don't believe there's a single soul in the beyond who'd harm any living being; on the contrary, I think if they can prevent harm, they do. But even if there are strayed sheep stumbling around trying to hurt the living, they are few.

When Honoria died, I sent my sweetheart, Ramón, a telegram asking him to come to me. But to achieve his ambition to become a soldier he'd vowed to hold a vigil before the Virgin the day he returned to Cuba, so instead of coming immediately when I needed him, he and his friends arranged to hold the vigil that night at his mother's house. It's true he had an obligation to the Virgin, and there was nothing he could have done for me, but still he should have postponed the vigil. It didn't have to be that very day. Anyway, he didn't answer the telegram but appeared two days later with my wedding gown, shoes, purse, and everything. I was burning up, not so much with anger as with disgust, and I wouldn't accept any apology. I thought he didn't sympathize with me and I didn't want him back. Well, he returned to the Isle of Pines and kept writing me from there but I never answered him. When he came back I gave him all the wedding presents—the initialed sheets, the tablecloths, and everything else I'd worked on—and called off the marriage.

Later I regretted my action. I would have been happy with Ramón and would have had a lot of children because he was just like me. He was the kind of man I dreamed about. But he'd hurt me so much, my pain at the time of my sister's suicide was so deep, I couldn't forgive him.

After that, I didn't know what to do or where to go. Four or five months later, Señora Mérida, who had moved from Colón to Havana and was visiting one of our neighbors, offered me a job as a servant. I accepted and moved to her home in Havana, where I did the shopping, cooking, and cleaning for 5 *pesos* a month, plus my food and free sewing lessons.

Señora Mérida owned a shop where ladies' dresses were made, and opposite this she owned a store where the dresses were sold. I learned to sew in her shop. Of course I already knew how to sew and knit, though I'd never studied dressmaking. But I'd made my own clothing from the time I was nine or ten, first by hand, then on my sister's machine, because I didn't like the way *mamá* did them. At the shop, Señora Mérida cut and laid out the dresses, a *mulata* sewed them, and I made the pleats and hems, sewed on the fasteners, and did all the simple things. The pay wasn't much, but they took me to the theater and everywhere else they went as though I were one of the family.

A few months after I came to Havana, I had my appendix out at the Calixto García Hospital. That was the only time in my life I've been hospitalized. I had lots of visitors at the hospital; all my relatives and neighbors came to see me. My ex-fiancé Ramón came too, but a lot of time had gone by and I was no longer interested in him. Besides, I knew he had another sweetheart.

Aside from appendicitis, I've never been ill except for a sore throat or the grippe now and then. I've never had an accident either—I have almost no scars. My health was always so good I never had to borrow money for doctors or medicines.

My older sister Alicia's death was another tragedy. She died in an auto accident in 1938. I was visiting *mamá* at Felicia's house, and Alicia, her husband, Claudio, and their little girl, Aida, were on their way from Havana to see us. Claudio fell asleep at the wheel and the car rolled over. Alicia was thrown into a ditch and the child onto the road. None of us blamed Claudio for Alicia's death. He hadn't wanted to drive because he'd just made a trip to Camp Columbia and had lost a lot of sleep. But my sister hadn't visited us since her marriage and was crazy to see us again.

Claudio was in Batista's army; he attended the Military Academy in Havana and later became a lieutenant. During the Revolution of 1933,[15] after the Army had occupied a number of towns, he was sent to the city of Manzanillo as advisor to the *comandante.* In 1934 he was transferred to Havana. After the Revolution Claudio stayed on in Cuba—I saw him recently at the Department of Finance when he was collecting his pension check. He was a major in the Army when he retired.

A year after Alicia's death my *mamá* died. She was about fifty-nine years old, but to look at her one would have thought she was very, very old—a little old woman with white, white hair and a thin body. She had diabetes and severe ulcerated varicose veins from bearing so many children. She could hardly do anything on account of her sick legs, but what finally killed her was heart disease, which she got after *papá* died.

Mamá was in the hospital in Camaguey for about a year. Gabriela and I visited her every week, bringing her cigarettes and things. She'd never smoked before because my *papá* didn't use tobacco, but when she was old she enjoyed smoking very much. It was a long trip by bus from Havana to the hospital. It cost almost 3 *pesos;* it wasn't a lot of money, but I was still working for the dressmaker in Havana and earning very little. Sometimes when people bought round-trip tickets and didn't use the return part, I'd ask them for it.

15. "The sergeants' conspiracy" of 1933, led by Fulgencio Batista, then a sergeant-stenographer in the Army. The coup was part of the power struggle that followed the overthrow of Machado's dictatorship. Batista did not become the official head of state until his election to the presidency in 1940.

Mamá never complained about a thing. She prayed a lot, and had her shroud all prepared for when she died—she was very foresighted. I was in Havana when the hospital notified us that *mamá* had passed away. Gabriela was with her at the time and soon the whole family gathered there. Funerals were not free then and my brothers paid for everything.

I'm always deeply affected when somebody in my family dies. Although I loved my *papá* more, I suffered very much when *mamá* died. I'd look at her picture every night and burst into tears. I cried so much I got sinusitis. We don't wear mourning nowadays but we did then; I stayed at home for a year or so, dressed in black.

My employer, Señora Mérida, and her sister were partners, and when they got married the business was divided up and I lost my job. I then found work in Vedado with a family named Ribadenira, taking care of a little boy whose *mamá* had been killed in an accident. I was paid 20 *pesos* a month and I slept in. My job was to take the little boy to school, to the movies, to play ball. I went everywhere with that boy. I even waited outside on a bench until school was over because his nerves were very bad. It was a good job, easy work, and the boy was fond of me.

The family was very nice; I was well treated and I never had complaints. No one took advantage of me because I always kept my dignity. The gardener and the chauffeur were Spaniards and a little forward, but I let them know they had to respect me, that I wasn't the same as the others. Some people thought a servant had to put up with anything.

After I'd been with the Ribadeniras for a year, the boy improved and no longer needed a nursemaid so I had to look for another job. I don't remember whether it was a friend of mine or the Ribadeniras who recommended me to Señora Zaldivar, but I went to work as her cook for two years. Besides me, she employed a housekeeper, chauffeur, waitress, laundress, and watchman, six servants in all. The señora was very kind; she paid me 20 *pesos* a month and whenever she went shopping she bought gifts for everybody—clothing, soap, powder, stockings, blouses, cloth.

The old lady lived alone and didn't work. She had breakfast late but we servants got up at 7:00 in the morning. I cooked for everyone. I didn't have to shop for food because the delivery boy from Minimax would come every morning to pick up the old lady's shopping list, or we'd phone and he'd bring it on his bicycle. Things were very different then.

Sometime between noon and 1:00 o'clock we had lunch, then I'd go to my room, which was fixed up very prettily, and stay there until 5:00 or maybe 6:00 in the evening. I'd sew and embroider clothes for my trousseau, as I was getting ready to be married. I worked in the kitchen again from 6:00 to 8:00 at night.

In the evenings my boyfriend, Reinaldo Serrano, would come to visit me out in the garden where the watchman was. I'd dress up and go sit on a bench with Reinaldo in the small plaza in front of the house. At about 10:00 we'd say goodbye and go home. I had every other Sunday off and on that day we'd go out.

I'd known Reinaldo Serrano Balseiro since 1939, the last year I worked for Señora Mérida. We met when he came to take the girl next door to a fiesta. He soon dropped her and began to send me postcards and call on me. That's how our courtship began. Reinaldo was a handsome boy with regular features; he was white with medium-brown hair and brown eyes like me, and a straight nose. Before we married he looked quite thin but afterward he filled out.

As for me, I'd always been considered *hermosa* but not *bonita. Hermosa* means you aren't thin or sickly; *bonita* means having a pretty face. But by the time I met Reinaldo, I think I was pretty. Everybody complimented me on my good skin and beautiful hands, and on my figure, too. I never worried about my looks, though, because I've always had such determination and ambition that I never thought about how tall or short I was or whether I was beautiful. I've seen very pretty women who were useless. At least I've been of service to everybody and have always felt satisfied with what I've done with my life, and I never had complexes about anything.

Reinaldo and I kept company for four years, and all that time he was very attentive, and a bit jealous, but he waited patiently for us to be married. He was rather severe in temperament and critical of everything—how I looked, the fit of my dress, or if my collar or my kerchief were right. We were really very different from one another.

Nor were Reinaldo's sentiments toward me all I would have liked. It's true that he always seemed to be in love with me, but he wasn't loving. Before we were married, I let him know all the defects I found in him and I said, "I don't think we're going to be happy on account of this." I faced him with it but he kept saying that when we were married he'd change.

Reinaldo worked as a dispatcher for a taxi company, and during our four years of courtship he earned a little over 1 *peso* a day. Out of this he had to give his mother money for his food—his family was worse off than mine—but with my earnings and what remained of his, we began to buy things for our future home. As soon as we'd accumulated 20 *pesos* we'd go off to the store to buy dishes, pots, sheets, blankets, and clothing. We kept the things at his mother's house in Santa Isabel.

About two months before we were married, an apartment in a little wooden house in a *solar* across the street from his parents became available. The old couple who owned it lived next door and were close friends of Reinaldo's parents. They needed the money and had to rent the apartment immediately. It had one room and a tiny kitchen. In back of the *solar* there was one toilet, without water, for all three tenants, and they had to bathe in the tiny kitchen, pouring water over themselves. Later a toilet and shower were added to each apartment.

Well, we rented the apartment for 5 *pesos* a month and decided to paint it and fix it up before getting married. Little by little we furnished it with a few pieces: a bed, two little tables, a chair, a china closet, and a used wardrobe in very bad condition. Later on we got a new bedroom set, hung curtains, and furnished it completely. We had everything, down to shoe cloths on which I'd embroidered Reinaldo's initials. A week before the wedding I stopped working so I could finish my trousseau and a few things for the house.

We were married late in 1943, when I was twenty-seven and Reinaldo twenty-nine. At 6:00 A.M. on my wedding day I washed my hair, got everything together, and started off with my nephew, who was to act as witness and as best man. We were married in the Toyo courthouse at 7:30 in the morning, and again in the church in the afternoon, because during the war, weddings had to be held in the daytime to save electricity.

Church weddings were very expensive—100 *pesos*—and as a matter of fact, Señora Zaldivar paid for it because she was religious and didn't want anybody to be married outside the church. She gave all her servants church weddings and also paid to send every one of their children to good Catholic schools. So she went and signed for me. Besides, she liked me very much. In fact, she was crazy about me!

For the ceremony at the courthouse I wore a jumper with a beige lace blouse, a brown bag and shoes, and a small hat. Reinaldo wore a light-brown suit. After the civil ceremony we had lunch at my sister Felicia's house in Los Pinos, where she'd been living since 1939. Later in the afternoon we went to the church. This time Reinaldo wore a light-gray suit with a white shirt and tie, and I wore all white. My gown was medium length but I wore a veil and a little tiara on my head and carried white gloves.

There were about fifty people at the church, including my in-laws and their neighbors. Señora Zaldivar and her niece came in their chauffeur-driven car. Most of my nieces, nephews, aunts, and uncles came, but my sister Felicia couldn't because she had to stay at home with her grandchildren. And Gabriela and Teodoro and Adolfo couldn't make it either, because at that time they were all poor and didn't have the money. My brother Luis Heberto came, but he'd have found a way even if he'd had to come on horseback or hitch a ride on the back of a truck. He was different. I wish all my brothers and sisters could have been there, especially their children, who were so fond of me. But everyone knew about the marriage and sent me gifts.

After the wedding we went back to Felicia's house for dinner. Later, friends and neighbors came over and had cake and refreshments and danced until 10:00 o'clock. Naturally I felt happy that day, with the radio on and everyone dancing. The guests stayed at the fiesta but Reinaldo and I left. One of his cousins drove us to our own home because we had no money to go to a hotel. Reinaldo didn't carry me across the threshold or any of that. He wasn't very romantic.

I was a virgin when I married, completely without experience. I knew only what my girl friends had told me. Reinaldo enjoyed it—he adored me—and treated me well that night, but he didn't make love tenderly. He wasn't really affectionate; he was hard and abrupt. That's the way he was and he never changed. He felt passion for me and still does, but I never did, nor did I ever feel much pleasure. Maybe that's why sex didn't mean much to me.

I'm not altogether sure I loved Reinaldo because I found it very difficult to adapt to his ways, though I was a good wife in every sense of the word. I'm sure that he was more in love with me than I with him. He wasn't a skirt-chaser; I've never known him to go with another woman. The main problem, I guess, was his character—our temperaments were very different. In my family we're affectionate, especially when we haven't seen each other for a while. But Reinaldo and his family are very cold and unexpressive; they love, but in their own strange way. They're very withdrawn and the brothers and sisters never kiss each other, not even their mother.

So I was very affectionate and Reinaldo wasn't. I looked after him and his things, I waited anxiously for his return, I called him pet names, like "Little Fatty" when he began to put on weight, but he had no such way of showing his love for me. And the times when I felt romantic and hopeful and most wanted him, he'd excuse himself by saying he had a headache or was ill, or he'd come home in a bad mood and begin to quarrel over the least little thing. But the day *he* wanted *me*, I had to give in no matter how I felt.

From the outset sex was when he wanted it, about once a week. I didn't want children by him so I used *Corome*, a Swiss contraceptive. He agreed to this because he's so self-centered he didn't like children. I had no guilt feelings about it, because I thought that it wasn't worth having a child who might grow up bitter and unsociable like his father. And feeling as I did that someday I would leave Reinaldo, it would have been foolish.

All through the courtship I knew we just didn't belong together, but I believed with God's help I could change him. It was my error, my weakness, not God's. I knew I shouldn't have married an atheist. It's unpleasant for me to admit these things, but I suffered so much with that man all my life, I don't know how I bore it.

Reinaldo is the kind of person you have to say yes to in everything.

"Do this, do that!" I'd always had somebody giving me orders and had never been free to say or do what I wanted. It turned out that after I married and had my own home, I was more a prisoner than ever. I couldn't even hang a picture where I wanted. It had to go where Reinaldo said. I had everything in the house so pretty, but it all annoyed him, even the china closet where I kept the glass wedding gifts. It bothered him so much we sold it. The curtains annoyed him, the flowers annoyed him, and little by little everything was replaced by what *he* liked. It was humiliating to have to always bend to his will.

Reinaldo's family was constantly on top of us, making things worse. He was very concerned about them, worrying whether one or another of his relatives needed this or that. They were never all in good shape; if one was working, there was another who was not, or someone was sick, and because we had no children we had to help them out. I felt sorry for Reinaldo's nieces and nephews because their *papá* earned so little. I deprived myself to buy them things and take them out. They became fonder of me than of Reinaldo, and still are to this day.

When I first began going with Reinaldo his family had never had a creche or even put up a Christmas tree! I went to the park, got a pine branch, and decorated it for them because I enjoy making life pleasant for others. After that, they set out a big beautiful tree each year, though Reinaldo never did because he didn't believe in anything. During the early years of our marriage it was customary for us to have Christmas supper at his parents' house, but the children annoyed him so we began to eat our fancy Christmas dinner at home alone and visit them afterward.

As a child Reinaldo had been very ill with asthma and parasites and lots of colds. He spent much of his time sick in bed, but he was simply coddling himself, complaining and saying this or that hurt. Tending sick people isn't something I enjoy—that's why I never wanted to work in a hospital. It disgusts me to see someone vomiting and I hate the smell of sickness and of medicines, though when *papá* was sick I felt differently about it. I wanted to be near him all the time.

Of course if there were no one else to do it, I'd take care of a sick person, as long as he didn't have tumors or other disgusting symptoms. I can't bear skin diseases. Reinaldo was always getting horrible rashes all over his body, and little by little that made him repulsive to me. The doctors said the rashes came from an allergy, but they never found out what caused it. All I know is that Reinaldo's feet were always rotten with fungus infections and he had some sort of rash in the groin. Or his eyes would get red and sore, or his lips cracked and peeling. He always had something disgusting the matter with him, but the doctors never really found anything wrong. He bought all kinds of medicines—that's his hobby—and if he read about a disease in a book, then he had it.

Reinaldo wasn't brought up by his mother but by a widowed aunt whose only daughter had died. As Reinaldo was the eldest, his mother sent him to live with the aunt, who fussed over him and treated him like an only child. Until he was nine he was never allowed to go out alone. And then he and his aunt spent all their time riding about in her car. It made him very helpless. To him everything seemed like a big problem, and every problem was a tragedy. If he went to hammer in a nail and it didn't go in right, he'd pull at his hair and say, "Shit on the hour I was born." It's an expression he always used. That's the way he was—a coward, lacking in determination; any little thing was a great operation for him.

I, on the other hand, let nothing stand in my way. I've always wanted people to treat me well because I don't treat anyone badly. I think I'm a very humane, helpful, sentimental, grateful kind of person. If someone is disagreeable, I try to avoid contact with him. I don't talk or shout or quarrel, I just suffer. The best thing is not to talk, because the more I say, the more I'm likely to offend. But at times this fortitude was useless. For example, when I'd curb my anger against Reinaldo and stop speaking or eating for days, or fixing myself up, he was quite satisfied to see me that way.

I'd say, "Well, I'll leave him," but there was something that kept me from taking the final step. I told myself that if I left him he'd kill me, that this or that would happen. It was all foolishness, because nobody goes around killing for a reason like that. It was just fear on my part. The trouble was that I didn't have any security worth a dime, nor anyone I could turn to.

Just one month after my marriage I went to see if I could go back to work for Señora Zaldivar, but she'd gone to Mexico on vacation and was away almost six months. The other alternative was to work in another private home, but I wouldn't have been able to find the sort of conditions I had with the Widow Zaldivar. Things had gotten difficult, with tremendous competition for domestic work. People were beginning to prefer men because they caused fewer complications. The only way I could get out of my situation in a hurry would have been to go back to Felicia's, where I didn't have any privacy or even a room of my own. I preferred dying to that.

When Señora Zaldivar returned, I told her about my situation and she said to me, "But Inocencia, listen to me. You were married in church so you believe in God. And when a person believes in God he must put up with things because life is like that." So I put up with my sentence. Little by little I got used to it. I felt I had no choice but to accept the inferior position Reinaldo forced on me. He never knew that if Señora Zaldivar had taken me back to work, I would have left him.

Every time I told my troubles to my sisters Felicia and Gabriela, they'd say that all men were alike, that you had to put up with a lot from all of them, that if it wasn't one thing, it was another. They were better off than I was but Gabriela's husband behaved miserably too. The three of us were long-suffering and put up with everything. Not all women are like that. I've seen some who tell their husbands to go to the devil. I don't know of anybody in our family who has that kind of disposition though, not even among my nieces. When they found out that their husbands had other women they weren't able to put up a fight.

I believe men are superior to women—that is, they're more intelligent and stronger—but that doesn't give them the right to do what they do. It's not that a woman is inferior, but she's weaker and easier to impress; there are times when she simply has to depend on a man. Women fall in love, have children, and have twenty difficulties men don't have, and no matter how intelligent a woman is, she feels more protected if she has a man. And yet, no matter how much I needed my husband and how hard I tried to please him, there's no moment I can think of and say, "Yes, he made me happy then."

Reinaldo was a bitter, jealous man. It annoyed him when the neighbors or even children were nice to me. He didn't like to share me with my family or friends; he wanted me to spend all my time on him. If he went to a store I had to go with him, but whenever I wanted to visit a relative of mine I had to wait for him to decide if he felt like taking me. I could never have meetings at my house, or birthday parties or a wedding. He always had some pretext, something hurt him or he was sick. He constantly looked for excuses to stay home; if he did take me somewhere, he'd be in a hurry to leave, especially if I was enjoying myself.

Reinaldo had a one-week vacation each year and we spent that at Gabriela's place in Camaguey. That was the only time we ever spent a night outside the house. We went to the beaches at Santa Fé, Jaimanitas, and Guanabo, but only for the day, no longer. I don't swim but I love to play in the sand with the children and give them piggyback rides. Whenever my sister-in-law took her son to the beach I'd beg Reinaldo to go along with her. Otherwise we'd never go to the beach because my husband didn't like to go by bus. After the Revolution we never took a vacation because Reinaldo didn't want to, even though he had the right to.

Reinaldo didn't like anything I liked. For example, he liked popular and old-fashioned Cuban music—*sones, guarachas*—and I don't. If there's one thing I detest it's Afro-Cuban music. What I love is the opera, all operas, and concerts too, and Spanish zarzuelas. I've heard some great singers, including Mario Lanza, who simply enchanted me, and Nelson Eddy. Ah yes! And also Jeanette MacDonald. But in the opera I preferred Lily Pons above all others. For me, her voice was the loveliest in the world.

Before I met Reinaldo, I went to most of the theaters in Havana. Oh, how I adored the theater! I saw all the shows that came from foreign countries, but what I most enjoyed and went to see whenever I got a chance was *The Merry Widow* with Rosita Fornés. If they were to show it a thousand times, I'd go to see it a thousand times.

I love the circus, but Reinaldo hated it so I had to stop going. I'd never seen a circus until I was twenty-one, although circuses had often visited the little towns where I lived as a child. Maybe they gave indecent shows or the conditions in them were bad, but no respectable people went to them, only the lower class. To me the circus was a delight. Before I married I went every time the Santos y Artiga circus came to Havana, but the Russian circus, which everyone said was even more magnificent, was the one I most wanted to see.

There were many things I enjoyed, like playing dominoes and checkers and a card game called *brisca*, although, except for the lottery, I never played gambling games. I found horse-racing fascinating but never could manage to go to the Hippodrome. Now, since the Revolution, such things don't exist. I've always loved to watch volleyball, basketball, boxing, and baseball. Why, I even played a little baseball with the neighborhood kids! I followed the baseball teams and knew the leading players, but I went to see the games only when Reinaldo was in the mood. If I had to stay home, I listened to them on the radio.

I feel that I missed so many things because of the man I married. I remember one time there was a big ship that would take people all over the bay for just 50 *centavos*. It was a pleasure boat, all lighted up, with a band playing on it. It looked so beautiful and I'd never been on a ship—unless you count the little ferryboat to Regla!—so I begged Reinaldo to take me on it just once. But he wouldn't because he was scared of the water. I couldn't go alone; he would have killed me if I had.

I loved the movies, and that was one thing Reinaldo enjoyed too, so we always went together. We took in a movie every night and saw some of them as many as three or four times, because the barrio movie houses were cheap and we could afford to go often. My favorite star is Ingrid Bergman; the first movie I saw her in was *For Whom the Bell Tolls*.

I think we went to every movie theater in Havana just to get out of the house. The truth is, we didn't have a comfortable home. It was a single room, with no TV or anything. After we got TV we hardly ever went to the movies. But I didn't enjoy television much because Reinaldo always turned to the programs he liked. There were four channels but he'd manage to choose something I wasn't interested in. Besides, he kept adjusting the picture, making it lighter and darker, so what I had to look at most of the time was not the program but him blocking the screen.

Reinaldo loved to read all types of books—love stories, detective stories, and some historical novels too—and occasionally he'd buy a book for 2 *pesos*, or 4. Of course he didn't buy them every day, only at the end of the month when he got paid. His father had been a tobacco worker, and every tobacco factory had its own library and a reader who read aloud to the workers while they worked.[16] His father borrowed books at the factory and took them home to read, so when Reinaldo was a boy he began to read books too.

When we first got married, Reinaldo gave me 60 *centavos* a day for food. It wasn't much, but he still earned only 1 *peso* a day. I'd plan the day's meals, and if it came to more than 60 *centavos* I'd start to figure all over again and plan something cheaper. We ate poor people's food— rice, beans, beef, macaroni—just common, ordinary food, because I couldn't stretch the money any further. I'd buy things such as rice, lard, coffee for the whole week, but I bought fresh bread, tubers, meat, and vegetables every day. Out of the remaining 40 *centavos* a day we had to pay rent, electricity, and buy movie tickets.

Later, under Batista, Reinaldo got a pretty big increase in wages, and I think the men were paid for forty-eight hours a week when they worked only forty-four. Then I began to receive 1 *peso* a day for the house; later on he gave me 13 a week and I was able to save a *peso* or so. That way I had a bit of a reserve and we could have something extra nice to eat now and then. All in all, we no longer lived in such miserable poverty. It wasn't only our meals that improved; I could get myself more clothes and we each bought a watch. And every week I'd buy at least four pieces of lottery tickets, or 1 *peso*'s worth, but I never won much—5, 10 *pesos* maybe—never enough to buy the little house of my dreams.

We still lacked a lot of things for our home. The bedroom set was of very poor quality, and I didn't have a sewing machine, a good pair of scissors, or many other necessary things. Then in 1944 the cyclone came and everything in the house got water-stained. Nothing was spared but our clothes, because I'd taken them to Reinaldo's aunt's house, where we stayed during the cyclone. There I had prayed and prayed. "Oh God, spare my little house because it's all I have." I said, "Walls, don't fall!" When I returned home after the storm, I found that the tarpaper roof had blown off. I thought, "I kept telling the walls to stay put and forgot to say anything to the roof, so now it's gone." That struck me as funny and I had to laugh.

I wanted to save up money to buy a house so I began to sew for others. Reinaldo didn't object to that. Señora Zaldivar, who kept track of me and came around regularly to see how I was making out, sent me to the

16. According to Fernando Ortíz, the custom of reading aloud to tobacco workers was introduced in the latter half of the nineteenth century, first to prisoners in their tobacco workrooms, then to factory workers. The readings and the libraries were initiated by the tobacco workers, who were among the first Cubans to form workers' associations. *(Cuban Counterpoint: Tobacco and Sugar* (New York: Alfred A. Knopf, 1947), pp. 89–91.)

homes of her nieces and other relatives. I'd arrive in the morning, sew, have lunch, and go home at about 4:00 o'clock to prepare dinner. I earned 1 *peso* a day.

Later Señora Zaldivar's nieces got me a job in El Encanto, a big department store. The only opening was in the boys' department and that's where I went. The first day they handed me some lengths of cloth to make samples of pockets for trousers. I knew nothing about this work but I was sure I could learn to do it. I've always felt self-confident. Perhaps it's my faith in God. When I haven't been able to deal with a problem, I've always turned to God and always with magnificent results.

I took the pieces of material, put them on top of the sewing machine, and looked around at everybody. I didn't know how to begin so I closed my eyes and asked God to help me. The machines were set up opposite one another and the woman in front of me said, "Don't you know how to do that?" and she made motions to show me. She didn't say a word because the forelady was a cross old maid who was very strict. I did what she told me to and I got the job. After a while I was their best pocket-maker. The women I worked with even gave me a little testimonial by pinning a make-believe medal on me.

In El Encanto they paid us by the piece. There were certain quotas to be met but we were never sure how much we made or how we were being paid. We just sewed and sewed and sewed, and when the pay envelope came around we had to accept their figures. I never said anything if I thought they were cheating me because I was afraid they'd fire me. I had a little notebook where I kept track of everything I made, as well as how much I was paid, thinking that it might be checked some day. But I never knew how much I'd earned until I got my envelope. One week it would be 9 *pesos*, another week 13. The most I ever earned was 19 *pesos* one week when I worked very hard.

One payday a girl told them she'd done a lot of sewing and they'd paid her very little. I said I thought I'd done about as much as she, and I'd been paid even less. So they checked up and gave us 5 *pesos* more. God knows how much had been held out before we protested. But because I'd finally complained they said, "Well, we don't want this one around," and they let me go. After that they called me only when they were in a jam. So I stayed home and waited until there was regular work. That was how it was for two years.

There were two unions in El Encanto, one communist, the other called the *Auténtico*.[17] I didn't belong to either one because I knew nothing of unions or communists except for the little I heard from Uncle Simón.

17. The Communist Party and the *Auténticos* (see Mónica, n. 5) were vying for control of the trade-union movement. In 1947 the *Auténticos* replaced the Communists as leaders of the *Confederación de Trabajadores de Cuba* (CTC), the Confederation of Cuban Workers.

Nobody else at home or in school talked politics. My family cared only about their work, just like everyone else in the countryside. But in the cities people were concerned about politics because it was a way of getting jobs and living better, or of getting one of those phony political jobs and not working at all.

I didn't like the communist union because they defended only the girls who were with them and never offered to help me in my work. They considered you a rat if you weren't one of them. The girls in the other union were just the opposite: good comrades, sociable, not political, and they got along with the rest.

In the forties the leaders of the Communist Party had fancy houses and cars so I didn't trust them.[18] One time at the shop, a girl who was a communist tried to talk to me about joining. I annoyed her by saying, "Listen, I put Lazaro Peña[19] in the same class as all the rest of the politicians because he rides around in a big black car and lives in style just as they do. So the Communist Party is a political party like any other."

I always compare the communists with the Jehovah's Witnesses. Both have the same idea—if you're one of them you're fine, if not, you're no good. When a cause is being advanced, it should hold good for everybody, shouldn't it? That's why I like the Revolution, because it's uniform and its laws are the same for all.

At first I handed over my pay to my husband because we had to pool both our wages to meet expenses. But he came to look upon taking my money as his right even when it was no longer necessary. I let him do it to avoid trouble. He'd even keep track of how much sewing I'd done. Later, when I was a saleslady, he also wrote down how much commission I received. On payday he was the one who got my money and decided what to do with it. Even the bank account was in his name, but those were *my* savings he took over because, actually, I was the only one who saved.

Reinaldo was always supervising me, asking how much I was going to spend and why. If I bought a birthday gift for someone, or wanted to take a child to an amusement park and spend 10 *pesos* or so, Reinaldo just couldn't see that. When I picked up some little things in the dime store, he'd tell me I was spending money on crap. One day I bought some flowers to put on the television set and he said, "How much money

18. Inocencia refers to the old Communist Party (PSP), dissolved in 1961. (See Mónica, n. 13.)

19. The black leader of the tobacco workers' union who was the first secretary-general of the CTC, serving from 1938 until 1947, when the *Auténticos* took control. Peña was one of the members of the old Communist Party who played a prominent public role in the Castro government. He held a variety of offices after 1959, including leadership of the CTC, but had no real power. Peña died in 1974.

do you want to throw down the drain?" But if *he* was interested in an antenna or a camera, he'd go and buy it for himself. He was piggish that way; any money he spent was fine, but I was always wasting money.

I kept my budget within my income and made do with what I had. I never pawned anything; when I needed a loan for some extra expense, such as a wedding present, I'd ask my brother Luis Heberto. He never refused me because he knew I couldn't get any money from that tightwad Reinaldo. I never borrowed more than 10 or 20 *pesos,* and my brother never wanted me to pay him back.

I quit sewing at El Encanto in 1949 because I was still only a temporary worker, without the right to retire on a pension. I found a job with the Phillips Company selling electrical appliances—refrigerators, television sets, radios, and sewing machines—on a commission basis. I got 20 percent on every sewing machine and 28 percent on the refrigerators. Selling was my passion—I'd sell anything, even if it were only a single sweet potato. It never embarrassed me to go to someone's house to sell something. When *papá* was a peddler he felt defeated and humiliated, but I was very proud of my work. I loved to win clients, overcome their resistance, and make a sale. Never before or after have I worked so hard or enjoyed it so much.

I even sold dolls once, plying my wares right out in the street. That was before I sold electrical appliances. My father-in-law had given a young fellow some money to invest, and the boy bought 250 baby dolls with stuffed cloth bodies and composition hands and faces. But then he and my father-in-law were worried because they didn't know what to do with them. Naked, the dolls wouldn't have sold. Suddenly my father-in-law had a bright idea: "Inocencia is the one who can solve this problem for us!" And he consulted me.

"Well," I told him, "you've already spent your money and we can't let it go to waste. Don't worry, I'll save it for you." So we went to the warehouses on Muralla Street, bought a lot of cloth remnants, and I spent a month making long robes for the baby dolls, designing different models and finishing them with braid. I dressed all the dolls and boxed them; then I went to a big hardware store where I knew the clerks and asked for permission to keep the dolls there until just before the Day of the Three Kings. When the time came to sell the wares my father-in-law and his partner were too embarrassed to do it. Real bourgeois types, those two. Reinaldo didn't even come near, he was so embarrassed. So I stood out in the street in front of the store until long after midnight, yelling, "Hey, here are your dolls for the Three Kings. You don't have to go any further. Baby dolls, 4 *pesos* each!" I was hoarse by the time I was through, but I sold every last doll.

My father-in-law got back his investment plus 200 *pesos'* profit and so did his partner. But do you know what *this* poor fool earned on that little

venture? A dress length they gave me as a thank-you gift! A sleazy bit of
cloth with a silky finish, Prussian blue with little white flowers, that was so
rotten I couldn't even sew it without tearing it. Some pay! Oh well, it was
one more experience!

The first equipment I sold for Phillips was sewing machines. I sold
them on the installment plan, 10 *pesos* down and 5 *pesos* a month. To
make things easy for clients I'd say to them, "Look, I'll make a special
arrangement for you, so much less down and so much less a month. You
may pay in this way, or else this other way. There are different
models...." I had to talk an awful lot! I fairly filled the neighborhood
and the barrio with my sewing machines. Yes indeed, all the women in
the neighborhood bought from me, some eighty or a hundred machines
in all—I still have the list—and I earned a commission of 10 *pesos* each. I
used that money to pay for a sewing machine of my own.

When I first started selling TV sets, I had a few disagreeable experiences. It took some time until the customers figured out how to adjust
the antenna and they thought I'd sold them defective sets. That's apt to
happen with electrical equipment, especially a TV. When I had a complaint I'd call the mechanics, and if a set was really defective I got company representatives to substitute it with another.

In 1951 I started selling frigidaires for General Enterprises, and after
that mattresses, radios, electric irons, record players, electric ranges—all
sorts of household equipment. I earned enough money to buy my
frigidaire, my sofa-bed, my dresser, and the table and chair. Everything
in the house was bought by me, including the china, tableware, and all
sorts of stuff, as well as my watch and ring. I still have the electric iron I
got at the time. And I paid cash for all of those things because I worked
to buy them. I never bought on credit.

My company offered us a very good record player at factory price and
Reinaldo gave it to me for our wedding anniversary. The speaker alone,
a very large Jensen, cost 100 *pesos* wholesale. We had a carpenter make
the cabinet for it and the son of a taxi driver we knew installed it. Then
we bought a lot of records—Reinaldo had his favorites and I had mine—
and some we borrowed from a friend. We heard the London and Minneapolis symphony orchestras in concert, but mainly we listened to
opera—*Faust, La Traviata, La Bohème*—all of them. The record player
eventually became a problem because Reinaldo seldom played the records I liked. He said they were so noisy they nearly shattered the walls, so
I had to put up with his lousy popular music.

Selling was not only my work, it was my social life too. I knew every
street and alley in the barrio and everyone who lived there. All the
neighbors were fond of me, and anybody I talked to was apt to become
my client sooner or later. The housewives were friendly when I called on

them because I never deceived them or took their money without delivering the goods, and I helped them as much as I could when they were in difficulties. Many of them were afraid to get in debt but I convinced them, not so much to earn a commission, but because I knew what I sold was quality equipment and would be useful to them. Many have me to thank that they learned to sew or that they have a frigidaire or some other piece of scarce equipment today. They're grateful to me now; the others regret that they didn't let me talk them into buying while the getting was good.

Chapter Three

Getting Involved

I DIDN'T BOTHER WITH POLITICS when I was young, but my awareness of the tragedies of others, especially those caused by economic misfortunes, caused me a great deal of suffering. I had a vision of a Cuban government led one day by a man who would do something more than play the usual corrupt politics, who had no personal interests or prejudices, and who would accomplish something for the people. It was like waiting for your dream prince—your lover—to come, like being in an ecstasy, expecting something good to happen.

It was not until 1937, during the Spanish Civil War, that I really thought about something political. I favored the Spanish Republicans and hated the fascist Franco, that *falangista* who wasn't interested in the people or their calamities. I did nothing about it, though, except read the newspaper every day. I was in Havana by then but I had no information and didn't know anybody who was in touch with the Republicans.

I hated Hitler too. He was surrounded by a lot of bad people. I believe he was crazy at the end, because sane people wouldn't have done what he did. The concentration camps were criminal. I didn't learn about them until after the war . . . the newsreels were horrifying. They shouldn't have treated the Jews like that, people who'd been driven out everywhere, but Hitler was their enemy and had no pity for them, and that's the truth. If you look around the world, you see that enemies are treated the same all over.

I didn't like Stalin, either. I considered him a "military boot," as we Cubans say, tough and authoritarian, a military man in the fullest sense of the word. He wasn't carrying on a true revolution for the people the way Fidel is. Nikita's policy was more democratic than Stalin's and would have unified the world more.

Fulgencio Batista was the man who sowed terror in Cuba, committing murders and all sorts of crimes. He took over power in 1952, two months before the election.[20] It meant that he was really chosen by the Army, not by the people, and that was a bad, dishonest thing. It never should have happened. If he'd been elected fairly and then turned out to be no good, at least the people couldn't say he'd been imposed on them.

People said that Batista's power had to come to an end. Groups gathered in the streets, and everywhere there were arguments about what should be done. The students marched in protest against his government and were beaten up and attacked with tear gas and fire hoses.

All these things upset me very much, but I finally became involved in politics because of my friend, Mario Ramón Ceballos,[21] who was an accountant for the General Enterprises Company. Here in Cuba everyone has his own motive for becoming a revolutionary—some were convinced by Fidel, others had trust in Camilo or Che. My motive was Mario.

I met Mario when I began to work for General Enterprises in 1951, while I was still selling sewing machines for Phillips. To sell on credit at Phillips, we had to investigate clients' finances and conduct to be able to guarantee them as responsible persons. We didn't sell to everybody. I had a client, a dancer at the Shanghai Theater, whom the Phillips Company wouldn't accept because, they said, she didn't have high moral standards. "Haven't you heard people talk of the Shanghai? It's a low theater," they told me.

I said, "Well, she may dance at the Shanghai for money, but on the block she's a very honest person and a good mother and she wants the sewing machine to make clothes for her children." But they insisted they couldn't accept her because of her bad moral conduct. Then they said, "Go and see Pereira. He might be willing to sell to her." Pereira sold furniture and was a subcontractor for General Enterprises, so I went to his place and he accepted my client. I guaranteed the payments.

Pereira also sold frigidaires; everywhere I looked I saw beautiful units. The man said, "Listen, if you're interested, I can let you have one on installments." I had a little trouble with Reinaldo, but we finally bought a frigidaire and I went to Pereira's office every month to make the payments. Then one day Pereira told me, "If you can get me sales, I'll give you a commission on each refrigerator and you can pay off yours that way." Well, I became a saleswoman for him then and there.

That's how I got to know Mario Ramón. He was one of the chief people in Pereira's office—he kept the books, the records of sales, the checks, and all that. I'd been selling refrigerators for almost a year and

20. The presidential elections scheduled for May, 1952, in which the *Auténticos,* party of incumbent President Prío, had nominated Carlos Hevia against the *Ortodoxos* candidate, Dr. Roberto Agramonte. Batista was a candidate without a party nomination.
21. One of the historical figures to whom we have given pseudonyms.

was getting a lot of commissions when Mario began to take me into his confidence. He told me Pereira was secretly involved with the *Ortodoxos,* Chibás's party, and was giving them money.[22]

"Oh," I thought, "this man will be using our money any day now and we'll be left high and dry." So I said, "You know, Mario, every time there's money coming to me, I wish you'd give me a check." After that, instead of letting my commissions accumulate, Mario would give me vouchers for 60 or 80 *pesos* and I'd apply them right away to what I owed on my frigidaire. I wanted to pay up as soon as I could because Reinaldo was always nagging me about this debt. I did pay every bit of it—my husband never put in a cent.

Mario was a wonderful boy, and very refined. Everybody who knew him said he was. He was responsible in his work and honest in his ideas, the kind of man who stood up for the workers and fought against wrongs. Once he even punched the manager in the face because of the man's methods, and from then on Mario Ramón was recognized as a good comrade who defended the poor.

At that time I don't think Mario Ramón or his comrades thought about communism, at least they never mentioned it. They worried about settling things in a good humane way, without coming to the point of communism. All Mario cared about was getting rid of Batista.

It was Mario Ramón who made me begin to care about the Revolution. He was inspired by the principles of the Twenty-sixth of July Movement and was involved in all their secret plans. He trusted me; he even gave me the telephone number of Haydée Santamaría's[23] house, where he met with Fidel and all the others, and I'd phone him when he was needed at the store. He had to be kept informed of all the sales, especially because it was installment buying. It was dangerous to belong to the underground and I never gave away anything Mario confided in me.

Because of Mario I knew about the plan to storm the Moncada garrison[24] just before it happened. You see, my next-door neighbor had bought some furniture on credit from the General Enterprises Company, but she hadn't paid for it and it was Mario's responsibility to reclaim it for the store. Since Fidel and the Rebels were leaving for Santiago de Cuba on Saturday, Mario came for the furniture on Friday. The following Sunday was July 26. Here in Havana they told everyone they were going to the regatta in Varadero, but they weren't going to any

22. The Cuban People's Party, founded in 1947 by Senator Eduardo Chibás (see Mónica, n. 20.) from a group of dissidents within the *Auténticos,* the party of President Grau San Martín. Fidel Castro was at one time affiliated with the *Ortodoxos,* but the Twenty-sixth of July Movement itself was organized independently of the party.
23. See Mónica, n. 21.
24. See Mónica, n. 11.

regatta. They were going to Santiago in Oriente and they had the plan for the Moncada attack all worked out.

Mario wanted to leave everything in order before taking such a step, because nobody knew how it would end. When he came to my neighbor's house to get the furniture, he stopped by to visit me. I was delighted and fixed him a grapefruit with a strawberry on top and he said, "This is the most delicious dish I've ever eaten." I guess he was a little sentimental.

Then he told me what they were going to do in Santiago. Imagine how I felt! I didn't think he had a chance. It seemed like a crazy dream that could never be realized. How could a small movement to overthrow the government begin by attacking a military garrison like the Moncada? It seemed impossible, a useless action. But I was mistaken. Though it failed and he and many others lost their lives, the spark was struck. Their attempt to improve the situation in Cuba remained a strong inspiration to our people.

It was a terrible blow for me that Sunday in 1953 when I read they'd been killed. My close friend Mario Ramón had become a martyr of the Revolution! That's when I really became a sympathizer of the Twenty-sixth of July Movement, a *patria o muerte*[25] revolutionary. My being a member of the poor working class had nothing to do with it. I'd have made the same decision had I been rich, if I had known Mario. That was crucial. Although I expected someone to turn up who could improve our lives, I never dreamed it would be Fidel. Mario's death woke me up. I said to myself, "If he died for this cause it must be something very good, therefore I too am willing to die for it."

With the storming of the Moncada the real struggle began. I was part of it because after Mario's death I pledged to do everything I could. Furthermore, I'd come to believe in the principles of the Revolution and I had faith that they'd win. From then on I cooperated with the Movement. The events of the Revolution itself convinced me even more, for if they hadn't been honest and good I would have had to break away.

After Moncada, when Fidel and the others were in jail on the Isle of Pines, I followed everything in the newspapers. I even saved the photographs of them the day Fidel and Raúl got out and came to Havana, each with his suitcase in hand. Then there were the meetings in Fidel's apartment and the *compañeros* who went to them, and all that. I knew every move they made. I remember when they left for Mexico, voluntarily, to prepare the invasion from there. Fidel knew it was more difficult to attack from inside Cuba because he was constantly being watched and persecuted.

I was full of confidence when Fidel and his men returned on the

25. "Fatherland or death," an expression used to characterize an ardent revolutionary.

Granma in 1956.[26] I believe he did the right thing, even though they were attacked and only a few of them were left. If he hadn't done what he did we wouldn't have been able to make any headway. We'd still be making compromises, trying to stay on the safe side just to keep from taking that one drastic step. And it had to be drastic because this country was an orphan in every way, poor in everything.

After Fidel went to the Sierra Maestra, Reinaldo and I got together with my father-in-law and other relatives who lived near us, to hear the broadcasts of *Radio Rebelde*. We played dominoes as an excuse if someone walked in on us. We knew the Batista government gave out false reports, because we learned from the Rebels that things were just the opposite of what the government said.

During the struggle my husband was afraid to attend meetings, although he was a sympathizer and a lifelong communist. He'd been a member of the Communist Party since 1937 or 1938, before I met him. He had his membership card and he'd attended meetings before the Batista presidency. He got out because he couldn't meet all their demands and at the same time support his family. He was still with the communists in his ideas, but as time went by he grew further and further away from them. Perhaps that's why he did nothing for the Twenty-sixth of July Movement. Or maybe he didn't think it was going to lead to communism. Anyway, he was a very cowardly man of no conviction, and he was afraid of Batista's persecution. I myself was not able to do much for the Movement because I lived under my husband's thumb. Had I not been married, I would have followed my heart and gone into the mountains.

The leader of the Twenty-sixth of July Movement for my zone was Rivas. My husband's youngest brother, Marcos, was the treasurer and a real revolutionary. He sold bonds and distributed pamphlets and *Revolución*, the paper that told what was going on in the Sierra. The pamphlets were passed from hand to hand among all the *compañeros*. I wasn't afraid to talk or to pass out a leaflet, and I told the *compañeros* what *Radio Rebelde* was saying. But I wasn't planting bombs or doing sabotage or things like that. Naturally, the more determined of us did, and the consequences were severe.

Once a *compañera* asked me to locate two boys hiding in a rented room so they could be warned that the police were after them. I looked in the rooming houses and everywhere, but it was no use. It wasn't until after they were killed that I learned they'd been living only two blocks from

26. *Granma* is the name of the launch that brought Fidel Castro and eighty-one other members of the Twenty-sixth of July Movement to Cuba from exile in Mexico. The *Granma* landed on Las Coloradas Beach in southwestern Oriente Province on December 2, 1956. The twelve survivors of the landing escaped to the Sierra Maestra and formed the nucleus of the Rebel Army.

my house. I was so furious at the police I threw on my clothes and started to go out, but Reinaldo stopped me.

In our neighborhood there were three secret meeting places: in Pepe's house, in Isidro's, and in Sixto's. They had to be kept secret or the *compañeros* would have been killed. Whenever there were meetings to train the Rebels in the use of weapons, the *compañeros* would notify me to keep an eye open for the police. I'd walk through the streets and if I noticed anything I'd warn the men. And they never were surprised. That's the way the struggle went on, until finally Fidel struck in the Sierra Maestra and the Revolution won out. Later, Sixto disagreed with its going communist and left for the United States. The rest of the *compañeros* stuck with Fidel.

When victory came, we hung out Twenty-sixth of July flags, scaring and surprising a lot of people. When they saw my flag they said, "How do you like that! Inocencia belongs to the Twenty-sixth." A group of us women began holding meetings at each other's houses, and when an order came to close all stores to prevent looting, our entire group went through the streets with flags, closing up the shops. The next step was to take over the police stations, so our group occupied the neighborhood station and stayed there every night until things returned to normal.

I was at home on January 8, 1959, when Fidel rode into the city. I had to see the whole thing on television because my husband wouldn't let me go out. I never went to any mass meetings or anything. Nor could I join the women's militia at that time because he didn't want me to stand guard. But I *was* a member of the Twenty-sixth of July from 1959 through 1961, and I *did* support the Revolution.[27]

The CDRs, the Committees for Defense of the Revolution, were set up on September 28, 1960.[28] Fidel told us we had to keep watch on the counterrevolutionaries because the enemy worked from inside. At first the CDRs practically didn't operate, because we had no idea how they were to function. Very few people were involved, about six or seven per block in most neighborhoods. Many just sat back and waited to see if the Revolution would win out or not, so they could go along with the winner. Anybody who wasn't a revolutionary kept quiet about it.

Some CDR people came around asking us housewives to join the women's militia to guard our own block, but that involved a certain amount of danger because guards were sometimes attacked and mur-

27. In 1961, the Twenty-sixth of July Movement, the old Communist Party (PSP), and all other revolutionary and socialist organizations, were incorporated into the ORI (*Organizaciones Revolucionarias Integradas*). A new alliance, PURS (*Partido Unificado de la Revolución Socialista*), succeeded ORI in 1963, before the founding of the new Communist Party in 1965.

28. See Pilar, n. 13.

dered. Guard duty was done in pairs, and Reinaldo objected to this partner and that, so there was no one I could do guard duty with. If I did it, it had to be with him. If anything happened on our block, I couldn't get up and go out unless he did. He wouldn't let me be active in anything. I felt I wasn't accomplishing much for the Revolution because of him. A lot of husbands still feel the way Reinaldo did then. There's plenty of jealousy, though most of the marriages are stable.

I heard about the Playa Girón attack on the radio. They announced that invaders had come into Las Villas Province through the Zapata Swamp. Our side mobilized the troops and then stopped broadcasting news. The three days that followed were terrible—we were completely cut off from them, without a word over the radio. Enemy planes had dropped bombs on Tejas Street before the invasion, but Reinaldo wouldn't let me go to the Plaza to see it. Then they announced on the radio that bombs had also been dropped somewhere in Miramar.[29]

I'd never seen war that close. I had terrible thoughts—I certainly was afraid! Nobody went to bed; we were all out on the street together, waiting. We knew how powerful the enemy was. They could wipe us out if they wanted to because Cuba is very small. It would be ridiculous not to admit it no matter how strong we were. I wasn't sure we were going to make it, though it wasn't really one country against another but a matter of Cubans against Cubans. True, they invaded under the protection of the Americans, but that's not the same as if the Americans wanted a war with us.

After the attack, the government sent men around to pick up anybody who had a car or who'd belonged to Batista's government. They had to watch carefully for people who might turn against the Revolution and cause other killings. So everybody suspected of not being for the Revolution was arrested and imprisoned. I knew a lot of the people who were arrested, including a man who'd been a police lieutenant under Batista. The neighbors disagreed about his arrest because he was old, but the ones who came to get him didn't let that stop them. They just said, "Here's a former military man and he has to be taken away." In my block, Eladio Zamora, the tailor, was taken. He'd never caused trouble but he did hang around with vagrants and counterrevolutionaries and was not integrated in the Revolution.

It was a bad situation. Women and whole families were taken away, which was unjust. They were all locked up for about a week. There were a lot of complaints about large numbers being packed together and not being fed. But, as a matter of fact, those of us on the outside didn't eat either. No one ever bothered to think about food. People were in a state of anxiety and nerves and there was such an atmosphere of insecurity

29. See Gracia, n. 21.

that they didn't know what they were doing. The people in prison were having a bad time but all of us suffered, especially those out there fighting.

The invasion came as a surprise, and at that time everybody was new and scared. Imprisonment was the only measure they thought of. We had to assume those people were guilty because we had no idea what their reaction was going to be. Now things are different. It's easy to tell who's against the Revolution, elections or no elections, because they request a visa to leave Cuba, or because they don't join any organizations and are isolated from all revolutionary activities. We know who everyone is, what he's liable to do, and who is incapable of harmful actions. Today, even if you're not with the Revolution, so long as you don't go against it, the Revolution won't go against you either. That has come with experience and maturity. If we know that a particular neighbor is not going to do anything, of what use is it to arrest him? But we *should* arrest known terrorists. Worse than imprisonment would have been a war among the people, because then innocent people would have been killed.

Nobody blamed Fidel for the war. People never said, "Fidel is deceiving us." No, nothing like that; everybody was behind him. And three days after the invasion we knew we'd won. In the days that followed, everyone was desperate to get news of relatives in the Army and to know what was going on. Finally we heard that two of our neighbors had been killed. When they brought back the bodies, I went to the wakes at the funeral parlor.

I hate war; it never settles anything. We didn't want war but we'd never accept defeat. If it had been announced that we had to fight the world, I think everybody would have come out and fought, even the children. Naturally, the minority against the Revolution wouldn't, but they can't move even a finger because they're watched everywhere.

I believe we should feel compassion for people on either side of the struggle at Playa Girón. Both we and the invaders were fighting for a cause each believed in. Those who died—all the young men on both sides who shouldn't have died—were equally mourned by their mothers and relatives. The men who came to kill us may have been impelled by beliefs they didn't stop to analyze. If they had, they would have realized that they had no reason to come.

After all, those who wanted to leave Cuba were allowed to. They went to countries where they could work and live in accordance with their own beliefs and ambitions, under a system they approved of. That's all right, but they shouldn't come here and force their ideas on us. We who stayed have done so willingly, knowing we'd have to make sacrifices.

No matter what division there is between us, the losses of both sides are irreparable. That's true in any war. The death of a Vietnamese and that of a young American soldier are equally tragic. As soldiers they're both doing what their countries order them to do. What makes it tragic is that there's no sense to it. Every country, including Cuba, should conform to its own way of life and settle its own problems, and not intervene in the affairs of any other nation.

After Playa Girón, vigilance was needed more than ever. A Party member, Federico Araya, was assigned to help our district reorganize the CDRs. He called an orientation meeting to decide what had to be done. Committees had been set up on a neighborhood or a block basis, but with a different Committee for each side of the street. That was a mistake, because there was always bad blood between the two Committees about who did what, who didn't, and so forth. There was no unity.[30] Then a new order came out to set up a single Committee for both sides of the street. These block Committees became the standard unit because the neighborhood level was too difficult to manage.

Well, Committees were appointed; I don't know whether it was by the Communist Party but Party members more or less predominated, because after the Revolution people from the Twenty-sixth of July Movement went back to their jobs and kept away from politics. So the old communists began to run the units and the Committees.[31]

In my barrio a boy named Patricio, who was married to a neighborhood friend of ours, organized us. First he spoke to me about joining the Committee, but I told him to come back later since Reinaldo was the one who decided our activities. He did come back, and Reinaldo and I joined as ordinary members with no special job assignment. At that time the only CDR officials were a chairman or president and a Vigilance officer, with members volunteering for guard duty.

The first big CDR activity was the lard census, which was the first food census in Havana.[32] Lard was rationed and the census had to be done to

30. The first CDRs had no set organizational base or structure. They were sometimes organized on a neighborhood level, sometimes on a block level, or in schools, factories, or other work centers. Richard Fagen reports that at the time of Playa Girón (April, 1961) there were 8,000 Committees across the country with a total of 70,000 members. After Playa Girón, the government set a goal of establishing 100,000 CDRs with an additional half-million members. The achievement of this goal was announced in August, 1961. However, the Committees still had no formal base structure, national organizational hierarchy, well-defined functions, or criteria for membership. (*The Transformation of Political Culture in Cuba*, pp. 74–75, 247 n. 14.)

31. The CDRs were being organized under the direction of the ORI (see n. 27), which, from its creation in the summer of 1961 until March, 1962, was largely controlled by the old-line communist Aníbal Escalante and associates from the old PSP. As David Booth has pointed out, the old Party members had organizational skills which were at a premium in the first chaotic years of organizing the new system. In March, 1962, Castro removed Escalante as head of the ORI and denounced him for using his office to strengthen the position of the old-line communists relative to members of the Twenty-sixth of July Movement. ("Neighbourhood Committees and Popular Courts," p. 35.)

32. Part of the "census of consumers," carried out by the CDR for MINCIN (Ministry of Domestic Trade) beginning in July, 1961. Rationing began in 1962.

find out how much of it would be needed. There was a shortage because we never had a hog-raising industry in Cuba; it was cheaper to import lard from the United States. So hog-raising had to be introduced and it wasn't easy. It took proper planning.

The census was quite complicated. It worked like this. After we set up a CDR, we'd tell the members, "Look, make a list of all the families living in each building on the block to show how many adults and children there are." All the available CDR members were sent from house to house to collect the information, and they'd turn in their lists at the neighborhood social center where the group heads met. If there was no CDR on a certain street and no possibility of setting one up, those of us in charge would have to go there ourselves and register each family.

The lists were then handed over to the local grocery stores to which the families were assigned.[33] Each individual was allowed 1 pound of lard per month, and with this list the warehouses knew that in one store they needed 300 pounds, in another 200 pounds, and so on. Sometimes there'd be a surplus in one store and a shortage in another, and we'd have to juggle the lard to distribute the ration properly.

The Revolution began new fronts or campaigns as it required them. After the lard census we were busy with the vaccination drive. Later the Public Health Front was organized. It had both a clean-up and educational function. Then an education campaign was set up to deal with children who were absent from school, and I participated in that too. We visited parents to discuss the reasons for the absence.

I really began working with the CDR when they organized the sectionals. My sectional was a small one with thirty-seven CDRs. There were also government-appointed district directorates. A district was very large and covered many *repartos* or neighborhoods.[34] When they opened the sectional headquarters, I went and cleaned up the house. It had belonged to a fellow who left the country. I cleaned it, helped put in the lights, and made that place look nice and neat. Like always, wherever I go I like things to look pretty. I wasn't really active yet because Reinaldo didn't want me to hold office. But I was always there anyway, helping them in any work they were doing, like making decorations or cleaning up the streets.

33. Cuban citizens were required to register at one neighborhood store of their choosing, where all food shopping had to be done. This requirement existed because most basic food items were rationed, and to facilitate the correct distribution of goods from the central warehouses, the state had to know the exact number of people who would shop at each store.

34. By 1962 the national directorate of the CDR had established a hierarchy of 6 provincial directorates, 150 district directorates, and 1,360 sectional directorates. Each Committee had a president and officers (*responsables*) in charge of each of the CDR fronts. These workers, as well as the coordinators of the sectionals, were volunteers. The district coordinators were paid, full-time cadre. (Fagen, *The Transformation of Political Culture in Cuba,* pp. 76–77.)

I helped organize the new block CDR,[35] and I called it the Mario Ramón Ceballos CDR after my martyred friend. Reinaldo was the president, and the corner groceryman, Abelardo Díaz, was in charge of Vigilance. The Committee met in my house. It began with nine members: Reinaldo Serrano, Inocencia Acosta, Carmelita Flores, Antonio Ruíz, Juan Alonso, Isabel Martínez, Josefina Santos, Adela Carrera, and Francisca Santiago. Antonio Ruíz was one of the first neighbors to join, and we had to let him even though he'd voted for Batista.

I devoted myself to the work of the CDR and was always ready to carry out any new directive or orientation that was issued. I had plenty of time; selling on commission had been abolished and I'd sold my last frigidaire two months after the triumph of the Revolution. I just looked after the house and did some sewing, although we had enough with what my husband earned and we no longer needed to save money for a house or for our old age or any such thing.

In 1962 I was indirectly involved in the Literacy Campaign through Reinaldo's sister's children, who lived next door. I practically brought up those kids. The boy was only eleven when he went to Camaguey as a volunteer teacher, but he was attending a parochial school and knew a lot. The same with the girls: they were in a convent school and very advanced, so they volunteered for the literacy brigades and were sent to Cárdenas.

We women got whatever supplies were available and sent things to them. They wanted a rag doll for each of the twenty-one little girls in the rural hamlet where they were teaching and we had to find the cloth, make and send the dolls, pick up clothing . . . there was always some task for us. Even Reinaldo thought my work for the Literacy Campaign was worthwhile, but he was indifferent to everything and really didn't pay much attention to it.

We realized that the children were risking their lives in that faraway place. It was terrible when those young teachers were killed by the counterrevolutionaries.[36] Imagine how worried we were. Sometimes the parents visited their children, but it was a difficult journey on horseback and across rivers. When the children returned, I was there with the parents and a whole group of neighbors to welcome them.

35. When Castro removed Escalante as head of the ORI, CDRs across the country were directed to hold "self-criticism" sessions to purge themselves of all members who had joined for opportunistic reasons, and to recruit new members. By the end of 1962, the Committees had been reorganized with 400,000 new members. The issuance of membership cards was also begun as a further method of tightening the organization of the CDRs. (*Ibid.*, pp. 77–78.)

36. Conrado Benítez, eighteen, and Manuel Ascunce Domenech, sixteen, both killed by counterrevolutionaries in the Escambray Mountains of Las Villas Province. Benítez, killed at the beginning of the campaign, is one of the most famous of all the Revolution's martyrs. Some of the literacy brigades trained after his murder were named for him, as were many schools, camps, projects, and work brigades.

I joined the militia the year of the Literacy Campaign. My training was in Civil Defense, for hurricanes or for giving aid in case of attack. For two months I was taught to use firearms, but they kept suspending classes because the militiamen and women had to go cut sugar cane.

Reinaldo's basic training was longer and more intensive than mine. He's still a permanent member of the militia and must go for additional training every time there are new weapons or a new program. He's in a combat battalion that participates in regular military mobilizations.

I was in the mobilization during the October missile crisis in 1962. It wasn't a regular mobilization. All we did was gather in one house, on the alert for orders from the CDR sectional office. It was a very dangerous time, setting us all on edge. It seems to me that the Russians didn't handle it well. As a great power the Soviet Union ought to have entered into discussions with other powers and declared that our rights had to be respected, with missiles or without. If not, they should have been ready to defend us in an attack. But Fidel took a strong line to show that nobody could tell him what to do.

I don't think the rockets would have settled very much for us in any case. If the United States wanted to, they could destroy Cuba in five minutes, whether we had rockets or not. What are we compared to them? If we were able to settle matters without getting shot at or without us shooting, so much the better. If only it hadn't turned out to be a motive for keeping us from defending ourselves! Better if they had never brought those missiles in! I'm not interested in rockets but I *am* concerned about respect.

We should try to get Russia to prevent war and eliminate the differences between Cuba and the United States. The American people have nothing to do with the government. There are people in the United States just like us who don't want war. Nobody wants war. We'd like everything to be settled everywhere in peace. I'd like to see Cuba develop with everybody helping us and with us helping everybody else, within our limitations.

When I first tried to join the Federation of Cuban Women in 1963, I had trouble being accepted. I was told by a *compañera* that to be a member in good standing I had to take a turn at guard duty. So I said, "Suppose my husband doesn't let me?" The *compañera* replied, "Well, then you can't join." She allowed me to contribute 1 *peso* a month as a voluntary donation, but wouldn't grant me membership. The fact is, this comrade was politically uneducated and deficient in understanding other people's problems. Furthermore, as I learned from a schoolteacher member of the Federation, she was mistaken in denying me membership, because only those who can freely stand guard are required to do it. The schoolteacher then made me a member of the Federation.

As a volunteer for both the Federation and the CDR, I've always gone to the Sunday activities of both groups—the CDR in the morning and the Federation in the afternoon or at night. But all along I've been more devoted to the CDR, which is highly political. Just the same, I'm the secretary-general of my delegation in the Federation and of the whole bloc,[37] too. I like it because it has an Education Front. Finances and education are the activities I'm always involved in. In fact, when I went back to school, I was the president of the school board and was in charge of raising all the money and getting the school supplies.

My personal affinities aside, I must admit that though some of the CDR and Federation fronts are the same, the Federation's work is more effective because it always has some specific, practical purpose in mind, like helping a comrade, or sewing kitchen cloths and aprons for the nursery schools.[38] Maybe because it's composed entirely of women, the Federation has greater unity than the CDR.

In 1964 the CDRs were reorganized again. The treasury was formed at that time and they started to collect membership dues.[39] Everybody felt that I should be in charge of the Finance Front and become the treasurer of both my CDR and the sectional, but Reinaldo objected. I was on the slate for two months before he finally gave in and let me accept the office.

None of the thirty-seven block CDRs in my sectional had a treasurer, and I went to each CDR to select them. It wasn't difficult since I knew practically all the mothers—that's why almost all the treasurers were women. My selection was based on my own personal judgment of them, particularly of their sense of responsibility, not on whether they were revolutionaries. Almost nobody in the barrio was revolutionary then; we were all beginning from scratch.

I went to each likely person and said, "Listen, I want you to be treasurer of your CDR." Among those I chose were Eva Mejías and Miranda Madrazo, whom we call Musa. She's black. They're both married and live with their mothers, who take care of the children. Neither Eva nor Musa has a job so they can devote time to the sectional. They were the type of woman I looked for. They were both good treasurers.

When I finished selecting all the treasurers, I sent in their names. Then I asked each for a list of their CDR members so I could apply for

37. The organizational level above a delegation. In 1969 the FMC's 1,192,843 members were divided into 23,990 delegations, 4,088 blocs, and 8 projects. (*Granma Weekly Review*, Jan. 25, 1970, p. 5.)

38. The overlap in function between the CDR and the FMC is mainly in the areas of education, public health, and recruiting volunteers for productive labor.

39. In 1964 old membership cards were turned in and new ones issued. These cards were updated by issuance of membership stamps, receipts for dues paid. Dues were collected monthly by the *responsable* of the Finance Front.

enough membership stamps; there were 752 members in the sectional and they all paid me their dues. It took me just one week to settle the whole problem and turn in the lists. Then I called on each CDR twice a month, once to bring them the stamps, the second time to collect the money.

Mine was the best coordinated campaign and I was credited with 752 dues-paying members. Of course they were already members, but I spoke to everyone personally to convince them to pay dues. Anyway, I came out first and they made me a Vanguard Worker in Finance and, in the presence of all the treasurers and members, gave me a testimonial and awarded me a diploma.

Naturally Reinaldo was there. I never went anywhere, even to buy panties, without him trailing after me. And as usual, he was jealous because everybody liked me more than they liked him. Of course! He never had a smile or a good word for anybody, but just ask around about Inocencia and everybody will have something nice to say. I was toasted with soft drinks, presented with a corsage, and asked to speak. I got up and said that the prize was not really mine, that it belonged to the thirty-seven treasurers who made it possible to fulfill the task. I still have a copy of the official programs drawn up that day. It was the only testimonial given. I was very moved, although it wasn't the first testimonial I've received in my life. I've always had them in school, at El Encanto, in the CDR—everywhere I've worked, I've been singled out.

As a reward, I was shifted to the CDR district directorate. The day I got the greatest kick was when Marta, the district coordinator, came to the house to tell my husband that because of my good work the district needed me. I was in the kitchen washing dishes and heard him tell her he'd think it over. I knew he was opposed to it. He wasn't a person who'd put himself out for me or for anybody. When he was called on to join the Party in 1962 or 1963 he said he couldn't because of his health. He didn't mind becoming a tobacco worker when his job as a taxi dispatcher was eliminated, but the only productive labor he volunteered for at his work center was office work—typing, writing, filing papers—which he enjoyed. He also did the required guard duty at the factory, but he never went to cut sugar cane, and of course he objected to everything I undertook.

Reinaldo said he wanted me to work only at the block level, near home. We began to argue because I felt it was my duty as a revolutionary to work for the district or for whatever came up. I was very absorbed in the Revolution by then and wanted to move ahead in its ranks. So I told Marta I'd accept. I was sent to the district and I worked for them for two or three years.

In spite of all I had to do, I never neglected my housework. Before leaving home, I prepared breakfast and dinner and pressed Reinaldo's clothes. But nothing satisfied him, and I went through a very difficult time for two years, from 1964 to 1966, trying to do the right thing in both places.

At that time the CDRs were truly revolutionary and carried out whatever task they were assigned. Now it takes more work to get the members going, because those who joined recently don't cooperate with the same spirit, they merely follow along. But I've always worked with great zeal and I've had many interesting experiences.

I remember particularly a clean-up competition which generated much enthusiasm.[40] The idea was to demonstrate that for hygienic reasons cans and refuse should not be strewn around the street. All of us went to a paint factory with the Public Health *responsable* and got green paint. We painted the big garbage cans, including the covered ones, on every block in the zone, and the big containers along the boulevard. After that we bought cloth remnants from a textile factory and made 300 small and medium-sized flags for the garbage cans and 195 big flags for the big containers. It was very colorful and there was a lot of enthusiasm. All the residents dumped their garbage into the cans and the garbage squad came and collected it. It was lovely, though the enthusiasm didn't last long. Not all the comrades have the proper spirit.

To my mind there's something basically wrong with the way things are organized. As soon as a comrade distinguishes himself in an activity somewhere, he's moved to another place that's in bad shape. I don't like that because his original area just backslides, though some people say that cadres have to be moved to be developed. But what good is it to develop cadres if other things go bad and get out of control?

As a Vanguard Worker I personally suffered from this approach when I was shifted to the district level. There were nine paid functionaries, each with a special job, and several of us volunteers. Those on a salary lived very well and ate heartily but they were really exploiting the Revolution. All they did was show up at headquarters and throw their weight around. In other words, I had to work with a group of parasites who collected their pay but didn't work.

Only four of these nine district workers were Party members. They were Rubén Araujo and Adalberto Cevallos, in charge of Finance, Clemente Nieves, organizer, and Osvaldo Chávez, in charge of Revolutionary Instruction. I found out later that before the Revolution Osvaldo had defrauded the Party by stealing Party funds for his women and for drunken sprees. And now this comrade was directing us! The

40. An emulation, a technique widely used in all production units and mass organizations in Cuba to improve worker performance. In an emulation, workers do not compete against one another but work to fulfill a goal, standard, or objective which they often help to set.

other district workers were from the provincial and regional CDRs and their salaries were paid by the provincial directorate.

There used to be two elements here: members of the Twenty-sixth of July Movement, who had no selfish interests, and the old Communist Party members, which is the same as saying people who were insincere. They made no sacrifices and I for one never had any faith in them. The communism they practiced was merely a form of organized politics, not true socialist humanism. As soon as the Revolution won they wanted to take over everything and wipe out the Twenty-sixth of July Movement. From the day I started working with these full-time professionals, I kept an eye on what they were doing. I wrote everything down, figuring that some day history would tell.

These men were paid according to what they'd earned in their previous jobs. For instance, if they were taken out of the cigarette industry where they made 300 *pesos* a month, that's what they were paid for their CDR work. However, it wasn't because of their salaries that they were living better than others. They had ration books like everybody else, but they ate in restaurants and pizzerias and charged everything to organizational expenses. They went everywhere in taxis, or they exploited a comrade who had a car, letting him put in the gasoline to drive them around. If they paid for it, they'd turn in the gasoline receipt and charge it to the organization. They never took a bus or walked—it would have been too much of a sacrifice for them.

Those nine men simply went too far. They lived only for themselves and were abusing their positions. For example, they were constantly draining off money that they never accounted for. The CDRs had a certain amount for expenses—official ceremonies, testimonials, buying books—and they raised money for these and other projects by giving dinners and fiestas. In addition, those district people were always asking the sectionals for money for something. If 100 *pesos* were collected, 40 would be spent and nobody ever knew what happened to the other 60. That's what I observed all the time. These men were spending right and left while they sat back ordering people around, not thinking of going out to work with the comrades.

The house of Araujo, one of the functionaries, had been damaged in 1963 in Hurricane Flora and was close to collapse. The neighbors said that later he finished knocking it down himself, because as district coordinator another house would be built for him. There was a meeting and all the CDRs were requested to donate money to build Araujo a house or to help with building materials, steel rods, cement, or anything usable. Besides that, on Sundays all the other coordinators contributed their personal physical labor.

One Sunday afternoon, when I arrived for guard duty at district headquarters, I saw thirty-five bags of cement. I said to my *compañera,*

Celina Rosas, another good boot-licker, "Isn't it nice that we finally have the cement to fix up the district office? This is a sign that they're beginning to spend money on something useful."

She said, "No, that cement is for Araujo's house."

"What do you mean, for Araujo?" I asked. Here, I thought, was one more proof of their wrongdoing. It was impossible to get cement anywhere; they must have requisitioned it and carted it over in a truck, claiming that it was to fix up the district office.

Among the comrades there was a lot of dissatisfaction with the goings-on. They grumbled, but most of our revolutionaries are still not mature enough to come out with the truth at a given moment. Various *compañeros* came to me and said, "Listen, Inocencia, you're on the inside; explain why they're collecting money for Araujo's house. What's it about?" All I knew was that it was dishonest. Had they been collecting for a school, a hospital, or a needy family, I'd have been delighted! But they shouldn't be taking people's money to re-build the house of a single individual, coordinator or not.

Then, one day a beautiful set of office furniture was delivered to the district office. It had cabinets, a desk, a swivel chair, and an easy chair. It must have belonged to some rich man and should have gone to *Recuperación de Bienes.*[41] But Osvaldo took the old furniture and switched it for the new set. The way he perched himself like a king in that easy chair you'd think he'd never sat in one. But there was no paper or document authorizing that furniture for the district office, and as far as I'm concerned he was stealing it and cheating the Revolution. The same thing happened with some typewriters that had been brought in by *Recuperación de Bienes.* No accounting was ever asked for, and I'd still like to know whether or not the coordinators were authorized to keep them.

In addition to being dishonest, these nine paid functionaries were inefficient. There was one school that had eighteen unused desks, and there was another school with no desk for the teacher. When I brought up the problem, I was told all the desks were needed where they were. A lot of things like that were going on!

Then a dinner was held to raise money to make improvements in the district office, which was located in an old school building that had been flooded by rain. I was filled with enthusiasm for the project and even brought my own dishes, also sheets to use as tablecloths, so everything would look nice. The dinner was successful, netting over 450 *pesos,* but the money disappeared. Misspent, I suppose, but that actually amounts to stealing. My spirit was crushed; it was the last straw. I reported the incident to my superior, but my complaint got no further because his

41. The agency for confiscation of property of emigrants, or recovery of property regarded by the state as unjustly gained.

hands weren't clean either. Time went by and nothing happened. The money never reappeared.

The Party has a policy of evaluating paid officials and it's one's civic duty to say if a mistake has been made. The truth had to be told, so I made a direct complaint. As a result of my accusations, a meeting was called and fifty or sixty people from all the Committees in the district were there. I can still visualize the scene. The Party comrade said, "I want you people to tell me what happened. Is it true that a plenary session was held here in the courtyard to ask the sectional coordinators for money to build Araujo's house?" There was silence. They all kept their mouths shut because corruption was so widespread that nobody was in a position to denounce anybody else. Finally I raised my hand, and then Adalberto the treasurer, who had asked for the contributions, said, "Yes, *compañero,* it's true, because we in the directorate agreed that the house was in such bad condition."

Everybody else kept quiet after that, but when my turn came I said, "Yes, comrade, a meeting was held but the directorate didn't consult us at all. If a house was to be built it should have been for the 400 *compañeros* whose shacks had been demolished and who were put up in Unit 14." Unit 14 was an old police station converted into a tobacco factory, and then into accommodations for many families after the hurricane. I went on to ask the comrade investigator what *he* thought of collecting money for one man when there were so many in need. I said, "Listen, you people don't know half of what's going on here."

He said, "Keep talking, Inocencia. Speak up and get everything off your chest."

I had a lot more things to say and that was the moment to do it. Well, I told them I had nothing personal against *compañero* Araujo, that my quarrel was with the district coordinator. Then I brought up the matter of the missing funds. "Right now," I said, "in the presence of the Party, I want the responsible *compañeros* to tell what they did with the 450 *pesos* raised at the dinner to fix up the district office."

They said, "That money was used to pay for literature sent to all the CDRs in the district." But they did it without the support or permission of the workers in the other fronts, who should be informed about how the money is to be used. When money is taken and not accounted for, that's embezzlement, I said.

I also criticized the preparation of falsified monthly work charts sent to the provincial office. Two days before the deadline, the 20th of the month, the functionaries would add extra figures to round out the numbers, to make it say 400 of this and 400 of that. It was all a lie. They were deceiving Fidel. And paid officials ought to justify their salaries, I said. I got it all out in the open—how they ate in restaurants, the money they spent, everything. How I, a volunteer worker, would never take a cent for bus fare or a piece of bread and guava because I felt the Revolution inside me.

Rubén Araujo was present at the meeting and I said it all to his face. In fact, he knew what I was going to say beforehand and he told me that somebody had to. Even he agreed about the immorality of their actions. Imagine! I guess the whole *reparto* was with me. But Araujo and the others I accused had the idea I'd been put up to it, that I wasn't acting on my own. They never thought me capable or brave enough to say all those things. I have courage when I need it. Why shouldn't I? When you speak the truth you fear nobody.

When the meeting was over, the Party comrade said, "Are you in agreement with what *compañera* Inocencia has declared here? If so, say something." There was dead silence, until finally Leonora Téllez, who had always been with me and was a 100 percent revolutionary, jumped up. It wasn't an easy thing to do, there was applause, and I was very, very moved.

Well, the corrupt ones were weeded out one by one, until they were all eliminated as leaders. What I don't agree with is that they're still members. The functionaries were just moved upstairs or placed under surveillance. They received no other punishment and that's what I didn't like then and don't like now. Others say, "No, they're still revolutionaries," but I say that a revolutionary who's guilty of such an error should at least be sent to a work farm or thrown out of his job. Imagine what kind of an example they set! And although they said it wouldn't happen, a year later they were back again as CDR functionaries. New Party comrades came to organize and direct, but Osvaldo Chávez stayed on in the district directorate, continuing to manipulate things for his own benefit.

By the end of 1965 or the beginning of 1966, it became obvious that some leaders at the national level were up to monkey business. You can fool a person just so long, then you can't get away with it anymore. Ultimately there's no deceiving Fidel. He realized that deception and dirty work were going on, and one after another he got rid of the old Party militants, all big wheels. *Bam, bam, bam . . .* out! The top ones first. He threw out Escalante, then José Matar, the national director of the CDRs, who had stocked up on supplies for his personal use and on hams and liquor from INIT.[42] Matar was barred from all organizations and

42. After Escalante was removed from ORI in 1962, Castro assigned him to a job in Moscow. When Escalante returned in 1964 he was given a minor administrative position, and over the next two years he apparently tried to build an opposition faction from the remainder of the old PSP. José Matar Frayne, who was associated with Escalante and the PSP, was dismissed as head of the CDRs and removed from the Central Committee in 1966, after a disagreement with Armando Hart over the future development of the Committees. Escalante was accused of errors in domestic policy and of working too closely with the U.S.S.R. In 1968 he was tried and sentenced to fifteen years in prison. (Thomas, *Cuba: The Pursuit of Freedom*, pp. 1458–59, 1468–69; Booth, "Neighbourhood Committees and Popular Courts," pp. 39–40.) INIT is the *Instituto Nacional de la Industria Turística* (National Institute of the Tourist Industry).

the CDRs were compelled to reorganize.[43]

Sure, Fidel fired the dishonest comrades at the national level. One by one they were expelled from the Communist Party and lost forever their right to be militants. But in places like my district? Maybe Fidel never even heard about my complaint because nobody came in from outside. Here the local leaders judge one another, then they judge the volunteers. The cases never get to the higher authorities so it all remains in the family. Thieves judging thieves.

All in all, I was very angry and disillusioned. These things caused me much suffering and affected my life deeply. I still feel cheated. What upsets me most was that the money had been collected in good faith from poor people. If their leaders did such things and weren't punished, I'd like to know why. Those men are still collecting their salaries and I'm sure they're stealing besides.

I haven't lost my enthusiasm for the Revolution and for the block CDR. After all, the government can't be expected to know every little detail in the lower echelons. Many of the errors were simply due to inexperience or lack of knowledge and to people being accustomed to a different way of living. Rarely have wrong things, such as the misuse of funds, been done deliberately in bad faith, and these weren't counterrevolutionary, merely dishonest. Not that I condone it. But I'm sure that the Central Committee has eliminated all personnel involved in injustice at every level. Had they punished only those on the lower levels, I wouldn't have liked it.

Just now I'm president of my CDR. There are twenty-seven members; only eight people on the block don't belong. The many contacts I'd made while selling appliances turned out to be very useful. Everybody in the barrio knows me. When the judges for the People's Courts[44] were elec-

43. In 1966 the district- and sectional-level organizations were abolished, and a new sectional structure (organized on the level of a *municipio* in rural areas), was created. In 1969 the structure was, from the top down: national directorate, provincial directorates (6, plus Isle of Pines); regionals (45); sectionals (360); zones (5,609), and base Committees (65,943). CDRs in work centers were abolished, making the block the sole organizational base and ending the practice of dual membership (work center and block CDRs). The reorganization was accompanied by a new recruitment drive, and by the early 1970s the CDRs had over 4 million members. Booth says, "One advantage of the new system was that it permitted CDR organs to establish direct liaison with equivalent units of government ministries, mass organizations, and the PCC." ("Neighbourhood Committees and Popular Courts," pp. 42–44.)

44. The *Tribunales Populares* were neighborhood courts, first established in Havana on an experimental basis in 1966 to hear minor civil and criminal cases involving "antisocial behavior" (e.g. petty theft, drunkenness, disorderly conduct, juvenile delinquency, health and sanitation code violations). The Courts were empowered to impose sentences of up to 180 days' imprisonment. The cases were heard by a panel of three lay judges who are popularly elected at the community level, after nomination by the CDR or the party. In 1974 the People's Courts were incorporated into Cuba's new judicial system. (*Granma Weekly Review*, Feb. 19, 1974, p. 3.)

ted, I was number one, the very first in my barrio to be chosen. I couldn't accept, though, because being a judge involved a lot of duties which Reinaldo wouldn't allow me to undertake. Those People's judges sometimes have to preside over a trial until the small hours of the morning. But oh, how I'd have loved to accept! It's too late now, that stage is past. They've already given the course of instruction and graduated a batch of judges, so if I wanted to become a judge I'd have to wait for the next stage.

The way the CDR is organized now, each sectional and zone has a coordinator and an organizer.[45] The organizer keeps track of the number of CDR members, the local CDR presidents, and whether the CDRs do or don't have money. It's her task to organize and coordinate the political activities and to exercise control. The coordinator must be alert to everything happening in the *reparto*. Her duties include attending district-level orientation sessions whenever there are new tasks. Following these orientations, presidents of the CDRs are called to the sectional office for a meeting and are told the priorities and advised how to accomplish the different jobs.

After that, the CDR presidents call a meeting at the block level and say, for example, "Next Sunday we must collect bottles and jars," or "clean up the streets," or "get a blood donation from every CDR member, or at least from four or five members without fail." In addition to organizing volunteer work, they recruit people to do productive labor.

The CDR zone coordinator and organizer are elected in a plenary assembly of all the block Committee members in the zone. The local CDR president tries to get his block Committee to attend the meeting in a group. Once in the assembly, suppose I say, "I nominate Eva Mejías." Then I'm asked, "Why do you nominate Eva Mejías?" I'd answer, "Well, because I've known her a long time and she's been a Committee member long enough. I also think she has the qualities necessary to be a good coordinator. She's young and enthusiastic and has the capacity to work on the zone level."

After that, everybody in favor of Eva Mejías is asked to raise his hand. If a lot of people raise their hands, they know she has a majority. If only a few do, two or three more nominations are made. All the nominees agree on basic things anyway, so they're only asked if they'll accept the nomination. The assembly discusses them and then they vote.

These elections are held whenever necessary. Suppose, for instance, that Eva Mejías has been coordinator for two or three years and then begins to lose interest, misses a lot of meetings, doesn't send anybody to do volunteer work on Sundays, falls behind in the assigned tasks—in short, has lost her enthusiasm. The superior organization, the sectional,

45. See n. 43.

then meets with the members of the zone's executive committee and says, "Look, Eva, we want to know why your zone isn't functioning as it should."

Eva might answer, "Well, the truth is, my child has been sick lately" or "I'm not in very good health." Then she's told, "In that case, Eva, we must find someone to substitute for you." A new plenary is called with the explanation, "Tonight there's a plenary assembly to elect a new coordinator because Eva feels ill (or whatever) and can no longer do the work she's been doing."

If a block CDR is not functioning well, Coordination calls a meeting of all the members to see what the trouble is. If the CDR president is responsible for the difficulties, the neighbors may decide that he or she should no longer hold that post, and a new president would then be elected.

Chapter Four

My Barrio

Barrio Santa Isabel is a very nice, peaceful working-class neighborhood with little violence and not much noise. Boys will shout when they're let out of school but you never hear the adults. It's so quiet that if anybody oversteps the bounds we all know it immediately. The streets are safe at any hour of the day or night. Sometimes I go home alone at 2:30 or 3:00 in the morning and I'm not a bit scared. In the wintertime the people are all asleep by 8:00 o'clock, just like a country town. Some of them don't even know how to get to downtown Havana; they travel on the bus within the *reparto* but they get lost if they go too far away.

Guard duty goes on throughout the entire zone to prevent robbery and other misdeeds. Everybody from the age of fourteen on is eligible to stand guard, though only exceptionally responsible teen-agers are ever assigned.

The first tour of guard duty, from 7:00 P.M. to midnight, is carried out by women. The second tour, from midnight to 5:00 A.M., is always done by men. At first there were guard posts on each block, but now we patrol several blocks at a time. This type of guard is never armed. If an assault occurs, we simply yell and the neighbors come out at once. Someone notifies the two people on alert at the special telephone in the zone office, and they call the police patrol. There are also guards at the block Committee office and special patrols—one if a man, two if they're women—who make the rounds to check with those standing guard.

One never sees policemen on the beat anymore. They used to be all over the place but now radio-equipped patrol cars circulate day and night. We've never had any criminal incidents in this barrio. We did have a fire in the grocery store once but it wasn't intentional, just plain stupidity. A grocery clerk tried to get rid of cockroaches in the frigidaire by pouring alcohol inside and setting a match to it. The electric wires caught fire. Those new girl clerks don't know a thing about the job.

Stealing is something Cubans have never accepted. God help anyone who should touch our belongings! And nowadays it's really extraordinary for someone to steal—it's simply not permitted. When our neighbor Máximo Meléndez was arrested, all the neighbors approved. They knew he was a thief and was bound to be caught. As for delinquency, well, one day at daybreak a young black fellow stole some chickens belonging to different neighbors. A policeman caught him and called the police patrol, who took him away. The neighbors had to go to the police station to claim their chickens, and the thief probably got thirty days in jail or on a prison farm.

Before the Revolution there were only two schools in my barrio, one public and one private, and very few children went to either. Now we have seven primary schools, each with a kindergarten, as well as a magnificent center run by the Worker-Peasant Schools. The center is a school for children by day and for adults at night.

In our barrio there are three *círculos infantiles,* which are nursery schools for infants and preschool children of working mothers.[46] There are also two *jardines infantiles* for preschool children.[47] These schools are small because not many housewives in my barrio go to work, and the ones who do are mostly black. Nursery schools are something new brought by the Revolution. Before that, we didn't even know what they were. All these new schools are a great and wonderful change for us. Whenever a rich family went to the United States and left one of those big comfortable old houses, the Ministry of Education had priority over it. If the house met the necessary requirements, it was turned into a school when one was needed. That shows how much the Revolution cares about education.

There are two parks in our barrio, one fixed up very nicely, the other for children to skate in. The Street Plan[48] for my neighborhood is set up a block away from my house. In the Street Plan, when Children's Week or Christmas or the Day of the Three Kings or any other special children's occasion comes around, a wide street is closed at both ends and

46. The *círculos infantiles,* children's circles or nursery schools, are part of a nationwide child-care center program under the jurisdiction of the Women's Federation since 1961. The *círculos* accept children from age forty-five days up to five years. The service, intended primarily for working mothers, has been free since January, 1967. In 1969 there were 44,245 children enrolled in 364 *círculos,* with thirty additional *círculos* under construction. (Figures quoted by Clementina Serra, former national director of the *círculos infantiles,* in *Granma,* July 4, 1969, p. 3.)

47. The *jardines infantiles,* a simpler, less structured, less costly type of nursery school, was established under separate direction in Havana in 1965. Consisting of a one-room prefabricated school built in a park or garden, the program was basically one of supervised outdoor free play. It accepted children from eighteen months to five years of age and also gave preference to those whose mothers were working. There were 164 *jardines* in 1968, mostly in Havana. (Ruth M. Lewis, unpublished study of the *jardines infantiles.*) In 1971 there were 178 *jardines* serving 6,000 children and the system had been incorporated into the FMC program. (Marvin Leiner, with Robert Ubell, *Children Are the Revolution: Day Care in Cuba* (New York: Viking Press, 1974), p. 106.)

48. See Gracia, n. 33.

parties are held for all the neighborhood children. Sometimes the children go to visit another neighborhood and vice versa. There may be 100, 200, 300 children—it's always increasing. This plan works very well because the *compañeras* of the Women's Federation take a lot of interest in it.

At the end of the school year the children give exhibitions and amateur shows in the schools. I participated in these programs before the Revolution and even more enthusiastically afterward, and I've gotten to know all the parents and pupils. I've never performed—I'm too shy—but I've always enjoyed organizing them, helping with the decorations, obtaining corsages for the girls, and so on. One school year I made all fifty-six corsages. Other times I arranged to get a piano, a singer, and a pianist to accompany him.

The two movie theaters in the barrio charge 40 or 50 *centavos,* as they always did. On Sunday mornings and sometimes during the week, children can go to the movies free. During Children's Week they also have a free afternoon show from 2:00 to 4:00.

Our barrio no longer has a drugstore because the only one we had burned down. Now we have to walk many blocks to get to the nearest drugstore. We do have two hardware stores and a barbershop, and on every corner of the barrio there's a grocery store. The grocery stores were expropriated by the government; the ex-owners continued working in groceries, but not in the ones they'd owned. They probably resent it though they don't express their feelings openly. A certain percentage of the value of the business was supposed to be paid to the owners but I'm not sure they ever received it. And even if they did, they could only be employees in their own stores. Imagine! They could never be with the Revolution—nobody could who'd lost his land and properties. But the storekeepers who were revolutionaries had voluntarily turned over their stores long before the government began expropriating them.

The four or five laundries in my barrio still exist but they no longer wash clothes. They just pick them up and send them to be washed elsewhere, causing a certain amount of discontent because it takes longer to get your laundry back. In the past, each laundry had a smaller work load and it could be done with hardly any wait at all.

At night there's plenty of light in the streets, though every now and then the lights go off for a little while. We pay for electricity in our homes but it's much cheaper than before. Even so, some people let four or five months go by without paying their electric bills. Then, of course, their electricity is cut off.

Water is clean and plentiful in Santa Isabel, and we have it day and night. Garbage is now collected without charge every day at 8:00 A.M., even on Sunday. The streets are much cleaner than they used to be, although street-cleaning has been a little disorganized lately because of the sugar harvest.[49] If there's garbage in the streets because the street cleaner's truck broke down or the personnel had to work at something else, the CDR members gather up and burn the garbage to keep away infection and rats.

We had medical services in the barrio even before the Revolution. An emergency clinic built by Batista's government was moved to a large estate and is now a sort of polyclinic. The National Hospital is about fifteen minutes away by bus. The Public Health Ministry has improved a lot since the Revolution. It's responsible for drinking water and drainage and Public Health representatives go from house to house checking to see if there are deposits of stagnant water or trash lying around.

The Public Health Front of the CDR also instructs the people about hygiene, telling them why they should cover their garbage cans, how to guard against infection in their homes, and when to boil the drinking water. This campaign is carried out mainly by distributing pamphlets and having meetings with mothers. If a mother is unable to attend, a CDR member brings her a pamphlet and reads it with her because the Ministry of Health wants everyone to get the information. Today there's no polio, and mumps, measles, malaria, and tuberculosis have been reduced to a few isolated cases. Nothing like this was done before the Revolution. I should say not!

The bus service in our barrio is good. The buses run on the same routes as before, some within the *reparto* and others along the main boulevard, which is in bad shape. Right now they're repairing some side streets in order to shift all the traffic over to them when they begin work on the boulevard. Not much new street construction has been done since the Revolution; only one new avenue, which was formerly a dirt road, has been put through my barrio. The other streets are just being maintained, holes filled in and so on.

In my barrio a number of the houses are very poor and in need of repair, but every house, regardless of size, has inside plumbing and electricity. And almost everyone here now owns his own home or apartment because of the Urban Reform Law of 1960, which said that after a person had lived in a house for twenty years it belonged to him. Houses built before 1940 were ours after five years under the law; those built after 1940 required a little more time to buy, and will be paid off in 1970.[50]

I've been in my house for twenty-six years now. I stopped paying rent

49. This was an occurrence peculiar to the Year of Decisive Effort, when many workers, including those in sanitation, left their regular jobs periodically to cut cane for the 1970 harvest.

50. Plans to abolish rent in 1970 and turn over all remaining house and apartment titles to tenants have been postponed. One of the principal reasons for continuing rent payments was to burn up the excess cash in circulation.

in 1963 and we were given the title deed. Reinaldo and I weren't very excited about it because it wasn't as though somebody had left us a fortune. I think we'd already paid about 1,000 *pesos* for this little one-room apartment and it seems to me we had a right to it, like a just reward. Besides, the rent was only 10 *pesos* a month and our income was about the same as before the Revolution, so the difference was hardly noticeable.

For most people, when the possession date arrives there's a great celebration. My friend Leida and her husband, Rafael Loza, who have five children, were very excited and happy. Rafael said it was the happiest day of his life. He'd never expected to own a house and now he had 40 *pesos* less to pay every month.

Housing is among the most pressing problems to be solved here. In some barrios there are married couples with eight children living in one room, while old couples, who could live in a more modest apartment, may have a whole house and patio to themselves. Great mansions shouldn't have been left in the hands of a few owners, but people say it wouldn't be humanitarian to take them away. Fidel is sentimental, as are all Cubans, and he's not likely to get over it. Undoubtedly his humanity and honesty bring more poeple over to his side than if he were callous. People wouldn't react well to different methods because no one can impose anything on Cubans.

Still, I'd like to tell Fidel my idea about this and other things. For example, every time I go down a street in the center of Havana and see all those closed shops, I think how much gayer and less gray it would look with families living in them. I've heard people say, "Just let me have one of these empty stores with its bathroom and running water and I'll find some way to patch up the woodwork and the brickwork and make it fit to live in."

With a little cooperation from Urban Reform, along with the efforts of other interested parties, we could have a beautiful and prosperous-looking Havana instead of a depressing one. However, people say, "The party takes care of these things and the Party knows what it's doing." Well, I think the Party is involved with a lot of matters and that everybody should contribute a little in the way of ideas.

A lot of repairs and alterations on private homes here in the neighborhood have been done by *Poder Local*.[51] They've also made a

51. Introduced in 1966–67, *Poder Local* (Local Power) was the national agency for coordinating local government functions. It was designed to decentralize administrative decision-making so that localized problems could be solved at the local level. Its administrative base was the sectional level in urban areas and the *municipio* in rural areas. The base-level offices were run by committees of delegates from local units of government ministries, the Party, and the CDRs. Two CDR delegates were elected (apparently in public assemblies at the zone level) from each zone in the sectional to serve as intermediaries between municipal administration and the people. *Poder Local* had jurisdiction over seven

little park across from the movie house. The people are pleased with the work done so far but more is needed. However, materials are scarce and it's been impossible to take care of every case. They attend to the most urgent cases first—houses with children or where there's a dangerous problem.

The *Poder Local* delegate in my zone is Pablo Salas. I didn't participate in the assembly that elected him, but in the neighborhood he's well known as a serious and responsible person. The last *Poder Local* assembly was about a year ago. It was decided then that each CDR should submit written reports on all the emergencies existing on its block. It's the job of *Poder Local* to visit the residents of houses most in need of repairs. Maintenance of the streets isn't up to *Poder Local* but to the Ministry of Construction.

On my block there are people of all kinds of religious beliefs, although there isn't one Party member. The churches in the barrio still post schedules on their doors and many people continue to attend the Catholic and Baptist churches. Fewer go to the Jehovah's Witnesses church, but they too hold regular services, and the sect has grown since the Revolution.

Santería[52] is also practiced here in the barrio. Fortunately, on my block only three people, all mulatto, believe in it. I don't believe *santería* is a religion, and though people have a right to believe what they please, they shouldn't be allowed to proselytize. Certainly the government shouldn't encourage such a degrading spectacle or allow them facilities for their ceremonies, but should gradually make them understand their backwardness and ignorance. I think *santería* is criminal.

The three neighbors who believe in *santería* are Magaly, her brother, and a boy named Genaro. Magaly is really a fine person, a good and helpful neighbor of whom I'm genuinely fond, but blacks always have their superstitions and she believes in witchcraft. Having worked in a jewelry store, she has the materials and the skill to make necklaces for different spells and she has no trouble selling them. Her brother practices all the *santería* rites. For the ceremony to become a *santero,* he recently paid 20 *pesos* each for hens and 70 *pesos* for cocks. A man like

---

administrative "fronts": commercial services, communal services, construction, economy, supplies, transportation, and organization. There was considerable overlap between *Poder Local*'s areas of responsibility and the "fronts" assigned to the CDRs, causing some rivalry between the agencies. (This description is based on Oscar Lewis's 1969 interview with a *Poder Local* official and on Booth, "Neighbourhood Committees and Popular Courts," pp. 56–57.) In 1974 the Cuban government was in the process of implementing a new administrative system, *Poder Popular* (People's Power), which will supersede the authority of *Poder Local.* Castro said the primary objective of the system is to control at the grass-roots level all production and service units that serve the community. (*Granma Weekly Review,* Aug. 4, 1974, p. 4.)

52. See Gracia, n. 35.

that, full of vigor and holding down a job, has no reason to believe in those things.

As for Genaro, there's an interesting incident involving his mother. One day in 1944 or 1945, Genaro's mother let loose some pigeons into the yard of her neighbor Emerida Lourido. That morning Emerida's son had gone to work in perfect health, yet the very next day he had a pain and three days later he died. Emerida suspected witchcraft and claimed Genaro's mother had killed her son with spells, even though the doctor said the boy died of cirrhosis of the liver. Still, the boy was only nineteen or twenty and was feeling fine. Because there was no proof, no formal accusations were made, but Emerida never spoke to Genaro's mother again and later moved away.

We white people on this block criticize Genaro, Magaly, and her brother quite a lot among ourselves on this *santería* business. We're not afraid of voodoo, but we're aware that believers are capable of all kinds of things so we can never really feel friendly toward them. In my case, I'm suspicious of all black people, though not the educated ones in the CDR and the Women's Federation, because they don't believe in voodoo. I think of them as whites just like us—so I suppose it's their beliefs that matter, not their color. But they are few, and even among them I don't feel entirely secure.

Living in barrio Santa Isabel for twenty-six years as I have, the neighbors get to be like members of one's family, although before the Revolution everyone kept to himself. There was none of that feeling of community, of sharing, that we now have. We have more contact with each other through meetings at the CDR, at orientation sessions, in the groceries, on guard duty. In the early days anybody not with the Revolution was considered a counterrevolutionary, but today it doesn't matter; revolutionary or otherwise, we all live the same way.

On my block there are now about six families who don't belong to the CDR but who, I think, wouldn't do anything against the Revolution. There are Engracia Quesada and Rodrigo Farías, a married couple with two sons in military service, who live right across the street. Neither Rodrigo nor the boys are integrated but they're decent, honorable people and good neighbors. Then there's Antonio Ruíz, who drives a truck for MINCON, and his wife, Martina Fernández. Both are white and they have one son. In the old days Antonio was a private chauffeur for some politicians. He's absolutely no good, not integrated at all, but he tried to make us think he was by joining the CDR when it was first organized. He's not a *gusano* but in private he says what the enemy wants to hear. No, he's not to be trusted.

Next door to me are two black men, Humberto and Genaro, who've lived here as long as I. Humberto Vega was the lover of Genaro's mother. About four years ago she died and Vega took over her son Genaro, who's abnormal and can't work. Now Vega supports him, does the shopping, cleans and takes care of the house. Vega is a wonderful man, decent, a hard worker, and very reliable. Neither Vega nor Genaro are integrated, nor do they belong to the CDR or any other organization, but Vega works at MINCON and is very responsible and efficient. He doesn't like communism but he tries harder with this government than with the past one. He's always talking about his work and never loses a day, even when he's sick with a fever. My goodness, I've been living next door to him for nearly thirty years and that man is my clock. When I have to get up early, I'll say to him, "Give me a call before you leave, Humberto," and he never fails. He's such a good person that I don't pressure him to integrate. He should do it when he wants to.

The Boróns were among the few counterrevolutionary neighbors I've had. They were Lebanese shopkeepers and the husband owned everything around him—stores, houses, tailor shops. His wife, Elena, was an English teacher, but because Lebanese men are very jealous, he made her stop teaching. He was good but strange, very closed to everyone, and he was a counterrevolutionary. After nationalization and urban reform, his capital kept shrinking until he had to work as an employee. That was very difficult for him because he hadn't inherited his money, he'd earned it after a lot of hardship.

Elena sympathized with the Revolution and listened to Fidel's speeches and bought all the government magazines. Every afternoon, after she'd bathed and dressed, she'd stop by to say hello. I'm not the kind to have a lot of close friends, but she'd tell me all her personal problems and I'd tell her mine. Basically, I'm reserved and would rather discuss matters concerning the Revolution. Here one lives through one's problems alone. Elena and I were exceptions.

Elena would cry about how she wanted to get out of the country because of her husband. It got to the point that when her son won a prize in school for a composition on the explosion of the ship *Le Coubre*,[53] it couldn't be shown to his father for fear of offending him. The family finally went north in 1966. She and I still write and occasionally she sends me photographs.

When she left, Elena's house was given to two abnormal people, Baco and his sister Carlota. They seem like ordinary people, but we know they're insane and mentally deficient because they've been in Mazorra.[54] Baco pays all the household expenses by working in the *Cordón de la Habana* cultivating coffee. He earns about 75 *pesos* a month. But as far as revolutionary activities are concerned, he and his sister can't be called

53. See Mónica, n. 29.
54. See Mónica, n. 2.

upon for anything. They spend all their time quarreling, making noisy scenes, beating each other, and talking nonsense. They scream, call each other dirty names, curse at the tops of their voices, and Carlota throws pots and pans around.

The situation has become unbearable. One day I went to talk to them, as a neighbor, not as a representative of the CDR, and I told them to watch their behavior and not make such a racket because the neighbors might bring them before the People's Court. Baco began to yell at me, "Report me. Call the police. Do whatever you want." So I told the neighbors that next time they'd all have to talk to him because I wasn't going to.

The point is that people like them can be controlled. When someone causes a disturbance, the CDR as a whole can bring a complaint before the People's Court just like any individual. That's why I told him I wasn't speaking for the CDR. If a doctor examines them, he may decide they have to be put away.

In the building next to Genaro and Vega lives Eladio Zamora, the tailor, whose wife married another man and went North. Eladio was allowed to do private tailoring as long as he didn't employ anyone, but the cloth ration for trousers and suits was stopped about a year ago so he now does only alterations and mending.

Eladio takes little interest in the Revolution. He's about forty-five and somewhat bohemian; he doesn't care much about his clothes or his living quarters. He's very poor; if he owns one pair of trousers and a shirt and has a bed with a mattress, it's a lot. After his wife left him he really went to pieces. Now life doesn't hold out much for him.

Another counterrevolutionary around here is Máximo Meléndez, a policeman from Batista's time. He's the neighbor who was arrested for stealing. After the Revolution Max drove police cars, but he smashed them all up so they put him on a truck for *Recuperación de Bienes*. He collected furniture from the houses taken over by the government. The furniture was supposed to be distributed to the poor, but instead, Max sold some of it and filled his own house with the rest. Finally he was caught and they gave him three years in prison. When he came out, he went to work driving a truck.

Max's family is a disaster. They're the only undesirable element on the block. At least his wife, Zenaida Palacios, is; not Max, because he has decent instincts and is a good person. Zenaida, who's white like Max, came here from Santa Clara after the Revolution and has caused nothing but trouble since. She fights with the neighbors, talks about everybody, and has taken up with other men. She usually goes elsewhere to do it but everyone knows about it, including Max. He's always had the horns pinned on him; in fact, of their five children, the eldest is by her first husband and the second is not Max's either, though he acknowledges her.

The problem with Zenaida is that she doesn't love her husband. All she's interested in is money and Max has to get it for her some way, even if it means stealing. She's very domineering and they fight constantly, using foul language in front of the children. She's a sick woman, very much out of hand. What she needs is a psychiatrist!

About three months ago investigators came to my house and said, "We need a CDR member to go with us to search a house in this street." I asked whose it was and they told me, "Máximo Meléndez's." I thought he'd been fighting again because he's awful that way. But it wasn't for that. Max had been going around with a false credential, committing swindles. He'd used his old policeman's badge and pad for writing fines that people paid him. So now he's in jail for the third time. He hasn't been brought up for trial yet. They say this time he's charged with being a counterrevolutionary and is going before the Revolutionary Tribunal.[55] The public doesn't attend those trials, only the authorities do.

They've already sent investigators to decide on how much monthly allowance to grant the family since Max was their sole support. They also checked up on whether Max's wife is treating the children properly. If not, the children would be put in boarding schools. If she were to misuse the allowance, they'd stop it, take the children away, and she'd have to go to work.

In a way Zenaida is a good mother. She sees to it that her children have their meals on time, and she really slaves over their clothes so they'll look neat in school. She's a very good housewife and makes sacrifices for her children. But it all depends on what mood she's in. When she's happy, nothing is too good for them, but when she's angry . . . !

The only way to control Zenaida would be for the CDR to send an official report to the superior level and take her before a People's Court. For the sake of the children we don't do it, and besides, we don't want to interfere in anybody's private life. And after all, taking that family out of this neighborhood would solve no problems. It would merely transfer them to another neighborhood. So we put up with them as best we can and try to get Zenaida to participate in the CDR and the Women's Federation.

Of the rest of the neighbors, some are actively involved in the Revolution, others are not. Matías Lozada is white, about thirty-five, divorced, and has been living alone for many years. He's a surveyor, educated, well

55. Revolutionary Tribunals are the only courts in Cuba that try persons charged with counterrevolutionary acts and the only courts that can impose capital punishment. The Tribunals try all charges of insurrection, sedition, treason, sabotage, etc., and fraud or embezzlement by government employees in their places of work, murder committed during robberies of homes, or armed robbery by persons in military uniform. Each province has one Tribunal with a rotating panel of judges chosen from the armed forces. Each case is heard by three judges—one officer and two enlisted men. Decisions may be appealed through the provincial director to the national director of the tribunals. (Jesse Berman, "The Cuban Popular Tribunals," *Columbia Law Review,* Dec., 1969, pp. 1317–54.)

dressed, always neat, clean, and perfumed. He likes to show off. He belongs to the CDR but isn't active.

Josefina Santos Guerrero, a good comrade, is a light *mulata* and lives with her daughter Eufemia next to Genaro's apartment. Josefina is separated from her husband; he occasionally visits his daugher, who's black like him. Josefina is a Baptist, but very humane. She's a charter member of my CDR and is now in charge of education.

Josefina is also the nurse for our street. She studied first aid at the polyclinic and was given the top rating in her courses. Medical work was her passion, like an obsession. For three years she worked in the polyclinic as a nurse's aid, without pay. Then, when it came time to issue the diplomas, she was told, "Josefina, we can't give you one because only those under thirty-five are qualified and you're thirty-eight."

It almost destroyed her. They'd told her nothing beforehand, not a word. She had a breakdown and took to her bed, lying there for months, practically dying of disappointment. She'd counted on working in the clinic to support her daughter. Instead she had to rely on a small government allowance, 30 *pesos* from her mother, 20 *pesos* from a brother, and contributions from Eufemia's *papá*. If Josefina wanted to demand more money from him she'd have to get a divorce, but she won't do that because of her daughter. So the neighbors help out and they manage.

Josefina has suffered a lot for the Revolution. If she hadn't been a true revolutionary she would have changed. But she's recovered and keeps right on carrying out her revolutionary assignments. She's intelligent and educated and loves what she's doing. When I have to be away, I leave my keys at her house and she takes over my revolutionary duties. And when they need help at the polyclinic, she still goes in as a volunteer. That's being a revolutionary!

Next door to Eladio the tailor there's a new couple, Jorge Bolanos and his wife, Celeste, who moved in only three years ago on an exchange of apartments. They have two children now, one of them in the *círculo*. The Bolanos are white, and good integrated revolutionaries. He works on leather for export and she's a presser in a dry-cleaning place. She belongs to the CDR and he's in the militia, but, as we say, he has one foot in the country all the time; that is, he leaves the factory to do agricultural work. Jorge and Celeste get on very well, without jealousies. When they get back to their little apartment after work, they both take care of the children and the household chores.

In the same building live Dominga Gayo and her mother and four-year-old daughter, who's in the *círculo*. Dominga is a pretty little *mulata* who's been in the neighborhood about four years. She left her husband, and the day he was to sign their divorce papers, he came to the house and put five bullets into her; she nearly died. What a tragedy! He's still in prison.

After she recovered, Dominga had to find work. The only jobs available were in the country, so she went into farm work as a *permanente* for two years. Then the doctor noticed a lung deficiency, an aftereffect of the bullets, and they took her out of farm work and put her in a mattress factory. Because of her devotion and enthusiasm, as well as her two years in farm labor, she was given membership in the UJC.

In the apartment next to Dominga there's a navy sergeant, Gustavo Estrella, and his wife, Emelinda Rasco. Both are black and they have two children. Before the Revolution Gustavo was on Batista's side and worked on a frigate. Many people worked for Batista's government because they had to support their families, not because they were in favor of him. Emelinda and I were good friends and she knew I was involved in underground work for the Twenty-sixth of July Movement, but she never betrayed me.

After the Revolution, Gustavo was sent to Russia for three years to complete his training as a torpedo-launch mechanic. Emelinda did quite well while he was away because his salary was sent directly to her and the neighbors were helpful with the children. We're like one big family, a real community, cooperating in everything and getting along.

Although Gustavo is integrated in the Revolution, Emelinda is not, because she was raised by nuns and is very Catholic. However, they don't quarrel over politics. She says she doesn't have to belong to anything to cooperate, and the day she wants to join the CDR or something else she will. Recently our CDR chose Emelinda as the "Exemplary Mother"[56] on the block because she's so good to all the children and takes care of them when their mothers work or do productive labor. She also takes part in other activities and calls on the mothers who don't send their children to school.

Lela, who's a very respectable single woman of about forty, lives alone in the front half of the little house where Matías Lozada lives. She's been there many years and has fixed up her apartment very nicely with a frigidaire, a sewing machine, a good set of bedroom furniture—all the comforts a person needs.

Lela worked as a domestic, but after the Revolution she went to night school and completed the sixth grade, besides learning to sew a bit. When the Women's Federation opened a workshop to wash bottles collected for perfume and medicine, I said to Lela, "Look, if you'd like to work near home, with no carfare to pay, just show up tomorrow for a trial." So she worked there fifteen days without pay, like everybody else, to see if she liked it. At first she thought the work was too hard, but when a store with better facilities was set up in Mariánao, she decided to stay.

56. A national campaign of the Education Fronts of the CDRs to increase parental involvement in their children's education.

She's very happy on her job now. She's a member of the CDR and the Women's Federation so she's integrated, but by the time she gets home from work it's already 6:00 o'clock, and after preparing dinner and doing her laundry, she doesn't have much time for anything else. She's a practicing Catholic who attends church regularly. Occasionally she goes dancing on Saturday, but she's working very hard now and is hoarding stuff for her family in Matanzas.

Of the rest of the neighbors there's not much to be said. An old couple, Ismael Vardalis and María Delgado, live behind Matías and Lela's house. Ismael is very integrated and María is not, but it doesn't matter. Frankly, she's a little dumb, in the sense that she's almost illiterate. She's not an emancipated woman at all. Next door there's an old maid who works and is integrated. That leaves one more close neighbor, Darío and his wife, Ilva, who are black. Darío is a good neighbor and has belonged to the CDR for a year, but he never does anything. The couple next door, Rosario Villegas, the CDR treasurer, and her husband, José Berrios, can always be counted on. They're black too. Almost everybody on my block is black.

Francisca Santiago was an original member of my CDR but she's not very active. In contrast to her, there are women like Eulalia Estévez, in whose house our first CDR sectional was installed. There's also the widow, Carmelita, another original CDR member, whose two older sons were not in favor of the Revolution and are gone, but she and her third son are both with the Revolution.

Since everybody in my neighborhood is poor, we all suffer more or less from shortages. Some go to relatives in the country and bring back lots of things. Others manage well because they eat lunch in the factory or their children eat in school. It's easier for families with many members because they get more food. It's the man who lives alone, like Eladio, who has it really rough, because he can't manage on his rations and has to eat out a lot. Antonio Ruíz gets better food because he's a diabetic and is entitled to buy a chicken once a month and extra milk, aside from his regular rations. He also gets extra vegetables, yams, lots of things; all sick people do, as well as children. Some people took advantage of this ruling—they'd get doctors to prescribe a special diet for them even if they were healthy—but the government investigated and put an end to that.

Chapter Five

Family Matters

THE CRISIS BETWEEN Reinaldo and me took place in 1966. I guess it was my being away from home so much that finished us off. I wanted a divorce but Reinaldo didn't because he would have had to contribute to my support. I would have divorced him anyway had it not been for my family; they said it was foolishness at our age, after having been together for so many years. But it was a big mistake on my part to have let them influence me.

I should never have put up with my marriage all those years. My life with him was impossible—like a nightmare—and every time I tried to change to suit him, it was worse. The woman who struggles to free herself and succeeds is more to be admired. Had I divorced my husband twenty years ago I wouldn't have been tied to a lie, to something I didn't feel and didn't want. Instead I waited for him to change, and of course he didn't. Such men don't change.

One of the reasons I didn't get a divorce before the Revolution was that I was afraid of some dirty work, such as someone making an accusation against me. He could have gotten a politican to do it for him. So I was very scared. But since the Revolution they play very clean here. If you're straight, nobody bothers you. Only wrongdoers are punished.

Instead of going my own way, I went on living in the same house with Reinaldo for three and a half more years, keeping up appearances, although our obligation to each other no longer existed. Only the members of the family knew of the separation; everyone else believed we were still married. During all that time I was very miserable, with nobody to confide in, no place to go, and nothing to do. Reinaldo didn't give me any money and he made life unbearable. He'd litter up the house, throw things on the floor, turn the place upside down. He kept it filthy. He tried to make life impossible so I'd be the one to leave and he wouldn't have to pay me alimony. If he'd been the man he ought to have been, he'd have gone to live in his aunt's or mother's house and I wouldn't have had to go through all that.

One day I did something the Revolution doesn't like. For the first time since I married, I went to church and confessed to the priest all that had happened to me. As the saying goes, "People remember God when it thunders." I was in such a state I muddled my confession, so I went back to confess again. The priest said it was more dishonest to go on living under the same roof with a man I didn't love or even like than to get a divorce. Well, actually he just said it was dishonest, not that I should get a divorce. They almost never advise divorce. But to me the priest's words came as a great truth and made me wish I'd gone to him twenty years earlier, though whether or not he'd have talked that way before the Revolution I don't know.

So I went home and said to Reinaldo, "I'm going to sue for a divorce." At first he didn't agree. Then, when everything looked blackest and he was treating me worse and worse and making the house a hell, I prayed to God. I was very confident that He would help me as He always has. I said, "God, You know I believe in You and Reinaldo doesn't. If You think I'm the one who should keep the house then do Your will. It may be nothing but a box but it's all I have." That's how I left it. Then one day out of a clear blue sky, Reinaldo told a friend that if I waived alimony he'd leave me the house. What did I need alimony for when I'd lived on practically nothing all my life? A few days later Reinaldo told me he was moving to his aunt's house.

I got together with my family and told them I was suing for divorce without alimony. I was capable of working, had worked all my life, and would continue doing so. Then, with the help of a lawyer, who charged me 40 *pesos,* I went to court and within sixteen days was divorced.

At the time I had 60 *pesos* that I'd saved at the rate of 2 *pesos* a week, in a bank account opened by the block CDR. I withdrew the whole amount to pay the lawyer and to cover my daily expenses. I'd always put away a bit of money for emergencies; in addition, before the Revolution, when I was working, Reinaldo managed to save nearly 1,000 *pesos* from our combined salaries. During the currency changeover[57] he banked 500 or 600 *pesos* in an account in his name with me as the beneficiary. It never entered my mind that if we happened to break up one day he'd be so mean as to keep all the money. But just before the divorce he opened a new account for himself. I received no part of the money and I didn't ask for any.

57. On August 4, 1961, the Cuban government issued new paper money and withdrew from circulation all paper currency then in use. Up to 200 *pesos* per person could be exchanged, with excesses to be deposited in "special accounts" in the National Bank. The exchange period ended on August 8, 1961, after which time individuals could make an initial withdrawal of not more than 1,000 *pesos* from the "special accounts" (business enterprises could withdraw up to 5,000). The rest could be withdrawn at the rate of not more than 200 *pesos* per month. Amounts over 10,000 *pesos* were to be confiscated. (Cuban Economic Research Project, *A Study on Cuba,* p. 647.)

When Reinaldo left, he took everything he said was "worth his while," including the refrigerator that cost me 579 *pesos,* paid off in eight months from my commissions. He also took the mahogany wardrobe that cost 195 *pesos,* the radio, the record player, the television set, and even the books. The only things he left were some furniture, the electric iron, the sewing machine with its new motor that cost me 120 *pesos,* and the house itself.

Reinaldo didn't claim the house because he knew the agony it had cost me to live with relatives. The title was transferred to my name and even though it's just a tiny room, at least it's my own. And as far as the divorce is concerned, I don't feel any guilt. It was like getting rid of a cancer that was destroying me. I'm very satisfied with what I did. After all, I fought to save our marriage and nothing that happened was my fault. In spite of everything, I was good to Reinaldo and affectionate, taking care of him up to the end in a way he never deserved and as nobody else had ever done. But his conscience will kill him, of that I'm sure.

It's been almost six months since I've been living alone and I feel very relaxed. At last I'm the mistress of my own home. When I was younger I never had a chance to spread my wings. I was always under someone's thumb. But now I have nobody to order me around, to tell me not to go out, to go to bed, or if it's raining, not to get wet. If I want to go to the movies, I go to the movies; if I want to cook, I cook; if I'm not hungry, I don't eat. I have something I've never had before, peace and freedom, and in that sense I'm very happy.

My greatest concern after the divorce was supporting myself. At first I did it by sewing at home. I received no cloth ration as I had no shop, so I could do only alterations. Otherwise I'd have had to pay the government a percentage of whatever I earned. Doing alterations, I sometimes earned as much as 30 or 40 *pesos* a week. It wasn't enough but I managed quite well.

My main problem then was food. As a single person I had a pretty hard time getting enough to eat. In a large family it's easier to stretch the rations; one day they can pool all the meat rations—three-fourths of a pound of meat per person per week—and the next day they pool something else. I got a two-burner electric stove and an alcohol burner for making coffee, so cooking wasn't any problem. But I'd have to spend a whole afternoon or evening queuing up to buy food, and I hated to do that. To eat out you needed a lot of money.

Before the Revolution I'd never eaten in a real restaurant. To me, eating out meant going to a relative's home, a cafeteria, the ten-cent store, or a street stand. There are no street stands left, but I've been to pizzerias and to some nice restaurants like the Rancho Luna, the Habana Libre, and my favorite, the Floridita. My friends Rafael and Leida have always invited me to those places and taken care of the check. Oh, how I love to eat out, especially in the Floridita! The music and the lighting are lovely. At places like Rancho Luna you can see the line outside and the people milling around and you eat nervously. But in the Floridita the atmosphere takes me completely away from all disagreeable things.

I didn't really lack food at home, because one neighbor would give me a plate of rice, another a can of milk, a third a banana, and a fourth something else. Or a friend who knew how fond I was of soup would call and say, "Cencia, I'm having soup for dinner, come eat with us." And my sister Felicia always brought me a can of milk, a bit of coffee, or some such thing when she visited. Occasionally friends came to dinner, pooling their rations with mine, or we all contributed food to celebrate a comrade's birthday.

I got along until self-employment was banned. Then, like it or not, everybody below the age of retirement, except for housewives and students, had to take a job. Each week a house-to-house census by ration cards was taken by the CDRs to determine the number of unemployed persons. In my *solar* I do the census in a book which shows everyone's age, work center, revolutionary activities—all the facts about each resident. I know all the information by heart so there's no need for constantly disturbing them. If a person is unemployed, he may be moved to another place, but if he refuses to do the work, another job is found for him. Many mothers don't feel the need to work because the Revolution provides their children with everything.

To get a job, I had to go to the Women's Federation, where I was classified as unemployed. I put down that I'd worked as a domestic and they said there were openings in the government protocol houses. As guests of Fidel, naturally not just anybody could be assigned to them. Honest, reliable people, good revolutionaries, were needed, so I agreed to take a job.

Today in Cuba it's no shame to be a servant, but nobody else I know who'd been one before the Revolution will do that kind of work anymore. The fact is, I enjoy doing housework. I pretend I'm in my own home doing the work for myself. I earn 85 *pesos* a month, the minimum wage, and I get a good lunch and dinner, which is a savings for me.[58] In the past I had no security at all as a maid, but now, the day I stop work in one place I'm sent elsewhere, so I'm never without a job. Soon I'll be getting a pension. I have to work until age sixty to qualify for retirement

58. In 1969–70 Cuba had several wage scales. Workers were classified by their occupational sector (i.e., agricultural, nonagricultural, administrative, or technical and executive), and by the skill level required in their jobs. Eighty-five *pesos* a month was the lowest wage (grade 1 skill level) in the scale for nonagricultural workers and administrative employees, but there were lower wages in the scale for agricultural workers. (Roberto E. Hernández and Carmelo Mesa-Lago, "Labor Organization and Wages," in Mesa-Lago, ed., *Revolutionary Change in Cuba*, pp. 224–35.)

at my full salary. Of course if I were very old, the government would pension me off right away, but I'm happy to work as long as I have the health and stamina.

And all my food problems are gone. Because I'm working full-time and must get up at 6:30 to be at work by 9:00, my neighbors make life easier for me by doing my shopping. I leave my ration book with a friend who picks up my meat and bread. At the end of the month I only have to buy soft drinks, my full ration of eggs, and the rest of my groceries. All in all I'm quite comfortable, though I have no savings.

Nothing about the shortages today really bothers me. I guess I'm not very demanding, though I do wish there were a larger supply of goods so everybody could have what he needs. But before the Revolution, when there were a lot more things in the shops, most of us couldn't afford to buy them. Now sometimes there's a line for food, but at least you know there's enough for everyone.

For manufactured goods, a certain group of people are given a number, say 3, and when it's the turn of no. 3, those people may go and buy.[59] If I have that number, I can assume that a lot of other people with no. 3 are going to be buying too and that they'll try to go early to get the pick of the stuff. If there's a shortage of blankets, for example, and only ten blankets are being sold for each number group and I'm eleventh in line, I know I'm not going to get a blanket until no. 3 comes around again the next week or month.

The problem is that it's "first come, first served." People with nothing much to do have the advantage because they're willing to waste hours standing in line. Furthermore, there are people who take along two or three ration books. Others see friends ahead of them in line and simply walk up and hand them their books, showing a lack of respect for the rights of all those waiting their turn. Of course the people object.

There are also certain other problems in connection with standing in line. If I have to step out of line a moment, say to go to the toilet—either at home or in the nearest polyclinic, police station, or CDR zone office where the toilets are open all night—I can get back into line if the people know I've been there earlier. That's why at a certain time, say 6:00 in the evening or 12:00 at night, everyone in line says, "Mark your place." This means you must check with persons in front of and behind you, so they know who you are. So if someone goes away he can say, "Inocencia was right in back of me. When she returns let her in the line." If I stay away so long that all those in front and immediately behind me have already

59. Unlike food, clothing and other goods could be purchased by Cubans at any store of their choice, provided the buyer had the ration coupon entitling him to the articles at that time. Each household was assigned a number and was entitled to buy only when that number came up, on certain days of the month. The numbers were posted in stores and announced over the radio.

bought and left, I'll lose my place. Neighbors take turns for two or three hours keeping each other's place in line, just like standing guard. This is allowed, as well as shopping for people who work or are ill. The only thing forbidden is to make a lot of noise and wake up the neighborhood.

Before the Revolution I shopped in all the big clothing stores, La Epoca, which was my favorite, Roseland, La Filosofía, El Telar, and El Elegante on Neptuno. My ration book is good anywhere in the city, so I haven't changed my shopping places much since the Revolution. On the days my number comes up, I go anywhere I like.

There's been a change, however, in the quality of clothes sold. Before, cloth used to come from France or the United States and there was a variety to choose from. Now there isn't enough available, it's of poorer quality, and there's very little selection. All the stores have about the same stock.

In shoes, too, there's not much choice of styles. There's one store where they sell custom-made shoes at very high prices, and of course they're much better than those you can buy in a regular shoe store for 10 or 12 *pesos*. If I have the right to a pair of shoes on my ration book, I can go there and order a pair for 50 or 60 *pesos*. Some people can afford them, but I can't.

I no longer worry about the future and have no intention of marrying again. I've gone through too much, I'm old, and besides I don't need a man. Yet my first Christmas alone after the divorce was very sad. I was invited to many homes but I refused them all and went to bed. Reinaldo and I had always gone together and I was embarrassed to show up alone. Furthermore, I couldn't contribute any food because on my single ration book I get so little. And Christmas is a bad day for going out anyway.

The one thing I really regret about the past is not having had children. I couldn't adopt any because I was never in a position to. Still, I have lots of godchildren—practically all my nephews and nieces and many of the neighbors' children. I'm the godmother of Leida's son Pancho, though he hasn't been baptized. His father is a revolutionary and doesn't approve of it. For me, though, and for Leida, ceremony or no ceremony, I'm the child's godmother.

My friendship with Leida began when we met in the CDR in 1964. Her husband, Rafael Loza, is a very bright man—he was an IBM technician before the Revolution—and their five children are lovely. I make clothes for my godson Pancho and give gifts to all of them. I even give them money to buy presents on Mother's Day, and they always find little gifts for me. I'm like a second mother to them and they act as if they love me dearly. When somebody asks them, "Whom do you love?" they always mention me first. They're a very important part of my life.

Every other Sunday their *mamá* takes one of the older boys to the station to catch the bus back to school and I stay with the other children. I take them out, usually to one of the two amusement parks, Coney Island or the Maceo. Riding the merry-go-round or roller coaster with kids is one of my favorite forms of amusement. Those kids are so affectionate to me, I'd give my life for them. When that family goes out anywhere, I go with them even if it's only to the Coppelia for ice cream. And whenever they give a dinner, I'm one of the guests. For them I come first. This year I'll spend Christmas Eve with them.

The fact is I'm never alone. When I'm sick my room is filled with people; black, white, young, old, everybody is there to help. Even on Mother's Day I have company. My nephews and nieces and the other children I know bring me gifts. They've always made Mother's Day a happy occasion for me. Reinaldo's relatives come around a lot too. His sister lives a block away, and whenever I need help she and her family come running, as though nothing had happened between Reinaldo and me. I feel the same toward them.

I work eight hours a day from Monday to Friday and a half-day on Saturday. Every other Sunday I volunteer for productive labor. I really don't like farm work but I don't mind going out to the country as a volunteer for a day. It's a lot of fun because people from the same neighborhood are picked up by the CDR truck and work together and have lunch picnic-style, like a family. Getting volunteers for hard labor is difficult—the majority make the effort, but we *habaneros* are not used to it.

Every day I get home from work around 5:30 or 6:00 in the evening. If I have time, I sew. If not, I cut out the material and get it ready for the following day. I have a lot to sew because I don't like to say no when someone asks me to make something. Most times I'm ashamed to ask for pay. After all, I'm drawing a government salary so why shouldn't I try to be useful to other people, especially to a friend who has a hard time finding her size in ready-made clothes, or whose husband is the only one in the family working and doesn't earn much. But if the person can afford to pay and is not a close friend, I charge a small fee. This helps me meet my expenses for the phone and the electricity and also for the medical society.[60]

Before the Revolution, and after, I was a member of a private clinic and got my medical care there, until it was closed. Now there's the

60. A phone cost about 8.50 *pesos* a month; electricity from a small house like Inocencia's would probably have cost from 4 to 8 *pesos* a month depending on the number of appliances used. (For medical expenses, see below.)

polyclinic, but I go to the medical society because there the doctor sees me the same day. If I ever have to be hospitalized it will be no problem.[61]

After I sew in the evening, I bathe, eat, and go out, usually to a meeting—of the CDR, the Women's Federation, or the study circle. The CDR study circle is something new. It's held by the zone Committee. Study circles were initiated at the urging of the superior levels and are used solely for political orientation. At first we studied works like *The Principles of Socialism* by Blas Roca[62] and *History Will Absolve Me* by Fidel,[63] as well as other political subjects connected with the Revolution. But now we discuss underdevelopment, sugar cane, agriculture, the position of women—things connected with our daily life. I really enjoy these meetings and I usually attend.

The study circle is directed by the comrade who's in charge of that CDR front.[64] He does his best to inform himself about the subject to be discussed, by reading books and by talking with people who know more about it than he does. About twenty to forty persons attend each meeting, and after he presents the topic they give their opinions. The men hardly ever speak up; they don't much like meetings, you know, and there are always some people who are shy about talking into a microphone. I often stand up and say something, especially if I feel strongly about a subject. I'm not timid. Not all CDRs have someone able to orient the group and answer all the questions, so it isn't always possible to have study circles every week. Sometimes experts are invited, because if none of us knows anything about the subject how can we explain it?

I'm an active *miliciana* and once in a while I have to attend militia

---

61. The services Inocencia subscribed to were not necessarily better or more extensive than those provided by the state at no direct cost. But some persons believed they could get attention more quickly at a private clinic than at a polyclinic, and some wanted to continue going to the private clinics of the mutual-benefit associations they belonged to before the Revolution. Another of our informants, Mercedes Millán (*Neighbors*, Part III), was a member of a private clinic and paid a monthly fee of 3.50 *pesos* for each adult and 3.75 *pesos* for each child. Mercedes said these private clinics were grouped and regulated by the government under a plan called *Clínicas Mutualistas*.

62. *Los Fundamentos del Socialismo en Cuba* (Havana: Editorial Páginas, 1944.) Blas Roca Calderío was an early member of the old Communist Party (PSP) and its secretary-general in 1933. As head of the Party, Blas Roca followed a policy of working within the system, strongly supported the alliance with the Batista government during World War II, and denounced the attack on the Moncada as adventurism by "bourgeois factions." (Thomas, *Cuba: The Pursuit of Freedom*, p. 842.) Even after 1959, Blas Roca was no admirer of Castro (and apparently even less so of Guevara), but he was elected to the new Party's Central Committee in 1965. From 1969 to 1975 he headed the Law Study commissions, which revised the Civil and Penal codes, reorganized the judicial system, and drafted a new Family Code and a new Constitution for the Republic. In 1975 Blas Roca was elected to the Political Bureau.

63. The self-defense statement Castro made in Santiago de Cuba on October 16, 1953, at his trial for the attack on the Moncada garrison. Published in book form as *La Historia Me Absolverá* (Havana: Ediciones Populares, 1961).

64. The Political Education Front.

meetings. I've completed my military training by going to military training classes at night. I finally learned to shoot a rifle, to take it apart, clean
it, and put it back together again. Learning how to handle arms is necessary so we can protect ourselves in case of aggression. I'd enjoy it if we
were given lighter weapons. The rifles we use are so heavy I can hardly
pick them up.

I do guard duty with the militia. Those on guard at the police station
are given a submachine gun instead of a rifle. I used to be at the station,
sitting at the entrance post, from 9:00 to 12:00 in the morning, but now
I've changed to the 6:00-to-9:00 shift in the evening.

I also go on street patrol in my neighborhood—for the CDR—at least
twice a month. The zone notifies a block CDR one day before it has
guard duty and the person in charge of the Vigilance Front rounds up
the patrol. The volunteers then go to the zone office for instructions.
There they're told, "Now, your beat is from this block to such-and-such."
Reinaldo used to be the Vigilance leader for our CDR, but now that he's
gone, I have to organize it myself.

On the evenings when there's no meeting or guard duty I visit a
comrade, or I may go to the movies, though I very seldom do anymore.
During the three years Reinaldo and I were separated, when everyone
believed we were still married, I couldn't go alone. It's not customary
here for married women to step out alone. Since the divorce, I go only if
I hear that the movie is especially good. I detest Cuban movies and have
seen only one or two based on revolutionary themes. Anyway, I'm not
nearly as interested in movies as I used to be. I have other things to do
and to think about now. That's been a real change in my life since the
Revolution.

As a matter of fact, I've been to the theater only once since 1959. I
didn't go because I couldn't get tickets. And now that I'm free to stand in
line all night to buy a ticket, the problem is that nothing special comes
here. About a year ago I went with Leida and Rafael to the National
Theater to see Alicia Alonso dance in *Swan Lake*. Marvelous! I adore
classical ballet; in my opinion modern ballet is a disfigurement of the art.

Occasionally I go to Leida's house to watch television. I like "Bat Mas-
terson" and "Frontiers"—things like that. Then there's "Behind the
Facade" with Consuelito Vidal, and lots of other Cuban entertainers I
used to see in the Amphitheater before the Revolution.

I don't have much time for entertainment anymore. Of the many
sports I've liked, I've followed only big league baseball since the Revolution. I haven't been to see a game, though admission is free, but I listen
on the radio. When the Cubans play abroad I don't miss a game. The day
they played the Americans, I had my ear glued to Leida's radio. I felt as
though I were right there in the stadium.

The last time I went to any sports event was about a year ago when I saw Fidel play volleyball at Sports City.[65] It certainly was worth going. Seeing Fidel as a *comandante,* then as a sportsman, is like seeing two completely different men. He plays like a boy, the way he gets excited—a real amateur. He doesn't tire fast, like Llanusa, the Minister of Education, for example.[66] Fidel is very boisterous and determined when he's trying to win and he fights like a lion. He doesn't expect favors because he's the chief—just the opposite. He's really beautiful, and he loses that austere air he has as a leader. Someone should make a movie of him playing. It would be wonderful.

In spite of the fact that I live alone, I get along. For example, I find it perfectly easy to get things fixed. Once I needed some boards to replace some rotten ones on the porch wall. The house was falling apart and Reinaldo wouldn't fix anything after we decided to separate. On the contrary, if something fell down, he'd smash it so I couldn't get it fixed. Well, after the divorce I decided to repair the wall myself, and I asked a boy I knew in *Poder Local* for boards 4 meters long. He got me six boards from a house that had been torn down, and he also got me some pink paint. I didn't even have to pay for the boards, because when a house is condemned, the materials from it are distributed where they're most needed. A friend of mine, the driver of an ice-cream truck, picked up the boards for me. Everybody is so helpful here.

Reinaldo had taken most of the nails, but before he left I filled a jar with some of every kind, so I was able to do the job properly. I don't know if it was good luck or my self-confidence, but those 4-meter planks fit that wall as though they were especially cut for it.

I've done a lot of household repairs myself. If the sewing machine is dirty or needs oiling I can take it apart and assemble it again. But if a part is broken I have to call the central repair service to replace it. The repair *consolidado* is very efficient. They usually come right away.

The one thing I don't repair myself is the electric wiring, because I'm terribly afraid of getting a shock. There's a man in the neighborhood who can't work because his nerves are a bit shaky; he's very useful to all us neighbors because any time we need a socket or a cable installed or something like that, he comes right over and does it. Of course it's against the law to work privately and we know he won't charge us, so we figure out how much the job is worth and say to him, "Here, take 3 *pesos* to buy yourself some medicine." We never let on that we're paying for the job, but pass it off as a courtesy gift.

There are no private plumbers either, so for plumbing repairs I have to call *Poder Local,* or a neighbor who knows about such things. There

65. A stadium built in the 1950s near the Las Cañas section of Havana.
66. Llanusa, a former national director of sports, was replaced as Minister of Education by Belarmino Castillo Mas in 1970. The present Minister is José R. Fernández.

aren't many good plumbers but we manage one way or another. Everybody knows a little of everything and neighbors help each other without thinking of money. In these times Cubans are plumbers one day, masons or electricians the next.

Other than plumbing, *Poder Local* hasn't made any repairs in my home. The house gets soaked every time it rains, but whenever I go to *Poder Local* to ask for roofing paper they tell me it isn't my zone's turn for it. I don't have time to hang around all morning so I haven't been able to get them to do anything so far.

My main pleasure in life is looking out for others, helping those in need. Aside from constantly making clothes for my neighbors and little friends, I give away my own things. Though I may not have enough, I like to see that others do. I still keep up the practice of never going visiting with empty hands. Even if I can't give a box of powder, a bottle of cologne, a toilet set, or a few handkerchiefs, I improvise something and keep on the right side of people. When a person is thoughtful, anything can be considered a gift, even a bunch of flowers that doesn't cost very much. Reinaldo's nieces and nephews usually bring me flowers. I suppose they're my favorite gift because they reveal a person's sentiments and upbringing.

The Revolution just doesn't leave time to see family, except by chance at mass rallies, or here and there. I'm much too busy to visit my relatives in Camaguey and Matanzas. But their economic situation has improved 100 percent. Everyone is working, and I can rest easy knowing they don't lack anything. True, there are many shortages but we're all affected equally.

My relatives have been somewhat divided in their ideas about the Revolution, but almost everyone in my family who is still in Cuba is with the Revolution, *patria o muerte,* and belongs to mass organizations. Even my sister Felicia, who is a Jehovah's Witness, belongs to the CDR and the Federation like Gabriela and me, though I'm the only woman in my family who does productive labor. The younger ones can't because they have to stay home with their children. However, many of my nieces and nephews do other volunteer work. The men have all been active since the beginning of the Revolution and most of them are now in the sugarcane fields for the 10-million-ton mobilization.

Before the Revolution my entire family were workers, every one of them, but now some of my cousins have become teachers, professors, officials. A nephew of mine and two of Gabriela's grandsons were sent to Russia to learn the language and study there. The nephew became a diplomat and the two younger boys are interpreters.

Gabriela is a widow now, sixty-seven years old, but she's strong and hardworking and still lives on a tiny farm in Camaguey. Before the

Revolution six of Gabriela's sons were farmhands. The only son who didn't work in the cane was Emiliano, the town barber. When the Revolution began, he joined the Twenty-sixth of July Movement and all his brothers followed suit. After the Triumph, the boys returned and joined the Revolutionary Army. Now only the eldest is still in the Army; all the others are working at different jobs.

Gabriela's children had only a fourth- or fifth-grade education but all her grandchildren will probably go through high school. I don't know whether or not they'll enter professions because boys and girls marry so young these days. However, their parents are concerned about their education and believe it's very important.

Gabriela raised my younger brother Teodoro's two sons. Teodoro died just four months after the Revolution. We were told that he'd hanged himself, but I didn't believe he'd committed suicide and I still don't. True, they concluded that he did, but the doctor was from the village and his investigation wasn't thorough because of all the upheaval of the Revolution. It's always been painful to me that his death was not explained.

Teodoro had worked on a farm in Camaguey and had married there, but his wife died two months after the second boy was born. My brother didn't talk much but I think he suffered greatly from his wife's death. For the four or five years Teodoro lived after his wife's death, he kept in close touch with Gabriela and the boys. He visited them and never failed to bring them money on payday. It seemed strange that it happened just before payday without my brother even leaving a note. I said to myself, "No sir, not without going to see the children."

His children were Teodoro's one pleasure. Besides, he was a Catholic. He was timid and retiring and looked like a sad old man, although he was only twenty-eight. He wasn't active or very interested in politics, but he sympathized with the Revolution and had sold bonds during the insurrection. I've always suspected that someone involved in the Batista regime hanged Teodoro, maybe because he was afraid my brother might denounce him.

Gabriela's sons helped Teodoro's boys get scholarships and they later applied to continue their studies. The government gives Gabriela a monthly allotment of 60 *pesos* for the two boys. With it she buys their dress clothes and puts the rest in the bank for them, because on their scholarship they get tuition, food, and school clothing. For the past two years one of the boys has been getting an additional 25 *pesos* a month, which Gabriela deposits in their savings account.

My brother Adolfo went to Oriente to work as a cane-cutter and he married there. He still works in sugar cane but has his own small farm, on which he grows crops and raises livestock. He belongs to various revolutionary organizations and occasionally comes to Havana. His two children are also revolutionary and had scholarships to study in Havana, but they preferred to leave school and get married.

My brother Luis Heberto lives with my sister Felicia in Havana. He has one child but never married. Luis Heberto works in dairy products, and though he's old and about to retire he's a Vanguard Worker and has won emulations in the regional office of the Ministry of Domestic Trade. He's also active in his CDR, as *responsable* of the Education Front and as a member of the Finance Front. He's a *permanente* in the sugar harvest and once won a vacation in Varadero for his cane-cutting. He wasn't interested in it, though, and said it should be given to a honeymoon couple.

Felicia, with whom I still don't get along very well, is seventy-four years old. Her husband Emigdio's flower stand was a good business until the Revolution abolished street stands. Then he had a hot-dog cart until they were taken out of circulation. Now he's a foreman in a soft-drink bottling factory, but he's old and his job simply requires him to keep an eye on the storage shed. He and Felicia had five sons and tried for a daughter, but the doctor told Felicia she shouldn't have any more children. Fourteen years later she had four girls in a row, one each year, and then another boy, Efrén. She's not a good sister but her children were innocent and I loved them all.

I was especially fond of Marcelo, Felicia's eldest son, who died in August of 1969. He was working at a store in Vedado, but just before his death he'd been cutting sugar cane in Camaguey. He'd worked in four or five previous sugar-cane harvests, but this time, since it was the Year of Decisive Effort, he remained four months. Soon after he returned, he had a heart attack. Well, it was the Decisive Year for him too, poor thing.

The ambulance and the medical care were free, but we had to pay the limousine and burial costs. These are now free too. About a hundred people attended the funeral. The service wasn't religious and there was no Mass, like at my mother's funeral. I like these old customs very much, especially the vigil by candlelight, but people have become afraid and do things by halves. Even the traditional wake is disappearing!

In general, the family was satisfied with Marcelo's funeral, but I wasn't. Marcelo had sacrificed himself for the Revolution, and when a dedicated revolutionary passes away, it's the practice for the revolutionary organizations to send delegates, yet none came. They didn't even send wreaths or flowers. After all, for many years Marcelo had been director of a sectional office of the *Recuperación de Bienes,* and he was a distinguished, popular figure in other organizations. I simply don't understand it.

Felicia has two other children who are *patria o muerte* revolutionaries. Crispín, her third son, left Cuba with his wife because she had big ideas

and didn't want to stay here. Cindo was a militiaman who belonged to
the Twenty-sixth of July Movement and fought with them. He separated
from his wife when she wanted to leave Cuba, but she kept after him
until they settled their differences and departed together.

Felicia's older children are Catholics but she and the younger children
are all Jehovah's Witnesses. When I was married in 1943, Felicia was
already converted and she and the children tried to convert me, but I
didn't like the idea. They gave me books and lectured me, yet all I know
about their religion is that they don't believe in the saints or anything
else, just in God.

None of us had every heard of the Jehovah's Witnesses until Felicia's
daughters became interested in it. The eldest daughter, Ofelia, came to
Havana to study and won a lot of prizes as an outstanding student.
Around 1940 she met Clara, an American Jehovah's Witness, who gave
English lessons. Clara introduced Ofelia and Felicia's younger children
to the religion. Felicia let herself be influenced to keep up with their
interests. She says they need her more than her older, revolutionary
children do because they're the ones who now have problems.

At an international assembly of the Jehovah's Witnesses held here in
Havana, Ofelia met Dennis, the American who married her and took her
to the United States. They have a great big house in Florida now and live
very well indeed. Felicia's daughters Demetria and Mima also went to the
United States just before the break in relations. They too are Jehovah's
Witnesses and have become religious notables and missionaries.

Felicia's older children were always very much opposed to this change
in religion. They believe that the Witnesses use their religion to get an
easy living out of other people. Their youngest sister, Petra, and her
husband still live in Felicia's house and are registered in the family ration
book, but they don't have jobs though they're strong and husky. Their
older brothers call them *gandozos*, lazy parasites. Actually Petra and her
husband don't spend much time at home. They go around from house
to house preaching and distributing religious tracts in spite of the fact
that the Revolution is opposed to missionary work. They receive a salary
from their Church and stay in the homes of other Witnesses when
they're away.

The older sons thought it a shame that their sisters wasted their youth
preaching instead of continuing beyond high school. And none of the
Jehovah's Witnesses contribute to their mother's support. With that faith
nothing is important except their religion and they put all their energies
into it.

The Catholics in the family are revolutionaries and the others aren't.
Their political differences didn't matter until the younger ones left the
country. Now politics has divided the family, and when the ones up

North write, the others don't even read the letters or ask after them. But I'm not that way. I always ask whether they've written and I read their letters. To me, their religion or their politics don't matter. They're my nephews and nieces wherever they may be.

Efrén, Felicia's youngest child, was the only one in the family who went to jail. He isn't a counterrevolutionary—neither he nor the other Jehovah's Witnesses are interested in politics—and usually the government leaves them alone. But when he was twenty-four he had to undergo compulsory military service and he refused to accept army discipline. In Cuba no one can be excused from army service or discipline. What one believes or feels doesn't matter, nor does being married or the sole support of children. Whatever the situation, whatever the pretext, the regulations must be obeyed.

In Efrén's military unit there was a whole group of Witnesses who refused to salute the flag or wear the uniform, or eat the festival supper on Christmas Eve. These rebels were all arrested. At first they were kept incommunicado. After two months they were allowed to send telegrams to their families, then for a few months they were in La Cabaña prison. Later they went to a work farm.

Efrén got into good shape and even gained weight on the work farm. The family was allowed to visit once a month and brought him sweets and whatever he wanted. He was happy there. Felicia and Emigdio and Efrén's wife took turns visiting him—only one relative was allowed to go at a time—but his older brothers never visited or sent him food because they didn't sympathize with him. They agreed with the government that the laws of the country are to be respected and they thought Efrén got what he deserved.

My nephew was sentenced to six to nine years but was released after four. Though he had no real complaints, neither he nor the Jehovah's Witnesses can be rehabilitated, nor can they be integrated into our society. I don't know why it is—they've been workers all their lives but they don't like the Revolution. At the time of his release, Efrén's wife, three children, and mother-in-law left the country, and he thinks he'll receive his visa soon because his sister Ofelia is sponsoring him.[67] Felicia says she and Emigdio will leave when Efrén does.

I've often wondered why only some of Felicia's children are revolutionaries while all of Gabriela's are. Both my sisters were good mothers and struggled hard for their children, so I can't attribute it to their mothers' differences in character. I think the change of religion in Felicia's family may have had something to do with life under Batista, a kind of looking for a way out. Certainly they'd seen the faults of the Catholic Church, the way it was against the poor with all the privileges

67. Efrén did receive his visa and is now in the United States.

given to the rich. The Jehovah's Witnesses religion isn't like that; it's quite humane. The brothers, as they're called, are very closely knit throughout the world and help each other and share whatever they have. For example, when a Jehovah's Witness arrives in the United States, the brothers get everything ready for him—a house, beds, towels, children's things. So to me, that religion is a type of Christianity and a form of communism, with its members joined in Christ the way the comrades here are joined in socialism. They operate in a different sphere but basically their goals are the same as ours. True, they're opposed to the Revolution and they want everyone to join their religion, but I personally believe they do nobody harm.

Chapter Six

One Foot in the Past

I'VE ALWAYS BEEN religious although I've never been much of a church-goer. Nor did I have faith in the saints, or visit shrines, or join any Catholic organization. All I did for the Church was sometimes make an altar cloth or bring a vase of flowers for the altar. I went to Mass once in a while to please my employer Señora Zaldivar. I went to Communion only about once a year during Holy Week or sometimes at a Sunday Mass, and I went to confession only when I had some problem, for consolation.

You see, my husband didn't believe in anything and constantly ridiculed me about God and religion, and that discouraged me. But when I finally stopped going to church, it was because most people had stopped. I thought, "Why should I go if it offends the Revolution?" It's not that I'm afraid to take part in religious ceremonies for fear of being seen by some revolutionary. When I'm asked to be a child's godmother, I still accept. If I'm invited to a church wedding, I go. I no longer pray the rosary or even own one, but that's merely a change in customs, not in principles. I still say grace before meals and pray before going to bed, and every time I begin a new task, whether for the Revolution or for myself, I place it in God's hands.

I still observe Christmas Day. Everyone who observed it before the Revolution has kept it up, even if they celebrate with only rice and beans. Some people go on outings, some to church, and some manage to have a big dinner. They still set up a pine branch in a corner with electric bulbs and a creche of the Child Jesus, and there is Santa Claus, too. Everyone finds little gifts to put under the tree, although with rationing it's not possible to give much. Each year, however, more items are becoming available. Mainly, Christmas is a time for families to get together. On Christmas Eve all my relatives in Camaguey still have midnight supper at Gabriela's house. Her in-laws live in the country and send her a dressed suckling pig for the occasion. My relatives in Havana also get together, each one contributing something—wine, candles, whatever he can.

Now that Christmas has been officially changed to July this year, I tell everybody that I'm going to celebrate Christmas Eve twice, in July and in December. "You can't do that, Inocencia," my comrades say, "we'll denounce you!" Declaring there'll be no Christmas in December is just a tall story of Fidel's. Oh, people will have to work as if it were a common, ordinary day, but who's to prevent us from having a special supper? And nobody can stop me from thinking about God that night.

So it isn't that I've stopped feeling religious. Not at all. But I have faith only in God, not in the Church anymore. In the Catholic Church one is well taken care of only if one pays. The Church gives everything—baptism, the marriage ceremony, and burial—for money. A person's poverty isn't taken into consideration. This made me realize that the Church is a business like any other. Also, a lot of people were involved in the Catholic Church just to live well and be part of high society. They lived in a man-made fantasy world. One who truly practices the faith doesn't care about money but acts out of his inborn feelings. People like that can't be bought anywhere.

Despite my doubts about the Church, I was very drawn to Pope John XXIII. I felt his death deeply and thought the world had lost a great man. He was humane and cared for his fellow man as Fidel does. I believe it was through Pope John's intervention that Church land and other properties were sold and put at the service of the people. I often think of one of his sayings, "I pray, feeling that everything depends on God, and I work, feeling that everything depends on me." He had great understanding of the world and was free of selfishness and would have done much for humanity.

I'll go on believing in God up to the last moment of my existence. I don't know what happens to us when we die, but I consider death to be beyond all things. Not even doctors are able to prevent it. It's not a punishment but nobody escapes it. That's when one's good and bad deeds are accounted for. A person who behaves right dies in peace. Without a clear conscience one can only die in a state of anguish. It must be terrible to die like that.

I'm not afraid to die; faith assures a peaceful death. At the moment of death I feel certain I'll confess and I'd like very much to receive Extreme Unction. If there's no priest, then I'll confess to myself. As for Heaven and Hell, I don't think about them at all. It doesn't worry me in the least.

I have no clear idea of what the soul is—I believe there is nothing after death. We pay here on earth for everything; that's what kills people, what makes them suffer and frightens them. A person's behavior decides his destiny. If he's bad and plants bombs and is against the Revolution, he must be punished.

I must admit that there are many confusing contradictions between religious faith and the Revolution. Sometimes I wonder if there isn't a conflict between those two allegiances. But I can believe in both at the same time because what is now called communism I've always practiced and learned as the principles of the Church. The difference is that now these principles and practices are general, whereas before, not many followed them. At the same time, many people make the mistake of believing that to be in favor of the Revolution is to be against God.

When I joined the Women's Federation nobody asked whether I believed in God and there was no conflict. The first thing I did as a member of the Federation was to cooperate in making layettes for Mother's Day. That was nothing new to me. All my life I'd been taught by the Church to give clothes to those in need. When we heard that a poor woman was expecting a baby, we sewed shirts and baby blankets for it. To this day, half the things I sew for people I do for free.

After all, it was God who said you shouldn't wish on your neighbor what you don't want for yourself. And He always spoke of doing good to others and sharing what you have. What is that if not true communism? Doesn't the Revolution require you to sacrifice yourself for others? And isn't that what religion is all about—kindness? So where's the conflict? I can't see how anybody can be required to renounce God in order to follow God's doctrine.

A big change since the Revolution is the increase in the religious practice of *santería*. Before the Revolution, *santería* was confined to Afro-Cubans because the whites were scared to death of it, but since the Revolution many poor, ignorant whites have become mixed up in voodoo. Now, one sees them dressed like *santeros,* in white from head to toe and wearing red seed necklaces. Maybe they join because they believe it will help them escape from the Revolution!

The whites who follow *santería* are not the ones who cast the spells. It's the black priests who have the power—the whites are just dupes. They're only the novices, the believers who are initiated because of pressure—the way Catholics go to church—or because of fear of sorcery or of becoming an invalid. It's the blacks who are the real magicians and exploiters, who use the rites for their own profit to harm others.

I believe the *santeros* will stop at nothing to harm a person they're really out to get. If they had access to Fidel or any of the other leaders, they might try it, with their potions and other preparations. Some claim they can hurt a person just by having him step on a powder they throw on the ground. Now that's really stupid! But if something toxic is put in a drink, it might really do harm.

A person who believes in God doesn't think like a *santero*. I'm fifty-four years old and have never thought about getting cancer or being paralyzed or anything of the kind. Why should I? If I have faith and something like that happens, that's the way it has to be, and nobody can prevent it, not by killing a hen or a cock or by spending 300 or 500 *pesos* on a necklace made of seeds or stones. And why should the *santeros* go through their elaborate pantomimes to ward off illness when there are so many fine doctors and surgeons and medicines? People who go to *santeros* end up in the hospital just like anyone else. Now *that* shows their belief is false.

To me, and to any civilized person, *santería* is a terribly backward cult. If it were just a legend or an account of what people believed in times past, I'd find it interesting, but I'm against keeping it alive. Furthermore, I don't believe the government should protect practitioners as it does, allowing them to buy things for their sorcery rites—the white clothing, the fruit, the stones that look like eyes that they hang on the wall next to the saints, and the goats and other animals to be sacrificed. If the *santero* can't buy animals in a store, he buys them at high prices on the black market. The thing is, they get them somehow. Killing animals not for food but to extract blood is a heresy against humanity.

They say the *santero* himself makes the necklaces and blesses them, but I know they're strung together by just anybody, perhaps the woman next door. They were sold openly until a short time ago; for all I know, they still are. Otherwise one wouldn't see so many of them around. The government has now eliminated all the hole-in-the-wall shops, but in the past that stuff could even be sold from porches.[68]

Those *santeros* and their guests carry on fiestas for two and three days at a time, doing their dances and other idiocies. That stupid dance! It depresses me, and so does that drumming of theirs that goes on day and night. Personally I'd prohibit *santería* absolutely, and I say so anywhere, any time the subject comes up. I don't limit the expression of my opinions in any way because I feel strongly about it. If my friend Magaly, who's a *santera,* brings up the subject, I tell her exactly what I think. After all, we have freedom of speech, and if she can say what she likes, so can I. I'm not attacking her, only disagreeing with *santeros,* just as any of them might disagree with the Revolution. We simply have opposite points of view.

I'm not quite as scared or distrustful of blacks as I was before the Revolution, but I can't see them as complete equals or treat them exactly as I would a white person. Certainly I'd never marry a black or mulatto man. Oh, never, never! Not unless I went blind first. When I see a married black and white, I'd like to have them both shot. I don't feel that way about the Chinese, but for me, black and white intermarriage is downright unforgivable. I was taught that in earliest childhood and I never will accept it, not here, in Russia, or anywhere else in the world, communism or no communism. I say there must be a reason why people are different colors. Perhaps I'm being stupid, but there it is.

68. See Mónica, n. 55.

I think my attitude is more a matter of religion than anything else. I've never met a black who was really Catholic or who genuinely believed in God. Never. If I met one who was truly Christian I might feel differently toward him. I've heard that there are Protestant *evangelista* blacks in other countries but there are none here. In Cuba, as soon as anybody beats a drum, all the blacks jump up.

I don't believe in spiritism either. If there were such a thing, my loved ones who are dead would have found some way to communicate with me. I always dream about them and I've never had any kind of revelation from them. A person with even a little intelligence who has reached any level of culture can't believe in such nonsense. Spiritism and *santería* are inventions of man. They're businesses that operate on the basis of money, and they're against the Catholic religion because they twist the truth, which is God. I also believe they're a manifestation of opposition to the Revolution.

I've always loved school and I wanted very much to complete my education. But if you were to add up all the months I attended before the Revolution, it wouldn't amount to more than two or three years. I got as far as a bit of the fifth grade. So in 1963 or 1964, when I heard an announcement from a sound truck inviting people to come to the new EOC night school, I enrolled along with Reinaldo. He'd gone to the fourth grade, and we were both put in the same class in fourth grade to catch up. From there we went through fifth and sixth grades and the EOC Secondary School.

The Worker-Peasant Secondary School wasn't a regular high school with the same standard of excellence. It's only a one-year school with a simplified course covering the rudiments of five subjects. I studied physics, chemistry, Spanish, mathematics, and plant biology, and I really enjoyed them. I got higher marks than Reinaldo because he has a poor memory; he failed the final examinations and didn't get his diploma. He still considered himself superior, though, and liked to humiliate others. When he left school I had to leave too. I wanted to go on to the pre-university and study mathematics, but he wouldn't let me. I gave up the idea and now I no longer yearn for more education.

When we were attending school, Reinaldo and I bought textbooks and a better dictionary and also some revolutionary pamphlets. Other than that, I've never bought a book in my life, though I've received a number as gifts. One of my English teachers gave me the story of *Madame Butterfly*. I was also given *The Diary of Che Guevara* and a booklet about a conference of Fidel's in the United States.

Novels seem a little fantastic to me although I've read a few. I prefer books that are true and will teach me history or something about other countries. I like to read Cuban history best, especially about the great Cuban heroes of the time of the War of Independence. Now they say that everything in the old history books was a lie, but, well, I've read the biographies of our patriots such as Carlos Manuel de Céspedes, Maceo, and Panchito Gómez, too, and I really liked them. I also read all of José Martí's poems and books.[69]

I've read all Fidel's published works. My favorite was *History Will Absolve Me.* I like it because of the courageous way he spoke out, and so well too, like the lawyer he is. It's impressive, the way he defended himself and called for justice. I used to read everything by El Che because there was always such deep feeling in it. And while I've not studied Marxism, I know something about the history of Russia and the Communist Party because I've been given revolutionary books by the CDR sectional in reward for good work. From them I've learned about Marx, Lenin, the Russian Revolution, Stalin, the stages Russia went through to achieve socialism, the Cuban Revolution, the emancipation of women, and so on.

I don't like poetry much except for the poems of Gabriela Mistral.[70] Before the Revolution I went to a lot of poetry recitations especially to hear her work. I don't go to readings anymore because my revolutionary chores keep me so busy, even though there are many new revolutionary poets writing now.

Some people say that a poet or an intellectual should write only to orient and stimulate young people to do what the Revolution wants them to. I don't agree. I believe that an intellectual should write about things as he sees them. Books and poems are very personal things; they must spring from the mind of the author, from his own knowledge, and should not be written for the purpose of helping or hurting anybody else.

If a writer limits himself to writing only what would help the Revolution, he has a very limited talent. All he's doing is repeating the revolutionary pamphlets. The Party has plenty of organizations for orienting and stimulating youth. And people who believe in the Revolution don't need to be talked into going along with it. When I read something against the Revolution, it doesn't affect me in the least. I might even find it funny. But I think if that's the way the author feels, he should say it. I don't believe a writer can harm the Revolution by expressing his true feelings.

69. All leaders of the Cuban independence movement. Carlos Manuel de Céspedes, a commander and president of the Rebel Republic, was killed by the Spaniards in 1874. General Antonio Maceo (1848–96), a mulatto, was a principal military leader of the War of Independence (1895). He and his brother José were commanders of the predominantly black *mambí* army; both were killed in battle. Panchito Gómez, son of the famous General Máximo Gómez, was an aide to Antonio Maceo and died in the same battle. José Martí y Pérez (1853–95), Cuba's most famous nationalist and philosopher, was an organizer of the Cuban independence movement. He also died in battle, in May, 1895.

70. Pseudonym of the Chilean poet Lucila Godoy Alcayaga (1889–1957), whose collections of poems—*Desolación, Ternura,* and *Tala*—won the nobel Prize for Literature in 1945.

I don't have much time to read anymore. Before the Revolution I read newspapers, pamphlets, and magazines to keep up with fashions, movies, news, and everything that was going on, not only in Cuba but all over the world. My favorite pieces were stories about actors and actresses and popular singers. Since they discontinued all the other newspapers, I read only *Granma* now, for news. That's the only one there is. But I don't even have an hour to spare anymore, and when I do, I sew.

When women's liberation was the topic in our study circle, it stirred up so much controversy we had to continue the discussion in another session. Some husbands thought one thing, others another, and the women were also divided. Some of the women equated the function of a housewife with that of a servant. They believe that men should help with the dishes, housekeeping, and so on. And some of the men said they usually help their wives with general housecleaning, that they often wash dishes and sweep floors. But I don't like to see a man doing that kind of work, unless a woman is ill. Otherwise, I think it's a woman's duty to organize her housework so she'll have time to engage in revolutionary tasks. The trouble is that many women start gossiping with neighbors and it gets to be 10:00 in the morning and they haven't made the beds. By noon they're rushing around like mad. Naturally!

Personally, I would never renounce woman's work though I wholeheartedly approve of women's liberation. I do any work I can for the Revolution, cutting cane or whatever, but I enjoy housework so much I don't want to be freed from it. I suppose I differ from most women in that respect. Of course I like to go to movies, to a party now and then, but I also like to have my clothes nicely ironed and I prefer to do the work myself. When a housewife says she's no better than a servant in her own home, it seems to me she doesn't love her husband or her children or her home. In fact, I think she's disappointed in being a woman.

To me, women's liberation means that a woman shouldn't have to submit to a man while he runs around doing whatever he pleases. Also, that women have the right to participate actively in the Revolution and to work outside the home, though I don't believe that the mother of young children should go off and work on a farm. But the Revolution would never ask that of her.

The truth is, women in Cuba are rarely integrated into the Revolution and most of them don't have jobs.[71] Aside from male prejudices, conditions here make it difficult for them to work. Women run into an infinite number of problems if they want their children to be fed in school or in public dining rooms, or to attend nursery schools or kindergarten, or to

71. See Introduction, pp. xviii–xix.

have laundry done outside the home. Such facilities are readily available only in cases of urgent need, like when a woman must work to support three or four children. Still, I believe that every married woman should have as many children as her health and circumstances permit.

As old-fashioned as it may seem, I also believe that a woman should obey her husband, within reasonable limits. Every woman with a home and family is aware of her duties and responsibilities and need not be dictated to, as I was. It's not necessary to tell her, "Do this, do that." That's a kind of slavery. Instead, mutual understanding and agreement ought to be involved in everything a couple does.

A woman has the right to demand faithfulness of her husband. No woman can accept her husband having an affair with someone else. However, I don't go along with those who see women's liberation as equality with men. A woman should be free to form her own opinions and make her own decisions, but that doesn't mean she has to act like a man and have one lover today and another tomorrow. She should never under any circumstances have two men at the same time. Some women claim they stay with their husbands for the sake of the children, and then secretly carry on with other men. I think that's wrong. When a woman stops loving a man she should give him up. So when I speak of women's liberation I don't mean sexual freedom or freedom derived from use of the pill or the ring. I don't think they've had much of an impact here. We've been brought up to believe that a man loses nothing by being promiscuous but a woman loses everything.

If a woman has to work because there's a task to be done and she has good health and no impediments, then she should go out and work. The problem is that men, Cuban men anyway, have a one-track mind. They think that when a woman has a bit of freedom she only uses it to look for another man. That's the kind of thing we Cubans ought to rise above. Of course, there's always the possibility that one or two may start an affair—from the beginning of time some wives have been unfaithful—but that shouldn't interfere with men and women belonging to the same organizations or the same Party. I, for one, feel as though my male comrades are brothers. What's more, I believe that the more freedom a woman has, the easier it is for her husband to discover whether or not she really loves him.

As much as I'm in favor of women's liberation, I believe a girl should complete her studies before becoming fully liberated or marrying. Cuban mothers are much more permissive now. Nothing is forbidden nowadays. It used to be that girls weren't allowed to go out alone any-where; now they go all over the place, with no chaperone. I don't mean to imply that they do anything bad, but from the time they're mere children they get used to acting for themselves and relying on their own point of view, uncontrolled by their *mamás*.

From what I've observed at meetings and other organized activities, the problems of our young people go deeper than the simple lack of social graces. Our youth, except for the Young Communists, who've reached a higher level of development, are still weakly organized and irresponsible at work. In the country, for instance, the old people work while the young ones stroll around or simply disappear. During a big mobilization they give a lot of orders but never become fully engrossed in the work, or at meetings they fool around and don't pay attention to what's going on.

It's true that our young people can't contribute much to the Revolution because they must give most of their time to studying and self-improvement, but they're much more idealistic than older people. Their knowledge is limited to the struggle for the new life, while the older generation is still backward in some ways. But young people haven't as yet found their way and must be guided by their teachers and by older people.

I suppose our young people are just not serious enough, and I blame this situation on the way they're being reared. A normal child who grows up in a good home and isn't allowed to hang out with bad company isn't apt to become a delinquent. One way to cure a delinquent is to separate him from his parents and put him in the hands of a psychiatrist or in a good school where he'll be taught sound principles.

If a boy kills someone, different measures must be taken because he's dangerous and might kill again. If he has a normal brain, it probably means his instincts are bad and he should be sent before the firing squad. For instance, in a recent case, a youth with a bad criminal record who had murdered a defenseless little old man was declared to have evil instincts and to be unrehabilitable and was sentenced to death. Nobody that perverse should be turned loose again. But minors are never sent to face the firing squad in Cuba, only people twenty years old or more.

What the problem boils down to is that nowadays in Cuba we put children first, bring them up to do as they please, and make no demands upon them. As a result, they don't strive for excellence. They're not exactly spoiled and selfish but they're willful and disobedient and, well, lacking in rectitude. In my time it was unusual for a teacher to punish a pupil. Children were respectful and behaved themselves in school. Today, students talk back to the teacher and say, "You can't hit me. I'll do what I please." They even talk like that to their parents! Perhaps I'm an old woman who doesn't understand newfangled ways, but I like to see young people show some respect for their elders. I'd certainly want my children to act as properly as I did to my parents.

It's not that I object to young people trying to be different or asserting their own personalities. Take hippies, for instance. I don't mind seeing a young boy with long hair and a beard. I think they're kind of cute. Some of them look downright handsome. Every generation of young people has made itself ridiculous in its own way, mainly I suppose to attract the opposite sex. And where's the harm in it? I like the Beatles[72] and just about everything else pertaining to youth.

The kind of thing that disturbs me is to see young, strong men in minor posts that could be filled by women. Why should a big, strapping fellow sit like a bump on a log when a skinny, sickly woman is out cutting cane or picking coffee?

Still, I must admit that much of the fault I find with young people holds as true for older folks. For example, in a restaurant one sometimes sees a dishwasher take an hour to wash a glass or two. Then it takes another hour for the glass to reach the desperate customer. No wonder people waiting in line become nasty. Seeing those waitresses taking their time setting a place or wiping the counter, you can tell they don't want to work. I say, if a person doesn't feel like working, she shouldn't work. If she does, she should do her best.

I had a very shocking experience with this type of thing when I worked for two months under temporary contract in a government clothing shop. There were fifteen or twenty male clerks in the shop, sitting around on the counters doing nothing but chatter. In the past, employees thought they had to make noise to show they were working, so when they had nothing to do they'd pull the drawers in and out. Today, unfortunately many people still have the same mentality. At the clothing shop there were times when we ran out of thread or needles and had to wait around idle for a couple of hours because the man assigned to supplies was busy with something else and couldn't go to the next floor for it. The others just sat and wouldn't get it themselves. I just can't go along with such apathy. This kind of behavior is the fault of the administrators. They should be more vigilant.

The CDRs and other organizations do manage to accomplish something, but even there we don't find complete honesty. Not everybody has a social conscience. A lot of people in the CDRs don't realize what their function ought to be, and not everybody works. If they're asked to clean up a street or do something for the benefit of others, they simply don't show up.

It would be interesting to talk with Fidel about some of these things. Recently when the *Fruti-Cuba* stands were set up in all the neighborhoods, we were told we were going to have fruit and I don't know what all. Well, there wasn't any fruit—there wasn't anything. The people in charge had misled Fidel by giving him the wrong information. If the fruit hasn't been grown, why put up stalls?

---

72. The Beatles' music was semiofficially disapproved of at the time of this study and was not played on Cuban radio and television.

Good administration has to start in the fields. When we go with the CDR to weed coffee plants, we ride along the highway where the strips of coffee bushes are neat as a pin. But farther in, the weeds are so thick we can't see the coffee. This means they keep up the area people see and don't bother about the rest, proving that the *responsable* in charge hasn't been paying proper attention to the job.

Just the other day I was saying to a friend of mine, "I agree that things here in Cuba should be attractive, but I don't think it's right that Fifth Avenue[73] is cleaned and the shrubbery pruned so often, when just around the corner the rubbish heaps reach up to the level of the roofs. And how long was there a leak in that sewer pipe in one of those dormitories where the scholarship children live?"

I say things like that amount to deceiving Fidel, because if he should go by Fifth Avenue he'd probably say, "How beautifully these streets are kept up!" Not everything should be left to Fidel, who has the entire nation on his shoulders. He can't be into everything, so there are always slip-ups. I say others must take some responsibility for getting things done.

Here in Cuba there's been a great deal of discussion of a profound issue—the person of the future whom we call the "new man." I'm not very intelligent, but to me the "new man" in a socialist country is one who's freed himself from all the old prejudices, such as the subjugation of women and the desire to live for himself alone. The "new man" must have a highly developed social conscience. He must be without egotism and must act for the general good, not for his own or for his family's benefit. The "new man" should devote himself not to his individual development but to that of the whole world. Never should he say, "I'm going to build a house for myself," but "We're all going to get together and build this house for someone who needs it more than we do. Let's help those with the most serious problems so that everybody can live peacefully and well."

Of course, I don't mean that everybody should spend all his time, or even most of it, doing productive labor or building houses. Suppose, for instance, a girl wants to be a pianist. Before she knows enough to become a good performer or teacher she must practice for hours every day. That's time well spent. After all, we can't live like beasts of burden, simply to eat and work. People need culture, relaxation, fiestas. But that very same girl who's studying piano will be sent by the government for two or three months every year to cut cane or do some other kind of agricultural work, and that, too, is as it should be. The pianist, the

---

73. A main boulevard through the residential section of Miramar and Marianao.

doctor, the teacher, the student should be trained just like every other comrade to help in any emergency, including war.

Take me, for example. Suppose I'd done nothing but housework, washed clothes, ironed, given all my time to making the house look pretty. I'd never have learned how to cut a bunch of bananas or when coffee should be planted or watered or picked. All these things should be learned by doing. Books aren't enough. The memory of something read may grow cold or be forgotten, but experience is never forgotten. The conditions of the country must be learned in practice, not merely in theory. And the "new man" must be ready to solve Cuba's problems and not depend on another country as we used to. He must develop our land so we can produce all we need and have a surplus for trade.

This concept of the "new man" is wonderful, and when conditions are right I believe the "new man" will arise. At this stage we're trying to create the conditions, though there's still confusion about the changes that have taken place. I've seen the qualities of the "new man" in some of the older *compañeros*, but I've not found them in our youth, not even in the young militants. It may be that our young people, like their elders, are still partly the product of one stage and partly of another. Perhaps it will be *their* children who are the "new men," though I have my doubts.

I don't think the "new man" should be like El Che and fight in other countries. No! Every country should solve its problems according to its resources and should develop by its own efforts as Cuba is doing. I didn't agree with Cubans going to Bolivia. If the Bolivians want to follow our lead, let them do the fighting themselves. And I don't think it was the government's policy to send Cubans there. No, that was Che's idea, to take off on an adventure, just as he did in coming to Cuba. The Cubans who went with Che weren't sent by Fidel; they were a guerrilla group, not a government contingent, otherwise there'd have been more security measures and more defensive weapons. In Bolivia Che's men were fighting with practically nothing. Still, we were following a dangerous policy in South America and the United States was very angry about it, although the whole world would be glad to see the South Americans fighting for their freedom the way we did.

I think Che made a serious mistake in Bolivia. It's tragic that people sacrifice themselves like that. What did he gain there, after all? If he wanted to direct a movement, he could have been its intellectual leader without endangering his life. He could have done the groundwork, studied the project, created the conditions for a movement before going into action. As it was, he solved nothing. But I suppose he believed it was his duty, and duty is above everything else. It's only by doing our duty that we'll gain true freedom. What's the use of freedom for its own sake? It should be used in the creation of a better world.

These are my opinions, not necessarily Fidel's. I loved Che—he had an exceptional brain—but I love Fidel more. Above all things and all men is Fidel. True, we're enduring hard work and scarcity, but we're solving our problems, as Russia and China and other countries solved theirs. We've had to begin from nothing, because the technicians and professional people were the first to leave the country and it has cost us an enormous effort to overcome that loss. But little by little we'll resolve our difficulties and we won't need rockets to do it.

Before the Revolution, everything here was from the United States. Whatever they had, we wanted too. We lived as if we were a city of the United States. Now we don't have to anymore. And to be free of the Americans, I don't believe we must subject ourselves to Russia or China or any other country. We've shown our independence by our open disagreement with Russia about letting Che go to Bolivia. The Russians want to avoid trouble with the Americans, and if Russia openly supported a Latin-American revolution they'd be risking a big to-do with the United States. Of course we have obligations to Russia and the other countries we trade with—France, Spain, Mexico, Canada, England, Japan, Vietnam, China, even with some Latin-American countries—but I don't think Fidel would allow us to be subservient to any of them. He knows that what his people want is to be really free even if we have to go hungry. Let others live in their countries and let us live in ours, the way we want.

We don't even have to be concerned with democracy here because the masses now govern Cuba. Everyone except a small minority is in favor of the present government, otherwise they'd have taken action against it. We don't need elections, because whenever there's something to be discussed, everyone is invited to gather at the Plaza de la Revolución and hear about it. The enormous crowds that attend each time Fidel speaks prove that. And a million more stay home and watch the meeting on TV. But nobody stays home on July 26 or January 2. Take a turn around the barrios and you'll see how all the streets are deserted. The only ones at home are old people and a few mothers with small children, and they listen to Fidel's speech on the radio.

People aren't forced to listen to our leader as they were in Batista's time. True, now whole schools are sent to meet an important diplomat, but the students go because they want to. In fact, many don't go. Here, even children are free to choose. Next door to me there are school children whose *papá* is a policeman, yet they never go to meetings. And many more don't attend because their mothers think they're too young. But those are isolated cases. Most children love to go.

Someday, perhaps, it will be necessary to hold elections.[74] Fidel himself will say so when we least expect it. He'll speak at a mass meeting and

74. See Gracia, n. 28.

say it's time to choose a new leader. Raúl is Fidel's rightful heir but there are others capable of directing the country—Almeida, Dorticós, Armando Hart, Llanusa, and all the other members of the Central Committee.[75] I have full faith in all our principal leaders. Naturally I wish Fidel could be with us always—he's our beloved national leader—but we're prepared. We're all mortal and death might surprise anyone, morning or night.

There is no constitution in Cuba now. When we had one, nobody paid any attention to it, least of all those in the government.[76] There it was on paper, mocked at by everyone's actions. What's the point of a piece of paper if it's not respected? The Revolution here has its own laws, its own human rights that must be respected, and it makes sure that they are. We citizens of Cuba have firm faith that nothing can happen to us as long as we obey the rules, and there's no need to have it written on a piece of paper.

As I see it, what we have is true democracy, the certainty that we can sleep in peace at night because no law, no judge, nobody can punish us unjustly. A person who insists on a constitution and elections and doesn't accept the revolutionary laws must be against the Revolution. Such people think only of themselves and their own welfare, not of mankind. They're in a very small minority, but they must also obey the law of the land and adapt to it.

Before the Revolution I didn't feel any great love for my country. Of course I felt a kind of love for my province, Matanzas, the love anyone feels for home. No matter where I might be, I'd feel that. But since the Revolution, I've changed completely toward the country. Now I feel for all of Cuba because I know the country is everybody's equally, and not in the hands of a monopoly or of someone who just wants to get rich or ride roughshod over the rest of us.

We Cubans will solve our difficulties little by little. Despite the problems, I have no fears for our future. On the contrary, I'm enthusiastic about the way things have progressed since the government took steps to increase agricultural production. There was a great deal of turmoil at the beginning, but the government has become more mindful of conditions in the countryside and the economy has improved. Our land is very

75. Comandante Juan Almeida Bosque, Armando Hart Dávalos, and Dr. Osvaldo Dorticós Torrado, all members of the Political Bureau. Dorticós is President of the Republic. José Llanusa Gobel, former Minister of Education, is no longer a member of the Central Committee. In 1976 he was director of the Matanzas cattle-breeding project.

76. In 1975, a new Constitution for the Republic was drafted to replace the Constitution of 1940 (incorporated into the Fundamental Law of 1959), which, as Inocencia says, was never enforced. The new Constitution received overwhelming endorsement (97.7 percent, 5,473,534 of 5,602,973 votes cast) in a referendum held on February 15, 1976. (*Granma Weekly Review*, Feb. 29, 1976, p. 1.) The text of the Constitution appeared in *ibid.*, Mar. 7, 1976.

productive, and if we work hard enough we can produce practically every agricultural product. Soon we won't have to depend on imported foodstuffs. After the 1970 sugar harvest, I expect the food situation to be much better here. The housing situation will also improve, but our energies should be directed to the production of cement and other building materials.

If we weren't blockaded our development would be more rapid and efficient. But in spite of obstacles I believe that Cuba's future will be prosperous and happy, with all Cubans cooperating with each other and sharing everything. I also have confidence in the Communist Party now that it's putting Fidel's ideas into practice. I know that he needs a lot of good people on his side. Perhaps now that the stage of persuasion is completed, we the people, along with the Central Committee, will be able to help Fidel achieve everything he wants.

Abbreviations

ANAP	*Asociación Nacional de Agricultores Pequeños* (National Association of Small Farmers)
CDR	*Comités de Defensa de la Revolución* (Committees for Defense of the Revolution)
CTC	*Confederación de Trabajadores de Cuba* (Confederation of Cuban Workers), reorganized as *Central de Trabajadores de Cuba* (Central Organization of Cuban Trade Unions)
CUJAE	*Ciudad Universitaria José Antonio Echeverría* (José Antonio Echeverría University City)
FEU	*Federación Estudiantil Universitaria* (University Student Federation)
FMC	*Federación de Mujeres Cubanas* (Federation of Cuban Women)
INIT	*Instituto Nacional de la Industria Turística* (National Institute of the Tourist Industry)
INRA	*Instituto Nacional de Reforma Agraria* (National Institute of Agrarian Reform)
MINCIN	*Ministerio de Comercio Interior* (Ministry of Domestic Trade)
MINCON	*Ministerio de Construcción* (Ministry of Construction)
MINED	*Ministero de Educación* (Ministry of Education)
MINREX	*Ministerio de Relaciones Extranjeras* (Ministry of Foreign Affairs)
OFICODA	*Oficina de Control para la Distribución de Alimentos* (Office for Control of Food Distribution)
PCC	*Partido Comunista de Cuba* (Communist Party of Cuba)
PSP	*Partido Socialista Popular* (Popular Socialist Party)
UJC	*Unión de Jóvenes Comunistas* (Union of Young Communists)
UNEAC	*Unión Nacional de Escritores y Artistas Cubanos* (National Union of Cuban Writers and Artists)

Glossary

barbudos	literally "the bearded ones," a term used for members of Castro's Rebel Army
botella	literally "bottle," used idiomatically to mean a sinecure, usually obtained by political appointment
caballería	land measure, approximately 33⅓ acres
círculo infantil	nursery school
colonia	sugar-cane farm; some were independently owned, others were company-owned but operated by tenant farmers
colono	sugar-cane farmer; refers to all cane growers whether they owned or rented their farms
comadre, compadre	terms used by a child's parents and godparents in addressing or referring to each other
consolidado	a general term of reference for any consolidated enterprise
Cordón de la Habana	the cultivated greenbelt that encircled Havana
décima	Spanish stanza of ten octosyllabic lines
guajiro (a)	Cuban peasant
guayavera	a pleated shirt-jacket popular among Cuban men
gusano	literally "worm," used in Cuba to refer to anyone who does not support the Revolution, from passive opponents to active counterrevolutionaries
jardín infantil	open-air nursery school
kilo	a *centavo*
"patria o muerte"	"fatherland or death," an expression used to characterize an ardent revolutionary
permanente	long-term volunteer for productive labor
peseta	one fifth of a *peso,* or 20 *centavos*
peso	Cuban currency maintained by the Castro government at the pre-1959 rate of 1 *peso* = 1 U.S. dollar until 1974, when the rate was changed to 1.25 *pesos* = 1 U.S. dollar

reparto   a suburb or subdivision of a city

responsable   person in charge of, or responsible for, a particular task
                           or area of activity

santería   Afro-Cuban saint cult that combines Yoruban and
                           Roman Catholic beliefs and traditions

santero   priest-practitioner of the *santería* cult

solar   a low-rent multiple-family structure, usually one story
                           high, with one or more rows of single rooms or small
                           apartments opening onto a central patio

Selected Bibliography

BIBLIOGRAPHIC NOTE

In a study such as this, the most important source materials are, of course, the interviews from which the life stories are constructed. However, due to the special nature of the Cuba project and to the peculiarities of doing field work in a socialist system, secondary sources and supplementary field materials took on special importance. Since this latter group of materials is not cited in the bibliography, we want to mention those which were most important in helping us better understand the life stories and write footnotes to the texts. Among supplementary field materials we most relied on were: observations of the CDRs in five *repartos* and interviews with officers and members; a conference with officials and interviews with eleven judges of the People's Courts and reports on six observed trials; a pilot study of the *jardines infantiles* and interviews with the program's directors; interviews with officials of *Poder Local;* interviews with Armando Torres, who led the drive to eliminate organized prostitution in Cuba; and special studies of household budgets and material inventories. Finally, there were the approximately 12,000 pages of interview material from informants not included in the three volumes of this series; these interviews verified and elaborated upon some of the information provided in the published life stories. All of the above-mentioned sources were of great value in providing details on the mechanics of daily life under Cuban socialism, which, as far as we know, are unavailable in published sources.

The following works from the appended selected bibliography have been of particular value to us. For historical background we relied most heavily on Hugh Thomas's *Cuba: The Pursuit of Freedom,* a study of the island from the English expedition in 1762 through the missle crisis of 1962, with heavy emphasis on the twentieth century. We consulted Philip Foner's two-volume study of Cuba from 1492 to 1895 (part of a projected multivolume series on Cuban-U.S. relations) for additional information on slavery, colonialism, and the War of Independence. Other sources of background information were: the classic study of the sugar and tobacco industries by Fernando Ortíz, one of Cuba's most famous sociologists; *Rural Cuba* (1950) by the North American sociologist Lowry Nelson; and Verena Martínez-Alier's study of Cuban women in the nineteenth century (1974). For understanding the terminology and explaining certain rituals and practices of the Afro-Cuban sects, the works of Lydia Cabrera and Romulo Lachatañere were especially helpful. A good general discussion of education and social-welfare policies in Cuba during the first three decades of this century can be found in *Problems of the New Cuba; Report of the Commission on Cuban Affairs* (1935).

The *Atlas Nacional de Cuba,* a magnificent work compiled by the Cuban and Soviet academies of sciences, was most useful to us, particularly as a source for changing place names. Included among its many maps are graphic summaries of some of the Revolution's major achievements. In 1971 its text was translated from the Spanish and reprinted (without maps) by the U.S. Department of Commerce, Joint Publications Research Service.

For information on the general direction of the Revolution's social and economic policies during the first decade we consulted the following: the speeches, writings, and published interviews of Ernesto Guevara, Minister of Industry during the early 1960s; the firsthand account of this period written by Edward Boorstein, then an economic advisor to the Cuban government; and Theodore Draper's *Castroism: Theory and Practice* for its discussion of the early attempts (under Guevara's direction) at industrialization. The Cuban Economic Research Project (*A Study on Cuba,* 1965) published a concise, yet quite detailed, study of the direction of economic development under the Revolution (including some economic statistics for the period 1959–64) in a larger work that includes an economic history of the colonial and republican periods.

For the period 1959–69, the work of Carmelo Mesa-Lago (including that with Roberto Hernández) and that of Lionel Martin (the *Guardian's* Cuba correspondent) were invaluable for an understanding of Cuba's labor policies. Richard R. Fagen's study of the CDRs is the most comprehensive single English-language work on that organization for the period 1961–65. For additional and more recent information on the CDRs, as well as the People's Courts (and information on other mass organizations, such as unions) we are indebted to David K. Booth for sending us his excellent unpublished Ph.D. thesis (University of Surrey, 1973), which was based on field work carried out in Cuba in 1969.

In Bonachea and Valdés's *Cuba in Revolution,* Ricardo Leyva's article on health care and Valdés's article on education were especially helpful. Government publications acquired in Cuba in 1969–70—general information bulletins, statistical reports, texts of laws, for example—provided invaluable detail, particularly on education policy. Finally, and most important, were the speeches and writings of Fidel Castro, from 1953 (*History Will Absolve Me,* which contains a comprehensive statement of the Twenty-sixth of July Movement's original objectives) to 1976. Castro's speeches were a principal source of information to us on social and economic policies, for details on the implementation of laws and programs as well as on their successes and failures.

Because this series places great emphasis on daily life under the revolutionary system, we found especially helpful journalistic accounts which re-created the general atmosphere in Havana, and elsewhere in Cuba, during the first ten years and after. The most outstanding single work of this kind is *Castro's Cuba, Cuba's Fidel* by the photo-journalist Lee Lockwood. This very readable and informative book, which is based on Lockwood's lengthy interviews with Castro, serves as a good introduction to revolutionary Cuba. Ruby Hart Phillips, the *New York Times* correspondent in Cuba for almost thirty years, wrote two books describing changes in Havana during the two years after the Triumph. The first of these, *Cuba: Island of Paradox* (1959), an evocative account of the first weeks after the victory, was written before Ms. Phillips became a militant anti-Castroite. Three other notable journalistic treatments of life in Cuba in the mid- and late 1960s are Sutherland's *Youngest Revolution* (1969), Yglesias's *In the Fist of the Revolution* (1969), and Reckford's *Does Fidel Eat More than Your Father?* (1971). Overall, Sutherland's work is enthusiastically sympathetic, but it contains good, quite realistic appraisals of race relations and the women's movement during the Revolution's first eight years.

For the purpose of updating information in the life stories, the single most valuable source was the *Granma Weekly Review* (1971–76), an official compilation of each week's most important speeches and news stories, translated and reprinted from *Granma*, the official daily of the Communist Party. Cubanists who are interested in every nuance in the printed media that might indicate changes in policy or leadership will certainly prefer *Granma*, but the *Weekly Review* does contain the complete text of most major speeches, laws, and declarations, as well as articles on Cuban history (particularly on martyrs and revolutionary battles), coverage of international relations and visiting dignitaries, and sports news. The *Weekly Review* has the obvious disadvantage over the daily paper of being a collection of articles selected especially for foreign audiences, and the minor disadvantage of utilizing often stilted official translations.

BOOKS AND PAMPHLETS

Anuario Estadístico, Curso 1966–67. Havana: Ministry of Education, n.d.
Area Handbook for Cuba. Washington, D.C.: Government Printing Office, 1971.
Atlas Nacional de Cuba. Havana: Academy of Sciences of Cuba and Academy of Sciences of the U.S.S.R., 1970.
Bonachea, Rolando B., and Nelson P. Valdés, eds. *Cuba in Revolution*. New York: Anchor Books, 1972.
Boorstein, Edward. *The Economic Transformation of Cuba*. New York: Monthly Review Press, 1968.
Booth, David K. "Neighbourhood Committees and Popular Courts in the Social Transformation of Cuba." Unpublished Ph.D. thesis, University of Surrey, 1973.
Cabrera, Lydia. *El Monte*. Miami: Rema Press, 1968.
Castro, Fidel. *History Will Absolve Me*. Havana: Book Institute, 1967.
Los CDR en Granjas y Zonas Rurales. Havana: Dirección Nacional de los CDR, 1965.
Chapman, E. E. *A History of the Cuban Republic*. New York: Macmillan, 1927.
Constitución de la República de Cuba. Havana: Compañia Editora de Libros y Folletos, 1940.
Cuba: A Giant School. Havana: Ministry of Foreign Affairs, n.d.
Cuba: El Movimiento Educativo, 1967/68. Havana: Ministry of Education, 1968.
Cuban Economic Research Project. *A Study on Cuba*. Coral Gables: University of Miami Press, 1965.
Debray, Regis. *Revolution in the Revolution?* New York: Monthly Review Press, 1967.
Draper, Theodore. *Castroism: Theory and Practice*. New York: Praeger, 1965.
———. *Castro's Revolution: Myths and Realities*. New York: Praeger, 1962.
Fagen, Richard R. *The Transformation of Political Culture in Cuba*. Stanford, Calif.: Stanford University Press, 1969.
———, Richard A. Brody, and Thomas J. O'Leary. *Cubans in Exile*. Stanford, Calif.: Stanford University Press, 1968.
Ferguson, Erna. *Cuba*. New York: Alfred A. Knopf, 1946.
Foner, Philip S. *A History of Cuba and Its Relations with the United States*, vols. I (1492–1845) and II (1845–95). New York: International Publishers, 1962, 1963.
Fundamental Law of Cuba, 1959. Washington D.C.: Pan American Union, 1959.
La Educación en los Cien Años de Lucha. Havana: Book Institute, 1968.

Gillette, Arthur. *Cuba's Educational Revolution.* London: Fabian Research Series 302, June, 1972.

Halperin, Maurice. *The Rise and Decline of Fidel Castro.* Berkeley, Calif.: University of California Press, 1972.

Horowitz, Irving Louis, ed. *Cuban Communism.* New Brunswick, N.J.: Transaction Books, 1970.

Jahn, Jahnheinz. *Muntu: An Outline of the New African Culture.* New York: Grove Press, 1961.

Karol, K. S. *Guerrillas in Power.* New York: Hill and Wang, 1970.

Kenner, Martin, and James Petras, eds. *Fidel Castro Speaks.* New York: Grove Press, 1969.

Lachatañere, Romulo. *Manual de Santería.* Havana: Editorial Caribe, 1942.

Lavan, George, ed. *Che Guevara Speaks: Selected Speeches and Writings.* New York: Merit, 1967.

Leiner, Marvin, with Robert Ubell. *Children Are the Revolution: Day Care in Cuba.* New York: Viking Press, 1974.

Ley de Reforma Agraria. Havana, 1959.

Lockwood, Lee. *Castro's Cuba, Cuba's Fidel.* New York: Vintage, 1969.

MacGaffey, Wyatt, and Clifford R. Barnett. *Cuba: Its People, Its Society, Its Culture.* New Haven: HRAF, 1962.

Martínez-Alier, Verena. *Marriage, Class and Colour in Nineteenth Century Cuba.* Cambridge: Cambridge University Press, 1974.

Matthews, Herbert L. *The Cuban Story.* New York: Braziller, 1961.

———. *Fidel Castro.* New York: Simon and Schuster, 1969.

Memorias de CDR, 1962. Havana: Dirección Nacional de los CDR, 1963.

Memorias de CDR, 1963. Havana: Dirección Nacional de los CDR, 1964.

Mesa-Lago, Carmelo. *Cuba in the Seventies.* Albuquerque: University of New Mexico Press, 1974.

———. *The Labor Force, Employment, Unemployment and Underemployment in Cuba: 1899–1970.* Beverly Hills, Calif.: Sage Publications, International Studies Series, 1972.

———. *The Labor Sector and Socialist Distribution in Cuba.* New York: Praeger, 1968.

———, ed. *Revolutionary Change in Cuba.* Pittsburgh: University of Pittsburgh Press, 1971.

Nelson, Lowry. *Cuba: The Measure of a Revolution.* Minneapolis: University of Minnesota Press, 1972.

———. *Rural Cuba.* Minneapolis: University of Minnesota Press, 1950.

La Ofensiva Revolucionaria: Asamblea de Administradores Populares. Havana: Dirección Nacional de los CDR, 1968.

Ortíz, Fernando. *Cuban Counterpoint: Tobacco and Sugar.* New York: Alfred A. Knopf, 1947.

Phillips, Ruby Hart. *Cuba: Island of Paradox.* New York: MacDowell, Obolensky, 1959.

———. *The Cuban Dilemma.* New York: Ivan Obolensky, 1962.

Plan de la Escuela Semi-internado, El Cangre. Havana: Ministry of Education, n.d.

Problems of the New Cuba; Report of the Commission on Cuban Affairs. New York: Foreign Policy Association, 1935.

Randall, Margaret. *Mujeres en la Revolución: Conversa con Mujeres Cubanas.* Mexico, D.F.: Siglo Veintiuno Editores, 1972.

Reckford, Barry. *Does Fidel Eat More than Your Father?* New York: Praeger, 1971.

Silverman, Bertram, ed. *Man and Socialism.* New York: Atheneum, 1971.

Semi-internado de Primaria, Valle del Perú. Havana: Ministry of Education, 1968.

Superación y Recreación para Maestros de Montaña en Varadero. Havana: Ministry of Education, 1968.

Suaréz, Andrés. *Cuba: Castroism and Communism, 1959–1966.* Cambridge, Mass.: MIT Press, 1967.

Sucklicki, Jaime. *University Students and Revolution in Cuba, 1920–1968.* Coral Gables: University of Miami Press, 1969.

Sutherland, Elizabeth. *The Youngest Revolution.* New York: Dial Press, 1969.

Taber, Robert. *M-26: The Biography of a Revolution.* New York: Lyle Stuart, 1961.

Thomas, Hugh. *Cuba: The Pursuit of Freedom.* New York: Harper and Row, 1971.

Valdés, Nelson P. *A Bibliography on Cuban Women in the Twentieth Century* (reprinted from *Cuban Studies Newsletter,* June, 1974).

Yglesias, José. *In the Fist of the Revolution.* New York: Vintage, 1969.

Zeitlin, Maurice. *Revolutionary Politics and the Urban Working Class.* Princeton: Princeton University Press, 1967.

ARTICLES

Berman, Jesse. "The Cuban Popular Tribunals," *Columbia Law Review,* Dec., 1969.

Butterworth, Douglas. "Grass-Roots Political Organization in Cuba: A Case of the Committees for the Defense of the Revolution," in Wayne A. Cornelius and Felicity Trueblood, eds., *Latin American Urban Research: Anthropological Perspectives on Latin American Urbanization,* vol. IV (Beverly Hills, Calif.: Sage Publications, 1974).

Dumont, René. "The Militarization of Fidelismo," *Dissent,* Sept.-Oct., 1970.

FitzGerald, Frances. "A Reporter at Large (Cuba)," *New Yorker,* Feb. 18, 1974.

Fox, Geoffrey E. "Cuban Workers in Exile," *Transaction,* Sept., 1971.

Leiner, Marvin. "Cuba's Schools, Ten Years Later," *Saturday Review,* Oct. 17, 1970.

Martin, Lionel. A series of articles on the Vanguard Worker program and union reorganization, *Guardian,* May 10–July 5, 1969.

Mesa-Lago, Carmelo. "Economic Significance of Unpaid Labor in Socialist Cuba," *Industrial and Labor Relations Review,* Apr., 1969.

Morgan, Ted. "Cuba," *New York Times Magazine,* Dec. 1, 1974.

Nicholson, Joe, Jr. "Inside Cuba," *Harpers,* Apr., 1973.

Yglesias, José. "Cuba Report: Their Hippies and Their Squares," *New York Times Magazine,* Jan. 12, 1969.

———. "A Cuban Poet in Trouble," *New York Review of Books,* June 3, 1971.

JOURNALS AND PERIODICALS

Bohemia, 1968–70.

Centro de Estudios del Folklore del TNC, 1961.

Cuba Internacional, 1969–70.

Cuba Review, 1974–76 (*Cuba Resource Center Newsletter,* 1972–73).

Cuban Studies Newsletter, 1972–75.

Ediciones CDR, 1969–70.

Etnología y Folklore, 1966–68.

Granma, 1969–70.

Granma Weekly Review, 1971–76.

Obra, 1961.